The Economics of the European Union

The Economics of the European Union

Policy and Analysis

Third Edition

Edited by

Mike Artis and Frederick Nixson

OXFORD

UNIVERSITY PRESS

Great Clarendon Street, Oxford OX2 6DP

Oxford University Press is a department of the University of Oxford.
It furthers the University's objective of excellence in research, scholarship,
and education by publishing worldwide in

Oxford New York

Athens Auckland Bangkok Bogotá Buenos Aires Cape Town
Chennai Dar es Salaam Delhi Florence Hong Kong Istanbul Karachi
Kolkata Kuala Lumpur Madrid Melbourne Mexico City Mumbai Nairobi
Paris São Paulo Shanghai Singapore Taipei Tokyo Toronto Warsaw

with associated companies in Berlin Ibadan

Oxford is a registered trade mark of Oxford University Press
in the UK and in certain other countries

Published in the United States
by Oxford University Press Inc., New York

British Library Cataloguing in Publication Data
Data available

Library of Congress Cataloging in Publication Data
Data available

ISBN 0–19–877640–3

Typeset in Stone Serif and Argo
by RefineCatch Limited, Bungay, Suffolk
Printed in Great Britain by
Bath Press Ltd., Bath, Somerset

10 9 8 7 6 5 4 3 2 1

Contents

List of figures

List of tables

List of boxes

Abbreviations

AASM	Association of African States and Madagascar
ACARD	Advisory Council for Applied Research and Development
ACOST	Advisory Council on Science and Technology
ACP	African, Caribbean, and Pacific
AMS	aggregate measure of support
ATM	Agreement on Textiles and Clothing
BAE	Bureau of Agricultural Economics
BMFT	Bundesministerium für Bildung und Forschung (Federal Ministry for Research and Technology)
BSE	Bovine Spongiform Encephalopathy
BTG	British Technology Group
CAC	Command and Control
CAD	Computer-aided Design
CAP	Common Agricultural Policy
CBA	Cost Benefit Analysis
CBD	(United Nations) Convention on Biological Diversity
CCIR	International Radio Consultative Committee
CEC	Commission of the European Communities
CEEC	Central and Eastern European Country
CEFTA	Central European Free Trade Association
CEPR	Centre for Economic Policy Research
CET	common external tariff
CFCs	chlorofluorocarbons
CFSP	Common Foreign and Security Policy
CI	Community Initiative
c.i.f.	cost, insurance, and freight
CJD	Creutzfeldt-Jakob Disease
CMEA	Council for Mutual Economic Assistance
CNC	computer numerically controlled
CO_2	carbon dioxide
COAPRI	Official Association of Industrial Property Agents
CQS	Community Quota System
CREST	Comité de la Recherche Scientifique et Technique (Scientific and Technical Research Committee)
CSF	Community Support Framework
CTP	Common Transport Policy
DAC	Development Assistance Committee
DFG	Deutsche Forschungsgemeinschaft (German Research Association)
DG	Directorate-General
DoT	Department of Transport
DPI	Department of Primary Industry

DRS	domestic rate of substitution
DRT	domestic rate of transformation
DTI	Department of Trade and Industry (UK)
EAGGF	European Agricultural Guarantee and Guidance Fund
EAP	Environmental Action Plan
EC	European Community
ECB	European Central Bank
ECE	Economic Commission for Europe
ECJ	European Court of Justice
Ecofin	Council of Economics and Finance Ministers
ECSC	European Coal and Steel Community
ECU	European Currency Unit
EDC	European Defence Community
EDF	European Development Fund
EEA	European Economic Area
EEC	European Economic Community
EFTA	European Free Trade Association
EIB	European Investment Bank
ELDO	European Launcher Development Organization
EMI	European Monetary Institute
EMS	European Monetary System
EMU	European Monetary Union
ENA	Ecole Nationale d'Administration (National School of Administration)
EP	European Parliament
EPO	European Patents Office
EPU	European Payments Union
ER	export refund
ERDF	European Regional Development Fund
ERM	Exchange Rate Mechanism
ERP	European Recovery Programme
ESA	European Space Agency
ESCB	European System of Central Banks
ESF	European Social Fund
ESPRIT	European Strategic Programme for Research and Development in Information Technology
ESRO	European Space Research Organization
ETUC	European Trade Union Confederation
EU	European Union
Euratom	European Atomic Energy Community
EUREKA	European Research Coordination Agency
FAST	Forecasting and Assessment in Science and Technology
FCCC	(United Nations) Framework Convention on Climate Change
FEAP	Fifth Environmental Action Plan
f.o.b.	free on board

FEOGA	Fonds Européen d'Orientation et de Garantie Agricole (EAGGF)
FP1	Framework [programme] 1
FRT	Foreign Rate of Transformation
FTA	Free Trade Area
GATT	General Agreement on Tariffs and Trade
GDP	Gross Domestic Product
GNP	Gross National Product
GSP	Generalized System of Preference
HDTV	high-definition television
IATA	International Air Transport Association
ICP	International Comparison Project
IGC	intergovernmental conference
IICA	inter-institutional collaborative agreements
IMF	International Monetary Fund
IPR	Intellectual Property Right
IP	investment premium
IT	information technology
ITCB	International Textiles and Clothing Bureau
JHA	Justice and Home Affairs
JIT	just in time
JRC	Joint Research Centre
JNRC	Joint Nuclear Research Centre
LAC	long-run average cost
LDC	less-developed country
LTA	Long Term Arrangement
MAC	Marginal Abatement Cost
MB	Marginal Benefit
MBI	Market-Based Instrument
MC	Marginal Cost
MCA	Monetary Compensatory Amount
MDS	Maximum Divergence Spread
MEC	Marginal External Cost
MEP	Member of the European Parliament
METS	minimum efficient technical scale
MFA	Multi-Fibre Arrangement
m.f.n.	most favoured nation
MIP	minimum import price
MITI	Ministry of International Trade and Industry, Japan
MMC	Monopolies and Mergers Commission
MNPB	Marginal Net Private Benefit
MPTC	marginal pollution treatment cost
MPV	multi-purpose vehicle
MRD	marginal reduction in damage
MSC	marginal social cost
NAFTA	North American Free Trade Agreement

NATO	North Atlantic Treaty Organization
NGACE	Nomenclature Générale des Activités Éonomiques des Communautés
NGO	non-governmental organization
NIEO	New International Economic Order
NIS	New Independent States
NRDC	National Research Development Corporation
NSI	national systems of innovation
NTB	non-tariff barrier
NUTS	Territorial units for statistics
OCTS	overseas countries and territories
ODA	Official Development Assistance
OECD	Organization for Economic Cooperation and Development
OEEC	Organization for European Economic Cooperation
OFT	Office of Fair Trading
OP	Operational Programme
OPT	outward-processing traffic
PAC	Pollution Abatement and Control
PEG	Production Entitlement Guarantees
PP	Precautionary Principle
PPP	purchasing power parity
P-P-P	Polluter Pays Principle
PPS	Purchasing Power Standard
PSE	Producer Subsidy Equivalent
PSRE	Public Sector Research Establishment
R&D	research and development
SDI	Strategic Defense Initiative
SEA	Single European Act
SEM	Single European Market
SF	Structural Funds
SME	small and medium-sized enterprise
SMU	Support Measurement Unit
SPD	Single Programming Document
SPRU	Science Policy Research Unit
Stabex	System for the Stabilization of Export Earnings
Sysmin	System for Safeguarding and Developing Mineral Production
TENS	trans-European networks
TEU	Treaty on European Union
TIP	Technology Integration Projects
UNDP	United Nations Development Programme
UNECE	United Nations Economic Commission for Europe
UNICE	Union of the Industries of the European Community
VER	voluntary export restraint
VHSIC	very high speed integrated circuits
VIL	variable import levy

VLSI	very large scale integration
VSTF	very short term financing
WTO	World Trade Organization

List of contributors

Mike Artis	Professor of Economics, European University Institute, Florence
Giuseppe Bertola	Professor of Economics, European University Institute, Florence
Robin Bladen-Hovell	Professor of Economics, University of Keele
Simon Bulmer	Professor of Government, University of Manchester
David Colman	Professor of Agricultural Economics, University of Manchester
Roy Gardner	Chancellor's Professor of Economics, University of Indiana
Stephen Martin	Professor of Economics, University of Amsterdam
Lynden Moore	Senior Associate Member, St. Antony's College, University of Oxford
Frederick Nixson	Professor of Development Economics, University of Manchester
Hedwig Ongena	European Central Bank
David Pearce	Professor of Economics, University College, London
David Purdy	Senior Lecturer in Social Policy and Social Work, University of Manchester
Peter Stubbs	Professor of Economics, University of Manchester
Gabriele Tondl	Associate Professor of Economics, Institute for European Affairs, University of Economics, Vienna
Nick Weaver	Teaching Assistant, University of Manchester
Bernhard Winkler	European Central Bank

Introduction

Mike Artis and Frederick Nixson

It was remarked in the Introduction to the previous edition of this book that 'The momentum towards "ever closer union" in Europe—despite the setbacks associated with the upheavals in the currency markets in 1992 and 1993—has been little short of impressive. The development of the EC6 to the EC12, the adoption of the 1992 Single European Market (SEM) programme, the inauguration of the European Union (EU) in November 1993 and its subsequent enlargement to fifteen Member States are markers of that progress.' Now, a prominent further marker has been added in the shape of the formation of the European Economic and Monetary Union, which started with eleven members on 1 January 1999 and has since admitted an additional member, with the participation, from the start of this year, of Greece.

As the economic significance and scope of policies decided at the level of the EU have increased and as the integration of the economies of the EU members has proceeded, so the need for sustained study of the development and impact of those policies has grown.

The basic aim of this book is to provide, for the intermediate-level student of economics, a comprehensive account of the economics of the EU. It contains a blend of theory, analysis, and application relating both to the EU as a whole and to a number of its constituent Member States. It is, therefore, intended to be of relevance and interest to university students in all the Member States of the Union.

The political context of the subject under study is of particular importance to its economic understanding and for this reason the first chapter in the book is devoted to a political analysis and history of the EU. The second chapter then sets out key statistical information relating to the economies of the EU and its Member States, together with comparative data for Japan and the USA to provide the broader economic context. The theory of customs unions and preferential trading areas—which is essential to the economic analysis of the European experiment—is laid out in the third chapter. This chapter not only covers classical theory but also takes a critical look at some more recent developments, notably the imperfect competition-based approach used by the European Commission to evaluate the benefits of the Single Market Programme. Chapter 4 is concerned with aspects of the enlargement process as the EU is set to expand considerably with the accession of new member countries. These four introductory chapters are succeeded by eleven further chapters which are devoted to the description and analysis of particular problems and policy areas.

Chapter 5 deals with the best-known and, in terms of money spent, much the largest economic policy area of the EU: the Common Agricultural Policy (CAP). It evaluates each of the main agricultural policy instruments that have been used, the reform process, and the future prospects for the CAP. Competition policy has always been seen as an essential element in the process of European integration: it is reviewed in Chapter 6. Chapter 7 contains an analysis of science and technology policy within the EU. First, it examines the case for government support of science and technology, then it considers national policies for science and technology in the UK, Germany, and France, and, finally, it describes and evaluates the development of a Science and Technology Policy within the EU.

Regional Policy is the subject matter of Chapter 8, which briefly reviews the history of EU regional policy then analyses in detail the aspirations and likely impact of the new programme adopted for 2000–6. The environmental policy of the EU is reviewed in Chapter 9, including an exposition of the basic principles of a rational environmental policy and an analysis of the extent to which European Union policy has adopted and applied those principles. Since the notion of 'sustainable development' was introduced in the Amsterdam Treaty and has become a major force in driving EU policy goals, it is afforded particular emphasis in this chapter. Chapter 10 is concerned with the role of social policy within the EU. To this end a typology of social-policy regimes is presented and explained (traditional, liberal, conservative, and social democratic), which is then used to explain the development of EU social policy and the forces which have constrained its scope.

The trade policies of the EU *vis-à-vis* third countries are studied in Chapter 11. The discussion analyses the use of non-tariff barriers such as anti-dumping duties and voluntary export restraints (VERs) to limit competition from third countries in certain product areas and describes EU commitments, under the Uruguay Round, to phase out these restrictions. There is a detailed examination of the key areas of protection, ranging from steel and textiles to cars and electronic products. Chapter 12 discusses the analytics of monetary union and describes and analyses the set-up of the European Monetary Union. A discussion of the first two years of experience of the new currency area is included in this chapter.

The formation of the EMU has prompted a greater concern for Member States' fiscal policy than existed before. The externalities of individual Member States' fiscal policy for other states have been sharpened by the creation of the monetary union and the delegation of monetary policy to a single, central actor; the European Central Bank. An immediate consequence has been the creation of the Stability and Growth Pact (SGP). This, and the surrounding issues, are the subject-matter of Chapter 13. Chapter 14 provides a description and analysis of what has in recent years been regarded as Europe's highest-priority problem, namely that of unemployment. Finally, Chapter 15 examines the foreign aid and external assistance afforded by the Member States of the EU and the development of policy at the Union level through the Lomé Conventions.

A set of discussion questions and references appears at the end of each chapter, together with suggestions for further reading and chapter notes.

The editors are most grateful to Dorothea Detring for helping to keep the editorial process in good order.

Chapter 1
History and Institutions of the European Union

Simon Bulmer

1.1 Introduction

The European Union (EU) formally came into existence on 1 November 1993 after final ratification of the Treaty on European Union (TEU or, colloquially, the Maastricht Treaty). From one perspective the TEU was just one step amongst several undertaken from the 1980s onwards that have been designed to make the integration process more attuned to contemporary challenges. From another perspective, the TEU sought to make a quantum jump in integration beyond its predominantly economic character to give it more explicit political functions, especially following the end of the Cold War. Up to that point it was the economic activities of the European Community (EC) which had been the main focus of attention. However, European integration had always had political objectives. And it is the purpose of this chapter to show that a knowledge of the wider context—historical, political, and institutional—is essential to an understanding of the economic activities.

The peaceful integration of the European national economies has been a development specific to the post-1945 era. The integration of Europe was proposed as early as the fourteenth century, but it was not until the period of economic, political, and military reconstruction following the Second World War that it was put into practice. The form taken by integration was strongly influenced by the historical experiences of its founding fathers. Hence they sought to avoid the excesses of nationalism and of the nation–state system that had been demonstrated by the German Nazi regime. They also sought to open up the national economies as a means of avoiding the protectionism that had characterized inter-war Europe. Poor economic performance was widely perceived to have provided a climate of political instability conducive to the growth of Fascism in Europe.

Economic integration has also been rooted in a particular European geography. This, too, has a historical explanation, namely in the division of Europe through the Cold War.

Thus the history of economic integration in the EC, until the 1990s at least, was *West* European history. Only with the collapse of Communism in Eastern and Central Europe at the end of the 1980s did the EC need substantively to develop economic relations with the other half of the continent.

If the division of Europe has major contextual importance to economic integration, so in particular does the division of one state, Germany. After the Second World War France was concerned that the revival of the German coal and steel industries might trigger expansionism. The principal objective of the European Coal and Steel Community (ECSC) was to allay fears of a 'military–industrial complex' fuelling renascent German nationalism. The roots of economic integration through what we may call the 'Community method' (see below) thus lay in the need to find a political solution to the turbulent past of Franco-German relations.

There are many other ways in which historical circumstance has shaped the pattern of economic integration. In particular, it can explain the tortuous way in which the UK has come to grips with the integration process, as a reluctant participant seeking to come to terms with its 'descent from power'. Similarly, the persistence of non-democratic forms of government in Greece and on the Iberian peninsula isolated those states from the EC until their domestic political transformation permitted membership, as part of a second wave of enlargement in the 1980s.

Thus history has conditioned the process of economic integration. But what of the politics and institutional framework of economic integration? These, too, are important.

Economic integration has not evolved as the result of some functional logic. Nor has it developed as the result of some 'natural' economic law enforced by Adam Smith's 'invisible hand'. Functional and economic determinism fail to explain both the setbacks to integration and the relaunches; economic integration has not been a smooth process following some scientific logic. Rather, it has been dependent upon political and institutional dynamics.

At the level of the major integration developments—from the Schuman Plan creating the ECSC to the signature of the TEU in 1992—the need to create a package deal satisfying the participants' national interests has been paramount. Without satisfying all Member States, no deal can be achieved. However, where the agreement amounts to a new treaty or a treaty amendment, even consensus between the member governments may be insufficient. The French National Assembly's actions in August 1954 led to rejection of the European Defence Community Treaty and the collapse of that initiative. The need to satisfy domestic political concerns was demonstrated most dramatically with the Maastricht Treaty—the TEU. The Danes' need to hold a second referendum following the Treaty's initial rejection by a narrow margin of voters in June 1992; the successful referenda in the Irish Republic and in France; and the tortuous ratification process during 1992–3 in the UK House of Commons: these all demonstrated the contingency of treaty amendments on domestic politics. Thus major integrative developments require not only agreement between the member governments but an ability on the part of the latter to ensure domestic approval.

On a more routine level, integration may be less publicly politicized. However, the political dynamics of policy-making are no less important. The EU is not like the many international organizations on the world stage. Uniquely amongst European and international organizations, it has supranational characteristics. These are concentrated overwhelmingly in the institutional arrangements concerning the economic 'pillar' of activity. It has its own body of law which has direct effect in the Member States, and takes precedence over national law. It has institutions with autonomy from the Member States. The most prominent of these are: the European Commission, which serves as an executive civil service; a parliamentary assembly which has been directly elected since 1979; a European Court of Justice (ECJ) which makes rulings on matters of law. Balanced against these three are two powerful institutions representing the interests of the member governments, namely the Council of Ministers and the European Council. The former is comprised of national ministers; the latter of heads of government or state. The EU is not like other international economic organizations in a further respect: namely, in the way that economic integration has been a continuing process of evolving goals from the first steps undertaken with the ECSC to the TEU and beyond.

Above all, however, it must be remembered that economic integration has never been an end in itself. It has always served as a means towards the end of political integration. The ECSC involved the integration of the coal and steel sectors as a means towards Franco-German reconciliation and towards creating a new system of post-war European relations. Similarly, an important motivating factor for some states, in particular France, in negotiating the TEU was to strengthen integration in the context of German unification in 1990. The French government feared that a more powerful Germany might become less predictable in European politics; it sought to pre-empt this through closer integration. These political objectives set the path towards the EU apart from the paths of more modest organizations, such as the European Free Trade Association (EFTA).

In reviewing the history of the EU, we explain the key developments summarized in Table 1.1. To do so, we need to commence with the situation in 1945, at the end of the Second World War.

1.2 Economic integration in historical and political perspective

Why European cooperation and integration?

Although European integration was not an idea new to the post-1945 era, it was propelled initially by a distinctive 'mix' of circumstances and impulses. These comprised

- the defeat of Nazi Germany and of the Axis powers;
- the wish to avoid a repeat of the excesses of nationalism and of the nation-state system by creating a new system of European international relations;
- the economic dislocation caused by wartime destruction;
- the emergence of two global superpowers with competing political and economic ideologies;

Table 1.1 Key stages in the development of the European Union

Year	Key developments
1951	Treaty of Paris is signed, bringing the European Coal and Steel Community into effect from 23 July 1952. Membership comprised Belgium, the Federal Republic of Germany, France, Italy, Luxembourg, and the Netherlands.
1957	Treaty of Rome is signed, bringing into effect the European Economic Community and the European Atomic Energy Community from 1 January 1958.
1965	Merger Treaty is signed, with the effect of merging the principal institutions of the three communities from 1967. Henceforth the three communities are known collectively as the European Community.
1973	Denmark, the Irish Republic, and the UK join the EC on 1 January.
1981	Greece joins the EC on 1 January.
1986	Spain and Portugal join the EC on 1 January. The Single European Act is signed, coming into effect on 1 July 1987, and introduces the first systematic revisions to the founding treaties.
1992	Treaty on European Union is signed (following broad agreement in December 1991 at a meeting in Maastricht in the Netherlands). It entails systematic revisions to, and extension of, the existing treaties. Following ratification, the TEU comes into effect on 1 November 1993. Within the European Union, the EC represents one 'pillar' of activities: the others relate to foreign and security policy; and justice and home affairs.
1995	Austria, Finland, and Sweden join the EU on 1 January.
1997	The Amsterdam Treaty is signed, coming into effect on 1 May 1999.
1999	Stage 3 of Monetary Union, including the launch of the euro, takes effect.
2000	Treaty of Nice agreed, signed in 2001: implementation will occur following national ratification.

- the division of Europe and the wish in the West for security from the Soviet threat;

- the need to base Western security and defence on economic reconstruction and well-being; and

- the desire for Franco-German reconciliation as the bedrock of stability within Western Europe.

In short, European integration was motivated by political, economic, and security considerations.

The protagonists of cooperation and integration were by no means of one view on how to address these issues. *Federalists* placed primary emphasis on the superseding of the nation-state with a larger democratic structure. Their roots were frequently in the European resistance movements, and, in 1944, at a meeting in Geneva, they had already drawn up a plan for a federal European order based on a written constitution.

A second category of protagonists may be termed *functionalists*. Like the federalists, they were strongest in continental Europe, but they lacked the federalists' organization. They shared the federalists' objective of a united Europe but adopted a more pragmatic approach to its realization. They saw the need for economic cooperation as a starting-point for achieving their political goals. The Frenchman Jean Monnet was the most prominent figure in this camp. Other political figures, especially from the Low Countries, shared this approach. By 1944 the exiled governments had already agreed on the establishment of Benelux, a customs union to comprise Belgium, the Netherlands, and Luxembourg.

A third category may be termed the *nationalists*. Although they did not display nationalism in its negative sense, these figures did not see any need to participate in a new political order. The nationalists were strongest in those Member States which had either escaped invasion during the Second World War or had remained neutral, and fiercely retained national political traditions. Hence they were strongest in the UK, Scandinavia, the Irish Republic, and Switzerland.

For the UK, the allied victory was seen as the source of heightened pride in national institutions; it had, moreover, galvanized relations with the USA. The resultant 'special relationship', together with the Commonwealth, represented powerful alternative poles of attraction for post-war UK foreign policy. Both the main parties in the UK opposed participation in any integration schemes which would jeopardize national sovereignty.[1] Winston Churchill, regarded in continental Europe as one of the protagonists of a federal Europe, was most supportive of integration when out of power. However, he saw the UK's relations with the strongest protagonists as 'with them but not of them'. The nationalists were prepared to participate in a number of European organizations, but these were characterized by cooperation between sovereign nation-states. It was not until the 1960s that the position began to change, as nationalists came to realize that this approach offered very limited opportunities for joint policy action.

A final set of protagonists—and one which must not be forgotten—was comprised of *external actors*. Essentially this was the political élite of the USA. The US position was to support cooperation and integration, both through exhortation and through financial and political assistance. The European Recovery Programme (ERP), popularly known as the Marshall Plan, played a major role in facilitating economic reconstruction. US leadership within the North American Treaty Organization (NATO) provided the security framework within which economic integration could flourish.

By the early 1950s a small group of six Member States had emerged that had shared objectives and a willingness to sacrifice national sovereignty to achieve them. These were the states which launched the process of supranational integration (see Table 1.1). A wider group—which also included these six—was willing to cooperate on various economic, political, or security-policy goals. However, states in this group were unwilling to go further. It was the different response to post-war circumstances on the part of the six which led them to favour *supranational integration*, whereas the wider group was unwilling to go beyond *intergovernmental cooperation* between sovereign states. Accordingly, the European organizations established in the post-war period tended either to be limited to cooperation or to entail the formal transfer of sovereignty that characterizes supranational integration.

The international organization of the West European economies

The first attempt to organize the European economies in the post-war period was made with the establishment in 1947 of the Economic Commission for Europe (ECE), created under the auspices of the United Nations. However, its pan-European nature was to be its undoing, for the emergence of the Cold War rendered it unworkable as a body aimed at facilitating the reconstruction of Europe as a whole. From this point onwards we are concerned with Western European integration. The Eastern European economies were brought together in the Soviet-led Council for Mutual Economic Assistance (CMEA), which was set up in 1949.

The emergence of the Cold War overshadowed cooperation and integration at the end of the 1940s. In consequence, this was a period when the USA showed leadership in promoting West European developments. The scene was set when President Truman pledged US support for 'free peoples who are resisting attempted subjugation by armed minorities or by outside pressures'. The specific trigger for the 'Truman Doctrine' had been Communist destabilization in Greece, but the declaration was a broader commitment to contain Communism.

The Marshall Plan was announced in June 1947. The US Administration recognized that the objectives of the Truman Doctrine could best be attained if Europe's democracies were based on sound economies. Hence the initiative made by Secretary of State George Marshall was a response to the continued economic dislocation and food-rationing in Western Europe. Although notionally offered to all European states, Marshall aid was in fact accepted only by those in the West. In defence policy the counterpart to the Marshall Plan was the signature, in April 1949, of the Atlantic Charter, which created NATO as the principal organization for the defence of Western Europe. The USA was to play the leading role in NATO.

US leadership was not confined to the European arena. The principles of *international* monetary cooperation had already been established at the Bretton Woods conference of 1944, which led to the establishment of the International Monetary Fund (IMF) and the World Bank. In October 1947 the General Agreement on Tariffs and Trade (GATT) was created, providing the guiding principles of liberalization in the trade arena, namely through tariff reductions. The economic principles embodied in these organizations were to have an important impact on economic cooperation within Western Europe.

The first step towards economic integration came at the start of 1948 with the creation of the Benelux customs union, complete with the introduction of a common customs tariff. Benelux was to serve as a precursor to the European Economic Community (EEC).

Of wider geographical significance was the foundation, in April 1948, of the Organiza-tion for European Economic Cooperation (OEEC). This was the organization entrusted with implementing the Marshall Plan. Disbursement of US aid was very much a matter to be organized by the European states themselves through the OEEC and its key governing body, the Council of Ministers. The OEEC was essentially an intergovernmental organ-ization, characterized by cooperation between states. It ensured fulfilment of the US condition that reconstruction should be coordinated, and that tariff reductions should be implemented. Its activities were concentrated on facilitating the reconstruction of the national economies, and reducing quotas on inter-state trade and tariffs. Under its umbrella were established other, more specialized, bodies and arrangements such as the European Payments Union (EPU). Established in 1950, the EPU was designed to facilitate a multilateral system of payments for trade until initial liquidity problems were alleviated.

The OEEC, having overseen the task of reconstruction, was succeeded in 1961 by the

Organization for Economic Cooperation and Development (OECD), an agency no longer confined to the West European economies. The OEEC and Marshall aid had facilitated the construction of an economic platform, upon which supranational integration could be founded.

For some states the OEEC was not enough. It neither took on ambitious tasks nor had any political component. The May 1950 Schuman Plan was an attempt by France to seize the reins of integration and take a different direction. Conceived as a Franco-German scheme, it was nevertheless open to other states to join. However, there was a condition: the principle of supranationalism, i.e. of relinquishing national power, had to be accepted. This precondition (and other factors) had the effect of ensuring that the UK did not participate in the negotiations.

The Schuman Plan, named after the French foreign minister, had in fact been elaborated by Jean Monnet. Its principal concern was with ensuring that reconstruction in the western part of Germany should not endanger peace. The heavy industries of the Ruhr had been under allied control, but this could not continue indefinitely. The proposed arrangements were also welcomed from the German side, for they offered a route to its regaining control over its key industrial sectors, as well as to international rehabilitation.

Thus the Schuman Plan was an explicitly political proposal; it offered a breakthrough into supranationalism; and it followed a functional approach of sectoral integration but with wider objectives in view. These features have come to characterize the 'Community method' of integration. The plan was favourably received in Belgium, the Netherlands, Luxembourg, and Italy as well as in France and West Germany. These six states were to become the sole participants of the Community method until 1973 (see Table 1.1).

Before the ink was dry on the April 1951 Treaty of Paris, which established the ECSC, proposals had already been made for further integration in the shape of a European Defence Community (EDC). Conceived at the height of the Cold War, and with an eye upon the hostilities in Korea, the EDC proposal was designed to facilitate the rearmament of Germany through supranational control, since a German contribution was seen as indispensable to West European security. The French National Assembly's failure, in August 1954, to ratify the Treaty represented the first setback to supranational integration. German rearmament was achieved in May 1955, through the intergovernmental Western European Union.

Those favouring further supranational integration were undeterred by this setback. The reasons for French non-ratification were varied but did not represent a rejection of supranationalism. Rather, there was a feeling that a supranational defence community was proceeding too far too fast. The death of Stalin and the end of the Korean War had also reduced the urgent need for the EDC. By 1955 new ideas were being floated for developing integration beyond the coal and steel sectors. Milward (1992: 120) points out that these proposals were not an attempt to relaunch integration *after* the failure of the EDC. Moves for a wider European customs union had already been mooted.

The forum for initial discussions on the proposals, which were advanced in particular by the Benelux countries, was to be the Messina conference of June 1955. This was attended by the foreign ministers of the EC6. The proposed areas for further integration comprised the creation of a common market (i.e. beyond the coal and steel sectors), a common transport policy, and integration in the energy sector. These ideas received broad support, and, in consequence, a committee of governmental representatives was set up, chaired by the Belgian Paul-Henri Spaak.

The UK was invited to participate in the negotiations; it accepted the invitation but then withdrew from the Spaak Committee, once again because of outright opposition to the proposed supranational form of integration. Negotiations between the EC6 were quite protracted, because of several thorny issues, and some matters were barely resolved by the time the EEC Treaty was finalized. Hence the Treaty contains quite limited indications as to the direction to be taken in the integration of agricultural policy and social policy. Nevertheless, negotiations during 1956 and early 1957 led to the two Treaties of Rome: the EEC Treaty and the Treaty establishing the European Atomic Energy Community (Euratom). They were signed on 25 March 1957. Following ratification, they came into effect from the start of 1958.

One further development must be referred to before examining the three European Communities in more detail. Having withdrawn from the Spaak Committee, the UK government began to reappraise its policy. Following a UK initiative, a committee was set up within the framework of the OEEC to examine the creation of a European free trade area. Although the resultant report deemed such a development feasible, there was considerable suspicion on the part of the EC6 that the UK initiative was designed to undermine their much more ambitious plans for a common market and a supranational political system to supervise it. It was only once the Treaties of Rome had come into effect, and the EC6 had gone their own way, that the negotiations on a free trade area gained momentum. They culminated in the signing, on 4 January 1960, of the Stockholm Convention creating the European Free Trade Association (EFTA). The founding members were the UK, Norway, Denmark, Sweden, Austria, Portugal, and Switzerland.

EFTA was a classic intergovernmental forum for economic cooperation. There was no threat to national sovereignty. As such, it suited the instincts of UK politicians. EFTA was centred around trade in industrial goods; agriculture was largely excluded. As a free trade area, each Member State was free to set its own external tariff. This enabled the UK to continue its trading relations with the Commonwealth countries.

Until the 1970s the EC6 and the 'EFTANs' comprised two distinct camps within Western Europe. With the first EC enlargement of 1973, it was agreed to reduce tariff barriers on industrial trade between the two groupings. By the late 1980s a much closer relationship was proposed: the European Economic Area (see below).

The two camps corresponded quite neatly to the two different political approaches to integration that were identified earlier. The EC6 comprised those states which were prepared to transcend the nation state by means of supranational integration. By contrast, EFTA was composed of those states which preferred more limited arrangements and the maintenance of national sovereignty. How, then, did integration through the Community method shape the form of integration pursued by the EC6?

Integration through the community method

The ECSC

The ECSC, which commenced operations in July 1952, was the starting-point of the Community method of supranational integration. Its provisions were set out in the Treaty of Paris, which runs to 100 articles. The ECSC had three key features.

First, it proposed a degree of economic integration that went beyond anything developed in the other existing European organizations. It was not concerned with the lowest level of economic integration (a free trade area) but with the higher goal of a common market, albeit confined to the coal, steel, and related sectors. Nevertheless, given that these sectors were then regarded as the 'commanding heights' of the economy, the ECSC was concerned with core activities of the EC6. The ECSC's chief aims were to ensure security of supplies through the removal of quotas and customs duties over a five-year transitional period; the rational expansion and modernization of the industries; and the provision of mechanisms for managing serious shortages or gluts. The ECSC sought to restrict Member States' use of discriminatory state subsidies and it provided a common external commercial policy relating to the two sectors.

It is worth pointing out that the economic philosophy behind the Treaty of Paris was more interventionist than that behind the later EEC Treaty. This *dirigisme* owed much to the influence of the French; it was no coincidence that the author of the Schuman Plan, Jean Monnet, was head of the French Commission for Economic Planning. Moreover, the Treaty of Paris spelt out most of the detailed arrangements, thus reducing the need for secondary legislation. The ECSC's activities were financed by levies on coal and steel production.

The second key feature was that these detailed arrangements were subservient to the political goal of providing a framework for Franco-German reconciliation. One indicator of the success of this was the relatively smooth reintegration of the Saar into (West) Germany in 1956, after some ten years effectively under French control.

The third key feature, and central to the Community method, was the set of strong, supranational central institutions associated with the ECSC. These provided a model which was later employed for the EEC and Euratom.

The ECSC comprised five institutions:

- the executive, known as the High Authority (equivalent to the European Commission of today);
- the Council of Ministers, comprising representatives of the member governments;
- the Consultative Committee, consisting of representatives of employers/industry, trade unions, and consumers concerned with the ECSC's activities;
- the Assembly, composed of a total of sixty-eight delegates from the six national parliaments;
- the European Court of Justice (ECJ).

These institutions were all located in Luxembourg, thus explaining why some services of the EU are located there.

The High Authority had a considerable degree of autonomy in carrying out the tasks entrusted to the ECSC. It was headed by nine members who were appointed from the Member States but were to act independently in carrying out their duties. Fittingly, the first president of the High Authority was Jean Monnet. Beneath the 'Members'—equivalent to present-day EU commissioners—the High Authority was staffed by an independent civil service. The independence of the High Authority and its staff from the national governments was a characteristic of the supranational approach to integration.

A Council of Ministers was created to allay the concerns of the Benelux countries. They were worried that the ECSC might be dominated by French and German interests. They were also concerned that the High Authority might pursue an excessively *dirigiste* form of economic policy. The Council of Ministers was thus a check against the realization of these worries. Although a check on supranationalism, the Council could not be compared with similar bodies in, for example, the OEEC. This was because the ECSC Council was able, under specified circumstances, to take decisions by qualified majority voting and simple majority, as well as by the conventional method of unanimity.[2]

The Consultative Committee and the Assembly were much less important institutions, confined to advisory roles. The ECJ, however, had a more important function. It was responsible for adjudicating on disputes relating to the ECSC's activities.

In operation, the ECSC was regarded initially as successful. Production and inter-state trade in coal and steel increased markedly, although how much of this could be attributed to the ECSC's existence is open to question. The initial success was followed by a period of less progress. The coal crisis towards the end of the 1950s was caused by falling demand owing to cheap oil imports. The High Authority's attempt in 1959 to declare a 'manifest crisis' in the coal industry, so as to obtain powers of intervention in the market, failed because it could not obtain the necessary majority in the Council of Ministers. The ECSC was regarded as having failed its first real test. This was the first of numerous challenges by national interests to the supranational principles of the Community method. It indicated that the ECSC was not so supranational in practice as it was designed to be.

The ECSC retained its separate existence until implementation of the Merger Treaty in 1967. This resulted in the High Authority's absorption into the EC Commission. The Assembly and the ECJ had already been shared with the other Communities from 1958. The Consultative Committee continues to retain its separate identity.

Following the creation of the EEC and the merger of the three European Communities, activities based on the ECSC Treaty have tended to be overshadowed. In the coal sector activities have concentrated on combating the effects of declining demand. A more effective role has been hampered by the absence of clear provision for an EC energy policy. There was greater prominence in the management of surplus capacity in the steel sector, where severe problems emerged in the 1980s.

Euratom

The Treaties of Rome expanded the area of joint activity considerably. Of the two, the Euratom Treaty was of much less significance. It was largely the product of French pressure. France had begun to develop a civilian nuclear programme and saw Euratom as a way of obtaining financial support for its extension and of developing a market for French technology.

In fact, Euratom was rather a failure. Differences between the Member States resulted in Euratom having little control over the development of the nuclear sector. Measures have been undertaken on health and safety in the nuclear industry, to promote joint research, and so on, but the core activities of civilian nuclear power have remained in the hands of the Member States.

The EEC

The establishment of the EEC was a most significant development in supranational integration. The ECSC's model of identifying functional bases for joint policy was continued. European integration retained a political objective, although no longer centrally concerned with fears of renascent German power; and the EEC Treaty followed the supranational model already established, albeit in a moderated form.

The activities and arrangements covered by the EEC Treaty can be seen from a summary of its structure (see Table 1.2). The EEC's policies are considered in detail in succeeding chapters. Remarks here are confined to general observations; an outline of the institutions of the EU is given later in the chapter.

The EEC Treaty was distinctly more market-oriented in ideology, compared to its rather *dirigiste* predecessor, the ECSC. Accordingly, the centrepiece of the Treaty was the

Table 1.2 Contents of the EEC Treaty

Contents		Articles
Preamble		
Part One.	Basic principles	1–8
Part Two.	Foundations of the Community	
Title I.	Free Movement of Goods, including creation of the customs union, elimination of quantitative restrictions	9–37
Title II.	Agriculture	38–47
TItle III.	Free Movement of Persons, Services, and Capital	48–73
Title IV.	Transport	74–84
Part Three.	Policy of the Community	
Title I.	Common Rules, including on competition policy, state aids, tax provisions, and the harmonization of laws	85–102
Title II.	Economic Policy, principally commercial policy	103–16
Title III.	Social Policy	117–28
Title IV.	The European Investment Bank	129–30
Part Four.	Association of Overseas Countries and Territories	131–36
Part Five.	Institutions of the Community	
Title I.	Provisions Governing the Institutions	137–98
Title II.	Financial Provisions (concerning the EEC budget)	199–209
Part Six.	General and Final Provisions	210–28

Note: The details relate to the 1957 EEC Treaty. They do not incorporate changes introduced by subsequent treaty amendments.

creation of the common market. The deadline for removing interstate tariffs was set down in the Treaty as 31 December 1969, but this had already been achieved by 1 July 1968. The deeper integration needed to achieve a common market received a boost with the Single European Market programme, launched in 1985. The target date for passing legislation at European level was the end of 1992.

If the greater market orientation signalled a decline in French influence on negotiations, this was redressed by the EEC's Common Agricultural Policy (CAP). The French made agricultural provisions a prerequisite for agreement to the Treaty, although this was not their priority from the start, as conventional wisdom has it. It is also worth noting that the agricultural 'title' of the Treaty does not specify the highly regulated and protectionist policy which the CAP became. This was the product of secondary legislation— i.e. subsequent legal acts implementing the principles set down in the Treaty. A further area of the Treaty which particularly reflected French interests was Part Four, conferring associate status on colonies and former colonies of the EC6. The arrangement ensured minimal disruption to France's existing trading patterns.

One or two policy areas provided for in the EEC Treaty have not had the impact that one might assume from their presence in it (see Table 1.2). Transport-policy developments were minimal until the 1980s. Similarly, the social-policy provisions were of a very limited nature, and it was not until the end of the 1980s that attempts were made to extend their range. Finally, it is worth drawing attention to one of the final provisions of the Treaty, Article 235. This article states:

If action by the Community should prove necessary to attain, in the course of the operation of the common market, one of the objectives of the Community and this Treaty has not provided the necessary powers, the Council shall, acting unanimously on a proposal from the Commission and after consulting the Assembly, take the appropriate measures.

The importance of Article 235 is that it has facilitated EC action beyond the immediate provisions of the Treaty. For example, the EC12 used Article 235 to agree four environmental-action programmes before they were given explicit constitutional authority to do so in the SEA![3]

A final observation relating to the overall shape of the EEC Treaty is that it was principally concerned with setting policy principles. By contrast, the ECSC Treaty itself provided most of the detailed arrangements for the supranational governance of the coal and steel sectors. With the exception of the provisions relating to the establishment of the customs union and to the institutions, the EEC Treaty provided only a framework. Thus a vast amount of secondary legislation has been necessary in order to put into practice the Treaty's objectives.

The 1960s: consolidation and challenge

The period from 1958 to 1969 may be seen as one of consolidation and challenge. The consolidation derived from making progress in putting the EEC Treaty into operation. The challenge was provided by General de Gaulle. He became president of the Fifth French Republic in 1958, in the first year of the EEC. Attempting to re-establish French credibility after the instability of the Fourth Republic, he sought to rebuild the prestige of the nation-state. This put him on a collision course with the supranational EEC.

Putting the customs union into operation was achieved early on, as already noted. The institutions were put into practice, although the (enlarged) Assembly and the ECJ were shared from 1958 with the ECSC and Euratom. The first president of the EEC Commission, Walter Hallstein, was a forceful individual and gave that institution activist leadership. In 1965 the first constitutional amendment was agreed: the Merger Treaty, which came into effect in 1967.[4] This merged the three Communities, with the creation of a single Commission being the principal result. The Treaties were not merged, however, and a few features remained distinct, such as the separate budgetary provisions for the ECSC.

A number of important legal developments occurred during the 1960s, also with a consolidating effect. These emerged in judgments on specific cases brought before the ECJ but that had wide-ranging implications and strengthened the EC's supranational character. Two cases were of particular importance. In its 1963 judgment on the *Van Gend en Loos* case, the ECJ established the principle of direct effect, i.e. that EC law confers both rights and duties on individuals that national courts must enforce. The effect of this was to make it possible for private individuals or companies to use the national courts to oblige governments to implement treaty provisions. Had this principle not been established, in what was an expansionist judgment on the part of the ECJ, progress towards the common market would have been much more difficult. The ECJ has made a number of major judgments facilitating the creation of the internal market. However, it cannot make these judgments until a case is referred.

A second important legal principle, that of the primacy of EC law over national law, was also established in the 1960s: a feature which had not been specified in the Treaty. This principle was enunciated in *Costa* v. *ENEL* (case 6/64) and in other ECJ judgments. The effect was to reinforce the supranationalism of the EEC. Added to the earlier case establishing the principle of direct effect, this facilitated a process of integration through law. So, whilst the 1960s are often characterized as a period of resurgence in national interests, as demonstrated by the 1965 crisis (see below), important legal developments were under way which had the opposite effect. They have also been of major importance in the realization of the economic objectives set out in the treaties.

Consolidation was also achieved through the translation of treaty objectives into secondary legislation. This was particularly necessary in the agricultural sector, for the whole regulatory structure of the CAP had to be introduced. Given the level of French interest in this policy area, it is not surprising that this was one of the principal battlefields for de Gaulle's assault on supranationalism.

De Gaulle's policy was based on a nation-state-centred view of world politics, and his particular wish was to strengthen French grandeur. His policy generated three specific flashpoints regarding the development of integration. The first resulted from his proposal for a 'Political Union'. Far from being an attempt to advance supranational integration, this was to be organized along traditional intergovernmental lines. The other Member States regarded it as a threat to the successful supranational Community method. His proposal failed. The second occurred as a result of a reconsideration by the United Kingdom of the merits of membership. The Conservative government of Harold Macmillan had already applied for membership in 1961. Applications were also made by Ireland, Denmark, and Norway. However, in a dramatic move, de Gaulle unilaterally rejected the UK application (and by extension the others) at a press conference in January 1963. De Gaulle clearly did not want competition from the UK for the leadership of the EEC. His actions irritated the other five governments both procedurally and substantively. In 1967 he vetoed the second UK application, this time made by the Labour government of Harold Wilson.

The third and most dramatic clash came with the 1965 crisis. Its immediate cause was the creation of the system for financing the CAP. Hallstein sought to link this provision with the creation of a self-financing, or 'own-resources', EEC budget. For de Gaulle, Hallstein was becoming too much like a government head. In addition, a step towards budgetary autonomy was a further (for de Gaulle, undesired) reinforcement of supra-nationalism. In the background, but at least as important, was the projected 1966 introduction of qualified majority voting in the EEC Council of Ministers. This was also regarded by de Gaulle as a major threat to national sovereignty, for that would mean that French interests could be overridden in the Council. The result was that in June 1965 France withdrew from the workings of the Council of Ministers. It was not until January 1966 that a solution was found in the so-called Luxembourg Compromise. While this had no status in EC law, it established the convention that, on matters of 'vital national interest' to one or more Member States, discussions would continue until consensus had been reached. The Luxembourg Compromise was important in practice, for it led to integration being dictated by the pace of the most reluctant Member State.

The result of the Luxembourg Compromise was a slowing-down of decision-making in the Council of Ministers. The need to satisfy all national interests contrasted with what was supposed to happen, namely decisions being taken by qualified majority vote. The Commission became less ambitious and the Community's supranationalism was in decline. This situation was not really reversed until the 1980s and the SEA. The Luxembourg Compromise is now considered to have been superseded in the economic domain of integration.

Revival through summitry

It was not until de Gaulle's resignation that the political will of the EC could be revived. Even so, Gaullist ideas continued to influence the policies of his successor as president, Georges Pompidou. Pompidou initiated a meeting with the heads of government of the other five states. Designed to give the EC new momentum, the summit initiated a number of developments:

• the opening of negotiations for enlargement of the EC;

• re-examination of the financing of the budget;

• the creation of a system of foreign-policy cooperation; and

• the drafting of proposals for an Economic and Monetary Union.

The enlargement negotiations were successful and, on 1 January 1973, the UK, the Irish Republic, and Denmark joined the EC. Norway, which had negotiated its terms of entry, rejected membership in a referendum held in September 1972. An 'own resources' system was introduced for the EC budget through two treaty amendments (1970 and 1975). The new system was fully operational from 1980. A foreign-policy cooperation procedure was set up in 1970 and has developed considerably over the intervening period. Finally, the Economic and Monetary Union initiative was launched as a response to currency instability in the EC at the end of the 1960s. The proposals failed because of the collapse of the Bretton Woods international monetary system and the impact of the 1973 oil crisis.

Subsequent summits in 1972 and 1974 were less successful, although providing some initiatives. The 1972 Paris summit, for instance, placed environmental policy on the EC's agenda. The 1974 summit, again held in Paris, was more noteworthy. On the institutional front there were two key achievements. The first of these was agreement to the principle of holding direct elections to the European Parliament (EP). This distinctly supranational step, aimed at giving European parliamentarians their own source of democratic legitimacy, was first put into practice with elections in 1979. The second was the agreement to hold regular summit meetings, known as the European Council, at least twice each year. In the period since 1975 'most of the major political decisions in the EC have been taken in the European Council' (Bulmer and Wessels 1987: 2). The main policy decision was agreement on the establishment of the European Regional Development Fund (ERDF).

With two former finance ministers at the heart of the European Council—Chancellor Schmidt of Germany and President Giscard d'Estaing of France—it was scarcely surprising that international monetary affairs should feature strongly at its meetings. Thus in 1978 Schmidt launched the initiative for the European Monetary System (EMS) at the Copenhagen European Council. After elaboration of its operation by a group of three experts, it came into effect in March 1979. It was to be one of the main achievements of this period.

The period from 1979 to 1984 was dominated by the UK budgetary problem. Mrs Thatcher's Conservative government was intent upon achieving a lasting solution to what it perceived as an inequitable system. It had been anticipated from the outset of membership that the EC's own resources budget would not favour the UK (see Scott 1992). However, the economic recession induced by the oil crisis resulted in few of the predicted trade benefits of membership accruing to the UK. It was only after protracted negotiations that a settlement was reached at the Fontainebleau European Council in 1984.

This agreement was part of a typical 'package deal' of EC negotiations. Not only did the meeting provide a solution to the UK budgetary crisis, increase the size of the budget, and provide for limited CAP reform, it also decided to look at the institutional structure of the EC, the start of the process leading to the SEA. A further part of the package was to give approval in principle to Spanish and Portuguese enlargement. The two states joined on 1 January 1986; Greece had joined from the start of 1981. The southern enlargements were motivated essentially by political considerations: namely, the wish to strengthen these new democracies, for the three states' economies were at a relatively low level of development.

The SEA and renewed dynamism

The SEA was signed in February 1986 and came into effect on 1 July 1987. It had been negotiated within an intergovernmental conference (IGC) under the supervision of the European Council. The SEA's significance was that it amounted to the first comprehensive revision of the treaties. The motivations for it included:

- a recognition of the need to overcome the 'Eurosclerosis' that had characterized the EC economy compared with its global competitors;
- a wish to provide a stimulus to the European economy by means of the liberalization associated with completion of the internal market;
- a wish to bring the treaties into line with actual practice in the EC;
- a wish to relaunch supranational integration because of a realization that decisional weakness had impeded the collective interest; and
- a recognition of the need to make the EC more politically responsive if the Iberian enlargement were not to create political sclerosis.

The content of the SEA can be divided into two: namely, the policy and the institutional provisions. The policy developments took two broad forms. Some of the treaty revisions were largely concerned with formalizing the EC's competence—for example, in environmental policy, 'monetary capacity', and research and technology policy. In these cases the treaty revisions gave clearer competence for EC action. The codification of foreign-policy cooperation, including enhanced institutional provision, had a similar effect, but this development was contained in a separate part of the SEA. The main contribution of the SEA, arguably, was to making the single market programme achievable. Already agreed to in June 1985, this programme had been set out in a Commission White Paper, *Completing the Internal Market*, drawn up by the UK commissioner, Lord Cockfield. The White Paper was based on a threefold strategy:

- a relatively small legislative programme (under 300 items) aimed at setting the essential requirements, by the end of 1992, for completion of the internal market;
- reliance on the principle of mutual recognition of national product standards as established in ECJ landmark decisions, especially the 1979 *Cassis de Dijon* case; and
- the 'new approach' of devolving decisions on creating new European standards from the Council to standard-setting agencies.

To this programme the SEA contributed by including provision for increased use of qualified majority voting in the Council of Ministers, thereby limiting the obstacles to achieving the White Paper's legislative programme.

Other institutional changes comprised increased provision for qualified majority voting in other policy areas, increased powers for the EP, and the creation of the Court of First Instance as a means of alleviating the backlog of work facing the ECJ. Initially regarded as rather modest in nature, the SEA succeeded in developing renewed momentum for integration, not least by the establishment of the 'end-1992' deadline for completion of the SEM (see Armstrong and Bulmer 1998).

In the aftermath of the SEA, the European Council became concerned with various 'flanking measures', especially relating to economic and social cohesion. The first of these became important in the negotiations surrounding the 'Delors package'—a set of measures designed to help the less-developed EC economies, and those regions suffering from industrial decline, to contend with the competitive challenges posed by the SEM. Agreement was finally reached at the 1988 Brussels summit to provide the finance for such measures, including through new restrictions on CAP spending. The wish to avoid the SEM being developed at the cost of declining social provision lay behind the so-called Social Charter. This whole area was highly contested, as symbolized by the UK government's refusal to sign the charter at the December 1989 European Council in Strasbourg. Subsequently, in the negotiations leading to signature of the TEU in 1992, the UK secured an opt-out from the Social Protocol, an arrangement designed to put the Social Charter into practice.

The momentum for integration was maintained by a revival of interest in European Monetary Union (EMU), culminating in the June 1988 decision of the European Council to establish a committee under the chairmanship of Jacques Delors to report on its feasibility. The subsequent Delors Report, and the broad support to take discussion of EMU further (a position not shared by the UK government), contributed to the wish to engage in a further round of constitutional reform which culminated in the Maastricht negotiations and the TEU.

The Treaty on European Union (TEU)

Whilst the initial momentum for reform was largely attributable to EMU, this was rapidly joined by other major political impulses. These derived from the collapse of Communism in Eastern Europe and the new role expected of the EC in international relations after the Cold War. There was also a recognition that the number of applications for EC membership would consequently increase, and that work should commence on reforming the institutions to facilitate an effective political process within a Community of some twenty members. German unification in October 1990—creating the EC's first enlargement without formal accession—reawakened strong concerns about German power. For some states, especially France, the solution lay in containing this power through the deepening of European integration. Hence the support of its government and of President Mitterrand for the goal of EMU. Finally, there was a wish, as with the SEA, to tidy up constitutional provisions and make substantive policy changes beyond EMU.

The resultant Treaty, which was finalized at the Maastricht European Council in December 1991, had been prepared by two parallel IGCs. The structure of the Treaty is usually described as resembling a temple. Hence the 'roof', which sets out various broad objectives in the so-called 'common provisions', rests on three pillars. The first pillar consists of the EC activities, i.e. comprising the three Communities as further enhanced by the TEU itself. The second pillar provides for a Common Foreign and Security Policy (CFSP). The third pillar covers Justice and Home Affairs (JHA), i.e. police cooperation, combating drug-trafficking and fraud, regulating immigration from third countries, and similar matters. The policies contained in the last two pillars are given greater prominence than before, and are strengthened, but retain an intergovernmental basis under the

TEU. Finally, the plinth of the 'temple' consists of detailed relationships with the existing treaties, ratification arrangements, and so on. There are also eighteen protocols (e.g. the UK 'opt-outs' on EMU and the new social-policy provisions) and over thirty declarations.

The first of these pillars is of principal importance to economic integration. Once again the new provisions can be divided into policy provision and institutional provision. The most prominent policy development concerned the conditions and timetable set for achieving EMU by the end of the 1990s. In return for agreement to this, the economically weaker Member States insisted on the creation of a Cohesion Fund to enable resource transfers to their economies; this was also provided for. The EC12 had sought to give a treaty base to the substance of the Social Charter. However, the UK opted out of this Social Chapter, thus leaving the other eleven states to legislate under rather messy arrangements. There were numerous other policy developments—for instance, on the EU's infrastructure, consumer protection, and industrial policy.

From Maastricht to Amsterdam

The TEU provided the EU with a fairly full policy agenda for the rest of the decade, not least with the timetable for EMU. However, there was considerable political fallout from ratifying the TEU: the initial Danish rejection of the Treaty in a referendum (first no, then yes), a very close referendum vote in favour in France and the difficulties of securing parliamentary approval in the UK House of Commons. This situation raised questions about the EU's legitimacy, about its remoteness, and specifically about how to proceed with one of the TEU's commitments, namely to hold another IGC in 1996 to consider further treaty revisions. Despite these questions an IGC was opened in March that year. Its objectives were moderated somewhat and the entire exercise became rather protracted. On the one hand, there was an effort to undertake a more widely consultative exercise to try to pre-empt the questions of legitimacy and remoteness associated with the TEU. On the other hand, the UK government of John Major was politically unable to support significant moves for deeper integration owing to its small majority. Eventually the IGC was extended into mid-1997 so that it was to conclude after the UK general election. The election of the Blair Labour Government, and with a landslide majority, facilitated the conclusion of the IGC in Amsterdam.

The Amsterdam Treaty was a rather low-key reform compared to the TEU. In terms of policy reforms the main change was the introduction of an employment chapter into the treaty provisions. This development, originating in a Swedish proposal, was seen as offering some counter-balance to a perceived bias in the EMU provisions against concerns with unemployment. Another development was that the Blair government acceded to the Social Chapter, thus eliminating the UK opt-out negotiated by the Major government. Other areas strengthened were: environmental policy, public health, and consumer protection (the last two partly in response to the 'mad cow disease' crisis). There were further efforts to strengthen the Common Foreign and Security Policy. Perhaps the key policy emphasis of the Amsterdam Treaty was in launching a programme towards an 'area of freedom, security and justice', which involved moving some of the activities introduced in the TEU from the third pillar to the supranational first pillar. The policy changes associated with the Amsterdam Treaty were thus quite slight; arguably the 1996

Stability and Growth Pact, which requires continued fiscal prudence after the commencement of EMU, was of greater significance for the economics of the EU than the Amsterdam Treaty.

Institutionally, the Amsterdam Treaty made some fairly significant reforms, notably through enhancing the powers of the European Parliament and increasing the provision for majority voting in the Council (see below). However, the member governments failed to reach agreement on reforming the institutions ahead of eastward enlargement. One final change needs to be noted. The Amsterdam Treaty entailed revisions to, and the re-numbering of articles in, the Treaty on European Union. In the case of the EC Treaty the revisions and re-numbering were more fundamental, creating problems for students of the EU using out-of-date textbooks! The Treaty was ratified over the following twenty months or so, and was put into effect in May 1999.

One further development in the 1990s requires attention, and had already occurred by the time of the Amsterdam Treaty, namely the EFTA enlargement. Austria, Sweden, and Finland left EFTA and joined the EU in 1995. Originally the EFTA states had sought to develop a closer relationship with 'core Europe', particularly in light of the single market, through an arrangement known as the European Economic Area. However, with the end of the Cold War and the break-up of the Soviet Union, these states decided that their historical neutrality would no longer be incompatible with EU membership. In consequence, the EEA has very limited importance, since it only comprises three states (Iceland, Liechtenstein, and Norway).

Our account of the EU's development is now complete up to the end of the 1990s; current issues and problems are considered below. We turn now to how the EU's institutions function, focusing on the EC pillar of activities.

1.3 Economic integration and its policy-making context

Economic integration is heavily dependent on legislation. Legislation takes one of two forms. *Regulations* are used chiefly to legislate on quite technical matters. They have direct effect in the Member States. *Directives* are used where there are different national traditions and it is felt more appropriate just to legislate on the objectives of policy. National legislation must then be enacted in order to translate these goals into national law. A third legal instrument is the *decision*. This is not so much a method of legislating as one of taking administrative decisions, such as on competition policy cases. A decision of this kind may be no less significant, especially if it imposes a substantial fine on a company in breach of European competition law. Resort to *recommendations* is another option for legislation, but these do not have binding effect; they are not part of EC law.

To explain how legislation is developed, attention is first of all paid to the various EU institutions, and then brief attention is turned to other policy actors.

The EC's structure comprises three supranational institutions which are independent of the national governments: namely, the Commission, the European Parliament (EP), and the European Court of Justice (ECJ). As a counter-balance there are two powerful institutions comprising representatives of the national governments: the European Council and the Council of Ministers.

The *Commission* has consisted since the 1995 enlargement of twenty members (commissioners), with specific portfolios. The commissioners are appointed by the national governments but are then expected to detach themselves from national loyalty. Each commissioner has a group of political advisers to act as his or her 'eyes and ears'; they constitute the commissioner's 'cabinet'. One commissioner is appointed president and there are two vice-presidents. The five larger Member States (France, the UK, Germany, Spain, and Italy) have two commissioners each (see column three of Table 1.3). The Commission is divided into Directorates-General (DGs), which deal with specific policy areas. In 2000 there were thirty-five DGs and specific services, such as the legal and translation services. The overall staffing of the Commission is some 20,000 but only about 14,000 fulfil executive and policy functions, once translation and scientific research centre staff are discounted.

In the economic policy domain (the EC 'pillar' of the EU) the functions of the Commission are:

- the proposal of legislation;

- mediating between governments to achieve agreement on legislation;

Table 1.3 The Member States' weightings in the EU institutions

Member State	Qualified majority votes in Council	No. of Members of the European Parliament	Commissioners	Population (m.)
Austria	4	21	1	8.1
Belgium	5	25	1	10.1
Denmark	3	16	1	5.2
Finland	3	16	1	5.2
France	10	87	2	58.0
Germany	10	99	2	81.6
Greece	5	25	1	10.4
Ireland	3	15	1	3.6
Italy	10	87	2	57.1
Luxembourg	2	6	1	0.4
Netherlands	5	31	1	15.4
Portugal	5	25	1	9.4
Spain	8	64	2	39.2
Sweden	4	22	1	8.8
UK	10	87	2	58.2
TOTAL	87	626	20	370.7

Note: the above institutional provisions will change with effect from 2004/5.

- management of technical details of policy;
- representing the EU, particularly in commercial policy negotiations (for instance within the World Trade Organization);
- acting as the defender of collective EU interests;
- acting as guardian of the treaties by ensuring that EC law is upheld.

The Commission's strength has varied over the years but achieved particular influence under the presidency of Jacques Delors (1985–94). The Commission's influence is challenged most when national interests are in the ascendant, and this happened in the aftermath of the Delors presidency. The British Prime Minister, John Major, blocked the appointment of Jean-Luc Dehaene, the Belgian Prime Minister, as the Commission President to succeed Delors. The Luxembourger Jacques Santer was eventually appointed as a compromise candidate to serve from 1995 to 1999. Santer and his team were the first to be subject to parliamentary hearings in the EP as part of the appointment process. Commissioners' appointments were also adjusted to a five-year term in order to coincide with the EP's electoral periods. In the event, the Santer Commission did not serve its full term. In 1999, following concern expressed in the EP, a report of independent experts found evidence of instances of mismanagement, favouritism in issuing contracts, and a general lack of vigilance by Commissioners (Nugent 2000: 103–5). The Commissioners—known collectively as the College—resigned *en bloc* before their term had expired. A new Commission was installed under Romano Prodi, a former Italian Prime Minister, and it was given the task of reforming its own organization in addition to its regular policy tasks.

The *European Parliament*, originally known as the Assembly, consists of members (MEPs) who, since 1979, have been directly elected by Member States on five-year mandates.[5] Following the 1995 enlargement, the number of MEPs was fixed at 626 (for the composition, see Table 1.3). Their election normally takes place at five-year intervals (most recently in June 1999). Turn-out for EP elections remains low by comparison with national elections. The EP plenary sessions are held in Strasbourg for twelve week-long sessions each year. Meetings of its committees, which generally 'shadow' one or more of the Commission's DGs, are held in Brussels.

The EP has ways of calling to account the Commission and, to a much lesser degree, the Council of Ministers. It has the power to dismiss the Commission but has never done so. The EP came close to dismissing the Commission in early 1999. Only after Commission President, Jacques Santer, had agreed to the appointment of a special investigating committee was the sting drawn from a parliamentary motion of censure. As the committee's report led to the Commission's resignation, the EP could claim its powers were enhanced by this episode. Its chief contribution to EU policy-making is through the legislative process. However, its influence is dependent on the policy area, for the latter determines the extent of its procedural rights.

- Under the consultation procedure, which originally applied to all legislation, the EP merely gave its opinion and had no effective sanction over the real decision-making agency, the Council of Ministers.
- Under the 1970 and 1975 budget treaties the EP gained important powers in this policy area, including the power to reject the budget outright.

- Under the SEA the assent of the EP is needed in respect of the accession of new Member States and for Association Agreements with third countries. The TEU extended this procedure.

- The SEA also introduced the cooperation procedure, as a result of which certain legislation undergoes two readings in the EP. This procedure has now largely been superseded by co-decision, following the TEU and Amsterdam treaties.

Following the TEU the EP gained a new co-decision procedure (Article 251, of the consolidated Treaty establishing the EC, TEC). This goes beyond the cooperation procedure in that the EP has the additional power to reject; thus it can kill legislation taking this route if it so desires. Originally applying to fifteen policy areas following the Maastricht Treaty, it was extended to encompass 37 by the Amsterdam Treaty. The co-decision procedure puts the EP in the place of co-legislator with the Council of Ministers.

The picture, as will be gathered, is highly complex but reflects a gradual extension to the EP of new powers, which that institution uses to full effect (see Jacobs, Corbett, and Shackleton 2000).

The *European Court of Justice* consists of fifteen judges and nine advocates-general. The ECJ does not formulate policy but, in line with provisions in the treaties for referral, the ECJ's judgments on matters relating to the interpretation and application of EC law are cumulatively of great importance to the operation of the EU. The ECJ is assisted by a Court of First Instance.

The *Council of Ministers* consists of ministers of the Member States. It meets about 100 times per annum but in different guises according to the subject matter. Hence the Council of Agriculture Ministers deals with the CAP, the Council of Economics and Finance Ministers (Ecofin) with monetary policy matters, and so on. These two Councils, along with the Council of Foreign Ministers, meet most frequently, although a separate Council now deals with monetary policy for the twelve full participants in EMU. Meetings are chaired by one of the Member States, which holds the 'presidency' of the Council for a six-month period. The UK last held this post January–June 1998. The presidency has become an important office facilitating the EU's operation. Meetings of the Council are prepared by the Committee of Permanent Representatives and an associated committee system. These meetings are attended by national civil servants and aim to pave the way for political agreement by the Council.

The Council is empowered to take decisions by qualified majority rather than unanimous vote in a number of policy areas. This was provided for in the original EEC Treaty but majority voting was rarely practised due to the Luxembourg Compromise. The practice of majority voting increased first from the 1970s, following treaty changes relating to the budget, then following the SEA, the TEU, and the Amsterdam Treaty. There remains a preference for decision-making with the consent of all governments, but no single state can pursue a blocking strategy without the risk of simply being out-voted where majority voting applies. The dynamism of the Council of Ministers determines the effectiveness of the EU. The increased provision for majority voting assisted the EU's decision-making speed, particularly to meet the 1992 deadline for the SEM. Each Member State has to recognize that it will, on occasion, be in the minority, with a negative effect on its national sovereignty. The Council of Ministers is no longer a classic intergovernmental body owing to the departure from unanimous voting.

The exact weighting of the individual Member States is as set out in column one of Table 1.3. A vote by qualified majority requires at least sixty-two votes of the total of eighty-seven. As can be seen, the number of votes over-represents the small states, since Luxembourg receives one vote for approximately every 200,000 inhabitants, whereas Germany receives one vote for about every eight million of its population! Put another way: France, Germany, the UK, and Italy represent more than two-thirds of the EU's population but under half of the votes in the Council. This issue has become contentious in the 1990s, since recent and projected enlargements involve smaller states, so that the weighting of the larger ones is decreasing and may do so further unless reform of the voting system is agreed.

The *European Council* has, since its establishment in 1974, become a very powerful body. Comprised of the fifteen heads of state or government, the fifteen foreign ministers, the Commission president and a vice-president, it has had a hand in all the major EU decisions in the intervening period (the creation of the EMS, agreement on the single market, supervision of the SEA and TEU negotiations, decisions on enlargement, reform of the budget, the launching of EMU, employment policy, and so on). The European Council meets at least twice a year. Its decisions are political; transposition into EC law is left to the Council of Ministers. The European Council is important to the strategic development of the EU and of other joint activities (i.e. the other two 'pillars' of the TEU). It is the principal institution of the EU, being common to all three pillars of activity. It has become a major 'media event', however, which can detract from its efficiency.

A number of additional institutions also exist. Arguably the most important, by virtue of its influence in a specific policy area, is the European Central Bank, located in Frankfurt and established with the move to the final stage of EMU in 1999. This body, headed by Wim Duisenberg, is responsible for the day-to-day running of monetary policy under the single currency, including decisions on interest rates for the euro-zone. The Economic and Social Committee, a kind of parliament of interest groups, is consulted on most economic policy legislation but is overshadowed by the EP. The TEU created a Committee of the Regions. Its role reflects the increased involvement of subnational government in EU activities, most notably in regional policy. The Commission has sought to allay concerns that it is a centralizing agency by promoting links with regional authorities, some of which have important powers in their domestic context.

Surrounding the EU institutions are numerous lobby groups. There are some 500 such groups, which chiefly focus their activities on the Commission. The Commission is comparatively open to such lobbying, not least because it has no field agencies in the Member States; hence it needs information. Thus lobbies are an important part of the decision-making framework.

The result of all this is that policy-making consists of a dense network of contacts. The nature of the contacts depends on the precise form that policy-making takes in the area concerned (e.g. which procedure in the EP; what type of voting in the Council?), as well as on the efficiency of lobby groups (and there may be several in competition with each other). The increasing complexity of policy-making led to calls during the ratification of the TEU for greater openness and more decentralization of power following the so-called subsidiarity principle.[6]

Two characteristics of the EU's institutional structure unify the complex structure. First, the predominant style of economic policy-making is a regulatory one: it provides a *framework* for economic and political action that is largely left to the Member States themselves to enact and administer. The lack of large-scale supranational budgetary resources reinforces this regulatory approach at the expense of macroeconomic or redistributive activities. A characteristic of regulatory politics is the conduct of policy-making in relatively closed groups of policy specialists. Thus, if decision-making at the more routine level has a relatively low profile, this does not mean that the political dynamic is absent; rather, it is present in discussions between specialist national civil servants, Commission officials, interest group representatives, and committee members of the EP.

Secondly, national interests still loom large in these technical discussions. Thus behind an apparently technical debate about standardizing axle weights for heavy goods vehicles may stand national motor industries with different interests, governmental authorities faced with divergent financial implications for road improvement programmes, and so on. However, at the technical level individual national interests are often challenged. The increased utilization of qualified majority voting can mean that decisions can be reached against the wishes of a minority of governments, and enforced by EC law, which takes precedence over national law. What is important here, then, is that there are *supranational* interests challenging national ones. The supranational institutions—the Commission, the ECJ, and the EP—have their own power resources and these often come into play at the technical level.

1.4 The EU in the 21st century

The EU continues to have an extensive agenda for change in the new millennium. As so often in the past the agenda can be seen in terms of the issues of widening and deepening the EU.

The principal challenge is that posed by enlargement. Past enlargements, such as to the southern countries (Greece, Spain, and Portugal) or to the EFTAns (Austria, Finland, and Sweden) appear relatively uncontroversial compared to tests posed by the queue of eastern and south-eastern states currently seeking admission to the EU. In June 1993, and reflecting these new challenges, the Copenhagen European Council set down three explicit and one implicit conditions for membership.

- Stable institutions guaranteeing democracy, the rule of law, human rights and the protection of minorities;
- a functioning market economy, including the ability to cope with the rigours of competition in the EU; and
- the ability to adopt the existing policy inheritance (known as the *acquis communautaire*), including the goals of political, economic and monetary union.

- Implicitly, enlargement was also conditional on the EU's ability to absorb new members (itself dependent on reform of a number of policies, such as of the CAP).

These conditions recognized that not only are there major disparities in economic performance between the applicants and the existing states, but that most of the applicants are contending with the economic restructuring needed to overcome the legacy of state-run economies from the communist era as well as developing a secure liberal-democratic underpinning. Moreover, some existing policies, notably the CAP, and the structural funds, will require major surgery in order to be viable in a pan-European EU. The EU made some advances in preparing the way for enlargement through reforms of the budget, the CAP and the structural funds in the so-called 'Agenda 2000' reforms, agreed in March 1999 at the Berlin European Council.

In addition to the central and eastern European countries in this category (see Table 1.4) there are three south-eastern applicants: Cyprus, Malta, and Turkey. These three states present their own problems: the need for some accommodation between Greece and Turkey to pave the way for Cypriot entry, and the issue of human rights in Turkey. Malta and Cyprus are micro-states, which highlights a set of institutional issues. The vast size of Turkey is also an issue, raising policy questions especially concerning the potential for considerable labour migration.

With progress towards enlargement confirmed at the December 1999 European Council in Helsinki, attention could focus on other issues, most notably the so-called 'leftovers' from Amsterdam. They essentially comprised the measures needed to prepare the

Table 1.4 Current applications for EU membership

Country	Date applied	Status
A. South-Eastern European Countries		
Turkey	April 1987	1989 application frozen; reactivated 12/1999
Cyprus	July 1990	Negs.
Malta	July 1990	Negs. 2/2000
B. Central and Eastern European Countries		
Hungary	March 1994	Negs.
Poland	April 1994	Negs.
Romania	June 1995	Negs. 2/2000
Slovakia	June 1995	Negs. 2/2000
Latvia	October 1995	Negs. 2/2000
Estonia	November 1995	Negs.
Lithuania	December 1995	Negs. 2/2000
Bulgaria	December 1995	Negs. 2/2000
Czech Republic	January 1996	Negs.
Slovenia	June 1996	Negs.

Notes: 'Negs'. denotes that the negotiating process ahead of entry was launched in 1998. These negotiations were commenced for a smaller group of states, deemed to be more advanced in their preparedness. Negotiations for a wider group commenced in February 2000.
 These data take into account decisions taken at the Helsinki European Council, 10/11 December 1999.

EU institutions for enlargement up to 27 member states. Unlike with previous enlargements, the scale anticipated meant that it would be impossible to keep extending the existing decision-making rules and institutions incrementally. On this basis there would be no building able to accommodate all the MEPs and there would not be enough portfolios for the large number of Commissioners. In addition, the over-representation of small member states in the Council of Ministers would become problematic, with the vast majority of applicant states falling into this category. It had been expected that all these issues would be resolved at Amsterdam but, in the event, these reforms proved too controversial. In consequence, a further IGC was convened in February 2000 to facilitate these institutional reforms. In brief, what was agreed at the Nice European Council, held in December 2000, to bring these negotiations to a conclusion?

There has been a further significant extension of provision for QMV in the Council in order to facilitate decision-making efficiency, but some areas could not be included owing to national objections, such as the UK blocking QMV on taxation. The weighting of votes has been re-balanced to take account of enlargement. In addition, the Council may be required to demonstrate that its decisions command majority support of 62 per cent of the EU's population: a new means of checking on the legitimacy of its decisions. The EP gained a small increase in its powers, notably through a small extension of its co-decision powers. The allocation of numbers of MEPs has been re-designated: a total of 732 is now provided for in an EU of 27 states. The new allocations will take effect with the 2004 elections to the EP. The Commission's size will be one Commissioner per member state until the EU's membership reaches 27. The Treaty of Nice made some other policy changes, of which the largest was the creation of a Common European Security and Defence Policy. The Nice Treaty needs to be ratified by all member states before it comes into effect—most likely in 2002.

The Treaty of Nice has prepared the EU for enlargement in the middle of this decade. This will be a major development for integration. But, in the nearer term, the introduction of the euro in 2002 will arguably be the development in economic integration that affects European citizens most directly.

Discussion questions

1 How far has economic integration within the EU been subordinated to the achievement of political objectives?

2 How far has the ceding of sovereignty to supranational institutions influenced the course of economic integration within Europe?

3 'The shape of the EU's institutions reflects the need to harness national and common interests to the pursuit of specific policy goals.' Do you agree?

Further reading

For accounts of the history of integration, see Dinan (1999) or Urwin (1995). McCormick (1999) provides a good introduction to the EU, whereas Cram, Dinan, and Nugent (1999) give a good review of current issues: both are written from a political-science perspective. On the institutions, see Hix (1999), Nugent (1999), or Richardson (1996). For analysis of the policy process in the EU, see Peterson and Bomberg (1999) or Wallace and Wallace (2000). Lynch, Neuwahl, and Rees (2000) offer a useful review of the reforms introduced in the Maastricht and Amsterdam treaties. For an introduction to the issues associated with enlargement, see Avery and Cameron (1998). Finally, Bainbridge and Teasdale (1998) is a useful dictionary of the terminology of the EU.

Notes

1   The history of Britain's relationship towards integration cannot be dealt with in detail here. For an account, see George (1998). For an interpretation, see Bulmer (1992).

2   Qualified majority voting is a system whereby the importance of larger countries in relation to smaller ones is reflected in voting through the assignment of a weighting. However, the system over-represents smaller states (see below). This system continues to operate: see the chapter on the Council of Ministers in Nugent (1999).

3   In 1999, with the implementation of the Amsterdam Treaty, the EC Treaty was consolidated and re-numbered (see below). Article 235 became Article 308. Already, and somewhat confusingly, at Maastricht the EEC Treaty had already been re-named the Treaty establishing the European Community (TEC). Separate treaties remain for the ECSC and Euratom.

4   It is from this date onwards that one can refer to 'the EC', i.e. referring to the three Communities.

5   When states join the EU between elections, they elect their MEPs at the earliest opportunity for terms of office expiring on the date of the next EU-wide elections.

6   The subsidiarity principle calls for collective solutions within the EU only where the national level cannot provide them. However, some see subsidiarity as a call for power at the regional, sub-national level.

References

Armstrong, K. and Bulmer, S. (1998), *The Governance of the Single European Market* (Manchester: Manchester University Press).

Avery, G. and Cameron, F. (1998), *The Enlargement of the European Union* (Sheffield: Sheffield Academic Press).

Bainbridge, T. and Teasdale, A. (1998), *The Penguin Companion to European Union*, 2nd edn. (London: Penguin Books).

Bulmer, S. (1992), 'Britain and European Integration: Of Sovereignty, Slow Adaptation and Semi-Detachment' in S. George (ed.), *Britain and the European Community* (Oxford: Oxford University Press), 1–29.

Bulmer, S. and Wessels, W. (1987), *The European Council: Decision-Making in European Politics* (Basingstoke: Macmillan).

Cram, L., Dinan, D., and Nugent, N. (eds.) (1999), *Developments in the European Union* (Basingstoke: Macmillan).

Dinan, D. (1999), *Ever Closer Union: An Introduction to the European Community*, 2nd edn. (Basingstoke: Macmillan).

George, S. (1998), *An Awkward Partner: Britain in the European Community*, 3rd edn. (Oxford: Oxford University Press).

Hix, S. (1999), *The Political System of the European Union* (Basingstoke: Macmillan).

Jacobs, F., Corbett, R., and Shackleton, M. (2000), *The European Parliament* (London: John Harper Publishing).

Lynch, P., Neuwahl, N., and Rees, W. (eds.) (2000), *Reforming the European Union: From Maastricht to Amsterdam* (Harlow: Longman).

McCormick, J. (1999), *Understanding the European Union: A Concise Introduction* (Basingstoke: Macmillan).

Nugent, N. (1999), *The Government and Politics of the European Union*, 4th edn. (Basingstoke: Macmillan).

Peterson, J. and Bomberg, E. (1999), *Decision-Making in the European Union* (Basingstoke: Macmillan).

Richardson, J. (ed.), *European Union: Power and Policy-Making* (London: Routledge).

Scott, A. (1992), 'Fiscal Policy' in S. Bulmer, S. George, and A. Scott (eds.), *The United Kingdom and EC Membership Evaluated* (London: Pinter Publishers), 45–56.

Tsoukalis, L. (1997), *The New European Economy Revisited* (Oxford: Oxford University Press).

Urwin, D. (1995), *The Community of Europe*, 2nd edn. (Harlow: Longman).

Wallace, H., and Wallace, W. (eds.) (2000), *Policy-Making in the European Union*, 4th edn. (Oxford: Oxford University Press).

Chapter 2
The European Economy

Mike Artis and Nick Weaver

2.1 Introduction

The primary purpose of this chapter is to provide the reader with a statistical illustration of some basic economic features of the European Union (EU) and its constituent members. Some comparisons between the EU as whole and the USA and Japan and a brief examination of some possible future entrants to the EU are also made. Whilst such a statistical picture of the European economy is useful, some discussion of economic policy is essential. A key event was the adoption on 1 January 1999 of a single European currency by all but four of the members of the EU. In producing a statistical picture it is always difficult to decide what to include and how it should be presented. Presenting data relating to all variables of interest, for all the countries and for all the years would result in an information overload. The approach taken here is to present figures and tables illustrating the major economic indicators in the most recent year for which a complete and consistent data-set is available and to look at the behaviour of some of the variables over a longer period.

2.2 Population

At 376.7 million the population of the EU is greater than that of either of the other major economies; the USA's population is 273.4 million and Japan's is only 127 million. The situation is, however, not static. Several countries are currently negotiating admittance to the EU and the USA, Canada, and Mexico have formed the North American Free Trade Agreement (NAFTA). In terms of population the most notable feature of the EU's constituent members is that most of the population lives in just a few big countries. Roughly 80 per cent of the people live in just five countries; Germany, France, Italy, the UK, and Spain. The remaining smaller countries—the Netherlands, Greece, Portugal, Denmark,

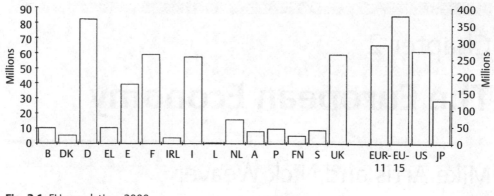

Fig. 2.1 EU population, 2000
Source: Eurostat (2000).

Ireland, and Luxembourg—together account for the remaining 20 per cent. As other countries join the EU, the dominance in terms of population of the Big Five will be reduced.

It is difficult to make any broad statements about population densities, but it is possible to discern a London–Milan axis around which are areas of relatively high density (more than 100 inhabitants per square kilometre). In contrast, much of Spain, Portugal, south and central France, the Irish Republic, Denmark, Sweden, Finland, and Greece outside the major urban centres, is relatively sparsely populated (less than 100 inhabitants per square kilometre).

2.3 **National income and expenditure**

There are various ways of measuring the size of an economy, with Gross Domestic Product (GDP) being the most commonly quoted. The GDP measure includes all goods and services for final consumption which are produced by the economic activity of producer units resident in an economy. It is a territorial measure. The other measure that is often used is Gross National Product (GNP). This measures the income earned by domestic citizens regardless of whether they earn their income at home or abroad. GNP equals GDP plus net property income from abroad. In fact there is only a small difference between GDP and GNP for most of the members of the EU (Ireland being the main exception) and for both the US and Japan.

A note of warning needs to be sounded about the use of either GDP or GNP as unqualified indicators of the size of an economy. Even in countries with advanced statistical services a large part of human activity goes unrecorded. Accounting techniques are not available to measure the value of un-marketed production (such as housework or DIY activities) nor to provide estimates of the costs of pollution and environmental destruction. Tax evasion and moonlighting give rise to a substantial 'underground' economy.

Despite the fact that the absence of broader measures has long been recognized as a serious problem, progress in this area is only slowly being made and as yet there is no widely available alternative to GDP and GNP that is consistently reported.

In order to make international comparisons GDP, which is initially calculated in terms of domestic currency, needs to be re-expressed in terms of some common or *numeraire* currency. Internationally this is usually done in terms of the US dollar, although any currency can be used. With the advent of monetary union this is increasingly done within the EU in terms of the Euro. However, the use of market exchange rates when making international comparisons has been criticized on the grounds that it gives rise to a systematic bias (Gilbert and Kravis 1954). Market exchange rates do not necessarily reflect the amount of goods that can be bought with a currency—that is, the purchasing power of a currency in terms of the volume of goods it commands. This is because the market exchange rate is the result of a whole variety of forces including not only the supply and demand for foreign exchange required to match the flows of real goods and services but also the speculative activities of foreign exchange dealers, capital flows, and so on. To the extent that these factors do not influence the purchasing power of the currency in a country, the market exchange rate will not be a good measure of the purchasing power of a currency in a country.

Various ways have been proposed to get around this problem. One simple method, proposed by the *Economist*, is the use of the 'Big Mac' index. This uses the relative prices of Big Macs in two countries to construct a new exchange rate. Big Macs are used because they are a standardized commodity whose price is widely known. However, price level differences between countries vary for different commodities and a more sophisticated measure using a similar principle to the Big Mac index but taking into account a larger basket of goods is required. Purchasing power parity estimates attempt to do just this, their aim being to provide an exchange rate that enables a proper comparison to be made of the quantities or volumes that can be purchased.

The measures of purchasing power parity (PPP) used in this chapter, Purchasing Power Standards (PPS), are produced by *Eurostat* (the EU's statistical office), which calculates them using methods established by the International Comparison Project (ICP) of the United Nations. They are calculated on the basis of a list of products chosen for their representativeness and comparability. For each product a price ratio is established and a weighted average across all the products in the list can then be calculated for each country. These weighted average price parities give an alternative (PPP) set of exchange rates that can be applied to the original national currency estimates of GDP to give PPP estimates of GDP. A scaling procedure ensures that the EU's total GDP in PPSs is the same as in Euros. Figure 2.2 shows GDP at current market prices in billions of Euros and in billions of Euros PPS for each of the fifteen member countries. It can be clearly seen that a comparison of the relative sizes of the countries is influenced by whether market exchange rates or PPS measures are used. Whichever measure of GDP is used the dominance of the five biggest EU economies—Germany, France, Italy, the UK, and Spain—is again clear. Together they account for roughly 80 per cent of the total GDP of the fifteen.

Scaling GDP by population gives us GDP per capita figures. Figure 2.3 shows GDP per capita in both PPS and Euros. Here the effect of adjusting the GDP figures for PPS is clear. All the countries having a below EU average per capita income (Portugal, Greece, Spain,

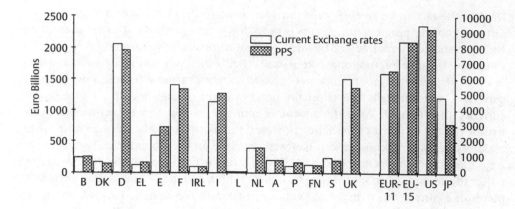

Fig. 2.2 GDP at current market prices, evaluated at current exchange rates and in PPS, 2000
Source: Eurostat (2000).

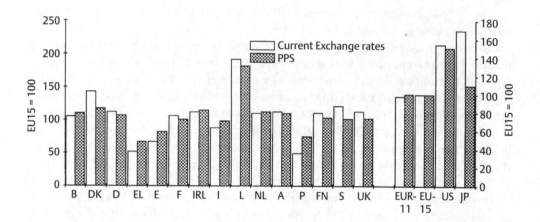

Fig. 2.3 GDP per capita in both PPS and Euros, indices
Source: Eurostat (2000).

and Italy) are in real (PPS) terms richer than would appear to be the case if market exchange rates instead of some measure of Purchasing Power Parities were used. This is the systematic bias that Gilbert and Kravis noted. The spread is still considerable, with the GDP(PPS) per capita in the richest country—Luxembourg—being roughly 2.7 times that in the poorest—Greece. In terms of the more populous countries, Germany, France, and the UK are above the EU average and Italy and Spain below it.

If one disaggregates the countries into regions the differences are even more marked. Inner London has a GDP per capita some 222 per cent of the EU average, while there are some 50 regions below 75 per cent of the average, including all thirteen of the Greek regions and all but Lisbon out of Portugal's seven regions. The others are mainly in the 'new' *Bundesländer* of Germany (nine), Spain (ten) and Italy (six, all in the south); there is one in Austria, one in Finland, and four in the UK. Over 20 per cent of the EU's population live in these regions. Pronounced differences can be found in Germany and the UK: in the latter, there are regions with only a third of Inner London's GDP per head, while there is even greater disparity between Germany's richest region—Hamburg—and some of the poorer regions of the east. Other countries have far less diversity. In Sweden, for example, there is no large difference between the highest—Stockholm (122 per cent) and the lowest—Östra Mellansverige (91 per cent).

2.4 **Economic growth**

In addition to looking at the static picture that the statistics discussed above provide, it is interesting to look at how the economies have grown. To study the change over time it is necessary to abstract from price changes so that comparisons in terms of volumes can be made. This is done by adjusting the GDP figures for changes in the level of prices; that is, for inflation. The most appropriate measure of inflation in this context involves a weighted basket of the prices of all products (not just those purchased by households). This measure of inflation, the GDP deflator, enables nominal GDP, which is expressed in current terms, to be converted into real GDP, expressed in terms of a constant base year.

Figure 2.4 shows GDP per capita growth over the last decade. Comparison with Figure 2.3 reveals that the countries with the lowest GDP per capita all grew faster than the EU average. Luxembourg, the richest, also grew fast—a factor directly attributable to the growth of the EU institutions located there. Since population growth in the EU countries has not been uniform, growth of GDP per capita tells a different story than GDP growth *per se*. Many of the faster growing economies have also been countries with faster growing populations. Greece, which was one of the fastest growing economies, falls far down the list when population growth is taken into account and per capita rather than growth *per*

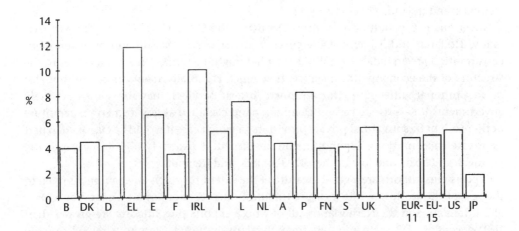

Fig. 2.4 GDP per capita growth, 1991–2000
Source: Eurostat (2000).

se is measured. Figures such as these enable us to examine the extent to which the levels of GDP per capita of the EU economies are converging. Here we must be aware that convergence of levels requires divergence in growth rates. Thus for GDP per capita to converge across the economies of the EU, the poorest countries must be expected to grow faster than the richer ones.

2.5 Disaggregation of GDP

GDP can, in theory, be derived in three ways: by finding the total expenditure, value added, or factor incomes in an economy. Each approach helps reveal different aspects of the economic structure of an economy.

The disaggregation of GDP by expenditure

Total expenditure in an economy can be found by summing private consumption (C), government consumption (G), investment (I), changes in stocks by businesses (ΔS), and the balance of trade (X – M).

$$GDP_{expenditure} = C + I + \Delta S + G + (X - M).$$

Private consumption is made up of household expenditure on food, clothing, housing services, household goods, transport, and health. Government consumption consists of expenditure on health, education, defence, and social security payments. Investment includes expenditure on machinery, transport equipment, and building construction. Exports of goods and services minus imports give the balance of trade. Figure. 2.5 shows GDP disaggregated by expenditure for 2000. As might be expected, private consumption figures for most of the countries are close to the EU average. The noteworthy exceptions are Greece, Portugal, and the UK, where private consumption is considerably higher, and Denmark and Ireland, where it is lower.

Government expenditure is high in Denmark, the UK, and Greece and low in Germany, Holland, and Belgium. Differences in the shares of private and of government consumption are an indicator not only of what might be termed 'real' differences in the structure of the economy (for instance, how much is actually spent on health) but also of institutional differences (for instance, health services may be almost entirely government-run—as is the case in Denmark—and classified as government expenditure or there might be substantial private provision, in which case it would be classified in part as private consumption). Expenditure on investment is relatively high in Luxembourg, Portugal, and Spain and low in the UK, Denmark, and Ireland.

Exports plus imports are a good measure of the extent to which an economy is open to the rest of the world. By this measure the most open economies are Luxembourg, Belgium, Ireland, and the Netherlands, all of whose exports plus imports are greater than 100 per cent of GDP. Spain and Italy are both relatively closed. Germany, Ireland, and the Netherlands all have positive trade balances whilst Portugal, Luxembourg, and Greece all have deficits.

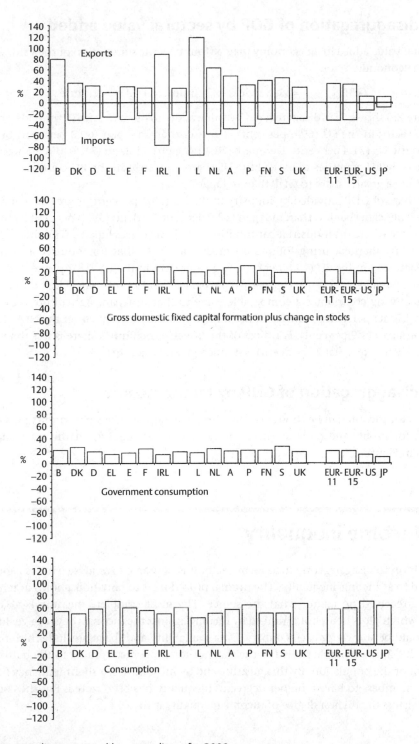

Fig. 2.5 GDP disaggregated by expenditure for 2000

Source: Eurostat (2000).

The disaggregation of GDP by sectoral value added

The total value added in an economy may be found by the summation of the value added of each economic sector.

$$\text{GDP}_{\text{value added}} = \text{VA Services} + \text{VA Industry} + \text{VA Agriculture.}$$

Figure 2.6 shows GDP disaggregated by value added. The share of GDP provided by the service sector in the EU (69.6 per cent) is greater than in Japan (60.2 per cent) but less than in the US (71.4 per cent). Denmark (72.1 per cent), Finland (71.5) and France (71.5) are the only EU countries to exceed the US share. In nearly all the EU countries services contribute a greater share to GDP than in Japan.

The share of GDP provided by industry in the EU (28.1 per cent) is greater than in the US (26.8 per cent) but less than in Japan (37.9 per cent). Ireland (39.3) per cent is the only EU country where the industrial contribution clearly surpasses Japan's. The share of GDP provided by manufacturing follows a similar pattern to that for industry as a whole. Manufacturing in the EU (19.8 per cent) is greater than in the US (18.2 per cent) but less than in Japan (24.3 per cent). Germany (23.6 per cent) is the only large EU country where manufacturing contributes a comparable share to that in Japan. Agriculture provides a slightly higher percentage of GDP in the EU (2.3 per cent) than in either the USA (1.8 per cent) or Japan (1.9 per cent). For most of the fifteen agriculture's share is less than 4 per cent. Only in Greece (at 12 per cent) is it much greater than this.

The disaggregation of GDP by factor income

Total factor income can be thought of as being made up of wages plus profits plus rents. Figures for profits and rents are notoriously difficult to acquire but the wage share is shown in Figure 2.7.

2.6 Income inequality

In addition to disaggregating income by factor it is desirable to analyse what is generally referred to as income inequality. The normal procedure is to rank households in terms of income received no matter what the source. The most complete measure is a Lorenz curve, which plots households ranked by income against the income they receive. Ideally one would be shown for each country. Data availability and space preclude this; instead Figure 2.8 shows a simple statistic—the share of total income accruing to the bottom 40 per cent of the population. By this measure and by most others, a slight tendency for the poorer members to have a higher degree of inequality has been noted. But the country that registers the highest degree of income inequality is the UK.

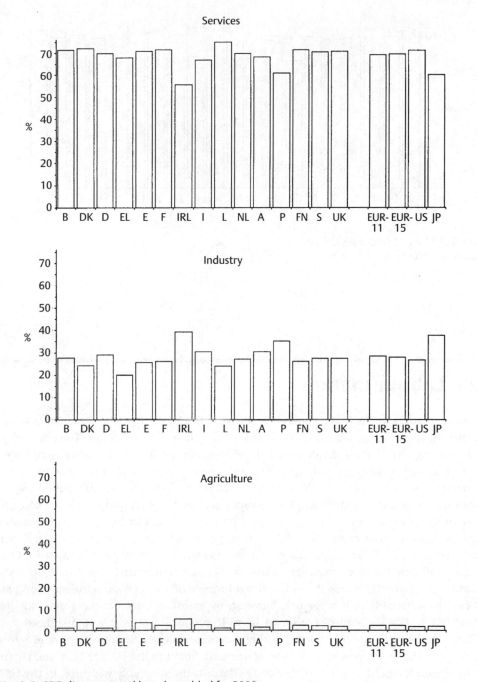

Fig. 2.6 GDP disaggregated by value added for 2000

Source: Eurostat (2000).

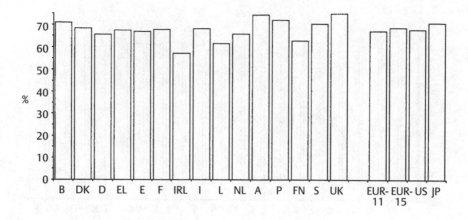

Fig. 2.7 Share of wages in GDP, 2000
Source: Eurostat (2000).

2.7 **Labour market**

The standard procedure when analysing the basic features of the labour market involves distinguishing the population of working age from the total population. The population of working age is then divided into three mutually exclusive and all-encompassing categories—the unemployed, persons in employment and the inactive. The unemployed plus the employed together constitute the labour force. From these categories various measures such as employment/population ratios (employment as a percentage of the population of working age), activity rates (the labour force as a percentage of the population of working age), and unemployment rates (the number of unemployed as a percentage of the labour force) can be calculated. International comparability is again difficult because countries' statistical services tailor their own data to their national requirements and the political significance of the statistics renders them particularly vulnerable to interference. Eurostat, by adjusting national measures with the help of an EU-wide labour force survey, aims to produce comparable standardized statistics. The most commonly quoted of these measures is the unemployment rate. Figure 2.9 shows the development since 1960 of unemployment in the EU, the USA, and Japan. The unemployment rate in the EU clearly contrasts unfavourably with that in the USA and Japan.

Figure 2.10 shows the current unemployment situation in the EU: at 9.2 per cent the rate is higher than in both the USA (4.4 per cent) and Japan (5 per cent). Unemployment rates vary widely between the EU countries, with Spain having the highest rates (15.8 per cent) and Luxembourg the lowest (2.7 per cent).

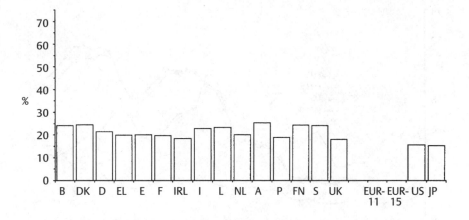

Fig. 2.8 Income share accruing to the lowest 40 per cent of households, 2000
Source: Eurostat (2000).

Figure 2.11 gives figures for male and female unemployment and youth unemployment. The unemployment rate for females is 50 per cent higher than for males in the EU, 10 per cent higher than for males in Japan and is 10 per cent less for females in the USA. Again there are wide differences across countries. The differences are greatest in Greece, Italy, Portugal, and Belgium, where the female rate is more than 100 per cent greater than the male rate. The UK is the only EU country where the unemployment rate for females is less than for males. Unemployment has particularly affected the young. Youth unemployment rates are generally far higher than the average. In Spain, Italy, Greece, and Ireland one in four of those aged less than 25 is unemployed. Only in Germany, with its exceptional training policy, is youth unemployment less than the national average. It is also interesting to note the regional variation in unemployment rates, with some countries having very marked imbalances: in Italy the rate varies between 3.9 per cent in Alto Adige in the North and 28.7 per cent in Calabria in the South.

2.8 **Trade**

A major economic justification for the establishment and growth of the EU arises from the expansion of opportunities to exploit competitive advantages that result from the removal of barriers to trade. The beneficial effects of the removal of such barriers in theory are that high-cost sources of supply are replaced by lower-cost sources. Such a process is referred to as *trade creation*. Undoubtedly, the establishment of the EU has led to

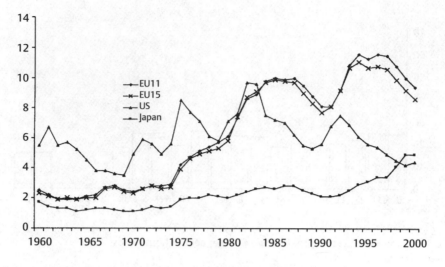

Fig. 2.9 Unemployment rates in the EU11, EU15, USA, and Japan, 1960–2000
Source: Eurostat (2000).

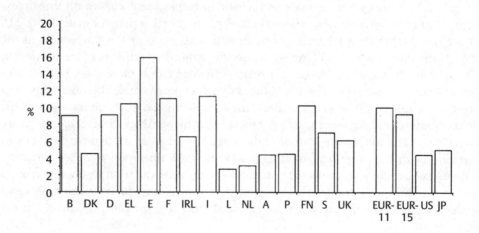

Fig. 2.10 Standardized unemployment rates in the EU countries, plus EU averages and US and Japanese rates, 2000
Source: Eurostat (2000).

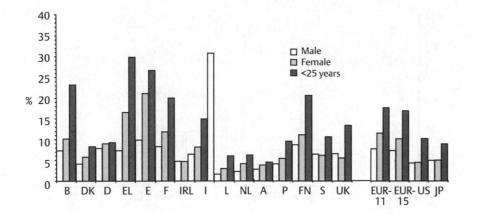

Fig. 2.11 Male, female and youth (< 25 years) unemployment rates, 2000
Source: Eurostat (2000).

substantial trade creation. There are, however, other less beneficial effects associated with these aspects of the EU commercial policy which have led to high-cost sources of supply supplanting lower-cost sources—a process referred to as *trade diversion*. (Chapter 3 provides a thorough analysis of these concepts.)

Figure 2.12 shows the degree of openness—as measured by Exports plus Imports as a percentage of GDP, divided by two. The degree of openness, measured in this way, shows that the EU-11 group (the original member countries of the Euro-area), and to an even greater extent the EU-15 as a whole, are only slightly less closed to the rest of the world than the USA and Japan. This is in line with the general rule that the larger the economy, the less open it will be. That 'law' is exemplified strongly with openness being highest in Luxembourg, the Netherlands, Ireland, Belgium, and Austria and of a similar and lower order of magnitude in the big economies the UK, France, Germany, and Italy.

2.9 Future entrants to the EU

The number of countries in the EU has grown considerably since its foundation, and, despite many problems, a number of countries are queuing up to join. At the time of writing most non-EU European countries are viewed as possible future entrants. They are often divided into three distinct groups on the basis of institutional and economic characteristics: the European Free Trade Association (EFTA) countries, the Central and East European Countries (CEECs), and the Mediterranean countries. Statistical data for EU applicants are given in Table 2.1.

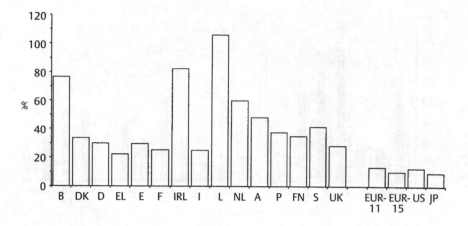

Fig. 2.12 Degree of openness in the EU, USA and Japan, 2000 (exports plus imports divided by two as percentage of GDP figures are for trade in goods only)
Source: Eurostat (2000).

Table 2.1 Central and East European and the Mediterranean applicants: GDP (€ bn.), GDP per capita, and percentage of employment in agriculture

	GDP bn. Euro	GDP/capita Index	Agricultural employment (%)
Bulgaria	11	23	25.7
Cyprus	8.1	78	9.6
Czech Rep.	50.1	60	5.5
Estonia	4.6	36	9.4
Hungary	42.4	49	7.5
Latvia	5.7	27	18.8
Lithuania	9.5	31	21.0
Malta	3.1	42	1.8
Poland	140.7	39	19.1
Romania	33.9	27	40.0
Slovakia	18.1	46	8.2
Slovenia	17.4	68	11.5
Turkey	175.8	37	42.3
EU15	7,585.6	100	5.2

The EFTA countries

The EFTA countries—Norway, Iceland, Switzerland, and Liechtenstein—are all relatively rich stable countries with economies roughly similar to the richer of the existing members of the EU. Switzerland and Norway have, for the present, decided against joining the EU, and Iceland, because of fear for its fishing interests, and Liechtenstein are unlikely to apply in the near future. However these countries already have most of the benefits of access to the EU's market through their membership of the European Economic Area (EEA). This aims to reduce frontier barriers and to allow the free movement of services, capital, and workers. Agriculture, notably, is excluded.

A Centre for Economic Policy Research (CEPR) (1993) report estimated that there may be some gain in terms of the EU's budget if EFTA countries were to become full members because their GDP per capita is something like 35 per cent higher than the EU average. The EFTA countries could expect to be net contributors and would be unlikely to receive structural funds allocated to poor regions. However the heavy dependence of the EFTA countries on the EU for trade means that there are potentially large gains to be made from participating in the single market. The CEPR report estimated that increased competition would reduce costs and boost productivity, raising EFTA's GDP by up to 5 per cent. Full membership would entail adoption of the EU's Common Agricultural Policy (CAP) by the EFTA countries. This could cause problems for the EFTA countries because their agriculture is even more heavily subsidized than the EU's (EU subsidies are roughly equal to 49 per cent of the value of farm output; EFTA countries' subsidies average 68 per cent of farm output and Swiss subsidies as much as 80 per cent.)

Within the EEA, the EU's competition policy must be applied to cross-border trade in manufactured goods. Full membership of the EU requires competition policy to be applied to a much wider range of domestic activities. This would restrict much of the state aid to industry and restrictive business practices that are common in the EFTA countries.

The Central and East European Countries

The Central and East European Countries—Bulgaria, the Czech Republic, Estonia, Hungary, Latvia, Lithuania, Poland, Romania, Slovakia, and Slovenia,—are all former communist countries and they are relatively poorer than the EU and have until recently had weak institutional links with the EU. Relative to the EU, the CEECs are all fairly poor. All these factors would make the CEECs eligible for large grants from both the Structural Fund and the CAP were they to become members.

The Mediterranean applicants

The Mediterranean applicants—Turkey, Cyprus, and Malta—have for a long time had close links with the EU but for a variety of reasons have not yet come close to membership. The EU–Turkey Association agreement of 1963 specifically mentioned the possibility of Turkey's eventual accession to the Community after a 22-year transitional period. As things stand both the EFTA countries and the CEECs seem to have pushed into the queue ahead of Turkey.

2.10 **European Monetary Union**

The Maastricht Treaty requires sufficient economic convergence to create the conditions for European Monetary Union (EMU). How 'sufficient' was to be defined was set out in criteria in relation to fiscal stance (budget deficits and debt burdens), inflation performance, interest rates, and exchange rate stability. How far these were met was judged by the European Council in May 1998 in part on the basis of a Convergence Report (1998) produced by the European Commission. Two countries, Denmark and the UK, had notified the Council prior to the meeting that they did not intend to participate in the single currency in 1999. Figure 2.13 illustrates the values used in the May 1998 decision.

The exact criteria are set out below, together with some relevant statistical information included in the Report. It is important to note that the notion of economic convergence associated with these criteria refers essentially to 'nominal convergence', which should be distinguished from what might be referred to as 'real economic convergence'. Real economic convergence is the process of equalization of national/regional GDP per capita and the convergence of economic structures and institutions.

Budget deficits and debt burdens

Budget deficits are the difference between government expenditure (including interest payments on debt) and receipts. Such deficits are financed either by borrowing, which is usually done by selling bonds, or by selling foreign-exchange reserves or other nationally owned assets including the privatization of publicly owned enterprises. Controlling the size of government has been the thrust of much policy. This has meant that, rather than just controlling deficits, policy has been aimed at trying to reduce government expenditure, partly because it has been thought that political expediency rules out increased taxation. The protocol on convergence criteria in the Treaty requires that 'at the time of the examination the Member State is not the subject of a Council decision under Article 104c(6) of this treaty that an excessive deficit exists' (CEC 1992: 185).

More specifically, an excessive deficit would be deemed to exist if the ratio of planned or actual government deficit to gross domestic product exceeds a reference value, unless either the ratio has declined substantially and continuously and reached a level that comes close to the reference value; or, alternatively, the excess over the reference value is only exceptional and temporary and the ratio remains close to the reference value (p. 27), where the reference value for the ratio of planned or actual government deficit to gross domestic product at market prices is 3 per cent (p. 183). Asset-selling can only be a temporary measure and continuous budget deficits lead to the accumulation of debt. Accumulated debt may become a problem if it tempts governments to 'inflate away' the burden of repayment and requires the assignment of resources to service the interest on it.

The second consideration, under the excessive deficit procedure, pertains to the level of government debt. Here the criterion is 'whether the ratio of government debt to gross domestic product exceeds a reference value, unless the ratio is sufficiently diminishing or

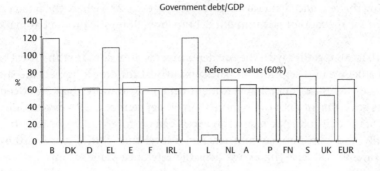

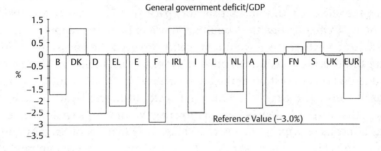

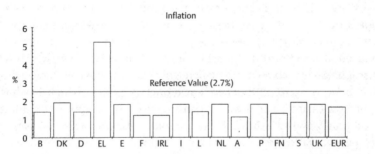

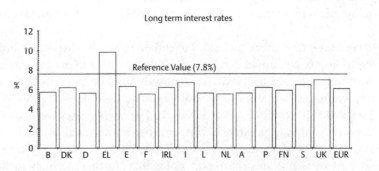

Fig. 2.13 Four measures of convergence in the EU countries at May 1998
Source: Eurostat (2000).

approaching the reference value at a satisfactory pace' (p. 27), where the reference value is '60 per cent for the ratio of government debt to gross domestic product at market prices' (p. 183).

Article 104c(6), together with the further protocols, indicates that the fiscal criteria are subject to a degree of discretion. In particular, whilst minimum targets are specified by the reference values—a general government deficit of no more than 3 per cent of GDP and a gross government debt of no more than 60 per cent of GDP—caveats are provided. In respect of the deficit it appears that an excess can be 'forgiven' if 'the ratio has declined substantially and continuously and reached a level that comes close to the reference value . . . or, alternatively, the excess over the reference value is only exceptional and temporary and the ratio remains close to the reference value'. In respect of the debt ratio, it appears that an excess can be forgiven if 'the ratio is sufficiently diminishing or approaching the reference value at a satisfactory pace' (p. 27). Should a Member State fail under one of these criteria, then the Commission would prepare a report which 'shall also take into account whether the government deficit exceeds the government investment expenditure and take into account all other relevant factors, including the medium term economic and budgetary position of the Member State' (p. 27). The intellectual rationale for these fiscal convergence criteria, whilst not spelt out in the Treaty, is to be found in the argument that excessive debt is a temptation to governments to manipulate a surprise inflation as a means of wiping out its real value. The analysis of Sargent and Wallace (1981) was responsible for suggesting that, at some point, a large enough ratio of debt to GDP implies monetization and inflation. Neither Sargent and Wallace nor the architects of the Treaty are able to indicate critical magnitudes for this ratio, and the reference values quoted in the Treaty have been heavily criticized (see, particularly, Buiter and Kletzer 1992; Buiter *et al.* 1992) for their apparent arbitrariness.

There is an additional point that must be borne in mind, however, which is the critical need for fiscal flexibility. In a context where governments have eschewed any ability to cope with shocks by resort to independent monetary policy (which is what monetary union implies: see Chapter 12), the fiscal convergence criteria appear to inhibit resort to a flexible fiscal policy as a substitute. There are some fundamental reasons why the 3 per cent and 60 per cent ratios are quite tough constraints aside from the incidence of below-average growth: public-service-sector productivity tends to grow less quickly than economy-wide productivity, implying that a greater level of expenditure is called for over time so as to maintain the same real level of provision (Leslie 1993); and taxes are always unpopular.

Five Member States (Denmark, Ireland, Luxembourg, the Netherlands, and Finland) were not the subject of a Council decision under Article 104c(6) on the existence of an excessive government deficit by 1998 and so already fulfilled the criterion. The Report noted that 'Government deficits have generally been brought down significantly during the second stage of EMU from the levels reached in 1993, when they were swollen by the effects of recession' and that 'Substantial further progress was made by Member States in 1997.' The deficits in 14 Member States in 1997 were either below or equal to reference value (3 per cent of GDP), and the report notes that 'further declines in deficits are expected in 1998.'

The government debt ratio was below the reference value (60 per cent of GDP) in 1997 in only four Member States (France, Luxembourg, Finland, and the United Kingdom), but all the other countries have succeeded in reversing the earlier upward trend except for Germany. This the report attributes to the 'exceptional costs of unification'. On this basis the Commission's Report recommended to the Council the abrogation of the excessive deficit decisions for Belgium, Germany, Spain, France, Italy, Austria, Portugal, Sweden, and the United Kingdom.

Inflation

The criterion on price stability referred to in the first indent of Article 109j(1) of this treaty shall mean that a Member State has a price performance that is sustainable and an average rate of inflation, observed over a period of one year before the examination, that does not exceed by more than one and a half percentage points that of, at most, the three best performing Member States in terms of price stability. Inflation shall be measured by means of the consumer price index on a comparable basis, taking into account differences in national definitions (CEC, 1998: 185).

The measure used to provide this comparable basis is the harmonized index of consumer prices (HICPs), which provides for greater comparability than national consumer price indices. The average rate of inflation for each country is calculated as the percentage change in the average HICP in the latest 12 months relative to the average index in the preceding 12 months. The reference value calculated in the Report was based on calculations done using the latest available information (i.e. January 1998), when the three best inflation performers were France, Ireland, and Austria, and the reference value was 2.7 per cent. All the countries—apart from Greece—had average inflation rates below this reference value and in the view of the Commission the structural changes (both institutional and behavioural) which have played an important role in achieving price stability and the developments in unit labour costs and other price indices gave strong reasons for believing that the current low inflation performance in all these 14 Member States would be sustainable.

Interest rates

One of the major ways of financing a budget deficit is by the selling of government bonds. These bonds are one of the most secure forms of investment and in most EU countries the market for them is one of the largest sectors of the capital market. Other 'private' interest rates will tend to be higher, indicating the greater risks. Different governments sell different forms of bonds and comparison is again complicated and the rather loose description 'long-term interest rates' covers a whole range of different bond yields.

The criterion on the convergence of interest rates referred to in the fourth indent of Article 109j(1) of the Treaty means that, 'observed over a period of one year before the examination, a Member State has had an average long-term interest rate that does not exceed by more than two percentage points that of, at most, the three best performing States in price stability. Interest rates shall be measured on the basis of long-term government bonds or comparable securities, taking into account differences in national definitions' (p. 186).

More precisely the assessment was based on the interest rates on comparable 10-year benchmark bonds, using an average rate over the latest 12 months with the convergence limit being the unweighted average of the interest rate in the three countries with the lowest inflation rate plus 2 per cent. These are, it must be emphasized, not necessarily the countries with the lowest interest rates, and this is a problem to the extent that, if the interest rates were being construed as an index of sustainable inflation performance, it might have been more appropriate to base the convergence limit on the countries with the best interest rate performance. In January 1998 the reference value was 7.8 per cent. Again, all the countries, aside from Greece, had average long-term interest rates below the reference value.

Discussion questions

1 What are the main problems involved in making international comparisons of countries' GDP? Illustrate with respect to the Member States of the EU.

2 Outline the Maastricht 'convergence criteria'. How closely did the EU countries meet these in the qualifying examination in 1998?

3 Describe how you would assess the level of development and the economic strength of an economy. Illustrate your answer by reference to the Member States of the EU.

Further reading

There is a variety of sources of data on the economies of the EU; noteworthy among these would be many of the publications of the OECD, the IMF, and several of the institutions of the UN. However, the statistics produced by Eurostat are incomparable as far as standardization and inter-country comparability are concerned. The institution, as well as producing a large number of annual, quarterly, or monthly reports, maintains a large statistical database. The most up-to-date source of information on these is the Eurostat home page on the Internet (http://europa.eu.int).

References

Anderson, V. (1991), *Alternative Economic Indicators* (London: Routledge).

Barrell, R. (1992) (ed.), *Economic Convergence and Monetary Union in Europe* (Association for the Monetary Union of Europe and the National Institute of Economic and Social Research; London: Sage).

Buiter, W., and Kletzer, K. (1992), 'Reflections on the Fiscal Implications of a Common

Currency', in A. Giovannini and C. Mayer (eds.), *European Financial Integration* (Cambridge: Cambridge University Press)., 221–44

Corsetti, G., and Roubini, N. (1992), *Excessive Deficits: Sense and Nonsense in the Treaty of Maastricht* (Discussion Paper No. 750; London: Centre for Economic Policy and Research).

CEC (1992), Commission of the European Communities, *Treaty on European Union* (Luxembourg: CEC).

CEC (1993), *European Economy*, No. 54 (Luxembourg: CEC).

CEC (1994), *Growth, Competitiveness, Employment*, White Paper (Luxembourg: CEC).

CEC (1998), *The Convergence Report 1998 Growth and Employment in the Stability-Oriented Framework of EMU* (1998 Annual Economic Report; Luxembourg: CEC).

CEPR (1993), Centre for Economic Policy Research, *Is Bigger Better? The Economics of EC Enlargement* (Monitoring European Integration 3, Annual Report, 1992; London: CEPR).

Eurostat (1985), *Purchasing Power Parities and Gross Domestic Product in Real Terms*, Results, 2 C (Luxembourg: CEC).

Eurostat (1988), *Labour Force Survey*, Methods and Definitions, 3 E (Luxembourg: CEC).

Eurostat (1989), *Labour Force Survey*, Results 3 C (Luxembourg: CEC).

Eurostat (1992), *Europe In Figures* (Luxembourg: CEC).

Eurostat (1993), *National Accounts ESA: Aggregates 1970–1991*, 2 C (Luxembourg: CEC).

Eurostat (1996), *Europe in Figures* (Luxembourg: CEC).

Eurostat (2000), http://europa.eu.int/comm/eurostat/

Gilbert, M., and Kravis, I. B. (1954), *An International Comparison of National Products and the Purchasing Power of Currencies: A Study of the United States, the United Kingdom, France, Germany and Italy* (Paris: Organization for European Economic Cooperation).

Leslie, D. (1993), *Advanced Macroeconomics: Beyond IS/LM* (London: McGraw-Hill).

OECD (1993), Organization for Economic Cooperation and Development, *Economic Outlook, Historical Statistics 1960–1990* (Paris: OECD).

—— (1994), *The OECD Jobs Study* (Paris: OECD).

Sargent, T., and Wallace, N. (1981), 'Some Unpleasant Monetarist Arithmetic', *Federal Reserve Bank of Minneapolis Quarterly Review*, 5/3 (Fall): 1–17.

UN and CEC (1986), United Nations and Commission of the European Communities, *World Comparisons of Purchasing Powers and Real Product for 1980; Phase IV of the International Comparison Project: Part I: Summary Results for 60 Countries* (New York: UN).

UNDP (2000), United Nations Development Programme, *Human Development Report* (New York: UN).

Chapter 3
The Economic Analysis of Preferential Trading Areas

Lynden Moore

3.1 Introduction

The EC was established in 1957 as a *customs union*: all tariffs and quotas were abolished in stages on trade between member countries, and a common external tariff (CET) was imposed on imports from outside. By the end of 1992, under the Single European Act of 1986, other non-tariff barriers with respect to standardization and public procurement had also been removed.

In 1973 the EC also formed a *free trade area* (FTA) in manufactures with the remaining members of the European Free Trade Area (EFTA). This involved the removal of all barriers to trade in manufactures between member countries, but the EFTA members retained their own level of tariffs on imports from third countries (that is, those outside the EC and EFTA). In order to avoid imports into an FTA coming through the member country with the lowest external tariff, an FTA agreement limits free trade status to member countries' products. These are specified by its rules of origin.

In this chapter we will begin by considering an economic analysis of the effects of such preferential trading areas, and calculations as to their magnitude. First, we consider the effect of the imposition of a tariff, and then examine the situation in which the tariff is removed on imports from the partner country. We will assume that the market for the product is small enough for us not to have to consider the effect of changes in consumption and production on the total economy. Thus we will be able to use supply and demand curves in a partial equilibrium analysis.

3.2 **Partial equilibrium analysis of tariffs**

The effect of a tariff on imports can be seen in Figure 3.1. The country is assumed to be 'small' and therefore faces an infinitely elastic supply schedule from the rest of the world S_W. The domestic supply schedule is shown as the upward-sloping supply line S_H and the demand schedule as the downward-sloping line D_H. Under free trade the price on the domestic market is the world price, P_W. Domestic consumption is Q_1 and domestic production is Q_2 with imports of Q_1Q_2. If a tariff is imposed on imports of t in percentage terms or d in absolute terms with

$$t = P_W P'_W / O P_W \quad \text{and} \quad d = P_W P'_W$$

it appears to domestic consumers and producers that foreigners are now only willing to supply the domestic market at P'_W—that is, it looks as if the foreign supply schedule has shifted upwards to $S_W{}'$. Domestic consumers and producers respond by reducing consumption to Q_3 and increasing production to Q_4 respectively. Imports fall to Q_3Q_4, both because production has increased by Q_2Q_4 and because consumption has fallen by Q_1Q_3. This involves a loss in consumer surplus of $P_W P'_W K L$. However, part of this represents a redistribution in favour of producers: there is a gain in producer surplus of $P_W P'_W J N$; and another part takes the form of a gain in tariff revenue (which could in principle be redistributed to consumers) of JKVR. The net result is an efficiency loss of the two triangles JRN, which is the additional cost of obtaining the extra output Q_2Q_4 from domestic sources instead of from the international market, and KLV, which is the consumer surplus lost on the reduction in consumption Q_1Q_3.

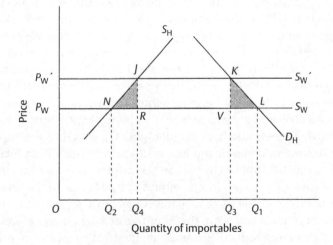

Fig. 3.1 Partial equilibrium analysis of a tariff

Preferential trade agreements: partial equilibrium analysis

The formation of a customs union or free-trade area was initially regarded as a movement towards free trade. But Viner (1950) pointed out that it also included an element of greater discrimination between member countries and non-member countries. He distinguished two aspects of the situation, one in which production is transferred from a higher-cost to a lower-cost source of production, say from the home country to the partner country, because tariffs have been removed from the latter country's products, which he termed *trade creation*. The other occurs when production is transferred from a low-cost source to a higher-cost source of production, say from a third country to a partner country because tariffs are no longer imposed on products from the latter—this he termed *trade diversion*. Trade creation he regarded as always beneficial, and trade diversion as detrimental (Viner 1950).

This is to look at benefits and costs entirely from the production point of view—Viner assumed that the commodities were always consumed in the same proportion. It was left to Lipsey to point out there was also a consumption angle. Indeed, the consumer benefits occurred in both cases and might even outweigh the losses in the case of trade diversion (Lipsey 1957).

To illustrate the effect on the market for a particular importable of a country becoming a member of a free-trade area or customs union we may consult a figure first employed by Kindleberger (1973) (Figure 3.2). The partner's supply schedule is also assumed infinitely elastic at S_P, but to lie above the rest of the world's supply schedule S_W; with a tariff, the partner's supply schedule is above S_W' and is not shown. The domestic supply schedule S_H is assumed to be upward sloping. The domestic demand schedule is D_H. Consumers are assumed not to differentiate according the origin of the product.

Before the formation of the customs union, all imports come from the rest of the world as they appear cheapest. The price on the domestic market is equal to the world price P_1 plus the tariff P_1P_2 and is thus OP_2. Consumers purchase a quantity OQ_3 and the output of domestic producers is OQ_4. Q_4Q_3 is imported from the rest of the world requiring a foreign exchange expenditure of ADQ_3Q_4 and providing a tariff revenue of $BCDA$.

If a customs union or free-trade area is formed, the tariff is removed on the partner's goods but not on those from the rest of the world and thus goods from the partner country appear cheaper at OP_3. If P_3 is less that P_2, prices on the domestic market fall. All imports are then acquired from the partner country and are greater in quantity at Q_6Q_5. There is therefore a diversion in the purchase of imports of Q_4Q_3 from non-members to the partner country. There is also trade creation of Q_6Q_4, which is now supplied by the partner country instead of domestic producers. In addition there is an increase in consumption of Q_3Q_5, which is supplied by the partner country. There is a gain in consumers' surplus of P_2CEP_3 and a loss in producers' surplus of P_2BFP_3 due to the lower price, and also a loss in tariff revenue of $ABCD$. In total this is equal to a net gain of $x + y - z$. z can be regarded as the cost of trade diversion, that is of transferring purchases from a low cost producer W to higher cost producer P. x and y are the familiar efficiency gains obtained from the reduction in tariffs.

Cooper and Massell (1969) challenged the assumptions underlying this particular argument. The comparison was being made between the pre- and post-customs-unions

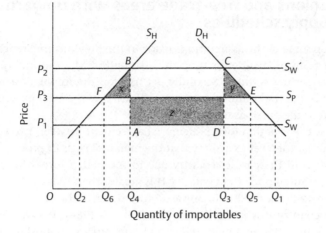

Fig. 3.2 Trade creation and trade diversion

position in order to assess whether it was beneficial. They argued that a comparison should be made between a discriminatory reduction of tariffs, as in the formation of a customs union or free-trade area, and a non-discriminatory removal of tariffs. A non-discriminatory removal of tariffs would always be superior and would avoid any trade diversion. Nevertheless, most economists carrying out applied work have continued to use the original framework and have compared the situation of the country before and after it joined the preferential trading area. This then is a theory of 'second best'.

From this theory some general principles can be deduced:

1. The benefits are likely to be greater the higher the original level of the tariff—the larger will be x and y.

2. Losses due to trade diversion are likely to be lower, the smaller the differences in costs of production between the partner countries and third countries—in the diagram the smaller P_3P_1 and therefore the smaller z.

3. A general principle not demonstrable from the diagram concerns the relative merits of unions between competitive and complementary economies. Two economies are complementary when they produce a different range of products. Initially a union between complementary economies was regarded as the most beneficial, but it provides the least scope for trade creation and the most for trade diversion. Competitive economies produce the same range of products and therefore there is scope for the low-cost producers to oust the higher-cost producers when barriers to trade are removed—that is trade creation. So if Britain forms a union with Germany, which has almost the same industrial structure, it provides considerable scope for trade creation. The actual benefits from this trade creation depend on the differences in cost.

Customs unions and free-trade areas with upward-sloping partner-supply schedules

Let us now drop some of the assumptions made in the previous theoretical analysis in a bid for greater realism. First, let us drop the assumption of an infinitely elastic supply schedule of the partner country. Secondly, let us drop the implicit assumption in the previous analysis that the common external tariff (CET) of the customs union is imposed at the same rate as the previous tariff.

Let us analyse the situation for a preferential agreement between two countries, H for home, and P for partner. Let us assume that the marginal costs of production are greater in the home than in the partner country due to the higher level of protection in the former. Thus the initial price T_H in country H is greater than that of the partner country T_P. Let us also make Robson's simplifying assumption that at the initial level of protection in the partner country it is just self-sufficient (Robson 1984). We will follow Robson's analysis and consider the final price and equilibrium that is established, the changes in welfare, and the effect on trade with the rest of the world (Robson 1984).

Free-trade area

Each member country can retain its previous tariff on imports from outside the area. However, it is now possible for the high-priced home country H with a price level initially at OT_H,(see Figure 3.3b), to import goods duty free from the lower-priced partner country P with an initial price level O_PT_P (see Figure 3.3a). The maximum that the home country can import from the partner country will be the whole of the latter's *production*. The price in the country will come down to the world price plus the tariff in the partner country OT_P if the latter can supply all the home country's requirement at that price. This

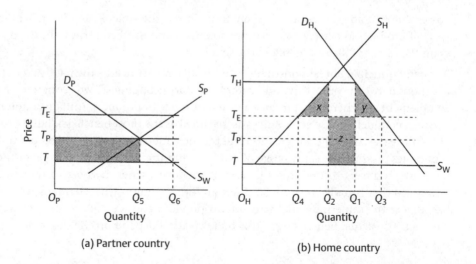

(a) Partner country

(b) Home country

Fig. 3.3 Free trade area

involves what is termed *trade deflection*. The partner exports its own output to the home country, and imports from the rest of the world to supply its own consumers.

The overall effect depends on the relationship between the supply schedule of the partner country S_P and the import schedule (demand minus supply) of the home country. If equilibrium can only be achieved at a price above that initially existing in the partner country such as T_E then the partner producers will expand output from O_PQ_5 to O_PQ_6 and will gain from extra profits; the partner country consumers will continue to purchase O_PQ_5 as before because they can import any amount at the world price plus tariff O_PT_P. Tariff revenue will be earned in the amount indicated by the cross hatched area due to the switching of consumption from domestic to third-country sources.

The net effect in the home country is that it obtains the efficiency gains of x and y due to the trade creation and consumption effects respectively but with the loss of z due to the trade diversion effect of obtaining Q_2Q_1 imports from the partner country rather than from the rest of the world. As the partner country now imports O_PQ_5, the imports of the free-trade area as a whole from the rest of the world have increased by $O_PQ_5 - Q_2Q_1$. There has been trade creation through the intermediation of the partner country.

Customs unions

To comply with GATT rules the level of protection in a customs union should be no greater than before. Thus, the EEC decided to set its CET at the arithmetic average of the previous tariffs of member countries. This therefore raised the level of protection against third countries in those members with liberal trade regimes and lowered it in the more protectionist ones.

Let us return to the analysis of two countries assuming the CET is the average of previously existing tariffs with the resulting tariff-distorted price denoted by CET in Figure 3.4. The ceiling price becomes that at which imports can enter, that is the CET price throughout the union. In the home country shown in Figure 3.4*b* the reduction in the apparent price of imports from OT_H to the CET level will lead to an increase in imports from Q_2Q_1 to Q_4Q_3 and to the familiar trade creation gain of x and consumption gain of y. There will also be the welfare cost z of diverting Q_2Q_1 imports from the rest of the world to the higher-cost partner country.

In the partner country, see Figure 3.4*a*, prices will rise due to increased protection. Thus, there will be a reduction in consumer surplus of $CETBET_P$, and a gain in producer surplus of $CETFET_P$ leading to an apparent gain of α. But this is inferior to the previous low level of protection by a net consumer loss β and producer loss γ. The ruling price will be at the ceiling if the partner country cannot supply, or can only just supply the amount required by the home country, $Q_6Q_7 = Q_4Q_3$. In the former case, there will be fewer imports from the rest of the world and in the latter none. However, the equilibrium price may be below the ceiling, with the partner country supplying all the imports of the home country and cutting out all imports from the rest of the world.

This analysis suggest that a customs union is inherently more likely to reduce trade with third countries than a free-trade area. This is because of our assumption about the CET which, though it reduces protection in one country, raises it in another: by contrast,

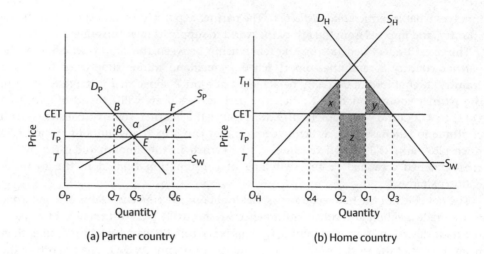

Fig. 3.4 Customs union

in a free-trade area the trade deflection effect lowers the price in the highly protected market without increasing the prices to consumers in the other.

3.3 **Applications of the theory**

The above theoretical analysis identifies the effects that would be expected from the formation of a customs union, assuming everything else remained constant. However, to work out the effect of the formation of the EC in practice, allowance must be made for changes in other economic variables; for instance demand and supply schedules may be expected to shift with changes in incomes and productivity. Herein lies the problem in calculating the economic effect of any institutional change, namely that in order to do so, an assumption has to be made about what would have happened in its absence. There are several approaches to that problem reflected in econometric exercises carried out to quantify the effect of the formation of the EEC and EFTA.

Balassa, in his investigation of the effect of the original six countries (France, Germany, Italy, Belgium, the Netherlands, and Luxembourg) forming the EEC, assumed that the income elasticity of demand for imports would have remained the same in the absence of its formation (Balassa 1974). By income elasticity, he meant the ratio of the annual rate of change of imports to that of GNP, measured at constant prices. Thus, the effect of integration was assumed to be the residual. He thus calculated this income elasticity of imports for the period 1953–9 before any tariff cuts were instituted and compared it with periods afterwards, 1959–65 and 1959–70, for total imports of the EEC, intra-area imports, and extra-area imports (see Table 3.1).

Table 3.1 Ex-post income elasticities of import demand in the EC6

Import Categories		Ex-post income elasticity of import demand		
		1953–9	1959–65	1959–70
Total imports				
0 + 1–07	Non-tropical food, beverages, tobacco	1.7	1.6	1.5
2 + 4	Raw materials	1.1	1.1	1.1
3	Fuels	1.6	2.3	2.0
5	Chemicals	3.0	3.3	3.2
71 + 72	Machinery	1.5	2.8	2.6
73	Transport equipment	2.6	3.4	3.2
6 + 8	Other manufactured goods	2.6	2.5	2.5
0 to 8–07	Total of above	1.8	2.1	2.0
Intra-area imports				
0 + 1–07	Non-tropical food, beverages, tobacco	2.5	2.4	2.5
2 + 4	Raw materials	1.9	1.9	1.8
3	Fuels	1.1	1.3	1.6
5	Chemicals	3.0	4.0	3.7
71 + 72	Machinery	2.1	3.1	2.8
73	Transport equipment	2.9	3.8	3.5
6 + 8	Other manufactured goods	2.8	2.9	2.7
0 to 8–07	Total of above	2.4	2.8	2.7
Extra-area imports				
0 + 1–07	Non-tropical food, beverages, tobacco	1.4	1.2	1.0
2 + 4	Raw materials	1.0	0.9	1.0
3	Fuels	1.8	2.5	2.1
5	Chemicals	3.0	2.7	2.6
71 + 72	Machinery	0.9	2.5	2.4
73	Transport equipment	2.2	2.4	2.5
6 + 8	Other manufactured goods	2.5	1.9	2.1
0 to 8–07	Total of above	1.6	1.7	1.6

Source: Balassa (1974: 97).

A rise in the income elasticity of demand from the earlier to the later periods for intra-area imports would indicate gross trade creation (due either to substitution for domestic or third-country sources of supply). A rise in the import elasticity from all sources would indicate true trade creation. A fall in the import elasticity from third countries would indicate trade diversion. Comparing the period 1953–9 with 1959–70 Balassa calculated that the overall income elasticity of demand for imports from all countries had increased from 1.8 to 2.1—this suggests trade creation proper. The import elasticity of demand from non-member countries had stayed the same, suggesting no trade diversion.

However, the results for the individual categories of goods were very different. The union appeared to have had no appreciable effect on trade in raw materials. This was not surprising as the initial tariffs on raw materials were zero or very low. There was a considerable amount of trade diversion in food, beverages, and tobacco. This was due to the Common Agricultural Policy (CAP). In fuels there was an increase in the import elasticity of demand from all sources. This was partly the result of the operation of the European Coal and Steel Community (ECSC) in the closing down of high-cost coal mines and the substitution of oil for coal. There was also an increase in the import elasticities of demand for machinery and transport equipment from all sources, in particular from non-members: they rose by respectively 1.5 and 0.3 from the earlier to the later period. The reduction in the income elasticity of imports from non-member countries after 1953–9 in chemicals and other manufactured goods (clothing, travel goods, scientific instruments, etc) indicated trade diversion.

At the time Balassa recognized that one of the problems with his approach was that some categories of goods were inputs into others. If, for instance, there was trade diversion in clothing (included in other manufactures) away from third countries this would increase the relative demands for inputs into it, leading to trade creation in those categories. However, any approach through input-output tables appeared very complex. He was also criticized by Winters for assuming that integration would lead to a change in an elasticity rather than a single (parametric) shift in trade between member countries (Winters, 1984: Appendix 2).

The European Free Trade Association (EFTA)

These problems were avoided by the EFTA Secretariat in their study of the effects of the formation of the EFTA (EFTA 1969). In this case imports were related to apparent consumption. The average annual change in the share of imports from 1954 to 1959 was extrapolated to the post-integration period 1959–65 and compared with the actual share of imports in apparent consumption i.e. output minus exports plus imports. This comparison was carried out for imports from all areas, imports from other EFTA countries, and imports from non-EFTA countries.

In so far as imports from non-EFTA countries were lower than estimated by extrapolation from 1954–9, this was regarded as trade diversion, and in so far as imports from EFTA countries were higher than the extrapolated estimate, this was regarded as trade creation. The results were that by 1965 the value of trade creation amounting to $373 million was less than the value of trade diverted of $457 million (EFTA 1969). This could be partly explained by the more complementary nature of the EFTA economies.

In both the Balassa and EFTA studies the whole of the difference between the estimate of what would otherwise have happened (the 'anti-monde') and what actually occurred is attributed to economic integration and thus is termed one of 'residual imputation'. This is generally regarded as producing rather high values.

Studies of the effect on the UK of its entry into the EC

The EFTA approach using shares in an export or import market has been used in assessing the effect on Britain of her entry into the EC, although some economists have just used total exports or imports. Most of these studies are of aggregate trade in manufactures. Winters (1987) criticized those that used the residual imputation method and endeavoured to model the situation more directly by including dummy variables for the effect of British entry in regression estimates.

The situation is complex because, while Britain by her entry gained free access to the EC market for her exports, she lost her preferential position in the markets of EFTA countries, Ireland, and the Commonwealth. These countries also lost their preferential position in the British home market as imports from the other members of the EC could then enter freely. But in addition the EC's Common External Tariff (CET) was lower for certain products than Britain's previous most-favoured-nation (mfn) tariff.

The author has calculated that from 1970 to 1987 the real value of trade with the Commonwealth, that is exports and imports, fell. Trade with EFTA increased, but that with the EC increased at a much faster rate, exports increasing by 172 per cent and imports by 250 per cent. For manufactures there was a fivefold increase in imports from the EC (Moore 1989). How much of this was due to integration? Winters investigated UK trade in manufactures with each of the main industrial countries (Winters 1987). He concluded that accession boosted exports to the EC by £4.5 billion but curtailed those elsewhere by £1.7 billion. More striking was the massive decline of £12 billion of sales by UK producers to their home market i.e. trade creation. He qualifies this estimate by then saying that £4 billion of this reduction might reflect a long-term secular decline. This still leaves a reduction in home sales of £8 billion which is only balanced by an increase in exports of £3 billion, leaving an increased manufacturing deficit of £5 billion. Even when modified to £3 billion this still represents about 1.5 per cent of GNP. There is an increase in consumer surplus to set against this; the question is whether it is large enough to offset it.

Both in these exercises and in subsequent ones the implicit assumption is that an appropriate means of assessing any economic integration is to compare what would have happened if there had been no reduction in tariffs with the effect of reducing trade barriers in the partner country. There is no comparison with the most efficient system of free trade.

Our exposition of the theory has been of the markets for individual products. The econometric work we have surveyed has taken a similar approach, although the categories considered have been very much larger. Clearly, on joining a preferential trading area, the different markets within a country would be affected differently. If the resulting changes in trade do not balance out, some adjustment of the exchange rate has to take place. The overall effect on resource allocation has been considered in terms of whether trade creation outweighs trade diversion. The effects on consumer and producer surplus were also considered.

However, from the point of view of the individual country entering a customs union there is also the effect on the rate at which exports are exchanged for imports, that is its 'terms of trade'. An improvement in a country's terms of trade may balance out negative efficiency effects. For an individual product this is illustrated in Figure 3.4*a*. However, to allow for the interconnection between markets we must employ a general equilibrium analysis.

3.4 **A simplified exposition of the general equilibrium theory of customs unions**

Let us now consider the general equilibrium approach to customs unions. Let us assume that there are only two products—manufactures and food. Perfect competition is assumed as are increasing costs. Thus the country is operating on the outer boundary of its production possibilities, the production possibility curve—see Figure 3.5. The slope of this curve at any point represents the domestic rate of transformation (DRT) between the two products, that is the amount of food that would have to be given up at the margin in order to produce one more unit of manufactures. Equilibrium in production will be reached at the point where:

$$DRT = \frac{\text{Price of manufactures}}{\text{Price of food}}$$

Demand is introduced into the picture by the use of community indifference curves. These are aggregates of individuals' indifference curves and thus represent the contour lines of utility for the community as a whole. Here they are taken both to show the response of consumers to changes in price, and as levels of welfare; they are therefore assumed not to cross, and problems of the effects of the distribution of income on welfare are ignored. If the country is closed to trade the maximum welfare attainable will be

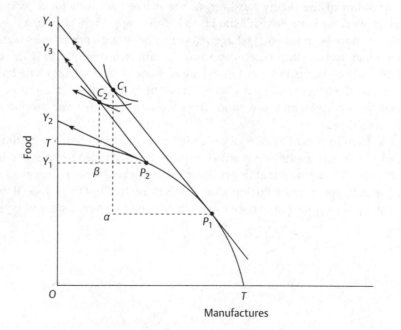

Fig. 3.5 Consumption and production with free trade and tariffs

where the production possibility curve just touches the highest possible community indifference curve with domestic prices indicated by their slope at this point.

If the world price of manufactures in terms of food is greater than the domestic one (the price line is steeper), then when the country is opened to trade, producers will have an incentive to increase their output of manufactures and reduce that of food. This will continue until the DRT is just equal to the international price as at point P_1, where the international price is given by the slope of Y_4P_1 equal to that of Y_3P_2, (see Figure 3.5). On the other hand, the higher relative price of manufactures will induce consumers to switch purchases from them to food. However, the increase in real incomes resulting from the trade will tend to increase the consumption of both goods assuming neither of them are inferior goods. The net result of changes in relative prices and incomes will be a change in consumption to point C_1 where the rate at which consumers are willing to substitute food for manufactures is just equal to the relative price of manufactures in relation to that of food, as indicated by the international price line.

Trade is the difference between production and consumption. The trade triangle $C_1\alpha P_1$ indicates that at an international price given by the slope of Y_4P_1 the country would export αP_1 of manufactures in exchange for $C_1\alpha$ of food. If the price of manufactures had been higher, the degree of specialization in manufactures would have been greater still, that is more manufactures and less food would have been produced.

An 'offer curve' showing the trade a country is willing to undertake at each relative price can be obtained by a plotting of the trade triangles as in Figure 3.6. OR represents a country's offer of manufactures for food. International equilibrium is reached when the country's offer curve intersects the offer curve of the rest of the world, assumed here to be infinitely elastic. At that equilibrium price OK the country wants to export OX_1 of manufactures in exchange for OY_1 of food.

Tariffs and subsidies destroy the equality between domestic and international prices:

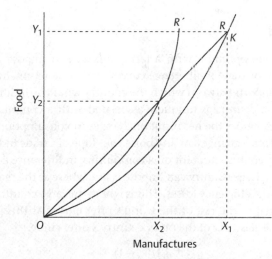

Fig. 3.6 Offer curve of a country exporting manufactures

see Figure 3.5 again. If tariffs are imposed on imports of food, both consumers and producers face a higher price of food indicated by the slope of Y_2P_2. This induces an increase in the output of food at the expense of manufactures, and production shifts from P_1 to P_2. This reduction in efficiency lowers real income. But the country as a whole can still trade at the ruling international prices, and thus its consumption possibilities are along Y_3P_2. Consumers will equate their marginal rate of substitution—indicated by the slope of their community indifference curve—to the domestic-tariff-distorted price; this would suggest consumption along Y_2P_2. But if the tariff revenue is redistributed back to them they will be able to consume along P_2Y_3 say at C_2. $C_2\beta$ food will be imported, βP_2 of manufactures exported. The overall effect has been a contraction of trade even though international prices remain the same.

Thus, a tariff has the effect of moving the offer curve depicted in Figure 3.6 inwards to OR'. If, as we have assumed, the country is small, the international price, equivalent to the rest of the world's offer curve, remains the same. Thus the effect of the tariff is a clear efficiency loss in a general equilibrium framework as in our previous partial equilibrium analysis.

However a large country is by definition one with some monopoly power in world trade. With free trade:

$$DRS = DRT = \text{International price}$$

but unlike the situation of a small country this is not equal to the marginal rate at which the large country can exchange manufactures for food on the world market, its foreign rate of transformation (FRT). A large country will face a less than infinitely elastic curve on the part of the rest of the world and will be able to improve its terms of trade by a tariff which leads to an inward shift in its offer curve. The welfare of a country is always assumed to increase with an improvement in its terms of trade, that is a rise in the price of its exports in relation to the price of its imports. Therefore a large country can set the gain in its terms of trade against its efficiency loss.

Optimum tariff

In order to consider the optimum tariff a large country can impose it is necessary to introduce the concept of trade indifference curves, each one representing the combination of exports and imports between which the country would be indifferent. Each trade indifference curve of a country is uniquely associated with a community indifference curve but the former includes the net result of changes in consumption and production on imports as relative price changes. At any point the slope of a trade indifference curve is identical to that at the equivalent point on a community indifference curve.

The optimum tariff a large country can impose is one where at the margin the terms of trade gains just equal the efficiency losses. This is where the large country's trade indifference curve is tangential to the rest of the world's offer curve. At this point the tariff is inversely related to the elasticity of the other country's offer curve.

$$t^* = 1/(e_w - 1)$$

where e_w is the rest of the world's price elasticity of demand for imports i.e.

$$e_w = \frac{\text{proportionate change in import volume demanded}}{\text{proportionate decrease in real price of imports}}$$

Thus when the rest of the world's offer curve is infinitely elastic the optimum tariff is zero.

Customs unions

Now let us turn to the analysis of the formation of a customs union. Let us simplify the analysis by assuming that there are three regions: A, the existing customs union or the country with whom membership is planned; B, the country whose interests we are considering; and W, the rest of the world. World efficiency will be maximized by free trade.

Calculations of the effect of the customs union will depend on the alternative scenario envisaged i.e. the anti-monde. Are we, for instance, comparing the country in a customs union with its position under free trade, or with a tariff, maybe an optimum tariff? Given this point of comparison the question is then whether membership of the customs union improves a country's terms of trade and who gains the tariff revenue; both will determine whether its consumers end up on a higher indifference curve than before.

Generally, it is assumed that both B and A specialize in the same products; in so far as Britain and the EC are taken as examples let us assume that they both export manufactures in exchange for food. The situation is depicted in Figure 3.7. 0W is the rest of the world's offer curve, and 0A + B is the offer curve of A + B with free trade. They can both be obtained by radial summation, that is by adding the amount each country in the group would export and import at any given terms of trade.

Free Trade

If A and B were to pursue a free-trade policy the equilibrium position would be T_1 and the terms of trade OT_1. A's trade position would be at a_1 and B's would be at b_1. Exports of manufactures by A and B would be OM_2 and OM_3 respectively, summing to $0M_1$. Imports of food would be a_1M_2 and b_1M_3 respectively, summing to T_1M_1. Thus

> International Price = Domestic Price = Slope of OT_1
> Exports of A + B = $OM_2 + OM_3 = OM_1$
> Imports of A + B = $a_1M_2 + b_1M_3 = M_1T_1$

Tariff imposed by A

If A, say the EC, then decided to impose a tariff on imports of food such that her internal domestic price is shown by the slope of Qa_2, this would induce a shift in her production from manufactures to food, and a substitution of manufactures for food in consumption. The offer curve of A would shift to A' and the overall offer curve of A and B would shift to $0A' + B$. This would increase the relative price of manufactures to food on the world market. Both would thus benefit from an improvement in their terms of trade, but B would be able to take advantage of it by expanding her trade, in particular increasing her exports from M_3 to M_5. To summarize:

> The Offer curve becomes A' + B

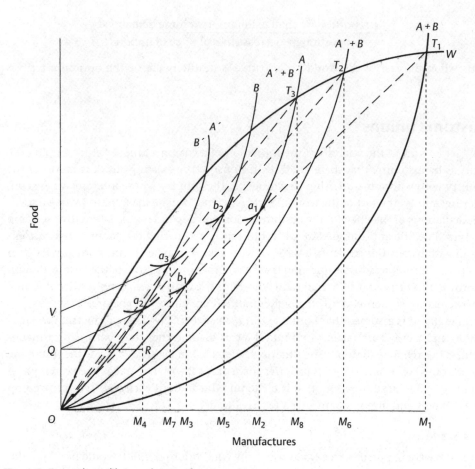

Fig. 3.7 General equilibrium theory of customs unions

International Price = domestic price of B = slope of OT_2 =

$$\frac{a_2 M_4}{OM_4}$$

Domestic price in A equals slope of Qa_2

The proportionate tariff t is placed on inputs of food.

∴ The price of food on A's domestic market is equal to $(1 + t)$ – international price of food.

$$\frac{QR}{a_2 R} = \frac{OM_4}{a_2 R} = (1 + t) \frac{OM_4}{a_2 M_4}$$

$$t = \frac{a_2 M_4 - a_2 R}{a_2 R} = \frac{RM_4}{a_2 R}$$

Imports of A fall from $a_1 M_2$ to $a_2 M_4$.

Exports of A fall from OM_2 to OM_4.
Imports of B increase from M_3b_1 to M_5b_2.
Exports of B increase from OM_3 to OM_5.

Thus from the figure it appears that although the imposition of a tariff by A has improved her terms of trade, her overall level of welfare may have fallen rather than increased, that is a_2 may be on a lower trade indifference curve than a_1. Whereas there has been a clear welfare gain by B: b_2 is higher than b_1.

B enters a customs union with A

Let us apply this argument by analogy to the position of Britain in relation to the original EC(6). The very high protection of agriculture within the EC(6) improved its terms of trade but constricted its exports of manufactures abroad. Britain, outside the EC, benefited not only from the improvement in her terms of trade but also from being able to expand her exports of manufactures.

Clearly it was in the interests of the EC(6) for Britain to join them and impose the same tariff on imports. Let us assume, that the combined group maintains the same internal relative price of food to manufactures. Let us also assume, for the sake of diagrammatic simplicity, that the new offer curve for B, B', coincides with A'. Their overall offer curve shifts to $0A' + B'$ (assumed for diagrammatic simplicity to coincide with the previous offer curve $0A$). The relative price of manufactures on the world market rises still further to the slope of $0T_3$. Thus, we can see from the diagram that:

The international price becomes OT_3.
The domestic price in A and B is assumed to be the same as A's previous price i.e. Va_3 is parallel to Qa_2.
Both A and B are assumed to export OM_7 $\therefore$ $2OM_7 = OM_8$.
    Both A and B are assumed to import a_3M_7 $\therefore$ $2a_3M_7 = T_3M_8$.

The variable a_3 now represents the trade indifference point of both A and B; it is clearly higher than a_2 and may also be higher than a_1—if it is not higher than a_1, A has not been pursuing an optimum policy.

On the other hand, B may or may not be worse off depending on the relative size of B in relation to A and the world market. Furthermore, the assumption so far made that the tariff revenue is redistributed back to the consumers of the country concerned does not apply to the EC, where it is transferred to the Commission. (Thus in Figure 3.5 instead of reaching consumption point C_2 the country would be operating on the budget line Y_2P_2. Under these circumstances consumers are always worse off. The actual change in the offer curve also depends on how the Commission spends the revenue.)

There are clear limitations to this type of analysis. One is that both A and B are assumed to purchase all their imports of food from the world market. However, Ghosh (1974) has considered customs unions of complementary economies. He evaluates the effect of union with respect to the prior tariff-ridden state of the constituent economies. He assumes that with a union between two countries one of them, described as passive, trades exclusively with the other. The active member trades its surplus with the rest of the world. The member that ends up with the more favourable terms of trade will gain and the other will lose. This situation most aptly reflects the entry of the smaller agricultural exporting countries into the EC such as Ireland, Portugal, and maybe Denmark, which have benefited greatly from an improvement in their terms of trade due to the CAP.

Thus, both partial and general equilibrium comparative static analyses show that entry to a customs union is not necessarily an improvement on a country's previous position. Furthermore in both cases, from the point of view of the world as a whole, it is an inferior position to a non-discriminatory reduction of tariffs or the optimum of free trade. This also applies to a free-trade area except, as explained, because the prices to consumers are not raised the cost of trade diversion is less.

However, there is a theorem by Kemp and Wan which states that if, in forming a customs union, the members keep their trade with the rest of the world at the same level and thus its welfare constant, it is always possible to improve the welfare of members of the customs union by a system of lump-sum or commodity taxation. That is regardless of the number of countries or number of commodities it is always theoretically possible for the formation of a customs union to be welfare improving. As more countries become members welfare will rise until they are all included when free trade is achieved (Kemp and Wan 1976, 1986). In practice taxation and transfers between countries have proved very difficult to negotiate. This is why so much emphasis is placed on the other benefits that are alleged to arise from preferential trading areas, in particular, benefits arising from the greater exploitation of economies of scale, which it is claimed that such arrangements encourage.

3.5 The concept of economies of scale

Speakers arguing for Britain joining the EC used to claim that she would benefit from being able to exploit economies of scale. Scale economies exist if average costs fall when a firm increases its output by investing in greater productive capacity, that is by increasing its scale of operations. It is shown by a fall in the long-run average cost curve, which is the envelope of the short-run average cost curves. Technological knowledge and the prices of factors of production, which include the rate of interest, are assumed constant for any given long-run average cost curve.

The economies are partly associated with the size of plant, that is production at any given geographical location. They may occur because capital costs do not increase proportionally with output—machines producing twice as fast may not cost twice as much. There may also be a spreading of indivisibilities associated with operating at any particular location in the form of secretarial and administrative services. These will be called plant economies. The actual shape of the long run average cost curve of a plant will depend on the relative factor prices of factors of production, and the way they are combined. For instance with a given plant, a doubling of the number of hours it is worked per year with the same manning levels, say from 4000 to 8000, would halve the capital costs per unit of output. The minimum efficient technical size of a plant with these longer hours would be different from one in which the increase in output had been obtained by continuing to work 4000 hours but building a larger size of plant. Thus what are called 'engineering' estimates of economies of scale must include some assumption about the number of hours a plant is worked.

There may also be economies associated with the length of production run. Each time the specifications of a product are changed turnround time is required for resetting machines. In so far as the production of a particular specification is carried out in only one plant these are often regarded as contributing to plant economies.

However, the economies of scale may also be associated with the size of firm, that is the unit of control and decision-making. In particular, for the high-technology industries an increase in the total output of a product reduces the research and development expenditure (R & D) per unit.

These are all internal economies the benefits of which may be appropriated by a firm. There are also external economies associated with the expansion of an industry which lead to the cost curves of firms within the industry falling as total output is increased. These may be due to the development of specialized services and the improvement in marketing facilities which may result from the expansion of industrial output.

The general approach in the theory is to assume that the firm discussed has only one plant and is the sole domestic producer of the product. Implicitly, the economies of both plant and firm are being considered.

Let us now consider how the formation of a customs union may lead to the greater exploitation of economies of scale, and the benefits and losses that will accrue to the member countries. We will first consider this within a comparative static framework which is a development and extension of work by Mead and Corden (Mead 1968; Corden 1972); this will be called Model T (for traditional). Then we will consider the imperfect competition model, termed Model M, which has been devised by Smith and Venables (1988).

Traditional analysis: model T

In the traditional model T the product of the home industry is taken as indistinguishable from that of the foreign partner firms or the rest of the world. If the home producer is the sole seller in the domestic market it might find it difficult to reach a profit-maximizing position because as the long-run marginal cost is below the long-run average cost curve, equating marginal cost with marginal revenue may lead to a firm making a loss unless the demand curve is relatively inelastic (although less than −1). A profit-maximizing firm would then either refrain from producing or produce the minimum possible. In order to avoid this the government often regulates the price. The presumption in much theoretical work is that a policy of average cost pricing is pursued. This we will call assumption (a) which is assumed to be a possibility even with trade.

However, if the economy is open, the firm is faced with two exogenous prices—on the one hand, the world price at which it can export the product; on the other hand, the tariff-distorted price at which products can enter the market from abroad. These represent its minimum and maximum price respectively. The general argument is that, if the country's cost curve is relatively low compared with that of the world as a whole, then it will expand production and export and will not need a preferential system to exploit economies of scale. No further mention will be made of this situation.

However, if the cost curve is high in comparison with the world price it may be assumed (as in Corden 1972) that a firm will maximize its profits by charging the maximum price, that is the price at which the product from abroad will just enter. If it can cover costs at this price it will produce, otherwise it will not. This is taken as assumption (*b*).

Therefore, in considering the outcome of a customs union formed between two countries whose long-run average cost curves exhibit economies of scale but lie above the world price, the important features are the pricing policies pursued, and whether the countries produce before and after the union.

For the sake of simplicity we will assume that the level of protection existing in the members of the customs union prior to entry was the same level as the common external tariff. To focus on the issues involved, the production function is assumed to be the same in the home and partner country, and is implicitly assumed to be that of an industry, maybe consisting of only one firm, maybe consisting of only one plant.

Three situations can be distinguished:

(*a*) No production prior to entry in either country

Prior to entry, imports provide for all consumption in both countries, OQ_1 in H and OQ_2 in P. Home market prices will be P_W' and the tariff revenue will be $P_WP_W'.OQ_1$ in H and $P_WP_W'.OQ_2$ in P. This situation is illustrated in Figure 3.8*a*.

After entry, if one country supplies the whole of the market, it can now produce at a lower average cost along LAC than P_W'. Let us assume that production is now carried out by H. There are two possibilities:

1. If prices are equated with average cost no producer surplus will be earned. The price within the customs union will fall to P_U with output OQ_3. There will be a gain in consumer surplus in both countries and a loss in tariff revenue. The net gain in each country will be the consumption effect, that is the consumer surplus on the increase in consumption, minus the cost of trade diversion from the low-cost world producers to the higher-cost home-country producer, which will be P_UP_W multiplied by the previous quantity of imports.

2. However, if prices remain at P_W' there will be no benefits to consumers. One country, assumed to be H, can now produce OQ_4 at a lower cost C than it can be purchased from third countries with the CET. If the partner country P now obtains all its supplies from H it suffers a loss of tariff revenue which represents its welfare loss; H also loses tariff revenue, but set against this it has profits of $P_W'C.OQ_4$

(*b*) Prior to entry there is production in home country H but not in partner country P

Prior to entry the partner country will import all its supplies OQ_2 from third countries at a foreign exchange price P_W', which with its tariff will appear as a price P_W'. Tariff revenue will be $P_WP_W'AC$. Again there are two possibilities, illustrated in Figure 3.8*b*.

1. If average cost pricing is assumed prior to entry, country H will produce all its

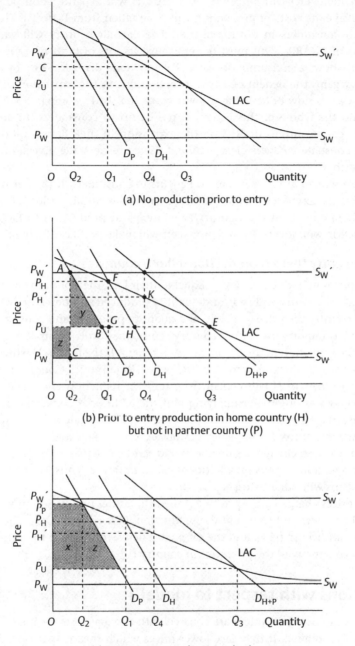

(a) No production prior to entry

(b) Prior to entry production in home country (H) but not in partner country (P)

(c) Prior to entry production in both countries

Fig. 3.8 Economies of scale in customs unions

requirements OQ_1 at a price OP_H. On entry H will expand its output to OQ_3 at a price P_U i.e. its costs of production will have fallen from P_H to P_U. There will be a gain to consumers in both countries. The partner country will gain consumer surplus of $P_W'ABP_U$. This must be set against its loss of tariff revenue of $P_W'ACP_W$. Thus it shows a consumption gain of y and trade diversion loss of z. The home country gains the benefit of a cost reduction due to the expansion of its industry. Thus, OQ_1 is now obtained at a lower cost—that is, P_U compared with a previous P_H—and the whole of this benefit is passed on to consumers. In addition, consumers gain a surplus of FHG on the expansion in their consumption. Thus, the home consumers have a clear gain and there are no trade diversion losses to set against them.

2. If prices remain at P_w' there are no benefits to consumers. If the partner country P transfers its purchases OQ_2 to the home country it sustains a loss of tariff revenue and welfare of $P_W'ACP_W$. Country H will expand production to OQ_4. Its cost of production will now be P_H' and producers will make profits of $P_W'JKP_H'$.

(c) Prior to entry there is production in both countries

1. If the prices in both countries are equal to their LAC then prior to entry the price in the partner country will be P_P and quantity produced and purchased Q_2, and in the home country the price will be P_H and quantity produced and consumed Q_1. There will be no imports into either country. This situation is illustrated in Figure 3.8c. With the formation of the union, assuming that it is the firm in H which expands to supply the customs union market, the price will fall to P_U. Country H will produce Q_3. Consumers in H will benefit from the cost reduction effect $P_HP_U.OQ_1$ on the amount H was originally supplying plus the additional consumer surplus on the increase in consumption that takes place because of the fall in price. The industry of the partner country P completely disappears due to the expansion of it in H. There appears to be an efficiency gain due to trade creation equal to the cross hatched area x, and a gain in surplus on additional consumption z. Thus, country P appears to show gains without any losses.

2. If the prices charged are equal to P_W' then the initial production in both countries would be lower and so would the production after entry at OQ_4. The final cost of production would be P_H and the difference between this and the price $P_W'P_H'.OQ_1$ would go entirely to the producers in country H.

Conclusions with respect to model T

Consumers only benefit if prices are equated with average costs, or if such an extreme assumption is modified, if they face lower prices which means that case (b) examined above does not hold. If a country is initially importing from third countries, entry into the customs union will always involve it in making a loss due to trade diversion. Thus, the only circumstances in which trade diversion costs are not incurred is when both countries are initially dependent on home production. In that case, expansion of production in one country leads to the disappearance of the industry in the other. This is not regarded as a loss in this type of marginal welfare analysis. But clearly, if this involved a number of industries in P or was important to country P's economy some adjustment to exchange rates would be required.

Because of the assumption that the LAC curves are the same in both countries the direction of trade is inherently indeterminate, although the country that can produce in the larger market will appear to have lower costs of production.

In all cases shown, the countries would be better off if they imported from the rest of the world.

Imperfect competition: model M

The Emerson report on the benefits the EC would obtain by removing their non-tariff barriers to trade by the end of 1992 approached the problem in an entirely different way (European Economy 1988) using an imperfect competition model developed and applied by Smith and Venables (1988a, 1988b). In the Smith and Venables model each EC firm is assumed to produce in only one EC country, and as in the previous analysis, implicitly in one plant. Each firm may produce several varieties of product, but the varieties are peculiar to it and cannot be produced by any other firm. The products of different firms within the same industry are imperfect substitutes.

Each firm can produce for its home market or can export its product; it will receive the consumer price in the former, but only $(1 - t)$ multiplied by the consumer price in the latter, where t represents the selling costs associated with exporting. It is assumed that because of the selling cost the firms will account for a smaller proportion of their export than home markets. A reduction in the selling costs, such as those associated with the removal of non-tariff barriers to intra-EC trade, will lead to greater exports and thus induce greater competition and lower prices in all markets. This will expand consumption and allow firms to further exploit their economies of scale.

The empirical basis of this Emerson report was a series of studies, in particular 'A Survey of the Economies of Scale' by Pratten (Pratten 1988). Much of the data referred to the 1960s (Pratten and Dean 1965; Pratten 1971). Pratten identified various factors which contributed to economies of scale and then listed the 'engineering' estimates. Most of these were associated with the size of plant or production runs, but some were also attributed to the spreading of Research and Development (R & D) expenditure over more units. The minimum efficient technical scale of plant (METS) is defined where costs cease to fall rapidly. The measurement of economies of scale is the percentage increase in costs at half or a third of the METS.

Smith and Venables initially propose a cost function with an initial fixed cost and a constant marginal cost. This then becomes modified by averaging it with another function with a declining marginal cost. They regard this as approximating Pratten's empirical findings on economies of scale. Each producer is assumed to maximize profits by equating marginal cost with marginal revenue. This is achievable because there are a number of producers which each individually face an elasticity very much greater than the elasticity of demand for the product itself. Smith and Venables considered the firms either to be making the 'Cournot' assumption in which each firm regards the sales of other firms as fixed, or the 'Bertrand' assumption in which each firm regards the prices of other firms as fixed. In both cases the elasticity of demand that the firm faces in its export market is assumed to be greater than that in the home market and therefore marginal revenue is a greater proportion of price in the former. As sales expand so does output and therefore there is a greater exploitation of economies of scale. If the less efficient firms are forced out by the increased competition this will enable those remaining to still further exploit their economies of scale.

Smith and Venables take production and consumption data for ten industries.[1] In order to apply this model they divided the world into six 'countries'—France, West Germany, Italy, the UK, the rest of the EC, and the rest of the world. They took ten industries, although some were broken up into sub-industries. Each of these industries or sub-industries was treated as one market. For each industry a matrix of production and consumption for the six 'countries' was obtained for 1982. The elasticities of demand for the products of the industries were available, but in order to obtain the elasticities of demand facing the individual firms information on concentration was required. This was constructed from the Eurostat data on the size distribution of firms using the Herfindahl index of concentration from which was 'calculated the number of 'representative' firms in each country. This is the number of equal-sized firms which would give rise to the same effective degree of market concentration as the observed distribution of unequal-sized firms . . . The minimum efficient scale [was] taken to be the size of the average "representative" firm in the EC.'(Smith and Venables 1988*a*: 5.9). The removal of non-tariff barriers was regarded as being equal to a tariff equivalent reduction of between 2.5 and 13.5 per cent. This was then regarded as a reduction in the selling cost of exporting to other EC countries.

Using these calculations the Emerson report shows the percentage reduction in cost from exploiting economies of scale and from restructuring, that is the disappearance of the less efficient firms. The greatest welfare gains were expected from the chemical industry at a rate of 7.7 billion ecu, electrical goods was put at 5.4 ecu, motor vehicles at 4.7 ecu, and mechanical engineering at 4.6 ecu (Emerson Report 1988; Table A.7).

Comparison of model M and model T

Clearly the assumptions underlying the two analyses of economies of scale, models T and M, are entirely different. In model T one industry or firm is assumed for each country, the production functions for different firms are the same (although this assumption could be modified) and the benefits and costs from the formation of a customs union depend on the reduction in the average cost obtained, and the pricing policy pursued. The absolute height of the tariff (or the tariff equivalent of non-tariff barriers), determines the maximum exploitation of economies of scale that can occur due to the customs union, because at the tariff-distorted world price imports could enter, and at the world price the country could export.

However, in model M because of the heterogeneity of product there is no 'world price'. Model M allows for several firms in each country and for differentiation of products. But these advantages of approximation to reality are thrown away by substituting a number of representative firms for the actual number and size distribution of firms. There is also a very limited concept of differentiation.

From the point of view of trade the question is whether in the long run the initial advantages of a country or firm are sufficient to determine trade flows. Thus, although in model T, H is assumed to have the lowest average cost and therefore to increase its output, in the very long run P would be just as cheap a location. The direction of trade flows is therefore indeterminate. In model M, where individual firms appear to have advantages specific to themselves, if these are specific to the firm as distinct from the country it is not clear why the firm should not relocate its production to the cheapest location within the EU or maybe abroad. This is precisely what worries trade unionists in the countries with higher wages and higher social security contributions.

Another aspect of the situation is the identification of economies of scale. The implicit assumption in both models appears to be that a one-plant firm is being considered; in particular, the Emerson report is perpetually slithering from a discussion of the METS and economies of scale of plant to that of a firm without distinguishing the two. However, Smith and Venables discount economies of scale associated with plant size by assuming that their representative firms are at the METS; it is not clear whether their cost function, which appears to allow for the further spreading of fixed cost, which they discuss in terms of R & D, is therefore only an economy of scale of a firm. If it is specific to the firm then the argument in the previous paragraph applies.

The greatest contrast between these models is in their treatment of trade with the external world. In model T it is assumed that if, by exploiting its economies of scale, a firm could produce at the world price, then it would have already expanded sufficiently to export. However, in the Emerson report, one of the advantages that is said to accrue from further exploitation of economies of scale is that as costs fall, European firms will become more competitive and it will increase their exports to the outside world. But in this case the argument used in model T, that they will already be exporting, appears just as applicable to imperfect competition. Furthermore there are considerable exports to non-member countries of all the products considered by Smith and Venables. This suggests that economies of scale of the most efficient firms are already being exploited.

Both models assume that the removal of barriers to trade between members of preferential trading area countries is likely to lead to trade diversion from non-member countries. Neither of the models allows for the multinational nature of the firms operating in the industry. In so far as these producers straddle national boundaries the assumptions about the bases of the competing firms do not hold. For instance, the choice is not so much whether the French and Germans buy French or German cars, but where the Germans wish to produce their cars. The concept of differentiation being associated with a firm producing in a particular country which then determines trade collapses. The location of production becomes determined by costs. Clearly, the fewer the barriers to trade the easier it is to locate production cheaply. That is why multinationals are always in favour of reductions in barriers to trade.

Conclusion with respect to economies of scale

The traditional analysis of the exploitation of economies of scale in a customs union has been in terms of a homogeneous product. In this case a firm may benefit and expand its output if its potential long-run average cost of production lies somewhere between the international price at which it could export and the tariff-distorted price at which imports can enter the union. The actual distribution of costs and benefits depends on which firms produce before and after the formation of the union, and the price policy being pursued.

The imperfect competition approach pursued by Smith and Venables for the Emerson report eschews all consideration of the level of protection. It is solely concerned with firms within the customs union. Each is assumed to be based in its home country, producing and exporting from it. In the Emerson report the economies of scale of plant are not distinguished from those of the firm. The more efficient firms are regarded as expanding at the expense of the less efficient. However both models exclude the possibility of firms choosing to shift production to lower-cost locations, which has occurred. It also ignores the great incentive to inward direct investment provided by high levels of protection.

The effect of PTAs on the rest of the world and multilateral liberalization

So far this chapter has been concerned with the benefits that members of a preferential trading area (PTA) receive from membership. But what effect does its formation have on the rest of the world? Has the establishment of the EU with its preferences for members and implicit discrimination against non-member countries been the inducement for the formation of NAFTA, Mercosur, and Asean? Has the formation of the EU therefore encouraged a retreat from the multilateral reduction of trade barriers through GATT and now the WTO? Economists have been discussing this over the past decade, their approach ranging from that of political economy to tightly specified mathematical models based on the terms of trade (Bagwell and Staiger, 1999). The government of a country is regarded as attaching greater importance to producer than consumer interests, for the latter of which prices are better kept down by free trade. Krishna (1999) argues that the impetus for the formation of PTAs comes from lobbyists representing industries that would benefit from trade diversion. De Melo *et al.* (1993) argue that one of the benefits of a PTA is the reduction in the influence of industries of individual countries within the larger group. Winters (1993) comments that this only occurs if the industries have conflicting interests; in the EU sectional interests within different member countries combine and become stronger.

Krugman (1993) constructed a simple model with a number of countries of equal size each specializing in the production of one distinct commodity which had a constant elasticity of substitution with other products. These countries were organized into a number of equally sized PTAs, each of which allowed free trade between its member countries but imposed an optimum tariff on imports from non-member countries. A reduction in the number of PTAs led to more trade creation because more trade occurred within blocs. It also led to more diversion of trade than previously occurred between blocs, and because each PTA was larger and therefore had more monopoly power, an increase in tariffs. One optimum appeared to be when there was a large number of PTAs with little monopoly power. If the number of PTAs fell, then world welfare declined until there were only three (say the EU, NAFTA, and Japan). It then rose until there was only one PTA, i.e. the world had reached free trade.

Bhagwati has argued that tariff reduction should be viewed as a process with the multilateral reduction in tariffs being carried out independently or interacting with the reduction of trade barriers within the PTAs. It may be easier to negotiate the reduction of tariffs between the few members of a PTA, than multilaterally with all members of the WTO. In that case the reduction of intra-PTA trade barriers may be the precursor of multilateral ones and may even assist them. Such a situation can be seen for services when under the Single European Act, non-tariff barriers were removed for trade between EU Member States, which was followed by the inclusion of services in the Uruguay round.

Ethier (1998) has argued that in the past joining a PTA was a substitute for insufficient multilateral liberalization, or, for some, to hold aloof from it. Now with the extensive reduction in tariffs through GATT and the abandonment of protection by less developed countries and Eastern Europe, the latter are endeavouring to enter regional blocs as a means of attracting direct investment and increasing their participation in the multilateral system.

The completion of the Uruguay round in 1994 demonstrated that developed countries were still interested in multilateral reductions in trade barriers. When the general mfn rates are lowered, the benefit of any reduction in them obtained by membership of a PTA is also lowered. 'Deep' integration, involving the removal of non-tariff barriers and adoption of technical standards, becomes far more important.

3.6 **Conclusions**

Comparative static economic theory suggests that the formation of a PTA by one group of countries will encourage others to form blocks of their own, and thus will tend to undermine the multilateral trading system. However, this ignores practicalities such as the difficulty of negotiating between large numbers of countries. The EU's success in removing non-tariff barriers to intra-union trade in services encouraged GATT to adopt a similar strategy for its Uruguay round of trade negotiations described in Chapter 11, which ultimately led to the multilateral General Agreement on Trade in Services (GATS).

Furthermore the completion of the Uruguay round in 1994 demonstrated that developed countries were still interested in multilateral reductions in trade barriers. Indeed, Sampson (1996) pointed out that 45 per cent of EU imports originated from non-preference receiving countries (17 per cent from the USA and 10 per cent from Japan). Under the Uruguay round 51 per cent of imports from non-preferential countries enter the EU under bound duty-free rates; the trade-weighted tariff average on manufactures from these countries became 3.1 per cent. Fifty per cent of EU imports from preference receiving countries enter duty free, and 24 per cent of imports from preferential countries did not benefit from preferential rates. Thus as mfn tariffs are reduced, the preferential rates become less important.

Discussion questions

1   Define a customs union and a free trading area. With the aid of diagrams explain how their formation results in trade creation and trade diversion, and the effect of these on the welfare of member countries.

2   Under what circumstances is a country likely to benefit from the greater exploitation of economies of scale by joining a customs union.

Notes

1   Smith and Venables take production and consumption data for ten industries as follows:

242	cement, lime, and plaster;
257	pharmaceutical products;
260	artificial and synthetic fibres;
322	machine tools;
330	office machinery;
342	electrical motors, generators, and transformers;
346	electrical household appliances;
351	motor vehicles and engines;
438	carpets, carpeting, oilcloth, and linoleum;
451	footwear.

In some cases these industries were divided up into a number of equal-sized sub-industries, for instance office machinery was broken down into two sub-industries, electric motors into three, and domestic electrical appliances, and pharmaceuticals into five. Each of these industries or sub-industries is treated as one market.

References

Bagwell, K. and Staiger, R. W. (1999), 'Will Preferential Agreements Undermine the Multilateral Trading System', in J. Bhagwati, P. Krishna, and A. Panagariya (eds.), *Trading Blocs: Alternative Approaches to Analyzing Preferential Trade Agreements* (Cambridge, Mass.: MIT Press), 505–29.

Balassa, B. (1974), 'Trade Creation and Trade Diversion in the European Common Market' Manchester School, June.

Bhagwati, J. (1993), 'Regionalism and Multilateralism: An Overview' in J. De Melo, and A. Panagariya (eds.), *New Dimensions in Regional Integration* (Cambridge: World Bank/ Cambridge University Press), 22–57.

—— Krishna, P., and Panagariya, A. (eds.) (1999) *Trading Blocs: Alternative Approaches to Analyzing Preferential Trade Agreements* (Cambridge, Mass.: MIT Press).

Cooper, C. A., and Massell, B. F. (1965), 'A New Look at Customs Union Theory', *Economic Journal*, 75: 742–7.

Corden, W. M. (1972), 'Economics of Scale and Customs Union Theory', *Journal of Political Economy*, 80: 465–75.

De Melo, J. and Panagariya, A. (eds.) (1993), *New Dimensions in Regional Integration* (Cambridge: World Bank/Cambridge University Press).

—— —— and Rodrik, D. (1993), 'The New Regionalism: A Country Perspective', in J. De Melo and A. Panagariya (eds.), *New Dimensions in Regional Integration* (Cambridge: World Bank/Cambridge University Press), 3–21.

Ethier, W. J. (1998), 'The New Regionalism', *The Economic Journal*, 108/449: 1149–61.

European Free Trade Association (1969), *The Effects of EFTA on the Economies of Member States* (Geneva: EFTA).

Emerson Report (1988), Commission of the European Communities, *European Economy*, 35. *The Economics of 1992*; referred to as the Emerson Report.

Ghosh, S. K. (1974), 'Towards a Theory of Multiple Customs Unions', *American Economic Review*, 64/1: 91–101.

Kemp, M. C. and Wan, H. Y., Jr. (1976) 'An Elementary Proposition Concerning the Formation of Customs Unions', repr. in J. Bhagwati, P. Krishna and A. Panagariya (eds.) (1999). *Trading Blocs: Alternative Approaches to Analyzing Preferential Trade Agreements* (Cambridge, Mass.: MIT Press), 201–6.

—— —— (1986) 'The Comparison of Second-Best Equilibria: The Case of Customs Unions', repr. in J. Bhagwati, P, Krishna, and A. Panagariya (eds.) (1999), *Trading Blocs: Alternative Approaches to Analyzing Preferential Trade Agreements* (Cambridge, Mass.: MIT Press), 207–13.

Kindleberger, C. P. (1973), *International Economics*, 5th edn. (Homewood, Ill.: Irwin-Dorsey).

Krishna, P. (1999), 'Regionalism and Multilateralism: A Political Economy Approach' in J. Bhagwati, P. Krishna, and A. Panagariya (eds.) (1999), *Trading Blocs: Alternative Approaches to Analyzing Preferential Trade Agreements* (Cambridge, Mass.: MIT Press), 453–77.

Krugman, P. (1993), 'Regionalism versus Multilateralism: Analytical Notes', in J. De Melo and A. Panagariya (eds.) *New Dimensions in Regional Integration* (Cambridge: World Bank/Cambridge University Press), 58–89.

Lipsey, R. G. (1957), 'The Theory of Customs Unions: Trade Diversion and Welfare', *Economica*, 24: 40.

Mead, D. C. (1968), 'The Distribution of Gains in Customs Unions between Developing Countries', *Kyklos*, 21; repr. in P. Robson (ed.), *International Economic Integration*, 1972 (Harmondsworth: Penguin).

Moore, L. (1989), 'Changes in British Trade Analyzed in a Pure Trade Theory Framework', in D. Cobham, R. Harrington, and G. Zis (eds.), *Money, Trade and Payments: Essays in Honour of D. J. Coppock* (Manchester: Manchester University Press).

Pratten, C. (1971), *Economies of Scale in Manufacturing Industry*, Department of Applied Economics Occasional Papers, No. 28 (Cambridge: Cambridge University Press).

—— (1988), 'A Survey of the Economies of Scale' in Commission of the European Communities Documents Research on the *Costs of Non-Europe*, *Basic Findings*, *vol. 2: Studies on the Economics of Integration*.

—— and Dean, R. M., (1965) *The Economies of Large-Scale Production in British Industry* Department of Applied Economics Occasional Papers, No. 3 (Cambridge: Cambridge University Press).

Robson, P. (1984), *The Economics of International Integration*, 2nd edn. (London: Allen and Unwin).

Sampson, G. P. (1996), 'Compatibility of Regional and Multilateral Trading Agreements: Reforming the WTO Process,' *American Economic Review Papers and Proceedings*, 80.

Smith, A. and Venables, A. J. (1988*a*) 'The Costs of Non-Europe: An Assessment Based on a Formal Model of Imperfect Competition and Economies of Scale', in Commission of the European Communities Documents Research on the *Costs of Non-Europe*, *Basic Findings*, *vol. 2: Studies on the Economics of Integration*.

—— —— (1988*b*), 'Completing the Internal Market in the European Community', *European Economic Review*, 32, 1501–25.

—— —— (1991), 'Economic Integration and Market Access', *European Economic Review*, 35.

Viner, J. (1950), *The Customs Union Issue* (Carnegie Endowment for International Peace).

Winters, L. A. (1984), 'British Imports of Manufactures and the Common Market', *Oxford Economic Papers*, 36: 103–18.

—— (1987), 'Britain in Europe: A Survey of Quantitative Trade Studies', *Journal of Common Market Studies*, 25/4: 315–25.

—— (1993), 'The European Community: A Case of Successful Integration?' in J. de Melo and A. Panagariya (eds.), *New Dimensions in Regional Integration* (Cambridge: World Bank/ Cambridge University Press), 202–33.

Chapter 4
The Enlargement

Roy Gardner

4.1 Introduction

The history of the European Union (EU) is a history of enlargement. The EU has grown continuously from the original 6 signatories of the Treaty of Rome to the current 15 members, with another 13 countries in various stages of negotiation for accession. The current projected enlargement is unprecedented, both in terms of the number of accession candidates and in their level of economic development.

EU enlargement entails many aspects—political, military, and security, and judicial, as well as economic. In this paper, we restrict attention to the economics of EU enlargement. This is not to say the other aspects are not important—they obviously are, especially to the architects of the enlargement at the European Commission. But to maintain focus on the economics, we only allude to the other aspects when their economic content warrants inclusion.

To anticipate our conclusions, we will argue that the EU is a club that provides benefits to its members, on whom it also imposes costs. Like any club, the EU has an optimal size, which is finite. The marginal benefits of adding the last member to the club just outweigh the marginal cost of adding that member. Applying this logic to the enlargement, we find that enlargement to 28 members may never occur, and if it does occur, such enlargement will take much longer than the political élites of the EU are currently willing to admit. Moreover, a corollary of our argument will be that current membership may not be eternal—today's EU may already be too large a club, where a restive member such as Austria is concerned.

4.2 **The economic theory of clubs**

Clubs produce goods and services for their members which are intermediate between private goods and public goods. The defining characteristics of clubs are excludability (like a private good) and non-rivalry (like a public good). (For a thorough discussion of the economic theory of clubs, see Cornes and Sandler, 1996; for a brief application to EU Enlargement, see Gros and Steinherr, 1995.) The EU obviously satisfies excludability—all non-members are excluded from membership. Non-rivalry may be a little harder to see. Here are three examples of goods and services produced by the EU which are non-rival in consumption by the members:

- Equal rights of membership: every member has the same rights of membership, and these rights do not impinge on each other.

- Equal access to the free trade area, customs union and single market: every member gains access to these three major creations of the EU, and that access is equal and non-rival.

- Equal right to participate in the monetary union: every member who is willing and able to participate in the monetary union may have the euro as its currency and enjoy the services of the European Central Bank.

These rights entitle the members to considerable benefits. For instance, the free trade area and customs union alone generate an extra 5 per cent of GDP each year to the members (see Chapter 3 for why this is so). That 5 per cent of bonus GDP works out to roughly 1000 euros for every inhabitant of the EU, annually.

Besides the benefits of membership, there are also costs. The following are cost categories that apply to each member:

- Maintain a substantial representation at EU installations, starting with Brussels: this human resource cost prevents postage-stamp countries like Monaco from belonging to the EU.

- Contribute to the EU budget: this includes automatic surrender of customs duties, a mandated value-added tax, a share of which is turned over to the EU, and supplemental payments as needed to balance the EU budget.

- Surrender of national economic policy to the supranational EU level: trade policy, agricultural policy, monetary policy (if in the monetary union), and industrial policy are all examples of policies surrendered by members to the EU.

So the EU satisfies the defining characteristics of a club.

Let us abstract for a minute from the diversity of EU members and potential members, and suppose that every country in Europe is exactly alike. This allows us to portray graphically the benefits and costs generated by a club, solely in terms of the number of members (see Figure 4.1). In Figure 4.1 the number of members (each identical to the rest) is portrayed on the horizontal axis. The marginal benefit and marginal cost of an additional member to each of the existing members are measured on the vertical axis. The

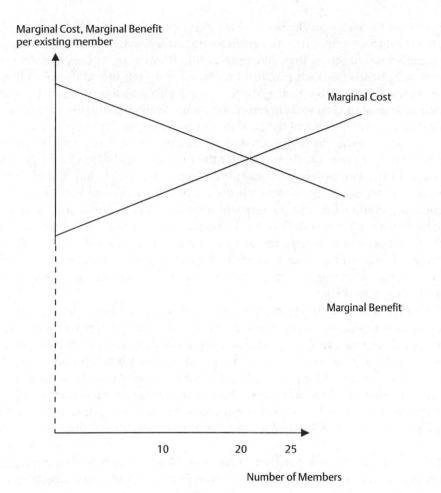

Fig. 4.1 Optimal club size

assumption that all the members are alike is what allows us to measure marginal benefit and marginal cost on a single axis. If every member were different, then we would need a separate axis for marginal benefit and marginal cost for each member. We will return to this assumption below.

Notice that marginal benefit decreases as the number of club members increases. This makes sense—the club begins to get crowded, the more members it has. The first members of the club are the most valuable; they bring the highest marginal benefit by joining. Later members are not so valuable. Notice also that marginal cost increases as the number of club members increases. This again makes sense. Just coordinating the activities of an additional member, together with those of existing members, drives the cost of an additional member up.

It pays to expand the club size as long as marginal benefit exceeds marginal cost—the existing club members will have an even better club, and the new member will also benefit from belonging. In Figure 4.1 we highlight three club sizes: 10, 20, and 25. At size 10, the club is too small—marginal benefit greatly exceeds marginal cost. Every one of the 10 members would benefit from adding an additional member. At size 25, the club is too large—marginal cost exceeds marginal benefit, and the club should reduce its member-ship. At size 20, the club is just right—the last member added just passed the marginal benefit/marginal cost test for being an economically justifiable addition to the club.

Of course, every member of the EU differs in many important respects: the size of its economy (as measured by GDP), population (the basis for the large/small distinction in the EU), and per capita GDP (the basis for the rich/poor distinction in the EU) among them. Germany has the largest economy and largest population, but is only average in per capita GDP, while Luxembourg has the smallest economy and population, but the highest per capita GDP. And the different members have different costs and benefits associated with enlargement. Germany is seeking to restore historic commercial links in Eastern Europe, which is much less of a concern to France. Both the UK and Germany welcome enlargement for what it will do to the CAP (see below), which is quite contrary to the position of France. So a model assuming identical members has to be taken with more than a grain of salt.

Nevertheless, despite the abstraction from detail of this simple model, it is still able to explain three basic facts we observe about EU enlargement. First, due to declining mar-ginal benefit and increasing marginal cost, the biggest gains accrue to the first members—which is precisely the experience of the original six members who form the core of today's EU. Secondly, as long as the EU is too small, no member will want to leave. If an EU with 15 members is too small, then those 15 members will surely want to stay in the EU. Thirdly, if an EU with 15 members is too small, then current non-members will want to join—up to the optimal size of 20. And this in a nutshell is the economic rationale for the enlargement.

This simple model is also powerful enough to explain two facts of EU history. First, no member after accession to the EU has subsequently tried to leave—and especially no core member. Secondly, the only members of the EU that have had second thoughts about membership—most recently, Austria—have been later accessions. For such members, the marginal benefit/marginal cost margin is rather narrow, and membership may not seem such a good deal. Indeed, in the latest polls, a majority of Austrians have rethought EU membership and favour leaving the Union, although economists almost uniformly agree that such a move would be detrimental to Austria economically. The model also allows us to make a prediction. If the EU should ever grow too large, beyond its optimal size, then we should expect to see members leave. The last to join are the most likely candidates to be the first to leave.

Of course the members of the EU are not identical, so one must be cautious in investing too much confidence in a model like that of Figure 4.1. Nevertheless, the lessons of Figure 4.1 carry over to higher dimensions, for instance when one considers marginal benefit and marginal cost to be functions not just of the number of members, but of a vector of numbers of different kinds of members. The simplest such extension, from number of members to number of members as categorized by large/small (in terms of population) and wealth, looks like the following:

Number of large/rich members: 4
Number of small/rich members: 8
Number of large/poor members: 1
Number of small/poor members: 2

Table 4.1. portrays the current membership in matrix form. The EU is primarily a club of rich members (12/15), and the dynamic benefits of membership are such that the current poor members project to become rich, at current growth rates, within a generation.

We now turn to the candidates for membership, where we see a very different picture.

4.3 **Candidates for EU membership**

According to the Treaty of Maastricht, 'Any European state may apply to become a Member of the Union.' (Article O). Although 'European state' is not defined in the treaty, one workable definition is membership in the Council of Europe, with 54 members. Take away the 15 current members of EU, and you still have 39 candidates. Take away the five postage stamp countries (Andorra, Liechtenstein, San Marino, Monaco, and the Vatican City), and you still have 34. Take away the three more members of EFTA (Switzerland, Norway, and Iceland) and you have 31. We should note that voters in Switzerland and Norway have voted against membership in the EU (twice in the case of Norway), so they are unlikely to join the ranks of candidate members any time soon. For the voters of Norway, and if a referendum were ever to be held, Iceland, opposition to the Common Fisheries Policy of the EU was a major reason to vote 'No'. The voters of Switzerland share many of the same concerns regarding EU membership as do the voters in neighbouring Austria.

Table 4.1 Current membership distribution

	Rich	Poor
Large	UK France Italy Germany	Spain
Small	Belgium Luxembourg Netherlands Ireland Denmark Sweden Finland Austria	Portugal Greece

Of those 31, 13 have applied for membership and their applications have been accepted. Applications are addressed to the European Commission, which then decides whether to accept or reject the application, in the context of the co-decision procedure. In the case of Morocco, the Commission twice rejected an application; in the case of Turkey, the Commission has had before it an application since 1962, which it only recently activated.

Table 4.2. lists the 13 candidates, by their vector of member types:

Number of large/rich candidates: 0
Number of small/rich candidates: 0
Number of large/poor candidates: 2
Number of small/poor candidates: 11

Two things stand out immediately: all the candidates are poor (13/13), and almost all are small (11/13). Should all 13 be admitted to membership, the EU would become a club of predominantly small countries (21/28), a majority of whose members are poor (16/28)—in other words, a very different club from at present.

This drastic difference has been pointed to with increasing frequency by the architects of the EU, most notably Jacques Delors, two-term President of the European Commission (1985–1995), who presided over both the single market and the run-up to the Treaty of Maastricht. In an interview with *Le Monde*, he expressed considerable caution about enlargement, noting it was wrong to think that what had worked in enlarging 'from six to nine and then to 12 is a good method for expanding to 27 or 32.' (*Financial Times*, 20 Jan. 2000). Delors went on to say that the expansion to the East was overly ambitious. Similar sentiments are routinely expressed by the political élites in the other large, rich countries, whose club the EU has traditionally been, along with their smaller but mostly rich neighbours. Interestingly, it was Delors who also presided over the Euro Summit in Essen, Germany, in 1995, at which the six 'front runners' among the candidates were

Table 4.2 Candidate members of the EU

	Rich	Poor
Large	–	Turkey Poland
Small	–	Romania Bulgaria Slovakia Czech Republic Malta Cyprus Slovenia Estonia Latvia Lithuania Hungary

Table 4.3 GDP per capita in candidate countries and in the EU (1996) in Purchasing Power Parity units, to the nearest thousand

Country	euros/person
EU	19,000
Cyprus, Czech Republic, Malta, Slovenia	10,000
Hungary, Poland, Slovakia	6,000–7,000
Bulgaria, Estonia, Latvia, Lithuania, Romania, Turkey	3,000–4,000

Source: Enlarging the European Union, European Commission, 1998.

invited to observe. These six candidates—the Czech Republic, Hungary, Poland, Slovenià, Estonia, and Cyprus—whose applications were accepted by the European Commission prior to 1998, often act as a group in public, even though the official position of the Commission is that all negotiations between the EU and candidates are on a strictly bilateral basis.

It is not just the qualitative difference of rich versus poor, but even more so the quantitative difference of just how poor the new candidates for membership are, that shows how the EU club could change (see Table 4.3).

It is clear from the table that the candidate countries fall into three types, by per capita GDP. The high-income type has per capita GDP of 10,000 euros—a little over half the EU average. The middle-income type has per capita GDP in the range 6,000–7,000—roughly one third the EU average. The low-income type has per capita GDP in the range 3,000–4,000, roughly one-sixth the EU average.

These numbers are somewhat abstract—they translate into poor, poorer, and poorest. To give them a wider context, consider the following thought experiment. Let the current members of the EU grow at an average rate of 2 per cent per year indefinitely; the candidate members are to grow twice as fast, on average at 4 per cent per year indefinitely. It would take almost 40 years for the high-income type like the Czech Republic to catch up with the EU average; while it would take the low-income type like Turkey a century to catch up with the EU average. In other words, even under very optimistic growth scenarios, these income differences can be expected to persist for a very long time.

4.4 Why does income matter to membership?

There is nothing in the rules that says only rich countries may apply for EU membership. Indeed, four times in the past a poor country has been admitted—Ireland in 1973, Greece in 1984, and Spain and Portugal in 1986. Ireland, by growing faster than the EU average, has just succeeded in leaving the ranks of the poor countries, a felicitous outcome which is testimony to the potential benefits of EU membership.

What the rules (since the Copenhagen European Summit of 1993) do require of candidates to be eligible for membership are the following conditions:

- a functioning market economy;
- a democratic political system;
- acceptance of the *acquis communautaire*.

It is clear, in view of the preceding discussion, that the higher a country's income the more likely that country is to satisfy these three eligibility criteria.

Consider first a functioning market economy. Although there is no theorem of mathematical economics to this effect, it is a strong empirical regularity that all rich countries are erected on a functioning market economy. This would seem to be a necessary, although not sufficient, condition for being a rich country. Ten of the candidates are in transition to a functioning market economy, after having been incorporated for various lengths of time in the Soviet colonial empire (the exceptions are Cyprus, Malta, and Turkey). These Central and East European countries have a long way to go to satisfy criterion one. The European Commission gives annual progress reports to each candidate; you can find the 1999 report cards on the Internet at http://europa.eu.int/comm/enlargement/report_10_99/intro/index.htm. For instance, the Czech Republic was rated as having made no progress in 1999 over 1998, in achieving a functioning market economy. When the richest of the transition countries is having trouble reaching this criterion, you can suspect that so are the rest.

Next consider a democratic political system. Again, the transition countries have overthrown Soviet-dominated one-party states and replaced them with multi-party democratic systems. However, these replacement systems all display what we shall call the 'Austrian problem'. Namely, they contain parties on the far right (nationalist) or far left (former communist, renamed) which are guaranteed to offend member state sensitivities, just as Austria's inclusion of such a party in its coalition government led to an EU crisis in February 2000. The Austrian problem, if anything, becomes worse the further east one goes in Europe. This consideration is one of the main reasons the marginal-cost-of-membership curve is rising. The more severe is the Austrian problem, the steeper is the rise in the marginal cost of membership.

It is not only the ten transition countries that have a problem with the second membership criterion: so do the three southern countries. Turkey has had three military governments the past 20 years, and remains a powder-keg of Islamic fundamentalism clashing with Atatürk's modernism for domination. Cyprus remains partitioned along the ceasefire lines of the 1974 war between Greece and Turkey; no democracy currently functions across the entire island. Malta is easily the most stable of these three. However, with its 200,000 inhabitants, barely half the size of Luxembourg, the EU will barely notice whether Malta joins or not.

Finally, consider the acceptance of the *acquis communitaire*, the some 80,000 pages of EU legislation all new (and existing) members are required to apply, implement, and enforce. Here it definitely pays to be rich, just to afford the lawyers required to wade through all this legislation. A significant part of this legislation deals with environmental rules and regulations. If the 10 transition candidates alone were to implement this legislation fully upon accession, the annual cost to them would be in the order of magnitude of 100 billion euros—roughly equal to the entire EU budget for a year. Clearly, that will not happen anytime soon—and particularly in poor countries where environmental concerns have a low priority compared to food and shelter (see Jovanovic (1999) for a longer discussion of this point).

If the three accession requirements are strictly applied, then none of the 13 candidates will enter the EU in the next five years. At the same time, the EU is publicly committed to an accession event no later than 2005. Clearly, something has to give here. What will probably take place is the accession of up to three transition countries (with Poland, Estonia, and Slovenia being the best bets) and one Mediterranean country (Cyprus) before the end of 2005, following the model of 1986, when Spain and Portugal entered. Both the latter were given long transition periods to reach EU levels of compliance with the *acquis*; the transition accession states will similarly be given even longer transition periods to reach EU levels of compliance.

4.5 Budget challenges to the enlargement

In 1947, the USSR and its Eastern European satellites were invited to participate in the Marshall Plan. The USSR rejected its invitation: in Molotov's words, the Marshall Plan was nothing but 'dollar imperialism'. But the Czechoslovak, Polish, and Hungarian delegations were ready to sign on in Paris, when they were called to heel by Stalin, and hurriedly boarded flights to Moscow (Gardner, 2000).

Thus, it is only historical justice, half a century delayed, when the EU offers a fractional Marshall Plan to its candidates for accession. The budget commitments, hammered out at the Berlin Summit of 1999, are detailed in Table 4.4.

Notice that the EU Budget provides for an accession event as early as 2002, as part of the Agenda 2000. It now appears exceedingly unlikely that any accession event will take place by then. However, an accession event no later than 2006 is a practical certainty, given the pressure from the budget to spend the money and get some results.

Pre-accession aid, available to all candidate members, is intended to defray the costs of

Table 4.4 EU enlargement, budget commitments (in billions of euros)

Year	Pre-accession aid	Available for new member countries
2000	3.1	0.0
2001	3.1	0.0
2002	3.1	4.1
2003	3.1	6.7
2004	3.1	8.9
2005	3.1	11.4
2006	3.1	14.2

Source: "Twenty-hour talk marathon ends in compromise" *Financial Times* 27/28 Mar. 1999.

preparing to comply with the *acquis communitaire*. This number is fixed annually throughout the period 2000–2006. It represents a lower bound to aid available for the enlargement. Relative to an EU budget of 100 billion euros, pre-accession aid is a commitment of 3 per cent. Since that EU budget is itself about 1 per cent of EU GDP, one can calculate that the smallest EU budget for enlargement is (3 per cent)(1 per cent) = 0.03 per cent of EU GDP. To put that number in Marshall Plan perspective, the Marshall Plan represented about 0.5 per cent of USA GDP per year. Thus, at a minimum, the EU is offering in terms of sacrifice a 1/16 Marshall Plan to its accession candidates.

Besides pre-accession aid, there is a variable category, comprising aid available to new members, accession candidates who have been accepted for membership. This category begins with 4.1 billion euros, and rises continuously to a peak of 14.2 billion euros in 2006. Of course, if no new members are admitted by that date, then these funds are not spent. In the event of maximum spending, the total available will be 3.1 + 14.2 = 17.3 billion euros, so in terms of sacrifice the EU is offering a 1/3 Marshall Plan to its new members and candidate members. Considering that the candidates are not recovering from the ashes of world war, as were the original Marshall Plan recipients, this order of magnitude of sacrifice seems not inappropriate.

These sums represent only the tip of the iceberg of the budget challenge the enlargement poses to the EU. Even at maximum spending, the enlargement category of the EU budget still ranks third behind spending on agriculture and structural operations. All the accession candidates have larger agricultural sectors than the EU average. The two big candidates, Poland and Turkey, have over 25 per cent of employment in agriculture, compared to the EU average of 5 per cent. If current agricultural programmes are left in place to apply to new members, then EU spending on this category will grow by between 50 per cent and 100 per cent, depending on developments within agriculture in the accession states.

Indeed, the implications of this possibility have not been lost on either current members or on candidate members. The former, especially Germany (the largest net contributor to the budget) and the UK, are pushing hard for reform of the CAP prior to enlargement. France, at the same time, is pushing hard for retention of the CAP in roughly its current form. In response, the six front-runners have all issued statements rejecting long transition periods and demanding full payment of current agricultural subsidies.

Structural operations are aimed exclusively at poor countries and poor regions. As we have seen, all the candidates are poor. Hence, they become targets of EU structural spending. Even a small enlargement, restricted to the front-runners, will still raise structural spending by 50 per cent at current rates. Needless to say, current beneficiaries of structural spending, chiefly Spain, are keen to defend the sums they receive against possible diversion to new members.

Considering that agricultural subsidies and structural operations account for three-quarters of the EU budget, a 50 per cent increase in spending here means a 37.5 per cent increase in spending overall. Add to that another 17 per cent increase in spending on enlargement, as detailed in Table 4.4, and one gets a number of around 55 per cent—a hefty increase in EU spending at a time when most of the members are practising fiscal discipline as part of their commitment to monetary union.

The budget challenge the enlargement poses to the existing members, in particular an increase in the EU budget of more than 50 per cent solely for enlargement, is fully consistent with the economy theory of clubs. It reflects the increasing marginal cost of membership. This cost increase will surely slow the pace of enlargement, compared to the quite optimistic projections of Agenda 2000. Whether the cost increase is enough to condemn the enlargement altogether is another matter. Economic calculations are by design narrow, compared to the broad political calculations that also find expression in the enlargement.

4.6 Economic integration challenges to the enlargement: even more variable geometry

When the EU was a tight-knit club of six or nine or even twelve members, the principle of unity of action was sacrosanct. Every member entered the customs union, or the single market, at the same time. Every member, even members such as Denmark, which had no intention of joining the monetary union, had to ratify the Treaty of Maastricht before any member could join that union.

Now that the monetary union has been launched, with a significant majority of, but not all, members, the EU enters a new style of economic integration: variable geometry. The EU no longer presents a single geometric object, but several such objects, whose variations add to the complexity of getting EU business done. As regards the variable geometry of the monetary union, there are three such objects:

- members of the euro zone (12);
- members of ERM II (1);
- members with floating exchange rates (2).

Enlargement promises to make this variable geometry even more variable. For example, if Estonia and Bulgaria, both of which have currency boards, join the EU and maintain their currency boards, then one immediately has a fourth object:

- members with currency boards (2)

If one were to ask when every member of the EU will belong to the monetary union, even without enlargement the answer must be 'Not for a long time'. With enlargement to 28 members, the answer is almost surely 'Many years hence'.

We might say that variable geometry exists to accommodate otherwise insuperable problems faced by the EU. The UK, Denmark, and Sweden do not wish to join the monetary union. If the principle of unified action were in place, then no monetary union could exist without participation by all the members. Thus, variable geometry allows a monetary union to exist with just a subset of the members. This is not the only such example: tax harmonization is another, and financial services regulation is a third. In the New Economy of Europe, we can expect to see variable geometry more as the rule than the exception in EU policy structures.

Given that the candidate members are poor, the four freedoms of the Single Market, and particularly Freedom of Labour, pose significant challenges to enlargement. Currently, any citizen of any EU country may work in any member country—the principle of establishment. Admitting poor countries with considerable rates of unemployment (the average level of unemployment in the candidate countries is somewhat above that of the EU) and low wage levels opens the single market in labour to a potentially large in-migration of labour. According to the theory of economic integration (Molle 1997), labour which is free to migrate moves from low-wage to high-wage areas, other things being equal. Just to take one example, consider a large front-runner like Poland: its accession would mean 10 million potential low-wage migrants, particularly from Polish agriculture. Even more worryingly, a porous eastern border of Poland opens the EU to ever larger migration from further east—Belarus, Russia, and Ukraine. Fears of such migration have led the EU to require visa regimes for potential border members like Poland with these countries.

It is worth pointing out another, more optimistic, view of labour migration. Labour migration from the poor countries already exists, much of it illegal. A better response is to prevent such illegal migration by making life better in the poor countries. And simply being on the road to EU membership promises to make life better, both in terms of direct EU pre-accession aid, as well as the ancillary growth effects that candidacy confers. For instance, being a candidate for EU membership is strongly correlated with investment climate (EBRD 1999), and investment is a major driver of economic growth.

Large-scale labour migration will almost certainly destabilize fragile coalition governments within the EU. The spectre of massive in-migration from eastern Europe to the current membership is already one of the factors driving political developments within Austria, and the growing popularity of nationalist parties throughout the EU. This is yet another reflection of the increasing marginal cost of membership with increasing size—here, the cost being the cost on the part of existing members of adjusting to large migrant populations. If the accession candidates were rich, then wages in the candidate countries would be roughly on a par with those inside the EU. In that case, labour migration would not be predicted, and this would not be an issue. It is the fact that all the accession candidates are poor, and some of them quite markedly so, that makes migration such a worrying issue—so much so that the Commission has announced a phase-in period of indeterminate length during which the freedom of labour to move is suspended for workers in new member states (for further discussion, see Chapter 14).

The upshot of the phase-in period for labour mobility is yet another dimension of variable geometry, with regard to the single market:

- members with full access to the single market (15);
- new members with restricted access to the single market (up to 13).

The picture that emerges is of a larger EU which has taken a large step backwards from hard-won integration gains by adding a large number of new members who are anything but integrated into the EU. And this picture can hardly appeal to the political élite that launched the enlargement in the first place.

This picture, together with the ongoing tension between the EU and Austria, has sparked a remarkable dialogue by members of the political élite within core states, especially Germany and France. Although the caution expressed by Jacques Delors, already mentioned above, might be dismissed as merely the words of a retiree, those of the German Foreign Minister or the President of France are not so easily dismissed. Both, during the year 2000, as pressure from candidates for accession builds, have called for a deepening of integration among the existing members before any new members are admitted. In the already famous phrase of German Foreign Minister Joschka Fischer, the EU is to move from 'confederacy to federation', and this, prior to further enlargement that widens the EU at the expense of its deepening. Fischer has repeated these words to the European Parliament, and other EU audiences. Moreover, the President of France, Jacques Chirac, has endorsed them in a speech to the German Parliament in Berlin, and made them a cornerstone of the French Presidency of the EU, during July–December 2000. The EU political élite, which, in 1995, set in motion the enlargement with the set of six front-runners, now faces the economic fundamentals, which hardly favour that enlargement—to say nothing of an even more ambitious enlargement of 13 candidates. If the EU indeed moves 'from confederacy to federation' before further enlargement, then that enlargement is pushed further back in time, well beyond 2003, before the next accession event takes place.

4.7 Conclusion

Although the EU has historically grown in size, that growth should not be taken as inevitable. Like any club, the EU has an optimal size, and that size is finite. In the event that the EU has already grown too large, then one should expect to see one or more restive members, who would prefer to leave the EU rather than stay as members. This is one, purely economic, interpretation of what is driving the unprecedented confrontation between the EU and Austria.

Even if the EU of 15 members is not too large, the margin between the benefits of adding a new member and the cost of adding a new member is not nearly as large in this enlargement as it has been in previous enlargements. This narrower margin is expressed in both marginal benefit and marginal cost. On the marginal benefit side, adding new members who are mostly small and poor does not greatly increase the gains to economic integration to the existing members. The accession candidates have little buying power, and are at a considerable distance from the core members of EU. At the same time, buying power and closeness to core members are the biggest determinants of increased trade, which in turn is the major source of marginal benefits of membership. On the marginal cost side, the poverty of all the candidate members, relative to EU average per capita GDP, makes them harder to integrate economically. This also makes them costly to the EU budget—which will go up roughly 50 per cent in the event of large-scale enlargement. Yet another dimension on the cost side is the possibility of large-scale migration of labour to the rich parts of the EU, especially from large poor countries (like Poland and Turkey) which have large, low-wage agricultural sectors.

The narrow margin between marginal benefit and marginal cost suggests that the EU is approaching its optimal size. It would be quite remarkable if that optimal size were 28 members. In a situation where the margin is narrow, then the risk of letting in too many new members becomes quite real, while the consequences of letting in too many members are hardly trivial. Those members will become restive—much more restive than Austria currently is—when they find that the costs of membership to them exceed the benefits.

In history, it is easy to see the hand of inevitability, even where no such inevitability existed, then or now. The creation of the EU, and its subsequent expansion, were not inevitable events. Although the theory of economic integration can explain why they were both beneficial, and how they have helped the affected populations enjoy some of the highest average standards of living in the world, this does not mean that the EU can grow ever larger. From the standpoint of the theory of clubs—of which today's EU is an outstanding example—an EU which is too large is an EU which is not optimal.

There are serious risks to a botched enlargement, risks which the EU political élite is now beginning to take seriously. Although prediction is a risky business, it would seem a safe bet that any enlargement prior to the next edition of this book is a low-probability event.

4.8 Postscript: the Nice Summit

Just as we are about to go to press, the European Summit held in Nice, France, December 2000, brings new information and a somewhat clearer vision of the scale and pace of the enlargement. After lengthy and sometimes tense debate, the EU made provisions for eventual voting weights on the re-weighted European Council for all 12 candidates. The largest candidate, Poland, is to receive the same weighting as Spain (27), 2 fewer than the 29 votes accorded to each of the 4 largest current members. Of course, these weights (indeed, all the outcomes of the Summit) have to be agreed by the member countries before they become official. The re-weighting of the European Council sends a strong signal to the 12 candidates that they will eventually be admitted.

Although the Nice Summit did not make any official decisions as to the date of the next accession, it is widely considered that the next accession will take place around 1 January 2004, nine years to the day after the last wave of accessions in 1995. Again, no official decision was made as to the identity of candidates that might accede on or about that date. However, based on the latest European Commission annual reports on the candidates, it is all but certain that Poland will be part of the next accession wave. The Summit raised the expectation in some quarters that not just Poland but all six of the first set of candidates might be admitted in 2004. Such a large accession remains unlikely.

In terms of the EU budget, the 2001–2006 budget commitments remain unchanged. This implies that if, as seems likely, Poland is admitted, then agricultural subsidies and structural/regional funds to all new members will fall below the levels to which existing members are accustomed. Once new members are present for budget talks, one can anticipate great debate over this discrepancy in the equal rights of membership. Such debate constitutes a marginal cost of membership for all involved. In a revealing twist, although structural/regional funds are henceforth to be decided by qualified majority vote, Spain, the only large poor member as of now, retains a veto on such funds until 2007.

Similarly, the question of access to the Single Market in labour by workers in newly admitted candidate countries was addressed. Such access will not be immediate, but phased in, starting no sooner than one year after accession. In another revealing twist, although visa regimes are henceforth to be decided by qualified majority vote, Germany, the member with the largest population of asylum seekers, retains a veto on such issues until 2007. Germany is expected to press for strict visa regimes on the EU's new eastern border in its capacity as veto player.

Taken as a whole, the results of the Nice Summit point to a wider EU, with at least 16 and probably 18 members by 2004—even if this widening comes at the expense of further deepening of the EU. And the broad contours, as well as the finer details, of the enlargement reveal the tensions we have pointed to in this chapter. Those tensions are real, and making the enlargement a success will be no mean feat for the EU and its leaders.

Discussion questions

1   What are the main challenges the current members of the EU face in the enlargement? What are the main challenges facing the candidates? Highlight the role of per capita GDP in your discussion.

2   Labour mobility is one of the principles of the Single Market. Discuss the role of labour mobility in an enlarged EU. In particular, describe some policies that might make for a smoother adjustment in labour-market conditions throughout an enlarged EU.

3   According to the economic theory of clubs, once a club gets too large, some of its members have an incentive to leave. Using this theory, assess the prospects of an even wider EU, containing not just the current members and candidates for membership but also the remaining Balkan states, Turkey, Russia, Ukraine, and Belarus.

Further reading

There is a variety of sources of data on the economies of the candidates for EU membership; noteworthy among these is the EBRD's annual *Transition Report*, the latest being for the year 2000. The European Commission has just produced a quite attractive

publication, *European Union Enlargement: A Historic Opportunity*. The latest reports on individual candidates' progress towards membership, as well as a great deal of other useful material, can be found on the Internet at:
http://europa.eu.int/comm/enlargement

References

Artis, M. and F. Nixon (2001), *The Economics of the European Union*, 3rd ed. (Oxford: Oxford University Press).

Cornes, R. and Sandler, T. (1996), *The Theory of Externalities, Public Goods and Club Goods*. (Cambridge: Cambridge University Press).

EBRD (European Bank for Reconstruction and Development; 1999), *Transition Report 1999* (London; EBRD).

European Commission, website address:
http://europa.eu.int/comm/enlargement/report_10_99/intro/index.htm

European Commission (1998), *Enlarging the European Union* (Luxembourg: Office for Official Publications of the European Communities).

Financial Times (1999*a*), 'Delors cautions on enlargement', 20 Jan.

—— (1999*b*), 'Twenty-hour talk marathon ends in compromise'. 27/28 Mar.

Gardner, R. (2000), 'The Marshall Plan 50 Years After: Three What-ifs and One When', in M. Schain (ed.), *The Marshall Plan: 50 Years Later* (New York: St. Martin's Press).

Gros, D. and Steinherr, A. (1995), *The Winds of Change* (Boston: MIT Press).

Jovanovic, M. (1999), 'Where are the Limits to the Enlargement of the European Union?', *Journal of Economic Integration*, 14: 467–96.

Molle, W. (1997), *The Economics of European Integration: Theory, Practice, Policy* (Brookfield, Vt: Ashgate).

Chapter 5
The Common Agricultural Policy

David Colman

5.1 Introduction

The Common Agricultural Policy (CAP) of the EU is a remarkably complex assembly of instruments and regulations covering such matters as trade controls, price-support measures, income transfers, production subsidies, investment grants, conservation policies, health regulations, and labelling standards. It entails a huge bureaucracy, most of it at national level, to manage and oversee its operations. Additional complexity continually emerges as the policy as a whole adjusts to the quadruple pressures of:

1. budgetary and consumer costs;
2. anguished responses by non-Member States whose trade interests are damaged;
3. concerns for the environmental damage caused by modern farming methods; and
4. protests about falling farm incomes despite the high costs of the policy.

In response to these pressures the CAP underwent a major change in 1992/3, which added to its complexity. These reforms, named after the then Agriculture Commissioner Ray MacSharry, involved a large reduction (phased in by 1995/6) in the commodity price support levels, and the introduction of a system of direct subsidies in compensation for these price cuts for those farmers prepared to reduce and limit input use (see Table 5.3 below for details). A further set of reforms was introduced in 'Agenda 2000', which deepened the MacSharry reforms and greatly increased emphasis on environmental protection and public goods output. In the wake of these changes, it is necessary to explain the 'old' system of price support, which has survived since 1957 but with diminished importance, and the 'new' system of compensation and income support which has been grafted on.

As explained in Section 5.3 below, there is no doubt that the course of CAP reform was greatly influenced by the negotiations on agriculture in the Uruguay Round of the

General Agreement on Tariffs and Trade (GATT), which commenced in 1986 and were finally concluded in 1994.[1] A significant contribution to achieving the final settlement was the negotiation by MacSharry in November 1992 of a bilateral agreement with the USA, the so-called Blair House Accord. He and the European Commission claimed that the EU could comply with the agricultural commitments in the Uruguay Round of GATT up to the year 2000 without breaking the bounds of the 1992/3 CAP reform package, a position which has proved to be substantially correct (Tangermann 1996).

One outcome of the Uruguay Round Agreement (URA) was the setting up of the World Trade Organisation (WTO) and agreement that a new 'Millennium Round' of trade liberalization negotiations should begin in 2000, in which agricultural policy is centre stage. From the EU standpoint this round is made more complex by the agreements to admit a number of Central and Eastern European Countries (CEECs) to membership of the EU.

In reflection of the situation sketched above, this chapter continues by exploring the economics of the main agricultural policy instruments which have endured since the founding of the European Economic Community (EEC) in 1957. This is followed in Section 5.3 by a brief review of the pressures which have helped to bring about the reform of the CAP. Sections 5.4 and 5.6 deal with the reforms themselves, starting first with reforms prior to 1992 and then proceeding to examine the 'MacSharry reform package' and that of Agenda 2000. This is followed by Section 5.7 on the agricultural policy problems of incorporating CEECs into the EU. Finally there is a brief discussion of possible future changes to the CAP.

5.2 The original system of CAP

The establishment of an integrated common market for agriculture by its original six Member States was a pivotal task in the formation of the EEC, and is the one which has persistently made the largest demands on its budgetary resources. Article 39 of the Treaty of Rome sets out a number of objectives, including ensuring supplies to consumers at reasonable prices, but the consistent emphasis of the CAP until the mid-1980s was 'to increase agricultural productivity by promoting technical progress' and 'to ensure a fair standard of living for the agricultural community'.

In the post-war period, when the memory of food shortages was relatively fresh, the productivist emphasis of the founding member countries was understandable. The dominant method of agricultural support had been import tariffs, which were an effective means of raising agricultural prices, since, in the early 1960s, the six Member States were net importers of cereals and oilseeds and only just self-sufficient in livestock products. With this background of external protection, the movement to a common external tariff (CET) for agriculture, as required by the Treaty of Rome, was a politically acceptable step towards the creation of a common market when accompanied by the abolition of customs duties on internal trade within the ring-fence of the CET. Importantly, for agriculture, instead of fixed tariffs, the EEC adopted a variable import tariff or levy system (which persisted until July 1995, when fixed tariffs were, in principle, introduced—see below). This entailed setting minimum import prices (MIPs) with variable import levies (VILs) equal to the difference between the minimum import price and the lowest c.i.f. price offered by importers at the Community's borders. In the case of cereals the MIP is now referred to as the *reference price* in the jargon of the CAP.

Because the MIP for all major products was (with minor exceptions in 1974 and 1978) consistently maintained above the c.i.f. international prices (P_m), at which imports were available, EU market prices of imported commodities have been forced upwards. Figure 5.1 shows the theoretical effects of this. EU supply is increased from S_m to S and demand is depressed from D_m to D. Thus the imported quantity falls from $(D_m - S_m)$ to $(D - S)$. This trade-distorting feature of the policy was, however, exacerbated from the standpoint of agricultural exporting countries by two attendant facts. One is that import demand $(D - S)$ became completely inelastic to changes in world prices. As P_m fell, the variable import levy (VIL) increased to ensure that no imports entered the EU at below the MIP; the EU market was completely insulated from all movements in international prices unless they rose above the MIP. The second is that international market prices are forced downwards; they would rise if EU price support and trade distortion was reduced and EU import demand was higher.

The increase in internal EU prices causes *producer surplus to rise* by the value of area A, as shown in Figure 5.1. *Budgetary revenues* equal in value to C accrue to the EU from import levies/tariffs and may be counted as a gain (less some cost for collection). These two gains $(A + C)$ are, however, more than offset by the *loss in consumer surplus* equivalent to areas $A + B + C + D$.[2] In fact, using this neoclassical economic calculus shows an overall *economic welfare loss* to the EU from the policy of $B + D$, reflecting a basic result of comparative static economic theory that free trade is optimal and that trade interventions result in a loss of economic welfare.

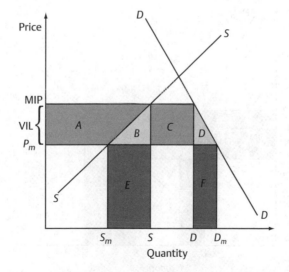

Fig. 5.1 Basic system of external protection for imported commodities

This last result can be confirmed by a dual calculation based on Figure 5.1. *Extra resource costs* of $B + E$ are stimulated by the price support to generate output which could be *imported at a cost* of E, thus registering a *welfare loss B*. Consumers have also reduced consumption which they value at $F + D$, but which cost them only F before the imposition of the MIP, resulting in an additional *welfare loss* of D and producing a total economic welfare loss or *deadweight loss* of $B + D$.

Because of rapid technical change in agriculture, further stimulated by prices supported above international levels, underlying agricultural supply growth in the EU has continuously exceeded domestic demand growth and resulted in the emergence of excess supply in cereals, beef, dairy products, wine, and some fruits. This has meant that the internal price support mechanism of *intervention buying* (Figure 5.2) played an important role when production of commodities in the EU moved into surplus. This internal support system operates through the process whereby national authorities operating the EU policy offer to buy produce of at least minimum standard quality at certain times of the year at the intervention price P_i. The latter is set in Euros at the Community-level EU's annual price-fixing round and is the basis of common pricing throughout the Community. In effect P_i acts as a floor price in the market,[3] and it has been consistently set above the f.o.b. export price, P_x which could be obtained by exporting the surplus. This form of price support has not been applied to all commodities covered by the CAP, but applies to wheat, barley, to milk in the forms of butter and skimmed milk powder, to beef, and to wine after distillation. In a modified form it applies to certain fruits and vegetables and fish, surpluses of which cannot be stored but have to be destroyed.

The effects of the internal price support policy are broadly as shown in Figure 5.2. The higher price and additional output stimulated (from S_x to S_i) results in increased *producer surplus* of $H + I + J$. Consumer surplus is reduced by $H + I$, as demand is cut from D_x to D_i. The

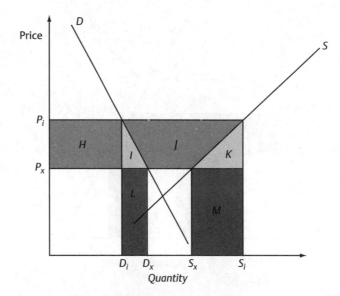

Fig. 5.2 Basic system of internal protection for commodities in surplus

amount by which supply exceeds consumer demand, $S_i - D_i$, is purchased into intervention stores, where it develops into the beef and butter mountains, and wine lakes, as they were often referred to in the media. It is conventional to explain the *budgetary costs* which arise from these intervention surpluses as being equivalent to areas $I + J + K$ in the figure. This is the cost which would arise if all the surplus $(S_i - D_i)$ is disposed of as exports with the aid of an *export refund*, or export subsidy, equal to $P_i - P_x$; alternatively it is the loss made by the intervention authority from buying the surplus at P_i and selling at P_x. In reality $I + J + K$ underestimates the budgetary cost of surplus management, since it does not allow for the storage costs or for the deterioration and wastage of product while stored. If, however, we accept this measure of budgetary cost and add the consumer surplus loss of $H + I$, it transpires that the producer surplus gain of $H + I + J$ only partially offsets it, and leaves an economic welfare loss of $I + K$. The same result is obtained by setting the increased export revenue $(L + M)$ against the resource cost $(K + M)$ plus the reduction in consumption value $(I + L)$.

A point which should be emphasized is that the system of intervention buying (Figure 5.2) cannot be operated without a minimum import price policy (as in Figure 5.1) if P_i exceeds P_m, which is how the CAP has been operated. Without an MIP in excess of P_i it would be profitable to import at price P_m in order to sell into intervention, which would be a completely unstable and untenable state of affairs. Thus, even though in the 1980s and early 1990s the primary instrument of agricultural price support has been intervention buying, the import-levy/minimum-import-price system has been necessary to protect its operation.[4]

5.3 The pressures for CAP reform

Budgetary pressure

The budgetary costs of the CAP provided a persistent source of pressure leading to the MacSharry reforms of 1992 (see below). They contributed significantly to the need to increase the total tax transfer from 0.77 per cent of the GDP of the nine members in 1980 to 1.03 per cent of the GDP of the twelve members in 1989. This was necessary to permit the expansion of spending on regional and social policy and for the percentage of total EU budgetary expenditure on the CAP to drop from 73 per cent in 1980 to 66 per cent in 1989. This modest change was only achieved by a continuous stream of *ad hoc* measures, as described in Section 5.4 below, to contain agricultural spending, and the periodic effects of a stronger US dollar which reduced the subsidy cost of exporting EU surpluses. The reforms which subsequently occurred have reduced CAP expenditure since 1993 to under 50 per cent of the total EU budget (see Figure 5.3).

It is the costs of agricultural surplus management which dominate the budgetary expenditure of the European Agricultural Guidance and Guarantee Fund (EAGGF).[5] Export restitution costs alone regularly account for over 30 per cent of total EAGGF cost, with the bulk of the 'other expenditure' being on costs for surplus storage and subsidized

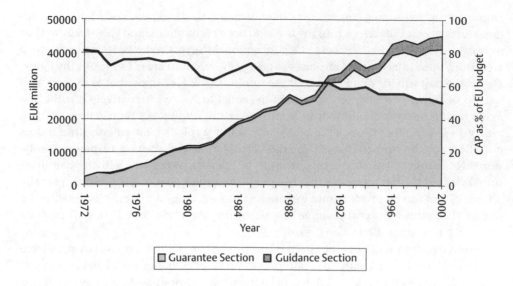

Fig. 5.3 EAGGF expenditure on the CAP: selected years (m. euros)
Source: Various issues of the *Official Journal of the European Communities.*

market disposal within the EU. As can be seen, Guidance Section expenditure on improving the farm structure of agriculture has (despite increases) remained small, with the vast bulk of budgetary resource diverted to market support under the Guarantee Section.

Some of the *ad hoc* measures to contain budgetary costs and surpluses prior to the 1992 reform package were very significant, such as the introduction of milk marketing quotas, which are discussed below, and co-responsibility levies. These measures failed to halt the relentless rise in the budget required for the CAP, and the reforms of 1992 became inexorable. It must be recognized that budgetary costs are *transfers*. Funds are paid as taxes by certain groups in society and paid out or transferred to others. In economic welfare terms, such transfers are not a complete loss of resource; this is evident from the analysis based on Figures 5.1 and 5.2 above, where the triangular areas of deadweight loss are much smaller than the budgetary and consumer cost transfers. In the case of the budgetary transfers, revenue is raised as a VAT levy at the country level, through direct national budgetary contributions and through import and sugar production levies; these are transferred to the EU in support of the principle of common financing of the Union's costs. These revenues are then used to finance storage and subsidized disposal of surplus products, and also the new forms of agricultural support detailed below. It follows that countries which import more agricultural products tend to contribute more revenue to the EU and that there is a net transfer to countries with greater surpluses to store and export. For example, in 1992 the largest net contributors to the CAP budget were (in billions of ecus) Germany (9.7) and the UK (2.4), while the main net gainers were Greece (3.6), Spain (2.7), Ireland (2.1), and Portugal (2.1).[6] Inevitably it has been the case that some countries have pressed for budgetary reform of the CAP with less enthusiasm than others, and that those which have pushed hardest, such as the UK, have sometimes been accused of lacking 'Community spirit'.

Consumer pressure

All the estimates of the costs of the original CAP system have demonstrated (unsurprisingly, given the assumption that any change in agricultural prices in the EU would be fully transmitted to food consumers) that the estimated transfer costs from consumers exceed the budgetary or taxpayer transfer by a significant margin. This is shown in the estimates for the EC by Roningen and Dixit (1989) in Table 5.1.[7] These are that in 1986 the cost to consumers in terms of higher food costs was over twice the budgetary cost of supporting agriculture and was almost equal to the net benefits to producers.

Various estimates have been made of the average cost imposed on EU non-farm families through higher prices and taxes to support the CAP. For 1984 the Department of Primary Industry (DPI)—Australia (1986: 1) estimated this at US $900 per family per year. This estimate of £600 (at an exchange rate of $1.5: £1), or £11.54 per week per family, compares with other estimates which range up to £16 per week per family of four depending upon the year considered. Since even non-taxpayers, the poorest members of society, may have to bear perhaps 60 per cent of this cost, and since larger farms and generally wealthier farmers benefit most, the CAP can be legitimately criticized for transferring funds from the poorest members of society (since all must eat) to some who are relatively well off; although there are also poor farmers in the EU. While this fact has been well recognized, the political lobby for consumers' interests has not developed the same weight of influence as the farm and agro-industry lobbies, which have a specified central place in agricultural policy negotiations. Thus it has been largely left to academics, and particularly economists, to argue for CAP reform on the grounds of excessive cost to non-farm families as both consumers and taxpayers (e.g. Brown 1989; BAE 1985: ch. 6; and Josling and Hamway 1972).

External pressure: the Uruguay Round of GATT

The CAP gave rise to progressive increases in trade distortion up to 1990. This was not even disguised by the incorporation of new Member States, which, by a process of trade

Table 5.1 Benefits and costs of agricultural support, 1986/7 ($ billion)

Countries	Producer benefits ($USbn.)	Consumer costs ($USbn.)	Taxpayer costs ($USbn.)	Net economic costs[a] ($USbn.)	Transfer ratio[b] ($USbn.)
USA	26.3	6.0	30.0	9.2	1.4
EC	33.3	32.6	15.6	14.9	1.5
Japan	22.6	27.7	5.7	8.6	1.5

a   Net economic costs: consumer costs + taxpayer costs—producer benefits.
b   (Taxpayer + consumer costs)/Producer benefits.
Source: Roningen and Dixit 1989.

diversion, switched a significant proportion of their agricultural imports from non-member to Member States. (This was particularly true of the accession to the EC of Eire, the UK, Spain, and Portugal). Table 5.2 confirms this general picture, showing, for several major commodities, either a substantial increase in EC net exports between 1973 and 1992 or, even more strikingly, a switch from being a net importer to a major net exporter. From the standpoint of non-member exporters of temperate zone agricultural products, not only have they suffered a severe contraction of their EU market as a consequence of the principle of community preference, but they have had to face intensified competition in other markets from the EU's subsidized exports. Australia and New Zealand were particularly badly affected when the UK joined the EC, and the USA (as the world's largest agricultural exporter) suffered particularly in the early 1980s, prior to the inauguration of the Uruguay Round of negotiations on GATT in 1986. As an indication of this, Figure 5.4 displays the dramatic changes in EU and US agricultural export volume in this period.

The USA's concern about the CAP, and about protective policies in Japan and elsewhere, can be gauged from the fact that, although it was at the USA's insistence that agricultural policy was excluded from earlier rounds of GATT negotiations and agreements, it was made the centrepiece of the Uruguay Round. Although agriculture was only one of fifteen negotiating heads, the USA stated that without a satisfactory solution on agriculture it would not sign an agreement. In seeking drastically to reduce agricultural support

Table 5.2 Net external trade in selected agricultural products, 1973–1993

Year	Product					
	Wheat[a] (mt)	Other cereals[a] (excl. rice) (mt)	Sugar[a] (mt)	Butter (000t)	Cheese (000t)	Beef and veal[b] (000t)
EC9						
1973	—	−10.8	−1.1	+204	+41	−913
1977	+0.9	−20.8	+0.1	+140	+84	−210
EC10						
1981	+10.7	−3.4	+3.3	+373	+213	+389
1983	+11.5	+0.5	+2.6	+250	+292	+165
1986	+11.9	+5.5	+2.6	+220	+269	+714
EC12						
1989	+18.3	+7.6	+3.3	+332	+324	+589
1991	+21.9	+7.4	+2.9	+275	+374	+804
1993	+20.2	+9.8	+4.7	+118	+415	+697
EU15						
1995	+10.5	+6.0	+3.3	+144	+446	+718
1996	+16.2	n.a.	n.a.	+97	+433	+646
1997	n.a.	n.a.	n.a.	+131	+400	+582

a Wheat, other cereals, and sugar data are for harvest years 1973/4 to 1996/7; other commodities data are for calendar years.
b Estimated: includes the carcass weight equivalent of trade in live animals.
Notes: Net imports are denoted by a minus (-) sign, and net exports by a plus (+) sign.
n.a. = not available.
Source: CEC, *The Agricultural Situation in the Community*; *Official Journal of the European Communities (various issues)*.

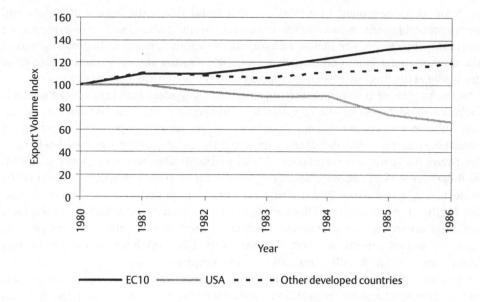

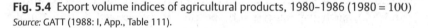

Fig. 5.4 Export volume indices of agricultural products, 1980–1986 (1980 = 100)
Source: GATT (1988: I, App., Table 111).

policies, the USA was backed by the so-called Cairns Group of agricultural exporting countries, which includes Australia and New Zealand.

In order to explain how the GATT negotiations influenced the 1992 reform of the CAP it is helpful to give a simplified account of the negotiating position of the USA and EU. (These and the positions of other groups are more fully summarized in Rayner *et al.* 1993). At the outset, in 1987–8 the USA demanded:

1. elimination of all trade-distorting subsidies within ten years;

2. elimination of all import barriers, including all health and non-health non-tariff barriers (NTBs);

3. changes to policies for individual commodities to permit the agreed phasing-out of government support;

4. increased market access; and

5. use of an aggregate measure of support (AMS) to establish initial levels of protection and to monitor progress with their elimination.

The importance of the last condition is apparent. In order to obtain a multinational agreement covering many commodities on reforming agricultural policy, there has first to be a common consent to use a particular measure of the distortion to be reduced or eliminated, and agreement as to its size for each commodity and each country. Then it is possible to negotiate timetables for reducing this distortion. The USA proposed a version of a measure called a Producer Subsidy Equivalent (PSE).

From the outset the EU accepted the need for an AMS but championed its own version, the Support Measurement Unit (SMU), which could reflect the impact of supply and support control measures taken in the second half of the 1980s. The EU, however, did not accept the objective of eliminating all agricultural support, proposing instead the notion of a short-term agreement on international market sharing and prices, with a long-term strategy of achieving more balanced support through reciprocal agreements.

In the process of negotiation that ensued, some key ideas emerged, two of which—*tariffication* and *decoupling*—deserve mention. One aspect of EU policy which was particularly abhorrent to other exporting countries was the variable import levies and export subsidies, since (as noted above) these insulated the EU market almost completely from short-term fluctuations in world prices. The key to *tariffication* was the expression of non-tariff barriers as tariff equivalents and the combining of these with specific import tariffs to create single, bound (i.e. fixed maximum) tariffs. This placed an upper limit on protection against imports and paved the way for fixed (as opposed to variable) tariffs and their reduction according to a negotiated schedule. In implementing the GATT Agreement, however, special conditions affect the way tariff reduction is applied for individual commodities. Tariffs do still change and are not completely fixed.

Given that the central issue is trade distortion, it can reasonably be argued that there is no fundamental cause for international dispute if a country chooses to support its farmers in ways which do not cause supply to exceed competitive free trade levels (S_m and S_x in Figures 5.1 and 5.2). Such payments might be said to be *decoupled* from supply response and not to be trade distorting. Academically the hunt has been on to identify forms of support which might be sufficiently decoupled. One proposal (Blandford *et al.* 1989) was for the introduction of Production Entitlement Guarantees (PEGs) whereby, for each commodity, farmers would be eligible for fixed payments on a quantity of output less than S_m and S_x in Figures 5.1 and 5.2. In that way, it might be argued, supply at the margin would be influenced only by the free-market price and would not be affected by the support payment offered. Another proposal (Tangermann 1991) was for an Income Bond, which would be given to farmers to compensate them for removal of all price support; the bond could either be retained as a source of annual income or sold to release capital.

Over the course of the Uruguay Round, the USA was forced to relax its position and it agreed to accept that certain types of support, modelled very much on its own policy at that time, were sufficiently decoupled to be exempt from the reductions in support levels required by GATT; that is, these measures were not included in the AMS finally agreed for reduction in the Uruguay Round Agreement. These so-called 'blue-box' measures are support payments for which farmers can qualify only by adopting certain supply-restricting measures such as *setting-aside* (taking out of production) a proportion of previously farmed arable land. The acceptance of this blue-box category, and agreement to place other environmentally related support payments in the so-called 'green box', proved critical in bridging the gap between the US position and that of the EU. It led, in November 1992, to the signing of the so-called Blair House Accord, a bilateral agreement between the two negotiating parties.

The Blair House Accord contained four critical elements to be phased into the CAP over the period 1993–9. These were, first, a commitment to *tariffy* all existing border measures and reduce tariff levels by 36 per cent (although an element of Community preference has been maintained by the EU via the so-called 'special safeguard clause'); secondly, an agreement to reduce internal support measures by 20 per cent from 1986–8 levels (with the blue-box compensation payments exempt for the reasons outlined above); thirdly, a commitment to reduce the value of export subsidies by 36 per cent and subsidized export volume by 21 per cent; and, finally, the acceptance of a 'Peace Clause' which lasts until 2003 and effectively limits both the EU and the USA from taking unilateral trade action against each other's farm policies until that date. This Accord, which formed the basis of the final GATT Agreement, paved the way for the European Council of Ministers to approve the MacSharry reforms of the CAP in 1992, before the Uruguay GATT Round was concluded, in a way which reduced the impression that the EU had been forced into reform by external international pressure.

The Uruguay Round Agreement (URA) was finally concluded in 1994, with the MacSharry reforms accepted as the basis for honouring the EU's commitments. These commitments, covering the period 1995 to 2000, and implemented by 2000, can be summarized as follows:

- Reduce the AMS of all trade-distorting, 'amber-box', measures by 20 per cent. Blue- and green-box measures to be exempted.

- Reduce existing and new tariffs by 36 per cent on average, and reduce tariffs by at least 15 per cent for each item.

- Reduce expenditure on export subsidies by 36 per cent and the volume of subsidized exports by 21 per cent.

Environmental pressure

As agricultural production has intensified since 1960, particularly in the northern EU countries, concern about its adverse environmental impact has grown. Increased use of inorganic fertilizer has resulted in high nitrate and phosphate levels in rivers and lakes, with consequent problems of excessive algae and bacteria in lakes and streams which kill aquatic organisms; it is caused by leaching of agriculture fertilizers. Field sizes have been increased by eliminating hedgerows and removing small woodlands and trees, with a consequent loss of wildlife. Wildlife has also been adversely affected by the heavy use of pesticides and herbicides, some of which cause a damaging build-up of toxic compounds in the food chain. Draining of wetlands and improvement of permanent pasture have caused serious habitat loss to birds, plants, insects, and amphibians. At the same time as these changes have occurred in areas of higher agricultural potential, more remote dis-advantaged areas have been struggling to maintain farming systems acknowledged to have high landscape value. For these, the underlying problems are agricultural decline and depopulation of some areas.

To the extent that most of the environmental concerns are the consequence of intensi-fication of production, itself stimulated by EU price support, diverse strong environ-mental pressure groups have emerged arguing for agricultural policy reform. The Commission's 1984 Green Paper *Perspectives for the Common Agricultural Policy* explicitly recognized that there was a 'need for agricultural policy to take more account of environmental policy, both as regards the control of harmful practices, and the promotion of practices friendly to the environment' (von Meyer 1990). However, despite this recognition, environmental measures introduced as part of the CAP prior to the 1992 reforms were limited. They have, however, been strengthened in the Agenda 2000 reforms (see Section 5.6, below).

The Agricultural Structures Policy Regulation 797/85 permitted the designation of *Environmentally Sensitive Areas* (ESAs) within which contractual payments were allowed to be paid to farmers to compensate them for profitability loss as a result of agreeing to de-intensify production and take measures to conserve traditional methods, features, and habitats. Limited to special protection areas, and depending on voluntary recruitment of farmers into the scheme, this policy initiative did little to alleviate the mounting environmental concerns. Moreover, the scheme violated the 'polluter-pays principle' adopted by EU environmental policy; instead, it provided compensation for not polluting and created a new form of agricultural support. Up to 1990, ESAs were implemented in only four Member States with a cost to the EC budget in 1989/90 of 10 million ecu out of the total CAP budget of some 30 billion ecu. However, as described in Section 5.5 below, the Agri-Environmental Programme which accompanied the 1992 CAP reforms has subsequently enhanced the role of environmental policies within the CAP.

5.4 The start of the reform process: the introduction of supply-control mechanisms

Throughout the existence of the CAP, its policy instruments and regulations have been adapted to meet changing economic and political circumstances. For example, during the 1970s, in response to the growing surpluses of some commodities, the EU introduced several new measures to the CAP designed to encourage domestic consumption; including subsidies to certain categories of final consumers, subsidies to industrial users of food products, and even 'denaturing premiums' (whereby product was dyed and in other ways made unfit for human consumption) to encourage the use of grain in livestock feed. Alternatively, the EU attempted to decrease the budgetary cost of an existing policy instrument—intervention buying—by changing its rules of operation; for many commodities supported by this policy instrument, the period of availability of intervention buying has been shortened and the quality standards for acceptance have been raised, whilst the price received for sales to intervention has been reduced to a so-called *buying-in price*, set some percentage points below the relevant intervention price. However, few, if any, of these *ad hoc* measures did anything substantial to alleviate the mounting pressures for more radical reform of the CAP.

It was not until the early 1980s that more significant changes to the CAP were initiated, with the introduction of three new supply control mechanisms—*marketing quotas*, *co-responsibility levies*, and *budgetary stabilizers*. The introduction of these supply-control mechanisms essentially marked the end of unlimited price guarantees, with each incorporating what has became known as the 'fourth principle' of the CAP, *producer co-responsibility* for surplus production. For commodities covered by such policy instruments, if production exceeded a certain fixed level (known as the guarantee threshold), action was triggered which ensured that at least part of the cost of the additional surplus disposal was borne by producers. The discussion below focuses on one mechanism which was retained in the May 1992 CAP reform package, namely marketing quotas.

The economics of marketing quotas

Marketing quotas were first imposed on EU dairy producers in spring 1984 against a background of long-term structural surpluses of dairy products, an extremely depressed world market, and escalating budgetary costs of milk support. Throughout the 1970s and early 1980s the milk regime accounted for the largest proportion of total guarantee expenditure of the CAP, although this fell from 29.7 per cent of EAGGF expenditure in 1984 to 18.2 per cent in 1992.

Prior to the introduction of quotas, in 1981 the EU had introduced a system of maximum guaranteed thresholds intended to operate in such a way that, should milk deliveries in any year exceed the (pre-fixed) quantitative threshold, action would be triggered to offset the additional costs of the regime caused by the excess production. As early as 1983 the guarantee threshold was exceeded by 6.5 per cent. The reduction in intervention price for dairy products which should have been triggered by this surplus was estimated by the Commission to have been in the order of 12 per cent—too large to be politically feasible. Instead, the EU chose to maintain the level of price support at its existing level and adopt a system of marketing quotas made effective by charging a very high tax, or *super-levy*, on excess deliveries beyond the quota.

Initially, each Member State was allocated a national quota or 'reference quantity' set equal to their 1981 milk delivery levels plus 1 per cent (apart from Italy and Ireland, whose initial reference quantities were based on the quantity of milk delivered during 1983). Quotas were then allocated to individual farmers, again on the basis of their historical production levels.

The welfare implications of quotas, as compared to those arising from a straight price support reduction for dairy products, are shown in Figure 5.5. Importantly, both sets of welfare effects are measured relative to a base scenario of surplus production and of the EU maintaining a support price at a level significantly above the world price for dairy products. In other words, the base scenario is intended to reflect the situation in the EC dairy industry at the beginning of the 1980s.

A straight reduction in the level of intervention price for dairy products from P_i to P_i' would cause consumers to increase their consumption from D_i to D_i' and farmers to decrease their production from S_i to S_i' by moving down the supply function SS. Consequently, the level of surplus production decreases from $(S_i - D_i)$ to $(S_i' - D_i')$, and the budgetary cost of disposing of the surplus through export refunds falls. A cut in the level of price support would *increase consumer surplus* by area $A + B$, *reduce producer surplus* by the area $A + B + C + D + E$, and *reduce the budgetary cost* of support by $B + C + D + E + F + G + I$, causing overall a net welfare gain relative to the base scenario of $B + G + F + I$.

In comparison, the imposition of a total quota at Q^* (which, for ease of comparison, is set equal to S_i') shifts the supply curve to SS^*. At output level Q^*, the supply curve is

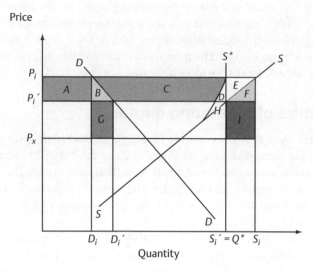

Fig. 5.5 Comparison of welfare effects of quotas and support-price reductions

perfectly inelastic, implying that the penalty for surplus production is severe enough to discourage any farmers from exceeding the production threshold and thus incurring the *super-levy*. Consumers are unaffected by the implementation of the new policy instrument—they continue to purchase the same level of output, D_i, at prices significantly above the world price of the commodity, P_x; thus *the change in consumer surplus* is zero. The figure suggests that farmers lose producer surplus equal to area $E + D + H$. Whilst area E is an unavoidable loss of surplus due to the output-restricting nature of the policy instrument, area $D + H$ is lost because of the manner in which quotas are allocated between individual producers. Distributing quotas purely on the basis of historical production levels rather than efficiency criteria means that some low-cost, efficient production is lost from the industry whilst some high-cost, inefficient production is maintained. If, following the initial allocation, transfer of quota is permitted, then it can be shown that low-cost producers would be willing to purchase or lease quota from high-cost producers and the area $D + H$ can be restored as surplus (Burrell 1989). Assuming that such trade takes place, total *producer surplus loss* to the dairy industry can be reduced to E.[8] The reduction in surplus production by $(S_i - Q^*)$ results in *budgetary savings* relative to the base scenario of $E + F + I$. Thus overall, Figure 5.5 suggests that the implementation of quotas results in a net welfare gain of only $F + I$ which is less than that of a price cut to P_i by $B + G$.

The preceding analysis begs the question; if a straight cut in support prices offered the greatest potential net welfare gains, why did the EU choose instead to implement milk quotas? The answer seems to be that quotas, whilst restraining the budgetary cost of milk support, minimized the dislocation caused to the farm sector. Analysis of previous CAP policy changes has suggested that the weight given to farmers' interests in the decision-making process is far higher than that afforded to consumers or taxpayers (MacLaren 1992) and, in this sense, the choice of milk quotas simply conformed with past precedent. However, quotas also helped nullify a widely held belief amongst CAP decision-makers—that in the short run reducing the support price of a commodity might not lead to a reduction in output of that commodity but may even cause output levels to increase. Whilst little empirical evidence has been found to support this idea of 'perverse' supply response, it is interesting to contrast the two alternative policy options from a producer's perspective. A straight reduction in price-support levels would keep the marginal revenue and average revenue of output perfectly elastic at the new (lower) price and retain the open-ended nature of support. Thus, it can be argued that it would offer individual producers an incentive to reduce costs per unit output but not necessarily their total output level. Surplus production has long been considered by the European Commission as the central problem of the CAP and it was consequently keen to introduce a policy instrument which gave it direct control over aggregate output levels.

The total quota for milk was periodically reduced from 103.7 million tonnes in 1984 to 96mt in 1991/2 for the EU10. It has subsequently been increased to accommodate the addition of five new member states and the federation of East with West Germany. The system, as noted above, has been fairly successful at reducing the budgetary cost of the milk regime, but its success has only been possible because of the way milk is marketed. Virtually all milk is sold from farms to a relatively small number of processing plants. This bottleneck in the marketing chain allows the output of each producer to be monitored and, if necessary, permits enforcement of the quota by charging appropriate individuals the super-levy on excess production. The same policy instrument would be ineffective if applied to the cereals regime, because no equivalent bottleneck in the marketing chain of cereals exists. Instead, during the 1980s, the EU adopted the other two types of supply control methods mentioned above—*co-responsibility levies* and *budgetary stabilizers*—to control the output level and budgetary cost of the cereals regime. Whilst both these mechanisms share the basic characteristics of quotas in that they penalize production in excess of some threshold quantity by imposing some kind of pricing penalty, they offer far less of an incentive to an individual producer to reduce output levels. As explained by Burrell (1987), a rational individual producer will respond to a quantitative threshold on output only if that threshold has been imposed directly on his own production levels. 'Otherwise he is a price-taker, and in spite of the threshold for aggregate output, he perceives the demand for his own output as perfectly elastic at the going price.'

The introduction and gradual increased reliance on supply-control mechanisms in the 1980s failed to stifle calls for yet more fundamental reform of the CAP. Thus, in May 1992 the CAP entered into a second stage of reform marked by the Council of Ministers' acceptance of the MacSharry reform package.

5.5 The MacSharry Reform Package

As intimated above, the MacSharry Reform Package owed much to the multinational trade negotiations and the pressure from agricultural trading partners to reduce the level of trade distortion caused by the CAP. Whilst the basic price-support mechanisms described in Section 5.2 above have been retained, reductions in the level of support prices significantly reduced their effectiveness. The impact of such price cuts for commodities in surplus can be ascertained by referring back to Figure 5.2. Consumers should benefit (assuming that reductions in the support price of raw agricultural products is passed on in the form of lower food prices); the budgetary cost of disposing of any remaining surplus production should decrease; and the farm sector, in the absence of any countervailing policy action, should suffer a loss in producer surplus. However, to compensate farmers for their potential loss in income, the EU has decided to give direct income payments to farmers provided they adhere to certain restraints on input use. For livestock producers, compensation payments are limited to a fixed number of animals based on historical herd sizes and contingent upon a maximum stocking density; whilst for arable producers, compensation is paid only if a farmer agrees to *set aside* (take out of production) a proportion of his/her arable land, the exact proportion being determined by the Council of Ministers each year.

By partly replacing price support with direct income payments, the correlation between the amount of support received and the amount of output produced has been weakened. In the jargon of the GATT negotiations, the MacSharry Reform Package marks a move towards *decoupled* farm income support.[9] The main changes to the commodity regimes of the CAP following the reform agreement are summarized in Table 5.3.

In addition to the changes in the various commodity regimes, a set of 'accompanying measures' were introduced as part of the CAP reforms to encourage farm forestry and farmer retirement, and to generalize and enhance existing agro-environmental policies. Previously, these types of measures were funded under the Agricultural Structures Policy, and they received little budgetary support. However, as part of the reform package, financial support was switched to the Guarantee Section of the CAP's budget and 6.2 billion ecu, or 5 per cent of the total Guarantee budget, was targeted at these issues. In particular, over half was earmarked for policies under the Agri-Environment Programme.

The introduction of the Agri-Environment Programme was significant in that it allows the implementation of policies at the national level to be flexible, with such policies being co-financed by Member States' governments. By the end of 1994, about 190 programmes, 12 national and 165 regional, had been approved. The changes suggest that more emphasis is being given to the long-recognized role of the CAP in securing environmental goals. This will have been consolidated by the subsequent 1993 Treaty on European Union (TEU) requiring all Union policies, including the CAP, to take environmental impacts into account. However, some Member States have been concerned that the reforms do not go far enough and are keen to see a more widespread introduction of *cross-compliance* within the CAP whereby the payment of all farm support subsidies is conditional on farmers complying with some pre-agreed environmental conditions. To some extent, some of the 1992 reforms do introduce an element of cross-compliance, for example, the limits on stocking rates associated with livestock subsidies. As is discussed in Section 5.6, this has been taken further in the Agenda 2000 reforms.

Table 5.3 Summary of the MacSharry CAP reforms.

Commodity	Cuts in support	Compensation and other gains	Production control
Cereals	• Target price cut by 29% from 1991/2 buying-in price. • Price reduction phased in over three years from 1993/4	• Per hectare compensation payments available provided set-aside is implemented. • Producers of less than 92 tonnes of cereals are exempted from set-aside. • Compensation payments based on historical yield levels for regions of the EU. • Co-responsibility levy abolished from 1992/3.	• Annual set-aside required for producers to receive compensation payments. • The minimum % of base arable area to be set aside varies from year to year. • Controls over which land can be set aside.
Oilseeds and pulses	• No price support 1993/4 onwards	• Per hectare area payments available but cut from 1992/3 levels. • Linseed added to list of eligible crops.	• Controlled by same set-aside schemes as cereal production.
Sheep	• Payment of ewe premium restricted by producer quota. • Producer quotas based on number of ewe premiums paid in 1991.	• Quota has market value. • Special extensification premiums for reduced stock levels. • Lower feed grain costs.	• If quota sold without land, 15% of quota taxed to national reserve. • No transfer of quota outside existing Less Favoured Areas.
Beef	• Intervention price cut by 15% from 1993/4. • 350,000t. limit set on intervention purchases by 1997.	• Beef and suckler cow premium increased but made contingent on stocking rates below minimum level. • Suckler cow quota has marketable value. • Lower feed grain costs.	• Beef premium limited by regional ceiling equal to number of premiums paid in 1991. If exceeded, producer payments reduced pro rata. • Suckler cow premiums restricted by producer quota. • Beef and suckler cow premium payments subject to stocking-rate restrictions.
Dairy	• 5% cut in butter intervention price by 1994/5.	• Milk quota and associated value to last at least to 2000. • Co-responsibility levy abolished from 1992/3.	• Cuts in quota may be made.

The economics of the new arable regime

The changes to the arable regime of the CAP are particularly significant, not just because of the introduction of land set-aside,[10] but because of the importance of cereals along with oilseeds and protein crops (the so-called COP crops) within the agricultural industry. Under the new arrangements, each COP farmer in the EU producing more than 92 tonnes of cereals faces a decision of whether (*a*) to use the whole of his arable acreage and receive the new (lower) market price for cereal output, or (*b*) to comply with the set-aside requirements and thus be eligible for compensation payments in addition to his market returns for output from land remaining in production.

For those who adopt the latter strategy and opt into the set-aside scheme, two types of compensation payments can be distinguished—price compensation on land farmed (the so-called arable area payment (AAP)) and set-aside compensation (SAP) on land set-aside. The planned levels of both payments over the transitionary period are shown in Table 5.4. The level of price compensation was intended to increase gradually throughout the transitional period, as the gap between the old buying-in price and new target price widened. Importantly, price compensation is converted from a tonnage to an area basis by applying a fixed yield factor. The yield factor has been calculated from historical data and varies between regions of the community. The table shows that, for England, the yield factor was initially set at 5.93t./ha thus implying that, by the end of the three-year period, every farmer who chooses to participate in the set-aside scheme would receive a payment of 266.85 ecus for each hectare remaining in production. In addition, participating farmers receive a compensation payment for land left idle. The level of this set-aside compensation was intended to be fixed during the transition period and was initially set equal to the level of price compensation in 1995/6. However, political pressures caused the set-aside payment to be raised in 1994/5 to 338 ecu/ha., and both the set-aside and arable area payments were raised in 1994/5 by around 20 per cent to adjust for major changes in the agrimonetary system which was in place at the time. The agrimonetary system came to an end with European Monetary Union in January 1999.[11]

The decision about whether or not to participate in the set-aside scheme depends on the market price of cereals and farms' actual yields. In particular, the decision depends on the value of compensation payments relative to the revenue which could be obtained by planting the area which would be set aside. When cereal prices are high, the opportunity cost of leaving land to stand idle is also high and a farmer is less likely to participate in the scheme. As the market price for cereals falls, the opportunity cost of idling land also falls. At some point, the value of the compensation payments from participating in set-aside

Table 5.4 Compensatory payments for the reformed CAP cereals regime, 1993/4–1995/6

	Marketing year		
	1993/4	1994/5	1995/6
A. 1991/2 Buying-in price (ecu/t.)	155	155	155
B. Target price (ecu/t.)	130	120	110
C. Price compensation [A–B] (ecu/t.)	25	35	45 (54)[a]
D. Yield factor (England) (t./ha.)	5.93	5.93 (5.89)[b]	5.93 (5.89)[b]
E. Price compensation (England) [C × D]	148.25	207.55	266.85 (320)[c]
F. Set-aside compensation (ecu/ha.) (England)	266.85	266.85 (338)[a]	266.85(405)[c]

a Adjusted upwards as a result of political pressure.
b Technical adjustment.
c Adjusted upwards to adjust for abolition of switchover.
Note: Figures in parentheses represent adjustments to the original planned scheme.

will exactly equal the profit that could be earned from planting the additional set-aside area. The price of cereals which gives rise to this equivalence can be called the 'indifference price', since at this price the farmer is indifferent as to whether he opts out of production and into set-aside—either way his total profit level is the same. If the market price of cereals exceeds the indifference price, a rational producer would choose to plant his full area. Alternatively, if the market price for cereals is less than the indifference price, a rational producer would participate in the set-aside scheme in order to be eligible for the compensation payments.

Because farms are not identical, indifference prices will vary between cereal producers. One would expect inefficient, high-cost producers to have a low opportunity cost of idling land and thus a relatively high indifference price. Conversely, one would expect efficient, low-cost producers to have a high opportunity cost of leaving land fallow and thus a relatively low indifference price. Taking such variability into account and aggregating across all producers in the industry, the supply curve for cereals under the new voluntary set-aside scheme would shift from its original competitive level, SS to the kinked curve $S'S$, as shown in Figure 5.6.

In Figure 5.6, P_{ih} and P_{il} represent the highest and lowest indifference price in the industry respectively. At any price above P_{ih}, the market return for cereals is sufficient to deter all farmers from participating in set-aside. Therefore, the total arable area would be utilized and the supply curve would coincide with the competitive supply curve, SS. However, once the price of cereals falls below P_{ih}, the least efficient, high-cost producers would choose to opt out of full production and into set-aside, idling the required proportion of their land and thus causing the supply curve to rotate to the left. As the price falls further, more and more farmers would opt into set-aside and more and more land would be withdrawn from production. Once the price has fallen to P_{il}, *all* farmers would choose

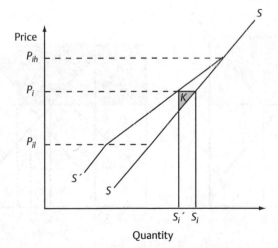

Fig. 5.6 Cereal supply curve under voluntary set-aside

to idle the necessary portion of their land in order to be eligible for compensation payments. In practice, market conditions are such that virtually all large arable farmers in the EU participate in the set-aside scheme.

The shift in the supply curve shown in Figure 5.6 allows us to identify the minimum value of set-aside compensation payments necessary to induce a certain reduction of cereal output. For example, if the EU had decided to implement a voluntary set-aside scheme with a fixed compensation payment per hectare without reducing the level of price support for cereals from its original level, P_i, Figure 5.6 suggests that enough farmers would opt into the scheme to cause output levels to fall from S_i to S_i'. It can be assumed, since the scheme is voluntary, that this would occur only if there were no overall reduction in producer surplus. In other words, the value of set-aside compensation payments must be at least equal to area K in the figure, which represents the amount of surplus lost from production.

The new supply curve with set-aside, $S'S'$, is replicated in Figure 5.7, where the changes in welfare and transfer effects of the MacSharry reforms of the old cereals[12] regime are investigated. From an initial buying-in price of P_i, the support price for cereals once the scheme is fully implemented falls to P_i'. The price reduction will cause demand to increase to D_i' and supply to decrease to S_i'. One result of this is a *reduction in the consumer surplus loss* of $(A + B) - (A' + B' + J)$, implying that, in principle, EU consumers should have benefited from this element of CAP reform.

The welfare effect for producers is less clear-cut. From a starting position of producer surplus gain of $(A + B + C)$ under the old regime, their surplus from cereal production is reduced to $(A' + B' + C' + D' + J)$. However, in addition, they receive direct compensation payments. As drawn, the new (lower) support price P_i', corresponds to the lowest indifference price of the industry. We can, therefore, assume that every eligible cereal producer is participating in the set-aside scheme,[13] and that area E is the budgetary transfer which is

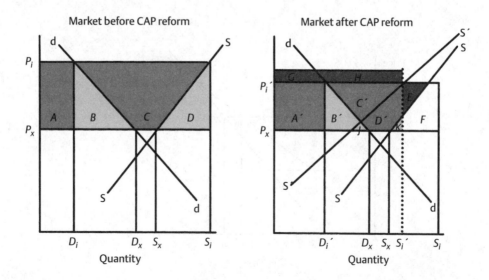

Fig. 5.7 The economics of the EU's arable set-aside regime

needed to induce this. Over and above that, the arable area payment (compensation) cost can be represented by areas $G + H$. That is, the cost is represented as a price subsidy averaged over output level S_i'. Thus the total amount of the arable area and set-aside payments can be shown as area $E + G + H$ in Figure 5.7, and the *change in producer surplus gain* (obtained by comparing the two panels in Figure 5.7) is given by $(A + B + C) - (A' + B' + C' + D' + E + J + G + H)$. Whether or not this is positive or negative depends on whether the value of set-aside plus compensation payments is larger or smaller than the loss in producer surplus from reducing support prices to P_i' and output to S_i'. As drawn it is smaller, to reflect the principle that the price compensation was intended to be only partial. However, in some years, such as 1994/5 and 1995/6, market prices remained above support price levels and therefore the 'compensation' was over-generous.

The impact of the new regime on the budgetary cost of cereal support is also not easily predicted. Whether or not the total budgetary cost of supporting cereal farmers decreases or increases depends upon whether the saving in terms of the disposal of surplus production $(B + C + D) - (B' + C' + D' + J + K)$ is larger or smaller than the value of compensation payments $E + G + H$. As drawn, the figure suggests a fall in the budgetary cost of support. However, in practice, this will depend upon the change in the world price for cereals and the extent of participation in the set-aside scheme. It also depends on any additional administrative costs incurred in administering the payments to farmers, something not explicitly represented in the diagram.

The reduction in net welfare loss caused by the policy reform appears less ambiguous (if we ignore administrative costs), and there is a welfare improvement. Taking into account the preceding analysis, the *net welfare loss is reduced* by $(B + D) - (B' + J + K)$. Importantly, as drawn, the MacSharry reforms reduce but do not eliminate the trade distortion caused by CAP support for cereal producers, with the level of exports falling to $(S_i' - D_i')$ but still remaining above the free trade level of $(S_x - D_x)$.

Whilst useful as an indication of the general welfare effects of the new CAP arable regime, the preceding analysis has ignored the more detailed aspects of the regime which will be critical in governing its effectiveness. For instance, no mention has been made of the problem of *slippage*, which is associated with any policy requiring that farmers set aside land. Slippage can be most easily described as the phenomenon whereby a certain reduction in cereal area does not necessarily lead to the same percentage reduction in cereal output. In terms of Figure 5.6 and 5.7, slippage would result in a smaller rotation in the supply curve for cereals to the left. There are many different reasons for slippage, including farmers using inputs more intensively on the land remaining in production, the setting-aside of less productive land, and increased fertility of land left to stand fallow, which would result in increased yields once that land is brought back into production. Alternatively, slippage may occur simply because of ineffective policing of set-aside, allowing farmers to plant more hectares than intended under the rules of the new regime. In addition, producers of less than 92 tonnes of cereals (equivalent to around 15 hectares) do not have to participate in set-aside to qualify for area compensation. The analysis has also ignored the fact that the rules of the regime are such that the base arable area of each individual farmer is defined to include land previously sown with oilseeds, potatoes, sugar-beet, and protein crops as well as cereals. Thus there will not be a direct correspondence between the change in cereal area and the area of land removed from production under set-aside, even before considering the complications of slippage. Again, the rotation in cereal supply curve shown in Figures 5.6 and 5.7 may be less pronounced than initially implied.[14]

In early 1996, the Commission proposed certain modifications to the arable regime described in Table 5.4. As well as adjusting the proportion of arable land to be set aside and hence the value of compensation payments, it also proposed to make the scheme more flexible. Whilst such modifications look set to continue, it is clear that the period of reliance of the CAP primarily on market price support is well and truly over.

5.6 **Agenda 2000 reforms**

The changes to the CAP agreed in the MacSharry reforms were basically allowed to run forward to 1999. The set-aside rate was adjusted from year-to-year, but target and intervention prices for cereals were maintained at the same level from 1995/6 to 1999/2000. There were simplifying modifications to the oilseeds regime, but essentially policy remained unchanged in the crop and livestock sectors.

For 2000/1 a new package of changes was agreed under the title Agenda 2000. For cereals there was a 15 per cent cut in the intervention price in two steps starting in 2000/1, with a partially compensating increase in the AAP and SAP payments. Support was also reduced for oilseeds, with the AAP and SAP payments converging to the cereals' level in 2002/3. For beef, a sector in crisis following BSE, the intervention price was reduced by 20 per cent over three years, and the various beef premium (headage) payments were increased in partial compensation. Thus the switch from price support to direct subsidies started in 1992 was deepened.

Surprisingly, the dairy regime survived Agenda 2000 largely unscathed. The milk quota regime was extended to 2006, and some countries and regions were granted small increases in quota from 2000/1 and the others from 2005. There are to be no cuts in intervention prices for butter and skimmed milk powder until 2005, when a phased three-year reduction of 15 per cent is planned. Significantly, the EU intends to introduce some form of compensation payment for these price cuts, probably on an area rather than a headage basis, as that would be more decoupled. This planned extension of direct subsidies is of considerable significance in relation to the new WTO Round and the problems of negotiating EU enlargement (see Section 5.7 below).

Agenda 2000 instituted some changes to place more emphasis on environmental objectives, and to move a small amount of the support for agriculture into the 'green box'. It required Member States by January 2000 to take appropriate environmental measures, by strengthening the environmental criteria for direct support payments; that is, it reinforced *cross-compliance*. It also provided Member States discretion over policy in a number of areas. One of these was for *modulation* (in effect, taxation) of direct payments, and for any savings achieved in this way to be redirected to environmental and other approved schemes such as early retirement.

All states were also required to produce seven-year Rural Development Plans (RDPs) formulated with a large degree of discretion within general rules. To illustrate this, England[15] has formulated an RDP for 2000–6, which incorporates *modulation* within it. The plan is to impose a 'tax' of 2.5 per cent on direct (AAP, SAP, and headage) payments in 2001, and to raise this in equal steps to 4.5 per cent in 2006.[16] The Treasury will then match this 'saving' pound for pound and put it into the budget for the RDP. By 2006 the plan is expected to cost £462 million, of which only £81 million will be from EU funds, the rest being provided nationally. The general principle underlying this approach to agricultural policy is highly significant. This is the principle of *subsidiarity*, whereby Member States finance an increasing proportion of the cost of support for farmers themselves with less of the funding coming from the EU budget. Any policies funded under this principle have to comply with EU regulations, but, as indicated above, new regulations provide discretion and flexibility about policy details. This discretion only applies to policy instruments which are in the green box and are judged to be decoupled; it does not apply to intervention purchases, export refunds, AAP, SAP, or most headage payments. Thus the discretion to spend more or less on policies in the Rural Development Plans should have minimal distorting effects on intra-EU trade, although no payment can be considered completely decoupled and to have no effect whatever on production.

Agenda 2000 may be seen as representing a step towards reducing central EU funding (and collective financial responsibility) for agricultural support, and a move towards renationalising agricultural policy. If, as expected, there are further reductions in price support measures and a switch to discretionary green-box measures, this may help reduce problems of negotiating EU enlargement.

5.7 EU enlargement

The EU has European Agreements with ten Central and Eastern European Countries (CEECs) plus Cyprus and Malta. Their potential membership of the EU raises major agricultural policy issues, and consequently budgetary ones (see Chapter 4 for more details on enlargement). The CEECs are more heavily dependent on agriculture than existing Member States. In the mid-1990s agriculture accounted for over 20 per cent of employment in Poland, Romania, Bulgaria, and Lithuania, and for more than 10 per cent of GDP in Romania, Bulgaria, Latvia, and Lithuania. The arable area of the ten CEECs is over 50 per cent of that of the EU-15, while the population is only around 28 per cent of that in the EU-15.

The fundamental issue is whether a *common* agricultural policy will survive enlargement, or whether a two-tier or even more fragmented policy will emerge. It is estimated (Tangermann 2000) that extending the post-Agenda 2000 CAP to just four early candidates for entry (Czech Republic, Hungary, Poland, and Slovenia), would raise the CAP budgetary cost by around 6.3 billion euros, equivalent to one-third of the current budget. The accession countries are keen to obtain this full package, given that it would entail significant net transfers. At the same time, to many it seems absurd to pay farmers in these countries arable area and headage payments designed to compensate EU-15 farmers for support price cuts, when in nearly all cases joining the CAP would mean higher support prices for the CEECs. The EU would have less of a problem with this issue if it had made the existing and planned compensatory payments subject to a time limit and had set them to progressively decline over time. To economists this would have been logical, but it has not been done, and Agenda 2000 has not helped. The reluctance of existing Member States to extend the full CAP to new ones, and the latters' insistence that this will be their right, now appears to be threatening the timetable for accession.

New members may have a long accession period in which to adjust, although they have already begun that process. As Swinnen (2000) has indicated, following the acute depression the CEECs suffered in the early phase of liberalization following the break-up of the CMEA, the CEECs have introduced agricultural policies which resemble the CAP prior to the MacSharry reforms. Joining the CAP will nevertheless in general lead to higher agricultural price supports, which in turn would lead to higher agricultural production and larger export surpluses. This compounds the EU's difficulties in the new WTO round of agricultural negotiations which began in 2000, as required by the URA. The CEECs themselves are signatories to the URA and joining the CAP may well lead to them violating their own undertakings on reducing support.

5.8 Summary and outlook

Changes which have been made to the CAP in the 1990s represent an uneasy compromise between continuing the traditional policies of protecting agriculture, through price supports and income aids, and the various pressures for reform discussed in Section 5.3. By compensating for commodity-price reductions through the introduction of direct income payments to farmers, reform has allowed a transfer of some of the cost of support from food consumers to taxpayers, which is socially progressive in reducing food costs to poor non-taxpayers. It also means that the costs of the CAP will be increasingly transparent, being revealed in budgetary accounts rather than being hidden away in the mass of consumer spending. Nevertheless, by retaining the basic mechanisms of price support and adding the new compensation payments, the operation of the CAP has been made even more complex. This is because the compensation payments are conditional upon compliance with a variety of qualifying actions, all of which should be checked before payment is authorized. Inevitably, this raises administrative costs and increases the size of the bureaucracy, while at the same time increasing the incentives and possibilities for fraud which are already a well-established consequence of the CAP.

Adding supply controls in the form of arable land set-aside and animal stocking rates to the existing marketing quotas for milk and sugar has been necessary to achieve an approximation to the decoupling of agricultural support and to help control budgetary costs. However, these actions reflect continued unwillingness to subject EU agriculture to the full rigours of free trade and open competition.

Several important factors mean that further reform of the CAP cannot be delayed for long. The new round of WTO negotiations began in 2000, and there is pressure for this to be concluded before 2003, when the 'Peace Clause' in the URA (which protects blue-box measures from certain challenges under WTO rules) expires. More pressure arises from the USA's 1996 Farm Bill, which made major changes to its system of agricultural policy and sets new challenges to the EU. In particular, the Bill ended the use of acreage set-aside controls within the USA and completely decoupled the link between production levels and government payments. In this way USA policy support for its crop sector shifted into the green box, while the EU's remains firmly in the contested blue box. However, the USA has devalued this negotiating advantage by offering large amounts of emergency aid to farmers, something not envisaged in the 1996 Farm Bill.

Despite the impending pressures in the WTO round to reduce support costs in the blue box, the biggest challenge to the CAP arises from the agenda to enlarge the EU-15 to include Central and East European Countries (CEECs) with a collective population of over 100 million. These countries are much more heavily reliant on agriculture than existing members, and the terms on which they are incorporated into the CAP are of great importance to them. There are signs of increasing concern in some EU-15 countries about the potential cost of offering them the current *common* policy terms, while Poland in particular (the largest of the applicant countries) shows increasing exasperation at the slipping timetable and lack of progress. Had the reforms of the 1990s described earlier been made more quickly and more boldly the problems of enlargement would have been easier to solve. As it stands, the likely terms of agreement on agricultural policy are unclear. Will a common agricultural policy, embracing a much larger EU, survive, or will subsidiarity be increased until price support is minimal and nationally funded rural development plans are the dominant policies?

Discussion questions

1   To what extent have the reforms of the CAP been driven by political and economic pressures within the expanding EU rather than by the external trade liberalization agenda set by the USA and the Cairns Group?

2   Why has the EU persistently favoured supply control and market regulation methods to free trade and uncontrolled price determination in agricultural markets?

3   What additional pressures are created by the potential expansion of the EU to include countries of Eastern and Central Europe?

4   Despite the costs to consumers and taxpayers, are there any justifications for continuing a policy of price support for agriculture?

Further reading

Readers wishing to explore issues related to the EU's agricultural policy further might wish to consult the book by Michael Tracy (1993), which provides an excellent overview; the new edition of *The Common Agricultural Policy* edited by Ritson and Harvey (1997), which provides up-to-date coverage; and the paper by Tangermann (1996) evaluating the implementation of the Uruguay Round of the GATT.

Notes

1   For a review of these negotiations and their substance, readers are referred to Rayner *et al.* (1993).

2   This assumes that all increases in the price of agricultural commodities such as wheat are passed through to the retail prices of bread, cakes, flour, etc.

3   For a whole series of reasons (see Colman 1985), the floor is not as rigid as portrayed in Figure 5.2, but it is an acceptable approximation for much analysis.

4   It may be noted that the position is more complex than this. For example, although the EU is a large exporter of soft wheat, it still has to import more expensive hard wheats for bread making. Import levies/tariffs calculated with respect to soft wheats result in hard wheats entering the EU at prices very much higher than the MIP.

5   This is also known by its French initials FEOGA, which stand for Fonds European d'Orientation et de Garantie Agricole.

6   For a fuller analysis of distribution of budgetary and trade gains and losses from the CAP, see Ackrill *et al.* (1994).

7   The numbers in this table are generated by a computable model, and reflect estimates of the reductions in cost which would arise if agricultural policy was reformed in a specific way. This is the standard approach to calculating the effects of any price support system which exists. The current position, with support, is known; the question is 'what would the position be if it was reduced or eliminated?'

8   This assumes that there are no inefficiencies in the quota market.

9   Under 'truly' decoupled income support, a farmer's decisions on levels of output would be based on the free trade price equivalents of commodities. Since, under the new CAP arable regime, the decision of whether or not to set aside land depends on the relative size of compensation payments *vis-à-vis* the new lower support price for cereals, the move towards decoupled farm income support is far from complete.

10   The option allowing EU farmers voluntarily to set aside arable land in return for compensation strictly dates from 1988. However, the impact of the initial set-aside scheme was extremely limited, with very low uptake levels in almost all Member States.

11   Those wishing to learn how this excessively complicated system worked might consult ch. 6 of Ritson and Harvey (1997).

12 In fact the set-aside policy applies to cereals plus oilseeds and protein crops (peas and beans), but for simplicity it will be discussed as if it is only applicable to cereals.

13 If this were not the case, it would be impossible to show the value of compensation payments in price/output space, as in Figure 5.5.

14 Yet another complication to measuring the effects of the new arable regime has been caused by farmers planting set-aside land with crops intended for industrial usage (e.g. linseed) or, alternatively, choosing to plant set-aside area with forage crops which has implications for other commodity regimes.

15 Because of devolution all four countries in the UK have produced their own plan to meet their own requirements, thus emphasizing both flexibility and subsidiarity.

16 The regulations allow for higher rates of modulation.

17 For comment on the Agricultural Strategy Paper, see Tracy (1995).

References

Ackrill, R. W., Suardi, M., Hine, R. C., and Rayner, A. J. (1994), *The Distributional Effects of the Common Agricultural Policy between Member States: Budget and Trade Effects* (CREDIT Research Paper, 94/1; University of Nottingham).

BAE (1985), Bureau of Agricultural Economics, *Agricultural Policies in the European Community* (Policy Monograph, No. 2; Canberra, Australia: BAE).

Blandford, D., de Gorter, H., and Harvey, D. R. (1989), 'Farm Income Support with Minimal Trade Distortions', *Food Policy* (Aug.): 268–73.

Brown, C. (1989), *Distribution of CAP Price Support* (Statens Jordbrugsokonomiske Institut, Report 45; Copenhagen).

Burrell, A. (1987), 'EC Agricultural Surpluses and Budget Control, *Journal of Agricultural Economics*, 38/1: 1–14.

Burrell, A. (ed.) (1989), *Milk Quotas in the European Community* (Wallingford: CAB International), ch. 8.

Colman, D. (1985), 'Imperfect Transmission of Policy Prices', *European Review of Agricultural Economics*, 12/3: 171–86.

DPI.-Australia (1986), *The Political Economy of Agricultural Policy Reform* (Canberra: Department of Primary Industry).

Greenaway, D. (1991), 'The Uruguay Round of Multilateral Trade Negotiations: Last Chance for GATT?', *Journal of Agricultural Economics*, 42/3: 365–79.

Josling, T. E. and Hamway, D. (1972), *Burdens and Benefits of Farm Support Policies* (London: Trade Policy Research Centre).

MacLaren, D. (1992), 'The Political Economy of Agricultural Policy Reform in the European Community and Australia', *Journal of Agricultural Economics*, 43/3: 250–97.

Rayner, A. J., Ingersent, K. A., and Hine, R. C. (1993), 'Agricultural Trade and the GATT', ch. 4 in A. J. Rayner and D. Colman (eds.), *Current Issues in Agricultural Economics* (Basingstoke: Macmillan), 62–95.

Ritson, C., and Harvey, D. (eds.) (1997), *The Common Agricultural Policy* (Wallingford: CAB International).

Roningen, V. O. and Dixit, P. M. (1989), *How Level is the Playing Field: An Economic Analysis of Agricultural Policy Reforms in Industrial Market Economies* (United States Department of Agriculture, ERS, FAE Report 239; Washington, DC).

Swinnen, J. (2000), 'Is the Emergence of Agricultural Protectionism in Central Europe Unavoidable' paper presented to the XXIV International Conference of Agricultural Economists, Berlin, August.

Tangermann, S. (1991), 'A Bond Scheme for Supporting Farm Incomes', ch. 10 in J. Marsh, B. Green, B. Kearney, L. Mahe, S. Tangermann, and S. Tarditi, *The Changing Role of the Common Agricultural Policy* (London: Belhaven).

Tangermann, S. (1996), 'Implementation of the Uruguay Round Agreement on Agriculture: Issues and Prospects', *Journal of Agricultural Economics*, 47/3: 315–37.

Tangermann, S. (2000) 'Eastern Enlargement of the European Union; A General and Partial Equilibrium Analysis' paper presented to the XXIV International Conference of Agricultural Economists, Berlin, August.

Tracy, M. (1993), *Food and Agriculture in a Market Economy: An Introduction to Theory, Practice and Policy* (Agricultural Policy Studies, La Hutte, Belgium).

Tracy, M. (1995), 'The Commission's 'Agricultural Strategy Paper': A Commentary', paper presented to One-Day Agricultural Economics Society Conference, London, 13 Dec.).

Von Meyer, H. (1991), 'From Agricultural to Rural Policy in the EC', in M. Tracy (ed.), *Europe 1993: Implications for Rural Areas* (Aberdeen: Arkleton Trust).

Chapter 6

Competition Policy

Stephen Martin

6.1 Introduction

Since before the Treaty of Rome, competition policy has been seen as an essential element of the ongoing process of European integration. In 1956 the Spaak Report, which laid the groundwork for the Treaty of Rome, said that (p. 55)

the treaty should provide the means to avoid situations in which monopoly practices block the fundamental objectives of the common market. In this regard, it is appropriate to prevent

- market division by agreement among firms;
- agreements to limit output or restrict technical progress;
- the absorption or domination of the market for a product by a single firm.

Such provisions appear in Articles 81 and 82 of the EC Treaty.[1]

Article 81(1) prohibits agreements that affect trade between the Member States and have the object or effect of preventing, restricting, or distorting competition on the ground that they are incompatible with the common market. Article 81(3) allows exceptions to the Article 81(1) prohibition for agreements that improve production or distribution, or promote technical or economic progress, provided among other conditions that a fair share of the benefits generated by the agreement go to consumers.

Article 82 of the EC Treaty prohibits abuse of a dominant market position by one or more firms. Examples of behaviour that have been found to constitute such abuse include restricting output, price discrimination, and using a dominant position in one market to limit competition in another market. If a firm is found to violate Article 81 or 82, the Commission may impose a fine up to 10 per cent of the firm's annual turnover. The Commission may also order that offending behaviour be ended.[2]

Articles 81 and 82 address themselves to business conduct. The 1989 Merger Control Regulation,[3] in contrast, deals with market structure. It gives the European Commission the authority to vet mergers and related types of business combinations that meet specified size and multinationality conditions. The European Commission may block a proposed merger entirely, or permit a merger to go forward on altered terms that are worked out with the firms involved.

Articles 81, 82, and the Merger Control Regulation set rules for different types of business activity. Articles 86, 87, and 88 of the EC Treaty, in contrast, set rules for actions of the Member States towards the business sector. Article 86 specifies that EU competition policy applies to public enterprises and to private enterprises that are given specific missions by a Member State. Article 87(1) prohibits as incompatible with the common market Member State aid to business, if the aid distorts or threatens to distort competition. Article 87(3) allows exceptions to the Article 87(1) prohibition for aid that promotes regional and other specified types of development. Article 88 obligates the Commission to monitor Member State aid systems to ensure continued compatibility with the common market.

The direct impact of EU competition policy is on market integration. Its deeper role is to maintain public confidence in the fairness of market processes, and therefore public support for integration on all levels. The bare bones of the provisions of EU competition policy are given substantive content in decisions of the European Commission, the Court of First Instance,[4] and the European Court of Justice. That content continues to evolve and adapt, as does the economy of the European Union. Particularly important changes in the application of competition policy are underway as the EU prepares for enlargement and for the deepening of integration that will come with the single European currency.

These changes are characterized by an increasing emphasis on the economic effects of different kinds of business behaviour. This emphasis reflects the increasing economic sophistication of the European Commission's Directorate General for Competition and general acceptance of the viewpoint that the invisible hand of the market place—independent decisions taken by independent firms seeking to maximize their own profit—will, over the long run, lead to the best allocation of resources that is attainable in the real world.[5]

In Sections 6.2 and 6.3 we discuss Articles 81 and 82, respectively, of the EC Treaty, including an examination of the process of market definition, which has considerable importance in all applications of competition policy. Section 6.4 deals with the Merger Control Regulation, while Section 6.5 considers a unique but vital aspect of EU competition policy, the control of aid to business by the Member States.

6.2 Article 81

Horizontal cooperation

Cooperation is said to be horizontal if it is between firms that operate at the same level of the production chain—between manufacturers, or between wholesalers, or between retailers. Some horizontal cooperation is virtually always found to violate EU competition policy: explicit collusion to raise price, to reserve particular geographical areas to particular firms (especially when markets are divided along national boundaries), or to raise barriers to entry for firms outside the agreement.

Before the Treaty of Rome, many Member States had an *abuse control* approach to cartels and collusion. Collusion as such was not illegal. Instead, cartels were obliged to register with the government and might be subject to legal action if they were found to act in some way contrary to the public interest. Given the contrast between these policies of benign neglect and the prohibition approach of Article 85(1), it is not surprising that many of the most flagrant examples of overt collusion in the history of EU competition law appear in the early years of the Community, before businesses had fully adjusted to the changed legal climate.

An example is the *Franco-Japanese ball-bearings* case.[6] Here representatives of Japanese and French trade associations and ball-bearing producers met in Paris in 1972 and agreed that Japanese firms would raise their prices in Europe from a level 15 per cent below the prices of European firms to no more than 10 per cent below, with an eventual increase to only 5 to 8 per cent below the prices of European firms. French participants prepared minutes of the discussions, and these minutes came into the hands of the European Commission during the course of its investigation. The result was a decision by the Commission that the agreements violated Article 85(1) of the EC Treaty.

Experience quickly teaches business executives with an interest in avoiding vigorous rivalry not to leave such clear-cut evidence of collusion as a set of minutes recording cartel meetings. The difficulty this creates for competition policy is that when the number of firms supplying a market is relatively small, they may in theory be able to obtain collusive results (restricting output, raising price) without engaging in collusive behaviour.[7] Competition authorities may well observe market outcomes that they feel certain reflect collusion, but to take successful legal action, they must have evidence of joint action that will be accepted by courts. Such evidence will often be difficult to obtain.

The European Court of Justice's 1993 *Wood Pulp* decision illustrates the issues.[8] During the period covered by this case, the European Community was supplied with wood pulp, an input for the production of paper, by firms located in North America and Northern Europe. The European Commission relied on several factors to justify its conclusion that the firms involved in the case had violated Article 81(1) (engaged in a concerted practice). Some US producers were members of an export cartel.[9] A number of firms were members of a trade association, based in Switzerland, which was the forum for regular meetings at which firms exchanged information about prices and formulated price policies. The Commission also relied on the fact that the prices set by different firms had a history of changing by more or less the same amount at more or less the same time, despite the fact that the firms in question were based in many different countries and kept their accounts in many different currencies:[10]

The fact that the addressees of this decision have coordinated their market conduct contrary to Article 81(1) of the EEC Treaty is proved by ... their parallel conduct in the years 1975 to 1981 which, in light of the conditions obtaining on the market ... cannot be explained as independently chosen parallel conduct in a narrow oligopolistic situation.

The European Court of Justice was unwilling to accept this conclusion. While parallel price changes might have been the result of collusion, they might also have been the result of a combination of a high degree of price transparency—prices widely known and news of price changes circulating rapidly—and the oligopoly structure of the market. For the Court, evidence of parallel pricing in combination with other factors might justify a finding of concertation, but in this instance the other evidence assembled by the Commission was not sufficient.

This is one example of the more general *oligopoly problem* facing competition authorities: when a market has an oligopolistic market structure, firms may be able to obtain collusive outcomes (restricted output, higher prices) without engaging in conduct that is collusive in a legal sense. The oligopoly problem raises at least two difficulties for competition policy. The first is one of proof: even if firms in an oligopolistic market are in fact colluding in a legal sense, it may be difficult to obtain sufficient evidence of that collusion. The second problem is one of remedy. If firms are colluding, they can be ordered not to collude, and they may be subject to large enough fines so that they decide it is in their own best interest not to collude. But firms in oligopolistic industries will often be able to refrain from tough competition without colluding; equilibrium market performance without collusion in an oligopolistic industry may be closer to monopoly than one would like. But if this is the kind of outcome that is produced by independent business decisions, there is probably not much policy-makers can do about it.[11]

Market structure is itself determined by market forces, and there are some industries[12] for which equilibrium market structure is oligopolistic. This observation suggests one clear implication of the oligopoly problem for competition policy. If there are practical difficulties in influencing business conduct in oligopoly markets, competition authorities should take care in policy towards market structure. Proposed mergers should be carefully vetted to ensure that they are privately profitable because they increase efficiency, not because they increase market power. We return to this matter when we take up the discussion of EU merger policy.

Collusion and concerted practices that have the effects of collusion are prohibited by Article 81(1). Other types of cooperation may be permitted under Article 81(3), and the Commission proposes to unify enforcement in this area.[13] The Commission's *Draft Guidelines*[14] take an economic approach to the analysis of inter-firm cooperation. Leaving naked collusion to restrict output and raise price aside, inter-firm cooperation typically has some effects that improve market performance and some effects that worsen market performance. If the combined market share of cooperating firms is relatively small (less than 20 per cent for specialization agreements, less than 25 per cent for R&D cooperation), the Commission takes the view that the beneficial effects of cooperation are likely to prevail, since effective competition from other suppliers will limit the exercise of market power. In such cases, the cooperation will benefit from a *block exemption* under Article 81(3).

Where cooperating firms have a combined market share that exceeds the 25 per cent threshold for a block exemption, it may nonetheless be exempted under Article 81(3). In this case, factors to be considered in evaluating the likely impact of the proposed cooperation on market performance (in addition to the market shares of the firms involved) include the degree of seller concentration,[15] the nature of entry conditions, whether suppliers or buyers are likely to exercise countervailing power, and other elements of market structure. If the conclusion of the analysis is that the net effect of the cooperation is positive, and that a fair share of the benefit will go to consumers, the cooperation will be permitted. In the trade-off between increased efficiency and market performance, priority is given to market performance: even great efficiency gains do not justify the complete elimination of effective competition (*Draft Guidelines*, ¶37).

The European Commission (1999*a*, 2000*b*) has proposed a fundamental change in the application of Article 81(3). At the dawn of the EC, the Commission faced the task of introducing a prohibition-based competition policy to a Community of six Member States, only one of which (West Germany) had a similar national competition policy. The others had either no explicit competition policy or followed an abuse control approach that viewed collusion as a natural and inevitable outcome of market processes. Under these circumstances, the European Commission reserved to itself the right to grant exemptions under Article 81(3).[16] To this end, cooperating businesses were obliged to notify the Commission of their agreement. In theory, such agreements might be permitted or not, depending on whether the conditions of Article 81(3) were or were not met.

In practice, some agreements were not notified to the Commission, and these were condemned if and when the Commission discovered their existence. Otherwise, the Commission was confronted with a flood of notifications that required some response but overwhelmed the resources available. One response was the block exemption system: formal policy statements outlining broad classes of agreements, typically based on market-share thresholds and other conditions, that automatically qualified for an Article 81(3) exemption. Another was the issuance of so-called *comfort letters* to notifying firms: statements that on the basis of the information before the Commission, the notified arrangement either did or did not appear to meet the conditions for an exemption under Article 81(3). The Commission issued comfort letters without formal action, and the European Court of Justice held that they did not constitute legally binding decisions.

At the start of the twenty-first century, the situation is vastly different. All EU Member States have national competition authorities; most have adopted national competition policies that are consistent with the approach of the EC Treaty.[17] The prospect is that the number of Member States will double in the near future. The advent of the Euro and monetary integration is likely to bring a further step forward in the process of market integration. Both developments will increase the workload of EU competition authorities.

The Commission therefore proposes to eliminate the requirement that it be notified of cooperative arrangements. Article 81(3) would be enforced by national authorities and before national courts, as is now the case for Article 81(1).[18] The Commission would then be free to devote its attention and resources to the most serious competition policy matters, leaving routine enforcement to national authorities.

The expansion of the European Union and the progress of economic integration make some change in the structure of competition law enforcement necessary and inevitable. The move to direct application of Article 81(3) at the Member State level will conserve EU resources and permit active enforcement of EU competition policy by Member State authorities. A necessary part of the reform, as the Commission acknowledges, is to ensure that enforcement at the Member State level is uniformly vigorous and consistent. Competition policy remains an essential element of the ongoing process of EU integration, and it will not fulfil its role if lax enforcement in a few Member States undermines confidence in its effectiveness.

Market definition

If cooperating firms have a combined market share that falls below the limits specified in the *Draft Guidelines*, they will be able to go forward with their cooperation without having to seek and obtain permission from the Commission or from Member State competition authorities. This approach reduces compliance costs for business and enforcement costs for the Commission. It also brings the process of deciding what the market is to centre stage: businesses need to know how the Commission thinks markets should be defined, for the purposes of competition policy, to decide if they need to seek explicit exemption for a cooperation agreement. As we shall see, the process of market definition is central to the application of almost all elements of competition policy.

For the Commission (1997*b*: 1)

The main purpose of market definition is to identify ... the competitive constraints that the undertakings involved face. The objective of defining a market in both its product and geographic dimension is to identify those actual competitors of the undertakings involved that are capable of constraining their behaviour and of preventing them from behaving independently of an effective competitive pressure.

In principle, the Commission emphasizes the demand side when it defines markets (1997*b*: 2): 'A relevant product market comprises all those products and/or services which are regarded as interchangeable or substitutable by the consumer' and (p. 3) 'the exercise of market definition consists in identifying the effective alternative sources of supply for customers of the undertakings involved, both in terms of products/services and geographic location of suppliers.' In practice, the Commission often considers supply-side substitutability along with demand-side substitutability when it defines markets.[19]

It is possible to carry out sophisticated econometric analyses of demand patterns to reach conclusions about the nature of the market. The time and data requirements of such tests often mean that they cannot be applied by the Commission when it defines a market. The Commission often looks at practical information about the nature of demand for a class of products (1997*b*: 8–10): historical substitution patterns, the views of customers and competitors, evidence of costs of switching from one brand or supplier to another, and whether there are distinctive national preferences or national (for example, tax or environmental) policies.

Vertical cooperation

Cooperation is said to be vertical if it is between firms that operate at different levels of the production chain—between a manufacturer and wholesalers, for example, or between a wholesaler and retailers. Manufacturers and distributors often agree to contracts that embody vertical restraints, including but not limited to

• exclusive territories (a manufacturer authorizes one and only one distributor for a certain area);

- exclusive purchasing (a distributor agrees to acquire all supplies of a certain product from a specified manufacturer);
- resale price maintenance (the distributor agrees to sell at, or not below, the price designated by the manufacturer).[20]

A manufacturer may also administer a selective distribution system (specifying minimum standards of certain kinds that must be satisfied by a distributor and supplying all or a subset of qualifying distributors). Franchise agreements typically involve some vertical restraints.

Vertical restraints typically restrict competition among dealers of a single brand (intra-brand competition). If a manufacturer finds it profitable to restrict competition among dealers of his brand, it may be because the manufacturer feels that those restrictions will lead the dealers to behave in ways that promote competition between his brand and other brands (inter-brand competition). In such cases, the vertical restraints have both pro- and anti-competitive effects, and the net impact on market performance is ambiguous.[21]

A fundamental purpose of EU competition policy is to promote market integration. The Commission has, therefore, consistently opposed vertical restraints that have the effect of splitting the Single Market along national boundaries. For example, national resale price maintenance systems do not come under the authority of EU competition law, since they do not affect trade between the Member States.[22] But the Commission has held that the existence of a legal national resale price maintenance system cannot be used to block shipments of a manufacturer's product from one Member State to another. If a German record producer supplies a retail distributor in France, the French distributor must be allowed to sell in Germany if it is profitable to do so, even if such sales are at a price below the fixed German retail price.[23]

The *FEG/TU* decision[24] is an example of the not uncommon combination of trade associations and vertical restraints in restricting competition. FEG, the Dutch association of electrotechnical equipment wholesalers, maintained an exclusive dealing system with an association of importers of such goods and with domestic suppliers, all of whom were bound to distribute their products through FEG members. Wholesalers that were not part of FEG were thus subject to artificial restrictions on their ability to obtain supplies; whole-salers located outside the Netherlands were not able to bring their products into the Netherlands using importers that were bound by the exclusive dealing agreement.[25] The Commission ordered that the exclusive dealing agreement be ended and levied fines of €200,000.

These cases illustrate the kinds of negative effects that may flow from vertical restraints: raising barriers to entry, foreclosing rivals from distribution channels, facilitating collusion, and impeding effective market integration. Possible efficiency effects include quality control and promoting distributor sales efforts in a way that increases inter-brand competition.[26]

The 1999 vertical restraints regulation[27] adopts an economic effects approach to the treatment of vertical restraints. Minimum resale price maintenance is prohibited. So are airtight exclusive territories: if a dealer receives a request from a customer located outside the dealer's designated territory, the manufacturer must allow the dealer to fill the request. Other types of vertical restraints are permitted under a block exemption if the manufacturer's market share is less than 30 per cent. If a manufacturer's market share exceeds 30 per cent, an exemption under Article 81(3) is possible, taking into account the same general elements of market structure—seller concentration and entry conditions, among others—that come into play for a horizontal cooperative agreement.[28]

The motor vehicle sector has long benefited from exceptional treatment under EU competition policy. A specific regulation[29] permits car manufacturers to sell only through designated dealers, to assign dealers to specific territories, to require various quality standards (for example, showroom size and post-sales service facilities), and to impose other restrictions. This policy is said to be justified (¶4) 'because motor vehicles are consumer durables which at both regular and irregular intervals require expert mainten-ance and repair, not always in the same place.' Importantly, the regulation also requires car manufacturers to allow a dealer to sell to customers or customers' designated representatives whether or not the customer is resident in the dealer's designated sales area.

Consumer groups have long challenged the idea that consumers benefit from the spe-cial car distribution regulation. It is seen as contributing to large and persistent car price differences among Member States (Mitchener 1999). Further, it appears that car manu-facturers have not honoured the part of the regulation that requires them to allow dealers to supply customers resident outside the dealer's home territory. In 1995, the European Commission fined Volkswagen AG €102 million on the ground that VW discouraged its authorized dealers in Italy from supplying cars to customers from parts of Northern Europe. From 1993 to 1995, exchange rate movements made it attractive for customers in Germany and elsewhere to consider buying cars in Italy. VW structured its dealer pro-grammes so that such sales did not count toward satisfying dealer quotas and did not help the dealer meet requirements for some bonus schemes. VW threatened to end the contracts of some Italian dealers if they sold to customers from outside their territories, and twelve dealerships were in fact cancelled. In July 2000, upon appeal by VW, the Court of First Instance allowed €90 million of the fine to stand.

In April 1999 the Commission suggested that Daimler–Chrysler had sought to keep some of its dealers from selling outside their territories. In September 1999 VW was the subject of a second investigation by the Commission for restricting dealers in ways inconsistent with the car distribution regulation. In September 2000 the Commission fined General Motors' Dutch subsidiary €43 million for seeking to block sales by Dutch dealers to EU residents from outside the Netherlands.

The car distribution regulation will expire on 30 September 2002. There seems to be a good chance that it will be renewed, if at all, only on substantially altered terms. If it is allowed to lapse, the car sector would be covered by the same vertical restraints rules that apply to other sectors of the EU economy.[30]

6.3 **Article 82**

The *United Brands* decision[31] illustrates the basic principles of EU competition policy toward abuse of a dominant position. The case dealt with conduct in the early 1970s, at which time the United Brands Company (UBC) was the leading banana producer in the world and more particularly in the European Community, with a market share of about 40 per cent. Its operations were vertically integrated from banana plantations through ocean shipping to destination markets. In those markets, it employed networks of banana ripeners and distributors that were subject to vertical restraints. These vertical restraints had the effect of partitioning the EEC into national submarkets. In at least one instance, UBC cut off supplies from a distributor that had supplied bananas outside its home territory. Prices differed substantially across Member States, although the costs of supplying the different markets were much the same.

A preliminary issue was one of market definition. United Brands argued that the relevant product market was that for fresh fruit, in which UBC's market share was too small to justify a finding that it had a dominant position. The European Commission viewed bananas as the relevant product market, arguing that bananas have distinctive characteristics that separate demand for bananas from the demand for other types of fruit. The European Court of Justice accepted the Commission's arguments and heard the case taking bananas to be the relevant product market.

For the European Court of Justice ([1978] ECR 207 at 277):

The dominant position referred to in [Article 82] refers to a position of economic strength enjoyed by an undertaking which enables it to prevent effective competition being maintained on the relevant market by giving it the power to behave to an appreciable extent independently of its competitors, customers, and ultimately of its consumers.

In this instance, the direct customers of UBC were the firms in its distribution network. The Commission argued, and the Court of Justice accepted, that UBC had a dominant position in the relevant market, based largely on its market share and the unique vertical integration of its operations. From this dominant position, UBC could maximize profit subject to few constraints from rival banana producers, from vertically related distributors, and from the final consumers of bananas.[32] The Court also found that UBC had abused its dominant position by dint of its conduct toward its distributors, which had the effect of partitioning the EC into submarkets along national boundaries.

The Commission also argued that UBC had abused its dominant position by charging prices that were both discriminatory and unfair. The facts of the case established that prices were in fact substantially different in different Member States. For the Commission, abuse lay in the fact that UBC had ([1978] ECR 207 at 296) 'applied dissimilar conditions to equivalent transactions with the other trading parties, thereby placing them at a competitive disadvantage.' The immediate victims of abuse, then, were UBC's distributors in countries where UBC set higher prices. They were, presumably, less able to compete with other types of fruit than UBC's distributors in countries where UBC set lower prices. To sustain these price differences, UBC was obliged to impose restrictions on the resale of green bananas by distributors across national boundaries—otherwise, distributors in low-price countries would export and under-sell distributors in high-price countries. The resulting partitioning of national markets was a distinct element of abuse of a dominant position.

The Commission also argued that UBC had abused its dominant position by charging unfair prices. As evidence, the Commission compared the lowest and highest prices set by UBC in different national markets, and argued that if UBC could profitably supply the low-price markets, its prices in the high-price markets must be unfair. The Court accepted the idea that charging unfair prices would be an abuse of a dominant position, but it also found that the Commission should have made a direct investigation of UBC's costs and reached a conclusion about unfairness by comparing costs and prices.[33] Thus the Court set aside the Commission's finding that UBC had abused its dominant position by setting unfair prices.

Price discrimination and partitioning the single market are considered to be abuses of a dominant position under EU competition law. Actions that have the effect of making it more difficult for rivals to compete on the merits also constitute abuse of a dominant position.

For example, in the late 1990s British Airways used incentive schemes for payments to travel agents under which the agents were paid more, the greater the increases in their customers' bookings with BA over the level of the previous year. This loyalty rebate scheme created incentives for travel agents to concentrate bookings on BA, and the incentive payments received by the agents were not directly related to efficiencies or cost savings, if any, generated by the higher booking level.

In its decision regarding the incentive scheme,[34] the Commission defined the relevant market as that for air travel agency services in the United Kingdom. BA disagreed, arguing that the market definition should take account of the fact that some final consumers purchase plane tickets without going through travel agencies (as, for example, directly from the airline over the internet). The Commission found BA to be a dominant customer in the product market (39.7 per cent of 1998 UK airfare sales through travel agents were for travel on BA). It traced BA's position as a dominant purchaser of travel agency services to BA's leading position in passenger air transport and its control of landing slots at major UK airports. The Commission also found that BA's loyalty payment scheme was an abuse of a dominant position, and fined BA €6.8 million. In this case, the nature of the abuse was interference with the ability of rival airlines to compete for the services of travel agencies. BA announced its intention to appeal the decision to EU courts.

The Commission's finding in the *BA* case is consistent with a long line of decisions which find that a seller with a dominant position may offer prices to consumers that are lower in proportion to lower costs of supplying the consumer, but commits an abuse if it offers lower prices solely for consumer loyalty. The BA decision applies the same logic—interference with the ability of rivals to compete on the merits—to the situation of a dominant buyer.

EU competition policy does not seek to limit the ability of dominant firms to compete. It does insist that such competition be based on efficiency rather than strategic anti-competitive behaviour (European Commission 1999*b*; 38). In this vein, the Commission has applied Article 82 to firms that enjoy a dominant position as a result of Member State legislation. The *Frankfurt Airport* decision[35] involved the market for the provision of airport facilities—services like baggage handling that must be performed for aircraft to land and take off—at Frankfurt airport. Under German law, the company managing the airport (FAG) had a legal monopoly, hence a dominant position, in the supply of airport facilities at the airport. The Commission determined that the market for the provision of ground-handling services constituted a distinct product market. It found that FAG had abused its monopoly position in the market for airport facilities by reserving the right to supply ground-handling services to itself, and ordered FAG to allow independent firms to supply ground-handling services.[36]

6.4 Merger control

Framework for merger control

Merger control came relatively late to the menu of European Community competition policy: control of collusion and of firms with dominant market positions dates to 1957 and the Treaty of Rome, merger control only to 1989. The founding fathers of what has become the European Union were explicitly concerned with preventing collusion and price discrimination along national lines, not with regulating market structure. Indeed, they may well have had some quiet sympathy for the idea of promoting EU champions to operate in world markets. It was only 30 years into the process of EU market integration that political support allowed the European Commission's Directorate General for Competition to persuade Member State representatives to adopt the Merger Control Regulation.

Amendments passed in 1997 sought to streamline merger control in the light of experience and of an expected further wave of mergers triggered by the introduction of the Euro and a hoped-for giant step forward in economic integration. On a procedural level, the 1997 amendments allowed the Commission to accept relatively early in an investigation a proposal (undertaking) from the parties concerned designed to make the nature of the post-merger firm acceptable to the Commission. Such adjustments (often involving divestitures) have been common in Commission enforcement of merger policy; the new rule makes it easier to put them into effect and economize on Commission resources.

Other changes with an efficiency motive altered the conditions that must be met for a merger to fall under the authority of the Commission, targeting mergers with cross-border effects (European Commission 1998; 60), so reducing the number of cases that firms need to report to competition authorities in several Member States.[37]

The focus of the Regulation is dominance (Article 2(3)):

A concentration which creates or strengthens a dominant position as a result of which effective competition would be significantly impeded in the common market or in a substantial part of it shall be declared incompatible with the common market.

Whether or not a concentration will create or strengthen a dominant position can be assessed only in the context of a relevant product and geographical market. For merger control, as for other aspects of competition policy, market definition is critical.

Collective dominance

The Commission stepped gingerly in the early years of merger control: between 1989 and 1995 only four mergers were blocked. More often, mergers were allowed to go forward, possibly on amended terms that eliminated the Commission's concerns about the creation of a dominant position.[38] Partly in connection with the treatment of joint ventures, the Commission has sought to introduce the concept of joint (oligopoly) dominance to EU merger control. As we have seen, the Commission has had only limited success in applying Article 81 to situations in which existing market structures allow firms in oligopoly to jointly exercise market power. Use of the concept of joint dominance in merger policy can be seen as an attempt to prevent the emergence of market structures that would allow firms in the post-merger market to non-cooperatively exercise market power.

Collective dominance arose in the Commission's *Gencor/Lonrho*[39] decision. The firms that proposed to merge were the leading firms in the world market for platinum and rhodium, with their principal mining operations in South Africa. A third firm, Amplats, would have become the second largest supplier in a highly concentrated market if the merger had gone forward. The European Commission estimated that in the post-merger market, Gencor/Lonrho and Amplats together would have had a combined world market share of 60–70 per cent. Taking the view that the merger would create a market structure in which the two survivor firms would be able to act as a dominant duopoly, the Commission blocked the merger.

The nature of post-merger market structure is then critical to application of the concept of collective dominance to merger policy. Market characteristics that might lead to a finding of joint dominance are high market concentration as well as (EC Commission 1999: 67) 'homogeneous products, transport, high entry barriers, mature technology, static or falling demand, links between suppliers, absence of countervailing buyer power, etc.'

With the September 1999 *Airtours/First Choice* decision, the Commission pushed the collective dominance doctrine further by blocking a takeover that would have reduced the number of leading firms in the UK travel operator market from four to three. The Commission estimated the combined 1998 market shares of Airtours and First Choice at 34.4 per cent, with the market shares of the next two leading firms being 30.7 per cent and 20.4 per cent respectively. If these market shares had remained unchanged, the post-takeover market would have been one in which the leading three firms had a combined market share of 85 per cent. For the Commission, this was sufficient to justify a finding of collective dominance (¶54):

it is not a necessary condition of collective dominance for the oligopolists always to behave *as if* there were one or more explicit agreements (e.g. to fix prices or capacity, or share the market) between them. It is sufficient that the merger makes it rational for the oligopolists, in adapting themselves to market conditions, to act—individually—in ways which will substantially reduce competition between them, and, as a result of which they may act, to an appreciable extent, independently of competitors, customers and consumers.

The economic logic behind this finding is impeccable. But the Commission's decision has been criticized both on the ground that its market definition is inappropriate and that it has pushed the collective dominance doctrine to the point where[40] 'It's a blank check to prohibit any merger in any industry.' Airtours has announced its intention to appeal the Commission's decision to European courts, and the final chapter in this line of development of EU competition policy remains to be written.

6.5 **State aid**

Perhaps the most prominent slippage in the culture of competition that has developed in the European Union is the persistent tendency for Member States to deliver financial support, often surreptitiously, to local firms. Such aid undermines the public faith in a 'level playing field' that is essential for EU integration: businesses in less-well-off Member States will not long go along with tougher competition in their home markets if they have reason to think that rivals from elsewhere in the EU are subsidized by governments of more-well-off Member States.

Member States have explored a wide variety of ways to deliver aid to business—direct subsidies, capital investment, selective tax breaks, loan guarantees, sales of assets to business below a reasonable market price, purchases from the company above a reasonable market price, and so on. The rule for EU competition policy is that state aid is present when public policy directly or indirectly gives a firm an economic advantage it would not otherwise have (Morch 1995). State aid, whatever its form, is forbidden by Article 87(1) of the EC Treaty, provided it distorts competition and affects trade between the Member States. Exceptions may be allowed under Article 87(3) if the aid serves some Community purpose.

General practice is codified and strengthened in the 1999 Regulation on State Aid Procedures.[41] Member States are required to notify the Commission in advance of aid projects. Aid projects cannot be put into effect unless and until approved by the Commission. Aid that is not notified to the Commission cannot benefit from the possibility of exemption under Article 87(3), and aid that is granted without receiving an exemption is to be recovered.

The 1999 Regulation increases the Commission's investigatory powers and makes clear that legal appeals before national courts are not to delay recovery of aid that has been denied an exemption. But 21 per cent of 1997 aid cases were not notified to the Commission (Sinnaeve 1998: 80). In many instances, firms kept aid after a decision that it was incompatible with the common market: 'Nearly 10 per cent of the recovery decisions are not executed *10 years* after they have been taken, in the majority of cases because of pending procedures before national courts' (Sinnaeve 1998: 80; emphasis in original).

The Commission continues to occupy itself with a wide menu of state aid cases. These include instances of aid by the German State Saxony to Volkswagen, aid by the UK government to BMW, loans allegedly made at below-market interest rates by Germany to a major construction company (Holzmann AG), and an allegedly indirect injection of capital by North-Rhine Westphalia to a state bank.[42]

6.6 **Conclusion**

EU competition policy began as the safeguard of the integration process. So it remains, even though the integration process has extended itself to dimensions that were only dreamed of in 1957. One hallmark in the development of EU competition policy is an enhanced role for economic analysis, with business and Member State conduct judged according to its effects in the marketplace, not its legal form. Another is a wave of procedural modernizations that seek to equip competition policy for the larger and more deeply integrated economy that it must serve in the immediate future.

One challenge that must be handled if this modernization is to be successful is to ensure consistent enforcement of horizontal restraint policy under Article 81 as that enforcement moves to the Member State level. Another challenge will be to shackle the tendency of Member States to aid firms that are placed in difficulty by the increased competition that comes with wider and deeper integration.

Discussion questions

1 Examine the role of market definition in the first merger proposal that was blocked by the European Commission, *Aerospatiale-Alenia/de Haviland*—Commission Decision 91/619/EEC of 2 October 1991; *OJ* L 334/42 5 December 1991; pp. 327–9.

2 Read Albæk *et al.* (1997). Discuss the role of information in sustaining tacit collusion.

3 What arrangements has the European Commission made to cooperate with the enforcers of competition policy in other countries? How have these arrangements been applied in practice?

Further reading

The web site of the European Commission's Competition Directorate http://europa.eu.int/comm/competition/ is the best source for tracking developments in EU competition policy.

Notes

1 The Treaty of Amsterdam provides for renumbering of the Articles of the EC Treaty. What are now Articles 81 and 82 were originally Articles 85 and 86 of the Treaty of Rome. Throughout this chapter, I have referred to Treaty Provisions by their current numbers, where necessary changing the text of older decisions and documents.

2 The Commission has proposed (EC Commission, 2000*b*) that it be given the power to break up firms that violate Articles 81 and 82, if structural remedies are the only way to end infringement. This proposal is likely to meet resistance from the business community.

3 Council Regulation (EEC) No. 4064/89 *OJ* L 395/1, 30.12.89, amended by Council Regulation (EC) No. 1310/97, *OJ* L 180, 9.7.97.

4 Established Oct. 1988.

5 There are, nonetheless, areas in which EU competition policy and the economic viewpoint conflict. One example is the traditional hostility of competition policy to price discrimination (a hostility that is shared, at least in a formal sense, by US anti-trust policy). In situations where price discrimination is privately profit-maximizing (which are the situations when one would expect to see firms engaging in price discrimination), it most often also increases economic welfare. But price discrimination by a dominant firm is considered an abuse of a dominant position under Article 82, no doubt because of its perceived negative impact on the integration process.

6 *OJ* L 343, 21.12.74: 19–26.

7 I refer to the theory of noncooperative collusion in repeated games. See e.g. Friedman (1983; ch. 5).

8 *OJ* L 85/1 26.3.85, 1–52; *Re Wood Pulp Cartel*; *A. Ahlström OY and others v. EC Commission [1988] 4 CMLR 901; [1993] 4 CMLR 407.*

9 Collusion with respect to the US market is illegal under the Sherman Antitrust Act. But under the 1918 Webb–Pomerene Act it is legal for US firms to collude with respect to export markets. The EC Treaty does not cover export cartels that do not affect trade between the Member States. However, the European Commission has been sceptical toward the possibility that firms could collude on export markets without some spillover effect on the EU internal market.

10 *OJ* L 85/1, 26.3.85: 16.

11 Around the world, the record of policy-makers in directly regulating markets is not a happy one.

12 Characterized, among other things, by relatively large fixed costs in relation to the size of the market.

13 At this writing (Nov. 2000), Commission policy on exemptions under Article 81(3) is embodied in a block exemption on R&D agreements, a block exemption on specialization agreements, and two notices on cooperative joint ventures.

14 See Lücking (2000), European Commission (27 Apr. 2000*a*).

15 As measured by the Herfindahl–Hirschman Index, the sum of squares of market shares of all suppliers in the market.

16 Council Regulation No. 17/62 *OJ* 13/204, 21.9.62, variously amended.

17 For descriptions of national competition policies in a representative sample of EU Member States, see Martin (1998).

18 In some Member States, national law would need to be amended to implement this approach. The Commission would retain the power to take a role in matters decided at the Member State level if it felt that such intervention were appropriate.

19 See Giotakis (2000) for an example. One might argue that market definition should be based on an assessment of demand substitutability, with supply substitutability a factor to be considered in evaluating entry conditions.

20 Rarely, resale price maintenance has involved the manufacturer specifying a maximum price rather than a minimum price.

21 Vertical restraints may also be part of a collusive scheme, restricting competition among brands; see the discussion, below, of the Commission's *FEG* decision.

22 Thus the EU challenged a resale price maintenance scheme that covered the retail book market in the UK and Ireland but not the separate application of such schemes within national boundaries. (More recently, the Commission has challenged resale price maintenance in retail book distribution in Germany and Austria.)

23 *Deutsche Grammophon* v. *Metro* [1971] ECR 487.

24 *OJ* L 39, 14.2.2000: 1; see also Ferdinandusse (2000).

25 The Commission also found that FEG was the forum for discussions and policies that limited price competition among its members. The Netherlands is one of the Member States in which cartels were legal (but obliged to register) before the EC Treaty, and the Commission suggests that the anti-competitive behaviour at issue in this decision resulted from an agreement that was the descendent of such a cartel.

26 Vertical restraints may eliminate the *free-rider problem*, which arises if some dealers under-provide sales efforts (from the manufacturers' point of view) and undersell other dealers who provide greater and therefore more costly sales efforts. If unchecked, free-riding leads to market failure in the market for distribution services and prevents that manufacturer from obtaining the level of sales efforts it finds most profitable (from independent dealers).

27 *OJ* L 336, 29.12.99; see also the *Green Paper on Vertical Restraints* (European Commission 1997*a*).

28 See the *Guidelines on Vertical Restraints* (European Commission 2000*c*) for examples.

29 Most recently, Regulation 1475/95 *OJ* L 145, 29.6.95.

30 As noted above, market structure is itself the product of market forces. If the car distribution regulation is allowed to lapse, one possibility is that car manufacturers will integrate forward into distribution and perform for themselves the function that is now carried out by independent dealers. Another possibility is that mergers or internal growth at the dealer level would lead to consolidation and the rise of 'super dealers' able to effectively bargain with manufacturers.

31 *United Brands Company and United Brands Continental BV* v. *EC Commission* [1978] ECR 207.

32 Like any firm with a position of some market power, UBC would be limited by the ability of its consumers to cease buying the product (la Cour and Møllgaard 2000). Following Lerner (1934), the monopoly price-cost margin is the inverse of the price elasticity of demand.

33 From an economic point of view, there is no clear definition of 'unfair prices'. In a free-enterprise system, businesses are expected to maximize profit, and the managers of a business may well have a legal obligation to stockholders to maximize profit. It is not clear in what sense profit-maximizing prices are unfair if they are set independently (without collusion) and without strategic behaviour to make it more difficult for rivals to compete. Indeed, in a market system, high prices (relative to costs) are a signal for resource reallocation that leads, in the long run, to an efficient allocation of resources across markets.

34 *OJ* L 030, 4.2.2000: 1–24; see also Finnegan (1999).

35 *OJ* L 72, 11.3.98.

36 In the *Aéroports de Paris* (ADP) decision, the Commission found that the firm operating two Paris airports had abused a dominant position by charging discriminatory fees to airlines that provided their own ground-handling services.

37 The 1997 amendments also modified the treatment of certain types of joint ventures. So-called full function cooperative joint ventures—those (EC Commission 1998: 68) 'having all the necessary resources in terms of funding, staff and tangible and intangible assets' to operate as a stand-alone economic unit—are now treated under the Merger Control Regulation rather than under Article 81 of the EU Treaty.

38 This was the result with the 1997 *Boeing/McDonnell Douglas* merger.

39 Judgment of the Court of First Instance of 25 Mar. 1999.

40 Frédéric Jenny, quoted in *Wall Street Journal Europe* (2000).

41 Council Regulation (EC) No 659/99, *OJ* L 83/1, 22.3.99.

42 It also seems clear that if state aid policy is interpreted in the usual way, the wave of selective tax reductions and fuel subsidies granted across Europe in the autumn of 2000 is a violation of EU competition policy. These fuel-price-related measures are under investigation by the European Commission.

References

Albæck, S., Møllgaard, P., and Overgaard, P. B. (1997), 'Government-Assisted Oligopoly Coordination? A Concrete Case,' *Journal of Industrial Economics*, 45/4: 429–43.

Christensen, P. and Owen, P. (1999), 'Comment on the Judgment of the Court of First Instance of 25 March 1999 in the merger case IV/M.619—Gencor/Lonrho', *Competition Policy Newsletter*, 2, June, 19–23.

Comité Intergouvernemental créé par la Conférence de Messine (1956), *Rapport des Chefs de Délégation aux Ministres des Affairs Etrangères (Spaak Report)*, 21 Apr. (Brussels).

la Cour, L. F. and Møllgaard, H. P. (2000), 'Testing for (Abuse of) Domination: The Danish Cement Industry', Department of Economics, Copenhagen Business School, Working Paper 10–2000

European Commission (1997*a*), *Green Paper on Vertical Restraints in Community Competition Policy*, COM(96) 721 final, adopted by the Commission 22 Jan.

—— (1997*b*), *Notice on the definition of the relevant market for the purposes of Community competition law*, OJ C 372, 9 Dec.

—— (1998), *XXVIIth Report on Competition Policy 1997* (Brussels–Luxembourg).

—— (1999*a*), *White Paper on the Modernisation of the Rules Implementing Articles 81 and 82 of the EC Treaty*, 28 Apr. (Brussels).

—— (1999*b*), *XXVIIIth Report on Competition Policy 1998* (Brussels–Luxembourg).

—— (2000*a*), *Draft Guidelines on the Applicability of Article 81 to horizontal co-operation*, 27 Apr. (Brussels).

—— (2000*b*), *Proposal for a Council Regulation on the implementation of the rules on competition laid down in Articles 81 and 82 of the Treaty and amending Regulations (EEC) No 1017/68, (EEC) No 2988/74), (EEC) No 4056/86 and (EEC) No 3975/87*, COM(2000) 582 final, 27 Sept. (Brussels).

—— (2000*c*), *Guidelines on Vertical Restraints*, OJ C 291/1, 13 Oct.

Ferdinandusse, E. (2000) 'The Commission fines FEG, the Dutch association of electrotechnical equipment wholesalers and its biggest member', *Competition Policy Newsletter*, 1, Feb. 17–18.

Finnegan, J. (1999), 'Commission sets out its policy on commissions paid by airlines to travel agents', *Competition Policy Newsletter*, 3, Oct., 23.

Friedman, J. (1983), *Oligopoly Theory* (Cambridge: Cambridge University Press).

Giotakos, D. (2000), 'The Commission's review of the aluminium merger wave', *Competition Policy Newsletter*, 2, June, 8–23.

Lerner, A. P. (1934), 'The Concept of Monopoly and the Measurement of Monopoly Power', *Review of Economic Studies*, 1 (June): 157–75.

Lücking, J. (2000), 'Horizontal co-operation agreements: ensuring a modern policy', *Competition Policy Newsletter*, 2, June, 41–4.

Martin, S. (ed.) (1998), *Competition Policies in Europe* (Amsterdam: Elsevier).

Mitchener, B. (1999), 'For a good deal on a British car, you'll need a boat', *Wall Street Journal Europe*, 19 July, 1.

Morch, H. (1995), 'Summary of the most important recent developments', *Competition Policy Newsletter*, Spring, 47–51.

Sinnaeve, A. (1998), 'The Commission's proposal for a Regulation on State Aid procedures', *Competition Policy Newsletter*, June, 79–82.

Wall Street Journal Europe (2000), 'European Commission aims to improve merger regulation', 15–16 Sept., 3.

Chapter 7
Science and Technology Policy

Peter Stubbs

7.1 **Introduction**

The first and most fundamental issue to address in considering EU science and technology policy is why nation-states and collectivities of nation-states should have a science and technology policy at all. Could we not leave the production and distribution of scientific and technological knowledge to the market mechanism, which, after all, ranges from the humblest individual worker to the largest international firm?

Not surprisingly, scientists and technologists tend to oppose such a proposition. Since Bernard Shaw vilified all professions as conspiracies against the laity, we might suspect self-interest in that opposition; governmental support means more jobs, more prestige, and more money for scientists and technologists. That area of economics known as public choice theory (Mueller 1989) examines the behaviour of interest groups, and acknowledges that bureaucrats have their own agendas, and are not simply dispassionate agents of government (Niskanen 1975). The same is likely to be true of scientists. However, most economists involved have agreed that, objectively, the scientists have a tenable and intellectually respectable case. The most powerful economic support was offered by Kenneth Arrow (1962), who was to become a Nobel laureate in economics in 1972. He observed that there are three categories of economic problems which make it inadvisable to leave the allocation of resources for invention (and, by implication, technological progress) to the market mechanism. They are uncertainty, indivisibility, and inappropriability, and they require some elaboration.

7.2 **Reasons for the support of science and technology**

Arrow applied neoclassical economic analysis to advocate government financial support for basic research. Basic research is the bedrock of technological progress: its accepted definition is provided by the 'Frascati Manual' as 'experimental or theoretical work undertaken primarily to acquire new knowledge of the underlying foundations of phenomena and observable facts, without any particular application or use in view' (OECD, 1993*a*: 29). Clearly, work of this sort is likely to be far removed from the market-place, yet it has the potential to yield immensely important advances such as the microchip or genetic engineering. For many private investors, including even large corporations, the uncertainty of such research as an acceptable pursuit of financial gain is a severe deterrent. The risks of failure are high, both because the research might lead to a dead end and because there is a risk that, even if it were fruitful, a speedier rival might beat them to the harvest. It also takes many years to recoup the investment, because basic scientific advances usually take much time and money to translate into saleable products or processes. Applying a typical commercial discount rate to compute a net present value for the speculative benefits of long-term basic research tends to disadvantage it when compared with less radical development work with a quicker pay-off.

Governments can pool these risks, since they are bigger than their national companies and may be able to consider longer-term benefits from the social rather than the private point of view: it does not matter to the government whether company *A* or company *Z* exploits the research findings, as long as they are exploited; but, if *A* contemplated doing the research itself, any prospect that *Z*, or *B*, or *C* could exploit it at the expense of *A* would be a disincentive. Notwithstanding, even nation-states can find basic research risky; but the funding of much basic research in most countries is a government responsibility.

There is a further benefit from public funding of basic research. Where a private research body would want to maintain its property rights—that is, 'keep hold' of its research results to cover its costs and make private profits—the public source can be more open. Basic research findings may be more likely to be translated into useful innovations if they can 'spill over' and be adopted and developed by a wide range of innovators. The prevailing ethic among basic researchers is for wide publication and circulation of their findings among their peer group, and this is most likely to be realized where there is no corporate restraint due to secrecy.

Indivisibilities present problems. Where markets are indivisible, there are problems both in assessing demand and in securing payment. A public-health research programme, analogous to a public-health investment such as urban drainage, can benefit a whole community, but, given the choice of whether to contribute to its costs, some people could become free-riders, enjoying the benefits without making any contribution to the costs. In this case it is better to fund and operate the project at community level.

There may also be indivisibilities in the process of research itself. Where an industry is atomistic, with many small producers, no single member may be able to afford a worth-while research and technical development (RTD) facility. In agriculture a multitude of competing farmers is most unlikely to do systematic RTD; individually they lack the assets, the expertise, and the incentive. Centralized RTD, supported by a levy on users, can overcome this problem; this solution can be applied to specific industrial processes or other small-scale industries by establishing research associations. Governments have sub-sidized these bodies permanently, or temporarily as a pump-priming exercise, until they becoming self-financing.

Inappropriability is a problem because the originator of the invention or technology may be unable to gain due reward, unless he or she can appropriate the returns to the effort. Ideas are easily stolen. If much of the originator's benefit is dissipated through copying and illicit application by others, there is no immediate social loss—indeed there may seemingly be social gain if the innovation is diffused more widely and more cheaply, as happens notoriously in the case of pirated computer software, which has been esti-mated to cost the industry £400m. a year in the UK alone (*The Times*, 22 Oct. 1993, p. 33). But, quite apart from the issue of legality, the loss to the innovator may prove a serious disincentive to the inspiration and hard work which RTD entails: short-run opportunistic gains would then compromise long-run technological progress. Most nation-states, therefore, protect the intellectual property of inventors through patents and copyrights granted upon original works.

A related issue concerns the benefits which accrue to users, as distinct from the innov-ator. Support for innovation may be given by governments on the grounds that there are social benefits from innovation beyond the private benefits which accrue through pay-ments to the innovator. Empirical studies of specific innovations by Mansfield *et al.* (1976) show that the social rate of return to innovation is usually higher than the private rate, sometimes helped by the spill-over effect noted above. The argument can be pressed further, in suggesting that there are second-order effects in enhancing industrial devel-opment and national competitiveness. If so, and the support improves dynamic resource allocation and the responsiveness of the economy, the effects can be subtle, profound, and long-lasting. However, it is very problematic to verify these effects in ways rigorous enough to persuade national treasuries to provide funding in the face of other less specu-lative and more populist claims for finance, though much generally positive evidence has accumulated over the past two decades.

Beyond these central issues of uncertainty, indivisibility, and inappropriability, there are other motives for government support of technology. It is often asserted that imperfect private capital markets restrict the funds available for RTD, that bankers are unappreciative of the full value of technological opportunities. In response to this view, governments have from time to time established mechanisms targeted at the provision of funds for technology, such as the National Research Development Corporation (NRDC) and its eventual successor, the British Technology Group (BTG), which was later privatized, and other measures in many countries to promote venture capital sources for technological small and medium-sized enterprises (SMEs).

Government may also act as a disseminator of scientific and technological informa-tion, and finance arbitration where there are conflicts arising from the use of new technology. Many governments have given support for communications technology in recent years, and there are well-known cases where they have funded inquiries into technological matters of public concern, such as the Sizewell B nuclear power station in the UK, or the links between bovine spongiform encephalopathy (BSE) and Creutzfeldt-Jakob Disease (CJD).

Finally, the view may be expressed that economic rationale alone should not rule the allocation of funds for science (in particular) and technology. This view rests on the belief that scientific investigation is a manifestation of advanced civilization with a justifiable ethic of its own, rendering it just as eligible for state support as the arts are. In this context, allocation to science is not simply to be regarded as an investment decision but also involves elements of desirable consumption. Indeed, some of the allocations to basic research face such high degrees of uncertainty and long gestation that it is difficult to apply to them any risk criteria where risk is understood in Frank Knight's sense of 'measurable uncertainty' (Knight 1921). However, even if this viewpoint is given some credit, there are problems of adjudicating between open-ended claims from the science lobby, and of deciding on the total allocation to the science sector.

Since Arrow made his contribution, a vast literature has grown as the full complexity of the many issues has emerged. Most contributors have employed a contrasting structuralist-evolutionary approach (Lipsey and Carlaw 1998) reflecting this complexity, though without supplanting Arrow's case for support. Rather, the debate has advanced, to address questions such as, how does RTD actually impact on industry (prompting some revision of its definitions), what form of support is required, and how do different measures perform? Researchers now stress the Schumpeterian pervasiveness of change rather than shifts between neoclassical equilibria.

In several advanced countries over the past decade, direct state support for science and technology has tended to decline. This arises in part from economic downturns and a general desire among governments to avoid increasing taxation, but also reflects the sentiment that since industry at large benefits from technological progress, some of its social benefits are internalized in the sector, if not in each firm executing the RTD. Also, the growth of inter-firm alliances and international corporate collaboration over high-technology ventures, which we consider later in this chapter, has enabled companies to pursue basic scientific research more enterprisingly than they could have done singly. However, it would be difficult to find many supporters for the proposition of Kealey (1996) that the entirety of scientific funding could and should be left to market forces, even if one concedes to him that grant-seeking scientists are as conscious of the pork-barrel as are any other professions.

7.3 National policies for science and technology

Before the advent of the EC, national policies for science and technology were inevitably separate. Though they shared a common focus of correcting market failures and enhancing scientific and technological performance in the search for improved economic performance and enhanced scientific prestige, there were evident differences among the nations of the Community, their national innovation systems, and their priorities and methods of support. Since there is a wide degree of independence to national policies, we need to examine briefly the national innovation systems and government policies that have developed. In the first edition of this book, we examined Germany, France, and the UK, as the three biggest performers of RTD in the EU (Stubbs and Saviotti 1994: 142–7). In the second edition we examined Italy, the Netherlands, and Sweden. We now return to cover recent developments in the original three. In aggregate, Member State expenditures on science and technology dwarf EU-level expenditures. Moreover, as M. Claude Allègre, the French Minister for Education, Research and Technology, noted in 1998, subsidiarity applies in science and technology, so that the EU should only operate in areas too expensive for nation-states to act in alone, and, presumably, where international collaboration might generate strong externalities. Thus national policies remain of paramount importance in the European picture as a whole. Some statistics concerning national science and technology performance are shown in Table 7.1 at the end of this section.

United Kingdom

Industrial and technology policies in the United Kingdom have been marked by pragmatism. The only attempt at a highly centralized industrial policy, partly inspired by earlier French planning experience, collapsed within a year in 1966. In the 1960s and 1970s the Ministry of Technology and the Industrial Reorganisation Corporation contrived to select national champions, encouraging growth by the merger of large firms, often of doubtful efficiency, which were intended to meet the challenge of the leading foreign firms which, by contrast, had usually grown by internal efficiency. Not surprisingly, the strategy failed dismally.

A right-wing government elected in 1970 dismembered the Ministry of Technology and introduced a 'customer–contractor principle' which sought to inject some market elements into government-funded applied research, decreeing 'the customer says what he wants; the contractor does it (if he can); and the customer pays'. Successive pragmatic interventions under governments of both political colours sought variously and without general success to improve industrial and technological development by interventionist policies under Heath, Wilson, and Callahan. Moreover, there were long-standing weaknesses in the national technological ethic which governments seemed unable to correct. Walker (1993) suggests that high (and technologically distracting) defence expenditure, poor technological training, short-termism emphasizing immediate profits rather than long-term strategic advantage, and a service rather than a manufacturing culture, all hobbled the optimum application of technology.

By the advent of the Thatcher government in 1979, it was clear that politicians and civil servants alike had lost any confidence they might have had to 'pick winners'—that is, to direct closely through chosen companies as national champions the strategic development of British industrial technology. At the same time, after years of poor performance in the nationalized industries, dogma and pragmatism combined to introduce privatization. Many industrial subsidies were phased out, moribund industries were allowed to disappear, and a more competitive managerial environment was urged.

Technology policy saw government expenditure on 'near-market' RTD trimmed back, as this was perceived as more appropriate for firms to fund and conduct; emphasis switched towards collaborative company programmes and longer-term research. Instead of picking company winners, which often meant an enervating relief from all domestic competition, emphasis shifted to generic technologies, such as robotics and microelectronics, which would impact across a wide range of industries, being adopted by their worthier members. Expert advice was provided by committees such as the Advisory Council for Applied Research and Development (ACARD) and later the Advisory Council on Science and Technology (ACOST).

After the 1992 election, government created an Office of Science and Technology and proposed changes to the structure of the Research Councils, as well as stressing the need for wealth creation, reaffirming the customer–contractor principle, and urging the need for cross-departmental coordination in science and technology. An important innovation was the Technology Foresight Programme, which brought scientific and industrial communities together in 16 panels to exchange views and help to explore consensually what future developments might be expected in science and technology.

However, the new market realism brought problems: it was wedded to the minimization of public expenditure, yet the shake-out of employment in inefficient industry placed a heavy financial burden on social services; the collapse of inefficient industries narrowed the base of British-owned manufacturing industry, though foreign direct investment filled the gap in key areas including motor vehicles and consumer electronics. In consequence, there was a steady reduction in government funding of RTD across the 1990s, and in university funding, which eroded their infrastructure for scientific research. RTD intensity declined at all levels of industry—high, medium-high, medium-low, and low technology sectors. RTD as a percentage of GDP fell from 2.13 per cent in 1990 to 1.8 per cent in 1997. The economy was more open than most other countries, with a higher ratio of trade to GDP than the USA, Germany, or France, but it was also more dependent on foreign capital and technology, with almost one-quarter of its business RTD financed by foreign principals in 1998, much more than any of its rivals. Without this foreign injection, the decline in RTD would have been significantly worse. While the UK has some areas of strength, such as pharmaceuticals, oil refining, and services, its innovative performance is weak compared to the USA, Japan, or Germany. An EC survey revealed that fewer British firms introduced innovations than did German ones, though they were ahead of the French and the EU average (Eurostat 2001). Only one-quarter of the innovating British firms conducted formal RTD, and it was observed that large firms were more likely to introduce innovations than small ones.

In 1997 a Labour government was elected under Tony Blair. Among other things it was pledged to maintain the general primacy of markets, but to emphasize education, health, and technology. During its tenure, it has introduced a wide range of technological initiatives. A second Foresight exercise was launched, following the success of the first, compounding the original 16 panels into 10. A Defence Diversification Agency was set up to capitalize on defence RTD. It seeks to make suitable recipients aware of available defence technology suitable for civilian use, draws attention to the Defence Evaluation and Research Agency's laboratories, fosters co-development and adaptation with civil partners, and makes information available to screened recipients of Ministry of Defence needs and on relevant technological trends, thus helping firms to appreciate the military scope for their products. In 1999, following a White Paper on Competitiveness, the Department of Trade and Industry stressed the need for innovation, widespread access to technology, and partnership between industry and the science base. A venture capital fund of £150m. was established, and innovative clusters predicated on California's Silicon Valley and the Cambridge complex in Britain were mooted, with biotechnology as a main focus, including eight enterprise centres to be based on universities. The Teaching Company Scheme was extended, to improve links particularly with small and medium-sized enterprises.

Funding for science has been augmented in a variety of ways. Following growing recognition of the decline in public-sector research establishments (PSRE) and university funding, and the consequent inadequacy of funds for laboratory infrastructure, government set up a Higher Education Innovation Fund with £140m. and a Science Research Investment Fund with £750m. The first White Paper on science for seven years appeared in 2000 (DTI 2000*a*), and the Science Budget for the following three years is to rise at 7 per cent a year in real terms. PSREs now have freedom to pursue commercial opportunities and to retain their subsequent receipts. Measures were also introduced to attract researchers from overseas, and SMEs were given tax credits for RTD expenditure, as an obvious incentive for the small business sector; but the budget in March 2001 extended the concession to businesses in general acknowledging that the UK lags behind its competitors in business RTD. However, the complexities of defining baseline expenditures against which incremental RTD expenditure will be credited, and of allowing for annual fluctuations, will delay implementation until 2002. Areas singled out for support programmes include post-genome medical research, advanced electronic communications, information processing, and nanotechnology.

Thus the intention is clear to improve innovative performance, but worries persist. University research staff are said to lack commercial awareness, government funding improvements are feared by researchers to be relatively short-term rather than strategic, and there is a long tail of SMEs which are not technologically oriented and will not be caught or improved by current policies. The strength in depth of German manufacturing, with its abler shop-floor workforce, is still lacking in the UK.

France

In the nineteenth century and the early decades of the twentieth century, French science and French industry lagged behind Germany's impressive progress (Chesnais 1993). After the Second World War, the French government was more *dirigiste* than its British or German neighbours, directing industrial policy much more closely, and with considerable success at first. From the late 1960s, like the British government, it promoted mergers to foster firms which it hoped would compete with large foreign rivals, of which the United States was perceived as the strongest and most dangerous. It lacked a large and sophisticated capital market, and it was not until the late 1980s that the stock market assumed much importance (Sharp and Holmes 1989: 3). The centralist bureaucracy applied equipment procurement policies to encourage selected industries such as telecommunications manufacturing, computers, and nuclear-power generation.

Many of the *Grands Projets* of the 1970s were high-profile successes technically, such as nuclear power and the TGV high-speed train, albeit rather opaque in their economics. But where Britain in the 1980s pursued privatization, deregulation, and the acknowledgement of market forces, the French Socialist government nationalized eight leading French firms as part of a strategy of state-inspired technological advance. The intentions were that continuous state funding would ensure efficient and effective research, and that the state could build bridges between public laboratories and industry, and balance small and big technology programmes. It was thwarted by economic recession, the reality of international market competition, and by the inherent problems which attend such intentions: even today they are still key items on the government agenda. Sharp and Holmes noted (1989: 220–1) that states could no longer carve out industrial territories, as market-led technology spilled out across industries and countries, and swamped many national ambitions. Minitel, the government-led video-link associated with domestic telephones, was outflanked by the privately developed modem that enabled personal computers to access the internet.

In the 1990s French government support for RTD faltered under the combined influences of economic slowdown, high interest rates, falling public expenditure and cutbacks in defence research. However the government diagnosed many of the earlier failings of the French innovation system, and set about reform in the latter 1990s. Many problems were identified for treatment. French research was rated good, technology rather less so. RTD was concentrated in high-technology projects in large firms, but was disappointing in information technology and in the service sector. In 1998–9, four major technology programmes were initiated, including life sciences and information technology, and the emphasis for support shifted from large companies, which were urged to finance their own research, to SMEs. Notwithstanding these changes, an authoritative report concluded 'the framework for innovation is still far from optimal' (OECD 1999a: 129). It noted that there was still too much centralization and concentration in the conduct of research. The 1999 Innovation Law set out to make French public research organizations less bureaucratic, more dynamic and entrepreneurial, through four key policies:

1. By encouraging the mobility of researchers and their freedom to act entrepreneurially.
2. By improving the public research/industry interface,
3. By improving the fiscal regime for innovative companies, especially SMEs,
4. By simplifying the legal framework for setting up high-technology firms.

A radical reappraisal of innovation policy was undertaken in late 1999 (Majoie and Remy 1999), drawing upon reports from multi-disciplinary groups. It recognized that SMEs needed guidance to inform the thrust of their research, possibly after the manner of the British Foresight exercises, and that there was a problem with the ageing profile of the population of researchers in public research organizations. Reforms followed: in April 2000 all state taxes on enterprise creation were eliminated, and new credits provided to enterprises working in new technology areas. The 2001 budget provisions favoured young researchers, and finance was given to help biotechnology, information and commmunications technology, and aerospace, including the A380 superjumbo Airbus.

Thus French government policy towards science and technology has undergone major, conscious change, consonant with the twenty-first century, and begun to address the problems identified by the OECD. Whether it will escape the traditional centralism of French administration remains to be seen but, interestingly, it has been suggested recently that a significant proportion of recent graduates of the prestigious civil service training school, the Ecole Nationale d'Administration or ENA, is entering the private sector, partly out of frustration at the rigidities of bureaucracy (*Financial Times*, 7 Mar. 2001, p. 23). Administrative, as well as scientific, labour mobility could be an important asset in France's advance towards the flexibility necessary in a modern economy.

Germany

German industry has long benefited from a strong national tradition of education and scientific research (Keck 1993). This has underpinned the impressive performance of its chemical and engineering industries, in which its export performance in the competitive US market was better than that of its EC partners in the 1970s and 1980s. In the 1990s it maintained a more positive trade balance in manufactures than France, while the UK and the US, had negative balances across the period 1992–8. In many respects the German economy appears technologically stronger than its British or French equivalents. It spends proportionately more on RTD than they do, more per head of population, and has almost as many business enterprise personnel engaged in RTD as Britain and France combined. Government support is directed more at science and technology infra-structure, and much less through government procurement, reflecting the lesser role of its defence industry. Its manufactured products are more up-market in their price-quality range, it has a significantly higher propensity to take out European patents, and excels in medium-high technology products. Its industrial strengths lie in industrial chemicals, machinery and electrical machinery, shipbuilding, motor vehicles, and scientific instruments, each with good export performance. GDP per head is well ahead of the British level, but the absorption of East Germany has pulled it back relative to France. It is less dependent on foreign capital than its two rivals, and on foreign technology.

However, there are some points of weakness. Despite success in the medium-high technology sector, it has not performed well in the high technology sector as such, where it has a negative trade balance in products such as office and computer equipment, as well as radio, TV, and communications equipment. Its corporate research is heavily concentrated in large firms defined as employing over 1,000 people, and there seems to be unexploited scope for technology-based SMEs (small and medium-sized enterprises).

Research funding is provided mainly by the federal government, but also by the state governments, or *Länder*. Federal support has gone mainly to business and private non-profit research institutes, and state contributions to universities. The dominant research institutions are the German Research Association (Deutsche Forschungsgemeinschaft, or DFG), the Max Planck Institute, and the Fraunhofer Association (FhF), which are supra-regional in scope with many out-stations, and for all of which there is extensive government support. The Federal Ministry of Education, Science, Research and Technology (Bundesministerium für Bildung und Forschung or BMBF) provided grant finance for a wide range of programmes in high-risk, long-term projects such as aerospace, and public-interest projects such as health and the environment.

After some slippage in research funding in the mid-1990s, by the end of the decade support was increased in real terms, and strategic areas identified for priority projects. These include health and medical research, molecular biology, biotechnology, laser technology and information technology, ecology and climate research, and transport. The Federal Ministry for Economics and Technology (BMWi) was given responsibility for technology-based SMEs, energy research and policy, aviation research, and multi-media issues.

Over the years there have been a number of criticisms of German research performance, notwithstanding the strength of the economy. Keck (1993) suggested that nuclear power research had been undertaken simply to secure research grants, without producing tangible applications, whereas privately funded work led to practical reactors. Later, Beise and Stahl (1999) concluded that while publicly funded research had stimulated some industrial innovation, it was not fully justified by the extent of identifiable transfers. Public research centres were meant to perform more applied research than universities do, emphasizing spin-off to industry, but they tended to concentrate on long-term research, locking in their staff so that there was limited transfer to industry. At a more general level, in a draft report of its latest country survey the OECD has criticized government for failing to liberalize its labour markets, and for wasteful investment in the economically depressed east (*Financial Times*, 7 Mar. 2001; 1). It highlights the need for more stringent investment criteria, a more competitive and accountable university sector, and the importance of lifelong training.

The research institutions mentioned earlier are, however, addressing many key issues in their spheres of interest. Over 40 per cent of the DFG budget is granted to individual research project applications and 26 per cent to collaborative research centres, emphasizing cooperation between universities and other participants. It has identified 129 priority programmes and has a commitment to promoting the public understanding of science. While it may be difficult for German industry to occupy the technological high ground alongside the USA and Japan, and there are concerns that other European countries have raised their technological profile, the strength in depth of the economy should assure its continued primacy in Europe.

Table 7.1 shows the national pattern of expenditure on RTD by selected nation-states, as percentages of GDP. Since some of the countries, notably USA, Japan, and Germany, have a much larger GDP than the UK, it is evident that in absolute terms their RTD expenditure is very much higher than that of the UK. UK expenditure on RTD has failed over the years to keep pace with its major competitors, and its positive technological balance of payments of the early 1980s was significantly negative by 1990, yet became positive again later in the decade. Japan has improved greatly, but the USA retains the strongest positive balance of payments on the technology account, partly though not wholly because the US Revenue Service is assiduous in requiring US companies to declare every conceivable element of their technology earnings.

Table 7.1 Statistics of national science and technology performance, 1998

RTD category	Expenditure on RTD as percentage of GDP					
	USA	Japan	UK	Germany	France	Italy
Gross RTD (GERD)	2.74	3.06	1.83	2.29	2.18	1.02
Civil RTD	2.3	n.a.	1.6	2.2	2.18	1.0
Government-funded civil RTD	0.84	0.59	0.51	0.82	0.87	0.52
Defence RTD	0.47	n.a.	0.27	n.a.	0.2	n.a.
Business RTD (BERD)	2.10	2.10	1.19	1.57	1.37	0.56
Industry-financed BERD	0.41	2.06	0.79	1.38	1.08	0.44
Higher-education RTD	0.39	0.4 [a]	0.35	0.41	0.38	0.26
BERD financed from abroad, %	n.a.	0.4	22	2.7	11	8.2

	Indicators of national size and growth					
	USA	Japan	UK	Germany	France	Italy
GDP (£bn. at PPP [b])	5,432	2,005	857	1,228	861	828
GDP growth rate, 1988–98 (% p.a.)	6.9	6.7	6.0	8.3	5.9	6.0
GERD (£bn. at PPP)	150.4	61.7	15.6	28.5	18.9	8.6
GERD growth rate 1988–98 (% p.a.)	6.8	8.6	4.5	6.0	5.6	4.4
Inventiveness coefficient [c] (1997)	4.5	27.7	3.1	5.5	2.2	1.2
Technological balance of payments (receipts/payments)	3.26	2.13	1.92	0.85	0.72	0.79

a   Estimated.
b   PPP = purchasing power parity.
c   Defined as resident patent applications per 10 000 population.
Notes: Definitional anomalies and rounding can cause seeming inconsistency within national figures.
n.a. = not available
Sources: DTI (2000a) and OECD (2000).

7.4 **The development of EU science and technology policy**

The original Treaty of Rome in 1957, signed by Belgium, France, Italy, Luxembourg, the Netherlands, and Germany, concentrated on the abolition of customs between the EC6 and on the adoption of a common external tariff (CET) on goods entering from other countries. Matters such as competition policy, freedom of movement for labour and capital, customs unions, state aid, and the harmonization of national laws fell within the Treaty's area of competence, so that one could say that there were components of an industrial policy but no overall framework, though there was a limited precedent in the experience gained in running the European Coal and Steel Community (ECSC), which had operated since 1951. However, there was no provision in the Treaty for science and technology in the then European Economic Community (EEC), or for the adoption of policy towards them.

However, there was some recognition of a technological issue, albeit very narrow, in respect of civilian atomic energy. At that time, atomic energy was perceived as one of the most dazzling and important frontiers of science, intellectually challenging and exciting. It was expected, in time, to provide very cheap power, that potentially could release Europe from its heavy dependence on coal and imported oil. It was an area where there ought to be economies in conducting RTD collectively. And there was an obvious European dimension, in that the USA and the Soviet Union were committed to nuclear energy programmes, but were secretive about their knowledge because of military security. Against this background, the European Atomic Energy Community (Euratom) Treaty was also signed in 1957.

Nuclear reactor designs and fuel technologies were expected to arise from the work of the Joint Nuclear Research Centre (JNRC), which was set up to conduct a five-year research and training programme. Inspired by the examples of Los Alamos and Oak Ridge in the USA and Harwell in the UK, JNRC was to be established on several sites. As Peterson notes (1991: 269), some commentators at the time foresaw a more influential future for Euratom than for the EEC. Harsh realities soon intruded upon these visionary intentions (Ford and Lake 1991), however rivalry occurred between the German and French nuclear industries, in the early climate of buoyant demand for nuclear power stations. The JNRC's reactor design, described as 'somewhat eccentric', was unsuccessful. Across the 1960s, oil provided increasing rather than shrinking competition, and the JNRC was left with nuclear scientists but little or no nuclear work to do. Gradually it mutated to become the Joint Research Centre (JRC), with its headquarters in Brussels, a main base and administrative directorate at Isprà in northern Italy, with others at Karlsruhe in Germany, Petten in the Netherlands, Geel in Belgium and, later, Seville in Spain, operating eight research institutes across five sites. The Ispra operation was long criticized for inefficiency, with one account reporting that only 30 or 40 people from a total staff of 1600 were qualified and scientifically active (Linkohr 1987). The JRC operation was described as being characterized by 'listlessness, apathy, lack of direction, and lack of conviction' (Ford and Lake 1991: 40). The failure of Euratom was critical: what should have been the flagship for European technology seemed to have run seriously aground. In 1993 its mandate was extended to conduct non-nuclear research, and Ecu 900m. was earmarked for it in the Fourth Framework Programme, as part of a strategy to make it more market-oriented and competitive. Since then there has been tangible improvement in the JRC, with major diversification out of its early specialization: currently it has 2400 staff engaged in 100 projects, and only 27 per cent of its annual budget of about Ecu 300m. now concerns nuclear matters, centred mainly on safety. Other research themes include food safety, the environment and sustainability, and European competitiveness, with a strong emphasis on interdisciplinary programmes and a conscious attempt to develop know-how clusters in the modern idiom.

The initial failure of this role-model for successful collective international research coincided in the 1960s with strongly interventionist national industrial policies in Europe, particularly in France and the UK (though the UK did not enter the EEC until

1972). The publication of an influential book by a French journalist, *Le Défi Américain* or *The American Challenge* (Servan Schreiber 1967), added to the pressures on governments to boost the capacity of European industries to counter the competition of powerful foreign concerns, typified by IBM, the then dominant US computer giant. The key weapons were mergers and subsidies, which were intended to afford the necessary resource and scale to match foreign competition. There were also several European collaborative initiatives, such as the Anglo-French Concorde airliner project, and the European Space Agency (ESA), independently of the EEC. Concorde was a technical success (until the Paris disaster in August 2000) but a commercial catastrophe from the outset: one commentator noted 'the advanced technologies of the 1960s provided suitable objects on to which the fantasies of European unity could be projected, while in reality they did not have any substantial long-term significance in contributing to a process of European integration' (Barry 1990, cited by Ford and Lake 1991).

More successful was the Airbus commercial airliner project, in which the consortium partners were France (38 per cent), Germany (38 per cent), the UK (20 per cent), and Spain (4 per cent). This has developed a family of airliners which has gained a very significant market share from the USA, though prompting bitter complaints from US manufacturers that it was unfairly subsidized. In the mid-1990s there was growing pressure, in the interests of internal efficiency and transparency of its accounting procedures, for the consortium to set up a public company, which it announced in July 1996. However, it has shown that European manufacturers can collaborate successfully in a high-technology area and compete with world leaders such as Boeing. In March 2001 Boeing announced that it would not compete with the latest Airbus A380 superjumbo, but would develop a radical, smaller, and faster alternative, leaving open the possibility that if they judge the market wrongly, their rival Airbus could monopolize an immense market.

Another technologically successful example in the space sector was not specifically an EC initiative. In 1962 two organizations were established to foster collaboration in space technology: the European Launcher Development Organization (ELDO) and the European Space Research Organization (ESRO). ELDO became a Franco-German initiative after the UK withdrew, but, with the merger of the two bodies in 1973 to form the ESA, a more pan-European stance followed. ESA fared better than its predecessors, for several reasons. First, inter-institutional collaboration was easier because governments and public agencies were the prime contractors; secondly, the specialized character of the technology led to a closely knit community of policy-makers, engineers, scientists, and industrialists; and, thirdly, its programme was designed so that all the fourteen Member States would share formally in the contracts let by the agency, under *juste retour*. In recent years, however, ESA has been strongly criticized for excessive bureaucracy.

The European Patent Office (EPO), founded in 1977 following the European Patent Convention of 1973, was another significant extra-EC development. It provides a single application process for the grant of a 'European patent', which is valid in all the signatory states for 20 years, and saves the administration and expense of applying individually to them. By 2001 membership comprised Switzerland, Turkey, Cyprus, Monaco, and Liechtenstein from outside the EC, plus fifteen members from within it. Patents issued grew from 1500 a month in 1980 to about 3000 a month in 1999. It has headquarters in Munich and the Hague, and sub-offices in Berlin and Vienna. The EPO also distributes patent information, which is an important function of any worthwhile patent system, and represents Europe in the World Intellectual Property Organization. Only recently a standard Community patent has been proposed, intended to be affordable and comparable in cost to a European patent.

Thus by the beginning of the 1980s it seemed ironic that the most successful examples of international collaboration were those deriving not from the EC, but from narrower combinations, like the Airbus, or wider ones, like ESA.

The shift of support from firms to generic technologies

Generally, the interventionist policies of support by national governments were seen to be unsucessful. By the mid-1970s, after the UK had joined the EC, it was apparent that this policy of 'picking winners' was beyond the capacity of governments: the phrase was heard increasingly that 'the business of government is not the government of business' (Lawson 1992: 211). If a government selected a firm (sometimes by the merger of former competitors) to be the national champion in an area of technological promise and to endow it with the size and subsidy to compete with the established champion of rival states, the most immediate effect was to remove its domestic competition and give it a comfortable, if temporary, feather-bed on which it might as readily relax as take up the bruising cudgels of foreign competition. However, competitive domestic markets tend to be an important precondition of the vigour required to compete internationally (Porter 1990: chap. 3).

In the 1970s the trend moved from selectiveness towards the identification and support of selected or 'generic' technologies, which might be expected to impact on a wide range of industries: electronics and biotechnology were the leading examples. Again, it was national governments rather than the EC which were prime movers in the new trend, but the first signs appeared of an EC policy towards science and technology.

On 14 January 1974 the Council decided to develop 'a common policy in the field of science and technology'. The scope of the policy was twofold: to coordinate the policies of the Member States and to implement research programmes and projects of EC interest. This sounds simple but is difficult in practice, since the finance available to the EC for implementation was between 1 and 2 per cent of the public funds spent by the Member States on RTD support. Three years later, the Commission produced objectives for the period 1977–80 (CEC 1977):

1. securing the long-term supply of resources—namely, raw materials, energy, agriculture, and water;

2. the promotion of internationally competitive economic development;

3. improvement of living and working conditions; and

4. protection of the environment and nature.

These pious if worthy aims posed a number of problems of implementation, apart from the modesty of financial resources already noted. How would Member States cooperate, given the record of national divergence discussed earlier in this chapter? Could EC policy be reconciled with the problems which the states themselves faced in their national science and technology policies? How should science and technology relate to other EC policies?

Criteria for EC support were itemized, four 'general' and eleven 'specific'. The general ones emphasized the need for rationalization and efficiency at EC level, the need for transnational action which would involve several countries, the economic need to spread development costs over several national markets, and the need to meet common national requirements. Specific selection criteria included cases where costs or required RTD capacity would be too high for a single nation to bear, or where there would be savings through joint efforts; cases where RTD was in an initial phase, where an EC programme would stand a good chance of competing internationally, as in new transport systems; cases where potential is real, such as new sources of energy, and where there was thought to be long-term potential, such as nuclear fusion. The need for standardization of measures and information systems was also noted.

The Scientific and Technical Research Committee (CREST) was responsible for the development of Community RTD policy and coordination at policy level with Member States, and included senior officials from the member countries as well as Commission officials. The Commission established an internally staffed pilot programme of Forecasting and Assessment in Science and Technology (FAST), to collaborate with outside bodies. The FAST programme helped to highlight shortcomings in Europe's capacity in capitalizing on basic research, which too seldom produced successful final products. The Commission also acknowledged the importance of evaluating the effectiveness of its research activities and programmes, which we examine later.

Thus by the late 1970s the Commission had begun to address some of the key issues concerning science and technology and establish tentative proposals for action, but these bore the stamp of a hesitant bureaucracy rather than the confidence which marked the Ministry of International Trade and Industry (MITI) in Japan.

The primacy of US and Japanese technology

Evidence accumulated in the 1980s that the 'technology gap' noted between US and European industry in the 1960s was widening, and that Japan was also outstripping Europe in many critical industries. One of the most visible industries was electronics, because its products could be seen to pervade industrial and domestic use, including the fashionable information technology (IT) sector. The national governments of France, Germany, and the UK had all supported their IT industries across the period from the mid-1960s to the early 1980s through subsidy, merger, and procurement preference in government purchases, to little effect (Sandholtz 1992). In 1975 the EC had a positive balance of payments in information technology, but it was in deficit by 1982. Europe's shares of world production in semiconductors and in integrated circuits were declining, foreign penetration of the European market was increasing, and European semiconductor manufacturing was unprofitable. Over four-fifths of the European computer market was held by US firms. Worse still, perhaps, was the fact that the USA and Japan were both pursuing ambitious research programmes in search of future IT supremacy, the former on very-high-speed integrated circuits (VHSIC), while the latter, after its successful very-large-scale integration (VLSI) programme, which had launched Japanese industry into the manufacture of mainstream memory chips in the 1970s, announced an initiative on fifth-generation computers intended, in popular parlance, 'to think for themselves'. Faced with this mounting challenge, a number of leading European IT firms had, with EC encouragement, already begun to collaborate in the late 1970s on 'pre-competitive' research—that is, research on innovations in principle rather than at the level of products for imminent commercial launch. As we shall see later, this concern over US and Japanese technological leadership is a recurrent theme, continuing today.

The emergence of Community programmes

In 1979–80 the Commissioner of DG III, the Directorate-General of Internal Market and Industrial Affairs, Viscount Étienne Davignon of Belgium, invited the heads of Europe's leading IT firms to form a Big 12 Round Table. They commanded more authority than more junior personnel who had attended earlier, less fruitful, discussions, and were well aware of the gravity of their industrial and collective circumstances. Sandholtz (1992) has suggested that 'in general, states will attempt unilateral strategies first and surrender the goal of autonomy only when unilateral means have proved to be impossible or too costly'. The participant national firms knew that unilateralism had failed, and this recognition generated a climate favourable to cooperation, and Davignon became the champion of new policies (Sharp 1993). Two years of talks failed to establish joint manufacturing companies along the lines of the Airbus consortium, but they did establish a consensus for collaborative research. Moral support also followed from the Gyllenhammer group, an informal gathering of twenty leading European industrialists, representing Gyllenhammer's Volvo, as well as Pilkington and Philips, which urged an end to national subsidies, intra-European trade barriers, and divided RTD programmes (Pearce and Sutton 1985: 53–4).

There was, however, potential conflict with EC competition policy, which forbids collaboration at the stage of developing products for an immediate market. However, Articles 85 and 86 allow collaboration for 'pre-competitive research'. Davignon's alliance of the EC and heavyweight industrialists, supported by the work of 550 industrial, scientific, and university experts (Sandholtz 1992: 14–15), overcame the doubts of national government officials, and established the European Strategic Programme for Research and Development in Information Technology (ESPRIT). The first outline proposal of September 1980 led a formal proposal, to establish a strategic collaborative IT research programme between the major European companies, together with smaller companies, research institutes, and universities, which was presented in May 1982, and approved by the EC Commission in December, with funding of Ecu 11.5m. (£8.5m.). Contracts under the pilot programme were signed in May, with 38 projects, chosen from over 200 proposals involving 600 companies and institutes, under way by September 1983. The twelve round-table companies won about 70 per cent of the funds. Davignon's gambit of pilot projects with a streamlined application and vetting procedure paid off in overcoming Member State reservations and led to a ten-year Ecu 1.5bn (£1bn) programme for 1984–93.

The first five-year phase, ESPRIT I, 1984–8, was to concentrate on pre-competitive research in microelectronics, advanced information processing, and software technology, as well as applications in computer-integrated manufacturing and office systems. There was an enormous response to the first call for proposals in March 1984, with only about one proposal in four winning acceptance. The 227 projects in Phase I involved about 3000 researchers from 240 companies (of which about 55 per cent were 'small', employing less than 500 workers apiece) and 180 universities and research institutes. Three-quarters of the projects involved firms and academic centres in collaborative work. Of the ten-year budget of Ecu 1.5bn., Ecu 1.3bn. had been committed by January 1987. The EC funded up to half of the project expenditure, and firms from at least two Member States had to participate.

The successful reception of ESPRIT I was heartening to Europeans, and the consequences were positive.

1. It created a useful European IT network of researchers, and allowed companies to economize on scarce technological personnel. They could commit one or two researchers to an ESPRIT project, and have their efforts geared up by the joint participation of other institutions' workers, with both short-and long-term benefits of collaboration and familiarity.

2. Because the research was pre-competitive, collaboration was more open than if it had been near market, when corporate secrecy would have inhibited the partners.

3. Collaboration across national boundaries, required intentionally, meant that the narrow horizons of 'national champions' had to widen.

4. In cases of industrial participation, industry met 50 per cent of the costs, thus enjoying effective subsidy from the EC.

5 Although the Commission identified priorities and broad areas of research, actual research projects were nominated by the applicants. Thus, within the restriction that they could not be too near-market, projects became more demand-driven.

6 Once agreed, each project was timetabled and monitored.

ESPRIT generated a new awareness of Europe's technological strengths, and provided a model for initiatives in other areas of technology. Indeed it helped establish the climate for the 'Framework' programmes, and produced a tribe of acronyms—RACE, BRITE, BRIDGE, BAP, ECLAIR, FLAIR, COMETT, and others.

Another consequence of the success of ESPRIT I was the need to find funds for the remainder of the programme's decade. The Commission brought forward the second phase, ESPRIT II, from 1989 to 1987. The Big 12 Round Table wanted to triple the budget and scope of ESPRIT II, but the proposal fell foul of UK and German government feelings that the EC RTD budget was too high. Compromises were struck over the Framework programme, and in April 1988 ESPRIT II was formally approved for 1988–92 with a budget of Ecu 1.6bn. (£1.07bn.), which was less than originally proposed but more than double the allocation for ESPRIT I. The Commission received about 1000 proposals and agreed to fund about half of them. Three principal areas were emphasized: microelectronics, IT processing systems, and applications technologies. The emphasis on pre-competitive research, however, still left the difficulty of how to capitalize at market level, and ESPRIT II went some way to address this issue by emphasizing 'demand driven aspects of the programme' (Sharp 1993), for example, Application Specific Integrated Circuit Technology, and Technology Integration Projects (TIP), which were intended to meld different elements of separate work and show how they linked together. Funds for ESPRIT II were all earmarked by the end of 1990, and the Commission launched ESPRIT III with Ecu 1.35bn. (£645m.) for 1990–4, to exploit seven areas—microelectronics, advanced business and home systems peripherals, high-performance computing and networking, technology for software intensive systems, computer-integrated manufacturing and engineering, open microprocessor systems, and basic research to 'contribute to the programme's main objectives from an upstream position' (DTI 1993: 9).

A further development in the 1980s deserves attention. This is the European Research Coordination Agency, or EUREKA, initiated by France and founded in 1985 as a European response to President Reagan's announcement of the Strategic Defense Initiative (or 'Star Wars' as it became popularly known) in the USA. It extended beyond the EC Member States to include the seven countries of the European Free Trade Association (EFTA), Turkey, and, latterly, Hungary; but it was managed and coordinated by the EC Commission. It was intended to help industry-led, market-driven projects involving the collaboration of at least two organizations from at least two EUREKA member countries. By March 1993 there were 623 projects involving Ecu 8.8bn. (£6.2bn.). No priority areas were specified but the project had to involve technical innovation, and so was closer to the market and more concerned with commercial applications than ESPRIT was allowed to be. In practice, most current projects fell into the following areas: communications, energy, environment, IT, lasers, medical and biotechnology, new materials, robotics and automated production, and transport. Specific concerns included high-definition television (HDTV), which has also been the subject of much Japanese RTD, the Prometheus initiative for automatic car navigation systems, and JESSI, the Joint European Structure on Silicon Initiative.

EUREKA has no central funding, simply acting as an umbrella mechanism for encouraging inter-firm collaboration: public funding is granted at the discretion of national governments, which usually follows any approval by the EUREKA programme. Thus EUREKA has a large nominal budget but no actual resource: the figures in Table 7.2 reflect a commitment to expenditure by Member States rather than effective expenditure. The partners negotiate the sharing of Intellectual Property Rights (IPRs), for which there are no general rules. EUREKA now operates a regime of continuous and systematic evaluation of its programmes, and Table 7.2 reports briefly some outcomes shown in the latest Annual Impact Report (EUREKA 2000).

EUREKA was conceived as a rival to ESPRIT and other Commission programmes; but, despite occasional overlaps, it has become more complementary, partly because its projects can be more applied than the pre-competitive ESPRIT projects. The two programmes, together with others listed in Table 7.2, raised the profile for research in the EC by the mid-1980s. Perceptions were also concentrated by the EC-wide acknowledgment of the technology gap, and of problems of the environment, and by a growing appreciation, through experience, of the benefits of inter-firm and inter-institutional collaboration. Peterson (1991: 270–1) has argued that 'the interests of public and private actors in promoting new collaborative RTD programmes converged as the Framework

Table 7.2 EUREKA project performance, 1985–2000

Project status	No.
Completed	708
Ongoing	874
Withdrawn	303
TOTAL	1,915
Project outcomes, 2000	**%**
Reporting 'excellent' RTD achievement	88
Reporting new product/process	69
Reporting knowledge acquisition	61
Expecting RTD commercialization	77

Source: EUREKA (2000).

programme and EUREKA were launched in 1985'. The instrument which allowed this fuller development of collaborative research was the Single European Act (SEA).

7.5 **The SEA of 1987**

The 1987 Act contained an additional section, called Title VI—Research and Technological Development, in which it set out in Article 130*f* the following credo:

The Community's aim shall be to strengthen the scientific and technological base of Europe's industry and to encourage it to become more competitive at international level.

In order to achieve this, it shall encourage undertakings including small and medium undertakings, research centres and universities in their research and technological development activities; it shall support their efforts to cooperate with one another, aiming notably at enabling undertakings to exploit the Community's internal market potential to the full, in particular through the opening up of national public contracts, the definition of common standards and the removal of legal and fiscal barriers to that cooperation.

In the achievement of these aims, special account shall be taken of the connection between the common research and technological development effort, the establishment of the internal market and the implementation of common policies, particularly as regards competition and trade.

The next Articles, 130*g* to 130*l*, spelled out the means. Research, technological development and demonstration programmes would promote cooperation between businesses, research centres, and universities. Cooperation would also be promoted with third countries and international organizations, as would the 'dissemination and optimization of results'. Training and mobility would also be stimulated. Member States undertook to coordinate amongst themselves policies and programmes carried out at national level, in liaison with the Commission.

The key provision was the adoption of a multi-annual Framework Programme setting out all the EC's proposed activities over a five-year period: it would lay down scientific and technical objectives, prioritize them, set out the main lines of activity and the amount of funding deemed necessary, including detailed rules for EC participation, and its distribution across the appropriate activities. The Framework would comprise specific programmes of fixed duration within each activity. An implementation mechanism worked at two levels: the Framework as a whole had to secure unanimous agreement among the Member States; and sub-programmes were to be adopted by the Council by qualified majority voting after consultation with the European Parliament (EP) and the Economic and Social Committee. Programmes subsidiary to the Framework were permissible involving certain Member States only, which could finance them subject to possible EC participation; and cooperation with third states and international organizations was also feasible.

This was a dramatic advance upon the 1956 Treaty of Rome, since it legitimized EC technology policy—as it did industry policy elsewhere in the Act. In fact, the Framework system had already been subject to discussions for two years when it was launched in 1987, in the hope of an earlier introduction. The motive of both the Commission and the EP was to break out of the stop–start cycle of *ad hoc* decision-taking and wrangling over the funding of research proposals. The First Framework Programme, now commonly labelled Framework 1, or FP1, was scheduled to run from 1987 to 1991. It was followed by others, with successive increases in funding, as shown in Table 7.3: the proportionate distributions of activity with the Framework programmes are shown in Figure 7.1. In the event, the take-up of funds for programmes was faster than expected; for example, the most important member programme, ESPRIT, over-ran its budget by Ecu 200m. in 1988, in the face of 'the high quality of the proposals, the industrial commitment underlying them and the urgency of the work proposed' (Peterson 1991: 282–3). A Second Framework Programme had been introduced to run across 1987–91, and by December 1989 the Research Council in Brussels agreed with Research Commissioner Pandolfi to establish a third-generation Framework programme: its funds were topped up in December 1992 from Ecu 5.7bn. to Ecu 6.6bn.

The total extent of the European programmes for new technology has been wide, and Table 7.4 lists some of the best known. Programmes often continued through successive

Table 7.3. Framework programmes of European activities in research and technological development, 1987–2002

Framework Programme	Period	Budget (Ecu m.)
FP 1	1984–8	3,750
FP 2	1987–91	5,396
FP 3	1990–4	6,600
FP 4	1994–8	13,215
FP 5	1998–2002	14,960

Source: CEC, various.

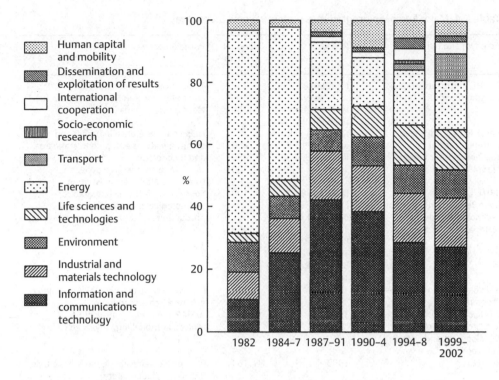

Fig. 7.1 Research and technical development priorities in Framework Programmes 1–5, 1982–2002

Source: CEC (1994) and author's estimates for FP5.
Note: In 1999–2002, Dissemination and Exploitation of Results is subsumed within the other categories.

generations of Framework—as in the cases of ESPRIT, COMETT, and SPRINT—though the emerging primacy of the Framework Programme has tended to mask the acronyms.

7.6 Evaluations of policy effectiveness

EU-sponsored research is important in both quantity and quality: some system of accountability is obviously necessary. Technically the Commission is accountable to the Council, which is made up of national ministers, and to the EP, which scrutinizes legislation and the drafting and execution of budgets. However, science and technology require expert examination of their effectiveness, as to both their scientific and their economic worth, to judge whether the work is worth doing in the first place and whether, once authorized, it has been well accomplished.

Thoroughgoing evaluation is exceedingly difficult (Georghiou and Roessner 2000). A range of issues arise, which can be characterized as follows:

• Ambit: how widely do benefits from support occur, through spillovers, research linkages, etc.?

Table 7.4 Major European programmes promoting new technology

Acronym and full name	Period	Budget[a] (Ecu m.)	Prime objectives
ESPRIT: European Strategic Programme for RTD in IT	I 1984–8 II 1988–92 III 1992–4 IV 1994–98	750 1600 1350	To promote EC capabilities and competitiveness in IT, especially micro-electronics systems
RACE: RTD in Advanced Communications Technologies for Europe	Definition 1985–7 RACE I 1990–4 RACE II 1992–4	21 460 489	Help EC competence in broadband communications equipment, standards, and technology
TELEMATICS	1990–4	380	Develop telematics in e.g. health, transport, public administration
BRITE/EURAM: Basic Research in Industrial Technologies/Advanced Materials for Europe	BRITE I 1985–8 EURAM I 1986–8 BRITE/EURAM I 1989–92 BRITE/EURAM II 1992–6 BRITE/EURAM III 1996–	100 450 663 1487	Support for RTD which upgrades technological or materials base of production
BAP: Biotechnology Action Programme	1985–9	75	Develop infrastructure in biotechnology, esp. research and training
BRIDGE: Biotechnological Research for Innovation, Development and Growth in Europe	1990–3	100	As BAP, but for large projects, e.g. molecular modelling, advanced cell culture
BIOTECH	1992–6	164	Pre-normative research, more basic than BRIDGE, includes safety
ECLAIR: European Collaborative Linkage of Agriculture and Industry through Research	1989–94	80	Applying advanced biotechnology in agro-industrial sector, esp. using raw materials from agriculture
FLAIR: Food Linked Agro-Industrial Research	1989–94	25	As ECLAIR, but food-oriented, in manufacture and processing
COMETT: Community Action	COMETT I 1987–9	30	Training programmes between university and industry, via enterprise partnerships and international staff exchange
Programme for Education and Training for Technology	COMETT II 1990–4	200 +30	
VALUE	VALUE I VALUE II 1992–4	66	Disseminate and exploit research results of Community programmes
SPRINT: Strategic Programme for Innovation and Technology Transfer	SPRINT I experiment SPRINT II 1986–9 SPRINT III 1989–94	9 90	Promote innovation and technology transfer, esp. among small and medium enterprises internationally. Merged with VALUE 1994
EURET	1990–3	27	Rail, sea, air transport research
STRIDE: Science and Technology for Regional Innovation and Development in Europe	1990–3	400	DG XVI programme to promote RTD in assisted regions
MONITOR	1989–3	22	Identify RTD policy priorities

a   The figures shown as budgeted do not include industrial contributions to ESPRIT and other shared cost programmes: in those cases actual expenditure involved in the programmes will approximate twice the budget figure shown above.

Sources: CEC (various publications).

- Horizon: how far into the future should benefits be counted? Can evaluation capture all the long-run effects and ramifications?

- Additionality: can it be demonstrated that support given to RTD raises the total spend, or does some of it merely allow recipients to substitute it for monies that they would have found themselves?

- Counterfactuality: relatedly, what would have eventuated in the absence of official policy? Does the support positively cause change, or simply accelerate it somewhat?

Hall and Van Reenen (2000) surveyed authoritatively the difficulties and findings of studies which attempted to quantify the impact of fiscal incentives for RTD. Results varied widely, but they were able to conclude that 'a tax price elasticity around unity is a good ballpark figure', that is, a reduction in the cost of research invokes an equi-proportionate increase in the amount of RTD conducted. Response to tax credits for RTD tends to be fairly small at first but increases over time. However, the intrinsic problems of cost–benefit approaches are exacerbated in the case of EU support by the complexity of cross-national involvements, so that qualitative review is favoured as more likely to capture major long-term benefits. Luukkonen (2000) suggests that Framework programmes were important as sources of finance for SMEs, but less so for large companies, for which new exchanges and informal contacts were more important. However, an ideal system of evaluation was a distant hope. The urgent need was to get something started as a discipline.

One early possibility was to employ FAST (Forecasting and Assessment in Science and Technology) in evaluations. But there seemed little enthusiasm at the top of the Commission to involve FAST: its resources were small for such a vast job, and independent outside judgement was deemed desirable (Holdsworth and Lake 1988: 424).

When the Third Framework Programme was adopted, the Council required the Commission to undertake an evaluation of all programmes which operated under the second programme, formally to provide 'an overall appreciation of the current state of execution and achievements of the specific programmes adopted under the second Framework . . . and to set out the principal lessons that have been learned from the execution of these programmes'. The main source of information was the reports of the independent evaluation panels commissioned to examine the operations of specific programmes. In addition there were reports from consultants commissioned to examine particular questions, internal Commission reviews drawing on the reports of panels or outside experts, reviews and reports of programme committees, plus findings from specially commissioned studies of the horizontal aspects of the effects of Community RTD programmes. An example of commissioned work was a study of the impact of EC policies for RTD on science and technology in the UK, which was prepared for the UK Office of Science and Technology and the Commission (HMSO 1993*a*).

The findings of these studies were generally positive: they chronicled good work and effective international and inter-institutional collaboration. A report from CREST was submitted to the Council in September 1992, giving an evaluation of the Second Framework Programme (CREST 1992). It addressed three major issues—the quality of programme results and their impact on competitiveness; management and cost-effectiveness of research; and consistency with EC policy and principles. It noted a substantial amount of state-of-the-art research, with a fair balance between incremental and more ambitious research, but intellectual property rights problems were an inhibition on dissemination and exploitation, for which there was, implicitly, more scope. While there were cases of RTD conferring significant technological advantage over international rivals, the most significant impact was felt to be in promoting the idea of collaboration across industry, academia, and the nations of the EC. There remained much scope for developing the harmonization of standards across the EC. Though there was general satisfaction over programme management, sometimes project assessment needed more attention, as did the lags between calling for proposals and beginning the research. Programme objectives could be more clearly defined and there was scope for closer and more transparent links with other DGs responsible for policy in areas such as transport, environment, energy, health, and agriculture. According to Pownall (1995), ESPRIT I raised 'European aware-ness' but brought less evidence of tangible and marketable results because of the pre-competitive nature of the work, but business and market factors were better considered in ESPRIT II.

With nearly 18,000 collaborative links in Framework 2, the UK was its most active participant. In fact, the UK fared well in the early Framework provisions, according to calculations by the Cabinet Office, reported in earlier editions of this book. UK views on Framework 2 were analysed by questionnaire and interviews among participants in aca-demia and industry (Georghiou *et al*. 1993). Academics were more positive, but two-thirds of industrial firms involved considered the benefits outweighed the costs, against 21 per cent who did not; and over three-quarters intended to reapply for future participa-tion. It was estimated that about half of EC RTD spending in the UK was 'additional'— that is, adding to the total of publicly financed RTD, and not just funding what would have been undertaken without EC monies. Moreover, EC programmes had a bigger impact than the 6 per cent of publicly funded RTD that they constituted, because they were approved by senior staff, they concentrated on recently established priorities, eased research-funding scarcities, and were geared up by EC participation. However, UK indus-trial participation in Framework 3 was disappointing in comparison with German and French industry. There were also complaints that project approval rates were low in the third programme and that there was not enough continuity, which is vital to long-term research work (*Research Fortnight*, 30 Nov. 1994, p. 12).

An independent panel of experts also found in favour of EUREKA's benefits (*Outlook on Science Policy*, 1993: 73–4). Most partnerships were vertical, between firms, customers, and suppliers, rather than horizontal. Collaboration worked best between partners of similar size, with smaller firms more product-oriented than large ones, which focused on longer-term research projects. Over 40 per cent of participants were found to expect substantial sales increases within three years, reflecting the near-market emphasis of EUREKA compared to Framework.

In the discussions leading to the Fourth Framework Programme, numerous lessons were drawn from earlier experience. The UK government submitted a policy paper in February 1992 (Cabinet Office 1992) drawing together the views of the UK science and technology community. It stressed the need for evaluation of Framework 2, for planning of annual commitments, for emphasis on generic technologies and dissemination of technology from research projects, as well as the need for consultation between DGs.

Some of these views were accepted in CREST (1992), but the Fourth Framework proposal was controversially received (Hill 1993: 16).

The programme proposed Ecu 13.1bn. of expenditure, but its adoption required a unanimous decision from the twelve Member States. However, the three biggest contributors to the EU—Germany, the UK, and France—sought against the wishes of the other nine to reduce the Framework budget by at least Ecu 1bn. One of the difficulties has been that the pay-off to Framework RTD is singularly problematic to assess in financial terms. Since it is not near-market research, it will take time to see clear financial benefit, and the advantages so far ascribed to it by expert analysts are inevitably qualitative rather than measurable in money terms. A cynic might observe that of course firms will welcome, and laud, Framework programmes if they bring handsome subsidies with them. The EU still seems to be lagging behind its US and Japanese technological competitors in many industries, but this can hardly be laid at the door of the EU programmes, which account for only a very small part of total RTD effort across the companies and countries of the EU. While Framework 4 remained directed, like its predecessors, at pre-competitive research, it was designed to complement national research efforts, and projects are expected to offer practical longer-term advances.

In 1995 the Research Commissioner, Mme Edith Cresson, proposed several taskforces to operate under Framework 4, focusing on the car of the future; educational multimedia; next-generation civil aircraft; the train of the future; vaccines for viral illnesses; clean technology; and socially useful applications of IT. Each taskforce was to consult with industry to set research priorities, to foster coordination, and to help garner resources. However, the distribution of effort in Framework 5 did not adhere absolutely to those priorities.

Framework 5 is now well advanced, and its priorities are shown in Table 7.5. There is greater emphasis on problem solving in areas of high social concern, with 'key actions' complementing generic research activities. Previous specific Programmes were rationalized into four thematic and three horizontal programmes, intended to help budgetary flexibility. These changes complicated the switch from Framework 4.

Several countries were concerned about its funding. Cost overruns on Framework 4 added to misgivings. Germany was keen to restrain public expenditure to meet the financial criteria set out in the TEU, and sought concentration on a small number of strategic industries, gaining flexible funding to make programmes more adaptable in the face of emerging needs, and seeking Article 169 'variable geometry' which would allow Member States to opt in or out of individual programmes. Pressure on research funds intensified in most countries: the UK capped its contribution to ESA in 1995, and EU-funded research by UK companies was balanced by a cutback of national government funds, acting as a considerable disincentive to the effort required to bid for them. The growth rate in funding, so pronounced between Frameworks 3 and 4, now slowed markedly.

The Framework programmes across 1994–9 were evaluated by an independent expert panel which reported in July 2000 (CEC 2000*a*). It drew on over 2000 questionnaire responses from participants in Frameworks 3 and 4, numerous reports from Monitoring and Assessment Panels, and interviews with key figures in the Commission and selected Member States. It assessed past activities positively, praising collaboration, networking, training-related activities, and the increased involvement of SMEs, and recommended

Table 7.5 Fifth Framework Programme, 1998–2002

Programme area	Budget (Ecu m.)	% RTD
Quality of life & resource management	2,413	16.1
User-friendly information society	3,600	24.1
Competitive & sustainable growth	2,705	18.1
Environment & sustainable development	1,083	7.2
Energy	1,042	7.0
Nuclear energy	979	6.5
Confirming research community role	475	3.2
Promotion of innovation & SMEs	363	2.4
Improving human research potential	1,280	8.6
Joint Research Centre	1,020	6.8
TOTAL	14,960	100.0

Note: Horizontal programmes are shown in italic.
Source: CEC website, 2001.

continued emphasis on social relevance, collective RTD projects, and emphasis on excellence and mobility of researchers. It recommended numerous changes to cope with future needs, several of which went beyond their remit but were considered to be vital . These included:

- Simpler, more understandable application procedures;

- Encouragement to propose riskier projects;

- A restructured and expanded Framework Programme, but no need for Programme Committees;

- A major review of systems and procedures to determine goals, specify delivery mechanisms, and implement programmes;

- Modification of existing management and admininstration structures and procedures to delegate tasks downwards in the Commission, or externalize them, to avoid needless bureaucracy.

The most important conclusion went beyond Framework, and was accompanied by others:

- Framework alone would not satisfy EU policy goals and a European RTD strategy was needed at the highest political levels;

- Science and technology budgets should rise to at least 3 per cent of GDP over the next ten years;

- Private sector RTD should be stimulated by indirect measures such as tax incentives;

- Urgent action is required to counter foreseeable skill shortages over the next decade;

- Centres of research and teaching excellence should be supported, though RTD support for expectant Central and Eastern European entrants to the EU would have to be channelled through existing Academies until new competitive science and industry structures emerged;

• RTD policies among the Member States need to reinforce rather than duplicate each other.

These proposals raise a host of issues, some of which we address at the end of the chapter. It will be interesting to see how they assess Framework 5, which has met widespread criticism that its attempt to combine thematic elements with horizontal factors spanning innovation, technology, training, and international cooperation has proved too complex to manage effectively.

7.7 Technology, industrial, and trade policies: tensions and contradictions

Industrial policy is traditionally concerned with matters such as influencing industrial and market structure and competitiveness, and encouraging the modernization of capital stock. It shares an uncertain border with technology and trade policies. For example, the structure of output cannot be decided independently of trade policies. If a country wishes to develop a new industrial sector in which other countries already have capabilities and experience, it may have to invoke the infant-industry argument and offer its industry a period of protection from unrestricted foreign competition. Subsidies to indigenous RTD may also be considered necessary. Technology, industrial, and trade policies clearly overlap here; perhaps the simplest theoretical discriminator is that industry policy emphasizes physical capital, whereas technology policy emphasizes the creation and utilization of knowledge.

However, it is a practical and not just a theoretical dilemma. Technology policy seeks to create productive capability, which often requires public sponsorship of RTD. Such support is only compatible with competition (which is a common goal of industrial policy) if the RTD is pre-competitive; but the boundary between pre-competitive and near-market RTD is fuzzy, at best. The tension between protectionism and enhancing capability is exemplified by European attitudes towards microelectronics and IT. European firms have persistently failed to compete satisfactorily in these sectors in spite of varied forms of protectionism, which are detailed in Chapter 11. How long, and by how much, is it necessary to support the development of European potential, before an infant industry can be weaned? Yet is it possible for the EU to achieve adequate economic performance and prospects for the future if these strategic industries are allowed to wither?

The tension between a protectionist Fortress Europa and an open, competitive EU of the sort which Porter (1990) would consider a prerequisite for efficiency, is reinforced by the institutional division of labour which assigns industrial, technology, and trade policies to different DGs. Each DG has its own routines, traditions, and power structure. Programmes, once initiated, are difficult to terminate and attitudes harden. Thus the rigidities and contradictions can persist if they are inherent in the priorities of different interest groups. It takes time and continuous effort to reconcile these conflicting forces and establish an acceptable balance of competition, protection, and capability enhancement. Further, one of the goals of EU policy is to enhance the science and technology capacities of Member States presently less capable in these areas. Resource is transferred via taxation from the advanced, efficient Member States to the disadvantaged. This may be acceptable in times of general prosperity and growth, but can create tensions if the advanced states face competitive pressures from non-Member States. As the EU accepts new members, and others join the queue for entry, additional pressures arise. The secretariat is presently unwilling to reveal how support under the Framework Programmes is distributed among Member States. Admittedly it is not an easy calculation because of all the split receipts among the international projects, but it is feasible; the bureaucratic coyness arises from fears that different countries are likely to object if their contributions run far ahead of their incomes. The principle of *juste retour* which seeks a balance between the two, as applied in ESA, is not applied to the Framework Programmes—hence the sensitivity.

Globalization and corporate alliances

As we have seen, EU technology policy has concentrated on sponsoring different forms of collaboration between European countries. Such forms of collaboration are not generally those which participants would choose spontaneously, otherwise the EU initiatives would have been redundant, having been implemented already by the market. In this context one should note the rise since the late 1970s of inter-institutional collaborative agreements or IICAs (Chesnais 1991; Mytelka 1991). They can be of very different scope, varying from licensing agreements, joint RTD, joint development of new products, and joint ventures in marketing and distribution, with or without joint equity. The Airbus consortium is just one of many possible manifestations.

The growth of IICAs poses a considerable theoretical and practical problem. From a theoretical standpoint, firms are not expected to collaborate. As they grow in size, we might expect them to integrate vertically and develop internal hierarchical organizational forms. Given the realities of market imperfection, firms tend to internalize functions (Coase 1937; Williamson 1975, 1985). Industrial RTD in particular is a function often internalized, because of the difficulties of establishing satisfactory markets in technology, given the complexities of valuation and the need for secrecy to ensure appropriability of returns to technological effort. The development of internalized RTD has been one of the most striking insitutional changes of the last century (Schumpeter 1943; Freeman 1982). In this context, inter-institutional collaboration might be considered the exception rather than the rule.

Why then do IICAs happen and why have they proliferated? Several authors have suggested contributory factors. One is the growing importance of knowledge in production, revealed by the growth of RTD in GDP and as a proportion of corporate turnover in many industries, and by the growing percentage of non-material investment (Mytelka 1991). Most IICAs are in relatively high-technology industries, such as IT, biotechnology, aerospace, or new materials. Other possible contributing factors were the productivity slowdown of the late 1960s and 1970s, and the observed shortening of product lifecycles, which implies more frequent innovation with its attendant costs and uncertainties. The decline of traditional mass production ('Fordism') and the rise of flexible manufacturing systems also place a premium on technological capability. Collaborative agreements can reduce the heavy fixed costs of entry, as well as facilitating exit by providing a partner to whom an interest might be sold. Another possible motive is a search for monopoly power. IICAs effectively reduce rivalry, and so represent a clandestine increase in concentration. If they enable players to raise their RTD game, they also raise barriers to entry. These have implications for economic welfare, but on the positive side the improved diffusion of knowledge which IICAs entail is valuable and effective. So long as technology continues to grow in complexity and expense, as seems certain, IICAs will figure prominently in the corporate landscape.

Collaborative agreements impinge upon technology policies. It might seem that they are in tune with the collaborative tenor of current EU technology policy; but IICAs are driven in opportunistic directions, not those favoured by state or community governments. Possibly the EU programmes may facilitate intra-EU IICAs; but collaboration outside the EU makes it more difficult to evaluate the pay-off to EU technology policy, and Sachwald (1993) has shown that major European firms tend to adopt a global rather than a Eurocentric view of their markets. In this context, it can make more sense for a European firm aspiring to a global presence to seek global, rather than European, partnerships. The 1990s witnessed a strong increase in foreign direct investment, prompting much talk of globalization. Europeans invested in foreign subsidiaries, and foreigners invested in European subsidiaries, as each sought to maximize the returns to their know-how. Provided that Europe maintains a strong science and technology infrastructure, and a dynamic economy, globalization can enhance her science and technology and her economic performance: it is much less a threat than an opportunity which, as Archibugi and Iammarino (1999: 265) put it, 'can allow a country to become an information crossroads, and thus acquire expertise in a wide range of technologies'. There is scant point in re-inventing other people's ideas; it is better to understand, adapt, and progress them.

National systems of innovation and EU technology policy

The concept of national systems of innovation (NSI) has gained much attention among leading scholars of technology (Freeman 1987, 1988; Lundvall 1988, 1993; Nelson 1988, 1990, 1993), who seek to interpret the persistence of areas of industrial and technological strength in national economies, and of very specific institutional configurations for very long periods of time. Such areas of industrial strength are chemicals, luxury cars, and machine tools in Germany; cars and consumer electronics in Japan; electronics, aircraft, and biotechnology in the USA. Furthermore, the institutions which control the generation and adoption of innovations in each country show a high degree of national specificity. Thus, not only do the degree of centralization and of state intervention, and the organization of universities and research institutes (to mention just a few factors), differ widely across countries, but these differences persist over time. Finally, what contributes still more to the specifically national character of the innovation system is the pattern of interactions between different institutions. There are powerful networks formed by research laboratories, government departments, and firms, which are extremely important and, again, very specific.

Pronounced differences exist at the level of national institutions; Lundvall (1988, 1993) laid particular emphasis on user–producer relations. These create institutional networks which communicate and interact, and define a system which may be highly country- or even region-specific, as Porter (1990) has noted widely. The role of MITI has been profoundly influential in defining industrial and technological priorities and coordinating firms' actions, stressing the role of forecasting and horizontal flows in organizations as significant elements of the Japanese national system of innovation (Freeman 1987, 1988). In particular, information flows in enterprises improve the relationship between RTD and production, in which the Japanese system has been singularly successful.

However, the observations of Sharp and Holmes (1989: 220–1) remain apposite:

The degree to which a nation state seeks to carve out for itself an area of 'industrial space' which it can dominate is now minimal. The growing interdependence of the economic and industrial systems of the nations of Western Europe means that actions pursued in one country spill over rapidly into others . . . the degree of autonomy available to the individual nation state for the pursuit of industrial objectives is severely constrained. . . . It is technology as much as political dogma that has put paid to the era of national champions.

In this context, EU-sponsored forms of inter-institutional collaboration across national boundaries establish valuable new networks, with links across the entire Union. This prospect prompts several questions. Will the networks be stable? How will they benefit the EU and Member States? Will there be conflicts between the EU and national systems of innovation? And there is the question of opportunity costs: will benefits be equitably distributed and will resources allocated to the EU system of innovation impair the performance of NSIs? In essence, this poses the question of subsidiarity on a technological plane.

Technology and public opinion

Among policy-makers, it is accepted that the development and application of technology are key elements of economic performance in advanced countries. The readiness of the general public to accept and embrace new technology can be influential, positively or negatively. The national enthusiasm to catch up with the West is held to have created a receptive attitude to technological change among the Japanese public (Williams and Mills 1986: 429–30), whereas the Chernobyl nuclear power plant disaster of 1986 strengthened the hands of the opponents of nuclear power in Germany and Sweden to the point where the state decided to phase out nuclear power generation altogether. Fear of untrammelled science is not new, as Mary Shelley's *Frankenstein* in 1818 clearly demonstrates, or as, more chillingly, does Robert Oppenheimer's quotation of Vishnu after witnessing the first atomic bomb test, 'I am become death, the destroyer of worlds'. Recently there have been many alarms involving technology, directly or indirectly, giving rise to legitimate public concern. Three Mile Island, Chernobyl, the Gulf War backwash, salmonella, genetically modified food, mad-cow disease, the foot-and-mouth epidemic in Britain, are incendiary fuel to the worries of the fearful, while para-scientific cults seem, to the scientifically literate, to gain adherents with undeserved ease. There is a danger that the limits of science at its frontiers, which all must acknowledge, may be used to raise unwarranted opposition to science and technology at their proven core. Such fears have been voiced by the British House of Lords, and within the EU itself, such that a major task of any technology policy is to dispel the wilder and more hysterical claims that may be made against science and technology.

Obviously there is a need for objective information about scientific and technological developments. Government officials need to ascertain which public fears are most widely and/or keenly held, how to address them, and what guidance might be offered to politicians. A recent national survey in Britain was commissioned jointly by the Wellcome Trust and the Office of Science and Technology, which is a constituent of the Department of Trade and Industry. The findings, which were reported in the latest UK science White Paper (DTI 2000*a*: 48–97) are too extensive to report fully here. On the whole there was public support for science and technology, but some misgivings were evident, as the following data reveal: they represent proportions of respondents who agreed or agreed strongly with propositions on a questionnaire, and exclude those who disagreed, disagreed strongly, or who felt neither way.

- 42 per cent felt science changes too fast;
- 36 per cent felt science was out of control;
- 41 per cent felt science was out of control of the government;
- 64 per cent felt the media sensationalized science;
- 70 per cent felt that scientists would do what they wanted behind closed doors, notwithstanding attempts to regulate them;
- 79 per cent felt that science and technology were important for competitiveness;
- 84 per cent expressed an interest in new medicines.

Interestingly, the leading interest in medicine and health mirrored the results of a French survey conducted about a year earlier, as did a strong interest in pollution and the environment.

National concerns may differ in degree, but there is an evident similarity overall in what concerns people. If a central tenet of EU science and technology policy is to do in common what it would be more expensive to do separately, then seeking and disseminating this sort of information is a natural function for it. The Joint Research Centre, which states as its main aim 'to help to create a safer, cleaner, healthier and more competitive Europe' (JRC website 2001), does relevant work. What is really needed, however, is bodies which can produce information which is independent, authoritative, transparent, and understandable. The European Food and Public Health Authority proposed in 1999 could be a prototype for inter-institutional bodies currently favoured to meet the public need.

7.8 **Summary and conclusions**

EU science and technology policy has now been in operation for a decade and a half. It sought to create new inter-institutional links and forms of collaboration, and to establish capabilities in specific industrial sectors. It was bound to be problematic, because the spontaneous development of the market would be unlikely to replicate those links. Yet it can be, and is, argued that the EU level of aggregation is the only possible locus at which adequate technological capacity can be established in certain industries or sectors, and that collaborative benefits and spillovers will occur which the market would ignore, to the cost of society at large.

The principle of subsidiarity still leaves the vast bulk of national RTD outside the authority of the EU, since the dominant Framework programme is only about 5 per cent of the total RTD expenditure of the Member States, and even with ESA, EUREKA, Cost, etc., about 13 per cent of the spend is supra-national. But it is surely significant that there is no pressure to abandon the Framework system, and revert to a combination of market-place and nation-state. The system is seen to have brought wide and approved benefits, albeit with an embarrassing abundance of bureaucratic irritations and shortcomings. To that extent it is a perceived but quite qualified success.

Morever there is widespread dissatisfaction that the EU still trails behind the USA and Japan in technological league-tables and that the gap has widened. In percentage of GDP spent on RTD, in patenting, and in the top ten technological corporations, Europe shows up poorly by comparison. Its research efforts are also more fragmented. Hence the search for improvement, which drove the establishment of a European policy twenty years ago, continues even more critically as Framework 6 approaches.

The Commission has called for a European Research Area, with a number of priorities (CEC 2000*b*). Broadly, it stresses the need for networking, centres of excellence, and targeted large-scale projects. Further strengthening of SME technology is called for, as well as increased end-user involvement to exploit RTD results more effectively, improvements to research infrastructure including electronic networking, and more open access to national programmes. Human resource development is prioritized, including cross-border mobility for researchers, the recruitment of more women into science, and the attraction of more foreign scientists into the EU. Science should attend dialogue with citizens, in the face of public scepticism, RTD should relate to broad EU goals, and programme and project management should be efficient and transparent, being subjected to systematic appraisal, monitoring, and evaluation, but with easier, decentralized procedures for SMEs. The British Office of Science and Technology generally welcomed the proposals (DTI 2000*b*), but with one or two hard-nosed observations. They noted that selection should concentrate on areas too large-scale for national programmes, and suggested that programmes of Euros 1–2 bn. could make a substantial difference to Europe's competitive position in areas such as biosciences, informatics, aeronautics, nano-technology, quantum computing, agile and intelligent manufacturing technology, and environmental goods and services including renewable energy. They should complement national programmes, and have inputs from 'customer' Directorates-General on

SCIENCE AND TECHNOLOGY POLICY

programme definition concerning issues such as environment, transport, food safety, and Common Agricultural Policy reform. Networked interdisciplinary centres of excellence were welcome, but 'substantial management and logistic competence' would be needed if tens of millions of Euros would be applied for long periods to some programmes.

Certainly, policy and its execution require a continuous scrutiny, both because the interaction of profit-seeking companies will always generate new forms of organization and collaboration, transcending the boundaries of nations and of blocs, and because the growth of EU-directed science and technology activity looks certain to increase in scale and complexity. Whether it can spearhead an acceleration of European RTD effort, however, remains an open if fascinating question.

Discussion questions

1 What sorts of activities in science and technology do you think national governments should support, and why? Illustrate, using specific examples.

2 Why have industrial policies for supporting 'national champions' proved disappointing in Europe? What lessons for technology policy can be drawn from such experiences?

3 Why has EU RTD effort lagged behind that of the United States and Japan?

Further reading

Arrow (1962) is the classic reference justifying the role of government in supporting science and technology. Freeman and Soete (1997) provide a valuable introduction to innovation in the real world, while Dosi et al. (1988) put innovation in a theoretical framework. Porter (1990) is an intriguing, if long, analysis of the basis of national competitiveness, and Nelson (1993) examines the importance of national characteristics and policies which underlie performance. Stoneman (1995) collects a number of authoritative contributors to recent debates in the area on technology, while Dodgson and Rothwell (1994) do the same with a more industrial focus. For recent developments and statistics in many official areas, there are very useful websites.

Department of Trade and Industry, Science and Technology site: http://www.dti.gov.uk/scienceind/index.htm

OECD Science, Technology and Industry site: http://www.oecd.org/dsti/sti

Community R&D Information Service: http://www.cordis.lu

Eurostat (CEC statistics source) http://europa.eu.int/comm/eurostat

UK National Statistics http://www.statistics.gov.uk

References

Archibugi, D. and Iammarino, S. (1999), 'The Policy Implications of the Globalisation of Innovation', in D. Archibugi, J. Howells, and J. Michie (eds.), *Innovation Policy in a Global Economy* (Cambridge: Cambridge University Press), 242–71.

Arrow, K. J. (1962), 'Economic Welfare and the Allocation of Resources to Invention', in National Bureau of Economic Research (ed.), *The Rate and Direction of Inventive Activity* (Princeton, NJ: Princeton University Press), 609–25.

Barry, A. (1990), 'Community and Diversity in European Technology', paper presented at the Science Museum.

Beise, M. and Stahl, H. (1999), 'Public Research and Industrial Innovations in Germany', *Research Policy*, 28: 397–422.

Cabinet Office (1992), *United Kingdom Paper on the Fourth Framework Programme* (London: Office of Science and Technology).

CEC (1977), Commission of the European Communities, 'Common Policy for Science and Technology', *Bulletin of the European Communities*, supplement (Mar.).

—— (1993), Working Document on the Fourth Framework Programme, 22 Apr. (Brussels: CEC).

—— (1994), *The European Report on Science and Technology Indicators 1994* (Brussels: CEC).

—— (2000a), *Five-year Assessment of the European Union Research and Technological Development Programmes, 1995–99* (Brussels: CEC).

—— (2000b), *Making a Reality of the European Research Area: Guidelines for EU Research Activities (2002–2006)*, COM (2000) 612 (Brussels: CEC); see also http://www.europa.eu.int/comm/research/area/com2000-612-en.pdf/

Chesnais, F. (1991), 'Technical Cooperation Agreements between Independent Firms: Novel Issues for Economic Analysis and the Formulation of National Technological Policies', *STI Review*, 4: 51–120.

—— (1993), 'The French National System of Innovation', in R. R. Nelson (ed.), *National Innovation Systems: A Comparative Analysis* (Oxford: Oxford University Press), 192–229.

Coase, R. H. (1937), 'The Nature of the Firm', *Economica*, 4: 386–405.

Dodgson, M. and Rothwell, R. (eds.) (1994), *The Handbook of Industrial Innovation* (Aldershot: Elgar).

Dosi, G., Freeman, C., Nelson, R., Silverberg, G., and Soete, L. (eds.) (1988), *Technical Change and Economic Theory* (London: Pinter).

DTI (1993), Department of Trade and Industry, *Innovation: A Guide to European Community RTD Programmes* (London: DTI).

—— (1996), Office of Science and Technology, *Forward Look of Government-Financed Science, Engineering and Technology*, Cm 3257 (London: HMSO).

—— (2000a) *Excellence and Opportunity: A Science and Innovation Policy for the 21st Century*, Cm 4814 (London: HMSO).

—— (2000b), *Making a Reality of the European Research Area: Guidelines for EU Research Activities (2002–2006)—UK response* (London: DTI).

EUREKA (2000), EUREKA Secretariat, *Fifth Annual Impact Report* (Brussels: EUREKA).

Eurostat (2001), *Statistics in Focus—Science and Technology: Community Innovation Survey* (Eurostat website).

Ford, G. and Lake, G. (1991), 'Evolution of European Science and Technology Policy', *Science and Public Policy*, 18: 38–50.

Freeman, C. (1987), *Technology Policy and Economic Performance: Lessons from Japan* (London: Pinter).

—— (1988), 'Japan: A New National System of Innovation?' in G. Dosi, C. Freeman, R. Nelson, G. Silverberg, and L. Soete, (eds.), *Technical Change and Economic Theory* (London: Pinter), 330–48.

—— and Soete, L. (1997), *The Economics of Industrial Innovation*, 3rd edn. (London: Pinter).

Georghiou, L., Cameron, H., Stein, J. A., Nedeva, M., Janes, M., Yates, J., Pifer, M., Boden, M., and Senker, J. (1993), Cabinet Office, *The Impact of European Community Policies for Research and Technological Development upon Science and Technology in the United Kingdom* (London: HMSO).

Georghiou, L. and Roessner, D. (2000), 'Evaluating Technology Programs: Tools and Methods', *Research Policy*, 29: 657–78.

Hall, B. and Van Reenen, J. (2000), 'How Effective are Fiscal Incentives for RTD? A Review of the Evidence', *Research Policy*, 29: 449–69.

Hill, A. (1993) 'RTD in a Tussle over EC Funding', *Financial Times*, 26 Oct., p. 16.

Holdsworth, D. and Lake, G. (1988), 'Integrating Europe: The New RTD Calculus', *Science and Public Policy*, 15: 411–25.

Kealey, T. (1996), *The Economic Laws of Scientific Research* (London: Macmillan).

Keck, O. (1993), 'The National System for Technical Innovation in Germany', in R. R. Nelson (ed.), *National Innovation Systems: A Comparative Analysis* (Oxford: Oxford University Press), 115–57.

Lawson, N. (1992), *The View from Number Eleven* (London: Bantam).

Linkohr, E. (1987), European Parliament document A-2 174/87, p. 18 (Brussels: CEC).

Lipsey, R. G., and Carlaw, K. (1999), *Taking Schumpeter Seriously on Structuralist Assessment of Technology Policy* (Working Paper, Industry Canada, Ottawa).

Luukkonen, T. (2000), 'Additionality of EU Framework Programmes', *Research Policy*, 29: 711–24.

Lundvall, B.-Å. (1988), 'Innovation as an Interactive Process: From User-Producer Interaction to the National System of Innovation', in G. Dosi, C. Freeman, R. Nelson, G. Silverberg, and L. Soete (eds.), *Technical Change and Economic Theory* (London: Pinter).

—— (ed.) (1993), *National Systems of Innovation: Towards a Theory of Innovation and Interactive Learning* (London: Pinter).

Majoie, B. and Remy, B. (1999), *Recherche et Innovation: la France dans la Competition Mondiale* (Paris: Documentation Française).

Mansfield, E., Rapoport, J., Romeo, A., Wagner, S., and Beardsley, G. (1976), 'Social and Private Rates of Return From Industrial Innovations', *Quarterly Journal of Economics*, 91: 221–40.

Mueller, D. C. (1989), *Public Choice II* (Cambridge: Cambridge University Press).

Mytelka, L. K. (ed.) (1991), *Strategic Partnerships and the World Economy* (London: Pinter).

Nelson, R. R. (1988), 'Institutions Supporting Technical Change in the US', in G. Dosi, C. Freeman, R. Nelson, G. Silverberg, and L. Soete (eds.), *Technical Change and Economic Theory* (London: Pinter).

—— (1990), 'Capitalism as an Engine of Progress', *Research Policy*, 19: 193–214.

—— (ed.) (1993), *National Innovation Systems: A Comparative Analysis* (Oxford: Oxford University Press).

Niskanen, W. (1975) 'Bureaucrats and Politicians', *Journal of Law and Economics*, 18: 617–43.

OECD (1993), Organization for Economic Cooperation and Development, *The Measurement of Scientific and Technological Activities* (Frascati Manual) (Paris: OECD).

—— (1999a), *Economic Surveys: France* (Paris: OECD).

—— (1999b), *Public Understanding of Science and Technology* (Paris: OECD).

—— (2000), *Main Science and Technology Indicators* (Paris: OECD).

Outlook on Science Policy (1993), 15 (July–Aug.).

Pavitt, K. and Patel, P. (1988), 'The International Distribution and Determinants of Technological Activities', *Oxford Review of Economic Policy*, 4: 35–55.

Pearce, J. and Sutton, J. (1985), *Protection and Industrial Policy in Europe* (London: Routledge & Kegan Paul).

Peterson, J. (1991), 'Technology Policy in Europe: Explaining the Framework Programme and Eureka in Theory and Practice', *Journal of Common Market Studies*, 29: 269–90.

Porter, M. E. (1990), *The Competitive Advantage of Nations* (London: Macmillan).

Pownall, I. (1995), 'The Capture of Internalisation as a Policy Tool: The Case of ESPRIT', *Science and Public Policy*, 22: 39–49.

Sachwald, F. (1993), *L'Europe et la globalisation: Acquisitions et accords dans l'industrie* (Paris: Masson Éditeur); English edn., *European Integration and Competitiveness: Alliances and Acquisitions in Industry* (Aldershot: Edward Elgar, 1994).

Sandholtz, W. (1992), 'ESPRIT and the Politics of International Collective Action', *Journal of Common Market Studies*, 30: 1–24.

Saunders, C. T., Matthews, M., and Patel, P. (1991), 'Structural Change and Patterns of Production and Trade', in C. Freeman, M. Sharp, and W. Walker (eds.), *Technology and the Future of Europe* (London: Pinter).

Servan Schreiber, J. J. (1967), *Le Défi Américain* (Paris: de Noel); English edn., *The American Challenge* (Harmondsworth: Penguin Books, 1968).

Sharp, M. (1993), 'The Community and the New Technologies', in J. Lodge (ed.), *The EC and the Challenge of the Future*, 2nd edn. (London: Pinter), 200–23.

—— and Holmes, P. (eds.) (1989), *Strategies for New Technologies: Case Studies from Britain and France* (London: Philip Allan).

—— and Pavitt, K. (1993), 'Technology Policy in the 1990s: Old Trends and New Realities', *Journal of Common Market Studies*, 31: 129–51.

—— and Shearman, C. (1987), *European Technological Collaboration* (London: Routledge & Kegan Paul).

Stoneman, P. (ed.) (1995), *Handbook of the Economics of Innovation and Technological Change* (Oxford: Blackwell).

Walker, W. (1993) 'National Innovation Systems: Britain', in R. R. Nelson (ed.), *National Innovation Systems: A Comparative Analysis* (Oxford: Oxford University Press), 158–91.

Williams, R. and Mills, S. (eds.) (1986), *Public Acceptance of New Technologies: An International Review* (London: Croom Helm).

Williamson, O. E. (1975), *Markets and Hierarchies* (New York: Free Press).

—— (1985), *The Economic Institutions of Capitalism* (New York: Free Press).

Chapter 8
Regional Policy

Gabriele Tondl

8.1 The development of EU regional policy

While regional policies were a common practice in the EU Member States in the 1960s and 1970s, for a long time no such policy existed at the Community level. With the Northern enlargement in 1973, Italy, which had to contend with the low development of its South, found a strong ally for requesting Community action in the UK, which itself faced considerable regional problems (in Scotland, Wales, and its old industrial areas). As a first step, the European Regional Development Fund (ERDF) was created in 1975. It provided transfers on the basis of national quotas to co-finance national regional policies. The financial contribution remained very limited, however. It took the Community more than another ten years to create its own regional policy. In view of the possible regional adjustment problems induced by the creation of the European Single Market 1992 programme and the increased income discrepancies arising with the Southern enlargement (Greece in 1981, and Spain and Portugal in 1986), the Community assumed the competence for its own regional policy with the European Single Act in 1986 (Article 130a–e Single European Act, after Amsterdam Articles 158–162 EC Treaty). Thereafter, a major reform of the Structural Funds in 1988 created EU regional policy in its present form, with respect to the financial framework as well as with respect to policy priorities and administrative procedures.[1]

   EU regional policy pursues two major objectives: (i) to assist the development of areas lagging behind, and (ii) to reduce regional imbalances in the Member States. The major concern from the perspective of the Union has been to reduce disparities between its Member States. Confronted with the wide gap in income levels and economic structures between the Western and Southern periphery, on the one hand and the core member states on the other, that arose in the mid-1980s (the so-called cohesion problem), EU regional policy gave highest priority to supporting the catching-up of lagging Community areas, comprising the so-called cohesion countries: Spain and Portugal, Ireland, and Greece, as well as the Italian South and East Germany after the German unification. (These areas also correspond to the Objective 1 area, which are regions with a per capita income of less than 75 per cent of the Community average. The cohesion countries, defined as countries with a national GNP per capita of less than 90 per cent of EU average, largely consist of Objective 1 regions.)

The major argument for Community action in favour of the development of lagging Member States goes beyond the common criteria for aid policies (equity and efficiency: see Molle 1997: 419–20). First, the Community justifies regional policy action as a matter of solidarity between rich and poor Community areas. Secondly, the major aim of a common regional policy was to alleviate the restructuring pressure on weak economic areas associated with the creation of the Single Market by assisting the modernization of their economic systems. This resulted in the 1988 Structural Funds Reform and the Delors 1 package, which fixed the spending of the structural funds for 1989–93 at 0.29 per cent of EU GDP. The request for consolidation of national budgets stipulated in the Maastricht Treaty (the so-called 'convergence criteria') led to a further demand for EU assistance satisfied by the Delors 2 package, which raised the Structural Fund spending to 0.48 per cent of EU GDP, where it remains. With the implementation of the European monetary union, which puts its members under a single monetary policy, regional policy has again come into focus as a means of alleviating asymmetric shocks (Bayoumi and Eichengreen 1993).[2]

The 1988 reform of the Structural Funds (the ERDF—European Regional Development Fund, ESF—European Social Fund, and EAGGF—European Agricultural Guarantee and Guidance Funds) created the principles of EU regional policy. First, the EU aimed to concentrate Structural Funds (SF) aid on the lagging areas (i.e. the cohesion countries and other Objective 1 areas). Secondly, EU regional policy was intended to target specific regional problems with policy priorities (Objectives 1, 2, 3, 4 and 5b), for which the EU defined policy strategies. Thirdly, EU regional policy should be effected by multi-annual regional development programmes. Fourthly, regional policy actions should be planned and implemented under joint responsibility of Member State authorities and EU bodies (the partnership principle). Finally, SF assistance was intended to complement national regional policy funds and not to replace existing policy support (the principle of additionality).

In accordance with the principle of concentration, Objective 1 regions received more than two-thirds of the SF in the two programme periods 1989–93 and 1994–9. In terms of GDP, the EU transfers amounted to between 0.6 per cent (for the richer parts such as Spain) and 2.4 per cent (e.g. for Portugal) on average in the period 1989–93 and between 1 and 3.2 per cent in the period 1994–96 (this excludes payments from the Cohesion Fund—see below). Transfers to the richer Member States remained much lower, even for those with substantial regional problems. For example, in 1994–6, the annual transfers to Germany (for the transformation of East Germany) reached only 0.14 per cent of GDP. In Italy (with its Mezzogiorno problem) transfers amounted to 0.24 per cent and in the UK (with Northern Ireland, Scotland, and numerous former industrial areas) they were 0.18 per cent (figures based on Court of Auditors, Eurostat). In 1993, a further financial instrument, the Cohesion Fund, was created to assist the lagging Member States to upgrade their infrastructures while consolidating their budgets to meet the Maastricht criteria. Countries with a GNP per capita of below 90 per cent of EU average should receive up to 85 per cent of project costs.

EU regional policy was intended to address five major policy priorities, the so-called 'objectives', which still exist with some amendments (see below). Objective 1 policies focus on the development of lagging regions with a GDP per capita of less than 75 per cent of the EU average. Objective 2 policies originally addressed industrial reconversion problems, largely in the richer member states. Objectives 3 and 4 were meant to address labour-market problems (youth unemployment, long-term unemployment, and the acquirement of new skills). Objective 5b targeted regional problems of little diversified, backward agricultural areas, as are found in all of the rich member states. With the 1995 enlargement, the new Objective 6 was created to address the sparsely populated, sub-arctic regions in Sweden and Finland. As the rich Member States were seeking to keep a large territory eligible for regional aid—which according to EU competition policy is restricted to regional aid in specified territories—and safeguard as high as possible EU transfers, the territory under Objectives 2 and 5b increased successively over the two previous programme periods. In 1999 Objective 2 regions accounted for 16.8 per cent and Objective 5b regions for 8.2 per cent of the population in the richer Member States.

To summarize, the central task of EU regional policy is to lay down common rules for structural aid in the Member States and to co-finance policy measures. The Union gives the broad guidelines of the type of policy measures for development and restructuring policies upon which Member States need to design—in cooperation with the Community authorities—regional policy programmes. The requirement for common rules arises from the principles of the Common Market. Meanwhile the much formalized procedural involvement of the Commission in planning, policy implementation, and monitoring arises from the wish to assure efficiency and to prevent misuse of EU resources. These procedures, however, have become sufficiently complicated so as to compromise efficiency themselves.

On the eve of the new programming period starting in 2000, the European Union has witnessed an impressive catching-up process in its periphery, to which the SF have certainly contributed. Some remarkable achievements, such as the formation of high educational attainment in Ireland and the creation of a modern infrastructure for key transport links in Spain, have been effected with EU regional aid. Without having solved the existing cohesion problem, the European Union will have to face a much bigger cohesion problem when Eastern European candidates, whose income levels fall below even the relative pre-accession income levels of the present cohesion countries, join the Union. (In 1999, GDP per capita relative to the EU 15 reached 22 per cent in Bulgaria, 37 per cent in Poland, 50 per cent in Hungary, 60 per cent in the Czech Republic, and 71 per cent in Slovenia.)

Following the policy guidelines of the Agenda 2000, which froze the existing financial level of support for regional development and attempted to simplify EU regional policy and to improve its efficiency, the European Council adopted new regulations for EU regional policy in the period 2000–6 in June 1999.[3] In principle, EU budget resources for regional policies were fixed at the Berlin summit in March 1999 at 0.46 per cent of EU GDP, equivalent to the level in the period 1994–9. In total, 213 billion Euro are reserved for structural policies for the present EU members, and some further 21.8 billion for pre-accession aid (1999 prices). Given the smaller financial means to be spent on the EU incumbents, a balanced reduction of EU regional policy support in all 15 Member States was necessary. Thus the eligibility of regions was much more strictly interpreted. Consequently, a number of regions slightly exceeding the threshold were put under a transitory scheme and assistance for areas which have already improved significantly (such as Ireland and Spain), was drastically cut. Practically all Member States have to face a reduction of SF support in financial terms (see Table 8.1).

In view of the large number of intervention schemes of the Structural Funds accumulated over the last decade, there was a desire to simplify the operation of the Structural Funds and reduce the number of priority objectives. The new EU regional policy pursues three principal objectives: Objective 1 will promote the development and structural adjustment of regions lagging behind in development; Objective 2 will promote economic and social conversion of areas facing structural difficulties; whilst Objective 3 aims to modernize education and training systems and employment policies.

The *Objective 1* policy continues to be the main emphasis of EU regional policy with its focus on assisting areas with a GDP per capita of below 75 per cent of the EU average. Nearly 70 cent of the SF are reserved for Objective 1 policies. Objective 1 areas which have passed the 75 per cent threshold receive a degressive transitional support until 2005. The previous Objective 6 policies for the sub-arctic regions in Sweden and Finland are now subsumed under Objective 1 policies.

Those areas which were covered under Objective 1 in 1994–9 and have meanwhile passed the 75 per cent income threshold comprise a number of catching-up regions in the

Table 8.1 Structural Funds transfers to member states 2000–2006 by priority objectives

	Total SF 2000-6[a] (€m.)	Average annual contribution		New Objective 1[b]	New Objective 2[b]	New Objective 3 (€m.)	Fisheries Instrument	Community Initiatives	Cohesion Fund	% share of SF receipts
		2000-6 (% GDP 1999)	1994–99 (% GDP 1994)							
Rich members:										
Belgium	2,037	0.12	0.15	625	433	737	34	209		0.9
Denmark	825	0.09	0.14	0	183	365	197	80		0.4
Germany	29,764	0.23	0.24	19,958	3,510	4,581	107	1,608		14.0
France	15,666	0.18	0.23	3,805	6,050	4,540	225	1,046		7.4
Italy	29,656	0.35	0.36	22,122	522	3,744	96	1,172		14.0
Luxembourg	91	0.07	0.15	0	40	38	0	13		0.1
N/lands	3,286	0.12	0.15	123	795	1,686	31	651		1.5
Austria	1,831	0.14	0.15	261	680	528	4	358		0.9
Finland	2,090	0.27	0.30	913	489	403	31	254		1.0
Sweden	2,186	0.16	0.13	722	406	720	60	278		1.0
United Kingdom	16,596	0.18	0.21	6,251	4,695	4,568	121	961		7.8
Cohesion countries:										
Ireland	3,974	0.64	2.53						720	1.9
Spain	56,205	1.18	1.62						11,160	26.5
Portugal	22,760	2.04	3.87						3,060	10.7
Greece	24,883	2.38	3.34						3,060	11.7
Total	211,850			54,780	17,803	21,910	906	6,630	18,000	100.0

[a] allocation from SF (objectives and Community Initiatives) and Cohesion Fund. [b] includes transitory assistance.
Source: Data from Eurostat, European Commission DG 16 and own calculations

periphery, such as the south-eastern region of Ireland, Northern Ireland, the Scottish Highlands and Islands, Cantabria in Spain, the Lisbon area, and Molise in Southern Italy. In the core Member States, East Berlin, Hainaut (Belgium), Corsica, and the objective 1 areas in Nord-Pas-de-Calais, and Flevoland (Netherlands) are phasing out from Objective 1. Roughly, each Member State lost an Objective 1 region in the new regional policy period. The Objective 1 areas which the northern Member States had gained in the policy period 1994–9 were classified back.[4] Evidently, the major assisted area change is in Ireland. In total, the Community's objective 1 territory drops from 27 per cent of the EU population in the period 1994–9 to 22 per cent.

The Cohesion Fund, the further operation of which was heavily questioned by the net paying member countries (Germany, the Netherlands, UK, Sweden, and Austria) since it was originally designed to facilitate qualification for the Euro—a goal the cohesion countries have reached—will continue its support. Once again, the 'Club Med' succeeded at the budget negotiations in bargaining its survival in exchange for the less drastic cuts in CAP support demanded by France. The Cohesion Fund will continue to assist Spain and Portugal, Greece, and Ireland in co-financing major projects for the environment and trans-European transport networks. As the threshold for entitlement to the cohesion funds is a GNP per capita of less than 90 per cent, even Ireland remains a beneficiary, although its allocations from the fund were cut. The new regulation foresees that support for a country must not only reflect its population size and income level, but also its growth performance. A review of further entitlement to the Cohesion Fund is planned for 2003. Since the Cohesion Fund was designed to assist previous high-deficit countries to consolidate their budgets while closing infrastructure gaps, it operates on the conditionality clause that funding requires to meet the convergence programme (Inforegio 4/2000).

As to the financial contribution of the SF to the cohesion countries/Objective 1 areas, Spain continues to be the major beneficiary in the current programme period with an allocation of 56 billion Euro (see Table 8.1). Portugal and Greece receive barely half of that amount, and now a rather small allocation is planned for Ireland. Regarding SF aid in relation to GDP, one can note a distinctly reduced support in all cohesion countries, but mostly in Ireland (Table 8.1). Until the changes, Ireland had always received the highest SF support in per capita terms, followed, with a distinct gap, by Greece and Portugal.[5] In the present programme period, however, Greece (337 Euro per capita) and Portugal (325 Euro) receive the highest support in per capita terms, Spain (207 Euro) and Ireland (150 Euro) will receive much less assistance (see Figure 8.1[6]).

The new *Objective 2* covers the previous Objectives 2 and 5b as well as structurally problematic urban areas and fisheries regions. It comprises:

1. industry-dominated regions with declining industrial employment and an above-average unemployment rate;

2. agriculturally dominated or sparsely populated areas with an above-average unemployment or continuing outmigration;

3. high unemployment urban areas with a high poverty and crime rate and low skills; and

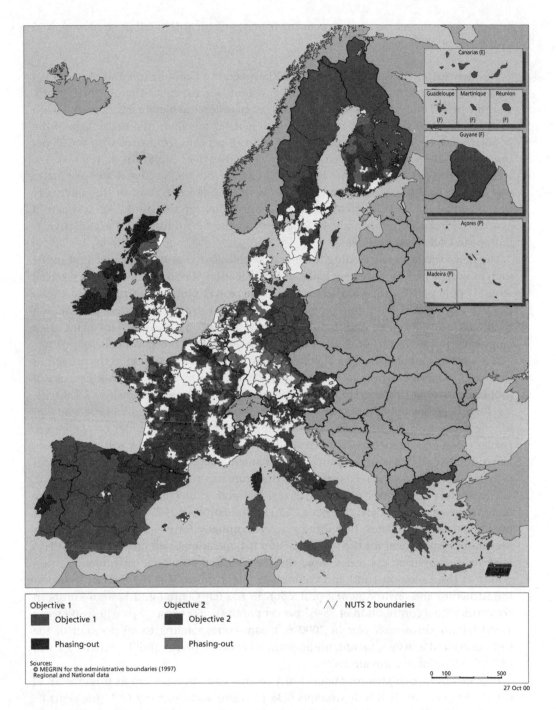

Objective 1

■ Objective 1

■ Phasing-out

Objective 2

■ Objective 2

■ Phasing-out

∧∕ NUTS 2 boundaries

Sources:
© MEGRIN for the administrative boundaries (1997)
Regional and National data

0   100   500

27 Oct 00

Fig. 8.1 Areas eligible for EU regional policy support, 2000–2006

4. regions dependent on the restructuring fisheries sector with a fall in employment in this sector.

The new list of Objective 2 areas, agreed between the Commission and the Member States in the first half of 2000, entitles fewer regions for assistance than in the last programme period under the old priority objectives. In order to achieve a reconciliation with the reduced EU budget funds available for present EU members, the percentage of the population covered by Objective 2 was limited to 18 per cent (compared with the 25 per cent of the EU population covered by the 'old' Objectives 2 and 5b in 1994–9). For eligibility, the seriousness of problems relative to the other Objective 2 Member States was decisive and no Member State should lose more than one third of the previously assisted areas. For previously covered areas, transitional support until 2005 was agreed as well. In financial terms, only 11.5 per cent of the SF are foreseen for Objective 2. (European Commission, 1999a).

The new *Objective 3*, succeeding the previous Objectives 3 and 4, takes account of the high ranking which employment issues and the creation of human capital have received with EU policy-makers due to the serious labour market problems in the 1990s. Under Objective 3, parts of the Community outside Objective 1 areas will effect programmes to modernize education and training systems as well as measures to adapt their employment system; 12.3 per cent of the SF are reserved for Objective 3 policies.

The wish to simplify EU regional policy finally led also to a reduction in the numerous *Community Initiatives*. These are regional policy operations in favour of a specific regional problem of strong Community interest. Several such initiatives for sensitive industries, e.g. for textiles or shipbuilding, existed. Their number fell from thirteen in 1994–9 to four for the present programme period, comprising Interreg III (cross-border co-operation), Leader (rural development), Urban (revitalization of poor urban areas with social problems), and Equal (equal opportunities in the labour market), for which no more than 5 per cent of the SF are now reserved (previously the figure was 10 per cent) (Inforegio 5/2000).

The Agenda 2000 introduced a set of regional policy interventions in favour of the Eastern European candidates. In total, 3.120 billion Euros, or 10.2 per cent of the SF for incumbent Member States, have been reserved annually for *pre-accession aid*. Phare, a preparatory instrument for the later ERDF funded operations, will provide 1.560 billion Euro to the applicant countries. Ispa, the pre-accession structural instrument, corresponds to the Cohesion Fund and co-finances major projects in the field of transport infrastructure and environmental protection in the ten Central and Eastern European countries with a contribution of 75–85 per cent of the project costs. Ispa will spend some 1.040 billion Euros each year in 2000–6, a sum corresponding to 40 per cent of the Cohesion Fund transfers. Sapard, the agricultural instrument for candidate countries, will provide 520 million Euros annually.

In general, the rich Member States clearly receive only modest support from the SF, at 0.1–0.2 per cent of GDP. Italy (receipts 0.35 per cent) and Germany (0.23 per cent) lie ahead due to the structural problems of the Mezzogiorno and East Germany (see Table 8.1). Practically all rich Member States, except for Italy and Germany, have to accept a modest reduction in SF support in 2000–6 compared with the previous programme period.

Financial support by the SF co-finances infrastructure, investment aid schemes, and training and employment schemes. Complementary to the financial support of the SF, policy measures have to be financed by national public resources (typical with infrastructure) and private resources (with industry investment aid). Support by the SF is provided through non-repayable grants. The rate of assistance varies according to the seriousness of the regional problem and the financial capacity of the Member State. Discussions about the appropriateness of the present support by grants in the perspective of efficiency and resource constraints have led the Commission to encourage the application of alternative financial support, such as interest subsidies for loans (European Commission 1999*b*).

The new financial guidelines have also led to some changes of aid rates. Thus, the new regional policy operates with a reduced *assistance rate* of the SF for profit-oriented investment projects. For purely public investment, the share to be financed by the funds remains at 75 per cent of total costs in Objective 1 areas and 50 per cent of total costs in Objective 2 areas, as before. For profit-oriented infrastructure investment, however, assistance by the funds falls to 40 per cent and 25 per cent respectively. Assistance to business investment, finally, is reduced to 35 per cent in Objective 1 areas (previously 50 per cent) and 15 per cent in Objective 2 areas (before 30 per cent). Clearly, the distortion for business investment created by subsidy competition will be reduced in this way, while the poorer Member States continue to receive a high share of co-financing to public investment (Inforegio 5/2000; European Commission 1999*b*).

The difficulties experienced with *programme planning*, *implementation* and *operation* in previous SF programmes were admitted by the EU in 1999 as a major reason for inefficiencies of the structural policies, a fact pointed out repeatedly by economists (e.g. Putnam 1993; Tondl 1998). Therefore, in order to improve the effectiveness of EU regional policy, the new regional policy regulations define precisely the tasks of programme management (programming, implementation, financial management, and monitoring), request the Member States to name the authorities and bodies assuming these responsibilities, and demand much stricter assessment and reporting than in the past.

The Member State has to appoint one principal *managing authority* at the national level. It acts as a co-ordinator and contact partner for the Commission. As to the organizational structure of programming, implementing, and operating structural fund programmes, it is up to the Member State to appoint the administrative units to effect these tasks. They may be located at the central government level or at the regional/local level. However, accounting for the *partnership* principle, all local and regional authorities, the economic and social partners, and environmental and equal opportunity representatives, have to be associated at the various steps of programme management at least via some form of consultation.

With the first two generations of EU regional policy programmes the absorption of allocated funds was often delayed and slow. With the regional policy programmes 1989–93, the payments rate of Objective 1 programmes reached 85 per cent on average at the end of 1993. For Objective 2 programmes, the payment rate was only 74 per cent of allocated funds on average at the end of the last programme year (European Commission 1994: 129, 39). With the last policy programmes 1994–9, at the mid-point of

1996, payments had reached just 30 per cent of allocated funds. After reprogramming, payments reached 61 per cent of allocations in 1998 with Objective 1 and about 50 per cent with Objectives 2 and 5b (European Commission 1999c: 39, 44). The organization of financial management and the documentation of funding turned out to be the main critical points for this unsatisfactory performance.

To raise the efficiency of SF interventions, the new regional policy regulations therefore aimed to assure a sound system of *financial management* in the Member State. It has to allocate responsibilities for the financial management of Community funds to its authorities with clearly defined tasks. It has to be assured that assistance is only granted to eligible projects and that irregularities are detected and corrected. In such a case the Commission would suspend payments. The Member State also has to submit an annual report on the funding activities of the financial authorities at various policy areas and regional levels. Clearly, Member States are now obliged to carry out a more detailed and timely documentation of financial support payments than previously. Government agencies are encouraged to employ joint computer facilities and data interchange for this task. This reporting will improve transparency and facilitate policy evaluation.

There is also a change in the way in which commitments and payments are effected, which will assure a more rapid implementation of regional programmes. First, it is foreseen that SF commitments for which no actual payments are effected within 2 years will be automatically decommitted. This will permit abandonment of badly performing policy measures and switching to other measures. Secondly, advance payments for funded measures are drastically reduced from a previous 50 per cent to 7 per cent in the initial stage of the programme. Thereafter, payments are only effected as a reimbursement of actual expenditures. Advance payments for programmes which have not actually started within 18 months need to be repaid (European Commission 1999a: 24). These new financial terms are in sharp contrast to the previous practice, where slowly starting programmes—either due to a mismatch of policy objectives or administrative incompetence—and lagging projects often remained unnoticed for too long. The new provisions force Member States to select projects more carefully and to monitor programmes tightly.

Finally, starting from the introduction of policy *evaluation* with the revision in 1993, the new regional policy requests an even more thorough assessment of regional policy programmes. Member States have to have their programmes evaluated ex-ante, at mid-term, and ex-post by independent consultants on the basis of a list of target indicators. This should not only provide accountancy to the public on the benefits of structural policies but also enable policy corrections. A performance reserve for each Member State of 4 per cent of the SF assistance is to be paid to best performing programmes on the basis of performance indicators after the mid-term evaluation in 2003.

8.2 **The cohesion problem**

In order to understand the priority which EU regional policy has obtained with EU policy-makers, one has to form a better understanding of the dimensions of the under-lying cohesion problem. In principle, the European cohesion problem can be character-ized as disparities in per capita income and in employment. These are considerable between Member States as well as between regions within those states.

With respect to per capita income,[7] the economic centres in the rich Member States exhibited a GDP per capita of between 120 and 170 per cent of the EU 15 average in 1996. The richest regions with a GDP per capita above 140 comprise the large metropolitan areas of Hamburg, Bremen, Darmstadt, Brussels, Île de France, London, Vienna, and Munich. Northern Italy, Salzburg, Southern Germany, Antwerp, Groningen, Berkshire/ Oxfordshire, Grampian, and the capital regions in Scandinavia showed a per capita income of between 120 and 140 per cent of the EU average in 1996.[8] The number of rich regions has slightly increased since 1988 (see Figure 8.2).

The core Member States predominantly consist of regions with a per capita income above the EU average. In particular this is the case in the North and Centre of Italy, in Germany, the Benelux countries, Denmark, and also the UK. On the other hand, in France only the Île de France, Haute Normandie, and the region Rhône-Alpes have an income above the EU average (see Figure 8.2).

The distribution of European regional incomes is skewed, with the peak in the income group 75–100 per cent of average income. The income frequency in the income group 100–124 per cent is much lower. In 1996 the largest part of Europe comprised regions with a per capita income of 75–99 per cent of the average lying in France, the Scandina-vian countries, the UK, Ireland, and the northern part of Spain. One has to note in particular the move of regions in the cohesion countries into this income group since 1988.

The income range of Objective 1 regions (those with a GDP per capita of below 75 per cent of the EU average) has narrowed since 1988. There are practically no regions in the EU 15 any longer with a GDP per capita of below 55 per cent (the remaining examples are Extremadura and Ipeiros). Nevertheless, a larger number of regions on the European southern fringe and the New German Länder have a GDP per capita below 75 per cent. All Portugal, the Centre and South of Spain, a rather stable number of southern Italian regions, and—also unchanged—the entire Greek territory are in this income group.

How have regional income disparities developed over the past decade? Is there any sign of diminishing regional disparities? If we look at the standard deviation of regional income among the EU-15—a common dispersion measure—several studies come to the conclusion that income disparities show a very modest tendency to decrease since the mid-1980s, despite an upward shift in levels due to the German unification (Dunford 2000: 88–89; Tondl 2001; European Commission 1999*d*). Empirical growth studies have shown that there is only a weak convergence process in the sense of neoclassical growth theory operating across EU-15 regions (Armstrong 1995; Tondl 1999; European Commis-sion 2000*a*; neoclassical growth theory postulates a higher growth performance of poor

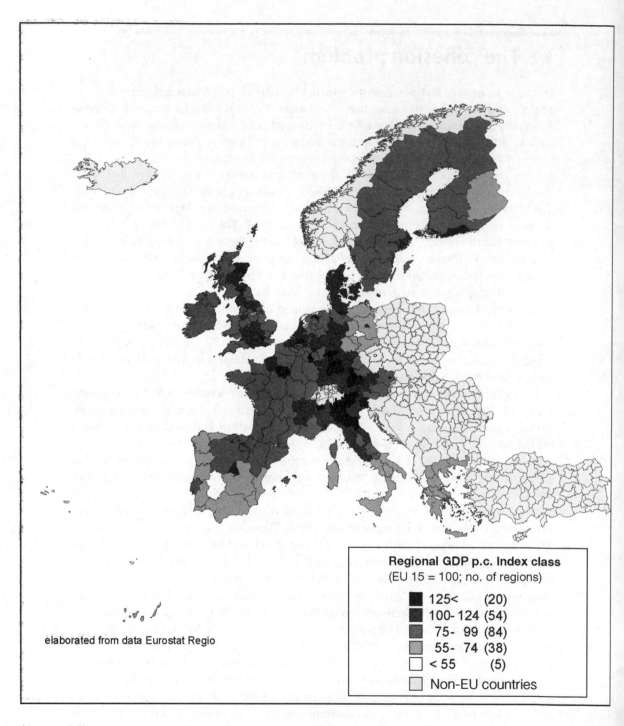

elaborated from data Eurostat Regio

Regional GDP p.c. Index class
(EU 15 = 100; no. of regions)

■ 125<   (20)
■ 100- 124 (54)
■ 75- 99 (84)
■ 55- 74 (38)
□ < 55   (5)
□ Non-EU countries

Fig. 8.2 GDP per capita of EU regions, 1996

regions, and thus a catching-up process: see Solow 1956; Barro and Sala-i-Martin 1995). Moreover, panel data studies show that regional steady-state incomes differ distinctly and are fairly stable despite such a convergence process (Tondl 1999, 2001). These econometric studies suggest that the reduction of regional income disparities is a cumbersome process, a fact which EU citizens and policy-makers have to face.

Notwithstanding this rather disappointing assessment for the EU, there are some very impressive catching-up experiences demonstrated by regions in the cohesion countries, particularly since the mid-1980s. There are several causes of this catching-up. Integration effects (FDI following endowment factors, investment to improve productivity under fiercer competition, and scale effects), initiated by the Internal Market programme and the accession of southern countries, have certainly induced considerable investment activity on the Iberian Peninsula and in Ireland, which initiated a dynamic growth process. On the other hand the lagging regions could also have benefited from a substantial increase in EU structural policies since the 1988 reform of the SF, which attempted to improve regional supply-side factors such as infrastructure and human resources. The likely contribution of EU regional policies for development, suggested by a number of macroeconomic evaluations (ESRI 1997; Roeger 1996), supports the demand for policy action at the EU level to assist regional development.

Besides the undesirability of large income differences across European regions, the European cohesion problem has a second major facet, namely unemployment. The bad message is that in general high regional unemployment problems coincide with a weak income position (Begg 1999; Tondl 2001: ch. 1; Fagerberg *et al.* 1997: 460). Moreover, they are equally persistent as income disparities (Baddeley *et al.* 1998: 205). Thus Objective 1 regions have a distinctly higher unemployment rate than the richer Member States (central and southern Spain 20–30 per cent; southern Italy 22 per cent; and East Germany 18 per cent in 1997: European Commission 1999*d*). The traditionally lower unemployment rate in Greece has increased with the transformation of agricultural areas and pressures to reduce public-sector employment. Greece had an unemployment rate of 9.6 per cent in 1997, while Portugal had the lowest of all Objective 1 regions with 6.7 per cent.

Clearly, the labour-market situation improved in most regions that experienced a catching-up process. In Ireland, unemployment dropped from 18 per cent in 1987 to 10 per cent in 1997 and turned into a labour shortage for certain skill segments by 2000 (European Commission 1999*d*). In Spain, where the Centre, South, and North-East experienced a catching-up process, employment showed an outstanding increase among the cohesion countries, without however reducing unemployment (European Commission 1999*d*: 78). (For econometric evidence on the nexus between regional GDP growth and employment growth see Fagerberg *et al.* 1997: 462 and Marelli 2000, who verify a strong relationship for European regions.) As economic theory would suggest, there are also cases where high growth coincides with a rise in unemployment, e.g. in the Algarve and Norte of Portugal, which is due to labour-saving productivity improvements. Evidently, technological change and labour-market characteristics make the growth–unemployment relationship less clear. (Bover *et al.* (2000), have shown that the persistence of high unemployment simultaneously with employment growth in Spain is a consequence of less diversified wage structures across skill categories, determined by the

Spanish trade unions.) On the other hand, it is also clear that a poor growth performance in the Objective 1 regions has aggravated unemployment problems, as, for example, in southern Italy.

In the richer northern Member States, regional unemployment rates are much lower, at around 6–9 per cent in 1997. Particularly difficult labour-market situations exist in the North of France (13 per cent unemployment in 1997) and its Mediterranean fringe (17 per cent in 1997); in the Objective 6 regions of Sweden and Finland (12 and 14 per cent respectively in 1997); and some other small industrial reconversion areas (European Commission 1999*d*).

In view of the large gap with the cohesion countries, southern Italy and East Germany, regional problems in the rich Member States are subordinate. We shall therefore devote the next section of this chapter to the Objective 1 regions. As mentioned in Section 8.1, northern Member States host a number of industrial reconversion areas with a large share of traditional industries and high unemployment. They face the requirement to establish new industries to absorb labour that has been set free, a process which often shows hardly any dynamism. Studies by the European Commission show that despite job creation in newly established small and medium-size enterprises (SMEs), job losses outweigh the gains (European Commission 1999*d*: 154). In 1997 the old Objective 2 areas had an average GDP per capita of 97 per cent of the EU average and an unemployment rate of 12 per cent (Begg 1999).

On the other hand, northern Member States have agricultural problem areas (old Objective 5b regions) which lack alternative economic activities and often suffer from a remote location, which in total results in labour-market problems, although generally less critical ones than in the old Objective 2 areas. Since the late 1980s, some advance in restructuring is discernible. An SME sector is emerging in production and services related to agriculture (European Commission 1999*d*). In 1997 Objective 5b areas had an average GDP per capita of 85 per cent of the EU average and an unemployment rate of 7.8 per cent (Begg 1999).

8.3 EU regional policy in the cohesion countries/ Objective 1 areas

Introduction

The Community's Objective 1 areas are generally large continuous territories, covering either practically the entire Member State (Spain, Portugal, Greece, and Ireland) or a large area of a Member State (southern Italy and East Germany). As mentioned above, the first group is also referred to as the cohesion countries. So far, two Community Support Framework Programmes have been effected in these EU areas in 1989–93 and 1994–9 (CSF I and CSF II).

For the cohesion countries in particular, the economic development of the whole economy has been the primary goal, given their generally low level of development and their overall need for modernization. Concerns for regional imbalances rank much lower. Thus EU regional policy in these parts of the Community has comprised predominantly national structural measures, and—to a varying extent—regional measures. EU regional policy has more of the features of a cohesion policy than of a regional policy (as in the rich Member States). Nevertheless, the European Commission has always put a strong emphasis on the pursuit of regional policies in the cohesion countries as well.

From a theoretical point of view there are strong arguments in favour of a country-level development policy. The Williamson hypothesis (1965) proposes that regional imbalances are originally low in a poor economy. In a first stage of development when the economy's income rises, regional imbalances increase. Thereafter, as the country becomes a high-income economy, regional income disparities successively disappear, a fact observed in Western European countries in the 1960s and 1970s. From this perspective, the preponderance of national-scale structural policy measures, which may even target the modernization of the most advanced regions—e.g. by assisting the development of advanced, innovative industries in these regions (the so-called 'growth pole strategy': Perroux 1955)—is highly important in the early stages of development of a country. Attention to the development of the most backward regions should be postponed to a later stage of development. This consideration is mirrored in the past SF programmes of the cohesion countries. In particular Ireland and Portugal effected virtually no regional development measures in CSF I and II. By contrast, Greece attempted to meet the Commission's request for regional development, which neither led to convincing regional improvements nor contributed to national development

The economic situation and policy requirements

The cohesion countries are by no means a homogeneous group, so big are the differences with respect to their development gaps and catching-up performance. After diverging from the rest of Europe for decades, Ireland accomplished a major step in development in the last decade, with an average annual growth rate of 7.5 per cent, soon being labelled the 'Celtic Tiger'. It succeeded in establishing an advanced industrial sector and in improving noticeably the skill level of the labour force. It transformed its unemployment problems into a labour shortage. Nevertheless, the development achieved has remained highly concentrated in the Dublin area (O'Leary; 1999, Government of Ireland 1999).

Spain and Portugal also achieved a favourable growth performance following the launch of CSF I in 1989. Both countries quickly integrated their economics into the European economy. Modernization of industry was an important requirement for both countries on the eve of EC accession in 1986. This process was then heavily supported by EU regional policy measures (such as the PEDIP programme for Portuguese industry) and by foreign direct investment inflows. Both contributed to a rise in industrial productivity and, in Spain, to a diversification of industrial activity. Spain took also full advantage of EU SF transfers to co-finance its ambitious infrastructure programmes.

An important problem for both countries is the qualification level of the labour force. For Portugal, the backlog in educational attainment comprises also general school education, in addition to a lack of professional education. In Spain, where general educational levels are much higher, poor vocational training and professional education have resulted in a lack of skills in the young labour force as well as among older workers, which is one cause of the extreme unemployment levels affecting Spanish society. In view of the size of the country, Spain hosts a number of regions with very different economic structures. Its north-eastern regions are leading in development and initially, after 1988, also accounted for the best growth performance. Since then regional imbalances have seemed to improve as development has settled also in the South and in the Centre.

Greece and the Italian Mezzogiorno are the other Objective 1 areas in the southern periphery, but their catching-up performance has been far less satisfactory. The Italian South now belongs to the richer Objective 1 areas while Greece fell back to the lowest EU income position.

The Italian South experienced a weak growth performance and rising unemployment throughout the 1980s and 1990s. Private investment fell heavily, whilst the region could never attract foreign direct investment on a noteworthy scale. However, there are some major multinational investments in the region and the rate of new firm formation in the SME sector has risen. Economic stagnation was also caused by the sharp decline in public investment by about 30 per cent. With the aim of reducing the national budget deficit, the Italian government reduced public transfers to the South, which led to an under-investment in infrastructure. Such a decline in infrastructure investment associated with deficit reduction did not occur in the cohesion countries, which received compensating transfers from the cohesion fund. A major problem for the Italian South is its persistently high unemployment rate, amounting to more than 20 per cent in 1997. Despite this general stagnation, the Mezzogiorno shows some positive developments as well. The region has significantly expanded its export activities and tourism. Another positive development is the decline of criminality (Ministero del Tesoro 1999a).

The chronically poor macroeconomic performance of Greece in the 1980s and early 1990s seems to have improved over the course of CSF II since the accession of the new government in 1996. This was manifested in higher economic growth of 3.8 per cent; a remarkable improvement in one of the worst European budget deficits to only −1.5 of GDP in 1999; and the stabilization of the exchange rate (CSF III Greece). Greece's private sector revealed a low investment propensity for years, impeding modernization of its specialization in traditional industries and new firm formation. Greek unemployment, together with that in Portugal, was surprisingly lower than in the other Objective 1 countries. Retarded agricultural restructuring and other forms of hidden unemployment kept unemployment low. In 1999, however, unemployment rose substantially. The poor qualification level of the labour force appears to be the main factor in this labour-market problem. The inadequate skills of labour-market entrants are linked to the poor education and training system of the country. The development of the Greek economy suffers from another important factor, namely its isolated location. Nor did the country succeed in creating an adequate internal transport infrastructure with the disposable EU funding. This also explains why economic activity is largely restricted to two major locations—the capital area and Central Macedonia.

The development process of eastern Germany has decelerated in the second half of the 1990s. Economic growth is weaker than in the former West Germany. With a GDP per capita of 63 per cent of the EU average, the New Länder show a lower economic

Table 8.2 Socio-economic characteristics of the cohesion countries/objective 1 regions

	GDP[a]	Growth[b]	Unemployment[c]	Agriculture[d]	Specialization[e]	Education[f]	R&D[g]	Investment[h]	Transport[i]
Ireland	**96**	**7.5**	**7.8**	**10.2**	—	**27**	**1.3**	**14.1**	**0.03**
Southern and Eastern Region	102		7.6	7.7	—	27	—	—	—
Border, Midlands and Western Region	70		8.4	17.6	—	25	—	—	—
Spain	**79**	**2.8**	**21.1**	**8.3**	**55**	**15**	**0.8**	**15.2**	**0.26**
richest regions:									
Madrid[j]	100	2.9	18.4	1.2	58	17	2.0	10.7	0.18
Noreste[j]	92	2.6	16	6.1	61	17	0.8	14.0	0.36
Este[j]	89	3.1	18.5	4.2	50	17	0.7	15.8	0.23
poorest regions:									
Sur	59	2.9	30	12.1	61	13	0.5	17.0	0.21
Noroeste	67	2.1	19.9	18.4	51	14	0.4	14.8	0.12
Centro	68	2.7	21.6	13.8	59	13	0.5	16.7	0.57
Portugal	**70**	**2.6**	**6.7**	**13.3**	**63**	**12**	**0.6**	—	**0.12**
richest regions:									
Lisboa[j]	88	1.3	7.9	3.8	52	17	0.9	—	0.15
poorest regions									
Acores, Madeira	50–54	—	5.4	12–16	74	9–10	0.2	—	0.0
Alentejo	60	4.9	10.4	14.2	62	9	0.5	—	0.08
Centro	59	5.9	3.4	31.9	60	9	0.7	—	0.18
South Italy		**1.1**	**21.6**	**12.6**	**57**	**29**	**0.5**	**22.0**	**0.20**
richest regions									
Molise	78	1.0	17.2	15.5	53	34	0.2	25.9	0.21
Sardegna	72	1.7	20.5	12.5	52	25	0.6	22.9	0.01
poorest regions:									
Calabria	59	0.9	24.9	13.1	58	31	0.3	23.5	
Greece	**67**	**1.9**	**9.6**	**19.8**	**59**	**32**	**0.5**	**12.9**	**0.05**
richest regions:									
Attika Notio	76.8	2.3	11.6	1.0	60	42	0.7	9.6	0.04
Aigaio, kriti Kentriki	69	4.0	4.3	24.0	65	25	0.4	10.6	0
Makedonia	67	2.1	9.2	19.5	73	31	0.5	11.2	0.06
poorest regions:									
Ipeiros	43.8	1.1	10.5	30.3	69	21	0.3	13.6	0.0
Voreio Aigaio	51.8	2.4	7.1	24.2	72	27	0.3	12.1	0.0
New German Länder	**63**	**9.6**	**18.2**	—	—	**63**	**1.7**	—	**0.48**
richest regions:									
Brandenburg	67	9.8	17.2	5.3	—	62	1.5	—	0.92
Sachsen	64	9.8	17.2	2.9	—	64	2.3	—	0.30
poorest regions:									
Mecklenburg-Vorpommern	61	8.5	18.8	6.5	—	62	1.2	—	0.49
Sachsen-Anhalt	61	8.3	20.6	4.4	—	65	1.6	—	0.42
Thüringen	61	11.7	17.6	3.9	—	63	1.7	—	0.26

a GDP per capita in PPS, 1996 (EU-15-100).
b Average annual GDP growth 1988–97 (East Germany 1991–7).
c Unemployment rate, 1997.
d Share of employment in agriculture, 1997.
e Industrial specialization: share of the three largest branches in total industrial employment. Figures for Italy 1995, Spain 1994, Portugal 1993, Greece 1991.
f Percentage of the population with upper secondary education, 1997.
g R&D rate: R&D expenditures in per cent of GDP. Figures Greece, Germany 1993, S-Italy, Spain, Ireland 1994, Portugal 1992.
h Average annual gross fixed capital formation as a percentage of GDP, 1985–92.
i Transport infrastructure indicator; km of motorways and double-track rail per 100 inhabitants, 1994/5.
j Not objective 1.
Source: Own calculations based on data from European Commission 1999d, Eurostat Regio database, Government of Ireland 1999, Cambridge Econometrics, unless otherwise indicated.

development than the poor cohesion countries. High wage concessions (wages reached 86 per cent of the West German level in 2000) undermine the competitiveness of East German industry, where productivity has hardly reached 60 per cent of the Western level and is only growing slowly. As a consequence of slow economic restructuring, unemployment remained fairly high (18 per cent: see Table 8.2) (Blien and Wolf 2000).

8.4 EU regional policy programmes: financial framework, policy priorities, and implementation

EU regional policy under Objective 1 endeavours to promote economic development, or economic growth and employment—the declared objectives of the Union—by measures in six policy priority areas:

1. Modernization and restructuring of the production sector, including agricultural, manufacturing, and service activities;

2. Upgrading of the economic infrastructure (transport infrastructure, energy, telecommunications);

3. Improvement of the general educational level of the population and vocational training to combat unemployment problems; improvement of research and innovation capacity to raise competitiveness; implementation of the information society;

4. Improvement of the environmental infrastructure (waste management, waste water treatment, drinking water supply, etc.);

5. Other additional measures important for some countries, such as the improvement of health infrastructure or safeguard of cultural heritage;

6. Policy measures to reduce regional imbalances.

These kinds of policy measures are considered to raise the competitiveness of regions. They should help regions to become an attractive location for enterprises, which ultimately will contribute to the economic growth and employment of the region (European Commission, 1999b).

Policy strategies of the CSFs 2000–6 of Member States give different weights to the various types of measures. Given the reduced amount of SF available, Ireland concentrates the funds on a few areas of its CSF and a substantial part of it receives no co-financing. The primary focus of the Irish programme is human resources and employment, as well as infrastructure; the productive sector receives practically no more SF. Ireland is gradually shifting its concern to regional inequalities and pursuing a truly endogenous development policy in the Borders and Midlands region. Spain is now pursuing a very balanced development strategy for its Objective 1 regions, placing equal weight on the production sector, infrastructure, and human resources. With CSF II, in contrast, infrastructure and production dominated.

Table 8.3 Policy priorities of objective 1 CSFs 2000–2006

	CSF Greece			CSF Spain			CSF Portugal			CSF Ireland		
	Total costs (€ m)	Co-finance rate	Priority share	Total costs (€ m)	Co-finance rate)	Priority share	Total costs (€ m)	Co-finance rate)	Priority share	Total costs (€ m)	Co-finance rate)	Priority share
Transport infrastructure	12,087	37.2	28.8	15,292	59.2	19.0	3,368	41.5	8.5	6,039	12.1	18.8
Competitive manufacturing & services	6,098	32.4	14.5	20,304	24.2	25.3	9,378	29.1	23.8	2,416	0.0	7.5
Agriculture & fishery	3,773	39.0	9.0	8,774	48.5	10.9	3,721	37.6	9.4	885	12.0	2.8
Human resources	4,480	73.2	10.7	9,797	74.7	12.2	4,487	61.8	11.4	13,041	6.9	40.7
Information society, RTD	2,839	60.0	6.8	8,911	35.0	11.1	1,582	49.3	4.0	3,381	9.3	10.5
Environment	1,811	70.9	4.3	9,495	65.9	11.8	456	72.8	1.2	963	12.8	3.0
Regional development	10,825	65.0	25.8	7,532	53.9	9.4	15,275	58.8	38.8	4,778	15.0	14.9
Technical assistance	85	74.1	0.2	274	74.5	0.3	108	75.0	0.3	10	50.0	0.0
Miscellenous							1,025	69.6	2.6	537	53.1	1.7
Total	42,000	50.8	100.0	80,379	48.7	100.0	39,400	48.7	100	32,050	9.9	100.0

Note: Total costs CSF include SF, cohesion fund and national public and private co-finance.
Source: CSFs 2000–2006.

The Greek CSF focuses on transport infrastructure and regional development as did CSF II. The development strategy pursued with the present southern Italian CSF differs greatly from its previous efforts and contains interesting new aspects. It favours local regional production systems, wishes to safeguard the natural and cultural heritage as a resource for tourism, and puts an unprecedented emphasis on training and education. In contrast, CSF II concentrated on infrastructure and productive investment (Ministero del Tesoro 1999*b*: 165). (EU regional support for East Germany consists of five sub-programmes planned and effected by the Länder themselves. At the time of writing, only one of them had been agreed.)

The productive sector

With respect to development policies for the productive sector, the SF co-finance investment aid schemes for the business sector, a traditional regional policy instrument in all Member States. In practice, the eligibility of investment projects may be very broadly defined in the sense that all projects leading to modernization and enhancing the competitiveness of industry are eligible. Investment aid schemes of the Mezzogiorno, Greece, and Spain commonly work on this basis (Yuill *et al.* 1996; CSFs 2000–2006). Alternatively, investment aid can be provided on a selective basis. This is practised for example by Ireland, which only assists investment in advanced industries. Such a focused investment support policy leads to a more successful development of economic structures and is now also proposed by the European Commission (European Commission 1999*b*).

Since 1994, the EU has wished to provide particular assistance to SMEs, reflecting the arguments of regional scientists (Cappellin 1991; Amin and Tomaney 1995) on the importance of a small-scale local enterprise sector that can assure the settlement and spread of a productive fabric in a region by its linkages with large-scale enterprises.

Traditionally, the investment support financed through the SF is granted by non-repayable capital grants. For the firm, this grant reduces the cost of the investment project (for the establishment of a new site and equipment investment). The size of the grant can be expressed as a percentage of the investment costs. Given the postulate of EU competition policy to limit investment aid to regional problem areas and to differentiate according to the seriousness of the regional problem, the permitted rate of assistance varies across Objective 1 areas (see Table 8.4). One can see that the rate of assistance for enterprise investment is generally quite high in Objective 1 regions. This has distortive effects and has led to a kind of 'investment aid shopping' across Europe by transnational corporations. Consequently, the European Commission now intends to employ alternative means of financial support, 'such as reimbursable advances, risk and venture capital, loan capital and revolving funds, mutual guarantee schemes, etc.' (European Commission 1999*b*).

What kind of experience have these countries had with investment promotion under the CSFs? Ireland achieved an annual expansion of private investment in the boom period 1994–9 of 14 per cent (Government of Ireland 1999: 26). Spain, Portugal, and East Germany did equally well. By contrast in Greece, at the beginning of CSF II, a weak investment climate, an unclear industrial development strategy, and complicated

Table 8.4 Investment aid ceilings[a] in Objective 1 areas/cohesion countries as applicable from January 2000

	Region	Investment aid (% of investment)
Ireland	Border, Midlands and Western	40
	Southern and Eastern	20
	of which Dublin	17.5
Spain	Andalucia, Extremadura, Galicia, and Asturia	50
	Cantabria, Castilla Leon (W), Castilla La Mancha (S), and Murcia	40
	Castilles (rest), and Aragon (S), Valencia,	30–37
	Pais Vasco, Rioja, Navarra, Aragon (N), and Cataluna	10–20
Portugal	Centro, Alentejo (littoral less)	50
	Norte, Algarve (littoral less)	40
	Lisbon	10
Southern Italy	Basilicata and Calabria	50
	Puglia and Campania	35
	Molise, Sicily, and Sardinia	20
Greece	Dytriki Ellada, Ipeiros, Pellop024nnisos, Voreio Aigeio, Anatoliki, and Macedonia	50
	Dytriki Makedonia, Kentriki Ellada, Ionia Nisia, Attika, Sterea Ellada, Notio Aigaio and Crete	40
East Germany	in general, excl. Berlin	35
	Berlin	18

[a]   Regional aid according to Article 87(3)(*a*) and (*c*) of the EC Treaty.
Source: European Commission, Regional State Aid Map 2000.

application procedures for investment aid resulted in a weak performance by industrial modernization measures (European Commission 1996b: 40, Petrakos and Saratsis 2000). Greece then shifted its attention to the assistance of SMEs and learned to provide aid through special agencies. In southern Italy, as a sign of general stagnation, industrial investment dropped significantly in the 1990s, picking up again only by 1997. Nevertheless, investment incentives are important to keep the rate above the northern Italian level. The recovery of investment led to a higher utilization rate of investment incentives and recourse to SF aid schemes (Ministero del Tesoro 1999a: 7; Svimez 1999: 419, 490).

The agricultural sector

With respect to the production sector, many objective 1 regions are still highly oriented towards agriculture or dominated by traditional industries. In terms of agriculture, Greece still has the highest employment share in agriculture of all EU members. In western Greece agricultural employment accounts for 20–30 per cent of employment (see Table 8.2). With all other Objective 1 areas except for East Germany, agricultural employment is less predominant but still fairly important, accounting for 12–18 per cent in Galicia and in the South and Centre of Spain, in Portugal's Alentejo (in Centro even 30 per cent), in the Midlands and Border regions of Ireland, and in southern Italy. All Objective 1 CSFs include measures to modernize agricultural production, to improve the processing and marketing of agricultural products, and to support the development of agricultural regions through related activities, such as tourism.

There is evidence, however, that these measures maintain dependence on agricultural activity. In Greece the CSF II provided assistance for modernization and compensation payments for agricultural small-holders, which were the best used allocations of the whole CSF (European Commission 1996b: 41). As another example, Spain has used a large share of its SF intended for agriculture in CSF II to modernize its fishing fleet (European Commission 1999e), its port facilities and product processing, which has only exacerbated the tensions underlying the European fisheries problem. Spanish SF commitments for modernization measures for agricultural production actually had to be increased, while measures aiming at diversification in rural areas were less in demand (European Commission 1999c). In contrast to these less admirable practices, Ireland has pursued a stronger diversification strategy, e.g. by using CSF III to develop small enterprises in the tourism sector and in aquacultures in its Border and Midlands region.

Specialization

The Objective 1 regions face another structural problem; their industrial sectors are dominated by traditional industries. Specialization is particularly high in Greece, where even the industrial centres (Attiki, Kentriki Makedonia) are highly specialized (the largest industries account for 60–75 per cent of industrial employment; see Table 8.2). Textiles, metal products, and the paper industry dominate. The other, poorer southern Objective 1 regions are also fairly specialized. The Centre and South of Spain, Portugal's Centre and the Alentejo, as well as Calabria show a specialization indicator of 60 (see Table 8.2). Many parts of the southern periphery have a large share of the food-processing industry, e.g. southern Italy, the East of Spain, and Norte and Lisbon in Portugal. The richer Objective 1 areas are less specialized, with a specialization indicator of hardly more than 50

(Table 8.2). Textiles, metal products, and food-processing industries dominate. In the Spanish and southern Italian regions some transport equipment industries can also be found. Consequently, the diversification of industrial production and the creation of advanced industries is a major challenge for these Member States, which they are pursuing under the CSF.

Foreign direct investment

An important vehicle for the development of advanced industries is foreign direct investment (FDI). Multinational enterprises are expected to establish modern plants operated with advanced managerial and organizational practices and to offer high-skilled jobs. Important spill-over effects are expected when multinational-trained workers share the local labour market and when foreign plant sites establish forward and backward linkages with local enterprises, which alone would not be able to operate in global markets (Amin and Tomaney 1995). In reality the actual experience of these expected effects has differed across countries. Objective 1 areas have been attempting to attract foreign companies with generous investment subsidies (see Table 8.4) co-financed under the SF programmes and permitted under EU competition law. The cross-European investment activity created by the Single Market favoured these attempts, but the strategy achieved varying levels of success. Ireland, Spain, and Portugal saw important investment inflows from abroad, reaching 5.4, 1.7, and 1.8 per cent of GDP in the period 1987–96 respectively (European Commission 1999*d*: 221). Equally, East Germany saw a boom in foreign investments. By contrast, the Italian South hardly participated in the investment inflows which entered into Italy; the investment largely went to the northern and central areas to strengthen their integration into the EU economy (only 10–12 per cent of inward FDI during 1985–95 went to the South; Iammarino and Santangelo 2000). Greece was also rather avoided by foreign investors, with inward FDI of only 0.5 per cent of GDP in 1987–96 (European Commission 1999*d*).

The experience of Ireland with FDI, which has been accommodated since the early 1980s by corporate tax rates as low as 10 per cent, is frequently cited by other Objective 1 countries as a strategy to imitate. However, this requires a closer look. Foreign direct investment did indeed play a significant role in the establishment of an advanced industrial sector (chemicals and electrical and electronic equipment) in the Irish economy, which was administered with a selective investment aid policy by the Irish Development Authority (IDA). Equally, in Spain and Portugal FDI led to new establishments in the transport sector as well as in the banking and insurance sectors and thus contributed to modernization. But Ireland's strategy was also criticized. Initially the investment of multinationals led to a dualistic structure in the Irish enterprise sector and the actual income effect of FDI was counteracted by repatriation of the profits of multinationals. At the present stage, however, multinationals have started to show the hoped-for effects. During the 1990s the linkages with the local economy became well established. Multinationals started their own R&D in Ireland and the indigenous sector has expanded into dynamic export branches as well, e.g. in the software industry, and establishing its own R&D activities (with a 1.3 per cent R&D rate, Ireland has reached Western European standards: Barry *et al*. 1999*a*; O'Sullivan 2000). Therefore, Objective 1 regions must be aware that the spill-over effects on the local economy are not certain and in any case are not immediate.

Measures falling in categories 2–4 of those outlined above should provide an improvement in supply factors which should make Objective 1 areas/cohesion countries more attractive for FDI.

Transport infrastructure

A modern transport infrastructure continues to be seen as a highly important factor for development by the European Commission, a view supported by a vast number of empirical growth studies stressing the importance of transport infrastructure (e.g. Aschauer 1989). The EU considers that local development potential increases when Objective 1 areas are linked to a high-capacity transport infrastructure. Preference is given to the construction of Trans European Networks (European Commission 1999*b*), which, however, need to be paired with investment in second-order transport infrastructure (Vickerman *et al.* 1999).

The infrastructure requirements and policy experiences differ between the individual countries. East Germany has a relatively better developed infrastructure than the southern periphery (see Table 8.2). Despite the policy efforts of the past, Spain and southern Italy still have infrastructure gaps: the infrastructure endowment of Italy's South reaches just half of the level in the North (Mazziola 1999).

Spain effected a very active and impressive infrastructure modernization programme with the help of the SF during CSF I and II, for which measures were very effectively managed at the national ministry level. The country tripled its motorway network in Objective 1 regions and modernized one third of its railways with CSF I (European Commission 1996*b*). Economists verified that this increase in public capital had a significant impact on Spanish regional growth (de la Fuente 1996).

The previous Italian CSF focus on transport infrastructure, by contrast, had little success. The output of construction dropped heavily in that period and execution of the infrastructure part of the CSF was one of the least successful. (Ministero del Tesoro 1999*a*: 7; 1999*b*: 168). Cuts in public investment to meet the Maastricht criteria, but above all the uncertainty of public administrative permissions, incompetent project management and interruptions of initiated projects were the causes cited (Svimez 199: 684, 709). The transport infrastructure gap is most significant in Greece and Ireland (see Table 2). Greece attempted in both previous CSFs to improve its infrastructure and started major projects such as the Pathe and Egnatia motorways and the Athens underground. Execution of these projects was much delayed until 1996 due to a poor project management and the unreliability of project contractors. Public procurement legislation was only then introduced (European Commission 1999*c*). The programme results should therefore improve with CSF III. The insufficiently developed transport network is considered a serious bottleneck for Ireland's further development (Fitzgerald *et al.* 1999), although the country advanced in this area and realized an annual increase in public investment of 11 per cent in the last programme period (Government of Ireland 1999: 26).

Education

Since the cohesion countries/Objective 1 areas have a general backlog in educational attainment and problems of skill adaptation in the labour force, education measures and vocational training have been an important policy area of the CSFs since their initiation. Professional training of labour-market entrants and young workers as well as continuous training have been the major policy measures financed by the SF. In addition, the policy measures aim at improving education and training structures as such, e.g. by supporting the training of teachers. Policy measures in the field of human resources lay the foundation for the development of a modern economy.

Ireland had a very sharp policy focus on human resources in its previous CSFs (Barry *et al.* 1999*b*; Tondl 1998). General education levels rose continuously from the beginning of the 1980s (Durkan *et al.* 1999; de la Fuente and Vives 1997) and general education levels have reached Western European standards. The present CSF will address only specific skill shortages in the labour market and long-term unemployment (Government of Ireland 1999). The experience of the other countries was less convincing and execution of the Greek human resources programme in CSF II has been rated as the least satisfactory of all (European Commission 1999*c*).

Living standards

Since the programme period 1994–9, the EU has included policy areas which should raise the social component of cohesion rather than only the economic components. Measures to improve environmental living conditions, to upgrade the national health system, and to prevent the social exclusion of unemployed and disadvantaged persons have been adopted since then. In the field of the environment, one can expect that actual measures, much required in the cohesion countries, will indeed be effected under CSF III, since 50 per cent of the cohesion fund transfers need to be spent on environmental projects. With the socially oriented measures aiming at avoiding discrimination, e.g. against disabled people, EU regional policy has also introduced a new policy focus that has so far been absent in the cohesion countries. Also new with CSF III, the EU regional policy suggests that the Objective 1 areas (southern Italy and Greece are prominent candidates) should make more use of their cultural heritage, and preserve and exploit their cultural sites as a source to develop tourism.

As for the institutional side of the regional policy programmes, the European Commission put forward the desirability of a multi-layer regional policy. Regional and local authorities should be closely involved in the programming and implementation process, together with the national level and the European Commission according to the partnership principle. In reality, however, Objective 1 policies are effected within somewhat different institutional arrangements in different countries.

In general, despite the requirement for regional involvement, Ireland, Portugal and Spain have relied on rather centralized programme planning and implementation structures. Southern Italy, Greece and the new German Länder, in contrast, moved towards a more decentralized system of programme management (see Table 8.5). Experience has shown that more centralized programme management yields a less complex and therefore faster programme implementation in small countries, as is apparent with Ireland and

Table 8.5: Organizational structure of the CSFs in objective 1 areas: Composition of national and regional operational programmes and CSF performance.

	Operational programmes 2000–2006				Operational programmes 1994–1999				
	Total	National	Regional	% regional	Total	National	Regional	% regional	SF spent[a]
Ireland	9	7	2	22	11	11	—	—	77
Spain	22	10	12	54	64	17	47	61	75
Portugal	19	10	9	44	18	10	8	21	72
S. Italy	14	7	7	50	35	23	12	48	55
Greece	24	11	13	33	32	19	13	32	61
East Germany	8	3	5	62	18	2	16	91	68

[a] Percentage of 1998 SF allocation effectively spent by 1999.
Source: Inforegio; European Commission 1997: 193–260; European Commission 1999c.

Portugal. Objective 1 areas with insufficient regional administrative capacities that attempted to practise strong regional devolution (such as southern Italy and Greece) met considerable delays and difficulties in EU regional policy management.

Ireland wished to pursue its development policies and the administration of the SF through the development of competent national institutions. Two such institutions played an important role in this context: the Irish Development Agency (IDA) in the field of aid policies and the Economic and Social Research Institute (ESRI), as a research body proposing and evaluating Ireland's development strategies. The present CSF, as was the case with the previous one, has a slim organizational structure, although Ireland's CSF now has a greater regional component due to the division into an Objective 1 area and a transitory assisted area. The highest managing authorities responsible for the top-level coordination of the programme are the Ministry of Finance and the Ministry of Enterprise, Trade, and Employment. Implementation is effected through ministerial departments and special agencies at the national and county level. There are also two newly established regional assemblies at the NUTS II level which participate in policy formulation. In view of the now more complex implementation structures the Irish authorities have already expressed their intention to look at the possibility of merging the implementation bodies.

The Greek and the southern Italian practices of EU regional policy programme management have met a number of difficulties in the past. These resulted from a high number of operational programmes under the CSF and the delegation of tasks to the regional level at which the administrative qualification required for programme management was poor. In Italy, regional governments were only created in the late 1970s, in Greece only in the late 1980s, in response to the wishes of EU regional policy-makers. The initial limited competence and capacity of Italy's regional authorities were challenged when the Rome government largely abandoned its Mezzogiorno support programmes and wished to delegate responsibilities to the regional level. The major share of the southern Italy CSF became effected by regional operational programmes—much as today, where 50 per cent of the CSF framework support will be placed under regional programmes. However, Italy's regional governments showed particular incompetence in the planning and execution of public investment projects as well as in the operation of aid schemes for the private business sector. A similar weakness appeared within the Greek EU regional policy administration, there also at the national, ministerial level. In general, the particular political style of these two Objective 1 areas, traditionally showing strong clientelism, is largely responsible for the weak performance of the public administration. As a consequence, both countries showed little progress of EU-funded public projects and could not attain a notable rate of new firm formation in the previous programmes. The payment ratio of the Italian CSF was only 55 per cent of allocated SF by the end of 1998, after a major reprogramming in 1997 (see Table 8.5). The Greek payment ratio was slightly higher at 61 per cent, after special agencies for public investment projects were created. With the new CSF, in contrast to a division of responsibilities between central and regional level in the last CSF, the Italian government wished to bundle the whole range of tasks under the responsibility of the regional governments, including programming, the budgetary competence, and project selection. An active top-level coordination will be effected by the Ministry of Finance. The strong devolution of competencies to the regional level appears also in Greece, where regional programmes are intended to be designed and implemented at the regional level. However, a much lower share of development support is located with regional programmes (33 per cent: see Table 8.5).

The CSFs of southern Italy and East Germany are the only ones which are predominantly effected by regional programmes under the authority of regional governments, which is mirrored by the share of SF for regional programmes (see Table 8.5). The high share of regional programmes within the Spanish CSF is somewhat misleading. Spain operates multiple regional operational programmes with large budgets at the level of the *comunidades autonomas*, but those programmes have a very similar policy structure and are administered by the Department for Community Funds and Regional Finance at the Ministry of Finance jointly with the regional governments. Spain still has a rather centralized institutional system to operate the SF programmes.

Another important feature of the current programmes should be noted. In general, the complexity of regional policy, as expressed by the number of programmes, has been reduced (although additional operational programmes may emerge during the programme period). Spain and the Italian South in particular have significantly reduced their number of operational programmes (see Table 8.5). This should have a positive effect particularly for the programme performance of Southern Italy. Greece and Germany also reduced the number of programmes they are to handle. Only Portugal did not reduce the number of its operational programmes.

Given the distinct amount of SF aid to Objective 1 areas, what is the macroeconomic impact of these transfers? Recall that CSF measures split into investment aid, public infrastructure spending, and education measures. Such policies entail demand-side effects (DSE) and supply-side effects (SSE). Investment aid reduces investment costs and thus should drive investment up. Demand for capital goods increases home production and imports (DSE) and leads to enhanced productivity (SSE). Public infrastructure spending equally increases demand for home production and imports (DSE) due to the additional demand for equipment goods and construction. A better infrastructure enhances endogenous growth potential (SSE) and increases the productivity of enterprises. Education measures lead to a better human-capital base, an important factor for endogenous growth (SSE): better-educated labour makes a more efficient use of capital and thus drives productivity up. Consequently, SF aid leads to Keynesian effects and endogenous growth type effects (on such growth models see e.g. Barro and Sala-i-Martin 1995). The first occur immediately; the second work in the longer perspective.

With respect to the main macroeconomic aggregates, one can thus expect SF aid to produce output growth effects, of which a part will be realized only after the CSF horizon. Additional growth will also induce employment growth, although to a lower extent, since a part of growth is due to productivity increases. A higher level of imports may cause the trade balance to deteriorate, in particular with the small countries. Due to the requirement of co-financing, the budget effect of SF transfers may be negative, although the Member State would have had to finance its investment totally on its own without transfers.

Under the postulate of accountability to the European Public, EU regional policy introduced macroeconomic evaluations as a part of CSFs after the first programme generation. The Commission developed the QUEST II macroeconomic model, which considers demand- and supply-side effects. Another macroeconomic model, the HERMIN model, was specifically developed for the cohesion countries under the lead of the ESRI in Dublin and particularly shows the medium and long-term effects (Roeger 1996; European Commission 2000a; ESRI 1997). Other macroeconomic evaluations have been carried out for the individual countries and are included in the CSFs. The results are generally very difficult to use for comparisons between countries since the assumptions of the models differ significantly. Table 8.6 shows the estimated growth effects of the CSFs 2000–2006 according to the QUEST II simulations and the HERMIN simulations.

With respect to the effects suggested by the QUEST II model, the additional GDP effect is much higher in the final CSF year 2006, when supply-side effects have already set in (expected to start in 2002), although the annual rate of SF transfers gradually decreases during the programming period due to phasing out. The growth effect differs considerably between the large recipients of SF—Greece and Portugal on the one hand, and Ireland and Spain on the other hand—which receive a small contribution from the SF in

Table 8.6 Estimated GDP effects of CSFs 2000–2006

	QUEST II		HERMIN	
	% additional GDP[a]		% additional GDP[a]	
	2000 (DSE)	2006 (DSE + SSE)	2000 (DSE)	2006 (DSE + SSE)
Ireland	0.6	0.5	1.1	1.8
Spain	0.5	0.9	1.5	2.2
Portugal	0.8	2.0	6.2	6.0
Greece	1.2	2.4	5.1	6.1
East Germany	—	—	4.4	4.0

[a] Additional GDP with respect to the baseline scenario, i.e. GDP in that year without CSF.
Source: European Commission 2000a: 215–16.

terms of GDP. For Ireland, due to the decline of the SF, the loss of DSE in 2006 hides the slowly growing SSE.

According to the simulations with the HERMIN model, the additional GDP generated by the CSF would be 2–3 times higher than the estimated effect using the QUEST model. The two models are differently specified but probably span the relevant range. Thus the actual GDP effect of the CSF may be assumed to lie somewhere between the two extreme results. The ranking of the countries would, however, be the same according to both models. (For the estimated impact of previous CSFs see e.g. European Commission 1999*d*: 155–7, 229.)

8.5 Problem areas and the outlook for the future of EU regional policy

Despite the persistence of income disparities one must note that the central concern of EU regional policy—the cohesion countries/Objective 1 areas—have visibly accomplished a major step in development. Multiple factors are responsible for that catching-up. Besides integration effects and improved macroeconomic stability, SF transfers also played an important role for development.

It can be foreseen that the present beneficiaries of EU regional policy will partly lose their status when new members enter into the Union. Accession of Eastern European countries will lower the EU average income. Applying the 75 per cent criterion and keeping budgetary resources fixed would automatically mean an enhanced phasing out of present Objective 1 areas after 2006.

It will become a matter of discussion whether EU regional policy in richer member states—the Objective 2 policies—should then be continued in the present EU managed framework. The large share of EU-imposed administrative procedures for a huge number of small EU programmes is highly inefficient (e.g. prolongation of start-up times and meeting costs) and appears redundant in view of the long experience of rich Member States with regional policies. Apparently, the Commission would also run into a capacity problem if it sought to participate in all programming procedures when new members have joined. Therefore, in the rich Member States more autonomy in regional policy formulation and area designation would be appropriate. Accountability for funding can be provided by the already established reporting tools (evaluation and monitoring).

The huge development gap facing the Eastern European candidates for membership will be a major challenge for EU regional policy-makers and the new Member States alike. It will be wise to benefit from the experience with structural funding in the cohesion countries. From their experiences, three major points have to be considered. First, support from EU regional policy has to start initially with a national development strategy and should not get lost within the manifold but minor regional problems (see the arguments of Williamson 1965). Secondly, it must be considered that stable macroeconomic policies, as later also required by the cohesion countries to qualify for EMU, are an essential condition to draw benefits from SF development policies (see Hervé and Holzmann 1998; Burnside and Dollar 1997). Thirdly, new Member States must be requested to develop an appropriate institutional framework which is capable of formulating policy strategies, implementing policies, and administering financial transfers. Otherwise they would risk losing much of the possible SF benefits as well as the willingness of other EU members to pay for interregional redistribution.

The European Union would be wise not to insist on a fully fledged regionalized institutional framework for the operation of EU regional policies. It should favour a flexible approach concerning the institutional framework in Eastern European countries. Programming and implementation of policies should mirror national particularities and requirements. Countries without regional policy competence should not forcefully implement regional programme management. Small countries should rely on national management. Countries in an early stage of development and with less developed administrative structures should favour national structural funds management. On the other hand, Eastern countries should not consider the requirements of partnership and programming as an excessive burden. It can be an excellent practice to identify the requirements of national and regional development, to build mutual trust, and to develop democratic procedures (Hooghe 1998: 469).

Discussion questions

1   Why should the European Union have a regional policy? Are the objectives of equal development among EU regions and solidarity of EU members justifiable?

2   Do you think that EU regional policy applies suitable measures and instruments?

3   What are the causes of the possible failure of EU regional policies?

Further reading

The development of EU regional policy over the past three decades is described at length in Bache (1998). A comprehensive discussion of the European cohesion problem and regional disparities, including also Eastern Europe, can be found in the *Second Report on Economic and Social Cohesion* of the European Commission, January 2001. Braunerhjelm *et al.* (2000), discuss in chapter 2 the possibility of core–periphery patterns of the new economic geography models, i.e. the persistence of regional disparities, in the EU. A review of empirical studies on regional convergence in the EU is given in Tondl (2001), chapter 2. The requirements of Eastern European countries with respect to the adoption of EU regional policy are discussed in Bachtler *et al.* (2000). The Commission's Directorate General for Regional Policy offers a useful website to follow up current developments; see http://inforegio.cec.eu.int/dg16 en.htm.

Notes

1 For the historical development of EU regional policy see e.g. Bache (1998), George (1991), and Allen (1996).

2 Apparently, EU regional policies have been the outcome of high-level bargaining, where lagging countries wish to secure a compensation for the potential negative effect of further economic integration (Allen 1996).

3 See Council regulation no. 1260/1999 laying down general provisions on the structural funds, Council regulation no. 1264/1999 amending regulation no. 1164/1994 establishing a cohesion, and Council regulation no. 1267/1999 establishing an instrument for structural policies for pre-accession.

4 On the revision of the SF in 1993, which brought very modest amendments, see Bachtler and Michie (1994), Tondl (1993).

5 During the programme 1989–93, Ireland received 253 ECU per capita, Portugal 171 ECU, and Greece 150 ECU. Spain with 91 ECU, Southern Italy with 82, and Eastern Germany with 62 ECU received considerably less. During the programme 1994–9, Ireland received 262 ECU p.c., Portugal 235, Greece 225, Spain 188, Southern Italy 117, and Eastern Germany 145 (European Commission 1996*a*; all at current prices).

6 Note that there are two area maps regulating the entitlement for regional aid. First there is the map of regions entitled for SF support under EU regional policy Objectives 1 and 2, which is decided by the Commission-Directorate 'Regional Policy' on proposals of the Member States for an entire programme period. Secondly there is the map of regions entitled to national regional aid under EU competition policy. It is decided by the Commission Directorate for Competition Policy. The current national assisted areas map was decided in 2000 and states the maximum aid rates of national regional aid. The two maps roughly coincide.

7 Due to data availability per capita income is commonly indicated by GDP per inhabitant. This indicator measures economic production in a region but does not include the income that a part of its population may earn in another (neighbouring) region. As a consequence, some Northern metropolitan areas with large surrounding residential areas, e.g. Hamburg and Vienna, have extraordinarily high income levels that are produced by commuters who live in the surrounding areas. GDP per capita also gives a distorted level of income in as far as it does not include social transfers which are particularly important in the poor regions of richer Member States (e.g. the Mezzogiorno and East Germany). To get a clearer idea of differences in living standards, it is common practice to measure GDP in PPS (see Dunford 2000).

8 Note that the income level of Groningen and Grampian is somewhat artificially high since it largely stems from North Sea oil production.

References

Allen, D. (1996), 'Cohesion and Structural adjustment', in H. Wallace and W. Wallace (eds.), *Policy Making in the EU* (Oxford: Oxford University Press).

Amin, A., and Tomaney, J. (1995), 'The Regional Development Potential of Inward Investment in the Less Favoured Regions of the Community', in A. Amin and J. Tomaney (eds.), *Behind the Myth of European Union* (London: Routledge), 201-20.

Armstrong, H. W. (1995), 'An Appraisal of the Evidence from Cross-Sectional Analysis of the Regional Growth Process within the European Union', in H. W. Armstrong and R. W. Vickerman (eds.), *Convergence and Divergence among European Regions* (London: Pion).

Aschauer, D. A. (1989), 'Is Public Expenditure Productive?', *Journal of Monetary Economics*, 23: 177-200.

Bache, I. (1998), *The Politics of European Union Regional Policy* (Sheffield: Sheffield Academic Press).

Bachtler, J. and Michie, R. (1994), 'Strengthening Economic and Social Cohesion? The Revision of the Structural Funds', *Regional Studies*, 28/8: 189-96.

Bachtler, J. *et al.* (eds.) (2000), *Transition, Cohesion and Regional Policy in Central and Eastern Europe* (Aldershot: Ashgate).

Baddeley, M., Martin, R. and Tyler, P. (1998), 'European Regional Unemployment Disparities: Convergence or Persistence?', *European Urban and Regional Studies*, 5/3: 195-215.

Barro, R., and Sala-i-Martin, X. (1995), *Economic Growth* (New York: McGraw Hill).

Barry, F., Bradley, J. and O'Malley, E. (1999*a*), 'Indigenous and Foreign Industry: Characteristics and Performance', in F. Barry (ed.), *Understanding Ireland's Economic Growth* (London: Macmillan), 45-73.

—— —— and Hannan, A. (1999*b*), 'The European Dimension: The Single Market and the Structural Funds', in F. Barry (ed.), *Understanding Ireland's Economic Growth* (London: Macmillan), 99-117.

Bayoumi, T. and Eichengreen, B. (1993), 'Shocking Aspects of European Monetary Integration', in F. Torres and F. Giavazzi (eds.), *Adjustment and Growth in the European Monetary Union* (New York: Cambridge University Press), 193-229.

Begg, I. (1999), 'Previsiones sobre convergencia regional en la Unión Europea', *Papeles de Economia Español*, 80: 100-21.

Blien, U. and Wolf, K. (2000), Regionale Disparitäten auf ostdeutschen Arbeitsmärkten, Informationen zur Raumentwicklung.

Bover, O., García-Perea, P. and Portugal, P. (2000), 'Iberian Labour Markets', *Economic Policy*, 30 (Oct.) 381-428.

Braunerhjelm, P., Faini, R., Norman, V., Ruane, F. and Seabright, P. (2000), 'Integration and the Regions of Europe', *Monitoring European Integration*, 10 (London: CEPR).

Burnside, C. and Dollar, D. (1997), 'Aid, Policies and Growth', *World Bank Discussion Papers*, no. 1777 (Washington, DC: World Bank).

Cappellin, R. (1991), 'Theories of Local Endogenous Development and International Co-operation', in M. Tykkyläinen (ed.), *Development Issues and Strategies in the New Europe* (Aldershot: Avebury), 1–19.

Community Support Framework Programmes (CSFs) (2000–6) for Ireland, Spain, Portugal, Greece, East Germany, and Southern Italy.

de la Fuente, A. (1996), 'Inversión pública y redistribución regional: el caso de España en la decada de los ochenta', *Papeles de Economía Española*, 67: 238–56.

—— and Vives, X. (1997), *The Sources of Irish growth*, CEPR discussion paper no. 1756 (Dec.) (London: CEPR).

Dunford, M. (2000), 'Regional Disparities in the EU through the Lens of Official Statistics', in G. Petrakos, G. Maier, and G. Gorzelak (eds.), *Integration and Transition in Europe* (London: Routledge), 60–99.

Durkan, J., Fitzgerald, D., and Harmon, C. (1999), 'Education and Growth in the Irish Economy', in F. Barry (ed.), *Understanding Ireland's Economic Growth* (London: Macmillan), 119–35.

ESRI (1997), *The Single Market Review. Aggregate and Regional Impacts. The Cases of Greece, Spain, Ireland and Portugal*, in European Commission (eds.), *The Single Market Review*, subseries VI, vol. 2 (Brussels: Office for Official Publications).

European Commission (1994), *Fifth Annual Report on the Implementation of the Reform of the Structural Funds 1993* (Brussels: Office for Official Publications).

—— (1996a), *First Cohesion Report* (Brussels: Office for Official Publications).

—— (1996b), *The Impact of Structural Policies on Economic and Social Cohesion in the Union 1989–99* (Brussels: Office for Official Publications).

—— (1997), *Sixth Annual Report on the Structural Funds 1996* (Brussels: Office for Official Publications).

—— (1999a), *Structural Policy Measures 2000–2006: Comments and Regulations* (Brussels: Office for Official Publications).

—— (1999b), *The Structural Funds and their Co-ordination with the Cohesion Fund; Guidelines for Programmes in the Period 2000–2006* (Brussels: Office for Official Publications).

—— (1999c), *10th Annual Report on the Structural Funds 1998* (Brussels: Office for Official Publications).

—— (1999d), *6th Periodic Report on the Socio-economic Situation of the Regions of the European Union* (Brussels: Office for Official Publications).

—— (1999e), *Mid-term Review of Structural Interventions Objectives 1 and 6* (Brussels: European Commission).

—— (2000a), 'The EU Economy: 2000 Review', *European Economy*, 71 (Brussels: Office for Official Publications).

—— (2000b), 'The Impact of Economic and Monetary Union on Cohesion', *Regional Studies*, 35 (Brussels: Office for Official Publications).

Fagerberg, J., Verspagen, B., and Caniels, M. (1997) 'Technology, Growth and Unemployment across European Regions', *Regional Studies*, 31/5: 457–66.

Fitzgerald, J., Kearney, I., Morgenroth, E. and Smyth, D. (1999), *National Investment Priorities for the Period 2000–2006* (Dublin: ESRI).

George, S. (1991), *Politics and Policy in the European Community* (Oxford: Oxford University Press).

Government of Ireland (1999), *National Development Plan 2000–2006* (Dublin: The Stationary Office).

Helliwell, J., and Putnam, R. (1995), 'Economic growth and social capital in Italy', *Eastern Economic Journal*, 21/3: 295–307.

Hervé, Y. and Holzmann, R. (1998), *Fiscal Transfers and Economic Convergence in the EU* (Baden-Baden: Nomos).

Hooghe, L. (1998), 'EU Cohesion Policy and Competing Models of European Capitalism', *Journal of Common Market Studies*, 36/4: 457–77.

Iammarino, S. and Santangelo, G. (2000), 'Foreign Direct Investment and Regional Attractiveness in the EU Integration Process', *European Urban and Regional Studies*, 7/1: 5–18.

Inforegio (various dates), newsletter of the European Commission, Directorate General for Regional Policy.

Marelli, E. (2000), 'Convergence and Asymmetries in the Dynamics of Employment: The Case of the European Regions', *Jahrbuch für Regionalwissenschaft*, 20/2: 173–200.

Mazziotta, C. (1999), 'Convergencia regional y dotación de capital público: El caso italiano', *Papeles de Economía Española*, 80: 136–48.

Ministero del Tesoro (1999a), *Il Mezzogiorno: Tendenze e Politica Economica* (Rome: Ministero del Tesoro).

—— (1999b), *Valutazione ex-ante del programma sviluppo del Mezzogiorno* (Rome, Ministero del Tesoro).

Molle, W. (1997), *The Economics of European Integration* (Aldershot: Ashgate).

O'Leary, E. (1999), 'Regional Income Estimates for Ireland, 1995', *Regional Studies*, 33/9: 805–14.

O'Sullivan, M. (2000), 'The Sustainability of Industrial Development in Ireland', *Regional Studies*, 34/3: 277–90.

Perroux, F. (1955), 'Note sur la notion de pôle de croissance', *Economique appliquée*, 1–2: 307–20.

Petrakos, G. and Saratsis, Y. (2000), 'Regional Inequalities in Greece', *Papers in Regional Science*, 79/1: 57–74.

Roeger, W. (1996), 'Macroeconomic Evaluation of the Effects of the Community Structural Funds with QUEST II', paper presented at the European Conference on Evaluation Methods for Structural Funds Intervention, Berlin, Dec.

Solow, R. (1956), 'A Contribution to the Theory of Economic Growth', *Quarterly Journal of Economics*, 70/1: 65–94.

Svimez (1999), *Rapporto 1999 sull' Economica del Mezzogiorno* (Bologna: Il Mulino).

Tondl, G. (1993), 'The Revision of the Structural Funds under the Principle of Cohesion of Maastricht', *Wirtschaftspolitische Blätter*, 5: 534–46.

Tondl, G. (1998), 'EU Regional Policy in the Southern Periphery: Lessons for the Future', *South European Society and Politics*, 3/1: 93–129.

—— (1999), 'The Changing Pattern of Regional Income Convergence in Europe', *Jahrbuch für Regionalwissenschaft*, 19/1: 1–33.

—— (2001), *Convergence after Divergence? Regional Growth in Europe* (Wien: Springer) (forthcoming).

Vickerman, R., Spiekermann, K., and Wegener, M. (1999), 'Accessibility and Regional Development', *Regional Studies*, 33/1: 1–15.

Wallace, H. and Wallace, W. (1996), *Policy-Making in the European Communities* (London: Wiley).

Yuill, D., Bachtler, J., and Wishlade, F. (1996), *European Regional Incentives, 1996–97* (London: Bowker Saur).

Chapter 9
Environmental Policy

David Pearce

9.1 Introduction

Action on preventing environmental degradation in the European Union is a relatively recent phenomenon. The original Treaties of Rome (1957) made no mention of the environment. This was not an issue of neglect. Rather it reflected the fact that, at that time, environmental awareness was generally low everywhere in the world. There had always been a conservation movement dedicated to protecting wilderness areas, but that movement did not become an environmental movement until the 1960s. Publications such as Rachel Carson's *Silent Spring* (1962), while much criticized, successfully raised the alarm over the impacts of human activity on the very life-forms and resources upon which humans depended. The early 1970s saw a number of iconoclastic publications forewarning of dire consequences if humans continued to behave as they did. Notable among these was the Club of Rome's *Limits to Growth* (1972), a flawed but extremely influential work. 'LTG', as it came to be known, drew attention to the finitude of the world's resources and to the limited capacity of the Earth to assimilate all the wastes being generated by economic activity. The central message was that there are 'bio-physical' limits to both population growth and to economic activity. Growth, as we knew it, had to end.

It is no accident, then, that the European Union's first foray into environmental policy also occurred in the early 1970s. The first Environmental Action Programme (EAP) was set out in 1973, following a 1972 Heads of State declaration that environmental issues should now be on the policy agenda for the Community. Subsequent Action Plans followed (see Box 9.1), each one tending to follow some basic themes. The more important of these may be summarized as follows:

- Preventive action is better than cure;
- Environmental impacts should be taken into account very early on in decisions;
- The polluter should pay;
- Actions in one Member State should not affect the environment in another Member State;

- The Community should act as one in international negotiations;
- Policy should be enacted at the appropriate level: some is best suited to action at the Community level, some at national level (the 'subsidiarity' principle);
- There should be co-ordination of national policies in the interests of avoiding competitive distortions.

The formal legal recognition of the importance of environmental policy did not come until 1987, however, when the Single European Act (SEA) included a new Title termed 'Environment'. Article 130R set out the Union's goals as:

(i)   to preserve, protect and improve the quality of the environment

(ii) to contribute towards protecting human health

(iii) to ensure a prudent and rational utilisation of natural resources.

These seemingly vague statements of principle effectively elevated environmental policy to a high level of importance, since it is hard to imagine a much wider agenda than that envisaged by the goals. For example, all economic activity, whatever it is, uses up natural resources, and all economic activity generates waste which is disposed of to various environments. Indeed, the first law of thermodynamics tells us that whatever resources we extract from the earth must reappear as waste, most of it fairly soon after it is extracted. If the waste exceeds the capacity of natural ecological systems to process that waste and render it relatively harmless, then there will be 'externalities'. An externality is a cost borne by someone who is not a party to the initial act that creates the externality, and who receives no compensation from the agent generating the problem. Thus, exhaust fumes from vehicles contain 'cocktails' of pollutants that reside in the air and which exacerbate human health problems. Some make respiratory illnesses worse, others are carcinogenic and can therefore kill. The person suffering the effect is not compensated by the vehicle driver and hence suffers an externality. Once we recognize the pervasiveness of waste and resource use in all economies, the EU's environmental goals are seen to imply the potential for extensive legislative action. And so it has proved, although simply enacting legislation at the EU-wide level is not enough. Conversion of central policy into national policies is required, and then those policies have to be implemented.

The Treaty of European Union (1992) (the Maastricht Treaty) further elaborated the role of environmental goals in EU policy. First, it revisited the terminology of the Treaty of Rome and spoke of the goal of 'sustainable growth respecting the environment' rather than the Treaty of Rome's 'continuous and balanced expansion', on the face of it 'greening' the whole Treaty. Secondly, the new Treaty spoke of the need to integrate environmental issues into all policies, whether environmental or not. As worded, policy-makers were compelled to adopt this approach, whereas before it was simply declared to be a component of good policy. This second provision is an explicit recognition of the pervasiveness of environmental impacts from all economic activity.

The Maastricht Treaty also introduced a further principle to guide environmental policy. This was the 'precautionary principle' (the PP). The PP effectively says that lack of scientific evidence linking cause and effect shall not be deemed sufficient reason to take no action when there are significant risks. In other words, however unsure we are of the

Box 9.1 **Environmental action plans**

1st EAP 1973–1976

Defines basic principles of environmental policy and sets out general goals as:

- Prevention better than cure
- Environmental impacts should be taken into account very early on in decisions
- The polluter pays principle
- Actions in one Member State should not affect the environment in another Member State
- Subsidiarity
- Co-ordination of national policies

2nd EAP 1977–81

- Repeats earlier goals
- Focus on preventive action
- Priority to water and air pollution and noise nuisance
- Environmental impact assessment
- First discussion of eco-labels
- Protection of nature and biodiversity

3rd EAP 1982–87

- Make most economic use of natural resources
- Harmonize national policies
- Polluter pays principle again
- Reduce pollution at source
- Subsidiarity principle restated

4th EAP 1987–92

- Environment and economic development to be made compatible
- Identify environmental problems from Single Market
- Environmental protection can create jobs
- Pollution issues require a multi-media approach

5th EAP 1992- Towards sustainability

- Sets sustainable development as the goal
- Targets climate change, acid rain and air pollution, urban quality of life, coastal resources, waste, protection of biodiversity, and management of natural resources
- Emphasizes the role of market-based instruments

6th EAP?

- Will probably highlight climate change, sustainability, and the implications of Enlargement of the Union with the Accession countries.

relationship between cause and effect, it is best to be safe and curtail the suspect activity. A final issue of importance is that the Treaty extended the EU's role into international and global environmental policy. Article 130R was amended to include 'promoting measures at international level to deal with regional or world-wide environmental problems'. This extension of the sphere of influence reflected growing evidence that some environmental problems could be tackled only at the global level (stratospheric ozone depletion, for example), that Europeans were affected by environmental problems well beyond their geographical boundaries (e.g. tropical deforestation), and that the well-being of Europeans was affected by environmental problems caused outside the EU, and vice versa (transboundary acid rain for example).

Finally, the Amsterdam Treaty of 1997 introduced the notion of the achievement of 'sustainable development' as one of the EU's tasks set out in Article 2. It had become clear that 'sustainable growth respecting the environment' had not raised the profile of the environment high enough, nor was it very clear what it meant. Sustainable development, which was however also not defined, took the place of sustainable growth. It was also clear that the previous attempts to get environment integrated into all policy actions had failed. The Amsterdam Treaty repeats the need for this integration to take place and declares that it is one of the means of securing sustainable development.

In what follows we set out the basic principles of a rational environmental policy and look at the extent to which the EU has adopted those policy components, especially cost–benefit analysis and market-based instruments. Because the 'precautionary principle' has entered into EU environmental policy it is discussed separately. Finally, the issue of 'sustainable development' is evaluated because, since the Amsterdam Treaty, it has become a major driving force of EU policy goals.

9.2 The principles of environmental policy

This section outlines the basic elements in the economic approach to environmental quality. In doing so, the conclusion must not be drawn that the economic approach defines the way in which environmental policy is actually set in the EU. Some economic principles have been followed, but many have not. In the early years especially, few Directives were subject to any form of appraisal of gains and losses. Indeed, it was often not known what the Directives would cost Member States in terms of the resources needed to implement them. While appraisals are far more common today, it is unclear whether they have much importance for the final design of policy. Environmental policy within the Commission is still promulgated on the basis of varied and often inconsistent principles and some legislation appears to have no particular rationale. To some extent this is as would be expected: the Commission is a bureaucracy and bureaucracies have many goals of their own. Additionally, EU-wide policy has to be a compromise between the interests of different countries at different stages of economic development.

To construct the economic basis for policy, consider Figure 9.1. There are two horizontal axes. The first is Q, the level of economic activity, say the output of a polluter. With

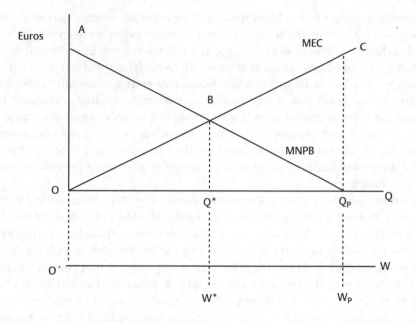

Fig. 9.1 The optimal level of pollution

each level of Q is associated a certain level of waste or pollution, W. The diagram implies that the bigger the output of the polluter the more waste there will be. Obviously, one of the aims of environmental policy is to try to increase economic activity whilst not damaging the environment. The ways in which this can be done are considered later, but if they are successful the effects of such policies would be to 'decouple' Q and W, i.e. there would no longer be a simple relationship between them. Nonetheless, making the assumption that the two are linked helps us understand the economic approach.

The vertical axis is measured in money units, Euros. Two lines are shown. The first slopes down from left to right. It is the marginal net private benefit (MNPB) line. It is easiest to think of it as the polluter's profit on the good he sells. But it is expressed in marginal terms, where marginal simply means 'extra'. So, as the firm's output expands, the extra profit on an extra unit of output declines. It does so until MNPB = 0 at Q_p. Total profit is the area under the MNPB curve, so at Q_p the firm maximizes profits. If this is the firm's aim, then Q_p is the profit-maximizing output and W_p is the level of waste the firm will generate.

The waste causes problems for third parties, e.g. downstream river users if the firm pollutes water upstream, or those suffering from respiratory illnesses if the firm emits air pollution. The loss of human well-being arising from these effects is known as an externality. Externalities can be positive or negative, but the focus is usually on the negative ones, i.e. on harmful effects. The marginal external cost curve (MEC) shows this damage to third parties, again in marginal terms. Here MEC is shown to be upward sloping because we assume that each additional unit of pollution causes more additional damage. In practice, the MEC line can take on many different shapes. Note that MEC is measured in monetary terms. Many methodologies exist for 'valuing the environment' in this way. An example might be the difference in house prices between houses in a quiet neighbourhood and houses in a noisy one. It is well known that amenity and disamenity affects the price of houses—think of houses with river views, for example, or houses next to factories. The extent to which house prices vary with a disamenity provides a first measure of the money value of that disamenity, a money value that is 'revealed' through prices in the housing market. This is an example of a 'revealed preference' approach to valuing pollution and disamenity. Another approach is perhaps more controversial but very useful. This involves asking people what they are willing to pay to avoid pollution, using a questionnaire. This would be an example of a 'stated preference' approach to money valuation.

The issue now is, how much pollution should we allow? If the firm was to decide and if it did not care much about the effects of its activities on others, the answer would be Q_p of output and W_p of waste. But it is easy to see that this is not optimal from society's point of view. The net well-being of the firm is given by the level of profits, so if the firm maximizes profits its total profits will be OAQ_p. But if it operates at that point it will impose a total external cost on the rest of society of OCQ_p. Subtracting the external cost from the profit gives us a net gain of OAB minus BCQ_p. It is easy to see that this could be a very small net gain or even a loss for society as a whole. Clearly, firms should not be allowed to maximize profits if they are polluters.

To find the optimum, look for the level of output where the net gains to society as a whole will be as large as possible. That turns out to be output level Q^* and waste level W^*. At that output, triangle OAB—the net social gain—is as large as it can be. It is easy to prove this by experimenting with different output levels and seeing if they generate bigger or smaller net social gains: in all cases the gains will be smaller than at Q^*.

From this analysis some very important conclusions emerge. First, the optimal level of pollution is not zero. It is a positive amount, W^*. This result needs to be compared to more popular, but erroneous concepts of environmental goals, such as 'zero pollution', 'zero risk', and 'waste minimization'. Figure 9.1 shows that these concepts are consistent with only one answer—zero output. But that would mean forgoing the net benefits OAB. Secondly, some means are required to force the polluter back to Q^* from Q_p, as he will not do this of his own free will. Hence the existence of externalities justifies policy intervention.

Thirdly, while the forms of policy intervention are discussed below, it is possible to see that polluter and sufferer could bargain with each other to reduce pollution to the optimal level. For example, suppose the property rights are vested in the polluter. Basically this means that the polluter has a right to pollute. The starting point will be Q_p. But at Q_p the sufferers experience a large loss compared to the polluter's small marginal profit. Hence it will pay the sufferers to 'bribe' the polluter not to pollute. The polluter will accept any sum bigger than MNPB at that point, and the sufferers will be better off if they pay him any sum less than the MEC at that point. Moving leftwards from Q_p it is easily seen that this process of bargaining would continue until Q^*,W^* is reached. Any further moves left would result in sufferers losing more in bribes than they would gain in reduced damage. Hence bargaining could avoid the need for government intervention.

Fourthly, an entirely analogous reasoning to the bribe case would show that imposing a requirement on polluters to pay compensation to the sufferers will also achieve the optimal result. This time the sufferer has the property right so we begin at the origin, O. If the firm has to pay compensation it will do so as long as its profits minus the compensation paid are still positive. Moving to the right from O, it can be seen that this will be the case until Q^*. After Q^* the firm would be paying out compensation sums larger than the profits it makes. It would therefore not go beyond Q^*.

Fifthly, to secure Q^* the government might simply order the firm to operate at Q^*. These kinds of output controls are very rare. Instead governments are far more likely to tell firms they cannot emit more than a certain amount of pollution or that they must use a particular type of clean technology. Setting emission or ambient standards and setting technology requirements is known as 'command and control'. The phrase is not a precise one and it is usually best to think of it as meaning that the government or regulator sets the goal and sets the means of achieving the goal. A technology-based standard has these characteristics because whatever pollution is still associated with the clean technology remains the goal, and firms are told what technology to use. Ambient standards are not strictly command and control because they set the goal but may well leave the firm free to decide how to meet the goal. In fact, in the EU, as in all other countries with pollution control policies, environmental policy tends to take these forms of regulation.

The bargaining solution is not wholly academic. People do bargain over pollution. Firms may pay compensation not because they are required to do so by law, but because they fear the pressure that affected parties might have on their public image. Sufferers may also pay polluters if the polluter is relatively poor. For example, some Eastern European countries pollute Scandinavia with acid rain. But rather than the Scandinavian countries forcing Eastern Europe to pay under the polluter pays principle (PPP), the sufferers may provide financial and technical help to upgrade sources of pollution in the emitting countries. This is an example of the 'victim pays principle'. This principle does not figure in EU legislation or goals. Rather, the EU is clear that sufferers have the property rights and firms must abide by the PPP. Nonetheless, it can be seen that bargaining has some potential, although the contexts in which it can be used are comparatively few (imagine what happens when there are many sufferers and when it is hard to identify exactly who is polluting and by how much).

But there are other ways of achieving Q^*, W^*. Figure 9.2 reproduces Figure 9.1 but adds a little further analysis. For convenience, the waste axis is removed. A new line through A and Q^* is drawn. The vertical distance between it and the MNPB line is a mirror image of the MEC line. The line reflects the level of tax that could be imposed on the polluter in order to 'internalize' the externality. Internalization means making the externality part of the internal costs faced by the firm. If it knows that it has to pay the tax it will look seriously at ways to reduce pollution. The tax is set equal to the MEC so at zero output the firm pays zero tax, but at Q_p the firm would pay a tax equal to Q_pC. The new line through A and Q^* is MNPB minus the tax, and this effectively becomes the firm's new profit line, i.e. profit after the environmental tax. If the firm is now left to maximize after-tax profits, it will automatically operate at Q^*, generating the optimal amount of waste, W^*. At this optimum the tax is seen to be equal to Q^*B, i.e. the marginal externality at the optimum. Such a tax is known as a 'Pigouvian' tax after Arthur Pigou, a Cambridge professor who first developed the approach in the early part of the twentieth century.

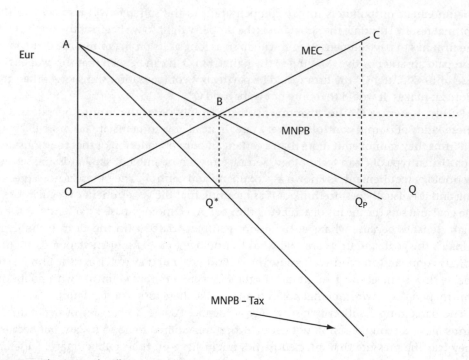

Fig. 9.2 The optimal pollution tax

A Pigouvian tax is an example of a market based instrument (MBIs). It contrasts with command and control in that the standard is set by comparing the costs and benefits of different standards, and operating with a financial inducement or penalty. Again, it is not easy to distinguish command and control from MBIs because command-and-control measures also impose a financial penalty, e.g. the cost of clean technology. Nonetheless, the literature usually reserves the notion of MBIs for environmental taxes and charges and a few other policy instruments.

There are very few examples of Pigouvian taxes, but many examples of environmental taxes. Recall that a Pigouvian tax has to be set equal to the MEC at the optimum. The only country in the EU to undertake studies to measure MEC as a basis for taxation is the UK. Two taxes are based on measurement of the externality: the landfill tax and the aggregates tax. The landfill tax is a tax on waste going to landfill sites. The tax is designed to divert waste from landfill sites into environmentally better outlets such as recycling and incineration. In its original form it was set equal to the externality costs of an average tonne of waste, but it has now risen above this due to the need to secure the landfill targets under the EU's waste strategy. The aggregates tax is a tax on materials extracted, such as gravel and sand, and is based on a stated preference study of what people were willing to pay to avoid the nuisance and disamenity from aggregate extraction sites.

The remaining environmental taxes in the EU tend to be more ad hoc in nature. Sometimes they are set in order to achieve a particular environmental target which may or may not have been informed by cost–benefit comparisons. Sometimes the taxes are the outcomes of compromises between polluters and the Commission, with the Commission usually preferring higher taxes and polluters seeking to reduce them. Such taxes are still potentially desirable, however, because they can be shown to minimize the cost of complying with regulations. Put another way, it generally costs polluters less to comply with a regulation backed by an environmental tax than it costs them to comply with command-and-control style regulations. Figure 9.3 explains why.

In Figure 9.3 the horizontal axis now measures the amount of pollution reduction. Two lines are shown: MAC1 is the marginal abatement cost curve of firm 1 and MAC2 is the abatement cost curve of firm 2. The meaning of these lines is that they show the extra cost of abating one extra unit of pollution. Note that the curves differ from each other, as one would expect. There is no reason to suppose that all firms would have identical cost curves. Let FG = GH by construction. Suppose each firm is subject to a command-and-control regulation which says each firm must secure OG pollution reduction. The total cost to firm 1 of achieving this standard would be OBG. The total cost to firm 2 would be ODG. Now suppose a tax is imposed to achieve the same level of pollution reduction, i.e. 2OG. The relevant tax is shown as t and t is set so that OF + OH = 2OG. Firm 1 will abate up to the point where t = MAC1 at point A. Beyond this it is cheaper to pay the tax. Firm 2 will likewise abate up to point E, beyond which it is cheaper to pay the tax. Note that the firm with the highest costs of abatement (firm 1) for any given level of abatement does the least amount of pollution reduction. The total cost of the tax in terms of compliance costs is seen to be OAF + OEH.

The cost of the regulatory stance is OBG + ODG and the cost of the tax is OAF + OEH. Subtracting the tax cost from the regulation cost gives a net difference of ABGF – GDEH. But, by construction, ABGF > GDEH, so the regulation costs more than the tax approach. This is the proof that taxes are least-cost solutions, even when they are not Pigouvian taxes.

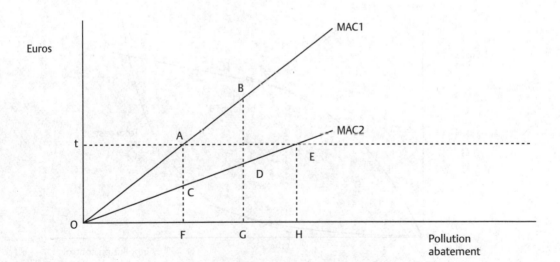

Fig. 9.3 Taxes as least-cost solutions

CBA
max ≠
between cost
& benefit
(MB=MC)

The final building-block of economic principles is the notion of cost–benefit analysis. Figures 9.1 and 9.2 actually include a cost–benefit analysis: the costs of reducing pollution show up as forgone private profits, and the benefits show up as reduced external costs. In Figure 9.3 there is again a comparison of costs and benefits, but in this case the costs and benefits of a tax versus a command-and-control approach. Cost–benefit analysis (CBA) is a formal procedure in which for any policy (or investment) the costs are compared with the benefits. Only if benefits exceed costs is the policy worthwhile in principle. If there are several ways of achieving the same policy goal, then the one with the largest net benefits should be chosen. Benefits are always defined as gains in human well-being. A gain in well-being is in turn defined in terms of individual preferences: if someone prefers A to B, their well-being from A is said to be higher than their well-being at B ('utility' and 'welfare' are often used interchangeably with human well-being). Preferences in turn tend to be revealed in the market-place. If someone is willing to pay more than the price of a good, then they must be experiencing a net gain in well-being. The problem with environmental goods and services is that they often have no market. This is why environmental economists seek to find out what individuals would be willing to pay for those goods and services if there were a market—so-called 'non-market valuation'. The house price and questionnaire examples given earlier are examples of non-market valuation.

The European Commission does carry out cost–benefit studies, but they have been a comparatively recent innovation. Section 9.5 looks at some of the experience; Figure 9.4 illustrates the basic idea of CBA. The horizontal axis in Figure 9.4 is shown as air pollution control as an example. There may be many different types of benefits: improvements to human health, reduced crop damage, reduced erosion of buildings and materials, reduced ecosystem damage. The TC curve shows the total costs of enacting the policy and these costs should include any losses in well-being that might arise. The TB curve shows

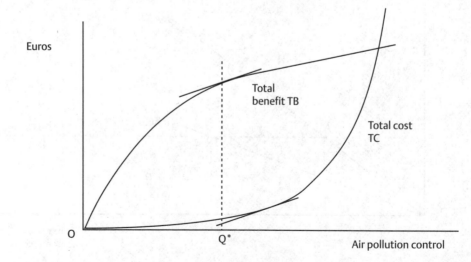

Fig. 9.4 Benefits and costs

the total benefits. The idea of an optimal policy is to secure the point where net benefits are greatest. This is at Q*. To find this point, construct gradients to the two curves and where they are equal is the optimum. These gradients are in fact the equivalent of marginal benefits (MB) and marginal costs (MC), so the requirement for an optimum is that MB = MC. Armed with this theoretical framework it is now possible to look at practical experience in the EU.

9.3 Cost–benefit analysis in the EU

Article 130R(3) of the Maastricht Treaty requires action to take into account four factors:

scientific data;
conditions in the various regions of the EC;
the potential benefits and costs of action or lack of action;
the economic and social development of the EC and the balanced development of its regions (emphasis added).

This article makes it clear that, whatever interpretation is placed on the measurement of benefits and cost, some comparison of them is required. This would appear to have been the original intention of the Commission, but the Intergovernmental Conference of 1987 considered that the phrase was too narrow in scope when translated into other languages. Thus, the phrase 'benefits and costs' remains in the English version but is, according to some commentators, translated as 'advantages and charges' in other linguistic versions. The term 'charges' is supposed to be wider in scope and encompassing 'in particular social costs'. By all accounts, then, the reference to benefit and cost appraisal imposes on the Commission an obligation to: 'weigh up the advantages and disadvantages of Community rules before drafting and adopting measures. This appraisal must include, *inter alia*, economic considerations' (Krämer 1995: 68).

Whilst accepting that the phrase 'benefits and costs' need not imply a full, monetized cost–benefit analysis, some form of risk assessment is clearly mandated by this provision. The 1992 Fifth Environmental Action Plan, *Towards Sustainability* is far more explicit: 'Valuation, pricing and accounting mechanisms have a pivotal role to play in the achievement of sustainable development. Economic valuations can help economic agents to take environmental impacts into account', while measures needed include the 'development of meaningful cost/benefit analysis methodologies and guidelines in respect of policy measures and actions which impinge on the environment and the natural resource stock' (European Commission 1992). The issue in question, then, is how the Commission has taken this requirement into account in formulating its own Directives.

Up to about 1990, EU environmental policy was, by and large, effected with little formal evaluation of policy taking place. An illustrative example is the Bathing Waters Directive. The Bathing Waters Directive dates from 1976 and hence predates the benefit–cost requirement in the Single European Act and Maastricht Treaty. This Directive has been controversial and attracted very low levels of compliance until the mid-1980s, when the Commission pursued Article 169 on infringements of Community law. Actions before the European Court of Justice for non-compliance continue to this day. It is known that the original 1976 Directive was drafted without the benefit of any form of risk assessment. Nor did the Commission adopt any risk-assessment procedure in evaluating progress under the 'old' directive, nor, more significantly, did it use risk-assessment procedures in the 1994 amendment to the Directive (6177/94). Yet the 1994 amendments should have been in compliance with the revised Article 130 of the Treaty. The aim of the 1994 proposals was to simplify and modernize the Directive. The Commission appears to have been aware of the potential criticism that no cost–benefit assessment had been undertaken, arguing that the revised Directive would 'on balance' reduce the financial burden on Member States since compliance would be less expensive, clean bathing waters would have financial benefits in the form of tourism, and would give rise to public health benefits. But no form of quantitative assessment of these impacts was available.

The most exhaustive inquiry into the Directive is that of the UK House of Lords (House of Lords 1994, 1995). Their analysis comes close to a benefit–cost assessment. They were themselves scathing in their criticism of the Commission for not pursuing some benefit–cost assessment: 'It is unacceptable that policy formulation has reached the stage of formal proposal from the Commission for revision of the bathing waters directive without the attachment of a menu of individually costed measures. The Committee deplores that a soundly based cost-benefit analysis has not yet been produced' (House of Lords 1995: para. 25). They added that: 'it is hard to see how the Commission could have thought that the new standard would not entail costly capital expenditure' (House of Lords: 1995, para. 15). The House of Lords' expert assessment of the proposed revised Directive was that there might be small gains in terms of reduced gastro-intestinal symptoms and eye, throat, and ear infections. Their view was that the benefits of the enterovirus standard, the most costly part of the revisions, were zero.

Table 9.1 gives some indication of the execution of formal appraisals by year, where formal appraisal is taken to mean some form of cost–benefit analysis even if all costs and benefits were not monetized. For completeness, however, studies of costs alone are included as shown. Impact studies, i.e. those dealing with the physical impacts of pollutants, are excluded. Needless to say, they are nonetheless a critical element in any formal appraisal.

Table 9.1 suggests some important results. First, some sort of formal appraisal was undertaken on water pollution and on the impacts of the Single Market before 1990. The number of studies indicated is deceptive, however, since they are often studies repeated for separate countries, or, in the case of water pollution, for different substances. Nonetheless, the fact that impacts were measured for individual Member States is an indicator of the importance of the issue. The multiplicity of studies on water tend to reflect the significant number of key pollutants involved in water pollution. Second, the other major targeted area for simulations of costs and effectiveness was the carbon-energy tax. In turn, this proposed Directive attracted probably the single largest opposing lobby of any Commission proposal, so that the studies are a natural outcome, anticipated or ex post, of that process.

It is clear that formal policy appraisal has emerged only recently in the context of European Union environmental policy. Given the extent of legislation over the past few *risk assessment, cost-effectiveness analysis, & CBA are routine in EU policy*

Table 9.1 Formal appraisals of environmental issues or directives in the European Union

Issue	Years	Number of studies
Biodiversity	1987–97	None
Common Agricultural Policy	1996–7	2
Internal Market	1988–9	15
	1992	1
Benefits assessment (general)	1989–90	2
Economic instruments	1988	1
	1990, 1992–3	4
Carbon-energy tax	1992–5	9
Air pollution	1987	2
	1991	1
	1994–5	3
	1996–7	2
Fifth EAP	1994	3
Costs of Control	1993	1
EIA	1995	1
Noise	1996	1
Water pollution	1988	1
	1989	9
	1992–6	17
Solid waste	1990	1
	1992	2
	1994–6	8
Priority setting	1996	1
	1999	1

Source: Author's research

decades, this neglect must have imposed significant economic costs on Member States, Directives having been issued without due regard to the costs to Member States of adopting them. Exactly what those costs are cannot be determined without detailed retrospective analysis, and even this appears to be extremely difficult given the non-availability of data, itself the result of the lack of appraisal. Since the early 1990s, the European Commission has changed its procedures to reflect the requirements of the Single European Act. Risk assessment, cost-effectiveness analysis, and cost–benefit analysis are now fairly routine. Exactly what role they play in shaping policy is open to question. There are some hints that findings that run counter to political wisdom may not survive the decision-making process. Nonetheless, while the findings of such appraisals will always be disputed, the process of undertaking them confers greater rationality on European environmental policy.

9.4 **The precautionary principle**

The Treaty of European Union 1993 added a further legal obligation to EC environmental policy which is relevant to environmental policy, namely the *precautionary principle* (PP). The PP had appeared in the Dublin Declaration of 1990 (The 'Environmental Imperative'), which had elaborated principles for environmental action and had included 'preventive and precautionary action'. The Fifth Environmental Action Plan (5EAP) of 1992 repeated the reference to a 'precautionary approach', but, like the Dublin Declaration, did not define it. Finally, the Maastricht Treaty declared that:

Community [environmental] policy . . . shall be based on the precautionary principle and on the principles that preventive action shall be taken, that environmental damage should as a priority be rectified at source and that the polluter should pay. Environmental protection requirements must be integrated into the definition and implementation of other Community policies.

Again, no definition of the PP is provided. What then might the precautionary principle be?

If individuals are very averse to environmental risk, it suggests a precautionary approach. The insights from risk experiments go a long way to explaining the attraction of a precautionary approach, particularly where there are low probabilities and potentially high damages, where the risk is involuntary (i.e. is 'imposed' by others), and where the risk is of loss rather than gain. The precautionary principle may take several forms. In its strictest interpretation it suggests that no action should be taken if there is any likelihood at all, however small, that significant environmental damages could occur. This likelihood may be independent of the scientific evidence. That is, unless there is certainty that there are no detrimental effects, actions should not be taken which, for example, release harmful pollutants into the environment. Perhaps the closest form of the strict PP in practice is the German *Vorsorgeprinzip*—widely translated as the precautionary principle—which is designed to secure *Umweltschutz*, environmental protection. *Umweltschutz* is a constitutional obligation in some German states, but not yet a Federal obligation. *Vorsorge* developed as a justification for state intervention as part of the social democratic movement and as a counter to the prevailing 1970s philosophy that limited environmental protection on cost grounds. *Vorsorge* requires that environmental risks be detected early (the research focus), that action be taken even without proof of damage when irreversibility is feared, that technology should be developed for preventive action, and that the state has the obligation of environmental protection. There appears to be no mention of cost in this interpretation of the *Vorsorgeprinzip* (Sand 2000). Indeed, much the same debate about cost occurred in the Rio de Janeiro Earth Summit of 1992, where the US insisted on precautionary action being 'cost-effective', whereas the EU proposed deleting the phrase (Sand 2000).

A second interpretation requires that there be a presumption in favour of not harming the environment unless the opportunity costs of that action are, in some sense, very high. Opportunity cost here refers to the cost of taking the precautionary action measured in terms of what has to be surrendered. Taking an extreme example, the cost of global conservation might be the sacrifice of part of economic development generally. Put another way, no significant deterioration of the environment should occur unless the benefits associated with that deterioration heavily outweigh the costs of the deterioration. Effectively, this *safe minimum standards* approach says that the benefit–cost ratio of any project or programme which incidentally damages the environment should be high. While this formulation is somewhat vague, it can be contrasted with the typical cost–benefit rule to the effect that the benefit–cost ratio should be greater than unity.

Clearly, on these interpretations, adoption of the precautionary principle could be expensive. If the benefits forgone are substantial and new information reveals that the measure turns out not to have been warranted, then there will be a high net cost to precaution. On the other hand, if new information reveals that precaution was justified, nothing is lost. This suggests that some balancing of costs and benefits still must play a role even in contexts where the precautionary principle is thought to apply.

These excursions into the meaning of terms are essential for an understanding of the extent to which policy appraisal is used in the European Union. It is far from clear that, by introducing the precautionary principle, the EU has embraced consistent environmental objectives. For the requirement now appears to be for some benefit–cost appraisal, albeit without defining what form this is to take, while at the same time invoking the precautionary principle. But the precautionary principle could be taken to imply that cost considerations are not relevant to environmental policy. If so, the Treaty contains an internal contradiction.

On other interpretations, the precautionary principle is relevant only when probabilities are small or unknown and damage potentially large, as with climate change. In this case, the irrelevance of cost is confined to only those environmental risks taking on a 'zero-infinity' characteristic. In all other cases, cost is relevant to risk assessment. A variation of this view is that the precautionary principle is relevant only when there is some suspicion of irreversibility, i.e. when some threshold is exceeded and the initial situation cannot be restored. Species extinction would be a case in point.

Sand (2000) is of the view that the PP requires that people understand the risks to which they are exposed so that they can make informed choices, and that the burden of proof of environmental and health harm rests with those who wish to introduce a new chemical or process, not with those who may suffer. If so, the PP would entail that the EU adopt free access to environmental and health risk information as in the USA and Canada.

A final interpretation is that the precautionary principle urges preventive rather than curative action and that benefit–cost comparisons of some form remain relevant in all contexts. But the analysis serves to show that apparently harmless phrases can easily be incorporated into guidance and even law without anyone having a clear idea of what it is they are committed to.

9.5 **Market-based instruments**

Table 9.2 suggests a typology for environmental policy instruments. The distinction is made between setting a goal for the sources of a given environmental problem, and telling those sources how to control the problem.

On this matrix, the term 'command and control' (CAC) is confined to regulations which tell the source what to achieve and how to achieve it. Prohibitions and bans of certain products and substances would be an example, as would any emission standard that is combined with a requirement about the technology to use, as would a fishing catch limit combined with a requirement on, say, net mesh size. The other three 'cells' are not so clear cut, but most of what are called market-based instruments (MBIs) would belong in the lower right-hand cell, where the regulator does not state goals and does not say how to respond to the regulatory instrument. Thus, a tax on pollution emissions fits this cell because, although the regulator will have some environment target in mind, and may state it, each individual source of pollution does not have a target and each source is free to respond to the tax as they see fit. In terms of response, they might alter their product mix, they might install abatement equipment, change fuel sources, practice material and energy conservation, and so on.

The matrix does reflect the key characteristics of MBIs. The first feature of MBIs is that they give the individual polluter more choice of the means to reduce pollution. The less choice there is, the closer we are to CAC along the 'how to' axis. The more choice there is, the closer we are to an MBI. The second feature is that MBIs give a greater chance of minimizing the overall costs of complying with the environmental objective of the regulator, a discussed earlier in Section 9.2. This feature of MBIs, economic efficiency, is extremely important for the following reasons:

1. It should help to minimize the impacts of regulation on competitiveness if the alternative is CAC. This outcome is essential to the goals of the EU since regulation should not harm trade within the Union, nor should the EU as a whole have its competitive position harmed by regulation.

2. It will potentially limit the opposition to future environmental policy, because it costs less than CAC and hence serves the goals of environmental efficiency and political feasibility. This argument is not one that is widely heard in the debate over EU

Table 9.2 A matrix of regulatory instruments

	Regulator SPECIFIES the goal to be achieved	Regulator does NOT SPECIFY the goal to be achieved
Regulator specifies HOW goal is to be achieved	Command and control	Technology-based standards
Regulator does NOT SPECIFY HOW goal is to be achieved	Most standard setting + most negotiated agreements	Most market based instruments + public information

Source: After Russell and Powell (1996).

environmental policy but would be stressed by, for example, approaches to regulation informed by game theory (the theory of strategic behaviour).

3. It could also serve the goal of equity because, relative to CAC, compliance costs are less and hence the costs shifted forwards to consumers could be less. The complication here is that industry may find it easier to pass a tax forward to consumers than to pass forward a rise in costs due to some other regulatory activity. Although the cost increases may be the same, the tax could provide an 'excuse' for price increases that consumers might perceive to be reasonable, whereas they might not see pollution control expenditures as a reasonable reason to raise prices. Price regulators might also take different views on taxes and cost increases. There is strong evidence that politicians fear the 'visibility' of tax increases in this context, preferring CAC because it tends to be invisible, even though it may be more costly.

Progress in introducing MBIs in the EU has been moderate. The OECD in Paris conducts regular reviews to see which countries have introduced MBIs, whilst the European Environment Agency in Copenhagen has similarly conducted reviews. The situation as recorded in the OECD surveys is shown in Table 9.3, which covers all MBIs other than environmentally related taxes.

Table 9.3 Market-based instruments in EU countries: number of instruments excluding environmentally related taxes

	Date of OECD survey and year of information		
	1989 for 1987	1994 for 1992	1999 for 1997–9
Emission charges		23	
User charges	58	22	81
Product charges		54	
Tradable permits	1	1	3
Deposit refund	9	14	16
Non-compliance fees	2	2	2
Performance bonds	0	0	0
Liability payments	na	na	8
Subsidies	na	na	49

Note: Coverage of countries varies. Only EU countries are recorded here. Significant use of tradable permits exists in the USA.

The 1989 survey covered the following EU countries only: France, Germany, Italy, Netherlands, Sweden, Belgium, Denmark, Finland. UK Comparisons are also limited by the fact that 'charges' in the early surveys included taxes whereas the tax coverage in 1999 is very detailed and is separated from the coverage of charges.

Emission charges are charges on emissions of pollutants; a user charge is a charge for the use of some collective service (e.g. waste collection); a product charge is a charge on the product causing the emission. Product charges can be very inefficient since they do not target the externality itself, but are successful where the externality is closely linked to the product, e.g. fuel. Deposit-refund systems operate by taxing the product when purchased and refunding the tax when the product container is returned. Non-compliance fees are simply penalties for not complying with regulations. Performance bonds are not used in the EU but involve a down-payment by the polluter before he can commence operations. The bond can be redeemed at the end of an operation (e.g. quarrying) but is forfeited if damage is done. Liability payments are payments under civil law for damage.

Sources: Adapted from OECD (1989, 1994, 1999) and Barde (1997).

The tax situation is recorded separately and in considerable detail. These data are not included in Table 9.3 because it is not easy to define the number of taxes. For example, Denmark records ten environmentally related taxes on vehicles through registration duty, and fifteen more on vehicle weight. But it is clear that environmentally related taxes are now widespread in the EU. Full details of such taxes, charges and fees in all OECD countries can be accessed on the OECD website at www.oecd.org/env/policies/taxes/index.htm.

There are some significant differences between Europe and North America in the use of MBIs. The USA, for example, typically has few environmentally related taxes, at least at the federal level. Europe, on the other hand, has a clear preference for such taxes. The USA has preferred to adopt tradable permits. A tradable permit works by having a regulatory authority issue a quantity of 'permits to pollute' and these are then issued to polluters, usually according to the historical record of how much pollution each polluter emits (known as 'grandfathering'). The sum total of the permits equals the environmental target in terms of tonnes of emissions of a given pollutant. Exactly the same procedure, but usually called tradable or transferable quotas, can be applied to natural resources such as water and marine fisheries. Each fisherman, for example, would receive a quota for an allowable catch and cannot catch more fish than this. In all cases, the essential feature is that polluters and resource users can 'trade' their permits and quotas. Consequently, permits and quotas have a market price. That market price is entirely analogous to a tax and the behavioural response of polluters is (theoretically) the same. Those with high costs of abatement will seek to buy permits and will do so as long as the price of permits is below their MAC. Those who find it easy to abate and therefore have low MACs will be willing to sell permits as long as the price they get exceeds their own MAC. As with the tax in Figure 9.2, abatement will be concentrated among low-abatement-cost polluters and permits will move towards high-cost abaters. The effect is to provide a least-cost solution to securing the environmental target.

Table 9.3 suggests very few tradable permit systems are in place in the EU. Why does the US have tradable permits but Europe does not? The explanation rests with political culture: US citizens tend to be very much opposed to taxes, as their difficulties in dealing with climate-change policies have shown. Europe is far more used to taxes. There are also problems within Europe in securing consensus on tradable permits. For example, the Second Sulphur Protocol produced by the United Nations Economic Commission for Europe (UNECE, not to be confused with EU institutions) in 1994 does enable countries to trade sulphur dioxide emission quotas. But analysis suggests that any trading would tend to have impacts on third parties, i.e. if countries A and B trade, country C may suffer. The result has been that no trades have taken place. This is in contrast to the USA, where trade in sulphur dioxide quotas has been immensely successful. Third-party effects are still present in the US system: states A and B may harm state C by trading. But the potential for harm appears to be tolerated in the USA (with some exceptions) whereas it is not in Europe. Note that this problem does not arise with trading of greenhouse gas emission permits. The reason for this is that the impact on global warming is the same whether the emission comes from location A or location B. Greenhouse gases are said to be 'uniformly mixed'. This explains why there is (now) far less resistance to tradable permits in greenhouse gases (see Section 9.6).

Europe has also entrenched itself within a complex and bureaucratic (and largely unsuccessful) control system for its fisheries, so that there is little scope for wholesale change in the system towards transferable fishing quotas. (Oddly, overproduction of milk in the EU is controlled by tradable milk quotas!)

Table 9.3 also reveals the extensive use of subsidies. In general, subsidies are best avoided because they tend to be difficult to remove. The outstanding example in the EU are the payments under the Common Agricultural Policy, the vast majority of which are environmentally damaging. Table 9.3 shows that the idea of subsidizing environmentally good behaviour is strong in the EU, mainly because of the presumption that 'development' comes first and the environment is something people have to be persuaded to care for. This contrasts with the rhetoric (and legal requirements) of EU environmental policy which, via constructs such as the precautionary principle, seek to shift the burden of proof on to polluters.

9.6 Climate change

In 1992 the Earth Summit at Rio de Janeiro produced two major international environmental agreements: the Convention on Biological Diversity (CBD) and the Framework Convention on Climate Change (FCCC). Both were intended to address the two most serious global environmental problems—the loss of biological resources and the diversity of those resources, and the increased surface temperature of the Earth due to the emission of 'greenhouse gases'. It seems fair to say that the CBD has been uncontroversial, although whether in fact it contains the means to slow the loss of biological diversity is open to dispute. The FCCC, on the other hand, has been immensely controversial, especially within the USA and the EU. The source of the controversy has not been the science, although that has been criticized, but the implications for environmental policy. Above all, it is difficult to see how greenhouse gas emission reductions can be secured without raising the price of energy significantly. The reason for this is that the main greenhouse gas is carbon dioxide (CO_2) which comes mainly from the burning of fossil fuels—natural gas having the lowest emissions, coal and oil the highest emissions. Reducing CO_2 therefore means reducing energy consumption, or switching to 'non-carbon' sources such as renewable energy.

The EU Member States accepted voluntary targets under the 1992 FCCC of reducing CO_2 emissions to 1990 levels by 2000. This constituted a reduction because emissions were expected to rise. The target was voluntary and hence none of the sanctions that could have been imposed by international law apply. In the event, very few EU countries have achieved the goal, the UK being the main one to be successful. Whilst politicians have claimed this as a success for the UK's climate change policies, in fact the reductions in emissions came about because of the unrelated policy of privatizing the electricity sector. Privatized utilities quickly ceased ordering coal-fired stations and switched to gas-fired stations, with a consequent fall in projected CO_2 emissions. The FCCC was followed by the 1997 Kyoto Protocol to the Convention. The Kyoto Protocol set emission reduction targets to be achieved by about 2010. The targets are set out in Table 9.4. They are again anchored on 1990 emissions, so that a reduction of, say, 8 per cent means that by around 2010 emissions must be 8 per cent lower than they were in 1990. Allowing for the underlying growth in emissions, the reductions compared to what emissions would have been are substantial in some cases. Projections vary but the EU total, for example, probably translates into only a 3 per cent reduction due to underlying reductions in emissions that are expected. But the situation within EU Member States varies. The EU acted as a single negotiating body at Kyoto, agreeing to a collective target of minus 8 per cent on 1990 emissions. It subsequently allocated that 8 per cent between Member States in a 'burden sharing agreement' as shown in Table 9.4. Whereas the Netherlands has a national target of minus 6 per cent on 1990 emissions, this translates to a probable 23 per cent reduction in what emissions would otherwise have been in 2010 (so-called 'baseline' emissions). The UK's 12.5 per cent target turns out to be a relatively modest 2 per cent cut on baseline emissions, but Greece's allowed *increase* in emissions of 25 per cent becomes a required cut of probably 14 per cent due to the rapid rate of growth in underlying emissions. Expressed as reductions in the baseline emissions, then, the Kyoto targets are tough.

One advantage of the EU having a collective target is that individual Member States who expect not to achieve their burden-sharing targets can 'trade' with other states. What this means is that a country that is likely to achieve reductions easily, could over-achieve the target and gain 'credits' from so doing equal to the tonnes of greenhouse gases reduced. Suppose country A's target of minus 10 per cent translates into X tonnes of carbon dioxide[1] but A achieves, or expects to achieve, 1.5X tonnes reduction. It can then sell its 0.5X tonnes 'overshoot' to other countries within the EU. A country struggling to meet its target, call them B, will be likely buyers. Indeed, it will pay country A to sell the credits so long as the price received for them exceeds the (marginal) abatement costs domestically. It will pay B to buy the credits so long as the price of the credits is less than the abatement costs in B. It is easy to see that a trade can quickly be established that has the effect of minimizing the costs to the EU as a whole of complying with the Kyoto targets. This is known as 'carbon trading' or, under the Protocol, a 'flexibility mechanism'. In fact there are several flexibility mechanisms under the Kyoto Protocol: the EU can trade within itself (the 'European bubble'); any country with a mandated target can trade with any other country, which effectively means that developed economies can trade with the economies in transition ('joint implementation'); and any country with a mandated target can trade with developing countries (the Clean Development Mechanism). Carbon trading is entirely analogous to pollution permit trading generally.

Although the Kyoto Protocol makes it clear that the onus is on emitting countries to cut emissions 'at home', the inclusion of separate trading mechanisms is a clear demonstration that trading was (and is) regarded as a vital ingredient of any approach to global warming control. The explanation for this fairly novel approach to an international agreement lies in one word: cost. Cost has two elements here. The first is simply the financial savings from investing in emissions reduction in countries where the cost of abatement is lower. The second is political cost. In the USA, in particular, there is strong opposition to ratifying the Kyoto Protocol. Table 9.4 reveals why. It can be seen that, compared to what carbon dioxide emissions would be on a 'business as usual' basis, the

Table 9.4 Emission reduction targets under the Kyoto protocol and the EU burden-sharing agreement

Country	Target[a]
Australia	+8
Canada	−6
Iceland	+10
Japan	−6
Liechtenstein	−8
Monaco	−8
New Zealand	0
Norway	+1
Switzerland	−8
USA	−7
European Union	−8
EU Burden sharing agreement	
Austria	−13
Belgium	−7.5
Denmark	−21
Finland	0
France	0
Germany	−21
Greece	+25
Ireland	+13
Italy	−6.5
Luxembourg	−28
Netherlands	−6
Portugal	+27
Spain	+15
Sweden	+4
UK	−12.5
Economies in Transition	
Bulgaria, Czech R, Estonia, Latvia, Lithuania, Romania, Slovakia, Slovenia	−8
Hungary, Poland	−6
Croatia	−5
Russian Federation, Ukraine	0

Notes:
[a] % reduction on 1990 emissions of 6 GHGs by 2008–12.

USA must cut CO_2 emissions by 28 per cent by around 2010. But carbon is pervasive to a modern economy since it is embodied in fossil fuels. All countries of the world are reliant on fossil fuels. 'Taking the carbon out' thus requires policy measures that will affect virtually all aspects of modern life, from resource extraction through production to consumption. No modern society has yet shown that it is willing to undertake this change in lifestyle.

Carbon trading provides the way out of this dilemma: a desire to do something about global warming, even if the efforts are modest against the scale of the reductions required, versus the economic and political difficulties of making that change. The cost saving from trading matters for at least two reasons:

1 If more resources are allocated to global warming control than are needed for any given target, there is a cost to the world as a whole in terms of the forgone activities that could have been undertaken with the wasted resources. Thus, if it costs $1 billion to control global warming efficiently, but $2 billion is spent because of an inefficient set of policies, then $1 billion worth of benefits are lost, e.g. in foreign aid or environmental protection, health care, etc.

2 If more resources are used than are needed, global warming control will be unnecessarily expensive and this will deter countries from agreeing to control emissions, or it may encourage them to defect even if they enter an agreement if they discover that emissions control is more expensive than they thought. In short, the very viability of the agreement is highly sensitive to the costs of complying with it.

For the Protocol to come into effect it requires that a minimum of 55 countries ratify it and that their combined carbon dioxide emissions must account for at least 55 per cent of all Annex 1 country emissions in 1990. The numbers place the onus on the USA, as the world's biggest emitter (33 per cent of Annex 1 greenhouse gas emissions in 1990) to ratify. But US ratification is extremely problematic. The Bush Administration has adopted an aggressive and negative stance on Kyoto, preferring to suggest that its own obligations be scrapped in favour of more vague and voluntary targets The rationality of the US position is clear: the financial and political cost of securing the US target is perceived as being large. Imposing that cost to secure a negligible change in the overall environmental impact makes the political task insurmountable. Moreover, only if developing countries come 'on board' is there even a chance that Kyoto will initiate a process of long-term change in warming. Arithmetically, the Protocol could come into force without US ratification, and it is not at all unusual for international environmental agreements to be effected without a US signature. But the political signals this would send to the developing world would fairly certainly lead to their refusal to sign up to commitments even for later Protocols. How the USA behaves is crucial for global warming control. And how far the USA can be persuaded to sign eventually will depend, in significant part, on how far the USA can buy carbon credits from other countries. The reality of trading is therefore the reality of the Protocol.

The EU's position on carbon trading has changed. Initially hostile to the idea, the EU sought to place 'caps' on the trades because of a feeling that emission reductions should take place 'at home' as indicated by the Protocol, and because the EU has been sensitive to developing countries' views that trading gets rich countries 'off the hook' in terms of lifestyle change. But the US position has been instrumental, and, in addition, there has been a growing realization that if the voluntary targets of the FCCC were not achieved, the mandatory targets under the Kyoto Protocol might be even more difficult to achieve.

One other factor explains the change of view within the EU. While it is possible to achieve some of the emissions reduction targets by various measures on energy efficiency, product standards, etc., there are really only two options for reducing emissions: placing a tax on energy or on the carbon content of energy, and carbon trading. In 1990 the European Commission proposed a 'carbon/energy tax', a proposal it took to the 1992 Rio Earth Summit. It was to be set at the equivalent of $3 per barrel of oil in 1993, rising to $10 per barrel of oil in 2000. The tax was a mix: 50 per cent was based on the carbon content of fuels and 50 per cent on energy. Whilst a pure carbon tax would tax only the carbon content, which varies between fuels, there were fears that such a tax would encourage too much 'switching' between fuels, e.g. from coal to gas, thus damaging the coal industries especially in Germany and the UK, and encouraging nuclear power, which was regarded with suspicion in some EU countries. The revenue implications of such a tax were formidable, amounting to around 1 per cent of EU GDP for the full tax. In anticipation of the opposition to it, the tax was to be 'hypothecated', i.e. none of the revenues would remain with governments. Instead, revenues would be used to reduce payroll taxes (taxes on labour and paid by employers). This was intended to stimulate employment by lowering the price of labour.

The carbon/energy tax proposal failed. The lobby against it was massive and unceasing. While environmentalists supported the tax, an alliance of two major players determined the outcome: industry and governments. Industry opposed the tax for obvious reasons—they were convinced it would harm the competitive position of the EU against other countries by raising EU costs of production. They also doubted the resolve of governments to honour the requirement to reduce payroll taxes as compensation for the tax. But governments had an altogether different concern, although some of them shared the concern over competitiveness. Their concern was that the uniform nature of the tax could only be established if the European Union extended its tax powers, a concern that has prevailed from the very outset of the Community and Union. Votes on taxation have to be unanimous.

In 1997 the Commission accepted defeat on the carbon/energy tax and proposed instead to restructure energy excise taxes, beginning with a proposed agreement on minimum levels of such taxes. But these are modest changes and would have little or no effect on greenhouse gas emissions in the EU. This explains why, with one major avenue of policy effectively closed to them, the Commission is looking at a wider menu of options, and also why opposition to carbon trading has diminished.

9.7 Sustainable development

Through the Amsterdam Treaty, the EU is committed to sustainable development. But what is sustainable development? As a political slogan it has come to mean all things to all men and has resulted in a rash of 'sustainable this' and 'sustainable that' as policy objectives. Economists have been more careful and have a clear definition and analysis of sustainability (Pearce and Barbier 2000).

Sustainable development refers to economic and social development that is sustained through time. The meaning of 'development' may not matter much, since there is good reason to suppose that what needs to be done to secure it will not vary much with the definition. To the economist, development would mean rising per capita well-being over time. The conditions for achieving this involve ensuring that future generations have more assets per capita than the current generation, since it is assets that produce well-being. But the assets in question are wide-ranging and include the traditional concept of capital as man-made capital (machinery, factories); human capital (the stock of knowledge and skills); natural capital (the environment seen as an asset yielding flows of services over time); and social capital (the sets of relationships between people and between people and institutions). It follows that the sum total of these assets must rise through time, in per capita terms, for there to be potentially sustainable development. This is known as the 'constant (or increasing) capital rule'. Note that the rule permits substitution between forms of capital—e.g. the environment could be sacrificed provided the proceeds are used to invest in other forms of capital. Similarly, technological progress will enhance the productivity of capital assets, whilst population growth will make the achievement of a per capita constant rule more difficult.

Not only does the constant capital rule make intuitive sense—it simply says that the total 'wealth' of an economy must rise through time at a rate faster than population growth—but it is capable of measurement. What is required is that, first, the level of savings in each economy be computed. The intuition here is that savings are the resources put aside from income and which become available to invest in assets for the future. But assets depreciate over time, so savings must be greater than the depreciation on all assets. It is easy to see that man-made capital and natural capital depreciate. For example, damage to ecosystems is effectively the depreciation of those natural assets. Social capital probably depreciates as well: social commentators have pointed to marked increases in violence, family breakdown, crime, etc. as negative indicators of social capital. Human capital and technological progress, on the other hand, tend to appreciate. Knowledge tends not to be lost. So, the 'true' or 'genuine' level of savings in an economy can be expressed as:

Genuine savings = Gross Savings – Depreciation on man-made capital – Depreciation on Natural Capital – Depreciation on Social capital + Appreciation on Human Capital + Technological Progress

To allow for population change, the formula:

$$\Delta (W/P) = W/P(\Delta W/W - \Delta P/P)$$

is required, where W = wealth (i.e. the sum of all the capital assets), P = population and Δ simply means 'change in'. (The right-hand side comes from differentiating the left-hand side as quotient.) Δ W is in fact genuine savings. Finding estimates of W, i.e. total wealth, is complex and Hamilton (2000) estimates it as the future flow of consumption all discounted back to a present value.

There are now two possible indicators of sustainability: genuine savings as an aggregate, and the expression inside the brackets of the above equation. The second is more difficult to calculate but is to be preferred because it explicitly acknowledges population growth. There are formidable problems in turning these categories into measurable entities but preliminary work has been done. Hamilton (2000), building on earlier work by Pearce and Atkinson (1993), has computed genuine savings for many countries. His results for the EU are shown in Table 9.5.

Table 9.5 suggests strongly that the EU is 'sustainable', i.e. it is saving more and investing more in other forms of capital than the loss of natural capital assets and the depreciation on ordinary capital. It is also accumulating wealth faster than its population grows,

Table 9.5 Sustainability in selected EU countries and the USA, 1997

Country	Change in wealth per capital $\equiv \Delta(W/P)$	Genuine savings as % GDP
Austria	1.1	17.7
Belgium	1.3	19.7
Finland	1.0	18.4
France	0.7	15.1
Germany	1.1	16.8
Ireland	2.0	31.3
Italy	1.2	16.3
Netherlands	1.4	23.5
Spain	1.1	17.3
Sweden	1.1	18.8
UK	0.6	11.6
USA	0.1	13.2

Source: Hamilton (2000).

a result reflecting the generally low magnitude of population change in the EU. From an environmental point of view, this may not be comforting, since it suggests that increasing environmental damage in the EU is justified by the increase in other capital assets. Indicators of sustainability of this kind may not therefore satisfy everyone's interests, and it is possible to look separately at the state of the environment and at social indicators to see if they are themselves improving or deteriorating. The high genuine savings rates in Table 9.5 reflect high gross savings rates in EU countries. The significance of gross savings can be revealed by comparing the EU results to that for the USA, shown separately in Table 9.5. While the genuine savings level in the USA looks acceptable, the change in per capita wealth is seen to be very low and not very different from zero. Even the development of rich countries, then, can border on being unsustainable.

Discussion questions

1   What are the respective advantages and disadvantages of market-based instruments (MBIs) for the achievement of environmental policy goals in the EU?

2   What are the advantages and disadvantages of using cost–benefit analysis to guide environmental policy choices?

3   What is 'sustainable development'? Is it consistent with damaging the environment?

4   What is the 'precautionary principle'? How might it be translated into practical guidance for decision-makers?

Further reading

An excellent text on the politics of environmental policy in the EU is Barnes and Barnes (1999). The advantages and problems of using market-based instruments are discussed at length in Panayotou (1998). Practical case studies of MBIs in Europe are contained in Gale *et al.* (1995) and Schlegelmilch (1999). The economics of sustainable development is comprehensively covered in Atkinson *et al.* (1997).

Note

1   There are in fact six greenhouse gases, but CO_2 is the main one.

References

AEA Technology (1996), *Economic Evaluation of the Draft Incineration Directive* (Luxembourg: European Commission).

Atkinson, G., Dubourg, R., Hamilton, K., Munasinghe, M., Pearce, D. W., and Young, C. (1997), *Measuring Sustainable Development: Macroeconomics and the Environment* (Cheltenham: Edward Elgar).

Barde, J.-Ph. (1997), 'Economic Instruments for Environmental Protection: Experience in OECD Countries', in OECD (ed.), *Applying Market-based Instruments to Environmental Policies in China and OECD Countries* (Paris: OECD), 31–58.

Barnes, P. and Barnes, I. (1999), *Environmental Policy in the European Union* (Cheltenham: Edward Elgar).

Bolt, C. (1993), *The Cost of Quality: Establishing Willingness to Pay in a Regulated Monopoly* (Birmingham: Office of Water Regulation—OFWAT).

Coopers and Lybrand, Centre for Social and Economic Research on the Global Environment (CSERGE), London and Norwich, and Economics for the Environment Consultancy, London (EFTEC) (1997), *Cost Benefit Analysis of the Different Municipal Solid Waste Systems: Objectives and Instruments for the Year 2000* (Luxembourg: Official Publications of the European Communities).

European Commission (1992), *The Fifth Environmental Action Programme: Towards Sustainability* (Brussels: European Commission).

Gale, R., Barg, S., and Gillies, A. (eds.) (1995), *Green Budget Reform* (London: Earthscan).

Hamilton, K. (2000), *Sustaining Economic Welfare: Estimating Changes in Wealth per Capita* (Washington DC: Environment Department, World Bank; mimeo). Available on www.econ.nyu.edu/dept/iariw.

Krämer, L. (1995) *EC Treaty and Environmental Law*, 2nd edition (London: Sweet and Maxwell).

—— (1989), *Economic Instruments for Environmental Protection* (Paris: OECD).

—— (1994), *Managing the Environment: The Role of Economic instruments* (Paris: OECD).

—— (1999), *Economic Instruments for Pollution Control and Natural Resource Management in OECD Countries* (Paris: OECD).

—— (2000), *Database on Environmentally Related Taxes*, at www.oecd.org/env/policies/taxes/index.htm.

Panayotou, T. (1998), *Instruments of Change: Motivating and Financing Sustainable Development* (London: Earthscan).

Pearce, D. W. and Atkinson, G. (1993), 'Capital Theory and the Measurement of Sustainable Development: An Indicator of Weak Sustainability', *Ecological Economics*, 8: 103–8.

—— and Barber, E. (2000), *Blueprint for a Sustainable Economy* (London: Earthscan).

Russell, C. and Powell, P. (1996), *Choosing Environmental Policy Tools: Theoretical Cautions and Practical Considerations* (Washington DC: Inter-American Development Bank).

Sand, P. (2000), 'The precautionary principle: a European perspective', *Human and Ecological Risk Assessment*, 6/3: 445–58.

Schlegelmilch, K. (1999), *Green Budget Reform in Europe* (Berlin: Springer-Verlag).

UK House of Lords, Select Committee on the European Communities, Session 1994–5, 1st Report, *Bathing Water*, HL Paper 6-I; and Session 1994–5, 7th Report, *Bathing Water Revisited*, HL Paper 6-I, London, HMSO.

Chapter 10
Social Policy

David Purdy

10.1 Introduction

When neighbouring states form an economic union, they give up unilateral controls over the movement of people, goods, capital, and enterprise across their borders and set out to create a single market with a single currency operating under uniform rules. The rules may be confined to product standards and competition policy or they may extend to employment, social security, and public services. In the EU, attempts to move towards the broad end of this range by harmonizing and upgrading national systems of social protection have so far made little headway. The consequence, many would argue, is that Member States are less effective than they once were or, at any rate, less effective than they should be, at preventing social exclusion, preserving social cohesion, promoting social justice, or pursuing other social goals that their citizens desire. The asymmetry between these two kinds of economic integration—market-making and market-braking—lies at the heart of debates about social policy in the EU.

The EU has always had social policies in some shape or form ever since its foundation, but no settled consensus has emerged either about what should be done or about who should do it. This is largely due to disparities of economic development and differences of policy regime among the Member States, but conflicts of ideology and interest have also played a part, for governments and other social actors hold divergent views about 'proper' role of the state in economic affairs and the 'proper' division of responsibilities and powers between national and supranational authorities. One of the aims of this chapter is to explain the origins and persistence of these disparities, differences and disagreements.

To prepare the ground, Section 10.2 provides an introduction to the study of social policy, analysing the concept of welfare, defining the welfare state, and invoking the distinction, first formulated by Marshall (1950), between three aspects of citizenship—civil, political, and social. Throughout the argument, it is stressed that economy and society form an integrated complex whose various elements need to be considered together if they are to be properly understood. Accordingly, attention is drawn to the ways in which the business, public, household, and voluntary sectors of the economy interact with and depend on each other, and it is suggested that the broad aim of social policy is to keep them in balance, though ideas about what this means and how it is to be accomplished vary greatly over time and across cultures. Section 10.2 concludes with an anatomy of the welfare state, distinguishing between in-kind services and income transfers and showing how different tax-transfer systems impinge on the distribution of income, work, and power.

Section 10.3 draws on comparative studies of social policy to clarify the concept of a welfare regime, to outline the principal regime-types which coexist in contemporary Europe, to explain why the differences between them matter, and to investigate the relationship between social policy and economic performance. Section 10.4 turns to the role of the EU as a social policy actor, noting the peculiarities of EU institutions, seeking to explain why the EU has not taken over the welfare functions traditionally performed by the nation-state, reviewing the evolution of EU social policy from the Treaty of Rome to the launch of the Euro, and examining the obstacles which have so far thwarted all attempts to harmonize standards of social protection.

Section 10.5 considers the domestic and global challenges facing national welfare states and shows how welfare reform has enabled some countries to combine high social spending with economic success. While welfare reform is primarily a matter for national governments and their social partners, there is much the EU can do to help, and the chapter concludes by outlining a proposal for graduated welfare benchmarking, both as a solution to the problems which have plagued the EU in the past and as the basis for a new global social framework.

10.2 The study of social policy

Social policy and the concept of welfare

As an academic discipline, social policy stands at the intersection between history, law, politics, economics, sociology, and psychology. It is roughly coeval, though not coextensive, with the study of the welfare state. The first nationally organized schemes of poverty relief were introduced in Europe in the early nineteenth century, but the term 'welfare state' did not appear until the 1930s and was not widely used until the 1940s. Conversely, even if the welfare state as we know it were to disappear, students of social policy would still find plenty to occupy them. International comparisons point to the same conclusion. Even in the poorest countries, action can be taken to improve standards of nutrition, sanitation, health, and literacy, to restrain population growth, and to widen access to credit, but only the twenty or so countries which belong to the OECD can properly be described as welfare states.

What, then, is meant by 'welfare' and when does a state become a 'welfare state'? These questions can be approached either from the standpoint of human individuals as welfare-experiencing subjects, or from that of the political community as a whole. Which political community is relevant depends on the locus of state power, for this is typically the focus of efforts in civil society to change or preserve the prevailing configuration of welfare-determining conditions. In contemporary Europe, the nation-state remains responsible for providing or financing social services and social transfers, the two main branches of the welfare state. The role of EU as a social policy actor is largely confined to regulating the consequences of economic integration for employment and social protection in the EU's Member States.

The word 'welfare' refers to the condition or state of a person, community, or society, and nowadays is normally applied to non-human animals as well, whether as individuals or as species. To promote someone's welfare is to establish or maintain conditions that enable them to fare well. There are various senses in which this can be understood. Bearing in mind that the word 'fare' derives from the Old English *faran*, meaning 'to travel or make one's way', and extending the metaphor of human life as a journey, we might distinguish: going in safety or security, without mishap or bad luck; arriving at some desired destination (i.e. attaining success according to some scale of values); fulfilling one's initial potential or developing one's capabilities on the way; and becoming empowered or achieving control over the course of one's life. These are all matters of degree and can all be judged by reference either to what people want or to what they need—I might, for example, want another cigarette, but need to stop smoking. Not surprisingly, therefore, the concept of welfare is apt to provoke controversy, even before one considers the various conditions that determine how much welfare, in any of these senses, each person experiences.

Only individuals can have experiences, not collective entities such as families or nations. Hence, the welfare of a group, considered subjectively, is the combined welfare of its individual members, not the experience of some supra-individual group-mind. But this does not imply that social conditions have no bearing on individual welfare. My welfare is likely to depend not only on my own personal situation, but also on that of other people around me, including total strangers, and on general features of the society in which I live, such as the state of civic amenities, the level of lawlessness, and the degree of social cohesion.

Welfare-determining conditions include not only *material circumstances*, such as physical health and personal income, but also *psychological states*, such as depression, addiction, and religious faith; *social connections*, such as friendship networks and family ties; and *cultural norms*, such as interpersonal trust and civic pride. Note also that besides describing a condition or state, 'welfare' is often used prescriptively, as when we commend some arrangement as welfare-enhancing. Clearly, in such cases, one should avoid conflating the value with the conditions intended to promote it. Critics of the welfare state need not be indifferent to human suffering and privation, any more than supporters value the welfare state for its own sake rather than as a means to certain ends. Of course, welfare is not the only social value: others are equality, order, freedom, rights, justice, and efficiency (sometimes called the economists' value). These various values sometimes conflict and, when this happens, people tend to disagree about which matters most, especially in modern pluralistic societies where no single moral outlook commands general assent. Only a hard-line utilitarian would insist that all other values are ultimately reducible to human (and animal) welfare.

Welfare states and social citizenship

Until the comparative study of social policy drew attention to the differences among welfare states, many writers failed to distinguish between the idea of a welfare state and the way this idea was embodied in specific national arrangements. Once it is accepted that there is no such thing as the welfare state in the singular, only welfare states in the plural, it becomes possible to frame a definition in terms of a lowest common denominator. On this basis, we might define a welfare state as a series of state-sponsored programmes, instituted within the framework of capitalism, and designed to ensure that all national citizens enjoy at least minimum standards of income, health care, education, and housing.

Three points stand out in this formulation. First, welfare states arose in countries with developed capitalist economies and strong nation-states. Having undermined earlier systems of mutual support based on family ties, religious precept, and parochial provision, capitalist industrialization eventually created the resources required to pay for nation-wide public services administered by the state. At the same time, the idea of the nation as a cultural community, bound together by ties of language, mores, character, and history, created opportunities for political actors, inspired by collectivist ideologies of varying hues, to forge connections between national success (however defined) and social solidarity.

Secondly, welfare states in capitalist societies are *market-limiting*, not *market-usurping*. To the extent that production and investment continue to be driven by the pursuit of profit and the accumulation of capital, the allocation of resources and the distribution of income continue to be determined by market forces, subject to the maintenance of certain minimum social safeguards. Of course, this does not preclude the pursuit of more ambitious social goals. Thus, besides preventing or relieving poverty, social security systems may be designed to redistribute income between generations or across the lifecycle, to redistribute income vertically from rich to poor, to offset the extra costs or special needs of groups such as disabled people or families with children, or to create a particular kind of social framework: for example, one in which people's shared identity as citizens tempers the sectional interests that divide them.

Thirdly, the welfare state is bound up with the institution of citizenship as it has developed over the past two centuries. In general, to be a citizen is to enjoy certain rights and to owe certain duties as a member of a political community. In the nation-states of the modern world, citizenship is an inclusive status, at least in a normative sense: over the long run, all denizens of the national territory tend to become citizens, though a good deal of cross-national variation is evident in the treatment of resident aliens and second-generation immigrants (Brubaker 1990). National citizenship is also egalitarian in the sense that it is a single status with no internal gradations. Historically, these two features imparted a powerful democratic logic to the politics of nation-states, slowly extending not only the scope of the demos, but also the range of the political agenda. Conceptually, the rights (and correlative duties) of citizens can be divided into three broad groups: *civil rights* comprising, on the one hand, the classic liberal freedoms—of thought, conscience, expression, movement, assembly, and association—and on the other, the 'possessive individualist' freedoms of contract and security of property; *political rights*, including—

notably—the right to stand for public office and vote in elections for national and local government; and *social entitlements* such as free education, access to health care, affordable housing and a guaranteed minimum income.

To be sure, the three dimensions of citizenship can come apart: some states confer rights without welfare (the USA and Japan), whereas others dispense welfare without rights (the former USSR and Singapore). And even in Western Europe where the principle of social citizenship is broadly accepted, the shape and scale of social entitlements continue to be contested, not least because they impose much heavier demands on taxpayers than civil and political rights. Nevertheless, there are strong grounds for arguing that without some form of collectively assured access to what Rawls (1972) calls 'primary goods'—the material and cultural prerequisites for becoming a moral agent with the ability to make choices and exercise judgement—the value of civil and political rights is diminished and whatever degree of equality citizens enjoy before the law or at the ballot box is largely bogus. As Anatole France observed, 'The law in its majesty permits rich and poor alike to beg in the streets, to sleep under bridges and to eat at the Ritz'. Nor do social entitlements benefit only individuals: institutions that bind society together into a (national) community of fate make it easier for society as whole to cope with difference, diversity, division, and conflict in a context of material scarcity.

Social reproduction and the remit of social policy

In contemporary social theory, a distinction is sometimes drawn between economic production and social reproduction, as if the economy were not part of society and played no part in reproducing it, or as if, conversely, institutions such as the family and the state helped to keep society going, but did not actually produce anything. This is a confused conception. Economic activity takes place whenever people devote their time, energy, and skills to producing objects or serving purposes which are of value to others, regardless of where they work, how their work is controlled, whether they are paid, what they produce, and whether it is marketed. On this basis, activities can be classified according to the role they play in reproducing human society, variously helping to replace (or increase) the human population, to maintain (or expand) productive capacity, to perpetuate (or reshape) social institutions, and to conserve (or transform) cultural patterns. In the case of welfare-capitalism, four broad sectors of activity can be distinguished: the *business sector*, in which profit-seeking firms employ waged labour to produce marketed commodities; the *public sector*, in which government and other public agencies employ waged labour to produce public goods; the *household sector*, in which individuals and members of families or other cohabiting groups perform unpaid provisioning and caring work; and the *voluntary sector*, in which a variety of membership organizations, charitable bodies, and civic associations employ both paid and unpaid staff to express shared values, promote shared interests, and cater to social needs that are either not met at all, or not met so well, by commercial or public provision.

Each sector depends on the others and all contribute to the development of society as a whole. Thus, just as the business sector produces commodities which the others buy and use in their respective spheres, so their activities in turn help to sustain the production of commodities and the accumulation of capital. The state, for example, operates an independent and predictable legal system, regulates the banking and financial systems, maintains or oversees the economic infrastructure, and seeks to promote macroeconomic stability. It also seeks to manage social conflict and legitimize the social order. What households, for their part, produce is people—both from generation to generation and from day to day—not, of course, as mere bearers of labour power, but as thinking, feeling human beings equipped with a more or less extended repertoire of ideas, values, habits, knowledge, capabilities, and skills. And the voluntary sector plays a vital role in the formation and maintenance of social assets such as interpersonal trust, social solidarity, and civic commitment, which not only improve the quality of life, but according to Putnam (1993), strengthen democratic governance and enhance economic performance.

In very general terms, social policy is concerned with trying to maintain a balanced relationship between the four sectors, whether in the negative sense that none creates dysfunctions for the others, or in the positive sense that they work together synergetically to promote certain generally agreed goals. What aspects of social life are perceived as problematic and what remedies gain acceptance among political élites and the general public vary greatly from one society and era to another. Transnational differences of policy regime are considered in the next section. Here it suffices to note the succession of policy paradigms which have influenced governments everywhere over the past fifty years. During the 'golden age' of welfare-capitalism from the end of the Second World War to the mid-1970s, the ethos of public policy was strongly collectivist. State welfare programmes, it was widely believed, were positively good for business because they helped to sustain aggregate demand, improve the quality of the labour force, legitimize capitalism, and reduce industrial conflict. With the onset of acute economic crisis in the mid-1970s and the subsequent persistence of 'stagflation', these ideas became discredited and were displaced by neo-liberal doctrines which held that the growth of the public sector in general, and of the welfare state in particular, were largely responsible for the deterioration in economic performance and needed to be reversed in order to restore monetary discipline, lessen the burden of taxation, create more room for the market, and remove the allegedly corrupting effects of social security on personal industry and responsibility. From the early 1990s onwards, there was growing disenchantment with the market revolution, which was widely blamed for causing or failing to prevent the growth of poverty, inequality, and social exclusion, for degrading the environment, and for imposing unacceptable levels of stress on workers, families, and communities. One response which found particular favour with the Democrats in the USA and with New Labour in Britain, was to seek out a 'third way', distinct from both traditional social democracy and free market liberalism, in a bid to reconcile economic dynamism with social cohesion (Giddens 1998, 2000).

Thus, social policy is an ideological battleground extending over a wide range of issues. Yet there are spillovers, linkages, interactions, and interdependencies between different policy areas. To take an obvious example, welfare arrangements designed for a world of managed exchange rates, full employment, regulated labour markets, stable marriages, traditional gender roles, and two-parent, one-earner families could hardly survive intact in a world of global finance, mass unemployment, flexible labour markets, rising divorce rates, gender convergence, and the growing diversity of family and household forms.

Clearly, whatever one's ideological stance, a coherent response to cumulative change calls for coordinated adjustments on several adjacent policy fronts: macroeconomic management, industrial relations, wage setting, employment policy, taxation, social security and provision for families and children.

Social services and social transfers

As noted earlier, welfare states provide both social services and social transfers. There are two main ways of providing services in kind: the state can create specialized public agencies which hire labour from the household sector and purchase commodities from the business sector; alternatively, it can contract out provision to private organizations in the business or voluntary sectors, relying on regulation, audit, and quasi-markets to secure equity, efficiency, accountability, and user choice. (In quasi-markets, service-providers compete for public contracts and service-users can choose among alternative suppliers; see Bartlett *et al.* 1998.) This distinction, of course, applies to all public goods, including defence, which can in principle be out-sourced to mercenary armies. Since the late 1980s, it has been especially relevant to the welfare state, where finance and provision, once tied together, have been steadily prised apart.

Because the state levies taxes on personal income and pays out social security benefits, it is necessary to distinguish between *original income*—what households get before taking account of taxes and benefits—and *disposable income*—what they end up with afterwards. In most EU countries, about 70 per cent of original income accruing to the household sector consists of wages and salaries paid to employees. Earnings from self-employment account for a further 10 to 15 per cent, and payments to property owners for the remainder. Both earnings and property income derive from market activity. If there were no welfare state, those who had nothing to sell or were excluded from the market would have to rely on their families, beg for charity, or turn to crime.

Given that only a few people own more than modest amounts of income-yielding property, most depend for their livelihood on continuous access to paid work, whether in their own right or as dependants of others who are continuously willing, or legally obliged, to support them. Regular employment confers various other advantages besides money income: experience and skills, friendship and contacts, self-esteem, social identity, public recognition, and political weight. In addition, regular job-holders are covered by *social insurance*. Employers, employees, and self-employed persons are all obliged by law to pay 'contributions' (or 'social security taxes') into one or more earmarked insurance funds, administered or regulated by the state. Typically, employees who meet the requisite contribution conditions are more or less adequately protected, both against temporary disruptions of earning power due to unemployment, sickness, and the demands of maternity, paternity, and parenthood, and against permanent loss of earnings due to incapacitation or retirement. Conversely, people who are not in stable, full-time employment throughout their working lives are less well served by social insurance. Indeed, unless the state provides credited contributions for unpaid work and keeps the threshold of admission to the insurance system low enough to include almost all forms of paid work, they may not be covered at all. The main groups at risk are the long-term unemployed, women who take time out of the labour market to bear children and provide unpaid care, and workers of either sex engaged in part-time, temporary, and other forms of 'non-standard' employment.

Most welfare states provide some kind of safety-net outside the framework of social insurance, but *social assistance*—to use a generic name for schemes which vary widely in operational detail—is almost invariably means-tested: benefit entitlements are determined by assessing how far the combined incomes and savings of the family or household unit fall short of some predetermined standard of 'subsistence'. In addition, able-bodied claimants of conventional working age, insured and uninsured alike, are normally expected to satisfy some kind of work test, of varying stringency. By and large, during the 'golden age', the unemployed were simply required to show that they were capable of, available for and genuinely seeking (paid) work. Over the past decade, such 'passive' arrangements have given way to 'active' measures targeted on specific, disadvantaged groups—the young unemployed, older workers experiencing long-term unemployment, lone parents, and others outside the workforce—who are, or risk becoming, disconnected from the labour market. The general aims of 'welfare-to-work' programmes, as they have come to be known, are to reduce welfare dependency by enhancing employability, to combat social exclusion by increasing labour-force participation, and to provide employers with an adequate supply of suitably skilled and motivated workers. Programmes vary in detail, but typically participants are interviewed, assessed, and counselled with a view to encouraging, helping, and, if necessary, driving them into the job market.

A prime example is the New Deal introduced by the New Labour government in the UK, with the reduction of youth unemployment as its main priority. On pain of forfeiting their benefit, unemployed persons, aged 18 to 24, are required to choose from four basic options: subsidized jobs (normally with a private employer), placements with voluntary organizations, enrolment in an environmental task-force, and remedial education or basic training. The New Deal is buttressed by various reforms designed to 'make work pay'. Besides introducing a National Minimum Wage, the government has revamped provision for low-paid family breadwinners, converting benefits which used to be provided through the social security system into *tax credits*. These are administered by employers on behalf of the income tax authorities and added to workers' pay packets. The aim is to strengthen the perceived link between family income and employment. Tax credits are also available to reimburse working parents for the costs of bought-in childcare and, more generally, offer a means of redistributing income in favour of working families which may be more acceptable to taxpayers and less socially divisive than traditional social assistance. Like all income-related transfers, however, tax credits create financial disincentives to the extent that low-income workers face high marginal tax rates because their entitlements fall if they earn more money by working harder, working longer, or moving to better paid jobs.

Contributory social insurance is designed to replace lost earnings; social assistance protects those with no earnings; tax credits protect those with low earnings. In addition, most welfare states provide *categorical transfers*, designed to meet the extra costs or special needs of designated categories of people. The best known example is *Child Benefit*, a cash grant payable to all parents and guardians for every child in their care from the moment the child is born until he or she leaves school. No state has yet introduced a *Citizen's Income*, a recurrent, lifelong transfer payable to every individual citizen, each in his or her own right, with no means test and no work requirement. There has, however, been a lively debate in recent years about the idea of redesigning social security arrangements on this basis (see Purdy 1994; Van Parijs 1995; and Robertson *et al.* 1996).

Besides using earmarked social insurance contributions and general tax revenues to pay for explicit transfers, governments also dispense implicit transfers in the form of *tax expenditures*, sometimes known as 'the hidden welfare state'. The effect of personal income tax allowances and reliefs is to drive a wedge between original income and tax-able income, thereby raising the disposable incomes of eligible taxpayers, just as cash benefits raise the disposable incomes of eligible claimants. Tax allowances play a useful role in maintaining work incentives for people on the margins of the labour force. In any case, it is not worthwhile collecting small amounts of revenue from low-income tax units. Tax reliefs, on the other hand, serve to subsidize favoured forms of expenditure, such as giving to charity, contributing to a private pension scheme, or taking out a mortgage to buy a home of one's own, and since they can seriously distort the markets concerned, while at the same time narrowing the tax base, they have generally fallen into disfavour with policy analysts.

10.3 Types of welfare regime

Welfare states come in various shapes and sizes. Box 10.1 summarizes the main institutional variants. It is tempting to think of a spectrum running from minimalist to more egalitarian modes of provision, but this is an over-simplification. Certainly, there is a difference between a 'lean' state that provides a low-level safety-net for market casualties and social misfits, while encouraging the majority of economically active citizens to take care of themselves, and a high-spending state that provides a wide range of first-class services for all. But consider two different social insurance systems: in one, benefits are paid at a flat rate to all eligible contributors; in the other, benefits are proportional to

---

Box 10.1 Welfare states: main dimensions of institutional variation

Coverage	selective/universal
Scope	restricted/expansive
Quality	minimal/optimal
Instruments	social transfers/in-kind services/regulation
Transfers	social assistance/social insurance/categorical transfers / tax expenditures/tax credits
Insurance formula	flat-rate/earnings-related
Finance	earmarked insurance contributions/general tax revenue
Redistribution	regressive/neutral/progressive

previous earnings. From a redistributive standpoint, the former will be more progressive than the latter, particularly if benefits are generous and contributions earnings-related. To complicate matters further, different states use different mixes of services, transfers, and regulation, and it is difficult to gauge the significance of any given provision without examining the wider context in which it operates. Australia, for example, has no system of social insurance, but relies entirely on means-tested social assistance. It does not follow, however, that the Australian welfare state offers workers and their families only minimal protection from the vicissitudes of the market. For one thing, if everyone depends on social assistance when times are hard, means-testing is less stigmatizing than in a system which discriminates between 'deserving' and 'undeserving' claimants. Moreover, (white) Australian workers have traditionally been strongly unionized and have enjoyed both high wages and high benefits, thanks to the country's unique system of wage regulation and, until the 1970s when they were dismantled, its protectionist trade barriers.

Thus, in comparing welfare states, it is necessary to consider not only the scale or growth of welfare expenditure, but also history, institutions, politics, and culture. In general, comparisons reveal both similarities and differences, but perhaps reacting against earlier universalist theories of modernization, comparative studies of social policy have tended to focus on differences. Until the 1990s, three main questions dominated the research agenda: How do welfare states differ? Why do these differences exist? And what effect do they have on social stratification and economic performance? More recently, two further questions have come to the fore: How are different welfare states responding to common domestic and global pressures for change? And what are the implications of globalization for social policy arrangements at both national and supranational levels?

In order to reduce the complexity of their task, researchers have attempted to delineate a limited number of models or ideal-types to which actual welfare states approximate more or less closely, it being understood that in reality welfare regimes contain various 'impure' elements and 'intermediate' forms. The empirical validity of the resulting typology can be assessed by devising suitable indicators of key characteristics such as those listed in Box 10.1, compiling data for various states and looking to see whether the data do, indeed, fall into distinct clusters, each with a notional centre of gravity corresponding to the relevant model.

Employing this procedure in a path-breaking study, Esping-Andersen (1990) distinguished three worlds of welfare-capitalism—the liberal, the conservative (or social Christian), and the social democratic—exemplified, respectively, by the USA, Germany, and Sweden. This schema has been widely adopted, but it also has its critics. Esping-Andersen was mainly concerned with the interface between employment policy, social transfers, and social stratification. But different clusters emerge when other social programmes are compared, such as health services or housing provision or, as Bonoli (1997) shows, when alternative empirical indicators are used. Several writers seek to extend Esping-Andersen's framework by creating additional regime types. Surveying welfare regimes in the EU, Leibfried (1993) argues that Italy, Greece, Portugal, and Spain defy classification in terms of just three categories and proposes a fourth which he calls the 'Latin Rim' or 'Mediterranean' model. Ferrera (1996) investigates this model in detail. On a wider canvas, Castles and Mitchell (1990) cite Australia as an instance of what might be called the 'Labourist' model, while Goodman and Peng (1996) discuss the so-called 'Confucian' welfare states of East Asia. Feminist critics such as Langan and Ostner (1991) and Lewis (1993) seek to recast Esping-Andersen's framework completely, arguing that it is gender-blind and neglects the role of public policy in shaping the sexual division of labour, reinforcing or countervailing traditional gender roles, as the case may be.

These are all valid points and it may be that no typology is suitable for all aspects of policy, all parts of the world, and all lines of social division, let alone all periods of history! Yet it is important to insist that without some comparative and historical framework, case-studies of single countries, specific programmes, or the experience of specific social groups fall short of their full potential. In any case, for all its limitations, the 'three worlds' thesis does help to explain the continuing diversity of welfare states. Reviewing trends in public spending, taxation, and employment in eighteen OECD countries, grouped according to regime type, Stephens *et al.* (1999) find that in social democratic regimes, taxes and spending are high as a proportion of GDP and the public sector is a major employer; in liberal regimes, the corresponding ratios are low; and in conservative regimes, they are somewhere in between. Admittedly, after 1979 regime-type performs less well as a predictor of fiscal developments, suggesting that differences between welfare regimes were more important in the 'golden age' than in the subsequent period of slow growth and fiscal retrenchment, when all governments found themselves wrestling with problems of public finance, regardless of the size of the public sector. But if 'hard times' have checked the growth of welfare spending everywhere, they have not (yet) reversed its previous expansion. And while all welfare states are being reshaped in response to common pressures, there is no sign of transnational convergence in the scale or design of welfare provision.

Liberal regimes

Liberal welfare states celebrate markets, property, and the work ethic. Echoing the early Puritan belief that the industrious would be saved and the idle damned, the presumption of liberal social policy is that all who are not incapacitated by age, disability, or illness have a duty to support themselves and their dependants. Accordingly, those with no private means of their own must be drawn or driven into the labour market. To this end, social transfers are strictly targeted, means-tested, and work-tested. Social services are similarly residual and the better-off are induced to opt out of state welfare, not least through the provision of tax relief on private pensions and health insurance. Thus, far from counteracting social inequality, liberal regimes impose a clear line of demarcation between self-reliant citizens and a dependent underclass, relying on free markets and coercive 'workfare' to contain the size and cost of the latter.

In the past, liberal regimes treated unpaid caregiving as a free service that women perform for the benefit of society as whole. This has changed with the growth of female employment, marital instability, and one-parent families, and nowadays 'neo-liberal' governments provide financial support for marketed childcare (incidentally discriminating against mothers who prefer to bring up their children at home). Even so, public provision for mothers and children in these states remains limited, whether in cash or in kind. Women may benefit from the deregulation of working hours to the extent that their gendered need to juggle commitments coincides with employers' competitive need for flexible work schedules. Over the past decade, alongside established practices such as part-time work, shiftwork, and homework, various new working-time arrangements have been introduced, including flexitime, annualized hours contracts, the compressed working work, and weekend working (Harkness 1999), and it is noteworthy that in the UK, where these developments have gone farthest, recorded rates of unemployment among women of all ages are lower than those found among men, in contrast to the pattern elsewhere in the EU (Nickell 1999).

Nevertheless, although the two-parent, one-breadwinner family is now quite rare, women still do far more unpaid work than men (Gershuny 1999). As a result, relatively few women are financially independent, either in the absolute sense that their personal income from all sources exceeds the official poverty line, or in the relative sense that they and their partners contribute more or less equally to household income (Lister 1990; Joshi *et al.* 1995). Without more 'family-friendly' employment practices, better nursery facilities, and more generous financial support for parents when their children are young, and without greater involvement by fathers in the care of their offspring, this basic situation seems unlikely to change.

Conservative or social Christian regimes

The watchword of *conservative* or *social Christian* regimes is the 'social market economy'. Capitalism is welcomed as an engine of economic growth, but social transfers are used to compensate market losers, uphold family values, and preserve social cohesion. Significantly, it was Germany, Esping-Andersen's exemplar country, which invented social insurance. The German model, however, is hierarchical. Instead of a unitary and comprehensive national insurance scheme covering all workers and all risks, Germany has a variety of occupational and sectoral schemes, and health insurance is funded and administered separately from retirement pensions and unemployment compensation. Each scheme is jointly managed by representatives of employers and workers, subject to broad requirements laid down by the state. Both for this reason and because insurance benefits are earnings-related rather than flat-rate, the system provides income security without disturbing established hierarchies of income and status. This makes it attractive to the affluent classes and fosters a corporatist approach to social policy.

Historically, the conservative model originated in the efforts of Bismarck to pre-empt the appeal of socialism by securing the allegiance of German workers to the newly unified German state. The influence of Catholic social thought is also evident: in the provision of 'family wage' supplements for (male) breadwinners; in the principle of *subsidiarity*, which accords a preferential role to the voluntary sector in the delivery of social services; and in a system of industrial relations designed to affirm the dignity of labour, prevent class conflict, and incorporate employee representatives in both enterprise management and national policy-making.

The continuing importance of these influences can be gauged by comparing responses to the sharp rise in unemployment that all countries experienced in the 1980s. Whereas the Anglo-Saxon countries sought to deregulate the labour market and restrict benefit entitlements, many continental welfare states adopted strategies of labour-supply reduction. In Germany, women were encouraged to stay at home, older workers to take early retirement, and foreign workers (*Gastarbeiter*) to return to their countries of origin. By lowering resistance to redundancies, this policy helped domestic firms retain or regain competitiveness through higher productivity rather than lower wages (Esping-Andersen 1994). Its continued viability depended on the willingness of employers and their remaining employees to accept higher taxes in order to meet the extra costs of family support and extended periods of pension entitlement, and this was sorely tried by the 'solidarity' taxes and high interest rates that were imposed on them in the early 1990s as the price of German reunification. In a parallel development, trade unions in the core EU states have repeatedly campaigned for a shorter working week as a means of creating more jobs. With the notable exception of the Dutch trade unions, however, they have not shown much willingness to accept commensurate reductions in weekly earnings. As a result, except in the Netherlands, employer resistance has been high and achievements have been modest, though negotiations over the staged introduction of a 35-hour week in France are said to have eased the way to more flexible working practices.

Social democratic regimes

Social democratic regimes are also committed to social insurance and social partnership, but as elements in an egalitarian scheme of social citizenship. In this model, the state is not a second or last resort, but plays a primary role in providing all citizens with the highest attainable degree of income security and a wide range of high-quality services. Esping-Andersen (1990) argues that such arrangements *decommodify* the labour market in the sense that they protect people's livelihoods from market contingency. This is true, but should not be taken to imply any antipathy to the wages system or the business sector. The social democratic model remains firmly wedded to employment as the pre-eminent form of work and, indeed, promotes it to the extent that the state becomes a major provider or purchaser of services that were once produced informally in the home. Likewise, the model rests on a concordat between capital and labour: workers accede to management control over the enterprise in return for business acceptance of the welfare state.

In the sphere of social transfers, all citizens are entitled to a basic retirement income as a matter of right. Additional income security is provided through social insurance. As in conservative regimes, contributions and benefits are earnings-related. But all employees belong to a common, unified scheme. Apart from its symbolic value, this inclusive arrangement pre-empts the growth of private pensions and insurance and raises the ceiling of tax tolerance, making it easier to maintain high income-replacement rates.

The viability of a system that guarantees paid work or generous transfers from cradle to grave depends on the maintenance of full employment, not simply as a condition of balance between labour supply and demand, but in the more vital sense that participation in the labour force is maximized, while frictional and structural unemployment are mimimized. It is, therefore, essential for the government to pursue an active labour-market policy, ensuring that workers made redundant are rapidly re-employed and drawing women into the labour force, if necessary by creating new jobs in the public sector.

This in turn requires an active childcare strategy offering all parents access to affordable day nurseries and instituting a system of paid parental leave so that both mothers and fathers can take time off work while their children are young, with generous replacement incomes and no loss of job rights.

The final limb of the social democratic polity—its Achilles heel, in fact—is some means of restraining money wages. Permanent full employment and low inflation are incompatible with uncoordinated wage bargaining. But government cannot avert the risk of a wage-price spiral single-handed: it needs the collaboration of trade unions and employers' organizations which are encompassing, unified, centralized, and disciplined. Moreover, having invited the 'social partners' into a regular process of negotiation over the whole field of economic policy, government must endeavour to reconcile conflicts of interest both between workers and employers and between different groups of workers.

This may not prove easy, even in a country like Sweden, where there is a strong commitment to consensus politics and the Social Democrats have been the senior partner in governing coalitions for all but nine of the years since 1932. Tensions were already apparent in the early 1980s, when Swedish employers rejected trade-union demands for a voice in corporate investment decisions. As the decade wore on, wage discipline began to break down, with schisms emerging between public- and private-sector workers, and the high fiscal cost of the active labour-market policy gave rise to further strains. Finally, in the early 1990s, mounting inflation, deteriorating international competitiveness, and pressure on the exchange rate forced the government to make deep cuts in public expenditure and unemployment rose sharply.

This was not, however, the end of the 'Swedish model'. For one thing, institutionalized solidarity makes it possible to impose even-handed welfare cutbacks on a scale that would be unthinkable elsewhere. Furthermore, in 1994 the Social Democrats were voted back into office and promptly set about raising income tax and reforming retirement pensions. Since then, thanks to a combination of economic recovery, fiscal prudence, and intensified labour-market activism, unemployment has fallen steadily. It is also striking that many of the ideas now advocated by proponents of the 'third way'—lifelong learning, 'welfare-to-work', childcare support, and social partnership—have long been practised in Sweden. True, it is sometimes claimed that the high cost of Sweden's active welfare state has retarded the country's economic growth (Lindbeck 1997). But Korpi (2000) casts doubt on the historical basis for this claim and comparative surveys fail to support the hypothesis that welfare policies are systematically and substantially damaging to economic performance (Atkinson 1995; Slemrod 1995).

To be sure, social policy affects social behaviour, if not always as its authors intend: but the ways in which people respond to taxes, transfers, and public provision in their various capacities—as workers, savers, taxpayers, and beneficiaries; as parents, partners, neighbours, and friends; as members of the multitude of interest groups that press their claims on available opportunities and resources; and finally, as citizens sharing certain rights and responsibilities in common—depend on the institutions, politics, history, and culture of the society to which they belong. In short, welfare regimes make a difference.

Social policy and economic performance

To conclude this section, Figure 10.1 presents a stylized overview of the relationship between social policy and economic performance, showing how seemingly contradictory claims may all be true in part, though none gives the full picture. The vertical axis measures some general indicator of economic performance, such as the level or rate of growth of per capita GDP. The horizontal axis measures welfare spending as a proportion of GDP. Curves A and B show what happens to economic performance as welfare spending grows, other things being equal, under two different welfare regimes. Both curves rise over a certain range, reach a peak, and then turn down. This can be interpreted as follows: as social democrats once argued, welfare states serve to improve economic performance by comparison with what would happen if they did not exist. But only up to a point: as the share of welfare spending rises, and with it, the tax burden, the gains from additional welfare spending gradually tail off until performance can be improved no further. Thereafter, if the welfare state gets any bigger, performance starts to deteriorate. This is the standard neo-liberal contention, though it needs to be borne in mind that GDP is not the only determinant of welfare, that welfare is not the only social value, that a marginal contraction of the welfare state is not the same as dismantling it altogether, and that the performance curves shown in the diagram are only heuristic devices, not well-founded empirical regularities.

Although the two curves have the same general shape, they occupy different positions: regime A performs better at every level of welfare-spending than regime B. This is the point stressed by those historians and comparative scholars who insist that it is not just the existence or scale of the welfare state that matter, but how it is organized, financed, justified, and supported. By the same token, while welfare regimes are not set in stone

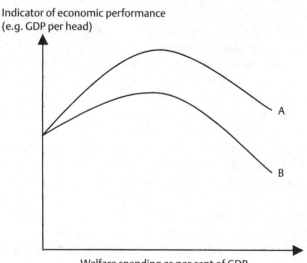

Fig. 10.1 Social policy and economic performance

and can be recast over time, political realignment, institutional renovation, and cultural change are hard to achieve and slow to take effect. Thus, even if the opportunity for reform arises and political leaders emerge with the imagination and will to seize it, a country which has inherited a relatively unproductive regime—such as that represented by curve B—will not find it easy to lift its performance towards the superior model which has evolved in country A.

10.4 Social policy in the EU

The role of the EU as a social policy actor

The EU is part of a system of governance in which political authority is shared between different levels: sub-national, national, and supranational. It is difficult to characterize this system in conventional terms. EU Member States retain far more autonomy than the constituent units of federal states such as the USA, Canada, and Switzerland: the extent of their reserved powers is greater and the Council of Ministers, where national governments pursue what they take to be their national interests, is the EU's central decision-making body. Neither, however, is the EU a mere confederation, empowered to act only at the behest of its members who, in turn, may secede with impunity. The EU's supranational agencies can and do act independently of national governments: the Commission is active in shaping the policy agenda and launching new initiatives, and the European Court of Justice exercises extensive powers of judicial review. Moreover, the Member States are constrained by the consequences of their own past commitments: restoring national sovereignty in areas where it has previously been ceded becomes progressively more difficult as social actors adjust to the new situation. And the relevant actors in this context include not only governments, but also organizations such as trade unions and employers' associations—the 'social partners' in EU jargon—which nowadays span national boundaries and are directly involved in EU policy-making.

As Leibfried and Pierson (1995) note, an inherent problem of multi-tiered governance is that disputes over what is to be done become intertwined with disputes over who is to do it. This greatly complicates the policy-making process. Policies must always serve two goals: resolving substantive problems and protecting institutional interests; and assembling a winning coalition may depend on scaling down policy ambitions to suit the demands of the least willing participant or, alternatively, on buying off opposition by means of side-payments. Such 'decision traps' have been particularly common in the field of EU social policy because the process of economic integration has continually raised questions about the appropriate division of powers and responsibilities between national governments and supranational authorities, without ever fully resolving them. The removal of barriers to trade and distortions of competition creates pressure for common EU social policies, whether to compensate prospective losers, to re-create the balance between market freedom and social protection that previously existed within each sovereign welfare state, or to build up the EU itself as an alternative to the nation-state.

Yet because welfare states came into being long before the EU was established, most of the available policy space is already occupied and national governments would strongly resist any transfer of core welfare functions to the EU, for this is one of the few realms where national autonomy still prevails and its loss would gravely weaken their fiscal and administrative capacity, diminishing their authority and standing more generally, and shifting the focus of political activity decisively upwards to the supranational level.

Thus, for the most part, the remit of the EU is confined to the edges of social policy space: that is, to areas which previously were not dealt with anywhere, or in which established arrangements have been disturbed, or which are only indirectly connected with social policy, such as the CAP and regional policy. Moreover, because it is unable to pursue ambitious social programmes of its own, in general the EU relies on *regulation* to establish common social standards. The legislative instrument most often employed is the *Directive*, which prescribes certain objectives or results to be achieved by Member States, but leaves them to decide how to achieve those objectives, as they see fit. Not that social policy-making is entirely, or even mainly, a matter of law-making and law-enforcement. Much of the work done by the Commission's Directorate-General (DG) V, which deals with Employment, Industrial Relations, and Social Affairs, consists of 'soft co-ordination' or 'communicative action': setting agendas, shaping the terms of debate, commissioning research, consulting other players—including the social partners—issuing opinions, building coalitions, and brokering agreements.

Why has this pattern of politics and power persisted? Why has the EU not developed a supranational welfare presence comparable, say, to the federal social security system that was introduced in the USA during the 1930s? One reason is that there is no constitutional basis for supranational welfare state-building. The main provisions of the Treaty of Rome relating to social issues, set out in Articles 117–28, have a very limited scope. In Articles 117 and 118, the signatories affirm their intention of seeking to improve living standards and working conditions, and charge the Commission with promoting cooperation in the social field. This, however, is confined to vocational training, employment, working conditions, occupational health and safety, social security, and collective bargaining—all matters that pertain to employees rather than to citizens. On these matters, moreover, the Commission's role is restricted to conducting research and offering opinions. The remaining Articles contain more substantial commitments: to ensure equal pay for men and women doing equal work; to facilitate the free movement of labour between Member States; and to establish a European Social Fund (ESF) with a view to expanding employment opportunities and helping displaced workers to find jobs. Even so, this is a narrow remit. With one exception, the underlying conception of economic integration is negative, focusing on the removal of restraints on trade and barriers to competition, rather than on harmonizing the rules under which markets operate. The exception is the equal pay provision. This was inserted into the Treaty at the instigation of France, where the law already prohibited sex discrimination with respect to rates of pay. The motive was strictly commercial: French employers were anxious not to be saddled with a competitive handicap. It was, nevertheless, an important precedent. In the years that followed, both the Commission and the ECJ exerted consistent pressure on Member States to equalize the terms on which women participate in the labour market (see Meehan 1993; Eurostat 1995; CEC:DG V 1999).

The EU's legal competence in the social field was widened by the Single European Act (SEA) (1986) and the Treaty on European Union (TEU) (1992), as Commission President Jacques Delors strove to give the single market a social dimension. This episode is described below. In general, however, while the process of market integration might be seen as adding a European layer to the civil rights of EU citizens, their political and, still more, social rights continue to be framed in national terms. Nor is there any popular demand for a European welfare state. On the contrary, notwithstanding the 'Ode to Joy', the starry blue flag, and the tears shed by central bankers at the launch of the Euro, the EU has signally failed to inspire the patriotism that was once evoked by the idea of the nation, binding its members together even as it set them apart from outsiders. The nation as an imagined community may be in decline, but it has not been replaced by any wider, supranational focus of popular loyalty and political mobilization. Except on the occasions when voters are asked to endorse abridgements of national sovereignty, EU politics is an élite business. The European counterparts of the coalitions and parties that once built and still defend national welfare states are, at best, weak and fragmented, and the link between parliamentary representation and executive power, which is the keystone of democracy in the nation-state, is missing from the institutions of the EU.

Finally, as we saw in the previous section, Europe's welfare states fall into three distinct clusters—four if one includes the 'Mediterranean' regime as a separate type—and their divergent institutions and norms inhibit the development of a federal welfare state. This was less of problem in the early years of the EC, when the six founding Member States formed a relatively homogeneous bloc approximating to the conservative model. But since then successive enlargements have introduced much greater regime diversity. It can, of course, be argued that despite this heterogeneity there is a 'European social model' and, in two senses, this is true. From a global standpoint, judged by criteria such as the level of spending, the scope of services, the extent of insurance cover, and the vigour of popular expectations, the various European welfare families have more in common with each other than with their distant relatives in North America, East Asia, or the Antipodes. Similarly, on the policy front, one can point to the growth of an EU-wide social policy network bringing together politicians, civil servants, interest-group functionaries, think-tank researchers, academic specialists, and media commentators, who tend to share the same intellectual outlook and policy ideas. But macroscopic affinities and 'epistemic communities' are no substitute for common institutions and norms. As Ferrera (1998) notes, even when policy experts in different countries use the same language, by the time buzzwords such as 'targeting', 'welfare dependency', or 'social exclusion' have been translated into the operational idiom of national social security systems, the 'European social model' looks far more heterogeneous that it appears from above.

The development of EU social policy

Besides being tightly circumscribed, EU social policy has developed in fits and starts. Sometimes it has been assigned a low profile, either by general consent or because any other course was politically infeasible. But there have also been periods of activism as those who favoured a collectivist, EU-wide approach to social issues—whether based on social Christian or social democratic principles—temporarily gained ground over the supporters of economic liberalism and national autonomy, groups which usually, though not invariably, coincide. In general, the policy activists include the Commission, the majority groupings in the European Parliament, and the European Trade Union Confederation (ETUC). This bloc is normally opposed by the Union of Industrial and Employers' Confederations of Europe (UNICE), which favours an internal market as free as possible from physical, technical, fiscal, and social 'distortions'. While the Conservatives were in power from 1979 to 1997, the UK government also took this view, sometimes gaining the backing of other Member States who objected to specific proposals or had decided to form an alliance of convenience. In the end, the fate of proposals for social legislation depends on the Council of Ministers. But the Council is a forum for national interests and hard bargaining, with voting rules that resemble the proverbial 'needle's eye'.

Given this unfavourable balance of forces, raising the profile of social policy has usually required the assistance of one or both of two conditions: an easing of the institutional constraints—as with the introduction of qualified majority voting for some of the issues within the EU's remit—or a change in the political complexion of the Council, usually as a result of national elections. Suitable conjunctures have arisen either at times when the EU is being enlarged through new accessions or when it is about to embark on some major new project, such as the single market and single currency programmes, the success of which can plausibly be shown to depend on strengthening supranational social regulation.

The evolution of EU social policy falls into four main phases: the early years from the Treaty of Rome to the late 1960s; the Social Action Programme of the 1970s; the struggle over the Social Charter which began with the signing of the SEA and ended with the collapse of the ERM in 1992; and the period since then in which European policy-makers have been preoccupied with globalization, monetary union, and welfare reform.

During the early years, as noted earlier, EC social policy was little more than a minor adjunct to market integration. The main concerns were to promote labour mobility and internal free trade, while mitigating any adverse impact on wages, working conditions, and social security. Some progress was made in redeploying redundant workers, especially in unskilled occupations, with the ESF being used to support resettlement and retraining schemes. But hopes that the Fund would benefit the less-developed regions of the EC proved unfounded: perversely, Germany emerged as the principal net beneficiary because the arrangements for reimbursing approved national expenditure depended on the scale of each country's training efforts. Hopes of harmonizing social insurance systems proved equally unrealistic. In part, this was because, even though the EC6 all belonged to the same welfare family, initial variations in coverage, scope, scales, finance, and eligibility were too wide to permit any easy or rapid convergence. But a more serious problem was that any uniform, Community-wide scheme would have entailed inter-state transfers on a scale that Germany, as the principal net loser, was unwilling to countenance. The alacrity and largesse with which the West German government subsequently absorbed the social security system of the former GDR provide a striking and instructive contrast.

Towards the end of the 1960s, the EC abandoned this low-key approach in a bid to change its popular image as a 'capitalist club'. At the 1972 Paris Summit, the Heads of

Government undertook to establish a Community regional policy, complete with its own Commissioner and a Regional Development Fund (discussed in Chapter 8), and instructed the Commission to draw up a Social Action Programme. This was finally unveiled in 1974 and spawned a stream of new Directives. Three of these conferred rights of information and consultation on employees in the event of collective redundancies, transfers of ownership, and corporate bankruptcies. Other Directives required Member States to guarantee women employees equal access to vocational training and social security, and imposed tougher standards of workplace health and safety. In addition, the ESF was given a larger budget and a new, more tightly specified list of priorities aimed at reducing unemployment, both in designated areas of rural underdevelopment or industrial decline, and among designated categories of people exposed to the risk of social exclusion, such as young workers, ethnic minorities, people with disabilities, and women seeking to re-enter the labour market. However, by the time these measures were implemented, the economic and political context had changed radically.

The recession which hit the advanced capitalist world in the mid-1970s marked the end of the long post-war boom and transformed both the nature and scale of the EC's social problems. Member States responded by seeking national rather than Community solutions, frustrating the Commission's efforts to promote common social standards by levelling-up. As Scharpf (1998) notes, the harmonization of national regulations has proceeded apace in certain areas—health and industrial safety, environmental risks, and consumer protection. But in the sphere of social protection and industrial relations, the conflicts of interest are too intense to be settled within the EU's institutions, especially when times are hard. The chief obstacles stem from disparities of economic development and differences of policy regime. Rich countries are reluctant to curtail their workers' established entitlements to benefits such as sick pay or parental leave. But the poorer EU countries, where output per worker is low, need to keep their wage and non-wage labour costs low as well, if they are to compete in the internal market. Thus, unless the richer Member States are willing to help them out, they cannot afford to agree to cost-increasing harmonization. As we have seen, inter-state redistribution was not a popular cause even in the booming 1960s. In the recession-bound 1970s and 1980s, it became a hopeless one.

Institutional differences are no less intractable. In the core EC states, the idea that workers have a right to be represented in the management of the companies that employ them was largely taken for granted. The UK, however, was steeped in the tradition of 'free collective bargaining' and even trade unions showed little enthusiasm for industrial democracy, in any guise. Throughout the 1970s, the Commission laboured to find an acceptable way of securing a common commitment to workers' participation in enterprise management. But even though it abandoned its initial preference for the German co-determination system and was prepared to allow for various alternative models from which governments could choose according to their national traditions, this effort failed. The ill-fated 'Vredeling' Directive of 1980 sought to extend the EC's disclosure laws to transnational companies, obliging them to inform and consult their employees on a regular basis and with respect to their global operations, not just those in the EC. The proposal aroused strong opposition from UNICE and was thrown out by the Council of Ministers after orchestrated resistance led by the UK.

The SEA and the Social Charter

After drifting into the doldrums in the late 1970s, EC social policy received a new impetus in the mid-1980s. The turning point was the Fontainebleau Council of 1984 and the appointment of Jacques Delors as Commission President. Displaying both vision and flair, Delors seized the opportunity to use the single market programme as a vehicle for extending the EC's social remit and introducing procedural reforms. Articles 100*a* and 118*a* of the SEA committed the EC to harmonizing and improving national regulations governing workplace health and safety, consumer protection, and environmental risk; Article 118*b* charged the Commission with promoting social dialogue between the social partners at the Community level; and Articles 130*a* and 130*b* sought to strengthen 'economic and social cohesion' through the use of reformed structural funds. In addition, except for certain reserved issues where unanimity was still required, the SEA introduced qualified majority voting in the Council of Ministers and strengthened the powers of the European Parliament in relation to the Council. (The regulation of pay, collective industrial action, and rights of association remain outside the EU's competence altogether.)

For a time, the 'social dimension' of the single market proved capacious and ambiguous enough to accommodate all major power-holders and all shades of opinion. Politicians and businessmen, impressed and alarmed by the dynamism of Japan and the East Asian 'tigers', sought antidotes to 'Eurosclerosis'. Trade unions and social democrats, devastated by mass unemployment and political defeat, were looking for new jobs and new horizons. Economic liberals saw in the 'social dimension' an opportunity to create a transnational labour market through improved communication and the mutual recognition of qualifications. Pragmatic realists, more alert to the potentially negative consequences of market integration, stressed the need to compensate those regions or groups who stood to lose from economic restructuring, and urged action to prevent 'social dumping'—the levelling down of established labour, social, and environmental standards which, it was feared, would result from the removal of barriers to pan-European competition. Finally, Euro-idealists saw the social dimension as a stepping stone towards a 'People's Europe' which would, in time, take over from the old nation-states as a focus of popular identity.

The Social Charter or, to give it its full title, the Community Charter of Fundamental Social Rights, was an attempt to strike a balance between these conflicting ambitions, establishing a common set of social standards which would be strong enough to satisfy social collectivists and Euro-idealists, but not so strong as to antagonize the neo-liberals. What emerged contained more symbolism than substance. The Charter was adopted at the Strasbourg Council in December 1989, with the UK as the lone dissenting voice, and subsequently formed the basis of the Social Chapter of the Maastricht Treaty under a compromise which allowed the UK to opt out of its provisions. As a result, three new objectives were added to Article 117 of the Treaty of Rome: 'proper social protection', social dialogue, and 'the development of human resources to achieve lasting employment'. In addition, the scope of qualified majority voting was extended to cover health and safety, working conditions, information and consultation, sex equality in the labour market, and the integration of persons excluded from the labour market. Yet for all the controversy surrounding it, the Charter was purely declaratory and had no legal force.

Most of its specific principles, such as the right to belong or not to belong to a trade union, had long been observed in most Member States or, as in the case of equal treatment for women at work, were actually enshrined in Community law. In addition, the Preamble contained a pointed reference to the principle of subsidiarity. This was a coded way of saying that EU standards should be consistent with national traditions.

The Charter did, however, serve as a standing reminder that what we call the 'labour market' is not a market like any other because labour is not a commodity like any other: the capacity for work is inseparable from the person whose capacity it is; human beings, unlike machines, care about what happens to them at work; and contracts of employment are continually being adjusted and renegotiated in the process of production. This doctrine was anathema to neo-liberals, while at a practical level, employers complained that some of the Charter's specific commitments would add to their costs or limit their room for manœuvre, notably: the requirement that the wages of non-standard employees should be set by reference to an equitable benchmark; the potential extension of disclosure rights through the establishment of European works councils; and the Commission's well-known and long-standing desire to establish Community-wide collective bargaining in transnational companies. Critics were also unhappy that the Commission was empowered to write an annual report on the application of the Charter in each Member State. Of course, there is little point in having a statement of principles without some way of monitoring observance. But recurrent monitoring does enable the Commission and its allies to keep social regulation permanently on the agenda.

The critics need not have worried. EU Directives are generally much less stringent than existing national laws. For example, the Working Time Directive adopted in 1993 (against UK opposition) provides for a maximum working week of 48 hours on average—including overtime—for minimum rest breaks during working hours and for four weeks' annual paid holiday. These standards are less restrictive than national regulations in every Member State except the UK, which has no law in this area. The Directive also allows for numerous exemptions. The process of European social dialogue, sometimes described as the 'second pillar' of EU social policy, is equally anodyne. Under the provisions of the Social Chapter, the Commission is obliged to consult the social partners before framing proposals for social legislation. The latter may indicate that they wish to negotiate an EU-level agreement on the issues in question, 'bargaining in the shadow of the law', as Bercusson (1992: 185) calls it. If the social partners manage to reach agreement, it is their proposal that is put to the Council of Ministers. Having examined five Directives enacted during the 1990s, Keller and Soerries (1999) conclude that where this procedure worked, it did not matter, and where it mattered, it did not work.

10.5 Globalization, monetary union, and welfare reform

Recasting the welfare state: pressures and responses

During the 1990s, Europe's welfare states faced an unprecedented combination of challenges. Not only were they having to contend, on the domestic front, with rising age-dependency ratios, increasing health care costs, high rates of open or disguised unemployment, the continued decline of employment in manufacturing and the rise of the service economy, pressure for more flexible labour markets and changing gender roles, but they were having to do so under a set of external constraints that severely limited their room for manœuvre and in an ideological climate that was still dominated by neo-liberalism. No social institution can be preserved in aspic and welfare states would have had to adjust to the cumulative effects of economic and social change even if national economies had not become more exposed to international competition, even if financial markets had not been deregulated, even if foreign direct investment had not grown in scale, and even if the EU had not embarked on the road to EMU. As it was, the effects of these developments, in the eyes of many observers, was to institutionalize neo-liberal ideology and politics, giving them a sharp global edge in the battle over the future of the welfare state and tipping the electoral scales against the electoral and interest-group forces which had hitherto managed to defend it.

Certainly, the liberalization of capital markets and the Maastricht convergence criteria diminished the macroeconomic autonomy of national governments, putting them under strong pressure to make central banks more independent and to announce pre-determined rules and commitments for public finance. Intensified competition began to affect sectors close to the state and hitherto protected by it, such as transport, telecommunications, public utilities, and financial services, forcing them to cut costs and shed labour. International tax competition coupled with domestic tax resistance made it harder for governments to maintain high rates of corporate taxation, payroll taxes, and personal income tax, squeezing public consumption, encouraging the middle class to defect from the welfare state, and damaging the framework of social solidarity. And the premium attached to international competitiveness increased the risk of social dumping, threatening a downward spiral of wages, working conditions, and social expenditure.

It is, however, important to distinguish between the logic of globalization and what actually happens. As Hirst and Thompson (1999) argue, the issue is how national governments respond to all these pressures and what scope exists to reform and protect the welfare state rather than allowing it to die. Some European governments have managed to maintain high levels of welfare spending, while improving the performance of their economies and bringing down unemployment. Denmark and the Netherlands are notable examples. In the early 1980s, both countries experienced double-digit unemployment and high fiscal deficits and, in both cases, centre-right coalitions introduced tough deflationary packages. But there was no assault on the legitimacy of the welfare state, the status of trade unions, or the practice of social partnership. Taking their cue from the government, employers accepted the need for social protection and were willing to engage in dialogue, while trade unions accepted the need for wage restraint and were willing to negotiate over patterns of working time and the reform of collective bargaining. The subsequent revitalization of social partnership set in motion a rolling process of policy innovation which, in the 1990s, extended to social security and the labour market. Repudiating retrenchment, both countries sought to make the work–welfare system more employment-friendly and both used active pressure rather than punitive sanctions to deter welfare dependency. The pay-off has been impressive: employment rates have grown—spectacularly in the Netherlands—long-term unemployment is low, and unemployed workers are not marginalized. More generally, disposable incomes are much less unequally distributed than in the UK or USA, and there are excellent public services which most citizens use, regardless of income or occupation. Thus, neither country has allowed a gulf to open up between those who pay for the welfare state and those who benefit from it (Hirst and Thompson 1999; ch. 7)

In a similar vein, Rhodes (1998) argues that while globalization inhibits welfare spending, national governments retain control over the design of welfare policy. Hence, given that untrammelled market freedom produces social dislocation, there is still a role for purposive state intervention to secure an acceptable balance between the interests of employers in not being over-regulated and over-taxed, the interests of employees in not being exploited or insecure, and the interests of non-employees in not being humiliated, poverty-stricken, or excluded. Rhodes particularly commends what he calls 'competitive corporatist' social pacts as a way of reconciling international market pressure with national social solidarity, citing, in addition to Danish and Dutch experience, ongoing negotiations over pension reform in Italy and the successive national accords which, since 1987, have helped to transform Ireland from a low-income, labour-surplus economy into a runaway 'Celtic tiger'.

Of course, these cases need to be treated with caution. They contain many path-dependent features and cannot be taken as models which other countries may emulate at will. But they do demonstrate that suitably refurbished, high-spending welfare states can survive in an internationalized economy. In so far as we can generalize about what is required to achieve this result, four broad precepts stand out: macroeconomic stability, responsive wage-setting, an employment-friendly tax and social security system, and 'flexicurity'. This last is a concept developed in the Netherlands embracing several related ideas: breaking down barriers between 'insiders' and 'outsiders' by relaxing job protection for the stable, full-time, core workforce, while giving better protection and support to casual, non-standard, and peripheral workers; promoting greater flexibility in work-time patterns, particularly by removing the legal and social security disadvantages attached to part-time status; pursuing active childcare strategies designed to reconcile employment and family commitments, especially through a system of paid parental leave; recognizing that it is better to expand labour-force participation than to reduce the supply of labour, whilst encouraging employers to introduce temporary job-rotation schemes and arrangements for sabbatical and educational leave as socially preferred alternatives to permanent labour-shedding; and stimulating the demand for unskilled labour by means of targeted wage subsidies and tax credits.

Pension reform

Social pacts can also facilitate the reform of retirement pensions, an area of policy where change necessarily takes time and policy-makers have to contend with vested interests and institutional inertia. Retirement pensions in Western Europe are predominantly state-organized, insurance-based, and earnings-related. The main exception is the UK, where private pensions account for 40 per cent of total pensioner income and the flat-rate component of the contributory state pension accounts for almost 90 per cent of state pension spending. Scandinavian pension schemes used to include a significant flat-rate element in the form of a tax-financed citizen's pension, but this is now being replaced by a means-tested minimum income guarantee (Olsen 1999). Whatever their structure, however, state pensions have traditionally been financed on a *pay-as-you-go* (PAYG) basis, whereby each year's payments are met from current contributions and income is redistributed from the working generation to the pensioners' generation. Private pensions, by contrast, are normally *pre-funded*: pooled contributions are invested in financial assets and individuals acquire entitlements in proportion to the size of their accumulated holdings.

PAYG systems are sensitive to the ratio between the number of retired pensioners and the number of employed contributors. If this ratio rises, either pension outlays must be reduced or contribution rates must be raised relative to average earnings. Over the past twenty years, to varying degrees in different countries, the ratio has risen thanks to rising life expectancy, high unemployment rates, and falling economic activity rates among older men—the result, in some cases, of voluntary early retirement, but more often, as Disney (1999) shows, a form of disguised unemployment—and over the next forty years it is set to rise still further as the baby boomers of the 1940s and 1960s reach retirement age. Given the reluctance of employers and job-holders to countenance higher contributions, governments have generally preferred to curtail pension commitments by variously raising the retirement age, lengthening the qualification period, scaling down earnings-related entitlements, and weakening protection for pensions in payment—for example, indexing pension scales to retail prices rather than average earnings or making annual adjustments conditional on the performance of the national economy. More recently, several governments have also taken steps to introduce or extend reliance on pre-funded pensions, either within what remains an inclusive state scheme, as in Sweden, or by altering the balance between state and private provision, as in the UK, where the role envisaged for the state by the New Labour government is confined to regulating the private sector, encouraging those who can afford it to subscribe to private pension plans, and providing a means-tested minimum income guarantee, uprated each year in line with average earnings, to supplement the incomes of retirees whose private holdings are inadequate (Department of Social Security 1998).

Pension reform is a fraught and complex business and governments cannot hope to build a broad consensus for change unless they consult widely, cultivate allies, and take pains to explain and argue for their plans. In Sweden, for example, after the breakdown of institutionalized pay restraint in the 1980s and the financial crisis of the early 1990s, the pension system was radically overhauled. This would scarcely have been possible without bi-partisan agreement. On returning to office in 1994, the Social Democrats proceeded to implement the proposals of an all-party commission which had been established by their 'bourgeois' predecessors. In Italy, it was the social partners who played a key role in persuading job-holders to accept the need for change. From 1992 onwards, with the public finances seemingly out of control and the post-war political order collapsing in the wake of corruption scandals, strong employer and trade-union organizations helped to legitimize the efforts of 'technocratic' governments to reduce the budget deficit and regenerate the republic, and remarkable progress was made in reforming a pension system that was not just financially unsustainable, but morally indefensible (Ferrera 1997; Pochet and Fajertag 2000). In the UK, by contrast, where social partnership remains the practice that dares not speak its name, a nervous New Labour government won little public understanding or support for its proposed new pensions contract and, with an election in the offing and its coffers overflowing, decided to abandon its principles, bow to popular pressure, and concede a hefty real-terms increase in the basic state retirement pension.

Social pacts and the role of the EU

Social pacts are primarily national affairs. Nevertheless, the EU has sought to promote the idea and disseminate good practice and there is more it could do to help. From the Essen Council of 1994 to the Lisbon 'dotcom' Council of March 2000, the process of 'soft co-ordination' mentioned earlier was consistently used to provide moral and didactic leadership on issues of employment and welfare reform. A Chapter on Employment was included in the Amsterdam Treaty agreed in June 1997, authorizing the Commission to monitor employment in Member States and, on an annual cycle, to publish reports, set guidelines, adopt targets, identify best practice and issue recommendations to any state whose performance in this area is judged to be deficient. This is a useful innovation, though so far the results have been modest. Pochet (1999) argues that too much attention has been paid to 'employability' despite the vagueness of this concept and the absence of good evidence that supply-side policies can do much to reduce unemployment on their own. He also notes that the EU still lacks comprehensive and standardized data on the various kinds and aspects of work, mainly because of the political choices that need to be made before one can assess policy performance. How, for example, should different kinds of work be classified and should data on work be combined with data on income? A further weakness is that until the Euro was safely launched in 1999, macroeconomic and labour-market policy were kept in separate compartments, though comparisons between Europe and the USA since 1980 strongly suggest that they are interdependent (Martin 2000). The greater the ECB's confidence that cheap money will not give rise to wage inflation, the less the risk of terminating growth by monetary stringency, the better the outlook for investment and jobs, the higher the public standing of the ECB, and the stronger the commitment of trade unions and workers to wage restraint. This, in turn, suggests the wisdom of regular multilateral macroeconomic dialogue involving the ECB, finance ministers, the Commission, and the social partners, as was finally recognized by the Cologne Council in June 1999.

It is also important to appreciate the dangers of a generalized strategy of competitive corporatism. If every state is striving to keep ahead of the game, with no supranational rules to keep competition within bounds, each may end up having to work harder to stay in the same place, and countries that start to fall behind may be tempted to resort to social dumping, holding back the 'progressive' states and creating an atmosphere of mutual mistrust. Admittedly, to date social dumping remains more of a threat than a reality. But that is no reason not to take it seriously, especially when building defences against it now offers important benefits at negligible cost in terms of resources expended or options foreclosed. As Mishra (1999) argues, standards of social protection should not be used as weapons in a competitive game, but must be part of the rules of the game. A precautionary, but conspicuous, demonstration of commitment to this principle would help to reassure people that welfare reform is not a euphemism for welfare retrenchment and would weaken the appeal of xenophobic, racist, and protectionist forces.

The problem is how to achieve this result. Hitherto, as we have seen, attempts to create an EU-wide social framework have been bedevilled by disparities of economic development and differences of policy regime among Member States, and by disputes of ideology and interest over the legitimate scope and appropriate level of social policy. These obstacles, however, are not insuperable. One possibility suggested by Scharpf (1997) is to have graduated systems of social and environmental protection, imposing higher minimum standards on rich countries than on poor ones. This would accommodate economic disparities, while ensuring that the level of social protection rises in line with economic growth. For example, taking the proportion of GDP that each state devotes to (some agreed definition of) social expenditure, plotting it against national per capita GDP, and determining the resulting regression line, EU Member States could fix an upward-sloping lower bound drawn so as to pass through or close to the position of the

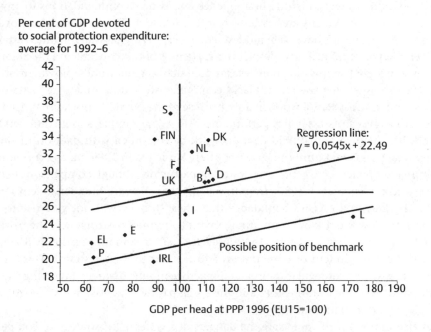

Fig. 10.2 Graduated benchmarks for social expenditure: an illustration

lowest outlier. National governments would retain control over the balance and design of social programmes, but would refrain from welfare cutbacks that caused their spending ratios to fall below this threshold. Figure 10.2 shows what such an agreement might look like. The percentage of GDP spent by each EU Member State on social protection is averaged over the five years from 1992 to 1996 and plotted against per capita GDP for 1996. The corresponding regression line determines the *slope* of the requisite lower bound; its ultimate *position* would be a matter for negotiation.

Such an agreement would, of course, mean abandoning any hope of transforming the EU into a federal welfare state, with substantial administrative and fiscal powers of its own. But this has always been a utopian idea and will not become any less so as the EU admits the former socialist states of Eastern Europe and a heterogeneous group of states in the Mediterranean basin, all of them much poorer than existing members. By contrast, a system of graduated welfare benchmarking would bring candidate states into the framework of negotiation at an early stage, whilst institutionalizing popular support for the welfare state in Western Europe through a binding convention against mutually ruinous competition. Indeed, as Mishra (1999) suggests, once established in the EU, the system could be extended to all members of the OECD and, eventually, to every country in the world. The process of reaching agreement would, no doubt, be arduous. But it would stimulate public debate about comparative welfare standards and the future of social citizenship by posing a question that concerns us all: if we accept that the poorest countries of Asia and sub-Saharan Africa should be able to provide all their people with primary health care, basic sanitation, safe drinking water, and adequate nutrition, what are the corresponding rights and responsibilities of citizens in the rich, industrialized states?

Discussion questions

1 Why has the process of economic integration within the EU not been matched by any comparable convergence in the field of social policy? Does this asymmetry matter? What, if anything, should be done about it?

2 What does the experience of the EU teach us about the problems of social policy-making in a multi-layered system of governance?

3 Analyse the challenges facing contemporary welfare states. How, if at all, should the EU help Member States to respond to these challenges?

References

Atkinson, A. B. (1995), 'The Welfare State and Economic Performance', *National Tax Journal*, 48: 171–98.

Bartlett, W., Roberts, J. A., and Le Grand, J. (1998), *A Revolution in Social Policy: Quasi-Market Reform in the 1990s* (Bristol: Policy Press).

Bercusson, B. (1992), 'Maastricht: A Fundamental Change in European Labour Law', *Industrial Relations Journal*, 23/3: 177–90.

Bonoli, G. (1997), 'Classifying Welfare States: A Two-Dimension Approach', *Journal of Social Policy,* 26/3: 351–72.

Brubaker, W. R. (1990), 'Immigration, Citizenship and the Nation-State in France and Germany', *International Sociology*, 5/4: 379–407.

Castles, F. and Mitchell, D. (1990), 'Three Worlds of Welfare-Capitalism or Four?', *Public Policy Discussion Paper* No. 21 (Canberra: Australian National University).

CEC: DG V (1999), *Women and Work: Report on Existing Research in the EU* (Luxembourg: Office for the Official Publications of the EC).

Department of Social Security (1998), *A New Contract for Welfare: Partnership in Pensions* (London: The Stationery Office).

Disney, R. (1999), 'Why have Older Men Stopped Working?' in P. Gregg and J. Wadsworth (eds.), *The State of Working Britain* (Manchester: Manchester University Press), 58–74.

Esping-Andersen, G. (1990), *The Three Worlds of Welfare Capitalism* (Cambridge: Polity Press).

—— (1994), 'Welfare States and the Economy', in N. J. Smelser and R. Swedberg (eds.), *The Handbook of Economic Sociology* (Princeton, NJ: Princeton University Press), 711–32.

—— (ed.) (1996), *Welfare States in Transition* (London: Sage).

Eurostat (1995), *Women and Men in the European Union: A Statistical Portrait* (Luxembourg: Office for the Official Publications of the European Union).

Fajertag, G. and Pochet, P. (eds.) (2000), *Social Pacts in Europe: New Dynamics*, 2nd edn. (Brussels: European Trade Union Institute and Observatoire Social Europeen).

Ferrera, M. (1996), 'The Southern Model of Welfare in Social Europe', *Journal of European Social Policy*, 6/1: 17–37.

—— (1997), 'The Uncertain Future of the Italian Welfare State', *West European Politics,* 20 (1): 231–249.

—— (1998), 'The Four "Social Europes": Between Universalism and Selectivity', in Rhodes and Meny, eds. *The Future of European Welfare* (Basingstoke: Macmillan), 81–96.

Gershuny, J. (1999), 'Gender Convergence and Public Regulation', in Hufton and Kravaritou, eds. *Gender and the Use of Time* (Amsterdam: Kluwer Academic Press), 281–95.

Giddens, A. (1998) *The Third Way: The Renewal of Social Democracy* (Cambridge: Polity Press).

—— (2000) *The Third Way and its Critics* (Cambridge: Polity Press).

Goodman, R. and Peng, I. (1990), 'The East-Asian Welfare States: Peripatetic Learning, Adapative Change and Nation-Building', in G. Esping-Andersen (ed.), *The Three Worlds of Welfare Capitalism* (Cambridge: Polity Press), 192–224.

Gregg, P. and Wadsworth, J. (eds.) (1999), *The State of Working Britain* (Manchester: Manchester University Press).

Harkness, S. (1999) 'Working 9 to 5' in P. Gregg and J. Wadsworth (eds.), *The State of Working Britain* (Manchester: Manchester University Press), 90–108.

Hine, D. and Kassim, H. (eds.) (1998), *Beyond the Market: The EU and National Social Policy* (London: Routledge).

Hirst, P. and Thompson, G. (1999), *Globalization in Question*, 2nd edn. (Cambridge: Polity Press).

Hufton, O. and Kravaritou, Y. (eds.) (1999), *Gender and the Use of Time* (Amsterdam: Kluwer Academic Press).

Keller, B. and Soerries, B. (1999), 'The New European Social Dialogue: Old Wine in New Bottles', *Journal of European Social Policy*, 9/2: 111–25.

Kitschelt, H., Lange, P., Marks, G., and Stephens, J. D. (eds.) (1999), *Continuity and Change in Contemporary Capitalism* (Cambridge: Cambridge University Press).

Korpi, W. (2000) 'Welfare States, Economic Growth and Scholarly Objectivity', *Challenge*, 43/2: 49–66.

Jones, C. (ed.) (1993), *New Perspectives on the Welfare State in Europe* (London: Routledge).

Joshi, H., Dale, A., Ward, C., and Davies, H. (1995), *Dependence and Independence in the Finances of Women at 33* (London: Family Policy Studies Centre/ Joseph Rowntree Foundation).

Langan, M. and Ostner, I. (1991), 'Gender and Welfare: Towards a Comparative Framework', in G. Room (ed.), *Towards a European Welfare State* (Bristol : School for Advanced Urban Studies), 127–50.

Leibfried, S. (1993), 'Towards a European Welfare State?', in C. Jones (ed.), *New Perspectives on the Welfare State in Europe* (London: Routledge), 133–56.

—— and Pierson, P. (1995), 'Multi-Tiered Institutions and the Making of Social Policy', in S. Leibfried and P. Pierson (eds.), *European Social Policy* (Washington DC: Brookings Institute), 1–40.

—— —— (eds.) (1995), *European Social Policy* (Washington DC: Brookings Institution).

Lindbeck, A. (1997), 'The Swedish Experiment', *Journal of Economic Literature*, 35: 1273–1319.

Lister, R. (1990), 'Women, Economic Dependency and Citizenship', *Journal of Social Policy*, 19/4: 445–67.

Marshall, T. H. (1950), *Citizenship and Social Class and Other Essays* (Cambridge: Cambridge University Press).

Martin, A. (2000), 'Social Pacts, Unemployment and EMU Macroeconomic Policy', in G. Fajertag and P. Pochet (eds.), *Social Pacts in Europe: New Dynamics*, 2nd edn. (Brussels: European Trade Union Institute and Observatoire Social Europeen), 365–400.

Meehan, E. (1993), *Citizenship and the European Community* (London: Sage).

Mishra, R. (1999), *Globalization and the Welfare State* (Cheltenham: Edward Elgar).

Nickell, S. (1999), 'Unemployment in Britain' in P. Gregg and J. Wadsworth (eds.), *The State of Working Britain* (Manchester: Manchester University Press), 7–28.

Olsen, G. M. (1999), 'Half Empty or Half Full? The Swedish Welfare State in Transition', *Canadian Review of Sociology and Anthropology*, 36/2: 241–67.

Pochet, P. (1999), 'The New Employment Chapter of the Amsterdam Treaty', *Journal of European Social Policy*, 9/3: 271–7.

Pochet, P., and Fajertag, G. (2000), 'A New Era for Social Pacts in Europe' in G. Fajertag and P. Pochet (eds.), *Social Pacts in Europe: New Dynamics*, 2nd edn. (Brussels: European Trade Union Institute and Observatoire Social Europeen), 9–40.

Purdy, D. (1994) 'Citizenship, Basic Income and the State', *New Left Review*, 208 (Nov–Dec), 30–48.

Putnam, R. (1993), *Making Democracy Work* (Princeton, NJ: Princeton University Press).

Rawls, J. (1972), *A Theory of Justice* (Oxford: Oxford University Press).

Rhodes, M. (1998), 'Defending the Social Contract: The EU between Global Constraints and Domestic Imperatives', in D. Hine and H. Kassim (eds.), *Beyond the Market: The EU and National Social Policy* (London: Routledge), 36–59.

—— and Meny, Y. (eds.) (1998), *The Future of European Welfare* (Basingstoke: Macmillan).

Robertson, J., Dore, R., Van Parijs, P., and Atkinson, A. B. (1996), 'Debate: Citizen's Income', *Political Quarterly*, 67/1: 44–70.

Room, G. (ed.) (1991), *Towards a European Welfare State* (Bristol: School for Advanced Urban Studies).

Scharpf, F. (1997), 'European Integration, Democracy and the Welfare State', *Journal of European Public Policy*, 4/1: 18–36.

—— (1998), 'Negative and Positive Integration in the Political Economy of European Welfare States', in M. Rhodes and Y. Meny (eds.), *The Future of European Welfare* (Basingstoke: Macmillan), 155–77.

Slemrod, J. (1995), 'What do Cross-Country Studies Teach about Government Involvement, Prosperity and Economic Growth?', *Brookings Papers on Economic Activity*, 2: 373–431.

Smelser, N. J. and Swedberg, R. (eds.) (1994), *The Handbook of Economic Sociology* (Princeton, NJ: Princeton University Press).

Stephens, J. D., Huber, E., and Ray, L. (1999), 'The Welfare State in Hard Times', in H. Kitschelt, P. Lange, G. Marks, and J. D. Stephens (eds.), *Continuity and Change in Contemporary Capitalism* (Cambridge: Cambridge University Press), 164–93.

Van Parijs, P. (1995), *Real Freedom for All* (Oxford: Oxford University Press).

Chapter 11

Developments in Trade and Trade Policy

Lynden Moore

11.1 Introduction

This chapter is primarily concerned with the development of the EU's trade policy. However, before confronting this issue, we should take a look at the overall picture of intra-EU trade, that is trade between the 15 Member States, and its trade with the rest of the world. Table 11.1 shows trade in the Major Product Categories in 1998. As can be seen from the last column the EU then had had net exports of manufactures of $107 bn. overall. These paid for its net imports of agricultural products, mainly food, mining products, and fuels. There was also a net positive balance in trade in services, which comprise transportation, tourism, financial services, etc. These do not add up to zero because of the other items in the balance of payments, namely the payment of interest and dividends, and capital flows, which we will not consider here. In the first category, of agricultural products, it

Table 11.1 EU15 trade in major product categories in 1998

Product groups	Total exports ($ bn.)	Export distribution (%)		Total imports ($ bn.)	Import distribution from rest of world (%)	Net exports ($ bn.)
		Intra-EU	Rest of world			
Agricultural products	221.23	72	28	247.8	35	−26.57
Mining products except fuels	45.52	72	28	67.55	52	−22.03
Fuels	49.71	68	32	105.95	68	−22.67
Manufactures	1,762.22	61	39	1,654.89	35	107.33
Services	488.22[a]			429.67[a]		17.19

[a]   Services are for 1997.
Note: Product groups are defined according to Revision 3 of the Standard International Trade Classification (SITC Rev. 3).
Source: WTO (1999).

can be seen that only 35 per cent of imports come from the rest of the world, whereas 72 per cent of exports from the EU go to other EU Member States. Later it will be argued that this is mainly the result of its protectionist Common Agricultural Policy (CAP).

For manufactures the situation differs between product categories, as shown in Table 11.2. The EU is a net exporter for the category as a whole, as mentioned previously, but it is a net importer of office and telecommunications equipment, clothing, and other consumer goods. The EU industries producing these and also iron and steel, and automotive products send around 70 per cent of their exports to other Member States. It will be argued that the ability of these EU industries to export to other Member States is not only due to the EU customs union but also to additional forms of protection against imports from non-member countries.

The EU faces a conflict when devising its commercial policy. On the one hand as a member of the international organizations regulating trade, initially the General Agreement on Tariffs and Trade (GATT), replaced in 1995 by the World Trade Organization (WTO), it is committed to the non-discriminatory treatment of other members of these organizations by the general application of most-favoured nation (mfn) tariffs, and to the abolition of quotas and the reduction of tariffs on international trade. On the other hand in the pursuit of economic integration the EU encourages its Member States to give each other preferential treatment; the first step in this direction was indeed by the establishment of a customs union between the original six Member States, France, Germany, Italy, Belgium, the Netherlands, and Luxembourg in 1968.

Table 11.2 EU15 trade in manufactures, 1998

Product groups	Total ($ bn.)	Export distribution (%)				Imports ($ bn.)	Net exports ($ bn.)
		Intra-EU	W. Europe	Other W. Europe	Rest of world		
Iron and steel	65.31	70	77	6	23	59.48	5.83
Chemicals	272.32	62	69	7	31	231.05	41.27
Other semi-manufactures	199.48	63	70	7	30	179.43	20.05
Machinery and transport equipment	910.37	59	65	6	35	838.78	71.59
Power-generating equipment	34.47	38	44	5	56	33.28	4.19
Other non-electrical equipment	221.57	48	55	7	45	151.33	70.24
Office and telecommunications equipment	202.35	66	71	5	29	253.39	−51.04
Electrical machinery	98.65	58	65	6	35	96.00	2.65
Automotive products	267.68	71	76	5	24	232.12	35.56
Other transport equipment	82.64	46	52	6	48	72.67	9.97
Textiles	60.60	62	69	7	31	56.38	4.22
Clothing	51.17	69	77	8	23	84.17	−33.00
Other consumer goods	202.96	42	67	25	33	205.61	−2.65
	1,762.22	61	67	7	33	1,654.89	107.33

Notes: Product groups are defined according to Revision 3 of the Standard International Trade Classification (SITC Rev. 3).
Source: WTO (1999).

11.2 **The EC Customs Union**

Article 3 of the Treaty of Rome of 1957 included provisions for

(a) the elimination, as between Member States, of customs and of quantitative restrictions in regard to the import and export of goods as well as of all other measures having equivalent effect;

(b) the establishment of a common customs [external] tariff [CET] and of a common commercial policy towards third countries;

This CET was from the point of view of GATT the mfn tariff.

These provisions were expanded in the following articles, but then in Article 36 it was stated that these

shall not preclude prohibitions or restrictions on imports, exports, or goods in transit justified on the grounds of public morality; public policy; public security; the protection of health and life of humans, animals or plants; . . . Provided always that such prohibitions or restrictions shall not be used as a means of arbitrary discrimination nor as a disguised restriction on trade between Member States.

Articles 100–2 provided the legal framework for 'harmonizing' these national restrictions if they affect trade.

11.3 **Conformity with GATT provisions**

Although customs unions and free-trade areas as Preferential Trading Areas (PTAs) appeared to conflict with the principle of non-discrimination, they were favourably regarded by GATT as leading on to greater liberalization in trade. But under Article XXIV they were required to comply with certain provisions; they should cover 'substantially all the trade between constituent territories', 'the (external) duties . . . shall not on the whole be higher or more restrictive than . . . prior to the formation of such a union' and they 'shall include a plan and schedule for (their) . . . formation within a reasonable length of time' (Article XXIV, GATT 1986).

The Treaty of Rome of 1957 was drafted with these provisions in mind. The EC was set up as a customs union with provision for the removal of all impediments to trade in goods and the establishment of a Common External Tariff (CET) for manufactures. Nonetheless, there was criticism of the setting of the Common External Tariff at the simple unweighted arithmetic average of the tariffs applied by each of the six EC member states on 1 January 1957. Inevitably, it raised tariffs on extra-EC imports into EC countries with previously low levels of tariffs (WTO 1995a) but then these tariffs were lowered by the following GATT rounds of tariff negotiations.

More serious was the *Common Agricultural Policy* (CAP), which while it provided for a free movement in goods also, under Articles 39 and 40 of the Treaty of Rome, provided for market intervention, i.e. raising the EC price above the world price to a 'target level' by the imposition of variable levies on imports from outside the EC, and if necessary stock-piling surpluses. These surpluses were often disposed of by the subsidizing of exports. The world market was thus affected by the EC's reduction in imports of agricultural products and the increase in its exports. However, as the developed countries initially agreed that agriculture was too 'politically sensitive' a subject to be included in trade negotiations, and there is not enough space to cover this issue here, it will only be mentioned casually in this Chapter.

The Council of Ministers determines the direction of trade policy and the Commission of the EC (CEC) carries out negotiations in the GATT, now WTO, rounds of tariff and trade negotiations. In practice the consultation of the CEC with the Member States adds to the complexity of any international negotiations.

In 1973 Britain, Denmark, and Ireland joined the EC. Britain and Denmark had previously been members of the *European Free Trade Association* (EFTA) and the EC then formed a free-trade area in manufactures with EFTA. By the time the EC had expanded to include Greece (1981) and Spain and Portugal (1986), manufactures could be freely traded, without the imposition of tariffs, throughout most of Western Europe.

Voluntary Export Restraints (VERs)

However, as the external mfn tariffs were reduced, the developed countries had frequent recourse to non-tariff barriers to trade, which were quite inconsistent with the ethos and legal requirements of GATT. Prominent among these devices was the 'voluntary' export restraint (VER), by which the importing country negotiates a physical limit on exports from a particular country. The VER is in effect a bilateral quota. It has a similar effect to a tariff in raising the price of the product on the market of the importing country. But no tariff revenue is gained. Instead, there is an 'economic rent' associated with the quota, due to the fact that the product is sold on the domestic market at a much higher price than it can command on the international market. Who gains the economic rent depends on how the quota is allocated. When VERs are imposed on developing countries those countries are generally given the entitlement to export and are therefore regarded as acquiring the rent from the quota.

Textiles and clothing

The most extreme use of VERs was in the limitation of imports of textiles and clothing from developing countries. In an endeavour to restrict their proliferation GATT negotiated the Short Term and then the *Long Term Arrangement on Cotton Textiles* (LTA) in 1961 and 1962 respectively, by which all quotas on imports of cotton textiles were to be increased by 5 per cent a year. This led the developing countries to expand their exports of clothing with a higher value per unit than textiles, and also that of textiles of other fibres or mixed with them. A more extensive *Multi-Fibre Arrangement* (MFA) was then negotiated in 1974, which provided for bilateral agreements between countries as before for the LTA. Quotas were set by the EC and other developed countries (excluding Japan) on imports of individual items of textiles and clothing from individual developing countries. These were to be extended by 6 per cent a year. The EC did not comply with this requirement. The CEC classified products according to 'sensitivity'. The most sensitive products were those in which the developing countries had achieved the highest degree of penetration in the EC market i.e. cotton yarn, cotton fabric, fabrics of synthetic fibres, T-shirts, pullovers, trousers including jeans, blouses, and shirts. The growth in quotas for these was the most limited, at 1–2 per cent a year. Initially the CEC also had to allocate quotas between the Member States. The 'burden sharing' was supposed to be arranged so that the EC countries with the lowest level of MFA imports took the greatest proportion of the increase in quotas. As Germany took 25.5 per cent and the UK 21 per cent they should have had the smallest increase (Keesing and Wolf 1980).

Anti-dumping and countervailing duties

In addition there was a widespread use by both the EC and the USA of countervailing and anti-dumping duties. Dumping is defined as the situation in which a product is sold in a market at less than its 'normal' value, which is regarded as either being

the comparable price . . . when destined for consumption in the exporting country, or, in the absence of such domestic price is less than either the highest comparable price . . . [of the] product for export to any third country . . . or, the cost of production of the product in the country of origin plus a reasonable addition for selling cost and profit. (Article VI, GATT 1986).

The importing country can levy an anti-dumping duty not greater than the margin of dumping on the exports of the firm. Alternatively, if the difference is due to a government subsidy, a countervailing duty may be imposed to offset it. Sometimes firms avoid anti-dumping duties by accepting a 'price undertaking', that is a minimum import price, by which the exporting firms lose their competitive advantage but gain a higher price. In 1999 the EU took 192 anti-dumping actions; 66 of these were initiations, 25 per cent were in the form of definite duties, and 15 per cent were in the form of price undertakings. The products most affected were iron and steel, consumer electronics, and chemicals (WTO 2000: 67–9 and Table III.8). A list of those applying to electronic products in May 2000 is given in Table 11.3. The duties are applied to specific firms and therefore a range of duties is shown for each country. Some of them are very high; even for commonplace items such as personal fax machines, they go up to 89.8 per cent from Malaysia, and for TV broadcast cameras they range up to 200.3 per cent. The EU also imposed six countervailing measures, five on imports from India and one on imports from Norway.

The problem with these non-tariff barriers is their arbitrary nature, the way they discriminate not only between countries but also, in the case of anti-dumping duties, between firms, penalizing the most efficient producers. In calculating the size of anti-dumping duties the EC is also accused of the dubious use of statistics.

Table 11.3 Definitive anti-dumping duties and undertakings in force on 15 February 2000

Product	Country	Duty or range (%)	Date of expiry
Personal fax machines	China	51.6	30.4.2003
	Japan	34.9	
	Malaysia	89.8	
	S. Korea	25.1	
Colour TVs (larger than 15.5 cms)	Malaysia	23.4–7.5	01.04.2000
	Singapore	23.6–0	01.04.2000
	Thailand	29.8–3	01.04.2000
	S. Korea	15.1–0	
	China	25.6	in force until outcome of review
Electronic weighing scales	Japan	31.6–15.3	28.4.98
Floppy discs	Indonesia	41.1	23.8.2003
	Taiwan	32.7–19.8	Review
	Hong Kong	27.4–6.7	Review
	S. Korea	8.1	Review
	Malaysia	46.4–12.8	14.04.2001
	Mexico	44–0	14.04.2001
	USA	44–0	14.04.2001
Large aluminium electrolytic capacitors	Thailand	39.4	—
TV broadcast cameras	Japan	52.7–200.3	10.10.2002
Microwave ovens	China	12.1	05.01.2001
	Malaysia	29	05.01.2001
	Thailand	27.3–14.1	05.01.2001
	S. Korea	24.4–3.3	05.01.2001

Source: Information supplied by the Department of Trade and Industry, UK.

11.4 Harmonization in trade between Member States

The EC Commission initially concentrated on the removal of tariff barriers between Member States, but it soon found other obstacles to trade. Under Articles 92–4 of the Treaty the EC Commission forbids national governments from subsidizing the direct costs of its domestic firms in a way that distorts competition between Member States. There are some escape clauses, but export aid is not allowed. In addition the differing regulations of Member States with respect to goods were regarded as constituting a barrier to trade. Thus was the EC Commission set upon the road to the 'harmonization' of these regulations, which proved to be very slow and arduous.

Soon after Britain joined the EC in 1973 instances of 'harmonization' aroused the ire of the British populace, as one consumer product after the other appeared to be under threat. British chocolate was one of these, because British manufacturers were not required, as on the Continent, to include cocoa butter, and generally used a cheaper vegetable oil as a substitute. The CEC proposed that Britain, Denmark, and Ireland should be allowed to use up to 5 per cent vegetable fat in their chocolate as an exemption from the 1973 directive (Maitland 1996). This was thrown out by the European parliament after an emotional appeal for 'pure' continental-style chocolate by the Belgian members. The compromise will be some form of re-labelling (Tucker 1997). This process culminated in a case brought by a German company, Rewe-Zentral, which was trying to import the French blackcurrant liqueur cassis, which had a lower alcohol content than required by German law. The European Court ruled in 1978 that consumer protection could have been achieved by a label indicating the alcohol content: the German requirement was not essential. The 'Cassis de Dijon' principle, essentially one of mutual recognition of standards, has become of increasing importance ever since.

However, there are areas in which the process of harmonization has been more fruitful, in particular with regard to the safety requirements for motor vehicles: the harmonization of 58 technical requirements for passenger cars became mandatory on 1 January 1996 and for other vehicles on 1 January 1998. In 1999 the EU adopted an agreement 'parallel' to that of the UN Economic Commission for Europe, setting global technical regulations for wheeled vehicles, equipment, and parts (WTO 2000: 102). Thus a car that complies with the technical requirements of one Member State automatically satisfies those of all the others. This cuts the costs of both EU and third-country car producers in supplying the market. There are other areas where agreements on standards have become very important and sometimes essential to communication, as for instance in the case of electronics and telecommunications, but generally these agreements are international.

11.5 The Single European Act (SEA) of 1986

Non-tariff barriers

By the 1980s there were still in being a large number of non-tariff barriers to trade. They not only applied to goods but also to services. The Single European Act (SEA) of 1986 set 1 January 1993 as the date by which these should be removed, establishing the Single European Market (SEM). Non-tariff barriers existed where Member States had retained their own individual non-tariff barriers on imports from third countries. With the SEM these should have disappeared, although in some cases they were replaced by EU non-tariff barriers. The MFA quotas were just replaced by overall quotas for imports of each item into the EC.

Member States' quotas on imports of *Japanese cars*, whether negotiated by governments or, as for Britain, between industry organizations, were replaced in 1991 by an agreement between the EU and Japan whereby there would be an overall import quota into the EU from Japan of 1.23 million units of cars and light commercial vehicles and trucks (up to 5 tonnes) calculated on a forecast market of 15.1 million vehicles for the EU as a whole. As agreed all restraints were removed by 2000.

Financial services

Freedom of establishment already existed but under different conditions in the different Member States. These were largely abolished and in 1989 a 'green passport' system was introduced under which a bank or financial firm authorized in one Member State, the 'home country', was automatically authorized in the others i.e. there was mutual recognition of licences. The 'home country' became responsible for supervising the banks activities wherever it operated (Second Banking Directive, 89/646/EEC).

Restrictions on international payments on the current account had been removed throughout Western Europe in 1958. Restrictions on capital account payments had been removed in the UK in 1979, and this action was followed in other EC countries. On 1 January 1999, 11 Member States[1] took the first steps towards the introduction of a common currency, the Euro. Its institution represents the completion of the Single Market in that it makes prices easy to compare and there will be no barriers to the transfer of capital.

Public procurement

One of the most important barriers to trade is that associated with public procurement. In 1987 public procurement accounted for 16 per cent of GDP (GATT 1991*a*: vol. 1, p. 15), and in 1984 a third of these were manufactures (CEC 1988). Traditionally, national firms considered they had a right to supply their own government and nationalized industries and therefore the proportion of public procurement supplied by imports was very much less than in the private sector. This is inconsistent with the ethos of the EU. Under the SEA public procurement orders have to be submitted for tenders which are open to suppliers in all Member States.

The privatization and liberalization policy introduced by the Conservative Party after it won the election in Britain in 1979, led to a conspicuous fall in prices of the previously state-owned industries. A similar picture appeared in the USA. This led the EC Commission to reverse tack in favour of similar policies throughout the EU. Previous state monopolies, as in telecommunications, were broken up and the possessors of the network were forced to open it up to newcomers. The scope for trade was increased, not only in the final products but also in the investment goods required for their expansion. Government procurement fell to 14 per cent of GNP (WTO 2000: 63).

However, the trade policy of the EU should be considered within the international context because, although much of the CEC efforts have been devoted to removing impediments to trade within the EU, there have been parallel developments on the international market. In tandem with the reduction in barriers to intra-EU trade, the GATT negotiations that took place under first the Tokyo Round (1973–9) and then the Uruguay Round (1986–94) included the proposals for opening up public procurement to international competition. In this forum, the EU endeavoured to maintain some degree of protection, a 3 per cent tariff, on tenders from outside the EU to supply the EC markets. This was rejected by the EU's trading partners in GATT and the area of public procurement subject to international competition agreed to in the Tokyo Round was extended by the Uruguay Round.

At both levels provisions have been extended to encompass trade in services as well as goods. Furthermore, the privatization of public utilities has been introduced in most countries of the world, thus opening markets to international competition most significantly in telecommunications. Even in areas where these have not been introduced there have been agreements to open up government procurement to international competition.

11.6 The Uruguay Round 1986–94

The Uruguay Round was the latest and most extensive of the GATT tariff negotiations. Its main provisions for trade in manufactures will be outlined, together with some comments on their significance for the EU.

The Common External Tariff

The mfn tariffs were further reduced such that the EU's CET on non-agricultural products[2] was reduced from 6.9 per cent in 1995 to 4.1 per cent upon implementation of the Uruguay Round Commitments (WTO 2000: 29). These agreements included the elimination of all tariff and non-tariff barriers on agricultural equipment, beer, construction equipment, furniture, medical equipment, paper, pharmaceuticals, some spirit drinks, some steel products, and toys (DTI 1994: 9).

Then under the *Information Technology Agreement* reached in 1997 in Singapore, it was agreed that by 2000 tariffs were to be removed on information technology products i.e.

1. computers (including accessories and components);
2. telecommunications equipment (including fax machines, modems, pagers, etc);
3. semiconductors;
4. semiconductor manufacturing equipment;
5. software (e.g. diskettes and CD-Roms);
6. scientific instruments (Williams 1997).

This had the effect of reducing the simple average tariff on non-agricultural products to 4 per cent.

The result is a considerable variation in the degree of tariff protection for different product categories; those with tariffs above 10 per cent are shown in Table 11.4. The highest tariffs in 1999 were on textiles, clothing and footwear, aluminium, and passenger cars (generally 10 per cent) with parts up to 22 per cent, all of which are now regarded as the products of 'sensitive' i.e. declining, industries. The tariff on vehicles for the transport of people is 16 per cent and of goods i.e. lorries is 22 per cent. Furthermore there are signs of escalation with tariffs on raw materials around 1 per cent, and for partially processed textile items 8.2 per cent, fully processed items 10 per cent, and clothing 11.6 per cent. But tariffs can also be high on electrical equipment—e.g. those on radio and TV sets are

Table 11.4 EU highest applied tariffs on imports of manufactures in 1999 by HS chapter

HS Code	Description	Simple average (%)	Maximum (%)	Imports (US$ bn.)
35	Albuminoidal subs., modified starches, glues, enzymes	9.1	39.1	1.0
38	Miscellaneous chemical products	5.5	20.1	5.3
39	Plastics & articles thereof	6.6	11.3	16.1
44	Wood & articles thereof	2.4	10.0	13.4
51	Wool/hair yarn/fabric	6.2	12.5	2.1
53	Vegetable textile fibre other than cotton and silk yarn/fabric	3.3	11.0	0.4
56	Wadding, felt, non-woven yarns	6.7	12.0	0.9
57	Carpets & other textile floor coverings	8.4	11.0	1.6
58	Special woven fabric, tufted, lace	8.8	11.5	0.7
59	Impregnated/coated textile fabric	6.8	11.0	0.8
60	Knitted or crocheted fabrics	9.9	10.0	1.0
61	Apparel accessories knitted/crocheted	12.3	13.0	17.0
62	Apparel accessories, not knitted or crocheted	12.4	13.0	21.5
63	Other made-up textile articles, sets	10.2	13.0	3.7
64	Footwear, gaiters, etc.	10.0	17.0	7.6
69	Ceramic products	4.8	12.0	2.1
70	Glass and glassware	4.8	11.0	3.0
76	Aluminium and articles thereof	6.3	10.0	9.7
85	Electrical machinery, equipment & parts thereof, sound recorders	3.0	14.0	87.6
87	Vehicles, other than railway/tramway parts/accessories	6.4	22.0	40.0

Source: World Trade Organization *Trade Policy Review – The European Union 1999* Table AIII.1 (WTO, Geneva, 2000).

14 per cent and also on organic chemicals and alcoholic solutions (WTO 1995*b*: vol. 1. pp. 52, 94, and 104; and WTO 2000: 99–100).

Removal of 'Voluntary' Export Restraints in the form of quotas

Under pressure from developing countries and the GATT Secretariat the developed countries agreed to scrap their MFA restrictions on imports of textiles and clothing, which were imposed as quantitative restrictions on imports of individual items from particular developing countries. As described these had been formulated in 1974 under the auspices of GATT, which had been trying to halt their proliferation. But they were quite contrary to the ethos of GATT. Under the *Agreement on Textiles and Clothing* (ATC) these MFA quotas were due to be gradually phased out from 1 January 1995 and eliminated by 2005. This was to be carried out in four stages, based on the quantity of imports in 1990. An importing country can choose the categories to be integrated, subject to the proviso that they must be selected from each of the following groups:

• tops and yarns;

- fabrics;
- made-up textile products; and
- clothing.

Let us assume that the growth rate of the quota for the non-liberalized product is G. The timetable comprises:

Stage 1 beginning 1 January 1995: 16 per cent of textiles and clothing trade in volume terms came under normal world trade rules, and the quotas of the remaining products were to increase by an additional 16 per cent a year for the next three successive years, that is by (G × 1.16) per cent p.a.

Stage 2 beginning 1 January 1998: an additional 17 per cent of trade must be completely liberalized and the growth rate of the remaining quotas must be accelerated by 25 per cent in each of the next four successive years, that is by (G × 1.16 × 1.25) per cent p.a.

Stage 3 beginning 1 January 2002: an additional 18 per cent of 1990 trade must be completely liberalized. Remaining quotas must be increased at a rate at least 27 per cent higher than under stage 2 in each of the following three years, that is by (G 1.16 × 1.25 × 1.27) per cent p.a.

Stage 4 end of transition: all quotas abolished (Khanna 1994).

However, the industrialized countries have dragged their feet: the USA, EU, and Canada started with products not currently subject to import restraints. As a result the quota restrictions were lifted relatively slowly, such that only 5.4 per cent of the 1990 EU's restricted categories had been de-restricted by 1999. At present the EU restrains more products, and restricts the growth of these quotas more from the dominant suppliers, i.e. Taiwan, China, Hong Kong and South Korea, to generally 0–2 per cent p.a., whereas it is more liberal with respect to its imports of clothing from India, Thailand, and the Philippines, allowing quotas to grow by 6–7 per cent. It has no quotas on imports of clothing from Bangladesh.

The CEC still appears to find the temptation to buttress the position of its domestic producers irresistible. In September 1996 it proposed, at the behest of Eurocoton, the trade body, to impose anti-dumping duties of between 3 per cent and 36 per cent on imports of undyed cotton fabric from India, Pakistan, Indonesia, China, Taiwan, and Egypt who were said to be undercutting German, French, and Italian weavers by between 28 and 36 per cent. Little cotton fabric is now produced in Europe, just over a fifth of the amount imported. The UK producers who dye, print, and finish the fabric, most of which goes into home furnishings, were furious and very anxious that their costs should not be raised as they were already facing increasing competition from finished imports (Luesby 1996).

The EU has also endeavoured to use the inducement of greater access to its market as a lever to open markets for its own exports. Indeed the clothing firms are beginning to show some sign of interest in further liberalization. The larger ones often supply their more inexpensive brands from producing units, which they may not own, in Asia. They may supply the design and the material according to the location. But they have realized that some of the fastest-growing markets are in Asia. They now appear to be willing to locate clothing production in a developing country provided they get in return some access for their up-market products into that country; at least that appears to be what is happening.

Special preferential agreements were also negotiated with Central and East European countries (CEECs), Bulgaria, the Czech Republic, Hungary, Poland, Romania, and Slovakia whereby textile and clothing import duties were to be abolished over six years and quantitative restrictions were to be removed at twice the rate as under the ATC (Winters and Wang 1994: 35). Thus these countries received preferential treatment in comparison to the MFA developing countries. By 1998 imports of textiles and clothing from these countries were increasing much faster than from Asia. Nevertheless, as the CEEC countries filled so little of their quotas it did not appear worth the paperwork to impose them and on 1 January 1998 they were scrapped (WTO 2000).

The EU has also removed some of the other quantitative restrictions it maintained under Article XIX of GATT 1947, and has scrapped the 'consensus' it had with Japan which limited imports of motor vehicles of Japanese origin into the EU.

Plurilateral agreement on government procurement (GPA 1994)

The new Agreement entered into by the EU on government procurement[3] provided for non-discriminatory and national treatment for products, services, and suppliers of another party to the Agreement with respect to the government procurement scheduled by each party. There was a tenfold increase in its coverage; for central government the threshold above which it comes into effect is round about £100,000, for local authorities in the region of £150,000, for public utilities around £300,000, and for construction contracts £3m. It has been drawn up on the basis of mutual reciprocity which has included a major bilateral agreement between the USA and the EU (DTI 1994; WTO 2000: 65).

General agreement on trade in services (GATS)

Services were brought into the negotiations for the first time. Those supplied in the exercise of government authority were excluded. The negotiations were with respect to trade in commercial services between members of GATT with the EU negotiating as one entity, that is one 'member'. They comprised the supply of a service:

1. from the territory of one member into the territory of any other member;

2. in the territory of one member to the service consumer of any other member;

3. by a service supplier of one member, through commercial presence in the territory of any other member;

4. by a service supplier of one member, through presence of natural persons of a member in the territory of any other member.

The General Agreement on Trade in Services (GATS)

This Agreement was then negotiated as a separate treaty. Each member was to accord mfn treatment to the services or service supplier of any other member. Further liberalization was then negotiated on the basis of a schedule of services each negotiating member put forward. Foreign suppliers could be accorded national treatment (i.e. no discrimination between national and foreign suppliers) and market access (i.e. freedom of entry and exit). Progressive liberalization was to be achieved over a period of five years. Under great pressure from France the EU took a derogation, that is an exemption, with respect to broadcasting services.

Negotiations were still continuing on many of the packages when the body of the GATS agreement was signed in 1994. The *Telecommunications Agreement*, reached in February 1997 under the aegis of the WTO, signed by 68 countries, including the EU, and accounting for more than 90 per cent of world telecommunication revenues, is one of the most important. The countries agreed to open their markets to foreign competition, allow overseas companies to buy stakes in domestic operators, and to abide by common rules on fair competition in the telecommunications sector. The agreement came into effect on 1 January 1998, when the world's biggest markets—including the USA, the most developed members of the EU,[4] and Japan—were liberalized. It covered all forms of basic telecommunication services including voice telephony, data and fax transmissions, and satellite and radio communications (Williams and Cane 1997). The final regulation for forcing the incumbent firms to open their exchanges to competitors for broadband services such as high-speed internet came into force on 1 January 2001 (Ward 2000). The liberalization of the telecommunications market was extended to all foreign operators with minor limitations on market access and national treatment (WTO 2000: 122).

It was estimated that competition would cut the cost of international calls by more than 80 per cent and the Institute for International Economics calculated that it could cut telecom bills by up to $1000 bn., equivalent to 4 per cent of world GDP. It would assist the development of the global information highway and boost foreign investment in modernizing and expanding the telecommunication network in developing countries (Williams 1997).

Mr Ian Taylor, the UK science and technology minister said the deal should usher in explosive growth in turnover and investment worldwide, "The market is already worth $600bn annually and is growing at 10 per cent a year. Some analysts predicted an extra £20bn worth of telecoms business for the UK alone over the next 10 to 15 years" (Williams and Cane 1997).

The WTO Financial Services Agreement

In 1997 102 countries agreed to open up their banking, insurance, and securities markets in varying degrees to foreign competition. The recent turmoil in the Asian currency markets, which revealed how primitive and inefficient were many of the financial systems in East Asian countries, persuaded them to join in order to restore stability and investor confidence. Developing countries in Asia and Latin America have agreed with the USA and EU to lower barriers to foreign suppliers of financial services, not just cross-border trade but in other ways such as by the establishment of local branches or subsidiaries. The 'single passport' principle for banks and finance corporations was adopted. This agreement covers 95 per cent of the world's multi-trillion dollar financial services market, involving $18,000bn. in global securities assets, $38,000bn. in international bank lending, and about $2,500bn. in worldwide insurance premiums. It came into effect in March 1999 (Jonquières 1997; Williams 1997; WTO 2000: 117).

TRIPS and TRIMS Agreements

In addition there was an Agreement on Trade-Related Aspects of Intellectual Property Rights (TRIPS), which involves the EU providing foreign companies with the same level of intellectual property protection as they afford EU companies, The Trade-Related Investment Measures (TRIMS) Agreement involves foreign firms operating in the EU being treated the same as EU firms. It prohibits the approval of inward foreign investment being dependent on its use of EU inputs or being restricted in its use of imported materials.

11.7 The EU's preferential agreements

In spite of its stated commitment to multilateralism the EC has entered into a wide range of preferential trade agreements (PTAs). Generally, these have been signed bilaterally with individual countries. The benefits the countries get from them depend not only on the degree of preference available but also on whether the products they produce conform to the 'rules of origin'. The rules of origin for preference schemes are that the product must be wholly produced or have undergone *sufficient transformation* in the exporting beneficiary country. A product using imported inputs qualifies 'if the four-digit tariff heading of final products differs from that of the inputs' (GATT 1991*a*: vol. 1, pp. 119–20). Sometimes the EU accepts cumulation between the output of the EU and the country, or between the output of several members of the same regional group. This makes it easier for a country, particularly a developing one, to meet the rules of origin requirements.

African, Caribbean, and Pacific (ACP) Countries

At the outset, the EC formed bilateral free-trade areas with the Overseas Territories— mainly former colonies and territories of the six original Member States. The membership of this scheme has been steadily increased by a succession of Lomé Agreements to 77 African (excluding South Africa), Caribbean, and Pacific (ACP) countries. For cumulation purposes the OCT and EC are regarded as one unit[5]—this in effect gives preferences to EC inputs. Despite this preferential access to the EU market the ACP's proportion of EU imports has fallen significantly since the 1980s (WTO 1995*b*: vol. 1, p. 27).

South Africa

The EU's Trade, Development and Co-operation Agreement (TDCA) with South Africa entered into force provisionally on 1 January 2000 with 95 per cent of EU imports from her being liberalized at the end of 10 years, and 86 per cent of South Africa's imports from the EU being liberalized at the end of 12 years. As South Africa is regarded as more advanced than the Lomé countries some reciprocity is required. She is most competitive in agricultural products and this is the area in which the EU is most reluctant to reduce its trade barriers (Buckley 1999).

Generalized System of Preference (GSP)

In response to the Developing Countries in UNCTAD the EC also established in 1971 a GSP by which they were permitted to export their manufactures tariff-free to the EC up to a certain limit (tariff quota), but this had to be renegotiated each year. In July 1999 this was replaced by a *revised GSP scheme* covering 146 countries and the entire industrial sector except for armaments. Under the general regime of the new GSP, tariff quotas are scrapped to be replaced by a degree of tariff preference which depends on the 'sensitivity' of the product being imported and the 'development index' of exporting countries. There are four categories of sensitivity:

1. 'Very sensitive' products (many agricultural products, textiles, clothing and ferro-alloys) for which the preferential rate of duty is 85 per cent of the mfn duty;
2. 'Sensitive products' (many agricultural products, chemicals, plastics and rubber products, leather goods, footwear, wood and wood products, paper, glass, copper appliances and motor vehicles), for which the preferential duty is 70 per cent of the regular duty;
3. 'Semi-sensitive' products for which the preferential duty is 35 per cent of the regular duty; and
4. 'Non-sensitive' products for which the preferential rate is zero.

'Graduation from GSP benefits applies to country-product category combinations, plus any country whose share of a certain products in the EU's imports exceeds 25%. As a result, "implicitly, the system disadvantages larger countries and . . . discourages countries concentrating exports to the EU in a narrow range of products"' (WTO 2000). The least developed countries benefit most and some South American countries get additional preference for combating drug production and trafficking. Special incentive may also be given to countries that adhere to internationally recognized labour standards, i.e. do not use child labour, and for environmental protection. Hong Kong, China, South Korea, and Singapore have been 'graduated', that is taken off the list of GSP beneficiaries, because of the degree of their development.

The EU argues that the new GSP system, although conceptually complex, '(has the advantages of) . . . transparency and stability, ease of implementation, reduced administrative costs and . . . the strengthening of the GSP as a Development tool' (WTO 1995*b*: vol. 1, p. 30). The author considers these objectives are buried by the complexity of the scheme.

The EU has now undertaken to grant tariff- and quota-free treatment by 2005 at the latest to essentially all products from the 48 Least Developed Countries. But the EU's sugar industry is lobbying against it, and some of the ACP countries that export sugar, rum, and rice at guaranteed high prices fear being squeezed out by the 39 ACP members and other poor countries that would benefit from the plan. Thus there has been some backtracking with respect to agricultural products and it remains to be seen what happens to manufactures (de Jonquières 2000).

Turkey

At the beginning of 1996 the EU entered into a customs union with Turkey, which thereby became part of the Single European Market and adopted the EU CET. There appear to have been some qualifications with respect to free trade in textiles and agricultural products. In 2000 the EU began negotiations for the liberalization of trade in services and government procurement. Cyprus and Malta have association agreements with the EU.

Eastern Europe

The breakaway of the Eastern European countries from the Soviet Bloc after 1989 faced the European Union with a quandary. On the one hand, it was anxious to assist the rehabilitation of these newly democratic states into the free markets of the western world. On the other hand, the industries in which the Central and Eastern European countries (CEECs) appeared most competitive were the 'sensitive' ones, that is the declining industries that the EU was doing its best to protect, in many cases by the imposition of quotas. Horticulture and textiles and clothing were the most important, but so also were coal and iron and steel.

The EU moved tentatively at first, extending to the CEECs (Bulgaria, the Czech and Slovak Republics, Hungary, Poland, and Romania) the generalized system of preference provisions it had instituted for developing countries. Then between 1991 and 1993, the EU negotiated with each of the six countries broadly similar agreements termed the Europe Agreements. The objective of these was the establishment of a free-trade area in goods and services between the EU and these countries within 10 years; they were allowed to cumulate value added over them and the EU. These Europe Agreements were then extended to Latvia, Lithuania, and Estonia and came into force on 1 February 1998 and for Slovenia on 1 February 1999. However, the position of these countries has changed now that they have become candidates for membership of the EU.

Mediterranean countries

The CEC considers that the Mediterranean countries need to obtain 'comparable accords', similar but not identical to the Europe Agreements. In 1995 it approved a plan to progressively establish a free-trade area in manufactures by 2010, and to liberalize trade in agriculture and services, and capital (WTO 1995b; vol. 2, p. 23). However, the agreement which was to have involved the 15 EU Member States and 12 Mediterranean countries[6] signing a charter for peace and security to be underpinned by a free-trade Mediterranean zone in 2010 with a €4.4bn. financial package to aid the economic transition has now run into difficulties in getting agreement between Israel and the Arab countries (Khalaf 2000).

Mexico

In 1999 the EU concluded a free-trade agreement with Mexico. It was anxious to gain access to the Mexican market for EU exporters equivalent to that enjoyed by those from NAFTA countries. In particular tariffs on cars would be reduced from 20 per cent to 3.3 per cent when the deal came into force and eliminated altogether in 2003. In addition 62 per cent of trade in agricultural products would be fully liberalized, although meat, cereals, and dairy products would be excluded. Trade in services would be progressively liberalized (Smith 1999).

11.8 Conclusion

The EU appears to be treating trade agreements as an instrument of foreign policy; a means of conveying benevolence to developing countries on the one hand, and on the other placating neighbours who feel that they are at a disadvantage in the EU market compared with Member States. However, it has been unsuccessful in satisfying the latter in so far as all the Eastern European countries and Turkey are queuing up to join the EU. When they do so the border of the EU will be shifted to that with Russia and the Ukraine and a similar problem will arise.

Has this process of removing barriers between EU Member States eventually been extended to the rest of the world and therefore been a stage towards multilateral liberalization, or has it just encouraged other countries to seek out their own areas of preference? We can cite the formation of NAFTA, the combination of Latin American countries to form Mercosur, and the Asean countries' contemplation of various forms of PTAs as instances of the better effect. On the other hand, negotiation is easier between a small group of countries, and the EU has blazed the trail with its removal of barriers to trade in services. Furthermore, what has become very clear is the process of globalization: transnationals in services as well as manufactures are taking a world view of their operations. For all the protectionism of the EU and its endeavour to maintain its car industry there is a clear shift of it eastwards to Eastern Europe and Asia in the pursuit of both lower labour costs and rapidly growing markets. The EU is very slowly ceding the production of textiles and clothing.

The EU officially adamantly maintains its support of the multilateral trading system and the launch of a new round of trade negotiations in WTO. It recognizes that Developing countries do not feel they have so far benefited from them and thus regards their integration into the world economy as of top priority. It also wishes to extend the WTO's activities into the regulation of investment and competition.

Discussion questions

1   Why did GATT, and now the WTO, which are devoted to the principle of non-discrimination, permit the formation of customs unions and free-trade areas and what conditions did they attach to these? To what extent has the EU complied with these provisions?

2   Explain what is meant by a 'rule of origin' and why it is important in preferential trading schemes.

3   What are the chief difficulties that the EU encounters in forming a free-trade area with Eastern European countries?

Notes

1   Austria, Belgium, Finland, France, Germany, Ireland, Italy, Luxembourg, the Netherlands, Portugal, and Spain.

2   WTO definition, excluding petroleum.

3   Signatories are Aruba, Canada, Hong Kong, China, Israel, Japan, South Korea, Liechtenstein, Norway, Singapore, Switzerland, and the USA.

4   There are delays for EU members Spain (December 1998), Ireland (2000), and Portugal and Greece (2003).

5   OCT = Overseas Countries and Territories associated with the EC.

6   Cyprus, Turkey, Malta, Egypt, Jordan, Algeria, Morocco, Tunisia, Lebanon, Syria, Israel, and the Palestine Authority.

References

Buckley, N. (1999), 'Push to Salvage South African Trade Accord', *Financial Times*, 10 Nov.

—— (2000), 'Confusion Surrounds EU Trade Pact with S. Africa', *Financial Times*, 7 Jan.

Commission of the European Community (CEC) Second Banking Directive (89/646/EEC) (Brussels: CEC).

CEC (1988), *European Economy*, Mar. p. 55.

Department of Trade and Industry (DTI) (1994), *The Uruguay Round of Multilateral Trade Negotiations 1986–94* Cm 2579 (London: HMSO).

GATT (1986a) *The Text of the General Agreement on Tariffs and Trade* (Geneva: GATT)

—— (1991a) *Trade Policy Review: The European Communities 1991*, i (Geneva: GATT)

Jonquières, G. de (1997), *Financial Times*, 15 Dec.

—— (2000), 'Brussels' Trade Plan for World's Poor May Change', *Financial Times*, 11 Dec.

—— (2000), 'Altruism with a Bitter Taste', *Financial Times*, 19 Dec.

—— (2000), 'Asian Ambition', *Financial Times*, 28 Nov.

Keesing, D. B. and Wolf, M. (1980), *Textile Quotas against Developing Countries*, Thames Essay No. 23 (London: Trade Policy Research Centre).

Khalaf, R. (2000), 'Mediterranean Voyage Becalmed by Age-Old Distrust', *Financial Times*, 15 Nov.

Khanna, S. R. (1994), 'The New Gatt Agreement: Implications for the World's Textile and Clothing Industries', *Textile Outlook International*, Mar.

Luesby, J. (1996), 'Textiles Makers Warn on Anti-Dumping Move', *Financial Times*, 17 Sept.

Maitland, A. (1996), 'European Commission Grapples with the Content of Chocolate', *Financial Times*, 20 Mar.

Smith, M. (1999), 'Brussels Backs Deal with Mexico to Drop Industrial Tariffs', *Financial Times*, 19 Jan.

Tucker, E. (1997), 'MEPs Reject Chocolate Compromise', *Financial Times*, 24 Oct.

Ward, A. (2000), 'EU Signals End to BT Monopoly', *Financial Times*, 5 Dec.

Williams, F. (1997), 'US, EU Vie for Credit on Telecoms', *Financial Times*, 17 Feb.

—— (1997), 'IT Accord to Scrap Tariff by Year 2000', *Financial Times*, 27 Mar.

—— (1997), 'New Rules for a Trillion-Dollar Game', *Financial Times*, 15 Dec.

—— and Cane, A. (1997), 'World Telecoms Pact to Slash Cost of Calls', *Financial Times*, 17 Feb.

Winters, L. A. and Wang, Z. K. (1994), *Eastern Europe's International Trade* (Manchester: Manchester University Press).

World Trade Organization (WTO) (1995*a*), *Regionalism and the World Trading System* (Geneva: WTO).

—— (1995*b*), *Trade Policy Review European Union*, vols i and ii (Geneva: WTO).

—— (1999), *Annual Report 1999: International Trade Statistics* (Geneva: WTO).

—— (2000), *The Trade Policy Review: The European Union* (Geneva: WTO).

Chapter 12

European Monetary Union

Mike Artis and Robin Bladen-Hovell

12.1 The birth of the Euro-area

At its meeting in May 1998 the Council of Ministers reviewed the data available up to March of that year, and on the basis of the match between these data and the criteria set out in the Maastricht Treaty (Treaty of the European Union) designated the initial participation of eleven EU member countries in the European Monetary Union.[1] Subsequently the area as a whole became known as the Euro-area, or sometimes as the Eurozone or Euroland. To begin with it comprised: Germany, France, Italy, Luxembourg, Belgium, the Netherlands, Spain, Portugal, Ireland, Austria, and Finland. Four EU members did not participate in this 'first wave': the UK, Denmark, Sweden, and Greece, but Greece subsequently qualified and became an active member of the monetary union from 1 January 2001.

The data on which the May 1998 decision was based are reported in Chapter 2 of this book, together with the actual text of the relevant Maastricht Treaty criteria against which they were judged. Less formally here we note that those criteria specified that to participate in European Monetary Union a member country which had not negotiated an 'opt-out' should have fulfilled the following conditions:

- It should have achieved an inflation rate over a period of two years before the examination of no more than 1½ percentage points higher than that of the 'three best inflation performers' (interpreted by the Council as the average of the three lowest inflation countries).

- Over the same period, it should have exhibited a long-term interest rate within 2 percentage points of the average of the three best inflation performers.

- It should have maintained its exchange rate, also over a period of two years before the examination, within the normal bands of the Exchange Rate Mechanism (ERM) without stress and without undertaking a devaluation.

- It should have fulfilled two fiscal criteria—its budget deficit (in ratio to GDP) should not have exceeded a reference value of 3 per cent, and the ratio of its government debt to GDP should not have exceeded 60 per cent. In both cases, some escape clauses were added, allowing infringement of the reference value in certain cases.

- Finally, the country should have a Central Bank which was independent of its government.

The decisions taken in May 1998 broke formally with the letter of the Treaty in respect of the exchange-rate criterion, since neither Italy nor Finland had been members of the ERM for two years by May 1998. The exchange-rate criterion had been written into the Maastricht Treaty at a time when the normal band of fluctuation was ± 2¼ per cent, rather than the much wider ± 15 per cent band which was introduced after the 1993 foreign exchange-rate crisis (see below for a brief history of the ERM). Since the criterion was supposed to indicate the desirability of a period of exchange-rate stability, the Council adopted another interpretation in its May decisions which implemented a performance-based criterion of stability for those countries which had been operating in the ERM.

The decisions with respect to the fiscal criteria also broke the rules; in this case some would argue the breaking of the rules was substantive. Nearly every country among those admitted to the Eurozone (the exceptions being France, Finland, and Luxembourg) showed a debt/GDP ratio above its reference value, in some cases very substantially so (e.g. Italy with a debt/GDP ratio of 121.6 per cent and Belgium with a ratio of 122.2 per cent) and in one case with recent movement in the 'wrong' direction (this was the case of Germany, whose 1996 ratio of 60.4 per cent increased to one of 61.3 per cent in 1997). The decision to press ahead with European Monetary Union thus combined some finessing of infractions of the criteria with a strong political determination on behalf of those concerned to move ahead with the project. The same combination of rule-bending, creative accounting, and political determination had shaped much of the convergence effort in the years since the signing of the Maastricht Treaty. Political determination to participate in the Eurozone was a highly significant factor in economic policy reforms in many countries (as well as a prompting for actual or attempted creative accounting in some cases) in the years preceding the birth of the Eurozone.

Replacement of national currencies

The May 1998 Council of Ministers also decided that the cross-exchange rates between the member countries of the Eurozone should be fixed, as of the formal beginning of European Monetary Union on 1 January 1999, at the central exchange rates of the ERM. The value of the new currency itself, the Euro, would not emerge until the last trading day of the old regime by virtue of the provisions of the Maastricht Treaty. The Treaty envisaged that the Euro would replace the Ecu, the 'cocktail currency' introduced with the initiation of the European Monetary System in 1979, and should do so without any discrete changes in its external value. Since the Ecu included three currencies of EU Member States not members-elect of the Eurozone (Greece, the UK, and Denmark), the 'market' would in effect decide not only the external value of the Euro on its introduction but also—given the cross-rates already specified by the Council of Ministers—the Euro-equivalence of each and every one of the individual member country currencies. The process was not guaranteed to produce nicely rounded numbers, and it did not. Box 12.1

> ## Box 12.1 Irrevocably fixed conversion rates for currencies participating in the European Monetary Union
>
> | | |
> |---|---|
> | 1 Euro = 1.95583 DEM | 1 Euro = 40.3399LUF/BEF |
> | 1 Euro = 166.386 ESP | 1 Euro = 2.20371 NLG |
> | 1 Euro = 6.55957 FRF | 1 Euro = 13.7603 ATS |
> | 1 Euro = 0.787564 IEP | 1 Euro = 200.482 PTE |
> | 1 Euro = 1936.27 ITL | 1 Euro = 5.94573 FIM |

shows what the Euro-equivalent rates turned out to be. The awkward numbers will increase the headaches that people will have in adjusting to the new currency as it physically displaces the old one in 2002: but electronic calculators are a great help.

The transition

The transition from May 1998 to the new regime seven months later was accomplished with a complete absence of tension or speculation in the foreign exchange markets. This seemed surprising to some observers, especially in light of the European foreign exchange rate crises of 1992 and 1993. The absence of such tensions has to be interpreted as testimony to the strength of the political determination to make EMU succeed. Only so was it possible for market participants to accept that exchanging lire for DM (say) in anticipation of a change in the pre-announced cross-rate would amount to no more than a swap of 'lire-Euro' for 'DM-Euro'. Since the Central Banks maintained widely different interest rates in May 1998 (the one-month rate in Ireland, for example, was over 6 per cent whilst that in the Netherlands was less than 3.5 per cent), and the start of the new regime would require just one rate, a carefully concerted convergence of these rates was also required; otherwise the market would misinterpret inappropriate interest differentials as evidence against the credibility of the cross-exchange rates fixed for the end of the year.[2] The authorities deserve some credit for successful management in this respect.

So, by the beginning of 1999, the scene was set for the introduction of a Monetary Union in which the great majority of EU countries were participants. It was the realization of a long-standing objective, spelt out as long ago as 1970 in the Werner Report, which had vainly targeted the realization of monetary union in Europe for 1980. It also represented an unprecedented degree of international cooperation and commitment. The possession of an independent currency and monetary policy is commonly considered to be a hallmark of political and economic sovereignty. Against this standard the voluntary founding by the Eurozone countries of their monetary union can be seen as a remarkable step, even if it was one that had been foreshadowed in earlier arrangements and aspirations. What does Monetary Union mean and what are the economic arguments for and against such an arrangement? This is the question studied in the next section.

12.2 **The economics of monetary union**

In forming a monetary union the participant countries in the Eurozone agreed, most importantly, that thenceforth they would share a single, common, monetary policy. This followed from the fact that from 1 January 1999 the exchange rates of the individual currencies against each other were irrevocably fixed; whilst the individual national currencies would continue to be used within national boundaries as before until the year 2002, during which notes and coins of the single currency would be issued, these individual currencies were in effect no more than 'non-decimal sub-denominations of the Euro' (as nickels and dimes are mere subdenominations of the dollar). The common monetary policy is conducted by the European Central Bank, which is at the centre of the European System of Central Banks, which comprises the central banks of the EU countries. What are the advantages of such a system, and what might be the drawbacks?

Optimum Currency Area theory

No discussion of this topic would be complete without reference to the relevant traditional economic theory—the so-called Optimal Currency Area (OCA) theory. This theory stresses that amongst the benefits of a single currency that the participant countries can expect to enjoy is the absence of the transactions costs of trading one currency for another as is required when currencies are separate. And, because there is no need to resort to the calculator to transform one currency price into another, there is a gain in 'transparency' in making price comparisons across the markets of the countries concerned. Both of these benefits will be bigger the larger the scale of trade between the countries. Over time additional gains should accrue as companies locate their productive plants in the lowest-cost locations and at the most efficient scale, free of the need to hedge against the possibility of exchange-rate changes. Later theorizing—spurred in part by the European example—has stressed that monetary union can offer an important additional benefit for participant countries to those just enumerated. If care is taken to design a constitution and a *modus operandi* for the Central Bank of the Union that can deliver results at least as good as those available to the individual countries before the monetary union is created, then there is a benefit for the conduct of monetary policy. In the context of the Eurozone, the Bundesbank (widely renowned for its excellent anti-inflationary record) was used as the template for the new Central Bank. Finally, some additional benefit might accrue to at least some members from the fact that through the creation of the new entity and the new currency some additional leverage on economic policy in the world as a whole might be obtainable. Some observers have seen with the creation of the Euro the emergence of a G-3 world in which Europe can speak with one voice in a small forum of dominant world economic powers (the USA, the Euro-area, and Japan).

What are the costs in moving to a single currency arrangement? The principal cost of joining a currency union is that of giving up the possibility of exercising an independent monetary policy. Here the chief concern of traditional OCA theory has been to stress that this would be a large cost if the shocks hitting the economy were different from those impacting the partner economies (the case of *asymmetric shocks*); for then a single monetary policy would not be appropriate. If on the contrary these shocks were largely *symmetric*, then the cost would be small. Thus the issue is whether the single interest rate set by the Union Central Bank might be too high or too low to meet the needs of an individual economy within the Union. It is in this spirit that a number of observers have examined the convergence of business cycles within the European economy to ascertain whether there is sufficient similarity of cyclical experience to suggest that the cost of a single 'one-size-fits-all' monetary policy might not be too high. Will half the countries in the Eurozone be in a boom while the other half is in recession, or will most countries be in the same business cycle phase?

The way in which monetary policy works suggests that the cost of forgoing the use of an independent monetary policy will decrease with the extent of integration of the economy concerned with those of its prospective partners. The logic is that the greater the degree of integration the more widely felt will be a change in the exchange rate, and the more likely it will be that trade-union pressure will cause wages to change in a way that offsets the exchange-rate change. Thus, a country which expects to be able to reduce its interest rate and depreciate its exchange rate as a means of fighting a deflationary shock, may find that its attempt to do so will be frustrated by a rise in wages which will match the rise in prices caused by the depreciation. This is the more likely the more widely imported goods figure in the consumer basket, i.e. the more integrated the economy is with its partners.

A cost–benefit analysis

These ideas can be represented in a cost–benefit diagram as in Figure 12.1. The diagram represents the situation facing a country which is contemplating entering a monetary union with a partner (the partner might be a block of countries). Benefits and costs (perhaps measured relative to GDP, as B/Y and C/Y) are measured along the vertical axis, whilst the horizontal axis represents the degree of trade integration of the economy with its partners (perhaps measured as the ratio of trade with those countries to GDP ((X + M)/Y)). The BB schedule slopes upward from left to right, reflecting the idea that benefits rise with the amount of integration. The cost schedules, CC and C'C', slope down from left to right, again for the reason articulated above (independent monetary and exchange-rate policy are less effective the more integrated the economy is). C'C' is drawn as lying above CC to represent the relevant schedule for an economy that is more 'out-of-synch' with its partners in terms of its business-cycle phase. The points T, T' represent points beyond which (to the right) benefits exceed costs and monetary union is worthwhile. The country with the 'out-of-synch' business cycle needs, by this logic, some extra gains to compensate it for the cost of forgoing a policy tool—independent monetary policy—which is more valuable to it than to economies which are more synchronous.

There is one more point to make about the diagram. It is clear that many of the benefits foreseen from monetary union are of a broadly political nature. Many of the supporters of monetary union in Europe regard the establishment of the Eurozone as a waymark to political union and it is clear enough that in taking economic policy decisions at the

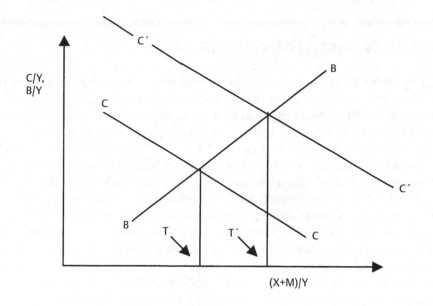

Fig. 12.1 Costs and benefits of monetary union

European level it is already necessary to think of Europe-wide interests, not solely of national ones. Depending on your view about this and related issues, the BB schedule, which embodies the total benefits of the joining decision, should be nudged higher if political union (or simply a desire to be among the forefront of Europe) is a desirable goal.

Core and periphery

When economists have tried to implement the criteria suggested by Optimal Currency Area Theory in the European context they have typically found that there is a core of countries for which the European Monetary Union is easy to recommend compared with some others for which the recommendation comes less easily: countries in the former category—referred to as the 'core'—can be contrasted with the countries in the latter category—the 'periphery'. The exact identity of the core and periphery changes from one study to another, although there are some constants: Germany, Austria, the Netherlands, Belgium, and Luxembourg are always in the core and the UK, Ireland, Sweden, Finland, and Greece are among the periphery; Italy and France 'float' from core to periphery from one study to another. Artis (2000) offers an entertaining view of this core–periphery distinction. This identification is not the same as that of the Euro-area 'Ins' (the eleven member countries participating in the first wave) and 'Outs' (the four member countries not participating), perhaps partly because political factors are not accounted for in empirical economic studies. This is discussed further below.

12.3 **The Maastricht criteria**

Given that, in the above, we have examined traditional economic criteria cast in a cost–benefit framework for guidance on the optimality of monetary union, it is time to ask where the Maastricht criteria come in. As we have already seen, these criteria, which were settled in the Treaty of European Union, were those against which membership of the Euro-area was settled at the Council meeting of May 1998. They do not refer to asymmetric shocks, the amount of trade or any such variables, but rather to a set of criteria which pertain essentially to the good running of monetary policy after the union has been formed. Thus the requirement that the central bank of the country concerned should be independent ensures that governments are not represented in the European System of Central Banks, whose task it is to oversee the execution of monetary policy after the Union has been formed. Equally, the criteria pertaining to fiscal policy can be regarded as a means of ensuring that the fiscal needs of governments do not result in undue pressure being placed on the European Central Bank. As discussed below, the Maastricht criteria paved the way for the Stability and Growth Pact to come into operation in conjunction with the Monetary Union. The exchange-rate stability criterion can be argued to be a requirement that, if fulfilled, shows that the country concerned can live in a regime in which its monetary independence is already reduced. The inflation requirement ensures that member countries can conduct their economic policy so as to bring about low inflation.

Maastricht as a contract

Viewed in this way the Maastricht criteria can be seen as a set of injunctions as to the features needed to run low-inflation economic policy. It is fair to argue that many EU countries profited from having an incentive to adopt the policies enjoined and that the political kudos to be gained from successful adherence to the Monetary Union (and the loss of reputation felt to be involved in a failure to qualify) was helpful in accelerating their adoption.[3] Perhaps most of all, the fiscal criteria, though arbitrary in the particular numerical expression given to them, were especially necessary in view of the high debt burdens that were accumulated in many countries. Viewed as a contract, the Maastricht Treaty was well conceived and clearly had a strong influence on economic policy formation and fiscal reforms in many countries: for a theoretical appraisal see Winkler (1999). The incentives created by the process were sufficiently sharp, however, as to occasion also some instances of creative accounting. Whilst fiscal accounting had to be approved by Eurostat, the EU's statistical organization, there were nonetheless a number of instances in which the pressure to bring the deficit and debt ratios down was sufficiently powerful as to result in some doubtful practices. Perhaps the most notorious of these was the case in which France-Telecom paid the French state a sum in the order of 0.5 per cent GDP to take over its pension liabilities—providing an immediate reduction in the deficit, but, of course, a source of deterioration in the finances in later years.[4] It seems likely that the final interpretation of the criteria to admit to the Eurozone as large a number of countries as eleven owed something to the unforeseen weakness of the German economy, which had to carry the fiscal burden of reunification in the face of recession. Whereas Germany had been the instigator of the fiscal criteria and had been responsible for continually reasserting their primacy, she was in an unexpectedly weak position, unable herself to meet the criteria to the letter when the decision time came (see Von Hagen and Strauch 1999 for an account of how this came about).

That the Treaty of Maastricht could set the criteria in the way that it did reflected a belief that the end-goal of European Monetary Union was desirable and that it was necessary to begin to lay the foundation for a sound combination of fiscal and monetary policy to prevail in the new regime. Not all countries fully shared the goal of monetary union—the United Kingdom being the principal exception—and the UK along with Denmark negotiated an 'opt-out' from the Maastricht Treaty to ensure that it was not obliged to participate in the Monetary Union.

The confidence of the remaining countries in the way forward that took expression in the Maastricht Treaty reflected not only a long-standing aspiration to monetary union but also the experience of the Exchange Rate Mechanism (ERM) of the European Monetary System. In the next section we take a look at this experience and the main lessons that were drawn from it.

12.4 The Exchange Rate Mechanism (ERM)

The European Monetary System and its key component, the Exchange Rate Mechanism, were launched in 1979. Its proximate aim was stated as being that of providing a zone of 'monetary stability' and its creation had much to do with a disillusionment with American leadership of global monetary affairs. It also appealed to the long-standing European objective of monetary union, and, although no such ambition was expressed in the preamble to the European Monetary System and its ERM, it is clear that experience of the ERM provided a kind of 'nursery' for European Monetary Union itself.

The ERM provided a set of central rates of exchange between participating currencies, expressed in terms of the European Currency Unit or Ecu. The Ecu was a 'cocktail currency' consisting of so many French francs, so many DM, so many pounds sterling, etc.—the combination being selected so as to reflect a weighted average of the participating currencies where the weights reflected a combination of GNP and trade. Currencies participating in the ERM were to maintain exchange rates *vis-à-vis* each other within +/− 2.25 per cent of the central rate, subject to a possibility of arranging a formal realignment.[5] With the benefit of hindsight it is possible to distinguish a number of important features of the development of the ERM up the crises of 1992 and 1993, as discussed below.

Evolution of the system

First, the system moved from an initial phase in which realignments were frequent, to a phase—called 'the hard EMS'—where realignments were rare. As Table 12.1 shows, the frequency of realignments was very high to begin with. The realignment of March 1983 was a particular landmark in that it represented the 'Mitterrand U-turn' in France; afterwards there was less resort to realignments. Indeed, after 1987 there was essentially no realignment until the crisis of 1992 (even the January 1990 realignment of the lira was in the nature of a technical adjustment as it coincided with the time at which Italy decided to reduce her wider + / − 6 per cent band of fluctuation to the normal narrow one).

The same picture is mirrored in data on actual exchange rates. Table 12.2, which is drawn from Gros and Thygesen (1998), focuses on the variability of the actual exchange rate against the original ERM-8 members. The figures shown are based on the standard deviation of the logarithm of bilateral monthly exchange-rate changes against the currencies of the ERM-8, weighted by Ecu weights. There is a very decisive decline (of between one-half and two-thirds) in this measure of exchange-rate variability between the first period and that of the hard EMS (1988–91), a fall which is shared by the four last countries listed, which were not members of the original ERM-8, though all of them were

Table 12.1 Realignments of central parities in the ERM: the original ERM-8

Date	Percentage realignment
Sept. 1979	DK (−3); D (+2)
Nov. 1979	DK (−4.8)
Feb. 1981	I (−6)
Oct. 1981	D (+5.5); F (−3); NL (+5.5)
Feb. 1982	B (−8.5); DK (−3)
June 1982	D (+4.25); F (−5.75); I (−2.75)
Mar. 1983	B (1.5); DK (+2.5); D (5.5); F (−2.5); IRE (−3.5); I (−2.5); NL (+3.5)
July 1985	B (+2); DK (+2); D (+2); F (+2); IRE (+2); I (−6); NL (+2)
Apr. 1986	B (+1); DK (+1); D (+3); F (−3); NL (+3)
Aug. 1986	IRE (−8)
Jan. 1987	B (+2); D (+3); NL (+3)
Jan. 1990	I (−3.75)
Sept. 1992	I (−3.5) Lira exits ERM
Feb. 1993	IRE (−10)
Aug. 1993	Fluctuation band widened to +/−15
Mar. 1998	IRE (+3)

Note: Figures show the percentage revaluation (+) or devaluation (−) against the Ecu.

Table 12.2 Nominal exchange rate variability against the ERM-8 currencies

	1979–83	1984–7	1988–91	1992–5	1996
Belgium/Lux.	0.91	0.40	0.33	0.87	0.46
Denmark	0.92	0.66	0.58	1.09	0.48
France	0.90	0.63	0.41	0.84	0.63
Germany	0.62	0.40	0.30	0.67	0.44
Ireland	0.92	1.02	0.41	1.60	1.59
Italy	0.94	0.80	0.55	2.55	1.45
Netherlands	0.74	0.52	0.46	0.77	0.52
Portugal	2.28	0.90	0.84	1.97	0.57
Spain	2.20	1.20	1.12	2.31	0.82
UK	2.98	2.24	1.64	2.13	1.96
Greece	2.77	2.10	0.77	1.13	0.86

Source: Gros and Thygesen (1998), p. 115. Figures show the weighted sum of the standard deviation of changes in the logarithm of monthly bilateral exchange rates (×100). Weights are the implicit Ecu weights as of 1991.

rehearsing in the last period of the comparison for their eventual formal membership of the ERM. The post-92 period shows how exchange rates then became more unstable, although by 1996 much of the previous achievement of stability had been restored. In the early phase, inflation was on average high and certainly varied a good deal across the region—accordingly, frequent exchange-rate changes were needed to preserve reasonably constant conditions of competitiveness (i.e., real exchange rates). In the later phase, inflation fell and variations across the region subsided.

Second, it was an important feature of the system that it combined the two features of preserving a degree of *nominal* stability in the short run with the preservation of reasonably constant *real* exchange rates in the longer run. To begin with, realignments of central rates were used to effect a reconciliation of the two objectives when inflation differentials demanded it, and for a while it proved possible to manage these without undue speculation. Over time, however, member countries used more disciplined counter-inflationary policies at home to realize the two objectives simultaneously.

A third important feature of the System was the acknowledgment, not present to begin with, that Germany formed the anchor for the system, and that this was not due simply to Germany's greater economic size, but to her low inflation. By aligning their currencies with the DM, through targeting a constant exchange rate against that currency, other countries were able in a sense to 'import' the Bundesbank's low inflation success. The key role of the DM and the dominance of Germany and the Bundesbank in the System implied that much of the paraphernalia of the System—the invention of the Ecu, the creation of the 'divergence indicator' and so on—was simply beside the point.[6] The EMS decades were a period when most countries decided to embark on a determined course of counter-inflationary policies and the ERM proved a convenient vehicle within which to conduct such policies. From the standpoint of economic theory the experience illustrated the operation of a policy regime in which the 'nominal anchor' was an external one—the DM exchange rate—displacing earlier nominal anchors (e.g. the money supply favoured by monetarists, incomes policy favoured by Keynesians). Over time, the System attracted new members, including the United Kingdom, for whom the incentive to join as a means of securing low inflation was particularly conspicuous.

The significance of the 'hard EMS'

The period of success of the hard EMS is significant for what it says about the determination of the member countries to defeat inflation—and their success in doing so—and also because it provides a stepping-stone to full Monetary Union. In fact, when considering the costs and benefits of monetary union, it is important to bear in mind that, for a time at least, the relevant counterfactual was not floating (as is implicit in most explorations of the costs and benefits of monetary union), but rather the hard EMS. With its narrow bands, infrequent realignments, and its orientation on the DM, participation in the hard EMS already implied that resort to an independent monetary policy would be marginal and exceptional; in fact, in some ways, the main advantage in moving from the hard EMS to EMU seemed simply to be that the domination of the Bundesbank over European countries' monetary policies would be diluted in favour of a collective sovereignty.

The ERM crises

However, after the exchange rate crises of 1992 and 1993 the option of a hard EMS effectively vanished. The crises shattered the illusion that the managers of the EMS had discovered a speculation-free way of realigning the central parities. They also dispelled any illusion that Germany, as the anchor country, would feel bound to support the System against attack by unlimited intervention in the foreign exchange markets. They drove two major countries—Italy and the UK (the former only temporarily)—out of the System altogether. Finally, the resolution of the second of these crises was to widen the bands of fluctuation to $+/-15$ per cent—little different from free floating one might have thought. Yet, in fact, the countries did not treat the new regime as tantamount to freely floating rates—in that they did not resort to widely differing policies and exchange rates did not in fact fluctuate a great deal more than they had done earlier. The crisis did not spell the end of aspirations to Monetary Union, as some had supposed—if anything, the opposite was the case. Informed opinion moved towards the position of saying that speculation would, sooner or later, wreck any system of quasi-fixed exchange rates and thus that full monetary union was the only viable fixed-rate solution. In this case, of course, the proper counterfactual to have in view when examining the costs and benefits of monetary union is, after all, that of free floating.

12.5 **The constitution of the European Central Bank (ECB)**

It was mentioned earlier as a potential benefit of monetary union that the creation of a new currency affords the opportunity to construct afresh a sound constitution for an effective Central Bank. The constitution of the European Central Bank was drawn up at the same time as the Treaty of Maastricht. It has been described as a constitution for the most independent Central Bank in the world. It can be seen to have been modelled on the constitution of the Bundesbank, with some features 'hardened'. That the Bundesbank's constitution should have been taken as a model is no surprise, from several points of view. First and foremost, the Bundesbank had been 'adopted' as the leader in the ERM by countries anxious to maintain a record of low inflation. Secondly, the Bundesbank's constitution had been written for a federation and the European Monetary Union would resemble a federation. Thirdly, the academic literature—following the influential analysis of Barro and Gordon (1983)—had come to place special emphasis on the need for a 'commitment technology' that would reliably produce low inflation; giving independence to the Central Bank was recognized as a means of achieving this. In this way the temptations to governments of short-term expansionary finance would be curbed.

Thus the European Central Bank (ECB) is placed at the head of the European System of Central Banks (ESCB); it is enjoined not to take instructions from any national central bank or organization of the European Union, nor to lend directly to national governments or organs of the European Union. It is given a mandate in the Treaty which forms the basis for its monetary strategy. The first part of that mandate indicates that the ECB's 'primary objective' is that of securing 'price stability'. The second part says that, without prejudice to that primary objective, the ESCB 'shall support the general economic policies in the Community'—which include a long list of 'desirables' (e.g. 'a high level of employment and of social protection'). The ESCB supplies the bulk of the composition of the Governing Council in the shape of the Governors of the National Central Banks, together with the members of the Executive Board which comprises a president, a vice-president, and four other members appointed by the 'common accord' of the EU governments for non-renewable terms. The independence of the ECB is bolstered by the fact that the National Central Banks must themselves enjoy 'Maastricht independence' of their governments. The ECB's independence could be decisively undermined if the governments were to adopt an exchange-rate policy for the Euro, since that would predetermine monetary policy. Again, the constitution appears to protect the ECB from such an eventuality by indicating that any such policy would have to be shown not to compromise the objective of price stability—and the belief is that the judge of that matter would be the ECB itself.[7] A final ingredient in the ECB's independence which should be mentioned is that its constitution also relieves it of the obligations that might arise if it carried the duty of prudential regulator and supervisor (these functions are left to national governments and central banks).

These features of the ECB's independence and its apparent dedication to the goal of price stability are by no means uncontroversial; in any case, whilst they exist on paper, they have to be worked out in practice. We return below to the way in which things have been working out during the first two years of the operation of the new regime.

12.6 The first years of a European monetary policy

The inception of the Euro was, not unnaturally, very closely observed—which may account for what might seem a sometimes hypersensitive and hypercritical reaction from outsiders to an institution charged with an exciting, but new and difficult task. It is pertinent to mention that the new Central Bank came into being at a time when, around the world, there was renewed interest in making more effective monetary arrangements. In particular, a number of countries (starting with the Reserve Bank of New Zealand and including among others the Bank of England, the Bank of Canada, and the Swedish *Riksbank*) had begun to experiment with a style of monetary policy called 'direct inflation targeting'. Paradoxically this fashion has helped to spread the gospel of 'transparency'. The paradox arises because the promise of a Central Bank to 'control inflation' at 'some time in the future'—which is what direct inflation targeting is—is so plainly non-transparent in the first place that Central Banks espousing this type of strategy have felt obliged, as it were in compensation, to be as open, direct, and precise as possible. The actions of the Bank of England, in particular, have raised these virtues to heights not previously witnessed in Central Banking, which for long has been associated with a certain mystical majesty. This inevitably raised expectations of what was to be expected of the European Central Bank.

From the start, though, the appointment of the President of the ECB struck a false note; appointed by 'common accord' to the positions of President and Vice-President, Duisenberg and Trichet were soon pictured as in disharmony when Duisenberg was prevailed upon to shorten his term from 8 to 4 years to allow Trichet to take over the reins earlier than otherwise. Subsequently disavowing that he had expressed any such intention, Duisenberg nonetheless gave the impression that his appointment had come under pressure from the French government (Trichet being the Governor of the Banque de France). This illustrated for many that the affairs of the ECB might not be so independent of governmental interference as had been suggested.

The monetary strategy

Perhaps of somewhat greater importance, however, was the way in which the ECB set about specifying its monetary strategy. The Treaty's mandate in respect of the primary objective given to the ECB was simply 'price stability'. The ECB defined this as an increase in the HICP (harmonized index of consumer prices) of less than 2 per cent. In initial presentations it was not made clear that zero was the floor, nor that the definition of 'price stability' as an increase in prices was derived as an implication of the view that consumer price measurement was biased upwards because of a failure to account fully for quality improvements. Subsequently it appeared that underestimated quality improvement might account for an upward drift in the measured price index of some 1.5 per cent per annum, suggesting that the ECB might be aiming for a maximum true rate of inflation of only 0.5 per cent. To some observers this seemed too low, although it could hardly be said to be the ECB's responsibility since the objective of 'price stability' is set out in the Treaty. Still, it is worthwhile mentioning that at least two lines of argument have been used to suggest that the ECB's policy aim might be too low. One is that if a low rate of inflation is achieved on average—through time and across countries—there must be a risk of periods of deflation (either overall, or in particular countries), and deflation is not an easy condition to manage. Secondly, it is frequently argued that because many prices— and wages, in particular—have a tendency to be sticky downwards, a condition of mild inflation is required to ease the adjustment of relative prices and wages to the market balance of supply and demand. A further problem with the statement of the ECB's strategy is that the objective of price stability is defined as one for the 'medium term'—leaving it unclear what kind of deviation, and for how long, might be acceptable. Yet another problem that has been raised is that the ECB only clarified its primary objective—perhaps seeing no need to amplify on the list of additional 'without prejudice' objectives that the Treaty mandate gave it.

The two pillars

The ECB went on to explain that it would endeavour to reach its primary objective by means of a 'two-pillar' strategy—the first pillar consisting in a reference value for the growth of the broad money supply (M3), and the second in a collection of forecasts and indicators of inflation. This also attracted a hostile reaction from critics, most of whom complained that the privileged position of the money supply was not justified.

In retrospect much of this followed from the ECB's understandable desire to inherit as much of the Bundesbank's strong counter-inflationary reputation as possible. This explains both the emphasis on price stability and the stress on the 'monetary pillar'. It also helps explain the lack of transparency, since the Bundesbank was able to operate with a degree of unchallengeable authority based on its past success that the ECB could not command, especially in the new conditions cultivated by the fashion for 'inflation targeting' around the world.

Accountability

These problems struck some other chords too. The alleged lack of transparency fed the image of a bank which had been given perhaps too much independence, as expressed for example in the phrase 'the political deficit', since neither national governments nor the European Parliament can call the ECB to account. Susan Lohmann (Lohmann 1995) has explained very well how a Central Bank preserves its independence—if it succeeds—by exploiting a political situation to cultivate a constituency of support, rather than by relying upon paper assurances. The ECB, on her account, is very vulnerable to threats to its independence because it has no natural constituency of support. An awareness of this may explain why it is that the ECB has in fact cultivated a number of avenues which allow it to account for itself, which exceed by far what is prescribed in the Treaty.[8]

These problems of presentation and interpretation can be resolved in large part by experience. Thus, whether the market understands or not, the ECB's strategy (hence whether or not the ECB has succeeded in clarifying its objectives) should be apparent from the reaction of the market to ECB actions. If these continually appear as surprises there is prima facie evidence that the ECB has not succeeded in communicating its policy.

The ECB's track record (up to December 2000, when this chapter was finalized) does not in fact suggest unreasonable or hard-to-understand policies—nor that any unreasonable government pressures were encountered. There have been few technical problems and none that have persisted. On the whole the problems are just those that could be predicted from the fact that the countries making up the initial Euro-11 were not all in the same business-cycle situation. Hence, for some, the ECB's policies were not appropriate.

One size fits all?

This problem is, of course just the mirror image of the costs of monetary union discussed earlier—how bad a fit is the one-size-fits-all monetary policy? Figures 12.2 and 12.3 are designed to explain further. Each employs the device of the IS curve, which relates the goods market equilibrium to the rate of interest, so that output is shown along the horizontal and the rate of interest on the vertical axis. As the ECB relies on setting interest rates, the customary LM curve can be omitted: the money supply will simply adapt to demand.

Figure 12.2, then, shows the position of a monetary union consisting of two countries—'France' and 'Germany'—in the face of a 'pure' asymmetric shock. Suppose the initial position to be one of equilibrium, where output is at its natural or equilibrium rate: this is shown by Y_e, determined by the intersection of the IS_0 curve for each country

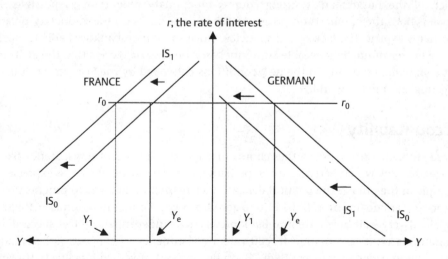

Fig. 12.2 A monetary union with 'pure' asymmetric shocks

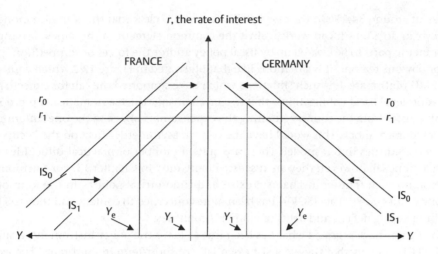

r, the rate of interest

FRANCE

GERMANY

r_0

r_1

IS_0

IS_1

Y_e

Y_1

r_0

r_1

IS_0

IS_1

Y_1

Y_e

Y

Y

Fig. 12.3 A monetary union with 'largely symmetric' shocks

with the interest rate, r_0. Suppose then that there is a pure asymmetric shock—one that is as expansionary for France as it is contractionary for Germany. The IS curves both move to the left, as shown by the schedules IS_1. Clearly, no single interest rate can reproduce the former equilibrium now. In France there is a positive 'output gap', i.e. actual output is above equilibrium output whilst in Germany there is a negative gap. Any movement of the rate of interest that reduces the gap for France will raise it for Germany, and vice versa. There are some other possibilities, however. One is a market adjustment: the positive output gap in France will tend to raise prices in that country whilst the negative one in Germany will tend to reduce prices there. In other words, conditions of competitiveness will tend to move in a stabilizing way. This might well be too small and too slow an adjustment, however. In that case, fiscal policy represents an alternative source of stabilization. A contractionary fiscal policy in France and an expansionary one in Germany will tend to move the IS curves back to their original positions.

For 'core' countries, though, most shocks should tend to be symmetric. An external shock, for example (say, a recession in the rest of the world) will tend to affect all countries in the union to some extent in the same way. Figure 12.3 illustrates this 'largely symmetric' case. The IS curves for both countries move inwards, though not quite to the same extent (as drawn, France is more badly affected than Germany by the external shock). With no policy response, the immediate effect is for output to move to Y_1 in both countries, well below the equilibrium rate in both cases, but the more so in France. This time, though, monetary policy can help quite a lot by reducing interest rates, for example from r_0 to r_1, which would enable output to rise in both cases. In fact, in this case, monetary policy could reduce interest rates even further, to the point where a positive output gap could open up in Germany compensating a still negative one in France. Since the policy is directed at European goals, the relative size of the two economies matters quite a lot: Irish conditions, for example cannot affect the European averages very much, since Ireland's weight is only 1.5 per cent. By contrast, Germany's (HICP) weight is much larger, at around 34.5%. In the case just illustrated it is clear that the common monetary policy can do a lot—it can work against the common element in the shock, leaving the asymmetric parts to be cleared up by fiscal policy and/or the forces of competition.

For obvious reasons, it is situations like that illustrated in Figure 12.2 which constitute the EMU nightmare. It is such situations which have supported the call for a mechanism of Union-level fiscal stabilization—that is, a mechanism, which automatically promotes a fiscal transfer from the country suffering the expansionary shock to the one suffering the contractionary shock. This would have the correct, asymmetric effect on the IS curves of the two countries in our model. There are quite a number of practical difficulties with such a proposal, however: they are discussed more fully in Chapter 13. For the moment, at least, no such transfer mechanism exists and Union fiscal policy—in the form of the Stability and Growth Pact (SGP)—has been more concerned to contain and then roll back the burgeoning deficits and debts of many EU countries.

The figures have assumed what has been true so far of the policy instruments available to the ECB, namely that these consist essentially of short-term interest rates. The execution of the operations in the money markets where these rates are made effective has been left to the National Central Banks acting on behalf of the ECB, which has specified three rates, two of which act as a floor and ceiling to the third—the so-called 'main refinancing rate'. Changes in the rates are announced at a monthly meeting of the Governing Council, with an explanation for the action (or for the lack of it) being given by the Governor at a press conference. These can be accessed on the internet at the ECB's website http://www.ecb.int/.

The ECB in action

When the EMU began there were widespread fears that the deflationary effects of the South-East Asian crisis would be severe, and the starting rate for EMU (at 3 per cent) reflected this. This rate was already significantly lower than the rate anticipated in the financial markets, say, in September 1998, when the general belief was that it would settle at around 3.75 per cent. There was a further cut in April, before it became clear that the deflationary effects were in fact less serious than had been supposed. Then, by late in the summer of 1999, there were some signs of an inflationary pressure and the rate was increased by 50 basis points in November, with two smaller increases following in March and April of 2000. By this time a European recovery was evident, commodity prices—notably including crude oil prices—were rising and the inflationary effects of the Euro's persistent devaluation were beginning to be felt. These pressures were to continue throughout the summer and autumn. In June 2000 the ECB mandated a further rate increase of 50 basis points, bringing the level to 4.25 per cent, which it followed up by introducing two further, smaller, increases of 25 basis points each in September and October. Table 12.3 shows the whole sequence.

Figure 12.4 shows the movement in inflation and GDP growth between the year to 1999 (the source of the arrow) and the year to 2000 (the head of the arrow). Data for the second year are largely forecast, being taken from the October 2000 issue of the *National Institute Economic Review*. The general recovery in output growth and an accompanying surge in inflation is obvious. It was mainly for the smaller countries (Ireland, Portugal,

Table 12.3 The ECB's main refinancing rate

With effect from:	Main refinancing rate (level)	Change from previous
1 Jan. 1999	3.00	—
9 April	2.50	−0.50
5 Nov.	3.00	+0.50
4 Feb. 2000	3.25	+0.25
17 Mar.	3.50	+0.25
28 Apr.	3.75	+0.25
9 June	4.25	+0.50
6 Sept.	4.50	+0.25
11 Oct.	4.75	+0.25

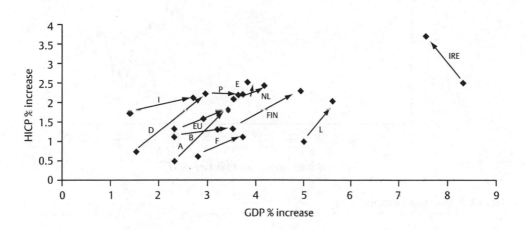

Fig. 12.4 Output growth and inflation in the Euro-area, 1999–2000

Finland, the Netherlands) that monetary conditions might have been too loose, with both output growth and inflation well above the Euro-area average.[9] It is clear, of course, that there will be some deviations around the average inflation rate: only traded goods prices are constrained to converge relatively rapidly and completely. Prices of non-traded goods and services in any given country can depart from the average more substantially and over a longer period of time. Some observers attributed the ECB's ability to allow monetary conditions to be quite accommodative in part to the fact that fiscal policy had been relatively restrained.

The Euro-exchange rate

A feature of the first two years of the Euro's existence—one that many found surprising, and some in need of correction, was the external weakness of the Euro. Figure 12.5 shows that the Euro declined almost continuously from its creation against the US dollar. A number of forecasts had been made that the Euro was at least potentially in the medium term a hard currency, and these predictions may have contributed to the fact that the

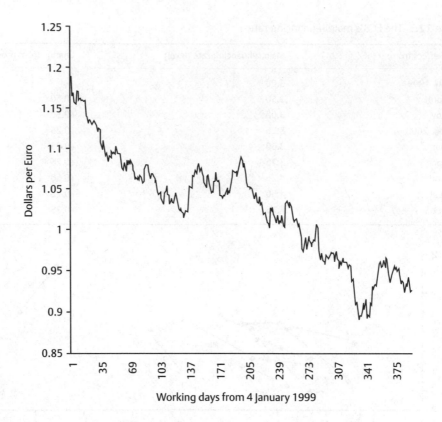

Fig. 12.5 The Euro exchange rates

Euro opened at quite a high rate. In any case the history of the Euro exchange rate thereafter was one of almost continuous decline; the values reached by the Euro in the course of 2000, not only in relation to the US dollar but also more generally, were perceived by economists as well below the values justified by the 'fundamentals'. Departures from the value warranted by the fundamentals are not unknown in foreign-exchange markets—in fact misalignments are a quite persistent phenomenon. Convincing explanations for the departure in this case are not easy to find, though one revealed regularity is that the rate with respect to the US dollar falls with the excess of expected US economic growth over that of the Euro-area (Corsetti and Pesenti 1999; IMF 2000). Hence the fall should be expected to reverse itself when the prolonged US boom slows and the recovery in Europe takes firmer hold. Consistent with the decline of the value of the Euro there was a substantial export of capital out of Europe—but cause and effect cannot be identified from this fact alone. The persistent decline in the Euro was a potential source of concern in two respects and a substantial bonus in a third. As a first, and objective, source of concern there is the fact that over a period of time the devaluation could be expected to disturb the price stability which is the ECB's principal target. Price increases due to the devaluation were mentioned by the ECB as a partial justification for the 50 basis-point rise in its main refinancing rate in June 2000 and for the further rises thereafter. Secondly, however unjustified, the decline in the external value of the Euro has been popularly treated as an indication of weakness, reflecting the shortcomings of the European economy at large and the ECB in particular. At a meeting of the G-7 in the autumn of 2000 the ECB was able to persuade its counterparts in the USA, Japan, and the UK that the weakness of the Euro was a feature of common concern, and from 22 September there was a brief period of concerted intervention in the markets. The action brought a short-term respite to the currency but, if it was designed to provide a floor to the rate that the markets would respect, it did not seem to succeed for very long. The concerted intervention was not sustained and the decline of the Euro continued. It may be, though, that awareness of the likelihood of a fresh round of concerted intervention prevented a faster fall and served to provide some bounds to the potential for further decline.

Despite these concerns and reactions, however, the weakness of the Euro was in fact substantially helpful in encouraging the recovery of the European economy, and in this respect could hardly have come at a better time.

So after two years of experience, the new monetary regime has survived. Its managers have steered the currency through an initial period of uncertainty and have made a beginning to the difficult task of building credibility and reputation. They have been lucky with the conjuncture, which did not turn out to be so unfavourable as was first predicted, and they have been fortunate that the fiscal managers have behaved themselves.

12.7 The 'Outs' and the 'Pre-ins'

The initial selection of eleven countries to form the first wave of the European Monetary Union left four member countries of the European Union outside. Two of these—the UK and Denmark—took advantage of the opt-out they had negotiated at Maastricht. Greece did not fulfil all the criteria in May 1998, whilst Sweden, in failing to participate in the ERM, in effect chose not to do so. The terms 'Outs' and 'Pre-ins' were coined to differentiate between those countries which, whilst not in the Union, clearly wanted to be so—the 'Pre-Ins'—and those which might very well not wish to join even at a later date—the 'Outs'. Greece was clearly one of the former and in fact joined the Union formally on 1 January 2001. For Denmark, the situation is somewhat different: although she also would be likely to qualify against the criteria, and whilst Danish government attitudes qualify Denmark as a Pre-in, her opt-out can only be withdrawn on the basis of a favourable referendum verdict for doing so. In September 2000 such a result was withheld by the Danish people.

Sweden and the UK represent cases of countries which, on the basis of the traditional OCA criteria, might not be well advised to join European Monetary Union, since their business cycles are substantially out-of-synch with those of the continental European countries and neither, historically, has shared to the full an enthusiasm for monetary or political union in Europe.

In the case of the UK this is graphically registered for many by the punishing 1992 crisis, when the UK would, for cyclical reasons, have liked interest rates lower than those that continued adherence to the ERM allowed. Public and business opinion in the UK remains very sceptical of the merits of participating in the European Monetary Union, and the government has made participation conditional on a favourable referendum result. The sceptical attitudes that prevailed through the first two years of EMU's life owed much to a perception that the EMU had produced a weak currency and that UK economic performance had been by contrast stronger—clearly factors that can easily be reversed.

In Sweden, in 1997 the Parliament took a clear decision to stand aside from the first wave of EMU in 1999. Economic reasoning (see Calmfors *et al.* 1997; Calmfors 2000) stressed Sweden's asymmetric business cycle position, her weak fiscal position, and unreformed labour-market institutions. Perhaps the main point was that it seemed difficult to imagine how Sweden could manage her asymmetric business-cycle position inside the EMU. In Spring 2000, however, the Social Democratic Party voted to join the EMU 'in principle', whilst still stressing caveats in relation to the same factors that were cited in the negative decision of 1997. Whilst there has been a clear improvement in relation to fiscal policy, the inspiration for the change in stance is probably attributable more to political factors: at any rate, this is the opinion expressed by Calmfors (2000), who has described this evolution of opinion as one that has gone from 'No, not now' to 'Yes, but not now'. In the meanwhile, the Riksbank has been credited with operating a successful monetary policy in the inflation-targeting mode.

Common to both the UK and to Sweden is a problem (probably more acute with the first country) with the exchange rate during transition. Whilst an 'ERM-2' arrangement has accommodated both Greece and Denmark, it is not clear that such an arrangement would be acceptable to either the UK or Sweden, or would be workable. Yet some period of exchange-rate stability prior to formal entry seems a likely requirement of entry into the Monetary Union in either case, and negotiating a safe passage looks very difficult (see Artis (1999) on the UK case and Genberg (1999) on Sweden's).

12.8 Conclusions

The formation of a monetary union in Europe is a remarkable achievement from many points of view. Many observers thought that the speculative crises in Europe's foreign-exchange markets in 1992 and 1993 had spelled the end of this ambition—whereas, as it turned out, they spelled only the end of an ambition to get to monetary union by way of fixed-but-adjustable exchange rates. More than this, perhaps the successful functioning of a monetary union requires a high degree of cooperation and discipline normally only forthcoming within the framework of a political union. Yet, to date, the union has worked with reasonable success. Still there are some problems. Not all EU countries are yet in the EMU. Early success owes something to good fortune, which may not last. The ECB has a difficult balancing-act to perform in front of many audiences, with different traditions of monetary policy-making, and its monetary strategy has not yet fully 'bedded down'. Perhaps most important, the ECB has yet to make of the independence granted to it by Treaty something that has a constituency of support with the European peoples.

Discussion questions

1   Describe the nature of the costs and benefits of EMU.

2   What are the key features of the statutes of the ECB? What is their economic significance?

3   Evaluate the success of the first two years of the ECB's monetary strategy.

Further reading

The subject matter of this chapter occupies several books. Those interested in the history of monetary integration in Europe should consult Gros and Thygesen (1998). The analytics of monetary union, with special reference to EMU, are dealt with by de Grauwe (2000). Kenen (1995) is instructive on the details of the Maastricht Treaty and the Constitution of the European Central Bank. Buti and Sapir (1998) discuss monetary and fiscal policy in the framework of EMU, as do Eiffinger and de Haan (200). An important text is the European Commission's 'One Market, One Money' (CEC 1990), where the Commission set out its views and estimates, where possible, of the costs and benefits of monetary union. The book edited by Artis *et al.* (2000) carries articles concerned with the impact of EMU on the development of the financial markets. Corsetti and Pesenti (1999) offer an early appreciation of the new system. To keep abreast of current developments, the ECB's Monthly Bulletins are highly informative; in this connection the ECB's website (http://www.ecb.int/) is a very useful resource. It also offers a lot of data that can be downloaded to your computer.

Notes

1   In doing so the Council had available to it the 1998 Convergence Report of the Commission (CEC 1998) and, in addition, a Convergence Report from the European Monetary Institute (EMI 1998).

2   The Uncovered Interest Parity (UIP) theorem maintains that the difference between the interest rates on securities of comparable maturity and risk but denominated in different currencies can be no more than the expectation of the depreciation of the one currency (the one with the higher interest rate) in terms of the other. Given current interest rates the market could easily compute whether the implied depreciation was consistent with the end-point exchange rate that the Council of Ministers had set.

3   It is clear, for example, that the Italian decision to accelerate its fiscal reforms in a bid to qualify for EMU was directly due to a perception that the Spanish government fully intended to do its best to meet the criteria by 1999. To have failed to qualify while Spain succeeded would have been seen as a political disaster in Italy (see Chiorozza and Spaventa 1999).

4   Germany attempted to improve the appearance of its fiscal position by having the Bundesbank's gold reserves revalued, a tactic the Bundesbank successfully resisted.

5   Some countries (e.g. at first, Italy, then later Spain and the UK) were allowed a larger $(+ / - 6\%)$ margin of fluctuation, at least in the early years of their membership of the System.

6   The System had in fact been designed with a very careful eye towards avoiding the domination of any one currency. Thus the invention of the Ecu circumvented the direct adoption of any existing currency, as anchor or even as numeraire for the System. The 'divergence indicator' in turn was a conscious attempt to build in a symmetrical early warning system under which the Central Bank of a strong currency would have been under equally strong pressure to adjust as the Central Bank of a weak currency, if it stood out from the rest.

7   On this issue in particular see Kenen's account (Kenen 1995).

8   In this connection the papers by Buiter (1999) and Issing (1999) are indispensable reading.

9   Among the larger countries, only Spain was similarly affected, the above-average inflation rate in Italy being unaccompanied by excess output growth.

Acknowledgements

The authors would like to acknowledge the helpful comments on an earlier draft of this paper from members of the EUI's Money Group as well as those of Andreas Beyer and Ton Notermans, also of the EUI. Naturally, none of these is responsible for the final draft of this chapter, which remains the responsibility of the authors.

References

Artis, M. J. (1999), 'The UK and EMU', in D. Cobham and Zis, G. (eds.), *From EMS to EMU: 1979–1999 and Beyond* (Basingstoke: Macmillan), 161–80.

—— (2000), 'EMU and Procrustes', in M. J. Artis, A. Weber, and E. Hennessey (eds.) (1998), *The Euro: A Challenge and Opportunity for Financial Markets* (London and New York: Routledge for SUERF).

——, Weber, A., and Hennessey, E. (eds.) (1998), *The Euro: A Challenge and Opportunity for Financial Markets* (London and New York: Routledge for SUERF).

Barro, R. and Gordon, D. (1983), 'Rules, Discretion and Reputation in a Model of Monetary Policy', *Journal of Monetary Economics*, 12: 101–21.

Buiter, W. (1999), 'Alice in Euroland', *Journal of Common Market Studies*, 37: 181–209.

Buti, M. and Sapir, A. (eds.) (1998), *Economic Policy in EMU* (Oxford: Oxford University Press).

Calmfors, L. (2000), Speech to the Unibank Seminar on 'Perspectives on European Integration', Copenhagen, 11 May.

—— Flam, H., Gottfries, N., Haaland Matlary, J., Jerneck, M., Lindahl, R., Nordh Berntsson, C., Rabinowicz, E., and Vredin, A. (1997), *EMU: A Swedish Perspective* (Dordrecht: Kluwer Academic Publishers).

CEC (1998), European Commission, 'Convergence Report', *European Economy*, 65: 23–162.

—— (1990), 'One Market, One Money: An Evaluation of the Potential Benefits and Costs of Forming an Economic and Monetary Union', *European Economy*, 44: 1–351.

Chiorozza, V. and Spaventa, L. (1999), 'The Prodigal Son or a Confidence Trickster? How Italy got into the EMU', in D. Cobham and Zis, G. (eds.) *From EMS to EMU: 1979–1999 and Beyond* (Basingstoke: Macmillan), 129–55.

Cobham, D. and Zis, G. (eds.) (1999), *From the EMS to EMU: 1979–1999 and Beyond* (Basingstoke: Macmillan).

Corsetti, G. and Pesenti, P. (1999), 'Stability, Asymmetry and Discontinuity', *Brookings Papers on Economic Activity*, 2: 295–358

De Grauwe, P. (2000), *Economics of Monetary Union*, 4th edn. (Oxford: Oxford Universty Press).

Eijffinger, S. C. W and de Haan, J. (2000), *European Monetary and Fiscal Policy* (Oxford: Oxford University Press).

EMI (1998), European Monetary Institute, *Convergence Report*, March.

Genberg, H. (1999), 'EMU and the Changing Structure of Macro Risks', *Swedish Economic Policy Review*, 6 (Spring): 7–34.

Gros, D. and Thygesen, N. (1998), *European Monetary Integration*, 2nd edn. (Harlow: Addison Wesley–Longman).

International Monetary Fund (2000), *The World Economic Outlook, October* (Washington DC: IMF).

Issing, O. (1999), 'The Eurosystem: Transparent and Accountable or "Willem in Euroland"', *Journal of Common Market Studies*, 37: 503–19.

Kenen, P. B. (1995), *Economic and Monetary Union in Europe* (Cambridge: Cambridge University Press).

Lohmann, S. (1996), 'Quis custodiet ipsos custodes? Necessary Conditions for Price Stability in Europe' in H. Siebert (ed.), *Monetary Policy in an Integrated World Economy: Symposium 1995* (Tübingen: Mohr), 139–60.

Winkler, B. (1996), 'Towards a Strategic View on EMU: A Critical Survey', *Journal of Public Policy*, 16: 1–28.

Chapter 13
Fiscal Policy in EMU

Hedwig Ongena and Bernhard Winkler

13.1 Introduction

The decision taken by the European Council on 10 December 1991 at Maastricht to form an Economic and Monetary Union (EMU) represented a milestone in the long process of European integration. On 1 January 1999, eleven Member States of the European Union (EU) adopted a single currency, the Euro, and entrusted monetary policy to a new institution, the European Central Bank (ECB). The adoption of the Euro means that there is a single unified European monetary and exchange-rate policy for the participating countries. At the same time the responsibility for most other areas of economic policy has largely remained at the national level. Nevertheless, it was recognized that monetary union also has repercussions on other policy areas. Most notably, a new framework for fiscal policy-making was established in parallel with the new monetary arrangements.

The relationship between fiscal policy and monetary union has been the subject of a long-standing debate. When proposals for a monetary union in Europe were first discussed in the 1960s and 1970s there was a widely held view, most prominently exposed in the McDougall Report commissioned in 1977, that monetary union would also require a significant centralization of fiscal policy and, in particular, a sizeable Community budget.

By the time the second—and ultimately successful—attempt to achieve a monetary union in Europe was launched in the late 1980s the angle on the implications for fiscal policy had shifted almost entirely. The Delors report, setting out a blueprint for the road to monetary union in 1989, on the contrary, placed more emphasis on the need to discipline national fiscal policies and to put constraints on government deficits and debts. Compared to the earlier period, concerns over macroeconomic stabilization of income and demand took the backstage. Instead, overriding importance was attached to the goal of price stability for monetary policy and the need for sound public finances on the fiscal side. These concerns were later reflected in the convergence criteria included in the Maastricht Treaty and in the rules and regulations on fiscal policy contained in the Stability and Growth Pact adopted by the Amsterdam Summit (European Council 1997).

One explanation for this shift in emphasis can be found in the policy experiences of the 1970s and 1980s. These called into question the earlier confidence in the ability of monetary and fiscal policy-makers to fine-tune macroeconomic developments. The shift in emphasis from concerns over short-term macroeconomic stabilization to the need for institutional mechanisms to safeguard stability over the medium-to-longer term also reflects developments in economic theory. At the risk of over-simplifying, broadly speaking Keynesian economics has been associated with a more optimistic view on the desirability and ability of 'activist' macroeconomic policy interventions to stabilize economic fluctuations and address market failures. By contrast, new classical economics as well as public choice or political economy approaches to economic policy-making, have tended to espouse a more pessimistic view, stressing the potential for government failure and the virtue of 'non-activist' or rule-based policy-making.

The basic philosophical divide between these two schools of thought has shaped the discussions about EMU in general and the role of fiscal policy in particular. Section 13.2 surveys the main theoretical building-blocks underlying the debate over the fiscal arrangements in EMU between those primarily concerned about preserving the flexibility and freedom of action of policy-makers and those stressing the need to limit the scope for discretion in the interest of credibility and longer-term stability. Against this background, Section 13.3 sets out in more detail the institutional framework that has been adopted under the Maastricht Treaty and the Stability and Growth Pact in order to promote sound public finances and policy coordination among Member States in the Euro-area. Section 13.4 looks at some of the fiscal policy issues that have arisen since the beginning of monetary union. Section 13.5 offers concluding remarks on how the Maastricht set-up for fiscal policy can be seen as reconciling the requirements for flexibility and credibility and includes some thoughts on future challenges.

13.2 Theoretical background

Optimum Currency Areas and the need for fiscal stabilization in a monetary union

The role of fiscal policy in a monetary union

The natural starting-point for a discussion of the role of fiscal policy in a monetary union is the literature on Optimum Currency Areas pioneered by Mundell (1961). His model is based on the traditional Keynesian assumption of fixed prices and wages. In such circumstances a region or country taking part in a monetary union which is hit by an exogenous shock (say reducing its export demand) can—by definition—no longer rely on its own monetary and exchange-rate policy to counteract such a shock (i.e. by lowering interest rates and depreciating its exchange rate). From this perspective the question of whether a collection of countries constitute an Optimum Currency Area will, in the first instance, depend on how important asymmetric shocks are, i.e. economic shocks that affect different regions differently. It also depends on the degree of wage and price rigidities in the economy. These are simply assumed to be present in the OCA framework, but if prices and wages are very flexible the economy might be able to adjust to economic shocks by itself and without the need for policy intervention. Traditionally factor mobility, i.e. the ability of labour and capital to move freely across the currency zone has also been stressed as an important criterion for an Optimal Currency Area, at least in the absence of sufficient price and wage flexibility.

With regard to labour mobility as well as price and, particularly, wage flexibility, European countries are usually argued to score quite badly, especially when compared to the USA. This leaves most of the argument on whether the Euro-area can indeed be seen to constitute an Optimum Currency Area centred around the question of asymmetric shocks. With respect to the topic of this chapter this also leaves a potentially important role for fiscal policy as the principal remaining national macroeconomic policy adjustment tool. Indeed, in the policy debate surrounding the Maastricht Treaty many economists steeped in the Keynesian tradition have argued against imposing constraints on fiscal policy and in favour of retaining maximum flexibility and an active role for national fiscal policies in monetary union. However, unlike when monetary union was first considered in the 1960s and 1970s, proposals for a centralized fiscal system—which would offer some sort of automatic insurance against (temporary) asymmetric shocks—were not seriously considered this time around.

Centralized versus de-centralized stabilization

The question of where stabilization mechanisms should be located, i.e. whether at the European or at the national level, can be seen as a special case of a more general debate over fiscal federalism, i.e. where to place tax and expenditure decision powers. However, the adoption of a European-wide stabilization scheme to provide insurance across countries need not necessarily involve a large central European budget, as had been assumed in the earlier discussions of European Monetary Union. Instead, a system of fiscal transfers could redistribute income from those regions within the monetary union which suffer from an adverse economic shock to those which experience favourable economic developments relative to the Union average.

In the proposal by Italianer and Vanheukelen (1993), the stabilization mechanism is based on year-on-year changes in countries' unemployment rates relative to the Union average. They argue that a sufficient degree of stabilization of country-specific shocks could be achieved with an estimated annual cost of only about 0.2 per cent of the Community GDP and without the need for sizeable budgetary flows. By construction such a scheme would be neutral with respect to the aggregate fiscal stance in the whole area. In the presence of a large centralized budget, such redistribution would, of course, be built in automatically, as higher tax receipts from better-off regions would coincide with relatively greater expenditures (e.g. on unemployment compensation) in worse-off regions.

A European-wide system—whether implemented through a central budget or a specific mechanism, as in the proposal by Italianer and Vanheukelen—provides insurance through redistribution of income across different regions at any point in time. By contrast, purely national stabilization has to rely on debt build-up (and run-down) in order to smooth income and consumption over time in the face of temporary shocks. A debt build-up in adverse times could have negative side-effects and it may also be difficult to reverse in good times (Perotti 1999). Moreover, inter-temporal smoothing may also be less effective compared to risk-sharing across countries and regions—if there are significant *Ricardian effects*. Under *Ricardian equivalence* tax-payers do not spend extra income that they may receive from debt-financed transfer payments since they anticipate an equivalent higher future tax burden in order to pay for the temporary debt build-up by the government (Bayoumi and Masson 1998). However, Ricardian effects tend to be small empirically, especially as long as deficits are perceived to be temporary and are seen as due to the normal operation of automatic stabilizers at the national level.

The role of market imperfections and moral hazard

More generally, the case for a centralized insurance mechanism rests on capital-market imperfections impeding private agents and/or national governments from lending and borrowing in order to achieve consumption-smoothing over time on their own account (Gros 1996). The evidence provided by Sørenson and Yosha (1998) indicates that capital-market integration within the EU is less than that within the USA. To the extent that there are obstacles to risk-sharing by private agents, a case can be made for government policies or insurance mechanisms to provide income stabilization on their behalf, be it at the national or the European level. However, it can be argued that EMU itself could spur greater capital market integration. In general, enhancing the efficient functioning of goods, labour, and capital markets will promote the resilience of economies to economic shocks and enhance their ability to adjust to them on their own account. This reduces the general need for government policy to perform a stabilization function and, in particular, the need to provide an insurance mechanism at the European level.

Moreover, there are a number of obstacles to the design of an effective and neutral central insurance mechanism. First, keeping responsibility for fiscal policy firmly at the national level may be preferable for reasons of accountability and differences in local preferences as stressed in the literature on fiscal federalism. Secondly, it is difficult to design any central insurance scheme in a way that avoids one of the classic problems in the insurance literature, i.e. moral hazard. Moral hazard means that insurance affects the incentives of the insured to behave in a way that limits risky behaviour. In our case fiscal transfers may encourage backward areas to attempt to profit from compensation for alleged unfavourable shocks instead of working to reduce their vulnerability to such shocks. Thirdly, in practice it is not easy to separate temporary and permanent shocks and therefore 'pure' insurance from the redistribution of wealth and income for other motives. Given such difficulties there is a case for continuing to leave national fiscal policies with the task of stabilizing local shocks, where necessary.

The need for fiscal discipline

From the perspective of the literature on Optimum Currency Areas, a monetary union entails the loss of one important tool of national macroeconomic stabilization policy which would need to be compensated by greater reliance on a second such tool, i.e. national fiscal policies.

During the 1970s and 1980s neo- and new classical schools of thought came into the

> ## Box 13.1 Fiscal stabilisation in a monetary union: Europe vs. the US
>
> One benchmark to evaluate the need for fiscal stabilization in a monetary union is provided by the experience of states or provinces within existing federal states, such as the United States or Canada, or of regions within more centralized, unitary states, like France or the United Kingdom (e.g. Mélitz and Zumer 1998). For example, empirical research on the USA has shown that there the federal budget performs a sizeable stabilization function in the order of 20 per cent of income shocks in most of the more recent studies (e.g. Bayoumi and Masson 1995).
>
> This does not, however, necessarily imply that the same stabilization function could not be performed equally effectively at the state level. Kletzer (1997) argues that stabilization through the federal budget in effect substitutes for stabilization through the budgets of individual states or countries. The opportunity to stabilize through accession to a federal system is thus primarily not a substitute for national monetary policy but for national fiscal policy. Thus, national fiscal policies in Europe should in principle be in a position to continue to perform a macroeconomic stabilization function in a decentralized way inside monetary union (c.f. Mélitz and Vori 1993; von Hagen and Hammond 1997). Moreover, the relatively large size of the state sector and of welfare and unemployment benefits in Europe, compared to the USA, also suggests that national automatic stabilizers should be more powerful (Allsopp and Vines 1996).
>
> Bayoumi and Eichengreen (1995) have estimated that the elasticity of the central government revenue/GDP ratio with respect to output (the percentage point increase in the deficit ratio associated with a percentage point increase in output growth) is in the order of 0.3–0.5 for a number of European countries, as a measure of the fraction of changes in disposable income that is offset by changes in government revenues. Buti *et al.* (1997) find that the elasticity of the budget balance for Europe as a whole is around 0.5 per cent; the IMF's estimates of the same elasticities (IMF 1997) are of the same order of magnitude. These elasticities are also often used to derive measures of cyclically adjusted budget balances as explained in Box 13.5.

ascendancy, not least, perhaps, favoured by the somewhat sobering results associated with Keynesian-inspired stabilization policies during that period. Models in the new classical mould or the re-emerging field of political economy reversed the basic premises of the previous policies. They placed relatively greater faith in the functioning of the market mechanism while being more sceptical about the effectiveness of policy interventions. The spotlight was moved away from 'market failure' towards 'government failure' and the need to provide appropriate incentives and institutions in order to improve policy-making.

The problem of time inconsistency and the value of pre-commitment

The seminal papers by Kydland and Prescott (1977) and later Barro and Gordon (1983) epitomize this change of emphasis, which went hand-in-hand with the rational expectations revolution in macroeconomic modelling. Their papers highlighted the problem of *time inconsistency* in discretionary policy-making. They showed that if policy-makers are left free to reconsider their policy plans at each point in time—i.e. act in a discretionary manner—this can lead to sub-optimal outcomes compared to a situation where policy-makers tie their hands and pre-commit to implement an *ex ante* optimal plan.

Most prominently, the problem of time inconsistency has been applied to monetary policy. Here governments are seen as subject to an *ex post* incentive to surprise-inflate in order to stimulate output and employment. For example, once social partners have concluded wage agreements, higher-than-anticipated inflation will reduce *ex post* real wages and thus increase output and employment. Such incentives to inflate will, however, be understood *ex ante* by a rational public, who adjust their inflation expectations accordingly. As a result, output and employment remain unaffected but inflation is suboptimally high. This so-called *inflation bias* of monetary policy has been proposed as an explanation for the high inflation rates observed in the 1970s and early 1980s, when monetary policies were no longer constrained by the Bretton Woods system of fixed exchange rates.

Problems of time inconsistency can also arise in the context of fiscal policy. In particular, a capital levy provides a non-distortionary form of taxation *ex post*, while the anticipation of such a levy would destroy the incentives to invest and accumulate capital *ex ante*. A similar argument can be made with respect to inflation, which can be seen as a tax on money holdings or as a capital levy on the stock of accumulated (nominal) government debt. In particular, a government that has run up a high stock of debt, fixed in nominal terms, will be subject to a strong temptation to reduce the real value of the debt burden through inflation. Again, the absence of an *ex ante* commitment not to impose *ex post* such an inflation tax on outstanding nominal liabilities of the government can lead to sub-optimal economic outcomes. The general message from this type of literature is that discretionary monetary and fiscal policies—instead of providing solutions to market inefficiencies—could themselves become a source of additional inefficiencies or instability. In such circumstances it can become beneficial to restrict the freedom of policy-makers.

Applying this line of reasoning it can be argued that the 'loss' of independent national monetary policy as a stabilization tool in a monetary union can actually represent a benefit to the extent that the new institutional set-up provides a more credible solution to the inflation bias problem than proved possible to achieve at the national level. A similar case could be made for fiscal policy if the institutions and incentives for fiscal policies which accompany monetary union mitigate against inefficiencies in fiscal policy-making at the national level.

The problem of 'deficit bias' and the sustainability of public finances

Apart from the time inconsistency problem *strictu sensu* (relating to the capital levy or the inflation tax), such inefficiencies in fiscal policy-making can be traced to incentives inherent in the institutions governing the political process. One example of such an inefficiency is provided by theories of a political business cycle, which link economic fluctuations to the electoral cycle. More generally, the political process may pay insufficient attention to the effects of policies that accrue in the distant future, or fall on constituencies which are dispersed and not well represented. These issues have long been emphasized by public-choice theorists (e.g. Buchanan 1977; Olson 1965). In such circumstances a politically induced 'deficit bias' under discretionary budgetary policy may arise in analogy to the 'inflation bias' that was identified in the case of discretionary monetary policy.

More specifically, such a deficit bias may be due to the strength of special interests pushing for public expenditure programmes relative to less-organized tax-payers. Moreover, future tax-payers are not represented at all in the democratic process, which favours the build-up of public debt to be repaid by future generations, and may also lead politicians to ignore the negative long-run growth effects of deficits via the crowding out of productive private investment. Government instability and a host of other political and institutional factors can be used to explain why the public finance performance of political systems has differed widely across countries (Roubini and Sachs 1989; Grilli *et al*. 1991; Corsetti and Roubini 1993; Alesina and Perotti 1995).

Over time the presence of such a potential 'deficit bias' or myopia in budgetary policy—whatever the source—would tend to lead to a build-up in government debt, which may ultimately cast doubt on the sustainability of public finances. Indeed, the experience of Europe in the 1970s through to the 1990s seems to lend support to the view that the accumulation of debt in this period cannot be fully explained as the outcome of optimal fiscal policies or tax smoothing behaviour over time. Instead, in particular in view of demographic trends and unfunded pay-as-you-go pension systems (Masson 1996), to a large extent it arguably represents an excessive burden on future generations. Empirical studies such as that by Artis and Marcellino (2000) also suggest that in the twenty years or so preceding monetary union, many EU countries did not appear to take sufficient heed of the constraint implied by the solvency condition in the inter-temporal government budget constraint.

This suggests a need to strengthen fiscal discipline in the national budgetary processes. Such a case could be made quite independently of the question of monetary union. To redress such inefficiencies countries might wish to reform their budget procedures or adopt mechanisms of unilateral self-commitment, e.g. by analogy to the constitutional balanced-budget amendment which has long been under discussion in the United States and is in widespread use at the state level there. However, unless international multilateral commitment is more credible than unilateral reforms, the adoption of mechanisms to sustain fiscal discipline in conjunction with a move to monetary union must be based on an additional set of arguments. In particular, monetary union might render the effects of any domestic deficit bias more damaging, allow fiscal problems to be 'exported' to a greater extent to partner countries inside the monetary union, or have negative side-effects on the single monetary policy. These issues are discussed in the remainder of this section.

The role of the 'no-bail-out clause' and bond markets for fiscal discipline

Monetary union means that countries are moving from a position in which they have both money-creating and taxing powers to one in which they are stripped of the former. Moreover, it is arguable that Member States' taxing powers may *de facto* also become increasingly confined to the extent that economic integration and liberalization promote the mobility of tax bases. Capital in particular may migrate and relocate to jurisdictions offering lower tax rates. From this angle monetary union could pose additional risks for government solvency, which in turn call for additional safeguards to promote fiscal prudence to be put into place. McKinnon (1994) has drawn attention to the potential danger that debt/GDP ratios which were sustainable in conditions where investors could be sure of the security of their assets, at least in the domestic currency of the issuing country, may not be sustainable when the countries concerned enter a monetary union and thereby abandon their money-creating power to an independent and area-wide central bank.

According to this line of reasoning governments that have accumulated a high stock of debt will—in a monetary union—no longer dispose of the ultimate recourse to the printing press. This means that governments lose the option of a monetary financing of their debt (i.e. reducing the real value of debt via inflation). All else equal, this raises the spectre of an increased probability of an outright default on government debt. Any suspicion of such a default could in turn precipitate a run on the government debt in question and provoke knock-on effects on the solvency of financial institutions with large exposures to such debt, and attendant contagion effects on the financial system at large. Eichengreen and Wyplosz (1998) regard this as the most serious reason for imposing fiscal constraints to pre-empt any such scenario from materializing in the first place. However, they consider alternative approaches, such as strengthening prudential measures to govern financial institutions' exposure to public debt and thus limit knock-on effects, to be more appropriate responses.

As in the earlier discussion of the costs and benefits of losing an independent monetary policy as a macroeconomic stabilization tool, the argument can be turned around. Losing the policy 'option' of a monetary financing of deficits and invoking the dire spectre of bankruptcy should sharpen *ex ante* incentives to avoid getting into an unsustainable fiscal position in the first place. In this context 'divorcing' and protecting monetary policy from the influence of fiscal authorities should have a disciplining effect on fiscal policies. In order for such 'deterrence' to be credible and effective it must not be possible for national fiscal authorities to rely on partner countries or union-wide authorities to help out countries that run into fiscal solvency problems. This is the rationale for introducing a 'no-bail-out' clause. If there were a perception of financial solidarity to help out imprudent national governments this would weaken incentives for fiscal discipline and create moral hazard problems similar to those discussed in the case of a central insurance mechanism for macroeconomic stabilization.

Central bank independence and a no-bail-out clause may, however, not be effective enough in providing adequate incentives for fiscal discipline in a monetary union (Beetsma and Bovenberg 2000). Additional rules or constraints may be required if governments judge the risks and consequences of a default as remote or too far into the future to affect current behaviour to a sufficient degree. Moreover, governments may judge a no-bail-out clause as not fully credible if a default also has systemic consequences for the financial systems in partner countries. Indeed, most federal states have some sort of restrictions on borrowing at the state level (Masson 1996), even if historically such restrictions have been introduced for a variety of different reasons (Eichengreen and von Hagen 1996).

In general, the effects of monetary union and a single capital market on the incentives for fiscal policy-makers go in opposite directions. On the one hand, the long-run budget constraint facing governments is hardened to the extent that a no-bail-out clause is credible and monetary financing of government debt by the European Central Bank is ruled out (Glick and Hutchison 1993). On the other hand, the short-run budget constraint facing national governments might soften to the extent that access to financing will be easier in the unified European capital market and (presumably) cheaper even for countries with a high debt and deficits. In a monetary union these countries are no longer subject to country-specific interest rate premia for devaluation and inflation risk. Abolishing national currencies removes the disciplining effect of international currency markets on national fiscal policies (Thygesen 1996) or, rather, detrimental effects from a lack of discipline by national policies will now affect the common currency and thus be shared by all countries inside the monetary union.

If a default risk on government debt were to appear one might expect bond markets to correctly price that risk (at least in the case where the no-bail-out clause is perceived as credible), which should in turn provide incentives for fiscal discipline. However, as long as countries retain sufficient taxing powers and control of the tax-base, the probability of outright default should be very small (Eichengreen and von Hagen 1996). By implication, any default risk premia are unlikely to be sizeable enough to act as an effective deterrent *ex ante*. Moreover, market reactions and political crises in response to fiscal problems tend to be discontinuous. They provoke a sudden and abrupt withdrawal of confidence which is difficult and costly to deal with *ex post* and thus may provoke attempts to furnish some explicit or implicit bail-out. For all these reasons it remains doubtful that market discipline by itself would be effective in offsetting any domestic political deficit bias (Lane 1993).

The need for fiscal policy co-ordination

The policy-making framework under EMU foresees that the basic responsibility for fiscal policy and most other areas of economic policy-making remains at the national level. The Community budget will remain too small to fulfil any significant role for macroeconomic stabilization and no additional insurance scheme was put into place. Thus a fundamentally decentralized fiscal policy regime is maintained alongside a unified supranational monetary policy and, accordingly, the task of macroeconomic stabilization of asymmetric country-specific shocks is left to national policy-makers.

This, first, raises the question of whether national fiscal policy is an effective instrument in a monetary union and can make up for the loss of an independent monetary and exchange-rate policy, when needed. A second question is the issue of policy coordination. This issue arises if there are significant spillovers among different national policy-makers or different policy areas which might not be taken into account in such a decentralized set-up.

A standard Keynesian open-economy framework like the Mundell–Fleming model can be used to assess these questions with respect to concerns over macroeconomic stabilization. In this context, the effectiveness of fiscal policy is enhanced in a fixed exchange-rate regime, such as monetary union, compared to a situation of floating exchange rates (Agell *et al.* 1996). Take the case of a fiscal expansion in one member country. In the case of a floating exchange rate the expansionary impact on output would be partially offset by negative effects on export demand due to an appreciating exchange rate. Inside monetary union any such counteracting effect would only occur to the extent that a national fiscal expansion affects the common external exchange rate.

The flip side of the enhanced effectiveness of fiscal policy for the purpose of national stabilization under monetary union is the reduced expansionary effect (spillover) from national fiscal policies on partner countries, since the (bilateral) exchange-rate channel is removed. Overall the effect on foreign output could become ambiguous, since the stimulation via greater import demand from a fiscal expansion might be offset by a dampening effect from higher common interest rates (and a higher common exchange rate) in the monetary union (Eichengreen 1997). From the simple Mundell–Fleming model one could thus conclude that the case for the coordination of fiscal policies is less strong in the presence of a monetary union than in its absence.

Most of the spillovers of fiscal policies are in any case not directly related to monetary union *per se* but rather rest on the degree of trade or financial market integration (Eichengreen and von Hagen 1996). However, should monetary union itself enhance economic integration and stimulate additional trade among countries inside the currency area this would, in turn, again increase the size of fiscal leakage and thus strengthen the *a priori* case for coordinated policy responses to shocks (Masson 1996).

Even if this should be the case, a number of obstacles to an effective implementation of macroeconomic policy coordination needs to be recognized (Winkler 1999).

First, the relevant spillovers need to be clearly identified. Even within a single model such spillovers are often ambiguous in sign; policy recommendations are even more prone to differ across different models, and the empirical evidence may not provide clear-cut answers either. For example there is not even agreement that fiscal retrenchment necessarily leads to a reduction in domestic output. Conceivably output could even be stimulated by fiscal retrenchment if budgetary consolidation restored confidence in public finances over the longer term (Giavazzi and Pagano 1990; Bertola and Drazen 1993; IMF 1997). However, the empirical evidence for such 'anti-Keynesian' effects appears to be mixed at best (Cour *et al.* 1996; Hughes-Hallett and McAdam 1996).

Secondly, all the reservations that apply to the experience with activist demand management policies at the national level as a destabilizing—rather than a stabilizing—influence on the economy apply with even greater force when it comes to attempts to organize such stabilization policies among actors with different interests. Timely agreement, action, and effective enforcement of coordinated policies on a case-by-case basis are difficult to organize in such circumstances.

Thirdly, a process of policy coordination might tempt policy-makers to shift policy actions or the responsibility for policy outcomes on to partner countries. This might weaken and dilute accountability with respect to national policy challenges. These include the role of fiscal policies in stabilizing country-specific shocks, which becomes more important in a monetary union, where monetary policy can only address area-wide developments. These also include the need for structural reforms to enhance the working of labour, goods, and capital markets to facilitate market-led adjustment to such shocks.

At the same time, in a monetary union participating countries are linked together via a common currency and the consequences of individual national economies policies will—for ill or for good—be shared among countries and reflected in common variables, such as market interest rates and the exchange rate. This gives rise to potential free-rider problems and a fundamental need to regard economic policies as 'of common interest' in a monetary union. Overall such free rider problems, i.e. substantial divergence between individual countries' self-interest and the common interest, seem less obvious in the case of concerns over macroeconomic stabilization. By contrast, the risk of undisciplined public finances in any particular country casting a shadow over area-wide financial, economic, and—ultimately—monetary stability seems to establish a much clearer case for minimal safeguards and common rules to be put into place. Therefore, pre-committing to a framework which promotes sound public finances should—at least *ex ante*—be in the interest of individual members of a monetary union.

Free-rider problems of the type described above could in principle be solved by establishing a central authority or some other mechanism to enforce coordinated policies in the common interest. Alternatively, constraints or sanction mechanisms could be imposed on decentralized policies in order to shift incentives in the desired direction on a durable basis. The latter is the basic approach taken by the fiscal rules embodied in the Maastricht Treaty and the Stability and Growth Pact.

The interaction between monetary and fiscal policy

Setting up an independent central bank means that monetary and fiscal policies are determined autonomously and potentially geared to achieving different objectives. The rationale for central bank independence is that overall such an institutional separation tends to achieve better economic results and higher welfare than if both policies were jointly determined. In particular, such an arrangement should provide better incentives to safeguard the objective of price stability. The basic rationale is that price stability can be regarded as a common good which is fundamentally in the interest of all members of society and is the foundation for the durable attainment and successful pursuit of other objectives like growth, employment, and overall welfare. However, unless sufficient institutional safeguards are put into place the common good of price stability may be vulnerable to political pressures and compromised by conflicts over redistribution or the pursuit of other objectives which may be conflicting in the short term. In particular, central bank independence can be seen as one way to avoid the time inconsistency problem and the associated inflation bias that can arise from such pressures and the pursuit of multiple objectives.

The clear assignment of monetary and fiscal policy functions to independent actors raises the question of consistency in the interaction of autonomous, but interdependent, policy areas. With regard to the shorter-term macroeconomic stabilization this points to the issue of the so-called 'policy-mix' between monetary and fiscal policy. With regard to long-term consistency it needs to be recognized that monetary and fiscal policy—even if they are determined independently—are nevertheless linked via the intertemporal public-sector budget constraint. Public-sector expenditures in any period can in principle be financed out of current taxes, by issuing debt or via seigniorage revenues arising from inflation as a tax on money holdings. The key question in this context becomes whether, in the case of conflict, the path of fiscal deficits or the path of inflation will ultimately give and adjust in the long run.

The separation of fiscal and monetary policy—while it is desirable to insulate monetary policy from fiscal pressures as much as possible—can, on the other hand, give rise to potential problems of consistency and lead to conflicts between both policy areas. Such conflicts could make it more difficult for monetary policy to maintain price stability in the short run and it may also place a question mark over the ability and determination of monetary policy to guarantee price stability in the face of fiscal instability over the longer run. In other words, additional mechanisms to ensure fiscal discipline may not only be desirable in their own right for the reasons discussed in the previous sections. They may also be seen as an additional safeguard to underpin central bank independence and avoid it being challenged by inconsistent fiscal developments (Beetsma and Uhlig 1999).

The game in Box 13.2 can be given economic interpretations both with respect to the long-run or the short-run strategic interaction between monetary and fiscal policy-makers. The long-run interpretation focuses on the intertemporal government budget constraint and the credibility of low inflation and no-bail-out promises. The short-run interpretation looks at the issue of the appropriate policy mix for macroeconomic stabilization. From this perspective fiscal constraints can be seen as an attempt to secure pre-commitment to the monetary dominance regime, i.e. select the better of the two possible equilibria and in particular to avoid costly conflict (leadership battles) between monetary and fiscal policy.

Introducing constraints on fiscal policy as a rough device and maintaining a clear separation of responsibilities may lead to an implicit solution to the coordination problem represented in Box 13.2. This solution may be greatly preferable to attempts at explicit and discretionary coordination between the two actors. Moving in the direction of a joint determination of policies, by contrast, would risk reintroducing all the problems of time-inconsistency and credibility that central bank independence was meant to solve.

Long-run credibility

Monetary and fiscal policy are linked via the intertemporal government budget constraint, which says that a stream of expenditures can be financed via taxes, issuing bonds or printing money. Here a regime of fiscal dominance assumes that the government can pre-commit to a path of net deficits and thus ultimately force the central bank to inflate in order to avoid insolvency as in the 'unpleasant monetarist arithmetic' of Sargent and Wallace (1981) or in the recent literature on the fiscal theory of the price level (Woodford 1995, 1998). Under 'monetary dominance' the central bank can commit not to inflate (no explicit or implicit bailout) and thus force the government to adjust its path of spending and taxes as in the 'unpleasant fiscal arithmetic' of Winckler and colleagues (1996).

In order to avoid fiscal and monetary policy being put on a collision course in the long run constraints on fiscal policy can reduce the risk of explosive or unstable debt dynamics. This can be done by placing a restriction or ceiling on the stock of debt (Pisani-Ferry 1996) or in the form of a feedback-rule on deficits that ensures that current deficits react to a debt build-up in a stabilizing manner (Canzoneri and Diba 1996).

Box 13.2: **The monetary-fiscal policy game**

Consider the simple illustration of the interaction between monetary and fiscal authorities in the game representation provided below. The pay-offs in this matrix are chosen for illustration. The first number in each cell refers to the utility obtained by the central bank from the particular combination of actions by the two players; the second number is the fiscal authorities' pay-off. The numbers chosen are meant to capture the value of fiscal and monetary policy paths to be coordinated in the short run and to be mutually consistent in the long run. Conversely, if policy-makers are on a collision course, pay-offs for both players are much lower. For example, a lax fiscal policy combined with tight money leads to an unbalanced policy mix, high interest rates, currency appreciation, and output losses. Note that both sides have an incentive to fall in line.

Faced with lax fiscal policy, monetary authorities may in the end give in and accommodate and accept the bottom-right outcome as the lesser evil. Likewise, when facing a tough central bank, fiscal authorities will prefer to 'chicken out' and accept discipline (the top-left outcome) rather than stick with zero pay-offs.

A Game of Chicken

		Fiscal Authorities	
		tight policy	lax policy
Central Bank	tight policy	4, 2	−1, −1
	lax policy	0, 0	1, 3

There are two Nash equilibria in this game, where neither of the players has an incentive to deviate. The central bank would prefer the 'tight' equilibrium (top-left) with tight monetary and fiscal policies, whereas fiscal authorities prefer the 'lax' outcome (bottom-right) with relaxed policies. The pay-offs are as in the standard 'game of chicken' (except here we make the 'tight' equilibrium the socially more attractive one). The two players have an incentive to coordinate their actions but differ over the preferred outcome. Therefore each side would like to pre-commit to a particular action in advance in order to induce its own preferred equilibrium. Depending on which side possesses strategic leadership in this simple game, we can distinguish two regimes; 'monetary dominance' and 'fiscal dominance' in the terminology of Canzoneri and Diba (1996).

Short-term credibility and policy-mix

In addition to the long-run compatibility of fiscal and monetary policy paths as reflected in the intertemporal government budget constraint, the choice of policy mix also becomes important in short-term macroeconomic management. Conflicts between fiscal and monetary authorities can be very costly, as the episodes of Reagonomics in the early 1980s and developments in the wake of German unification demonstrate. In both cases an expansionary fiscal policy collided with tight monetary policy and the real economy paid a high price for the re-establishment of the strategic leadership of the monetary authorities. In normal times, when monetary leadership is uncontested agents should be able to rely on the central bank to keep prices stable over the medium term. This should help to anchor expectations (especially for wage bargaining and financial markets) and contain economic uncertainty in the wake of shocks.

European countries' differing responses to the oil-price shocks in the 1970s illustrate the virtue of monetary dominance with respect to fiscal dominance. The long but unbalanced struggle of European economies to regain stability over the course of the 1980s can also be taken to illustrate the costs of an unbalanced policy mix (Allsopp and Vines 1996), resulting from an increase in the credibility of monetary policy (constrained by the European Exchange Rate Mechanism) which was accompanied by still relatively lax fiscal regimes. In general, if confronted with undisciplined fiscal policies (in the aggregate) the central bank would need to keep short-term interest rates higher than otherwise in order to contain inflationary pressures. If the central bank has to reassert its leadership (i.e. a regime of monetary dominance) in conflict with fiscal authorities this may entail greater real economic costs to society. Alternatively (if fiscal dominance prevails), the central bank may be forced to accommodate and monetary control over the price level may be compromised. Fiscal constraints can be seen as a (blunt) safeguard to limit the extent to which the central bank will be confronted with this dilemma and to avoid central bank independence being tested or contested too severely.

13.3 The institutional framework

The requirement of achieving fiscal discipline to join the single currency and of maintaining it once in EMU is at the core of the Treaty on European Union. Article 104 of the Treaty states that, in EMU, 'Member States shall avoid excessive government deficits' (see Box 13.3 for extracts from Article 104 of the Treaty on European Union). More specific requirements are set out in Protocol No. 5 on the excessive deficit procedure annexed to the Treaty.

Compliance with the Treaty's fiscal discipline requirement is assessed, *inter alia*, on the basis of the behaviour of the general government budget deficit in relation to the reference value of 3 per cent of GDP and by the evolution of the government debt ratio with respect to the 60 per cent of GDP threshold. The deficit criterion is satisfied when the government deficit ratio remains below the 3 per cent of GDP threshold or has fallen substantially and continuously and comes close to that level. All the eleven countries joining EMU on 1 January 1999 had a deficit at or below the 3 per cent reference value in 1997.

The Treaty allows the 3 per cent ceiling to be exceeded without causing an excessive deficit, but only under a highly restrictive set of conditions. The original cause of the rise of the deficit above the 3 per cent ceiling must be 'exceptional', the deficit must, in any case, remain close to this threshold, and must return promptly below it once the initial driving force has subsided. The range of events not giving rise to an excessive deficit depends on the degree of restriction with which these conditions are interpreted, but the Treaty does not provide any further indications to guide this interpretation.

The government debt ratio has to remain below 60 per cent of GDP or has to be on a clearly downward path towards that level. Government debt is defined as gross debt at nominal value outstanding at the end of the year and consolidated between and within the sectors of general government. Data availability and definitional problems as well as the fact that financial instability concerns are usually linked to gross rather than net debt motivated this choice.

When a country is subject to a Council decision on the existence of an excessive deficit, a procedure aimed at correcting this situation is initiated. This procedure includes several steps involving increasing pressure on the Member State through recommendations and notice to take effective measures to reduce the deficit. If such correction does not take place, the Maastricht Treaty foresees that sanctions may be applied to EMU members. Amongst the sanctions cited in the Treaty are non-interest-bearing deposits and fines. The Treaty, however, leaves a certain discretion to the Council on the application and the content of these sanctions and does not set time limits on the various steps of the procedure.

Gradually it became clear that the provisions of the Maastricht Treaty still left some leeway for interpretation. Moreover, the fear existed that countries, once admitted to monetary union, would be less inclined to maintain fiscal discipline thereafter. In November 1995, German Finance Minister Theo Waigel put forward a proposal for a Stability Pact for Europe. Waigel's pact presented a number of proposals to nail down a strict interpretation of the provisions regarding fiscal policy in the Treaty, but did not envisage a re-negotiation of the Maastricht criteria for participation in EMU.

The Stability and Growth Pact was adopted in Amsterdam in July 1997[1] (see Box 13.4 for extracts from the Stability and Growth Pact). It includes a Council Regulation on strengthening the surveillance of budgetary positions—the preventive arm of the pact— and one on speeding up and clarifying the implementation of the excessive deficit procedure—the dissuasive arm. These two legal texts were complemented by a European Council resolution on the commitments by all the actors to move swiftly and allow the use of sanctions in the event of budgetary misbehaviour.

Under the pact, EU countries are obliged to adhere to country-specific *medium-term objectives of budgetary positions close to balance or in surplus,* so as to allow them to respect the 3 per cent ceiling even during economic downturns. In the event of a harsh and persistent recession, the budgetary room for manœuvre between close-to-balance and a deficit of 3 per cent of GDP may not be sufficient to cushion the negative effects of the shock on economic activity. If the deficit overshooting takes place in the presence of a severe economic downturn, an 'exceptionality clause' can be called in.

An excess over the 3 per cent of GDP deficit limit is considered 'exceptional' if there is an annual fall of real GDP of at least 2 per cent. An annual fall of GDP of less than 2 per cent could nevertheless be considered exceptional in the light of further supporting evidence, such as the abruptness of the downturn or the accumulated loss of output relative to past trends. In any event, in evaluating whether the economic downturn is severe, the Member States will, as a rule, take an annual fall in real GDP of at least 0.75 per cent as a

Box 13.3 **Extracts from the Maastricht Treaty**

Article 104 (ex Article 104c) of the Treaty on European Union

1. Member States shall avoid excessive government deficits.

2. The Commission shall monitor the development of the budgetary situation and of the stock of government debt in the Member States with a view to identifying gross errors. In particular it shall examine compliance with budgetary discipline on the basis of the following two criteria:

    (a) whether the ratio of the planned or actual government deficit to gross domestic product exceeds a reference value, unless:

    —either the ratio has declined substantially and continuously and reached a level that comes close to the reference value;

    —or, alternatively, the excess over the reference value is only exceptional and temporary and the ratio remains close to the reference value;

    (b) whether the ratio of government debt to gross domestic product exceeds a reference value, unless the ratio is sufficiently diminishing and approaching the reference value at a satisfactory pace.

    The reference values are specified in the Protocol on the excessive deficit procedure annexed to this Treaty.

3. If a Member State does not fulfil the requirements under one or both of these criteria, the Commission shall prepare a report. The report of the Commission shall also take into account whether the government deficit exceeds government investment expenditure and take into account all other relevant factors, including the medium-term economic and budgetary position of the Member State. . . .

6. The Council shall, acting by a qualified majority on a recommendation from the Commission, and having considered any observations which the Member State concerned may wish to make, decide after an overall assessment whether an excessive deficit exists.

11. . . . the Council may decide to apply or, as the case may be, intensify one or more of the following measures:

    —to require the Member State concerned to publish additional information, to be specified by the Council, before issuing bonds and securities;

    —to invite the European Investment Bank to reconsider its lending policy towards the Member State concerned;

    —to require the Member State concerned to make a non-interest-bearing deposit of an appropriate size with the Community until the excessive deficit has, in the view of the Council, been corrected;

    —to impose fines of an appropriate size.

reference point. The excess of the deficit over 3 per cent of GDP will be considered temporary and thus allowed by the pact only insofar as the 'exceptional' conditions mentioned above persist. Therefore, the deficit has to move back below the 3 per cent threshold in the year following that during which these 'exceptional' circumstances occurred.

The pact put in place an early-warning mechanism under which Member States participating in the Eurozone have to submit stability programmes, while those not adopting the single currency have to present convergence programmes. The key feature of both types of programme is the specification of the national medium-term budgetary objectives. The Council will regularly examine both sets of programmes. The Council can issue a recommendation urging the Member State concerned to take adjustment measures, should significant slippage from the targets set in the programmes be identified. The pact applies to all EU countries but it does not impose sanctions on the non-EMU members.

The pact speeds up the excessive deficit procedure, set out in Article 104 of the Treaty. In order to avoid the imposition of sanctions, the Member State which has been put into excessive deficit needs to take immediate action and complete correction of the deficit in the year following the identification of the excessive deficit. Thus, in order to avoid sanctions, the Member State concerned should bring its deficit back below the reference value within two years after the occurrence of an excessive deficit and one year after its identification, unless special circumstances are given. The pact does not specify what these special circumstances are but it seems to be widely accepted that this clause could be relied upon in case of protracted or very severe recessions.

The pact also specifies the sanctions that may be applied in the event of persistent excessive deficits. The amount of the non-interest-bearing deposit in the first year of application of the sanctions is composed of a fixed component equal to 0.2 per cent of GDP and a variable component equal to one tenth of the difference between the deficit and the 3 per cent reference value. A ceiling of 0.5 per cent of GDP is set. The fixed component aims at providing an incentive not to incur an excessive deficit, while the variable component represents an incentive to limit the excess over the 3 per cent threshold. In each subsequent year, until the excessive deficit decision is abrogated, only the variable component will be applied. As a rule, a deposit is to be converted into a fine after two years if the excessive deficit persists. If no action is taken to correct the excessive deficit, sanctions can be imposed within the calendar year in which the decision on the existence of the excessive deficit is taken.

However, the pact did not clarify all the uncertainties surrounding the implementation of the excessive deficit procedure. It did not specify when deficits are *close to the reference value* of 3 per cent of GDP. The pact only provides more specifications on the interpretation of the deficit criterion and does not address the debt criterion.

The pact demands that EU countries present *medium-term objectives of budgetary positions close to balance or in surplus* in their stability and convergence programmes. In identifying a 'safe' budgetary position allowing the deficit to be kept below the 3 per cent of GDP reference value, the influence of cyclical fluctuations in economic activity on the budget balance needs to be examined. This influence depends on the size of cyclical fluctuations in output as well as on the sensitivity of the budget to the cycle. The

Box 13.4 **Extracts from the Stability and Growth Pact**

Council Regulation (EC) No. 1466/97 of 7 July 1997 on the strengthening of the surveillance of budgetary positions and the surveillance and coordination of economic policies

Article 3:

1. Each participating Member State shall submit to the Council and Commission information necessary for the purpose of multilateral surveillance at regular intervals . . . in the form of a stability programme, which provides an essential basis for price stability and for strong sustainable growth conducive to employment creation.

2. A stability programme shall present the following information:

   (*a*) the medium-term objective for the budgetary position of close to balance or in surplus and the adjustment path towards this objective for the general government surplus/deficit and the expected path of the general government debt ratio;

   (*b*) the main assumptions about expected economic developments and important economic variables which are relevant to the realisation of the stability programme such as government investment expenditure, real gross domestic product (GDP) growth, employment and inflation;

   (*c*) a description of budgetary and other economic policy measures being taken and/or proposed to achieve the objectives of the programme, and, in the case of the main budgetary measures, an assessment of their quantitative effects on the budget;

   (*d*) an analysis of how changes in the main economic assumptions would affect the budgetary and debt position.

Article 5:

1. Based on assessments by the Commission and the Committee set up by Article 109c of the Treaty [i.e. the Economic and Financial Committee], the Council shall, within the framework of Multilateral surveillance [. . .], examine whether the medium-term budget objective in the stability programme provides for a safety margin to ensure the avoidance of an excessive deficit, whether the economic assumptions on which the programme is based are realistic and whether the measures being taken and/or proposed are sufficient to achieve the targeted adjustment path towards the medium-term budgetary objective.

Article 6:

2. In the event that the Council identifies significant divergence of the budgetary position from the medium-term budgetary objective, or the adjustment path towards it, it shall, with a view to giving early warning in order to prevent the occurrence of an excessive deficit, address . . . , a recommendation to the Member State concerned to take the necessary adjustment measures.

Council Regulation (EC) No. 1467/97 of 7 July 1997 on speeding up and clarifying the implementation of the excessive deficit procedure

Article 11:

Whenever the Council decides to apply sanctions to a participating Member State . . . , a non-interest-bearing deposit shall, as a rule, be required.

Box 13.4 **continued**

Article 12

1. When the excessive deficit results from non-compliance with the criterion relating to the government deficit ratio . . . the amount of the first deposit shall comprise a fixed component equal to 0,2% of GDP, and a variable component equal to one tenth of the difference between the deficit as a percentage of GDP in the preceding year and the reference value of 3% of GDP.

2. Each following year, until the decision on the existence of an excessive deficit is abrogated, the Council shall assess whether the participating Member State concerned has taken effective action in response to the Council notice . . . . In this annual assessment the Council shall decide . . . , to intensify the sanctions, unless the participating Member State concerned has complied with the Council notice. If an additional deposit is decided, it shall be equal to one tenth of the difference between the deficit as a percentage of GDP in the preceding year and the reference value of 3% of GDP.

3. Any single deposit referred to in paragraphs 1 and 2 shall not exceed the upper limit of 0.5% of GDP.

influence of the cycle on budget balances can be removed by cyclically adjusting budget balances (see Box 13.5 and Figure 13.1 for a discussion and illustration).

The stability and convergence programmes are the main instrument for monitoring whether EU countries have attained such sustainable medium-term budgetary positions (European Central Bank, 1999). EU countries have to submit medium-term budget plans to the Council and the Commission, in which they set out their budgetary policies for the coming years. The programmes have to be updated each year.

The procedures for the submission and assessment of these programmes are spelled out explicitly in the Pact. The Pact specifies the information that needs to be included in the stability and convergence programmes. Member States have to present their 'medium-term objectives for budgetary positions close to balance or in surplus' in the programmes. The programmes also have to include information on the adjustment path towards these targets, on expected economic developments, on budgetary and economic policy measures envisaged to reach these targets, as well as a sensitivity analysis. Countries submitting convergence programmes also have to set out their medium-term monetary policy objectives. Member States also agreed, on an informal basis, to include more specific technical information in the programmes.

The programmes have to be assessed both by the Commission and the Economic and Financial Committee (formerly the Monetary Committee). To prepare these assessments, a technical evaluation of each programme is drawn up by the Commission services. Since the first set of stability programmes submitted at the end of 1998 and the beginning of 1999, a detailed examination of each programme is undertaken by the Council every year. The Council examines whether the medium-term budgetary objectives set in the programme provides sufficient room for manœuvre to ensure the avoidance of an

Box 13.5 **The cyclical adjustment of government budget balances**

Fluctuations in economic activity significantly affect government budget receipts and expenditure: tax receipts weaken and social transfers increase during recessions and show reverse movements during expansions. When government balances are cyclically adjusted, the effects of cyclical fluctuations on government budgets are filtered out and an underlying structural balance is identified. Cyclical fluctuations are determined by subtracting output trend estimates from actual output. The effects of these output gaps on the budget are then deducted to obtain the cyclically adjusted budget balance. When no active discretionary policy is undertaken, the government budget balance will automatically worsen during periods of economic hardship and improve during good periods and these automatic fluctuations in the budget will have a stabilizing impact on the economy.

Figure 13.1 presents a simplified illustration of the working of the automatic stabilizers. In this figure, the overall budget balance and its cyclical and discretionary components are pictured against the output gap. Here it is assumed that the government maintains a balanced budget position when the output gap is zero. The figure is drawn by assuming a neutral discretionary policy and a cyclical sensitivity of the budget of 0.5, which, according to the Commission services' calculations, is the average for the countries of the Euro-area (Buti *et al.* 1997).

In the Commission services' cyclical adjustment method (European Commission 1995), the Hodrick–Prescott filter is applied to calculate trend output over the cycles. Trend estimates are calculated by minimizing the fluctuations in actual output around the trend, subject to a constraint on the variation of the trend growth rates. This method is widely used at present as a simple technique of detrending time series. In common with all moving-average-based methods, the Hodrick–Prescott filter is sensitive to the lack of data at the extremes of the actual series.

Therefore, the actual output time series are extended with forecasts in order to ensure a symmetric filtering of the trend at the end of the actual series and to avoid end-point bias problems. Revenue and expenditure elasticities are applied to the output gap to estimate the impact of the cycle on government budget receipts and expenditure. The revenue elasticity is an average of specific elasticities per revenue category, weighted by the relative share of these categories in total revenue. Corrections for lags in the collection of corporate taxes have been introduced. The sensitivity of the budget balance to the cycle for the European Union as a whole lies around 0.5. This means that each widening of a negative output gap by 1 percentage point increases the government deficit by 0.5 percentage points of GDP.

The OECD and the IMF follow another approach and use a Cobb-Douglas production function for the estimation of potential output. Potential output is defined as the level of real GDP attainable with full employment of all production factors and sustainable over the medium-term at a stable rate of inflation. As the potential level of output tends to lie above the average output level, deviations of actual output from potential output tend to be systematically negative and asymmetric. This production function approach has a firm basis in economic theory but there remain significant problems with the estimation of its inputs. Under this approach, trend factor productivity, capital input, and full employment labour input are determined separately and plugged into the production function to obtain potential output estimates. The potential output estimates of the OECD and the IMF closely correspond to the Hodrick–Prescott trend output estimates because the Hodrick–Prescott filter is used to detrend the main inputs in the production function.

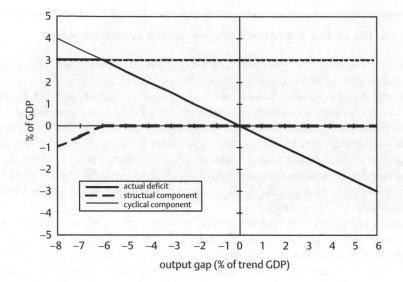

Fig. 13.1 Evolution of government deficit and debt ratios in the European Union

excessive deficit, whether the underlying economic assumptions are realistic, whether the measures announced in the programme will be effective in reaching the budgetary targets, and whether the policies presented in the programmes are consistent with the Broad Economic Policy Guidelines. Following this examination, the Council adopts an opinion on each programme on the basis of a Commission recommendation and after consulting the Economic and Financial Committee. The whole procedure has to be completed within tight time constraints: the Council has to carry out its examination and adopt its opinion within at most two months after the submission of the programme.

The assessment procedure for the updated programmes is less heavy. The updated programmes have to be assessed by the Commission and the Economic and Financial Committee, but a formal Commission recommendation and Council examination and opinion may not always be necessary. However, if the updated programme sets out a new strategy because there has been significant slippage from the targets set in the previous programme, or because there has been a change in government, recourse to the full procedure may be needed.

The pact introduced an early warning system in order to remind Member States of their obligation to respect budgetary discipline. In case Member States deviate from the budgetary targets set out in their stability and convergence programmes, a warning is issued by the Council that they should take measures to correct this deviation. Countries can only deviate from the figures of their programmes when this is attributable to the operation of the automatic stabilizers. In case there is a structural deviation from this path, a new programme has to be submitted that shows how the country plans to attain the initial target. At the first sign that budgetary positions tend to deviate from the safe level indicated in the programmes pressure is exercised on the country concerned to correct this.

The new system set up under the pact penalizes 'bad' behaviour rather more than it rewards 'good' behaviour. The Stability and Growth Pact foresees sanctions when the budget deficit exceeds the 3 per cent of GDP reference value. It does not foresee a reward when Member States achieve a balanced budget or a surplus during expansions. The EU countries often conducted pro-cyclical policies in the past. In particular, countries with high deficits and debts found it easier to take measures to prevent their budgets from getting out of hand during recessions than to make further progress in budgetary consolidation during periods of vigorous economic growth (Buti *et al.*, 1998). In practice, the new system does not restrain the tendency of many Member States to conduct pro-cyclical policies.

A certain adjustment fatigue has set in in recent years (Eichengreen and Wyplosz 1998) following a period in which substantial reforms and consolidation took place (see Box 13.6 and Figure 13.2). Most countries are back-loading the structural adjustment efforts that are necessary to reach safe budgetary positions by 2002 towards the end of the projection period. In addition, many countries are implementing important reductions of the tax burden. This could slow down the pace of the further budgetary consolidation.

13.4 **Policy debates**

The debate on policy-making in EMU and on the interpretation of the new rules did not subside with the start of monetary union. On the contrary, pressure increased on policy-makers with the slowdown in economic growth that took place in this period and the debate on the appropriate policy mix in EMU was re-opened. Many of these debates were followed closely by the financial markets. The proposals initiating these debates were often interpreted as an attempt to weaken the rules for budgetary discipline and thus as a threat to the credibility of the new system. The outcome of these debates was, however, that a strict interpretation of the rules of the Stability and Growth Pact needed to be maintained. These debates helped in this way to clarify the new rules and to improve the functioning of the new system.

Four main issues came to the forefront of the policy debate: whether, under the Stability and Growth Pact a country can be allowed to finance its government investment fully via deficits; what the safe medium-term budgetary positions are that countries have to attain under the Pact; whether a coordination of budgetary policies in EMU is necessary; and whether and when to introduce tax cuts.

The debate as to whether the EU budget needs to take over a number of functions from the national level took place some years before the start of monetary union. The question was raised in this debate whether a stabilization or transfer mechanism needs to be put in place at the EU level in order to dampen the asymmetric shocks that can take place in monetary union (Italianer 1993). The consensus on the political unfeasibility of such a transfer system was so large among EU countries that the debate on this issue was not re-opened.

The 'golden rule'

In a letter to the then Commission President Jacques Santer in October 1998, Mario Monti—at that time the Commissioner responsible for the internal market and tax coordination—raised the question whether the Commission should not encourage Member States to increase their government investment spending when they carry out their budgetary policies at the national level. The letter received a lot of attention in the press and was discussed in the European Parliament and the Ecofin Council. The letter was widely interpreted—unjustifiably so, to some extent—as calling for a more flexible interpretation of the rules of the Stability and Growth Pact and for a revival of the 'golden rule'.

Under the 'golden rule' of deficit financing, governments are only allowed to borrow in order to finance government investment. This implies that current expenditure cannot be financed via borrowing but must be funded directly out of tax receipts and other current revenue. The rule thus assumes that it is less imprudent for governments to borrow in order to finance investment than for them to incur deficits in order to fund government consumption and current transfers. The rule is based on the fact that, unlike government consumption, government investment spending leads to the accumulation of a stock of assets, which yield a stream of future returns (OECD 1998).

During the negotiations on the Maastricht Treaty, the golden rule was not retained as a primary criterion for assessing the budgetary position of Member States. The Maastricht Treaty only implicitly refers to the golden rule as an auxiliary criterion. The Treaty only specifies that the Commission, when initiating the excessive deficit procedure and drawing up its report, is required 'to take into account whether the government deficit exceeds government investment expenditure.[2] The golden rule is thus only taken into consideration when the Commission is determining whether or not a Member State is in a situation of excessive deficit. In such a case, the Commission has to examine not only whether the country in question complies with the golden rule but also has to take into account 'all other relevant factors, including the medium-term economic and budgetary position of the Member State'.

The golden rule is disregarded in the Stability and Growth Pact. While the Pact explicitly specifies what the exceptional circumstances are that may allow an overshooting of the 3 per cent of GDP limit, no mention is made of the golden rule in this respect. The Maastricht negotiators also decided to exclude the golden rule as the main budgetary criterion for EMU membership. The main objections that were raised against it during these negotiations were that it could constitute an incentive for spending ministers to increase their demands for expenditure and that it could create the impression of an encouragement for investment expenditure to be debt-financed, leading to excessive borrowing in the case of non-productive expenditure.

There has been a tendency in recent years for government investment spending to be reduced relative to GDP. This fall in government investment is partially due to the fact that a disproportionate share of the budgetary retrenchment that took place in the run-up to EMU fell on investment spending. Indeed, while government investment only makes up 5 per cent of total primary expenditure in the Union as a whole, around one-quarter of the improvement in the structural primary balance in the run-up to EMU fell on investment spending.

Box 13.6 **Evolution of government deficit and debt ratios**

In the run-up to EMU, important consolidation efforts were undertaken in the EU countries to meet the Maastricht budgetary criteria. The determination with which most governments undertook budgetary adjustment policies as well as the magnitude of these adjustments was quite remarkable. Even though the retrenchment process was difficult and gathered pace mainly towards the end of the period, it represents a genuine break with past budgetary behaviour and constitutes a major step towards budgetary discipline among Member States. In 1997, the year on which the evaluation of whether or not countries were deemed fit to enter EMU was based, no country had a deficit above 3% of GDP. Following a peak of 6 per cent of GDP in 1993, the average government deficit in the Union fell steadily in the following years, reaching 2.4 per cent of GDP in 1997. Many countries still had debt ratios above the 60 per cent of GDP reference value but in all those Member States, except Germany, the debt ratio declined in 1997 (European Commission 1998).

Due to strong economic growth and the strong decline of interest payments—the result of falling debt ratios and low interest rates—government budget balances continued to improve further over the period 1998–2000. For the Union as a whole, the deficit fell further to 0.1 per cent of GDP in 2000 (excluding proceeds from the sale of UMTS mobile phone licences). Many EU countries now have budget surpluses or at least a balanced budget position and only a few countries—Germany, France, Italy, Austria, and Portugal—still had deficit near or above 1 per cent of GPD in 2000. The debt ratio also continued to fall rapidly in all EU countries and by 2002 all countries, except for the high-debt countries Belgium, Greece and Italy, are expected to have a debt ratio below the 60 per cent of GDP reference value.

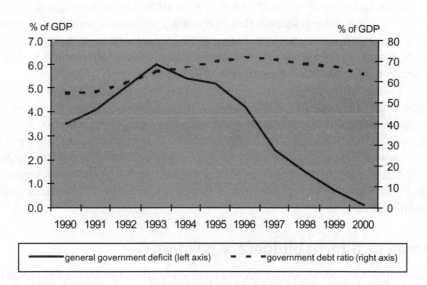

Fig. 13.2 Stylized budgetary behaviour over the cycle

Numerical budget rules, such as the Maastricht rules, often result in the reduction of expenditure falling predominantly on government investment during periods of budgetary consolidation. This has to do with the fact that it is politically easier for governments to cut down investment spending than expenditure resulting from legal or contractual commitments. The empirical evidence shows, however, that budget consolidations tend to be more successful if government investment is maintained (Alesina and Perotti 1996).

However, the appropriateness of government investment spending as a stabilization tool to stimulate demand is questionable. There is a lack of flexibility in the timing and implementation of this type of spending. In addition, unlike the operation of the automatic stabilizers, investment spending may be difficult to unwind during periods of economic expansion. There is ample evidence that in the past EU countries have not used government investment as a stabilization tool to sustain the cycle. If anything, investment behaviour over the past decades has been pro-cyclical. In a majority of the recession episodes that occurred in the EU countries, and especially during protracted multi-year recessions, cuts in government investment spending took place. Government investment has shown pro-cyclical behaviour especially in the high-debt countries. In these countries, the level of government investment was reduced during periods of negative output gaps, while it was increased during periods of positive output gaps.

There is a further reason why a strict medium-term objective of 'close to balance or in surplus', could deter government investment. Since it entails a transition from debt to tax financing of investment the current generation of tax-payers will have to shoulder fully the cost of new projects while also having to service past debts. Debt financing will no longer be available under the Pact to smooth the burden of investment over the generations of tax-payers receiving its benefit (Buti *et al.* 1998). The generation that profits from government investment is not the same as the generation that carries the costs. It is mainly the current generation that shoulders the costs to the advantage of future generations. The outcome could be that the present generation decides to reduce government investment. There is indeed evidence that government investment remains higher under a golden rule than under stringent balanced-budget restrictions. US States that are allowed to borrow to finance investment have a higher level of both capital and current expenditures than States that do not (Poterba 1995).

The outcome of the debate on the golden rule that took place at the end of 1998 and the beginning of 1999 was that a strict interpretation of the rules of the Pact needs to be maintained. It became clear that no consensus could be found for new and looser budgetary rules in EMU. Deficits higher than 3 per cent of GDP are no longer accepted, not even to finance government investment. The attention paid to government investment in this debate led most Member States to announce in their stability and convergence programmes that they plan to increase their spending on investment again or at least not decrease it further.

Safe medium-term budgetary positions

The Pact obliges Member States to achieve a medium-term budgetary position of 'close to balance or in surplus'. The resolution of the European Council on the Stability and Growth Pact confirms that 'sound budgetary positions close to balance or in surplus will allow all Member States to deal with normal cyclical fluctuations while keeping the government deficit within the reference value of 3 per cent of GDP.'

The reference value of 3 per cent of GDP is a ceiling that is the same for all Member States. The safe budgetary positions that are implied by the Pact differ from country to country. Lengthy discussions took place on the question of what these safe budgetary positions are for each individual country and how large the safety margins should be.

The Commission calculated minimal benchmark positions that would allow countries to cope with the effects on their budgets of cyclical fluctuations in economic activity without breaching the 3 per cent of GDP limit (see Box 13.7 and Table 13.1). The necessary safety margin depends on the size of the cyclical fluctuations in output and on the sensitivity of the budget to these fluctuations The Commission calculated that the maximum output gap that occurred in the Euro-area and in the Union on average over the past decades amounted to around 4 per cent of GDP. The average sensitivity of the budget to cyclical fluctuations is around 0.5 for the Euro-area and the Union as a whole; this means that a reduction in economic growth of 1 percentage point increases the government deficit in the Eurozone and the Union by 0.5 percentage points of GDP on average. Thus, a minimal government deficit of 1 per cent of GDP and a corresponding safety margin of 2 percentage points are necessary on average for the Eurozone and the Union to deal with the consequences of normal cyclical fluctuations, whilst staying within the 3 per cent of GDP limit.

The Pact says that EU countries need to aim for safe budgetary positions in order to limit the danger of being put into excessive deficit. The Pact only points out that when countries have reached such safe positions, they will be able to cope more easily with normal cyclical fluctuations. The Pact does not mention other factors that need to be taken into account. However, Member States have committed themselves to aim for larger safety margins, which allow them also to deal with other setbacks without breaching the 3 per cent reference value. The factors that need to be taken into account are: unexpected fluctuations in the budget due to interest rate shocks or tax shortfalls, the burden of population ageing, and a rapid reduction of the debt ratio for high-debt countries.

Detailed calculations to estimate the additional safety margin that is necessary to take into account these factors have not yet been carried out. The debate on this issue has not yet closed. Preliminary estimates show that an additional margin of around 1 to 2 per cent of GDP will be necessary for most countries. Member States will therefore have to aim for more ambitious positions than set out in their stability and convergence programmes. Countries that wish to implement active budgetary policies will have to foresee additional margins. These strict budgetary positions will have to be attained in the coming years. The rapid reduction of the debt ratio that will follow when more ambitious budgetary positions are maintained will lead to a reduction in interest payments and in this way will create some budgetary room to cope with population ageing.

Coordination of budgetary policies

An important policy debate took place on the question of whether the budgetary policies that are followed by the EU Member States at the national level need to be coordinated at

Box 13.7 **Minimal benchmarks**

The Commission services have calculated, for illustrative purposes, minimal budgetary positions that would allow countries to deal with the effects on their budgets of severe economic recessions (European Commission 1999, 2000). Figures for these minimal benchmarks are shown in Table 13.1. The first column of the table presents recent estimates for the sensitivity of the budget to the cycle for each individual EU country. Estimates for budgetary positions allowing countries to deal with the effects on their budgets of severe recessions are presented in the second column of the table.

The Commission's calculations showed that, from the point of view of keeping the budget balance within the 3 per cent of GDP reference value through a 'normal' cycle, it would be sufficient for Belgium, Luxembourg, and the Netherlands to aim for a structural budgetary position of between 0 and 1 per cent of GDP. For Germany, Greece, Spain, France, Ireland, Italy, Austria, Portugal and Sweden a budget deficit of around 1 per cent of GDP would be sufficient. Denmark and Finland would have to aim for a surplus, as the budgets of these countries have a high sensitivity to the cycle and their economies have in the past shown a high degree of volatility.

Similar results were obtained by the IMF and the OECD. The OECD (1997) calculated that for most EU member states a structural budget position of 1.5 per cent of GDP would be sufficient to deal with an increase in the output gap by 3 percentage points of GDP, the average value of the output gap that occurred during recessions over the period 1975–97. The IMF (1997) also reached the conclusion that structural budget positions of 0.5 to 1.5 per cent of GDP are sufficient for the EU countries to allow the automatic stabilizers to operate fully. The OECD also carried out calculations with a structural VAR model to measure the impact on the government budget of stochastic shocks (Dalsgaard and de Serres 1999). These calculations showed that it is sufficient for most EU countries to reach a budgetary position of 1.0 to 1.5 per cent of GDP in order to remain below the 3 per cent limit with a 90 per cent certainty over a period of three years. Structural deficits between 0 and 1 per cent of GDP extend this horizon from five to seven years.

The Commission's benchmarks only represent a minimal position. Extra room for manœuvre to deal with other factors of uncertainty and volatility in the budget should be envisaged. Several factors need to be taken into account in this respect. First, a supplementary safety margin around the medium-term budgetary position may be required to cope with unforeseen variability in the budget balance arising from non-cyclical factors, such as unexplained tax shortfalls, more rapid expansion of spending on entitlement programmes than expected, etc. Secondly, the high-debt countries need to secure a steady and rapid decline in their debt ratio. These countries therefore need to aim for a sufficiently ambitious level when setting their budgetary positions. Thirdly, Member States might want to aim for a more ambitious position or even a budget surplus in order to prepare for the future burden on their budgets of population ageing. Especially those countries where the financing of the pension system is based on a pay-as-you-go instead of a funded system should take into account these additional considerations. Finally, a supplementary safety margin would need to be ensured in case Member States want to pursue an active counter-cyclical budgetary policy (Artis and Buti 2000).

Table 13.1 Minimal benchmarks

	Sensitivity of budgets to the cycle[a]	Minimal benchmarks[b]
Belgium	0.6	−1.0
Denmark	0.7	−0.7
Germany	0.5	−1.1
Greece	0.4	−1.4
Spain	0.6	−0.4
France	0.5	−1.5
Ireland	0.5	−0.9
Italy	0.5	−1.2
Luxembourg	0.6	0.0
Netherlands	0.8	−0.1
Austria	0.5	−1.3
Portugal	0.5	−0.6
Finland	0.7	1.3
Sweden	0.9	0.8
United Kingdom	0.7	−0.1
Euro-area	0.5	−1.0
EU 15	0.6	−0.8

Notes:
a   Worsening of budget balance in percentage points of GDP following a widening of the negative output gap by 1 percentage point
b   Structural budget position that needs to be maintained so that the effects of the cycle on the budget balance can be accommodated
Source: European Commission (1999).

the level of the Euro-area or the Union as a whole. The debate centred in particular on the question of how budgetary policies that are determined independently at the national level can lead to a global stance that is appropriate for the Euro-area as a whole. If each Member State sets its budgetary policy in accordance with the economic situation at the national level, will the outcome at the aggregate level then be automatically appropriate? Or should a specific coordination mechanism be put into place forcing countries to take into account the overall economic situation of the Euro-area as a whole when setting their budgetary policies?

The EMU institutional set-up implicitly assumes the following typology of shocks and related policy instruments (Buti and Sapir 1998):

• Supply shocks need to be addressed via structural measures, while demand shocks, especially if they are of a temporary nature, can be met by macroeconomic stabilization policies;

• If the shock affects only one country—i.e. it is country-specific or asymmetric—the proper instrument is national budgetary policy and there is little or no case for a monetary response;

• If, on the other hand, the shock affects several countries at the same time—i.e. it has a high degree of symmetry—the appropriate instrument is monetary policy. In addition, if Member States let their budgetary stabilizers work, the system would have a considerable degree of built-in stabilization (OECD 1999);

- In the event of a particularly severe common shock, however, there might also be a need for discretionary budgetary policy beyond automatic stabilization in addition to the monetary policy reaction.

Table 13.2 shows the type of policy instrument that would be the most appropriate to deal with different types of shocks.

Within the EMU-framework it is assumed that EU countries can let their automatic stabilizers operate fully in order to stabilize 'normal' cyclical fluctuations once they have reached their medium-term budgetary position of 'close to balance or in surplus'. Under this 'automatic pilot' approach there is no need for an assessment of the budgetary stance at the level of the Euro-area as a whole and neither is there any need for an *ex ante* coordination of budgetary policies. Such an *ex ante* coordination only makes sense when discretionary policy is implemented. Thus, underlying the EMU set-up is the presumption that discretionary policy action is unnecessary during periods of 'normal' cyclical fluctuations and this is why a formal mechanism to coordinate budgetary policies has not been worked out in the Treaty.

However, the EMU framework does not prevent Member States from using discretionary budgetary policies to deal with exceptionally severe common shocks, such as harsh recessions or expansions. During such periods, monetary policy could be insufficient to stabilize the shock and may therefore have to be supplemented by budgetary policy interventions. Given the low frequency of such extreme shocks, however, no formal arrangements were included in the Treaty to deal with these circumstances and such discretionary policies should therefore be undertaken on an *ad hoc* basis.

In EMU, disincentives to implement discretionary relaxation policies during recessions may, however, be particularly strong. There are several reasons why countries may refrain from giving a budgetary stimulus during recessions. There are the traditional counter-indications to discretionary budgetary fine-tuning. Indeed, while active budgetary policy-making to sustain the cycle may be useful under particular circumstances, a number of undesirable features cannot be ignored: timing problems, non-reversibility of

Table 13.2 Type of shocks and associated policy instruments

Type of shock:	Small shock	Large shock
Asymmetric	• *Monetary policy*: no response by the ECB • *Budgetary policy*: operation of automatic stabilizers in country affected	• *Monetary policy*: no response by the ECB • *Budgetary policy*: in addition to letting automatic stabilizers play, the affected country could undertake discretionary budgetary action
Symmetric	• *Monetary policy*: response by the ECB • *Budgetary policy*: operation of automatic stabilizers	• *Monetary policy*: response by the ECB • *Budgetary policy*: discretionary budgetary policies possibly needed

Source: Buti and Sapir (1998)

budgetary expansions, model uncertainty, delay of structural reforms, etc. (Allsopp and Vines 1998).

In addition to these arguments, there exist a number of EMU-specific counter-indications. First, the effectiveness of budgetary policy is likely to be reduced in EMU because of increasing demand leakages. Secondly, countries might be unwilling to aim for more ambitious medium-term budget targets and to create the necessary room for manœuvre since the latter would only seldom be used. Lack of room for manœuvre and fear of sanctions under the Pact may lead to a wait-and-see attitude on behalf of each country. Thirdly, the system has a built-in pressure for tightening but not for expanding.

The need for coordination in monetary union crucially depends on whether or not budgetary policy affects the economies of the other countries and leads to spill-overs. Budgetary policy in one country affects other countries via direct demand leakages and through the impact on interest rates and the Euro exchange rate. If a country stimulates demand via an expansionary budgetary policy, its trading partners benefit from such a policy through increased exports. If it is a large country that carries out this budgetary stimulus, the danger of inflationary pressures in the Euro-area resulting from this increase in demand may, however, induce the ECB to tighten monetary policy and thus to increase interest rates (see Box 13.8).

If the actions of the budgetary authorities do not lead to an increase of the common interest rate, then the demand effect dominates. This could be the case especially if it is a small Member State that carries out such a discretionary relaxation, since such a policy action is less likely to create inflationary pressures in the Euro-area as a whole. The expected deepening of trade integration in EMU increases the external leakages caused by budgetary policies and the demand effects can therefore be expected to become larger.

An overall assessment of the budgetary stance at the level of the Eurozone as a whole is certainly a useful exercise. However, such a judgement of budgetary policies at the Euro-level should not imply that there is no longer any responsibility to meet the requirements of the Stability and Growth Pact at the national level. It does not imply either that the 3 per cent of GDP deficit criterion would only apply to the average deficit for the Eurozone as a whole, or that individual Member States could be permitted to overshoot the 3 per cent deficit ceiling as long as there are other countries with deficits well below 3 per cent. Thus, a 'compensation' between Member States cannot take place, and countries with deficits that are still close to the 3 per cent threshold cannot be allowed to exploit the larger room for manœuvre enjoyed by other countries (therefore, a system of tradable deficit permits as proposed by Casella (1999) is not compatible with the requirements of the pact).

In addition, the action that each individual country would need to undertake for the common good may be hard to implement if it goes against its own interest. In the case of a severe recession, a country will only be able to undertake a discretionary relaxation if it does not violate the pact and if this does not go against its own interests by worsening the policy mix at the national level.

Moreover, there is a risk that such debates lead to demands for co-ordination between monetary and fiscal policies. There is a clear allocation of responsibilities in the Treaty. The Treaty says that the primary objective of the ECB is to maintain price stability. Therefore, the ECB's monetary policy cannot be made conditional on the policies carried

---

Box 13.8 **The spill-over effects**

There is no agreement on the empirical size of the spill-over effects. As the effects go in opposite directions, the net effect is ambiguous. Most econometric simulations indicate that, whatever their sign, these spill-over effects are likely to be small in size in EMU.

Simulations with the Commission services' QUEST-model (Röger and In 't Veld 1997) show that if the three largest countries of the Euro-area—Germany, France, and Italy—introduce a reduction in labour taxes amounting to 1 per cent of GDP, to which the ECB reacts by increasing its interest rate, real GDP growth for the Euro-area as a whole will increase by barely 0.1 percentage points. Real GDP in the Euro-area also increases by only 0.1 percentage points if the budgetary stimulus is given in the form of an increase in government consumption, equally amounting to 1 per cent of GDP. The effects are significantly higher if, notwithstanding the budgetary relaxation carried out by the three largest countries, the ECB does not tighten its monetary policy. In such a case, real GDP growth in the Euro-area increases by 0.4 percentage points.

When the budgetary relaxation is assumed to take place in the smaller Euro-zone countries, the spill-over effects are even smaller. If a 1 per cent of GDP tax reduction is implemented by the remaining eight countries—Belgium, Spain, Ireland, Luxembourg, Netherlands, Austria, Portugal, and Finland—and the ECB keeps interest rates unchanged, then real GDP in the Euro-area increases by less than 0.1 percentage points. Real GDP growth increases by around 0.1 percentage points if these countries raise government consumption by 1 per cent of GDP. The effects are even lower in the case where the ECB decides to raise interest rates as a response to the budgetary relaxation undertaken by these eight countries. As the relative size of these countries is much smaller than that of the three large countries, the effects of their budgetary actions on the Euro-area as a whole are correspondingly smaller.

All scenarios show that the spill-over effects could remain small in EMU. The question can then be raised whether countries will find it worthwhile to undertake a budgetary relaxation for the common good if the effects on the other countries in the Euro-area remain so small.

---

out by the other policy actors. It is clear that the ECB neither seeks nor takes outside instructions and there can therefore be no question of co-ordinating policies *ex ante*.

Tax reforms and tax harmonization

As government budget balances were approaching balanced positions or even surpluses in the first years of EMU, EU countries turned their attention to new policy challenges. Many countries started to introduce significant tax cuts. These tax cuts were mainly geared towards reductions in labour and corporate income taxation and social security contributions. The aim of these tax cuts was to enhance the non-inflationary growth potential in the European Union. The tax burden in most countries is still far in excess of that of the main industrialized countries outside the Union. The tax cuts that are being introduced will therefore help to bring down these high tax burdens.

The tax reforms followed a common pattern. Most countries introduced significant corporate and personal income tax cuts, with the latter typically benefiting mainly the low and middle-income earners. The objective of promoting employment was also behind the social security contribution cuts. Overall, countries made some progress in making tax systems more employment-friendly. However, labour taxation still remains very high, by international standards, in many EU countries.

However, the danger exists that these tax cuts lead to a weakening of fiscal discipline if they are not offset by spending reductions in order to prevent government deficits from rising again. In order to avoid a reversal of the fiscal consolidation process, the Commission proposed that the tax cuts need to satify the following four criteria (European Commission 2000):

1. for countries not yet 'close to balance or in surplus' tax cuts need to be fully compensated by expenditure cuts;

2. tax cuts must not be pro-cyclical;

3. when implementing tax cuts, countries need to take into account the level of public debt and long-term sustainability; and

4. tax reductions should form part of a comprehensive reform package.

There was general agreement that these reforms should thus not jeopardize the achievement of a budgetary position consistent with the Pact and they should not lead to a pro-cyclical fiscal policy stance. Moreover, these reforms should not slow down the debt reduction process in the high-debt countries. Revenues arising from higher than expected economic growth should not be used to finance structural tax cuts. A strict control of expenditure growth is needed to ensure further progress in fiscal consolidation in a period of economic expansion. In this way, room is also created for supply-side-oriented reforms to taxes and social security contributions.

The spurt of tax reforms and tax cuts in the early years of Monetary Union can be interpreted as governments reaping the first fruits of the previous phase of budgetary consolidation which was necessary to regain some room for manœuvre. At the same time, such reforms are required to address longer-term structural challenges. These challenges, in particular, arise from the implications of ageing populations for pension and healthcare systems, and from the need to reduce tax burdens and improve conditions for profitable investment in Europe.

However, the spurt of tax reforms and tax cuts can also be seen as the result of increased tax competition between different jurisdictions inside the Monetary Union. Such increased tax competition and intensified pressures for reforms is widely regarded as beneficial, but in some areas it has also prompted a debate about a countervailing need for tax *harmonization*. One example of this is the debate over the taxation of capital income, which has differed widely across Europe. This is thought to have contributed to tax evasion or distorting capital flows away from higher tax regimes. Thus some balance will have to be struck between allowing for healthy tax competition while ensuring a minimum set of ground-rules. Such a balance would be consistent with the general Maastricht approach to fiscal policy coordination. It stops short of fully fledged harmonization, it retains national responsibility, but tends to provide some common minimum standards or constraints where needed. However, as the mobility of tax bases to migrate across Europe (and, indeed, beyond) increases, calls for greater harmonization may intensify and the balance may shift over time.

13.5 Conclusions and outlook

The Maastricht framework for economic policy-making under EMU features a basic asymmetry. On the one hand, there is a single, unified monetary policy for the Euro-area; on the other hand, the basic responsibility for most other economic policies—including, in particular, fiscal policy—remains at the national level. This gives rise to three sets of concerns. First, are market mechanisms and the policy instruments remaining at the national level sufficiently flexible to fulfil a stabilizing role and compensate for the loss of national monetary and exchange-rate policy? Secondly, to what extent is there a need to coordinate national fiscal policies within a single currency area? Thirdly, how can it be ensured that national fiscal policies are consistent with the single monetary policy, both individually and in the aggregate?

This chapter has provided an overview of the framework for fiscal policy-making inside EMU as established in the Maastricht Treaty, subsequent amendments to the Treaty, and the Stability and Growth Pact. This framework essentially preserves decentralized, national responsibility for fiscal policy choices but within a clearly defined set of common ground-rules, constraints, and procedures. This set-up can be seen to represent an appropriate institutional response to the challenges for the conduct of fiscal policy in a single currency area composed of a union of nation-states, where the principal locus of democratic accountability remains with national parliaments and national electorates. Thus the coexistence of a single independent monetary authority at the European level with a plurality of national fiscal policy actors, on the one hand, reflects the—to date—limited advances in European political integration. On the other hand, there are also good economic arguments for taking the view that the 'economic constitution' adopted at Maastricht provides a sound basis for the longer term.

In particular, the rules-based and procedural approach to cooperation in the field of fiscal policy combines the need for credibility with the benefits of flexibility. Inside monetary union it is even more important that the economic policy instruments remaining at the national level can be geared to the particular prevailing local economic conditions. By stabilizing the national economy, policy-makers can also make their best contribution to economic stability across the Euro-area as a whole, as long as spill-over effects remain limited. At the same time, the deficit ceilings introduced in the Maastricht Treaty (and backed up by the sanction mechanism included in the Stability and Growth Pact) provide a safeguard against potentially significant spill-overs which could arise from undisciplined fiscal policies. As in the context of monetary policy, placing constraints on fiscal policy can be helpful for credibility. Providing incentives for sound and sustainable public finances can be desirable even in the absence of a monetary union. Inside monetary union constraints on national fiscal policies also reduce the scope for gross inconsistencies and major tensions with the single monetary policy.

The experience with the Maastricht framework for fiscal stability to date can be judged to be broadly satisfactory. The Maastricht fiscal criteria were a crucial device in promoting policy convergence in the run-up to monetary union, despite much initial criticism among academics (e.g. Buiter and Roubini 1993). The multi-lateral budgetary surveillance procedure has been implemented successfully and is being refined further. Progress in deficit reduction has, however, slowed in many countries after their entry into monetary union, despite the favourable economic conditions in recent years. The credibility of the fiscal framework has not yet been tested in more adverse circumstances, and the sanctions procedure has not yet been applied. So the real stress-test for rule-based coordination is yet to come.

It is also too early to tell how far recurrent efforts to move to more ambitious forms of economic policy coordination will go. In particular, the hopes of those pushing for enhanced economic governance, if not a fully-fledged economic government, to accompany (if not to counter-balance) the European Central Bank on the European scene are pinned on a gradual upgrading of the informal Euro-Group of Euro-area finance ministers. The widely diverging responses of European governments to a common external shock as represented by the rapid rise in oil prices in 2000 provide some food for thought. It could be argued that the episode showed that greater coordination would be desirable. One could also conclude that it shows that any such ambitions remain premature.

Discussion questions

1 Why does a monetary union require both greater discipline and greater flexibility of national fiscal policies? What are the theoretical foundations for these two requirements and in which way have the Maastricht Treaty and the Stability and Growth Pact reconciled them?

2 Is there a need for greater fiscal policy coordination among the countries of the Euro-area or even some kind of 'European economic government'?

3 The Stability and Growth Pact says that countries need to achieve medium-term budgetary positions of 'close to balance or in surplus'. How is this clause to be interpreted?

Further reading

Buti, M. and Sapir, A. (1998), *Economic Policy in EMU* (Oxford: Clarendon Press).

Calvo, G. and King, M. (eds.) (1999), *The Debt Burden and its Consequences for Monetary Policy*. International Economic Association Conference, vol. 118 (London: Macmillan Press).

'Challenges for Economic Policy Coordination within European Monetary Union', *Empirica*, 26/3 (1999), special issue.

Eijffinger, S. and de Haan, J. (2000), *European Monetary and Fiscal Policy* (Oxford: Oxford University Press).

Hughes Hallett, A., Hutchison, M., and Hougaard Jensen, S. (eds.) (1999), *Fiscal Aspects of European Monetary Integration* (Cambridge: Cambridge University Press).

Van Bergeijk, P., Berndsen, R., and Jansen, W. (eds.) (2000), *The Economics of the Euro Area: Macroeconomic Policy and Institutions* (Cheltenham: Edward Elgar).

Useful Internet addresses: www.ecb.int for publications and press releases of the European Central Bank; europa.eu.int is the homepage of all European Union institutions. From there, there is a link to the website of the European Commission. The site of the Directorate General for Economic and Financial Affairs, europa.eu.int/comm/economy_finance, provides access to publications on EMU.

Notes

1 The Stability and Growth Pact consists of:

- Council Regulation (EC) no. 1466/97 of 7 July 1997 on the strengthening of the surveillance of budgetary positions and the surveillance and coordination of economic policies, published in the Official Journal L209 of 2 Aug. 1997, p. 1;

- Council Regulation (EC) no. 1467/97 of 7 July 1997 on speeding up and clarifying the implementation of the excessive deficit procedure, published in OJ L209 of 2 Aug. 1997, p. 6;

- Resolution of the European Council on the Stability and Growth Pact of 17 June 1997, published in OJ C 236 of 2 Aug. 1997, p.1.

2 The Protocol on the excessive deficit procedure — Protocol no. 5 — defines government investment as corresponding to gross fixed capital formation, as defined in the European system of economic accounts (ESA).

Acknowledgements

This chapter partly draws on previous work by the authors, in particular Artis and Winkler (1998) and Buti, Franco and Ongena (1998). The views expressed in this chapter are those of the authors and do not necessarily reflect those of the European Central Bank.

References

Agell, J., Calmfors, L. and Jonsson, G. (1996), 'Fiscal Policy When Monetary Policy is Tied to the Mast', *European Economic Review*, 40: 1413–40.

Alesina, A. and Perotti, R. (1995), 'The Political Economy of Budget Deficits', *IMF Staff Papers*, 42: 1–32.

——— ——— (1996), *Fiscal Adjustment in OECD Countries: Composition and Macroeconomic Effects*, Working Paper no. 5730, National Bureau of Economic Research (Cambridge, Mass.: NBER).

Allsopp, C. and Vines, D. (1996), 'Fiscal Policy and EMU', *National Institute Economic Review*, 158: 91–107.

—— —— (1998), 'The Assessment: Macroeconomic Policy after EMU', *Oxford Review of Economic Policy*, 4/3: 1–23.

Artis, M. and Buti, M. (2000), 'Close to Balance or in Surplus', *Journal of Common Market Studies*, 38: 563–92.

—— and Marcellino, M. (2000), 'The Solvency of European Government Finances' in Banca d'Italia (ed.), *Fiscal Sustainability* (Rome: Banca d'Italia).

—— and Winkler, B. (1998), 'The Stability Pact: Safeguarding the Credibility of the European Central Bank', *National Institute Economic Review*, Jan. 87–98.

Barro, R. and Gordon, D. (1983), 'A Positive Theory of Monetary Policy in a Natural Rate Model', *Journal of Political Economy*, 91: 585–610.

Bayoumi, T. and Eichengreen, B. (1995), 'Restraining Yourself: The Implication of Fiscal Rules for Economic Stabilization', *IMF Staff Papers*, 42: 32–48.

—— and Masson, P. (1995), 'Fiscal Flows in the United States and Canada: Lessons for Monetary Union in Europe', *European Economic Review*, 39: 253–74.

—— —— (1998), 'Liability-Creating versus Non-Liability-Creating Fiscal Stabilization Policies: Ricardian Equivalence, Fiscal Stabilization, and EMU', *CEPR Discussion Paper* 1984 (London: Centre for Economic Policy Research).

Bertola, G. and Drazen, A. (1993), 'Trigger Points and Budget Cuts: Explaining the Effects of Fiscal Austerity', *American Economic Review*, 83: 11–26.

Beetsma, R. and Bovenberg, L. (2000), 'Designing Fiscal and Monetary Institutions for a European Monetary Union', *Public Choice*, 102: 247–69.

—— and Uhlig, H. (1999), 'An Analysis of the Stability Pact', *Economic Journal*, 109: 546–71.

Buchanan, J. (1977), *Democracy in Deficit: The Political Legacy of Lord Keynes* (New York: Academic Press).

Buiter, W., Corsetti, G. and Roubini, N. (1993), 'Excessive Deficits: Sense and Nonsense in the Treaty of Maastricht', *Economic Policy*, 16, Apr.: 57–100.

Buti, M., Franco, D. and Ongena, H. (1997), 'Budgetary Policies during Recession: Retrospective Application of the "Stability and Growth Pact" to the Post-War Period', European Commission, DGII, *Economic Papers*, no. 121, May (Brussels: CEC).

—— —— —— (1998), 'Fiscal Discipline and Flexibility in EMU: The Implementation of the Stability and Growth Pact' *Oxford Review of Economic Policy*, 14/3: 81–96.

—— and Sapir, A. (eds.) (1998), *Economic Policy in EMU: A Study by the European Commission Services* (Oxford: Oxford University Press).

Canzoneri, M. and Diba, B. T. (1996), 'Fiscal Constraints on Central Bank Independence and Price Stability', *CEPR Discussion Paper* 1463 (London: Centre for Economic Policy Research).

Casella, A. (1999), 'Tradable Deficit Permits: Efficient Implementation of the Stability Pact in the European Monetary Union', *Economic Policy*, 29; 321–347.

Corsetti, G. and Roubini, N. (1993), 'The Design of Optimal Fiscal Rules for Europe after 1992', in F. Torres and F. Giavazzi (eds.), *Adjustment and Growth in the European Monetary System* (Cambridge: Cambridge University Press), 46–82.

Cour, P., Dubois, E., Mahfouz, S., and Pisani-Ferry, J. (1996), *The Cost of Fiscal Retrenchment Revisited: How Strong is the Evidence?* CEPII Document de Travail, 96–16 (Paris: CEPII).

Dalsgaard, T. and de Serres, A. (1999), *Estimating Prudent Budgetary Margins for 11 EU Countries: A Simulated SVAR Model Approach*, OECD Economics Department Working Papers, no. 216 (Paris: OECD).

Eichengreen, B. (1997), 'Saving Europe's Automatic Stabilisers', *National Institute Economic Review*, 159/1: 92–8.

—— and von Hagen, J. (1996), 'Fiscal Policy and Monetary Union: Federalism, Fiscal Restrictions, and the No-Bailout Rule', in H. Siebert (ed.) *Monetary Policy in an Integrated World Economy* (Tübingen: Mohr), 211–31.

—— and Wyplosz, C. (1998), 'The Stability Pact: More than a Minor Nuisance?', *Economic Policy*, 26: 65–115.

European Central Bank (1999), 'The Implementation of the Stability and Growth Pact', *Monthly Bulletin*, May: 45–72.

European Commission (1995), 'Technical Note: The Commission Services' Cyclical Adjustment Method', *European Economy*, 60: 35–90.

—— (1998), *Euro 1999: Report on Progress Towards Convergence and Recommendation with a View to the Transition to the Third Stage of Economic and Monetary Union*, March.

—— (1999), 'Budgetary Surveillance in EMU: The New Stability and Convergence Programmes', *European Economy*, Supplement A, n. 3.

—— (2000), *Public Finances in EMU: 2000*, May.

European Council (1997), 'Presidency Conclusions', Amsterdam European Council 16 and 17 June 1997 (repr. in *European Economy*, 64).

Giavazzi, F. and Pagano, M. (1990), 'Can Severe Fiscal Contractions Be Expansionary? Tales of Two Small European Countries', *NBER Macroeconomics Annual*, 75–111.

Glick, R. and Hutchison, M. (1993), 'Fiscal Policy in Monetary Unions: Implications for Europe', *Open Economies Review*, 4: 39–65.

Grilli, V., Masciandaro, D. and Tabellini, G. (1991), 'Political and Monetary Institutions and Public Financial Policies in the Industrial Countries', *Economic Policy*, 13: 341–92.

Gros, D. (1996). *Towards Economic and Monetary Union: Problems and Prospects*, CEPS Paper no. 65 (Brussels: Centre for European Policy Studies).

Hughes Hallett, A. and McAdam, P. (1996), *Fiscal Deficit Reduction in Line with the Maastricht Criteria for Monetary Union: An Empirical Analysis*, CEPR Discussion Paper no. 1351 (London: Centre for Economic Policy Research).

IMF (1997), *World Economic Outlook* (Washington, DC: International Monetary Fund).

Italianer A. and Vanheukelen, M. (1993), 'Proposals for Community Stabilization Mechanisms: Some Historical Applications', *European Economy, v. Reports and Studies: The Economics of Community Public Finance*.

Kydland, F. and Prescott, E. (1977), 'Rules Rather than Discretion: The Inconsistency of Optimal Plans'. *Journal of Political Economy* 85: 473–91.

Kletzer, K. M. (1997), *Macroeconomic Stabilization with a Common Currency: Does European Monetary Unification create a need for Fiscal Insurance or Federalism*, ZEI Policy Paper B97–04 (Bonn: Zentrum für Europäische Integrationsforschung).

Lane, T. (1993), 'Market Discipline'. *IMF Staff Papers*, 40, 53–88.

Masson, P. (1996), 'Fiscal Dimensions of EMU', *Economic Journal* 106: 996–1004.

McKinnon, R. I. (1994), 'A Common Monetary Standard or a Common Currency for Europe? Fiscal Lessons from the United States', *Scottish Journal of Political Economy*, Nov., 337–57.

Mélitz, J. and Vori, S. (1992), 'National Insurance Against Unevenly Distributed Shocks in a European Monetary Union', *Recherches-Economiques-de-Louvain,* 59: 81–104.

—— and Zumer, F. (1998), *Regional Redistribution and Stabilization by the Centre in Canada, France, the United Kingdom and the United States: New Estimates Based on Panel Data Econometrics*, CEPR Discussion Paper 1829 (London: Centre for Economic Policy Research).

Mundell, R. (1961), 'A Theory of Optimal Currency Areas', *American Economic Review*, 51: 657–65.

Olson, M. (1965), *The Logic of Collective Action* (Cambridge, Mass.: Harvard University Press).

OECD (1997), *OECD Economic Outlook*, Dec.

—— (1998), *OECD Economic Outlook*, Dec.

—— (1999), *EMU: Facts, Challenges and Policies*, (Paris: OECD).

Perotti, R. (1999), 'Fiscal Policy in Good Times and Bad', *Quarterly Journal of Economics*, 114: 1399–1436.

Pisani-Ferry, J. (1996), 'Fiscal Policy under EMU', *CEPII Newsletter* 6: 1–2.

Poterba J. M. (1995), 'Capital Budgets, Borrowing Rules and State Capital Spending', *Journal of Public Economics*, 56: 165–87.

Röger W. and In 't Veld, J. (1997), *Quest II: A Multi Country Business Cycle and Growth Model*, Directorate-General for Economic and Financial Affairs of the European Commission, Economic Papers, no. 123.

Roubini, N. and Sachs, J. (1989), 'Political and Economic Determinants of Budget Deficits in the Industrial Democracies', *European Economic Review*, 33: 903–38.

Sargent, T. and Wallace, N. (1981), 'Some Unpleasant Monetarist Arithmetic', *Quarterly Review* (Federal Reserve Bank of Minneapolis), Fall: 1–17.

Sørensen, B. E. and Yosha, O. (1998), 'International Risk-Sharing and European Monetary Unification', *Journal of International Economics*, 45: 211–38.

Thygesen, N. (1996), 'Should Budgetary Policies Be Coordinated Further in Economic and Monetary Union: and Is That Feasible?' *Banca Nazionale del Lavoro Quarterly Review* 196 (special issue): 5–32.

Von Hagen, J. and Hammond, G. (1997), 'Insurance Against Asymmetric Shocks in a European Monetary Union', in J.-O. Hairault, P.-Y. Henin and F. Portier (eds.), *Business Cycles and Macroeconomic Stability: Should We Rebuild Built-in Stabilizers?* (Dordrecht: Kluwer Academic), 171–88.

Winckler, G., Hochreiter, E. and Brandner, P. (1998), 'Deficits, Debt and European Monetary Union: Some Unpleasant Fiscal Arithmetic', in G. Calvo and M. King (eds.), *The Debt Burden and its Consequences for Monetary Policy*, International Economic Association Conference vol. 118 (London: Macmillan Press), 254–76.

Winkler, B. (1999), 'Co-ordinating Stability: Some Remarks on the Respective Roles of Monetary and Fiscal Policy under EMU', *Economica*, 26: 287–95.

Woodford, M. (1995), 'Price Level Determinacy Without Control of a Monetary Aggregate', *Carnegie-Rochester Conference Series on Public Policy*, 43: 1–46.

Woodford, M. (1998) 'Control of the Public Debt: A Requirement for Price Stability?', in G. Calvo and M. King (eds.), *The Debt Burden and its Consequences for Monetary Policy*, International Economic Association Conference vol. 118 (London: Macmillan), 117–54.

Chapter 14

Europe's Unemployment Problems

Giuseppe Bertola

14.1 Introduction

The dynamics of European unemployment, shown in Figure 14.1, are quite familiar from frequent references in the press and political debates. Against a background of fluctuations around relatively low levels in the USA and (until recently) even lower unemployment in Japan, the aggregate unemployment rate of EU member countries has increased almost continuously from the early 1970s to the present. The steady increase in European unemployment parallels the growth and consolidation of European

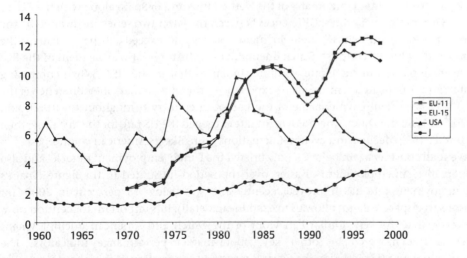

Fig. 14.1 Unemployment rate in the EU, USA and Japan, 1960–2000

Definitions and sources: Standardized unemployment rates, OECD *Economic Outlook* database. EU-11 is the Euro area: the aggregate of current EU members excluding the UK, Denmark, Greece and Sweden.

Community institutions. There is no reason to presume that any causal link runs from the latter to the former, but many important interactions can be identified between the economics of the EU and the performance of the member countries' labour markets. This chapter reviews the sources of high and persistent unemployment in many European countries' experience, tracing it back, first, to aggregate labour demand shocks in simple theoretical approaches focused on wage-setting behaviour; secondly, and recognising that labour is not a homogeneous factor of production, to the interaction of distributional shocks with institutional features which prevent formation of low-wage employment relationships. It also discusses the implications of EMU for European labour markets, and reviews policy approaches towards the increasingly unsustainable high-unemployment configuration of Europe's labour markets.

As in economic textbooks, and as in all industrialized economies, involuntary unemployment has been brought to European labour markets by incomplete wage adjustment in the face of labour demand shocks. To understand the resilience of European unemployment, however, it is important to analyse how institutional features prevent labour markets from delivering full employment, and how government policies address and, sometimes, exacerbate employment problems. In both respects, there is more than a single 'unemployment problem'. Behind an aggregate unemployment rate, one may find quite different configurations as regards labour-market participation rates, incidence along gender and age lines, wage inequality, regional dispersion of employment, and other disaggregated indicators of labour-market performance. In turn, labour-market performance is shaped by a wide variety of government policies and institutional features, such as minimum wages, unemployment benefits, contractual arrangements, and taxation.

To assess the relevance of institutional and structural factors, we may take advantage of the fact that not only is Europe as a whole starkly different from other advanced economies, but also European countries and regions are quite different from each other. Figure 14.2 plots the unemployment rates of the Netherlands and of Spain along with the EU-11 and US unemployment rates. Differences between the latter two series are dwarfed by the experience of Spain, whose unemployment reaches and exceeds 20 per cent over the 1980s and 1990s. By contrast, Dutch unemployment history—also an element of the EU-11 average plotted in the figure—is quite similar to that in the USA. When comparing Dutch and American unemployment experiences, the most remarkable difference is the relatively *low* unemployment rate of the European country throughout the 1960s and 1970s. In 1982 the Dutch unemployment rate exceeded the US rate for the first time, then featured a steep decline and cyclical fluctuations quite like its American counterpart.

We shall consider again below, if only briefly, the Dutch 'employment miracle' and also the Spanish 'unemployment disaster' over the period illustrated in the figure (Spain's unemployment rate has improved recently and was below 15 per cent in 2000, for reasons that space will not allow us to examine in detail). It is important to mention now, however, that the very similar behaviour of the Dutch and American unemployment rates is not mirrored by other key labour-market performance indicators. The unemployment rate plotted in the figure is measured as a fraction of the labour force, that is, of labour-market participants among the country's working-age citizens (the others study, work in the home, or are retired). In Figure 14.3, we see that a smaller fraction of

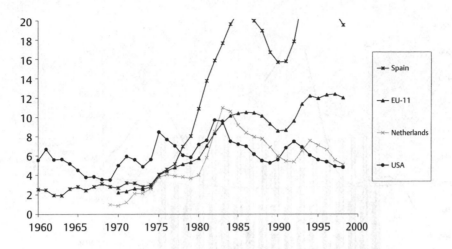

Fig. 14.2 Unemployment in the EU, Netherlands, Spain and the USA, 1960–2000
Definitions and sources: Standardized unemployment rates, OECD *Economic Outlook* database.

the working-age population is either employed or unemployed in the Netherlands than in the USA. We also see that the Dutch labour-force participation rate increases only slightly as that country's unemployment rate (like the US one) plummets from some 11 to some 5 per cent over the last two decades. Thus, important and quite persistent differences are observable in the two markets on the labour-force participation margin: even though measured unemployment behaves quite similarly, employment rates are and remain higher in the USA than in the Netherlands. A second, very important, difference between the two countries' labour-market performances pertains to the extent and dynamics of wage inequality indicators. The logarithmic ratio (or percentage difference) of wages earned by individuals in the middle and in the bottom of the wage distribution, plotted as black bars in the figure, is much smaller in the Netherlands than in the USA, and also not as steeply increasing over time. And the same is true, as illustrated by the lighter bars, when the wages at the top of the distribution are compared to those in the middle.

For workers, employment at very low wages can be just as unpleasant as unemployment, especially if the latter entitles one to some benefits as well as to leisure. High-wage inequality benefits those at the top of the earnings distribution, not those at the bottom of it, and is not an appealing labour-market feature for anybody who fears finding him- or herself in the latter situation. And wage inequality, like low labour-market participation and low employment rates, may or may not be a sign of poor resource allocation, that is, of an economy's inability to make the best use of its citizens' productive potential.

In general, a proper assessment of a labour market's overall performance should take into account many different indicators, and keep in mind that different economic agents may well evaluate different indicators differently. The following sections discuss how economic mechanisms link a labour market's structural and institutional features to the

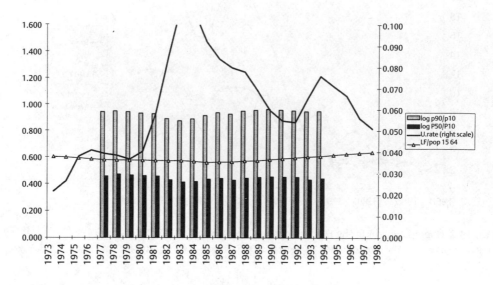

Fig. 14.3*a* Labour-market performance indicators in the Netherlands

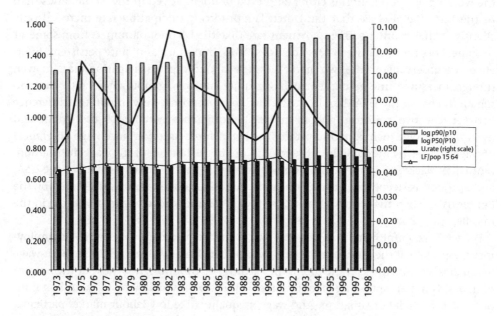

Fig. 14.3*b* Labour-market performance indicators in the USA

many relevant aspects of its performance; applies such theoretical mechanisms to further discussion of European evidence; and highlights how European policy-makers try to strike a balance between various desirable and undesirable features of their labour markets' configurations.

14.2 Employment and unemployment

The simple data above indicate that labour-force participation and unemployment both display substantial differences across countries and over time. Individuals may choose not to participate in the labour market when the wage they expect to earn is low relative to the opportunity cost of working, in terms not only of leisure, but also in relation to non-market activities such as schooling, housekeeping, and care of family members. Unemployed individuals, instead, by definition would like to work—provided the wage and the other characteristics of the job meet their expectations—and are taking at least some action towards finding that suitable job. Unemployment is *frictional* when the jobs being searched for actually exist, and it is only a matter of time and effort before they are found. But sometimes, and very often indeed when unemployment is as high and persistent as in many European countries, the jobs to which the unemployed aspire do not exist or, rather, are already occupied by workers who may only make them available when they retire. Such a mismatch between wage and employment aspirations and opportunities is the source of *structural* unemployment. We discuss next how labour supply and labour demand may become and remain different at the aggregate level.

Shocks

Why would a labour market ever feature involuntary unemployment? Figure 14.4 illustrates a possible answer. The mechanism, familiar from macroeconomic models, is based on a standard microeconomic approach to the determination of employment levels. Employers maximize their profits when the level of employment, on the horizontal axis, and the wage, on the vertical axis, identify a point on the downward-sloping labour-demand relationship plotted in the figure. A labour-supply schedule is also plotted, and for our purposes may be interpreted in terms of labour-force participation decisions. While nobody is available to work when the wage rate is lower than the horizontal segment of that schedule, at higher wage levels the labour force is positive and increasingly large. This relationship between the market wage rate and the size of the labour force reflect heterogeneous opportunity costs of working in the market we are considering. Prime-age males, for example, are more readily induced to work than younger individuals, who may prefer to study if the market wage is low. Poor individuals may similarly be more inclined to seek employment than similar individuals with substantial sources of non-labour income. (In reality, of course, the wage commanded in the labour market is also different across individuals. We shall consider the implications of such heterogeneity in Section 14.3 below, but it is helpful initially to view all workers as identically well suited to productive work.)

As drawn, the wage level is not compatible with full employment. Those who are willing to work (along the labour-supply schedule) are more numerous than those that firms find it profitable to employ (along the labour-demand schedule). Hence, some of

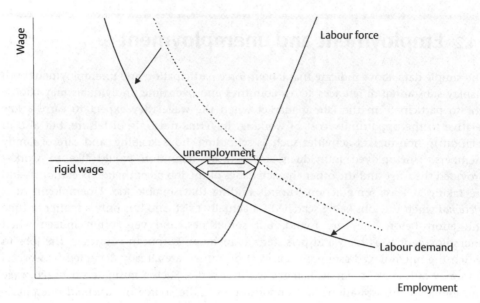

Fig. 14.4 Shock and unemployment

them remain unemployed. The arrows in the picture offer an explanation for why that may be the case. The prevailing wage would imply full employment if the dashed labour demand schedule were the relevant one, but some negative shock has reduced the number of jobs available at that wage. In the figure, the result is lower employment at an unchanged wage, rather than a lower wage rate and full employment of a smaller labour force.

Wages do indeed fail to adjust quickly to labour-demand fluctuations, because they are set before labour-demand conditions are known with certainty. The interplay of such wage rigidity with labour-demand shocks is important for European unemployment dynamics. When in the early 1970s the first oil shock reduced the amount of labour demanded at any given wage, unemployment began to increase. In Figure 14.1, further episodes of sharply increasing unemployment for the EU aggregate are apparent in the aftermath of the second oil shock in the early 1980s, when macroeconomic policy also imparted negative aggregate demand impulses. Unemployment increased further in the early 1990s, when policies of fiscal and monetary austerity were engendered by adherence to the Maastricht Treaty's criteria.

Macroeconomic shocks affect the position of the figure's labour-demand curve, and unemployment, in ways that are intimately related to inflation dynamics. Figure 14.4 fails to be explicit as to whether the wage on its vertical axis is measured in nominal or real terms. In a worked-out model of the mechanism that the figure is meant to illustrate, however, it is nominal wages that should be viewed as fixed, or 'sticky,' in the face of nominal labour-demand shocks. If nominal contractual wages are set before market conditions are known, hence on the basis of expected rather than actual prices, then real wages turn out to be excessively high when inflation is unexpectedly low. This is the rationale of Phillips-curve relationships between realized inflation and unemployment. If expected inflation could be viewed as stable over time, then a plot of actual inflation and unemployment should display a downward-sloping relationship when the latter origin-ates from dynamic phenomena of the type illustrated in Figure 14.4. More realistically, expected inflation should be viewed as variable over time, with higher inflation expectations resulting in vertical upward shifts of the Phillips relationship.

Figure 14.5a plots consumer price inflation against unemployment for the EU-11 coun-tries. The two are indeed negatively related over the 30 years considered in the figure, and it is also easy to glimpse in the picture some vertical or upward-sloping episodes which could be explained by shifts in the expected rate of inflation. Roughly speaking, 1970 may be interpreted as a lone observation on the low-expected-inflation Phillips curve prevalent in the 1960s, and 1974–8 may be viewed as observations on a new, outwardly shifted curve (two such curves are drawn in the figure). The 1980s and 1990s may in turn lie on yet other different curves (not drawn). Plots against unemployment of producer-price or GDP inflation offer similar, but different messages and, of course, so do country-specific plots of this type. Country experiences cannot be reviewed in detail here, but it is worth mentioning that national inflation and unemployment dynamics were import-antly affected by expectations of exchange-rate devaluation during the adjustable-parity EMS period. During periods of exchange-rate stability, unemployment was typically increasing in weak-currency countries, such as Italy, where fears of future devaluation would lead unions to request steep contractual wage increases aimed at preventing loss of purchasing power at times of exchange-rate realignment. As long as the feared devalu-ation was not realized, wage inflation reduced competitiveness, depressed labour demand and exports, while increasing imports, and ultimately sowed the seeds of unavoidable devaluation. Imperfect credibility of exchange-rate arrangements symmetrically affected strong-currency countries, such as Germany, where both unions and firms would loudly complain about loss of competitiveness when exchange-rate crises led to large exchange-rate realignments.

It would be misleading, however, to view inflation and unemployment dynamics in Europe in terms of Phillips curves shifted only by inflation expectations. The role of the latter in determining the level of pre-set wages makes it less than straightforward to ascertain the extent to which observed unemployment reflects the 'shock' mechanism illustrated by Figure 14.4. But one may suppose that past observations provide useful information. Most simply, suppose expected inflation is well approximated by past real-ized inflation. Then, unemployment should be higher when inflation decreases and pre-set wages are too high in real terms, and it should be lower when inflation increases. This idea motivates an 'accelerationist' version of the Phillips curve that relates unemploy-ment to *changes* in inflation. The intercept of such a relationship on the unemployment axis gives an indication of the labour-market conditions consistent with wage-setting practices, in the absence of unexpected changes in inflation. This 'non-accelerating infla-tion rate of unemployment', or NAIRU, need not be constant across countries and over time and is another source of shifts in the Phillips-curve relationship between wages and unemployment.

The NAIRU, while theoretically well defined as the steady unemployment rate

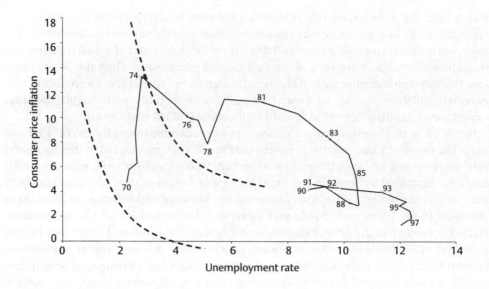

Fig. 14.5*a* Phillips curves for the EU-11 aggregate

Definitions and source: Unemployment rate and consumer price index inflation for the EU-11 aggregate, OECD *Economic Outlook* database.

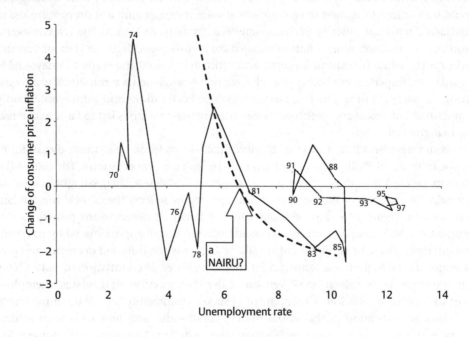

Fig. 14.5*b* Accelerationist Phillips curve for the EU-11 aggregate

Note: For definitions and sources see Fig. 14.5*a*.

consistent with a labour market's structural features, is not easy to estimate with any degree of confidence. It can be computed by a variety of more or less sophisticated methods, using different wage or price inflation series, and behaves in interestingly different ways in different countries. The plot in Figure 14.5*b* of EU-11 aggregate data illustrates the main features of the European inflation-and-unemployment experience. Europe's inflation did increase and decrease in spurts in the mid- and late-1970s, and decreased in the early 1980s and 1990s. Short-run unemployment dynamics were erratically related to inflation changes, however. One possible accelerationist Phillips curve is drawn in the figure, along with its NAIRU, but the intercept of such curves (and the level of unemployment consistent with a given inflation change) appears to have increased steadily over time.

As argued and empirically shown by Blanchard and Wolfers (2000), many institutions play a crucial role in explaining why wages may not decrease in response to high levels of unemployment, as they should if the latter were due to unforeseen shocks. We consider next how institutional features of the wage-setting process, and constraints on employers' freedom to choose the level of employment in the face of dynamic labour-demand shocks, may imply that unemployment and wages both remain persistently high.

Wage setting

Figure 14.6 illustrates a simple mechanism through which a labour market can persistently feature unemployment. In the figure, the wage level is so high as to imply that some willing-to-work individuals fail to obtain employment. However, it is also such as to yield a larger total labour income, net of disutility from labour-market participation, than at full employment. Indeed, loss of employment is more than compensated by the higher wage

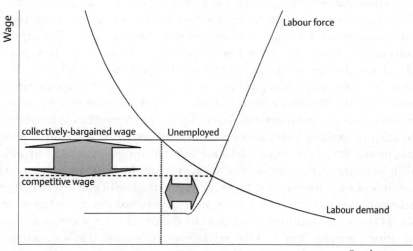

Fig. 14.6 Collective wage-setting and unemployment

paid to those who are employed, as illustrated (respectively) by the slim horizontal arrow and the thick vertical arrow. If wages are set collectively rather than individually, this labour-market outcome serves workers' interests better than the perfectly competitive one where labour demand and supply are equated at the margin. In fact, it is optimal for unions not to choose the wage that makes employment a matter of indifference at the margin. Since additional employment is associated with lower wages for all infra-marginal workers, unions should exploit their monopolistic market power and, as in Figure 14.6, choose a wage that is 'marked up' relative to the cost of offering labour in the market.

Any downward slope in the labour-demand schedule implies that if the wage is chosen so as to maximize the workers' total proceeds then there will be unemployment, as conventionally measured and defined. In Figure 14.6, some individuals would be quite willing to work, and do not. If they are bonded to their employed counterparts by loyalty, family ties, legal constraints (more on this below), and/or they receive non-employment benefits, their willingness to work at the going wage is not accompanied by a willingness to bid for work by accepting lower wages.

The extent to which these considerations bias employment downwards depends on the shape of the labour-demand function. It also depends on the degree of wage demand coordination across workers, and on the bargaining power of employers, who in the figure simply accept whatever wage is chosen by the union but in more sophisticated models—and in reality—have more of a say in wage determination. Thus, this perspective offers a rich set of reasons why labour-market outcomes may differ as much as they do in comparisons between EU countries and the USA, where unions and collective wage agreements are much less prevalent, and in comparisons among EU countries' different unemployment problems. It also offers useful insights from a time-series perspective, since workers' political power and union activity both increased substantially in the late 1960s and in the 1970s. The 'wage push' organized by labour in France and across Europe in 1968–70 took some time to result in lower employment, for reasons considered in the next sub-section, but certainly played a role in shaping Europe's unemployment experience. Oil price increases and slower productivity growth in the following years compounded the problem if, as is likely, workers took some time to realize that their real wage aspirations (albeit at the cost of lower employment) could no longer be based on the relatively favourable labour-demand conditions of the previous period.

By the simple mechanism illustrated by Figure 14.6, persistently high unemployment is the other side of a high-real-wage coin from the workers' point of view. Thus, cross-country differences as regards unemployment should be mirrored in real-wage comparisons. In order to compare wages across countries, however, one would need to account for labour productivity differences, which are both obviously important and difficult to measure. It is much easier to compare real wages over time for the same country. In Figure 14.7, an index of real compensation per employee (a measure of employers' costs, which is the relevant wage indicator if employment is determined along the labour-demand schedule of Figures 14.4 and 14.6) is displayed for the USA and some European countries: pre-unification Germany, Italy, and the Netherlands, for reasons that will become apparent below. The wage indicator's growth in EU countries parallels the increase in unemployment, relative to the USA, and slows down in more recent years, and does so particularly early and clearly for the Netherlands.

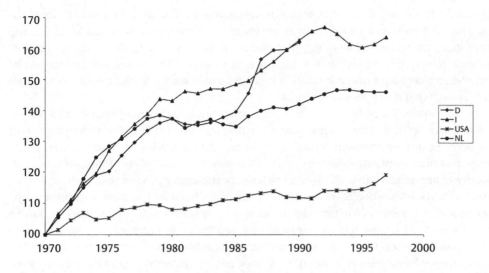

Fig. 14.7 Real total compensation per employee in the USA, Germany, Italy and the Netherlands
Definition and sources: Real total compensation of employees (includes all taxes and contributions, deflated by producer price index), OECD *Economic Outlook* database.

To the extent that high wages do appear to accompany high unemployment, the wage-setting mechanisms illustrated in Figure 14.6 arguably play a role in explaining European experiences. Before examining in more detail the implications of this and other relevant institutional features, it is important to note that even when 'real wage resistance' accounts for persistently high unemployment (a large NAIRU), economic activity can still respond to unexpected shocks. This has interesting implications for the joint behaviour of inflation, unemployment, and other macroeconomic indicators. As we know, unexpected inflation is associated with unemployment decreases by the 'accelerationist Phillips curve'. If market interactions deliver sub-optimally low levels of employment and economic activity, and nominal wages are rigid in the short run, then monetary authorities are *ex post* tempted to engage in expansionary monetary policy. If such behaviour is rationally expected *ex ante* by wage- and price-setters, however, then inflation expectations must be *ex ante* so high as to discourage further increases. Thus, in equilibrium permanently low levels of activity (or high unemployment) and high inflation coexist, resulting in a state of uniformly poor macroeconomic performance known as 'stagflation'. We shall return to consider these effects below, discussing in particular how the slope of the labour-demand schedule bears on them, how that slope depends on the intensity of product-market competition, and how the more or less 'credible' character of monetary policy may bear on incentives to increase wage demands.

Job security

If high wages are a conscious choice on the part of workers, it is a little strange to see many formerly employed workers ejected into unemployment by a negative labour-demand shock, as in Figure 14.4. As mentioned, collective wage-setting practices generally trade off high wages and low employment. The preferred point along the trade-off depends on features (such as the elasticity of the labour-demand function, and the opportunity cost of working) that need not vary systematically with the level of economic activity. Hence, there is little reason to expect that wage stability should be privileged over employment stability: a high and stable wage is attractive for workers, but less attractive if it implies job-loss risks.

In fact, workers need not accept the employment fluctuations implied by stable wages. From their point of view, *employment protection legislation* (EPL) serves the purpose of smoothing out employment fluctuations. In the labour market of industrialized countries, not only must individual dismissals be motivated (and subject to appeal), but collective dismissals are often also subject to lengthy and costly procedures involving formal negotiations with workers' organizations and with local or national authorities. The scope and stringency of such provisions varies widely across countries, sectors, and time. Most aspects of EPL are hard to measure quantitatively: for example, it is hard to put a price on advance notice or administrative requirements. Further, the difficulties encountered by employers when trying to shed redundant employment do not only stem from formal legislation: think, for example, of the attitude of labour courts towards wrongful dismissal constraints, or of the likelihood that collective lay-offs may result in a serious deterioration of industrial relations. It is possible, however, to formulate unambiguous qualitative rankings of EPL. Such rankings see Continental European members of the EU at the top among OECD countries.

From the point of view of firms, when firing employees is costly it is no longer a profit-maximizing strategy to choose employment levels that equate labour's marginal productivity to the wage, as in Figure 14.4. In the aftermath of a negative labour-demand shock, when employers contemplate shedding labour, redundancy payments and legal or administrative expenses have to be taken into account. Since firing costs imply a smaller reduction of labour costs if employment is reduced, firms behave as if the wage were lower (or labour demand higher) in the face of a negative labour-demand shock. Thus, they do not reduce employment by as much as they would in the absence of firing costs. Less intuitively, rational employers should also to some extent refrain from hiring in upturns if they expect positive shocks to be less than fully permanent. To the extent that additional employees increase the need to reduce employment in future downturns, in fact, the cost of higher employment includes not only the wage, but also expected discounted future firing costs. In terms of the familiar labour-demand figure, accordingly, firms behave as if the wage were higher (or labour demand lower) during cyclical upswings.

Hence, more stringent EPL should be associated with smoother dynamic employment patterns, and its contrasting effects on employers' propensity to hire and fire have ambiguous effects on average employment and wages. For a given degree of wage rigidity, unemployment should increase less in Figure 14.4 when job security is stringent, but it should also remain high more persistently. This prediction is confirmed by aggregate data. For example, the unemployment impact of the oil shocks was not as strong in the 'rigid' European labour markets as in the USA, and up until 1985 the (fluctuating) US unemployment rate was consistently higher than both of the EU measures shown in Figure 14.1. In the aftermath of negative shocks like oil price increases, or contractionary fiscal and monetary policies, US unemployment increases by more, and more quickly, than EU unemployment, but it also decreases more quickly and more substantially, while European unemployment fails to return to its initial level.

14.3 Distributions and flows

While the labour-market mechanisms discussed in Section 14.2 implied that some workers could be unemployed, they did not explicitly identify whether and how unemployed individuals could be different from their employed counterparts, and assumed an identical wage for all employed workers. In reality, of course, the employment and wage opportunities are very heterogeneous. This is true at a given point in time, since different individuals have different productivity as well as different opportunity costs of labour-market participation. Heterogeneity, however, is also important and realistic from a more dynamic perspective. At the same time as aggregate employment and unemployment vary over time in a whole country's labour market, relative labour demand and productivity also fluctuate across sectors and firms at finer levels of disaggregation. The following sections discuss how European labour-market institutions interact with such static and dynamic heterogeneity.

Wage inequality

Different workers have different skills and talents, hence different productivity. In a competitive market, their wages should result from supply-and-demand relationships like those plotted in Figure 14.4 for specific productive tasks and specialized skills rather than for undifferentiated, aggregate employment. Such market relationships imply a distribution of wages across jobs and individuals, plotted as a bell shape in Figure 14.8. The figure also features a vertical line, and supposes that employment relationships may only exist when market wages are higher than the level marked 'minimum'. If jobs that would pay low wages disappear (for one of the institutional reasons discussed below), then employment is lower and wages are both less dispersed and higher on average.

The most straightforward institutional constraint on the formation of low-wage relationships is indeed a legal minimum wage, which does exist in France, the United Kingdom, and other countries (including the United States, but not Italy, Germany, and other high-unemployment EU members). When low-wage jobs are outlawed, either unemployment or labour-force participation may be a counterpart of lower employment, depending on which institutional features enforce the 'truncation' illustrated in the figure. Those whose market wage is not high enough may be entitled to some benefits, either conditional on searching for work (to imply that they are counted among the unemployed) or on the basis of disability (and out-of-labour-force status).

Even in the absence of legal minima on wages, availability of non-employment benefits naturally prevents the formation of low-wage employment relationships.

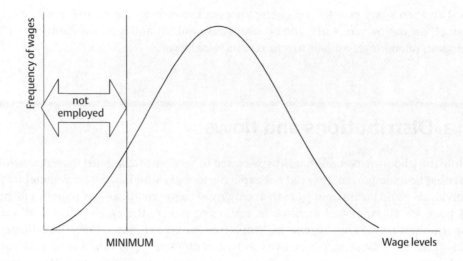

Fig. 14.8 Low-wage truncation and non-employment

Unemployment benefits, which are conditional on not working, may be justified by *ex ante* insurance considerations but can hardly avoid reducing the likelihood of job acceptance *ex post*. The generosity of unemployment insurance schemes is measured by the 'replacement rate' of previous wages, which are typically higher in EU countries than in the USA, and by entitlement rules, regarding both past work experience and length of unemployment.

A third important limit on the viability of low-wage employment relationships in many European labour markets is given by centrally negotiated employment contracts, which typically specify a narrow range of wage levels. Like legal minimum wages, centralized wage setting prevents relatively less productive workers from bidding for jobs when laws provide for 'administrative extension' of union-negotiated wages to all workers (whether members of the union, or not) within a sector and/or a region, or even a nation.

A fourth related cause of low employment rates is the existence of wide fiscal wedges between employers' labour costs and workers' take-home pay. For a given worker productivity, higher tax and contribution rates eliminate employment opportunities unless they are compensated by lower take-home pay. Individual workers may indeed accept lower wages when employment status affords benefits, such as old-age and invalidity pensions, which are financed by payroll contributions and only accrue on the basis of work experience. In the lowest portion of the pre-tax wage distribution, however, take-home pay would need to fall to levels that may either be unacceptable for the worker, or run into the legal and contractual minima discussed above.

The employment impact of low-wage truncation depends on the shape of the underlying distribution of productivities. Outlawing low-wage employment, or making it unappealing via subsidies or tax wedges, does not eliminate many jobs when the labour force is very homogeneous and market wages are quite concentrated. European countries differ importantly in this respect, especially in that labour productivity is more widely dispersed in large and heterogeneous countries (such as Spain and Italy) than in smaller, homogeneous ones (such as Denmark or Austria). The employment implications of wage compression may also become more serious, for a given distribution of skills and talents in the labour force, when the labour market tends to pay higher wages to relatively more skilled workers. Trade with less developed countries, where unskilled labour is abundant, and especially technological trends (such as the diffusion of computers and information technology, which also induces 'skill-biased' changes in wage distributions) can both have such effects. The increasing relevance of such phenomena over the last few decades has arguably played an important role, alongside macro shocks, in the dynamics of European unemployment (see Nickell and Bell, 1995, and their references).

Further, the shape of the wage distribution displayed in Figure 14.8 need not be invariant to truncation of its lower section. If different skills and groups of workers are substitutable, and wage-setting not perfectly competitive, eliminating low-wage jobs may make it easier for more productive workers to remain employed at higher wages. On the supply side, workers may be induced to upgrade their skills when they do not suffice to obtain a job, especially if education and training are subsidized. Both points are relevant to European Union policies in the relevant field, to which we shall turn after considering briefly some additional theoretical mechanisms and some empirical evidence.

Flows

In reality, workers lose jobs at the same time as other workers are hired. The time-consuming process of reallocating the labour force from old to new jobs is the source of frictional unemployment, resulting from shifts in relative labour demand across firms, or sectors, within an economy whose aggregate employment may or may not be changing. In the presence of such *idiosyncratic* (as opposed to aggregate) labour-demand shocks, wages result from the equilibrium of labour demand and supply in local subsets of the whole labour market, such as regions within a country, or industrial sectors. Thus, local labour-demand shocks imply wage fluctuations around the aggregate level, and wage instability over time for the individuals who supply their labour in such subsets.

As mentioned, the wage patterns that result from equilibrium of labour demand and supply in local labour markets need not be stable. When labour demand decreases in one region or sector relative to others, wages tend to decline, unless labour supply is appropriately reduced by mobility of workers towards other regions or sectors. Such mobility improves the allocation of resources, since workers move from low-productivity to high-productivity jobs. Labour mobility is far from costless, however, for the workers concerned, and European labour-market institutions typically tend to reduce labour mobility. Employment protection legislation reduces labour shedding by declining firms and sectors and, symmetrically, job creation by expanding ones; collective wage-setting agreements reduce wage variability across subsets of the labour market, and therefore the extent to which wages may serve as signals of reallocation needs; unemployment and non-employment subsidies, and some forms of public employment, also tend to reduce workers' incentives to exit depressed segments of the labour market.

Such resistance to change, sometimes called 'Eurosclerosis', tends to reduce the labour market's efficiency by preventing replacing of low-productivity jobs with high-productivity ones. Like collective wage agreements that trade off high wages for low employment, however, lower labour-market flexibility may be advantageous for workers, who may put less weight on aggregate efficiency than on their individual stressful job reallocation. As to employment levels, Eurosclerosis does not necessarily have adverse implications, because the effects of employment protection legislation are different from those of high wages and social security contributions. A firm must pay the latter to employ labour, but it can avoid paying firing costs if it reduces job creation and job destruction around a level that is on average just about the same as what it would obtain, for the same wage and contributions level, in the absence of job security provisions. Thus, higher firing costs reallocate employment across firms and sectors without necessarily changing its overall level. Their implications, in fact, are similar to those of a tax on profits, or on production factors other than labour.

The sources of wage lower bounds discussed above interact importantly with employment protection legislation, however. Firing costs introduce some slack in the relationship between current wages and labour demand. Since firms are reluctant to hire, workers who are not yet employed would need to work for wages that can be quite a bit lower than marginal productivity. They could in fact be willing to accept such low wages initially, looking forward to future times when (enjoying protection from dismissal) they will be able to negotiate wages higher than their actual productivity. Any lower bound on wages, however, can interfere with such plans, and effectively insulate employed 'insiders' from outside wage competition. Turnover and firing costs imply that involuntarily unemployed outsiders would need to bid for the insiders' jobs on a present discounted (rather than period-by-period) basis, and minimum wage constraints can prevent such bidding.

European experiences

Wage inequality statistics, like wage level statistics, are not readily comparable across countries. Sharply differentiated wages may reflect the coexistence of very differently educated workers, if wage equality reflects a homogeneous labour force rather than the kind of compression and truncation that would result in involuntary unemployment for relatively less productive workers. However, the message of the available data is quite clear. The horizontal axis of Figure 14.9 reports employment as a fraction of the population between the ages of 15 and 64: countries where this employment rate is high (because of low unemployment and/or high labour-force participation) also tend to display less wage differentiation, measured as in Figure 14.3 in terms of the ratios of median and high wages to low wages. As the figure indicates, this is but a general tendency, with many interesting exceptions. France's low employment rate, for example, is accompanied by substantial inequality in the upper portion of the wage distribution, and Sweden and Finland appear to achieve both low wage inequality and high employment: like other Nordic countries, they do so through 'active labour market policies' (on which more below).

It is especially interesting, however, to consider regional unemployment statistics from this perspective. In some of the larger Continental European countries, compressed wage

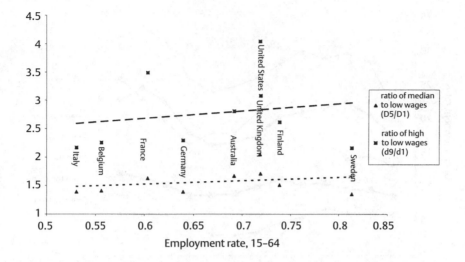

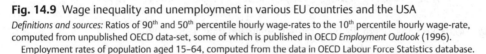

Fig. 14.9 Wage inequality and unemployment in various EU countries and the USA

Definitions and sources: Ratios of 90th and 50th percentile hourly wage-rates to the 10th percentile hourly wage-rate, computed from unpublished OECD data-set, some of which is published in OECD *Employment Outlook* (1996).
  Employment rates of population aged 15–64, computed from the data in OECD Labour Force Statistics database.

distributions are associated with extremely dispersed unemployment rates. Spain's unemployment rate dwarfs other countries' rates in Figure 14.2 but, as shown in Figure 14.10, it is in turn dwarfed by the unemployment rates of Spain's southern regions (Andalucia, Murcia, Ceuta y Melilla). And while the unemployment rate of Italy's large southern region Campania rivals Spain's, that of its Northern region Lombardia fluctuates around the same low levels of the Dutch miracle labour market. In both countries, contractual arrangements tend to prevent wages from adjusting to local labour-market idiosyncrasies, institutional features subsidize low-employment equilibria in relatively depressed regions, and workers have little incentive to move away from high-unemployment regions when job security provisions reduce hiring and job-finding rates even in low-unemployment regions. If the work that would be performed by the residents of less productive regions at low wages is demanded of high-productivity regions instead, this makes it easier for the latter to obtain employment at relatively high wages, in a large-scale version of the standard trade-off between the number of jobs and wage levels illustrated in Figure 14.6.

  Employment protection legislation, as mentioned, is ambiguously related to employment levels for given wage characteristics. It also tends to be more stringent in countries where wages are less dispersed and higher, however, and employment is lower. This is not surprising, since quantity constraints on employers' freedom to fire are largely motivated by the same considerations that make subdued wage competition attractive for workers. One specific effect of EPL deserves to be discussed. As we know, stringent EPL reduces flows both into and out of employment, and therefore tends to reduce the incidence of frictional unemployment at the same time as it lengthens the length of unemployment spells (especially when unemployment subsidies are generous). Some of the flows into

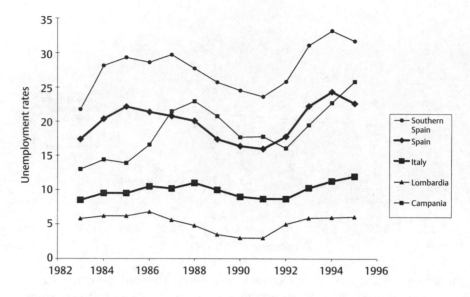

Fig. 14.10 Regional unemployment rates in Spain and Italy, 1982–1996

unemployment, however, are not reduced by EPL: while older workers are less likely to lose their jobs, young workers still flow into the labour market, and have worse job-finding opportunities when employers are reluctant to hire. Not surprisingly, the incidence of youth unemployment is somewhat higher in countries where flows into and out of unemployment are less intense, and job security provisions stronger. Figure 14.11 displays the youth and adult unemployment rates of EU member countries, ordered on the horizontal axis according to the stringency of employment protection legislation. Of course, this and other indicators of labour-market performance are influenced by many institutional features other than EPL; in particular, the relatively low unemployment rates of German and Austrian youth can be credited to those countries' efficient vocational training system. Still, countries with the most stringent EPL, such as Italy, do tend to have higher youth unemployment rates than countries where job security provisions are very mild, such as the United Kingdom.

Our discussion of institutional constraints on labour-market outcomes would not be complete without mentioning that 'black' labour markets flourish alongside heavily regulated formal labour markets in Europe. Enforcement of official rules on wages and conditions of employment is, not surprisingly, less careful where those rules are more binding. For example, in Italy nominal labour-market regulation is almost uniform across regions with very different levels of economic development, and the incidence of irregular employment is much higher in the South (28.4 per cent) and the islands (27.4 per cent) than in the North West (9.9 per cent), the North East (8.3 per cent), and the Centre (11.3 per cent). This does not imply that rules are completely non-binding, or that their low-employment implications may be disregarded. Rather, it simply signals that markets do try to circumvent constraints imposed on them, and put more effort into doing so when the constraints (whether well-motivated, or ill-advised) are tighter.

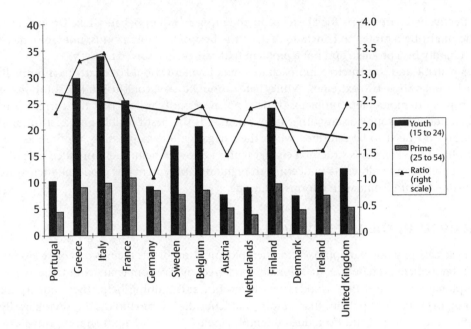

Fig. 14.11 Employment protection, youth and adult unemployment in various EU countries

Definition and sources: Unemployment rates for demographic groups, OECD *Employment Outlook*; countries are ordered on the horizontal axis according to the OECD *Employment Outlook* (1999) index of employment protection legislation stringency.

The line interpolates the ratio of youth to adult unemployment rates over this ordering.

14.4 Policy and attitudes towards unemployment

Why does high unemployment persist when it is not only unpleasurable for the individuals concerned, but also decried by unions, politicians, and public opinion? One might entertain the possibility that simple theoretical mechanisms such as those outlined above are not well understood by those who draft laws and set wages, so that unemployment is evil in the eyes of the same agents who (directly or indirectly, individually or collectively) are responsible for it. If this were the case, more economics education—or perhaps granting exceptional reform powers to a well-trained economist—could suffice to resolve all problems.

It is more satisfactory, of course, to maintain that rational agents understand the economy's mechanisms as well as, or even better than, we do. One may then be tempted to argue that unemployment, if it exists and persists, presumably is more palatable to a political majority than possible alternatives. Reducing regional unemployment by encouraging wage differentiation and geographical mobility, for example, could unpleasantly disturb the existing economic and political equilibrium of large countries. Eliminating unemployment subsidies could very well eliminate unemployment, but only at the cost of increases in poverty and possibly crime rates, and other phenomena collectively referred to as 'social exclusion' in European policy debates. Like Dr. Pangloss, one might be tempted to conclude that, in the best of possible worlds, unemployment can hardly be a problem and not a problem that can ever be solved anyway.

A realistic and constructive approach to unemployment should of course be intermediate between these two extremes. While there cannot be easy, cold-fusion-like solutions to Europe's unemployment problems, it does not necessarily follow that the current configuration of Europe's or any other labour market is the best possible one. Institutional features do need to be reformed when their negative effects (possibly unintended, or amplified by exogenous structural changes) offset or overwhelm their intended purpose. The public's and politicians' concern with high unemployment has produced increasing pressure towards some such reforms in Europe.

Activating the unemployed

An increasingly popular approach to unemployment problems focuses on active labour-market policies. These are traditionally preferred by Scandinavian countries, where employment services help workers search for jobs and training helps them qualify for them, over 'passive' policies that simply grant subsidies to unemployed individuals. By definition, such policies do reduce unemployment—if not by reintegrating otherwise long-term unemployed individuals into the labour market, at least by converting them into students and trainees. They are expensive, however, because administering 'active' instruments uses more resources (especially personnel, further contributing to their positive impact on employment rates) than simply paying unemployment subsidies. The choice of more or less 'active' approaches to treatment of unemployment problems depends on the balance of complex interactions between their costs and benefits.

A variety of such policies has indeed been adopted in different countries. At one extreme, unemployment may be reduced by direct job creation in the public sector. The costs of activation are, of course, particularly apparent in this case, and its beneficial effects particularly doubtful if public employees' wages need to be financed by taxing private-sector employment more heavily (thus increasing the wedge between employers' costs and employees' take home pay, and decreasing the employment generated by given labour-demand and labour-supply schedules). Less drastic active policies have qualitatively similar drawbacks. Whether those receiving training are permanently more employable is theoretically possible, but empirically doubtful, and training programmes may be more expensive than just paying moderate subsidies and leaving skill-upgrading strategies to individual choices. Other active policies are those that require unemployed workers drawing benefits to visit job centres, be interviewed by potential employers, and consult with specialized public employees. Such requirements, especially when combined with well-organized vacancy databases, may of course quite effectively improve workers' information as to their realistic employment opportunities and increase job-finding rates but, again, they are not without costs for the government—and for the unemployed.

A related but different approach is that of 'make-work-pay' policies, which aim at subsidizing employment by reducing the gap between the wage workers aspire to and their productivity. As mentioned above, low-wage employment relationships are often not viable because of minimum-wage provisions and/or unemployment subsidies. Even when benefits are not explicitly conditional on non-employment, they tend to create poverty and non-employment 'traps' when they are means-tested, that is, when they are granted only in the absence of other income sources. For example, single mothers and families with children are typically entitled to monetary and in-kind benefits when their income falls below a certain level. Incentives to obtain gainful employment are clearly very low if labour income is not only taxed, but also leads to loss of benefits: in effect, the combination of income-tested benefits and standard labour income taxation easily implies extremely high marginal tax rates, and very small incentives to seek employment. Make-work-pay policies try to restore employment incentives by modulating the progressivity of effective tax rates. For example, an 'earned-income tax credit' can be granted to workers whose labour income, if taxed at the standard rate, would be so low as to threaten benefit loss without net income gains. A form of tax progressivity is employment-conditional *negative* taxation of income: low-wage employment relationships are subsidized. If the individual in question commands a low wage in the labour market, but has positive productivity, the social costs of in-work benefits are lower than those of non-employment benefits. A single mother's productivity, net of her labour-market participation costs, may be very low (say, €200 per month); but it is still less expensive to 'top up' her income by €300 than to pay €500 in the form of social assistance.

The attractiveness of such fiscal instruments again depends on a variety of cost and effectiveness considerations. Like active policies, in-work subsidies can be expensive at the same time as creating additional employment: this is because of 'deadweight' effects, unavoidable in the absence of precise information as to individual productivity, whereby most subsidies are paid to jobs that would exist anyway. Employment subsidies may also be costly and relatively ineffective through 'displacement', whereby employers replace relatively better-paid workers with subsidized employees with little or no net increase in employment. Waste of subsidies is clearly problematic if fiscal revenue is scarce. In fact, if maximizing employment were the only policy objective, one would want to eliminate all labour income taxation, and perhaps subsidize not only low-wage, but all employment relationships. Eliminating or inverting the tax wedge certainly increases employment but, especially in Europe, making work pay *taxes* is also an important policy objective. And, just as benefits paid only to the unemployed obviously reduce incentives to obtain gainful employment, subsidies paid only to low-wage employment relationships obviously discourage workers and employers from engaging in education and training.

Social pacts and work sharing

Like glaciers and sunny beaches, unions are part of the landscape in many Continental European countries, if less so in the United Kingdom. Even when relatively few workers are union members, collective contracts cover a very large proportion of employment relationships: in the UK the *coverage rate* of collective bargaining agreements falls short of 50 per cent, but it exceeds 70 per cent in all other EU countries, ranging up to 98 per cent. Unions are organized coalitions of economic agents, not unlike political parties and government majorities. In the simple wage-setting diagram of Figure 14.6, collective wage-setting led to high wages and low employment. The economic role of unions, however, is more complex in reality. Here, we shall briefly review the role of unions (or lack of unions) in shaping employment and wage dynamics, illustrating some general insights with the experience of some European countries: the Netherlands (and Italy), the United Kingdom, and France.

The extent to which union negotiations are biased against high levels of employment depends importantly on the degree of centralization and coordination across sectors and regions. If wage negotiations are conducted at the firm level, then unions may believe that those among their members who fail to obtain employment when the wage is raised will still find jobs elsewhere in the economy. If every other firm-level union also raises wages, however, this belief is mistaken, and poorly coordinated wage demands can easily result in employment levels that are too low from the collective point of view of workers themselves. When wage negotiations are conducted at the national level, conversely, then unions can more easily see the employment implications of their wage demands. Hence, as argued by Calmfors and Driffill (1998), when workers bargain wages at the central level then labour markets can generate more employment than when workers, while not perfectly competitive, bargain wages at the firm or sectoral level.

'Social pacts', or more generally incomes-policy agreements, aim at ensuring that the employment effects and macroeconomic consequences of unions' wage demands are correctly taken into account. Recent labour-market developments in the Netherlands have been largely shaped by such policies. Recall that in Figure 14.9 the Dutch wage indicator stopped growing faster than the US one in the early 1980s. This was largely the result of agreement between the 'social partners' (unions, employer organizations, and the government). A pact, signed in Wassenaar in 1982, featured union concessions in the form of wage moderation and a relaxation of work rules, notably those regarding part-time arrangements. In exchange, employers committed to employment generation through investment, and the government contributed concessions in the area of social-policy intervention. The package of government policies included fairly generous early and invalidity retirement provisions, which play a role in explaining why in Figure 14.3 the decline of Dutch unemployment was not accompanied by an increase in participation rates.

In the Nordic countries, unions play a similar role, and even in Italy the objective of unions was broader than just current labour income. During the process that led that country to join EMU, the wage pressure-devaluation spiral mentioned in Section 14.2 was broken by a wage-moderation agreement in 1992, and macroeconomic stabilization was aided by further cooperative behaviour by unions throughout the 1990s. In the UK, by contrast, the role of unions in both wage determination and broader economic policy determination was eliminated by reforms of work representation rules during the 1980s, under Mrs Thatcher's governments. As a result employment rates increased in that country, which now relies on politically chosen unemployment and in-work benefits to regulate employment and maintain competitive pressure on wage rates.

In France, unions represent a very small fraction of the labour force, but they do exert considerable influence in the political determination of minimum wages and work rules. French law has reduced the standard work-week to 35 hours as of January 2000, and has done so in the context of extensive revision of provisions for employer–employee discussion of work organization. A reduction of individual work time can redistribute across the labour force the wage bill paid to its employed fraction in Figure 14.4, and this can be quite sensible from the union's point of view. If unit labour costs are unaffected, then output may be unchanged and leisure distributed differently, which may be a desirable outcome if the *ex-post* involuntarily unemployed workers of Figure 14.6 are prevented by legal minimum wages from bidding for employment, without being compensated by transfers. But the opposition of business organizations to a mandated (rather than negotiated) shorter work-week indicates that such legislation is expected to increase production costs, rather than simply facilitate work sharing (or, equivalently, unemployment sharing). Then, work-time regulation can be equivalent to higher hourly wages, and therefore reduce employment (in terms of hours worked) even as it increases, or leaves unchanged, the number of employed workers. In practice, the French law provides for several flexibility-oriented measures, and its effects need not be as simple as the above reasoning would make it.

14.5 Unemployment and EMU

The steady increase of European unemployment in parallel with the growth and consolidation of the European Community institutions does not imply a causal link from the latter to the former, and the different unemployment experiences of member countries indicate that it would be equally naïve to suppose that European Union membership somehow begets unemployment. The process of European integration, however, interacts importantly with the web of structural and institutional features that determine the extent and character of unemployment in the member countries.

One interpretation of stable low-employment labour-market equilibria views them as a conscious choice on the part of unions, governments, and more generally the collective organizations that choose the labour market's institutional configuration. From this perspective, unemployment and low employment may simply be the price paid by most European countries in order to avoid paying the price, in terms of more dispersed and unstable wages and jobs, of a more competitive labour-market configuration.

The EU process of international economic integration does bear on the desirability and the very feasibility of such arrangements. The reason why this is so is perhaps most clearly seen by considering the emphasis of EU integration on freedom of mobility for labour, and its implications for a caricature of a low-employment labour-market configuration. Suppose unemployment is prevalent among the children of high-wage employees, and out-of-labour-force status is prevalent among their spouses and older relations. Family links reduce the intensity of competition for jobs and redistribute the wage bill among the employed and non-employed members of the labour force, so this configuration may be stable and (in the absence of perfectly competitive financial and labour-market interaction) may also be preferable to a scenario of cut-throat competition in the labour market. But such a low-employment, high-wage labour market configuration is easily disturbed by increased labour mobility: newcomers to the market need not exercise the same restraint in bidding for jobs as those who used to be peacefully unemployed, and impose on employed members of the local labour force the unpleasant choice between lower wages and job loss.

Labour mobility is not intense within the EU, at least as regards member countries' citizens (immigration from non-community countries, and the prospect of enlargement to the poorer countries of Central and Eastern Europe, are however a source of keen political concern in many current member countries). But very similar challenges to low-employment equilibria are presented by more intense competition in the product market, and by mobility of factors other than labour (such as financial capital). In the simple mechanism illustrated by Figure 14.6, high wages and low employment may be attractive for workers when relatively few jobs are lost in exchange for substantially higher wages, that is, when the labour demand curve decreases steeply (is *inelastic*). Now, increased competition in the product market flattens the labour demand curve: if the wage-setting process tends to pay high wages to a small core of primary workers, that core tends to be very small indeed when firms that pay high wages are driven out of business. Nor does the wage-bill redistribution, whose feasibility is challenged by more intense competition, need to take place within families, as in the caricature above of a rigid labour market. Low employment (in certain regions, or of certain age groups through retirement schemes) is often subsidized by the revenue of labour taxes, but subsidizing the non-employed becomes impossible if production can be moved to other locations, where payroll taxes are low.

In general, the collective wage-setting mechanisms that account for low employment in Figure 14.6 are weaker when, through economic integration, competition for jobs extends beyond the boundaries of collective agreements. As we know from Figures 14.2 and 14.7, Dutch wage moderation was successful in decreasing that country's unemployment rate and increasing its employment. Given the strong economic links between the Netherlands and Germany, at least part of this success must have been gained at the expense of German employment. In Figure 14.7, German wages (and other labour costs, as summarized by the 'Compensation of employees' series) continued their rapid growth while Dutch unions were moderating their demands, and employment losses resulting from such stiff wage growth can only have been larger when production could take place just across the border than if Germany had been sealed to foreign competition.

Similar issues arise with regard to other labour-market institutions. For example, it is hard to imagine a small town introducing stringent working-time limits on its own. A short working week is pleasurable, of course, but may well reduce productivity—and probably does when it is imposed by law, rather than by an agreement between employers and employees. Lower productivity calls for a lower wage in order for jobs to remain profitable, and business not to leave our hypothetical small town; but a lower wage might easily result in the town residents taking on jobs in nearby, less regulated municipalities. The very idea of labour-market regulation at the town level is damaged by such considerations (though not necessarily killed, for some activities cannot easily migrate even across town boundaries: shop-opening hours can to some extent be set at that level). Not surprisingly, the discussion leading to introduction of 35-hour work-weeks in France envisaged similar provisions in other EU countries.

EMU and pressures for national reform

How does the process of European Economic and Monetary Integration bear on the sustainability of the member countries' labour-market configurations? As we have seen, European unemployment is best understood in terms of interactions between dynamic shocks and 'protective' institutions, and the higher intensity of competition entailed by the process of economic (rather than purely monetary) integration is expected to play a crucial role. Easier access to other countries' products, free mobility of capital, and incipient labour mobility should privilege economic efficiency, and make it harder to sustain existing levels of regulation. Contractual negotiations and legal requirements at a national (or regional) level face strong deregulatory pressure from 'competition among systems', in the form of lower unionization, wage moderation, increasing wage differentials, more nominal and real-wage flexibility, and a reduction of institutional barriers to interregional and inter-occupational mobility in the labour market. It might be misleading, however, to expect stronger product- and capital-market linkages automatically to lead to deregulation, and to view any such deregulation as an unqualified blessing for European labour markets. Increased market pressure may generate demands for continuing and perhaps increasing the current levels of labour-market regulation, particularly for specific socio-economic groups.

The monetary leg of the EMU process is also relevant to national reform incentives. Recall that labour-market problems interact importantly with macroeconomic policies when institutions tend to increase unemployment permanently (the NAIRU is high) and policy-makers attempt to reduce it by aggregate demand management. Such attempts, as mentioned, are futile when they are expected. Expansive monetary policy only results in high inflation, without reducing unemployment. Similarly, aggregate fiscal policy cannot permanently increase the level of economic activity when it reflects the economy's structural configuration, and expansionary fiscal policy will only increase public debt. Thus, low activity levels, excessive real wage aspirations, and time-inconsistent monetary policy should be targeted by appropriate structural reforms. These should aim at increasing competition and at fostering supply, while monetary policy should be explicitly and independently targeted to price stability only, and fiscal policy should stabilize fluctuations rather than trying to boost economic activity above the 'natural' level determined by structural and institutional features. National fiscal and monetary policies played an important role before the former was restrained, and the latter superseded, by the Employment and Stability Pact and by the adoption of a single currency in the Euro-area. For the Euro-area, monetary policy is conducted at the central level, and should be independent of national structural rigidities. Whether this fact may encourage or hinder the structural reforms envisaged by the standard prescription is controversial. Incentives for structural reform may be smaller when reform affects only local activity levels and not inflation. Further, the political feasibility of reform may be hampered by constraints on the extent to which monetary and fiscal macro policy can be used to smooth adjustment trajectories and buffer distributional implications in the aftermath of such reforms.

EU-level policy

For most of their history, EU institutions did not explicitly address labour-market issues. The *Acquis communautaire* harmonizes health and safety regulation, but labour-market institutions—and other social policy instruments—were viewed as 'subsidiary' policies, that is, policies whose objectives can be sufficiently achieved by the Member States.

In the context of the EU economic integration process some efforts have been made to preserve, through EU-level coordination, the protective character of many labour-market institutions. Within a fully integrated supranational economy, national unions can no longer perform their historical role—with the more or less desirable effects reviewed above on the level, composition, and cyclical behaviour of employment. Accordingly, it is not surprising that unions would try to join forces at the EU level. This tendency is known as the Doorn process, from the location of an international union conference in 1998. It has not made much progress, except perhaps in the metal sector of the German and BeNeLux economies, where geographical proximity and highly substitutable products would indeed make it very difficult for national unions to extract wage concessions. Just like the employees of a firm in a highly competitive industry, sectoral or national unions within a tightly integrated regional economy face a stiff trade-off between higher wages and the very existence of their jobs.

Coordination also looks attractive if one sees unemployment as the result of negative demand shocks (as in Figure 14.4), which may be offset by stabilizing macroeconomic policies. These may also spill over across national boundaries: to the extent that a country's aggregate demand stimulus influences macroeconomic conditions of other countries via trade spill-overs, each government may have insufficient incentive to provide macroeconomic stimuli (and simply hope that other countries will do so). Such spill-overs may stem from monetary policy, their sign depending on whether exchange rates are fixed or flexible. But monetary policy is now fully coordinated in the Euro-area, where there is only one monetary policy (whether the stance of the single monetary policy may be set so as to suit varied labour-market conditions around the Euro-area is not an issue, since the European Central Bank's mandate privileges price stability). While fiscal policy may in principle still be used to steer cyclical labour-market conditions, coordinated demand and wage management at the EU level has little political support. A document signed under the German presidency of the EU at the Cologne meeting of the Council on 3–4 June 1999 does no more than state general principles and set up a 'Cologne process', a forum for macroeconomic policy discussions among the EU's social partners and policy-makers.

Pressure for coordination or harmonization is also apparent as regards work rules, such as maximum working time. A directive on maximum working time was adopted in 1993. It guarantees workers minimum daily and weekly rest periods, maximum weekly working time (48 hours), and minimum paid annual leave (four weeks), with derogations for certain sectors with unusual production requirements. The specified levels were less restrictive than national ones in all countries except the UK, which had no law in this area and was opposed to the introduction of EU-level legislation. Such concerns are likely to be to the fore in the next few years as the process of deepening European integration proceeds apace, and the EU expands to embrace the countries of Central and Eastern

Europe with their significantly lower wage costs and very different institutional structures.

Employment problems are prominently featured in the 1998 Amsterdam revision of the Treaty on European Union, which incorporated in the full 15-country Treaty the provisions of the Social Protocol signed in Maastricht by only eleven countries (the then members of the EU, bar the UK). Article 2 states as the EU's first objective the promotion of 'economic and social progress and a high level of employment . . . through the creation of an area without frontiers . . . and the strengthening of economic and social cohesion.' In practice, employment-related policies remain subsidiary. A monitoring and coordination process is in place, however, named after the venue (Luxembourg) for the November 1997 Extraordinary European Council on Employment. The Luxembourg process is organized around four 'Pillars':

- 'Improving employability' (measures envisaged under this heading have an active labour-market policy character, particularly targeted towards training of young and long-term unemployed people);

- 'Encouraging adaptability of businesses and their employees' (through union-negotiated work reorganization);

- 'Strengthening the policies for equal opportunities' (mostly along gender lines—a long-standing concern of EU social policy intervention—but also as regards labour-market participation of disabled individuals).

- 'Developing entrepreneurship' (chiefly through deregulation and simplification of market access and operations by small firms).

Within each of the pillars detailed policy guidelines are listed, some in the form of precise quantitative targets. For example, Guideline 3 (within Pillar I) specifies that at least 20 per cent of the unemployed should be in training programmes or comparable schemes. This makes it possible to develop the monitoring dimension of the process. Every year, Member States are requested to submit National Action Plans (NAPs), setting out labour-market policies and their implementation in the context of the Luxembourg process. This framework allows the monitoring of national employment policies and their progress in principle. As a result of the Amsterdam Treaty, the Council is free to give recommendations to specific countries after consultation with the European Commission. Within the Luxembourg process, the European Commission plays an active role in monitoring and formulating recommendations. The outcome of the process is reported in the annual Joint Employment Report. Commission evaluation has increasing political weight in many Member States. Further, disbursement of European Social Fund line items is now decided in the context of the NAP review process.

The Luxembourg process is inspired by a fairly coherent approach to Europe's employment problems. These are viewed as a structural problem that should be tackled by reform efforts as existing institutions encounter unavoidable difficulties in a new macroeconomic environment. The guidelines, however, display a clear unwillingness to sacrifice the protective features of the current labour-market configurations. Pillar I largely conforms to the active labour-market policies of the Nordic tradition of social intervention, policies which try to reconcile the conflicting goals of generous protection and high employment with expensive public employment and training programs. Also, the concept of 'adaptability' is quite different to that of 'flexibility': it is required of employers as well as employees and, rather than relying on market incentives, envisages intense consultation among workers' and employers' organizations.

The Luxembourg recipe is careful not to dismiss the key features of European industrial relations. It does not advocate higher flexibility of wages, nor does it condemn the rigidity of employment relationships. It does, however, emphasize 'activation' of non-employed individuals. Passive unemployment subsidies are frowned upon by official reviews of country-level policies: help for the unemployed should come in the form of placement assistance as well as of cash handouts, which should be made conditional on search and acceptance of jobs. If a segment of the population is not employable within the existing wage and contractual structure, the Luxembourg guidelines envisage bringing them into the employable segment of the productivity distribution via training and job-finding assistance. In terms of Figure 14.8, this would mean upgrading the labour force so that a larger proportion of it clears the minimum-wage hurdle without, however, removing the legal, contractual, or fiscal features that underlie that hurdle and underpin earnings equalization, and without renouncing the job security afforded by employment protection legislation. As discussed above, this type of policy is attractive—especially when other, more traditional policies are troubled by increased competitive pressure in the labour and product market—but tends to be expensive.

Recently, documents prepared towards social-policy coordination under the Portuguese presidency of the EU have indicated higher employment rates (rather than lower unemployment rates) as a high-priority objective. This means that, for example, early-retirement provisions should not be as widespread as they have typically been in many EU countries (including, as we have seen, ones that have led a successful fight against unemployment, such as the Netherlands). Unemployment may once have been viewed in Europe as an acceptable side-effect of otherwise very desirable labour-market institutions, especially as it was concentrated among marginal segments of the labour force. This is no longer the case, and the European Union construction process has played some role in reducing the sustainability of status quo labour-market configurations. It remains to be seen whether EU labour markets will converge in terms of institutional structure and/or in terms of outcomes. The two types of convergence by no means imply each other, because the economic and social structure of EU countries is far from homogeneous (as regards, for example, the extent of regional underdevelopment and the political role of unions). To the extent that such structural differences call for different policy approaches, the policy harmonization envisaged by the Luxembourg process would result in different and possibly diverging labour-market performances.

Discussion questions

1 Which institutional features imply that unemployment increases sharply when labour demand falls? Which ones slow down subsequent declines of unemployment?

2 How do inflation expectations and labour-market structure determine shifts of the Phillips curve?

3 Which labour-market institutions prevent the formation of low-wage employment relationships, and when is it a particularly acute problem?

4 Can active labour-market policies reconcile high employment and wage equality?

5 How do EU-level policy guidelines relate to fundamental trade-offs between wage inequality, employment rates, and tax-and-subsidy policies?

6 What are the Luxembourg process, the Cologne process, the Doorn process? How are their objectives related?

7 How did the Social Charter and the Amsterdam Treaty reform EU objectives and institutions? Which country was reluctant to follow this reform direction?

8 What does 'adaptability' mean in a labour-market context, and is it different from 'flexibility'?

Further reading

Bertola (1999) offers a survey of more technical theoretical and empirical work on the interaction of labour-market institutions and performance. For recent discussions of the NAIRU concept encountered in Section 14.2, see Staiger *et al.* (1997), or McAdam and McMorrow (1999). Details on current UI arrangements can be found in OECD (1999); Atkinson (1999) and his references can be consulted for empirical evidence on their implications for labour-market performance. Nickell and Van Ours (2000) provide a detailed discussion of the Dutch and British labour markets' evolution; Bertola (2000) and his references discuss in some detail interactions between the degree of 'activism' in labour-market policy and structural characteristics of different economies, particularly as regards the availability of fiscal instruments. Bean *et al.* (1998) discuss the possible tensions arising from competition among systems of labour-market regulation in integrating economies. For discussions of interactions between labour-market institutions, reform incentives, and the new macroeconomic policy environment of European integration, see Calmfors (1998), Bean (1998), Burda (2000), and their references. Atkinson (1998) discusses the possible evolution of European 'social models' as a result of economic integration. For a detailed discussion of the current institutional layout of European policy-making in the relevant areas, see Bean *et al.* (1998) and Bertola *et al.* (2000). The 'Luxembourg process' documentation, which includes reports by the Member Countries on their own labour-market policies and performance, can be found at: http://europa.eu.int/comm/employment_social/empl&esf/ees_en.htm

References

Atkinson, A. B. (1998), *Poverty in Europe* (Oxford: Blackwell).

—— (1999), *The Economic Consequences of Rolling Back the Welfare State* (Cambridge, Mass: MIT Press).

Bean, C. (1998), 'The Interaction of Aggregate Demand Policies and Labour Market Reform', *Swedish Economic Policy Review*, 5/2: 353–82.

—— Bentolila, S., Bertola, G. and Dolado, J. (1998), *Social Europe: . . . One for All?* (London: CEPR).

Bertola, G. (1999), 'Microeconomic Perspectives on Aggregate Labour Markets', in O. Ashenfelter and D. Card (eds.), *Handbook of Labour Economics*, iii (Amsterdam: North-Holland), 2985–3028.

—— (2000), 'Making Work Pay: Policy Choices and Interactions with Existing Instruments', *OECD Economic Studies*, 31: 185–98.

—— Jimeno, J. F., Marimon, R., Pissarides, C. (2000), 'Welfare Systems and Labour Markets in Europe: What Convergence before and after EMU?', in G. Bertola, T. Boeri, and G. Nicoletti (eds.), *Welfare and Employment in a United Europe* (Cambridge, Mass.: MIT Press).

Blanchard, O. and Wolfers, J. (2000), 'The Role of Shocks and Institutions in the Rise of European Unemployment: The Aggregate Evidence', *The Economic Journal*, 110: c1–c33.

Burda, M. C. (2000), 'European Labour Markets and the Euro: How Much Flexibility Do We Really Need?' in Deutsche Bundesbank (ed.) *The Monetary Transmission Process* (Basingstoke: Macmillan).

Calmfors, L. (1998), 'Macroeconomic Policy, Wage Setting, and Employment: What Difference does EMU make?, *Oxford Review of Economic Policy*, 14/3: 125–51.

—— and Driffill, J. (1988), 'Bargaining Structure, Corporatism and Macroeconomic Performance', *Economic Policy*, 6: 14–61.

McAdam, P. and McMorrow, K. (1999), *The NAIRU Concept: Measurement Uncertainties, Hysteresis and Economic Policy*, European Commission, Economic Papers no. 136 (http://-europa.eu.int/comm/economy_finance/document/ecopap/ecp136en.pdf)

Nickell, S. and Bell, B. (1995), 'The Collapse in Demand for the Unskilled and Unemployment Across the OECD', *Oxford Review of Economic Policy*, 11: 40–62.

—— and van Ours, J. (2000), 'The Netherlands and the United Kingdom: A European Unemployment Miracle?,' *Economic Policy*, 31: 137–80.

OECD (1999), *Benefit Systems and Work Incentives* (Paris: OECD).

Staiger, D., Stock, J., and Watson, M. (1997), 'How Precise are Estimates of the Natural Rate of Unemployment?' in C. Romer and D. Romer (eds.), *Reducing Inflation: Motivation and Strategy* (Chicago: Chicago University Press).

Chapter 15
Foreign Aid and External Assistance

Frederick Nixson

15.1 Introduction

Increasing economic interdependence between national economies ('globalization') is leading to profound changes in both the global economy and in the economic relationships between rich and poor countries. The 1990s witnessed huge increases in private capital flows to less developed countries (LDCs) but many of the poorest countries failed to attract these flows and remain dependent on concessional flows of finance. Domestic savings remain the main source of finance for investment throughout the developing world (DFID, 2000: 84–5), but 'Development assistance is a vital resource that can help put in place the reforms necessary to attract inward investment, improve government services, boost economic growth, and equip them [LDCs] to take advantage of new opportunities in a global economy' (DFID, 2000: 84).

In this chapter, we consider various aspects of the development assistance policy of both individual members of the EU and of the EU itself. Historical circumstances have left the UK and France, in particular, with a network of economic, political, social, and institutional relationships with a large number of low- and middle-income economies, formalized through a variety of agreements, with the current Partnership Agreement signed in Cotonou (Benin) in June 2000. The development assistance that the members of the EU make available is thus a combination of national (bilateral) aid and assistance programmes, and the multilateral (EU) programmes through which member countries channel a part of their overall aid programmes and assistance.

Table 15.1 gives details of total net resource flows from DAC Member Countries and Multilateral Agencies to aid recipients for the period 1991 to 1998. Over the period 1991 to 1997, there was a significant increase in total net resource flows, both private and public, going to low income, less developed economies but there were equally significant changes in the composition of those flows.

Table 15.1 Total net resource flows from DAC member countries and multilateral agencies to aid recipients

	Current $ bn.								Per cent of total		
	1991	1992	1993	1994	1995	1996	1997	1998[p]	1991	1994	1998[p]
I. OFFICIAL DEVELOPMENT FINANCE (ODF)	84.5	78.3	82.4	84.5	87.6	73.5	75.3	88.3	61.2	37.5	36.9
1. Official development assistance (ODA)[a]	57.1	58.3	55.5	59.6	59.1	55.8	47.7	49.7	41.4	26.4	20.7
of which:　Bilateral	41.4	41.4	39.4	41.3	40.6	39.1	32.4	35.1	30.0	18.3	14.7
Multilateral	15.8	17.0	16.1	18.3	18.4	16.7	15.3	14.5	11.4	8.1	6.1
2. Official Aid (OA)	6.6	6.0	6.0	6.9	8.4	5.6	5.6	7.0	4.8	3.0	2.9
of which:　Bilateral	5.0	5.2	5.2	5.5	7.1	4.0	4.0	4.5	3.6	2.5	1.9
Multilateral	1.6	0.8	0.7	1.3	1.3	1.5	1.6	2.5	1.1	0.6	1.0
3. Other ODF	20.8	14.0	21.0	18.1	20.1	12.2	22.0	31.7	15.1	8.0	13.2
of which:　Bilateral	13.1	8.0	11.4	12.2	14.0	5.7	5.9	12.8	9.5	5.4	5.3
Multilateral	7.7	5.9	9.6	5.8	6.1	6.5	16.0	18.9	5.6	2.6	7.9
II. TOTAL EXPORT CREDITS	0.6	1.0	−3.0	6.3	5.6	4.0	4.8	4.0	0.4	2.8	1.7
of which:　Short-term	−0.8	0.5	−1.5	0.2	0.8	0.5	0.6	0.5	−0.6	0.1	0.2
III. PRIVATE FLOWS	53.0	80.1	86.3	134.7	176.0	291.7	244.9	147.2	38.4	59.7	61.5
1. Direct investment (DAC)	24.8	30.2	41.6	52.1	59.6	69.7	106.7	118.0	18.0	23.1	49.2
of which:　to offshore centres	6.5	9.5	9.4	10.8	6.3	16.7	19.1	20.3	4.7	4.8	8.5
2. Inernational bank lending[b]	10.7	34.6	4.8	32.1	76.9	86.0	12.0	−65.0	7.7	14.2	−27.1
of which:　Short-term	12.0	25.0	7.0	44.0	40.0	40.0	12.0	−70.0	8.7	19.5	−29.2
3. Total bond lending	4.9	7.5	28.7	32.0	30.0	96.6	83.2	39.8	3.5	14.2	16.6
4. Other (including equities)[c]	7.1	1.8	5.5	12.5	3.5	33.8	37.8	49.1	5.2	5.5	20.5
5. Grants by non-governmental organizations	5.4	6.0	5.7	6.0	6.0	5.6	5.2	5.4	3.9	2.7	2.2
TOTAL NET RESOURCE FLOWS (I + II + III)	138.1	159.4	165.7	225.5	269.1	369.2	324.9	239.6	100.0	100.0	100.0
Memorandum items (not included):											
Interest paid by aid recipients[d]	−75.9	−68.0	−64.6	−83.2	−105.0	−103.2	−114.0	−112.2			
Net Use of IMF Credit[e]	3.6	0.8	3.3	0.6	15.6	0.3	14.4	18.8			
Non-DAC donors (ODA/OA)	2.8	1.1	1.4	1.0	0.8	0.8	0.7	0.6			

a　Excluding forgiveness of non-ODA debt for the years 1991 to 1992.
b　Excluding bond lending by banks (item III.3), and guaranteed financial credits (included in II).
c　Incomplete reporting from several DAC countries (including France, the UK and the USA).
　　Includes Japan from 1996.
d　Excluding dividends.
e　Non-concessional flows from the IMF General Resources Account.
p　Provisional.
Source: OECD, 2000: Table 1, pp. 162–163.

Between 1991 and 1997, Official Development Finance (ODF) and Official Development Assistance (ODA) fell in both absolute and relative terms, although there was a rise in both ODF and ODA in 1998. Private flows expanded almost five-fold over the 1991–7 period. Direct Foreign Investment (DFI) rose from US$24.8 bn. in 1991 to $106.7 bn. in 1997 and rose further in 1998 to $118.0 bn. (that is, DFI was not adversely affected overall by the 1997 Asian financial crisis—inflows fell in respect of some affected economies and rose in the case of others). International bank lending, much of which was short term, rose dramatically up to 1996, fell equally dramatically in 1997, and collapsed spectacularly in 1998. Bond lending demonstrated a similar pattern although the post-1997 collapse was less dramatic. As Table 15.1 clearly shows, there was a major reduction in net resource flows in 1998. By 1998, therefore, Official Development Assistance (aid) accounted for only one-fifth of net resource flows to less developed countries. The 1980s and early-1990s had been characterized by pro-market and anti-government rhetoric, with major western donors expressing the desire to substitute private capital flows for

ODA (Thorbecke, 2000: 47). The 1997 crisis in effect prompted a fundamental re-examination of the role of aid, both with respect to bilateral and multilateral institutions and a new development agenda, with an explicit focus on poverty alleviation, dominated development discussions.

15.2 Foreign aid and development

Foreign aid or economic assistance consists of transfers of real resources to less-developed countries (LDCs) on concessional terms. It excludes, by definition, purely commercial transactions, and should also exclude military aid, which, although it is non-commercial and concessional, does not have as its main objective the promotion of economic development. Aid raises a number of fundamental questions about development and under-development and the relationship between rich and poor countries (although not all donor countries are rich: China has made substantial sums of aid available in the past to countries such as Tanzania). These include the following:

- Why do donors give aid?
- Why do poor countries accept aid?
- How should aid be given?

    loans versus grants;

    tied aid versus untied aid;

    bilateral versus multilateral aid;

    project versus programme aid.

- Which countries should be given aid?
- What is the impact of aid on the process of growth and development?
- What is the nature of the aid relationship?

Clearly, simple and straightforward answers cannot be given to these questions, and, even after fifty years of experience of aid, the debate continues (major contributions to the debate include Cassen *et al.*, 1986; Mosley, 1987; Riddell, 1987; more recent contributions are Tarp, 2000; World Bank, 1998; and OECD, 2000). Donors give aid for a number of reasons. Humanitarian motives may dominate, but more usually there are economic, political, and strategic factors that determine the amounts given and the countries selected by donors for assistance.

Equally, poor countries may accept aid for a variety of reasons—the urgency of the problems facing them, the domestic absence or shortage of the resources that aid can provide, the building-up of a relationship with a donor or group of donor countries for political reasons, and the role that aid can play in maintaining a particular regime in power and/or consolidating and extending its power.

Aid can be given in various forms—as grants or loans, technical assistance, or commodity (largely food) aid—and with various forms of conditionality attached. Aid may be given for a project (to build a road, for example) or be made available for a programme (e.g. in the transport sector). Bilateral aid is given by the aid agency of one country (the UK Department for International Development, for example) to recipients in another. Multilateral aid (through the EU, the World Bank, or various UN agencies, for example) is usually considered to be superior to bilateral aid, as it avoids the problems that can arise in bilateral one-to-one relationships. Bilateral aid is normally tied (either to a particular project or programme and must be spent in the donor country); multilateral aid may be project- or programme-tied, but, by definition, it cannot be tied to a particular country.

Aid can be tied in various ways (Bhagwati, 1967) through formal and informal restrictions, the use of export and import credits, and aid provided in the form of technical services and goods. There is general agreement that tied aid reduces its value to the recipient (lower-cost sources of supply in non-donor countries will not be allowed to bid for aid projects). Tied aid benefits donor-country enterprises and its extensive use has led in the past to allegations that aid policy is subservient to a donor country's commercial interests.

When we consider the effectiveness of aid, it is useful to refer to what Mosley (1987: ch. 5) has called the 'macro–micro paradox' This refers to the apparent paradox that, whereas the microeconomic evaluation of aid projects is usually positive, there appears to be no statistically significant correlation, either positive or negative, between inflows of aid and the rate of growth of the recipient economy. Mosley (1987: 139–40) and White (1992) suggest various reasons why this situation exists—inaccurate measurement and fungibility within the public sector (that is, if certain conditions are satisfied, aid can never be completely tied to a specific project: see Singer, 1965), and backwash effects from aid-financed activities that adversely affect the private sector.

These results have recently been challenged. The World Bank (1998) argues that: financial aid works in a good policy environment; improvements in the economic institutions and policies in the LDCs are the key to the alleviation of poverty and that foreign aid can provide critical support to such improvements; effective aid complements private investment (with sound economic management, foreign aid 'crowds in' private investment); the value of development projects is to strengthen institutions and policies in order to ensure more effective service delivery; the best aid projects change the way the public sector does business and that aid can promote reform in even the most adverse conditions (but it requires patience and a focus on ideas, not money).

OECD (2000: ch. 6) surveys a number of econometric studies which attempt to evaluate aid effectiveness. It concludes that development assistance has had a positive impact on growth, but in some cases it is minor and statistically insignificant. Sound and stable macroeconomic policies reinforce aid's positive effects, but aid is only one of many elements in the complex economic growth process. Hansen and Tarp (2000) argue that the micro–macro paradox is non-existent and that econometric results consistently find that aid increases aggregate savings and investment and that there is a positive relationship between aid and growth. They conclude (Hansen and Tarp, 2000: 124): 'the unresolved issue in assessing aid effectiveness is not whether aid works, but how and whether we can make the different kinds of aid instruments at hand work better in varying country circumstances'.

Despite the confidence with which these studies present their conclusions, there is still a great deal that we do not know about the impact of aid on the process of economic development. We cannot prove that aid is either necessary or sufficient for economic and social development, or that the relationship between donor and recipient countries is either advantageous or disadvantageous to the latter. Despite their policy statements, the aid programmes of most major bilateral donors are dominated by political and geo-strategic considerations. If humanitarian factors are not of the highest priority, it should not surprise us if we find it difficult to establish a positive causal connection between aid and development.

15.3 EU development policy

The development policy of the EU has a number of distinct components which have evolved separately over time. The four Lomé Conventions and the Cotonou Agreement represent the oldest and most fully developed area and are discussed in Sections 15.5 and 15.6. But the EU has also developed:

1. A Mediterranean policy, based on a series of bilateral agreements,[1]

2. A series of cooperation instruments linked to common policies (generalized trade preferences, participation in commodity agreements, and food aid); and

3. An aid system set up by the EU on a unilateral basis. This includes emergency aid given in the event of natural or other disasters, aid to non-governmental organizations (NGOs) working on development projects in the Third World, financial and technical contributions to development projects, and industrial cooperation by means of financial aid to enterprises.

The EU has emphasized the 'fundamental characteristics' of its development policy (Frisch, 1992). These include: contractual arrangements freely negotiated by the EU and African, Caribbean, and Pacific (ACP) economies; the creation of joint institutions to allow continuing dialogue; and the global approach to cooperation involving a wide range of instruments in the fields of both trade and aid. In the Cotonou Agreement and elsewhere, greater emphasis is placed on poverty alleviation and 'ownership' issues.

15.4 The ODA record of EU member states

Between 1992 and 1997, aid from DAC Member Countries to the developing world fell by 21 per cent in real terms. As a proportion of their combined national income, it fell by one third. As the OECD (2000: 67) notes, these were the largest declines in ODA since the inception of the DAC in 1961. The fall in ODA was halted in 1998. Total net official development assistance rose from US$48,324 m. in 1997 to US$51,888 m. in 1998 (in

Box 15.1 **A note on aid statistics: terms and definitions**

All members of the EU are members of the Organization for Economic Cooperation and Development (OECD). One of the specialized committees of the OECD is the Development Assistance Committee (DAC), the members of which have agreed 'to secure an expansion of aggregate volume of resources made available to developing countries and to improve their effectiveness'

The Commission of the European Communities (CEC) takes part in the work of the OECD and is a member of the DAC. All fifteen members of the EU are members of the DAC but Greece is not included in the DAC aid tables. Greece does contribute, however, to EU aid programmes and multilateral institutions.

Official Development Finance (ODF) includes:
1. bilateral ODA;
2. grants and concessional and non-concessional development lending by multilateral financial institutions and
3. other official flows which are considered developmental (including refinancing loans) but which have too low a grant element to qualify as ODA.

'Aid' or 'assistance' refers only to items which qualify as 'Official Development Assistance' (ODA)—that is, grants or loans:

- undertaken by the official sector;
- with promotion of economic development or welfare as main objectives;
- at concessional financial terms (if a loan, at least 25 per cent grant element).

Technical cooperation is included in aid. It consists almost entirely of grants to nationals of developing countries receiving education or training at home or abroad and payments to defray the costs of teachers, administrators, advisers, and so on, serving in developing countries.

current prices and exchange rates). This was a rise of 9.6 per cent in real terms, although the rise was smaller in relation to GNP, with the combined ODA/GNP ratio for DAC Member Countries rising from 0.22 per cent to 0.24 per cent. This recovery was in part due to the introduction of short-term measures to deal with the 1997 Asian financial crisis, but it also reflected policy decisions by a number of Member Countries to stablize or gradually rebuild their aid programmes.[2] Of the DAC total of US$51.9 bn. in 1998, the USA and Japan together accounted for US$19,426 bn. ($8.8 bn. and $10.6 bn. respectively). The fourteen EU members of the DAC accounted for US$27,462 m., that is approximately 52 per cent of the total. Further details are given in Table 15.2.

For DAC Members as a whole, ODA as a proportion of GNP fell over the 1980s from 0.35 per cent in 1982–3 to 0.33 per cent in 1987–8. As noted above it fell further over the 1990s, reaching 0.22 per cent in 1997 and recovering slightly to 0.24 per cent in 1998. For the fourteen EU Member States, the equivalent figures were 0.45 per cent in 1982–3 and 0.44 per cent in 1987–8, falling to 0.33 per cent in 1997, where it remained in 1998. The

Table 15.2 Net official development assistance from DAC countries to developing countries and multilateral organisations

	$ million							Per cent of GNP						
	1982–3 (av.)	1987–8 (av.)	1994	1995	1996	1997	1998	1982–3 (av.)	1987–8 (av.)	1994	1995	1996	1997	1998
Austria	197	251	655	767	557	527	456	0.30	0.21	0.33	0.33	0.24	0.26	0.22
Belgium	489	644	727	1,034	913	764	883	0.58	0.44	0.32	0.38	0.34	0.31	0.35
Denmark	405	890	1,446	1,623	1,772	1,637	1,704	0.75	0.88	1.03	0.96	1.04	0.97	0.99
Finland	149	520	290	388	408	379	396	0.30	0.55	0.31	0.32	0.34	0.33	0.32
France	2,979	5,356	8,466	8,443	7,451	6,307	5,742	0.56	0.59	0.64	0.55	0.48	0.45	0.40
Germany	3,164	4,561	6,818	7,524	7,601	5,857	5,581	0.48	0.39	0.33	0.31	0.32	0.28	0.26
Ireland	40	54	109	153	179	187	199	0.23	0.20	0.25	0.29	0.31	0.31	0.30
Italy	822	2,904	2,705	1,623	2,416	1,266	2,278	0.20	0.37	0.27	0.15	0.20	0.11	0.20
Luxembourg	4	16	59	65	82	95	112	0.09	0.19	0.40	0.36	0.44	0.55	0.65
Netherlands	1,334	2,163	2,517	3,226	3,246	2,947	3,042	0.99	0.98	0.76	0.81	0.81	0.81	0.80
Portugal	8	62	303	258	218	250	259	0.04	0.16	0.34	0.25	0.21	0.25	0.24
Spain	153	240	1,305	1,348	1,251	1,234	1,376	0.09	0.08	0.28	0.24	0.22	0.24	0.24
Sweden	870	1,454	1,819	1,704	1,999	1,731	1,573	0.93	0.87	0.96	0.77	0.84	0.79	0.72
UK	1,705	2,258	3,197	3,202	3,199	3,433	3,864	0.36	0.30	0.31	0.29	0.27	0.26	0.27
TOTAL DAC of which:	26,904	43,834	59,152	58,926	55,438	48,324	51,888	0.35	0.33	0.29	0.27	0.25	0.22	0.24
EU Members	12,318	21,374	30,416	31,358	31,293	26,612	27,462	0.45	0.44	0.42	0.38	0.37	0.33	0.33

Note: Net disbursements at current prices and exchange rates.
Source: OECD, 2000: Table 4, pp.168–169.

figure ranges from 0.99 per cent in the case of Denmark to 0.20 per cent in the case of Italy. Comparing the average for 1987–8 with 1998, the ratio fell for all the larger donors (in absolute terms)—France, Germany, Italy, the Netherlands, and the UK, as well as smaller absolute donors—Belgium, Finland, and Sweden. The ratio rose for a number of smaller doners—Austria, Denmark, Ireland, Luxembourg, Portugal, and Spain.

The accession to the EU of Austria, Sweden, and Finland in 1995 was seen as a positive move as far as development cooperation was concerned. In 1994 their total ODA amounted to $US2.9 bn. (Table 15.2), with Sweden alone contributing $US1.8 bn. The Finnish aid programme suffered massive cutbacks in the early 1990s, however, and both Austria and Sweden have cut back their aid programmes in the latter half of the 1990s.

A variety of burden-sharing indicators are presented in Tables 15.2 and 15.3. Table 15.2 includes data on ODA as a share of GNP, and we can note that in 1998 only Denmark, the Netherlands, and Sweden exceeded the UN target of a 0.7 per cent ODA/GNP ratio. That the EU average is above that of the DAC as a whole is largely owing to the very poor burden-sharing indicators of the two largest global donors—Japan (an ODA/GNP ratio of 0.28 in 1998) and the USA (an ODA/GNP ratio of 0.10 in 1998).

Table 15.3 gives details of two further burden-sharing indicators—the grant equivalent of ODA as a percentage of GNP, and ODA per capita of the donor country. The latter set of figures allows us to make some interesting comparisons. The largest EU donors (Germany, France, and the UK) tend to have low per capita figures. The Netherlands is in the middle of both rankings. The smaller EU donors, especially Denmark, Luxembourg and to a lesser extent Sweden, have the highest per capita contributions.

Table 15.3 Burden-sharing indicators in terms of net disbursements, 1997–1998 average

	Grant equivalent of total ODA[a] as % of GNP	Multilateral ODA as % of GNP[b]		Aid to LICs[c]	of which Aid to LLDCs[d]	ODA per capita of donor country 1997 dollars		Aid by NGOs as % of GNP	
				As % of GNP		Memo: 1987–8	1997–8	Memo: 1987–8	1997–8
Austria	0.24	0.05	(0.09)	0.10	0.04	44	61	0.02	0.02
Belgium	0.34	0.06	(0.14)	0.14	0.09	88	81	0.01	0.02
Denmark	1.01	0.33	(0.39)	0.49	0.31	222	316	0.02	0.02
Finland	0.33	0.11	(0.15)	0.15	0.08	114	76	0.03	0.01
France	0.47	0.05	(0.11)	0.16	0.08	120	103	0.01	0.00
Germany	0.31	0.04	(0.10)	0.11	0.05	78	70	0.06	0.04
Ireland	0.30	0.04	(0.11)	0.17	0.14	19	53	0.09	0.08
Italy	0.17	0.05	(0.10)	0.08	0.05	63	31	0.00	0.00
Luxembourg	0.60	0.09	(0.18)	0.28	0.16	55	242	0.00	0.03
Netherlands	0.85	0.16	(0.23)	0.36	0.22	182	192	0.08	0.07
Portugal	0.25	0.02	(0.08)	0.16	0.15	10	26	0.00	0.01
Spain	0.25	0.03	(0.09)	0.07	0.03	8	33	0.00	0.02
Sweden	0.75	0.20	(0.24)	0.37	0.22	207	189	0.07	0.02
UK	0.29	0.06	(0.12)	0.13	0.07	56	61	0.03	0.03
TOTAL DAC	0.24	0.05	(0.07)	0.10	0.05	72	62	0.03	0.02

Notes:
a   Calculated on a gross disbursement basis
b   In brackets, including EC. Capital subscriptions are on a deposit basis.
c   Low-income countries (LICs) comprise LLDCs and all other countries with per capita income (World Bank Atlas basis) of $765 or less in 1995. Includes imputed multilateral ODA. Capital subscriptions to multilateral agencies are on a deposit basis.
d   Least developed countries (LLDCs) are countries in the current United Nations list. Includes imputed multilateral ODA. Capital subscriptions to multilateral agencies are on a deposit basis.
Source: OECD, 2000: Table 7, p.175.

Although it is recognized that multilateral institutions have a key role to play in the development process, most donor countries, for the reasons outlined above, prefer to maintain direct control over their aid programmes through bilateral relationships. The early to mid–1970s saw a significant expansion in the role of multilateral aid, including a major expansion of aid from EC members through EC programmes. In the latter half of the 1970s, the proportion of ODA channelled through multilateral institutions levelled off, and in the 1980s the proportion, expressed as a percentage of GNP, actually declined (OECD, 1992: 42, Table V-5).

In the 1990s, the share of multilateral ODA in total ODA has risen in the case of Austria, Finland, Italy, and Sweden. Among the larger donors, it has risen in the case of France and fallen in the case of Germany. The figure for the UK has hardly changed in the 1990s. France is noteworthy in this respect, having the lowest ratio of any EU member, indicating that France maintains a tight bilateral control over its aid programme.

The percentage of multilateral ODA going through the EU varies widely, although there is no obvious pattern. Some small donors channel the larger part of their multilateral aid through the EU (for example, Portugal and Ireland); other small donors channel less (for example, Sweden and Denmark, who focus more on the United Nations Agencies). Some big donors, for example, France and Germany, channel 50 per cent or more of their multilateral ODA through the EU. The UK's share is roughly the average for the EU as a whole (see Table 15.4).

As noted above, aid can be either tied or untied. The tying of aid has always been a controversial topic, with critics arguing that tying reduces the value of aid and lowers its 'quality'. The other determinant of the 'quality' of aid is its grant element. This reflects the financial terms of a commitment: interest rate, maturity (interval to final repayment), and grace period (interval to first repayment of capital). The grant element measures the concessionality—that is, the softness—of a loan. The market rate of interest is conventionally taken to be 10 per cent. The grant element of a loan is thus nil for a loan with an interest rate of 10 per cent or higher and, by definition, the grant element of a grant is 100 per cent. The grant element will lie in between these two limits for a soft loan. Although maturity and grace periods are important, it is the interest rate that is the major determinant of the softness of a loan (OECD, 1992: A99–100).

As Hjertholm and White (in Tarp, 2000: ch. 3) note, (un)tying performance tends to change quite markedly over time, although as the data in Table 15.5 show, the second half of the 1990s has witnessed significant untying of bilateral ODA (multilateral aid, by definition, cannot be tied to individual donor countries) with some notable exceptions among the larger EU donors (France, Germany, and Italy). Changes in policy and performance over time in individual donor countries are a reflection of changes in political administration, changing budgetary priorities, and the result of policy reviews and changing priorities. The data in Table 15.6 show that EU Member States in general score highly with respect to the concessionality of their aid, with high grant elements in all cases.

The major uses of EU ODA are shown in Table 15.7. Social and administrative

Table 15.4 Multilateral aid indicators in terms of net disbursements, 1997–1998 average

	Multilateral ODA as per cent of total ODA[a]	Per cent of multilateral ODA going through EU[b]
Austria	36	49
Belgium	39	56
Denmark	40	16
Finland	47	35
France	27	50
Germany	37	59
Ireland	38	65
Italy	69	45
Luxembourg	31	54
Netherlands	30	34
Portugal	32	72
Spain	39	69
Sweden	34	18
UK	45	48
EU Average	38	47

Note:
a   Calculated from OECD, 2000: Table 4, pp.168–169 and Table 15, pp. 200–201.
b   Calculated from OECD, 2000: Table 15, pp. 200–201.

Table 15.5 Bilateral ODA commitments, share of untied aid, DAC donors; selected years 1981–1997 (%)

	1981	1985	1989	1993	1997
Austria	3.4	3.0	3.1	44.8	60.6
Belgium	29.0	37.5	n.a.	n.a.	49.9
Denmark	63.6	60.4	n.a.	n.a.	71.6
Finland	84.9	80.9	20.8	59.0	76.8
France	42.5	42.5	47.8	31.5	n.a.
Germany	74.3	3.7	33.8	47.9	n.a.
Ireland	n.a.	100.1	n.a.	n.a.	n.a.
Italy	71.6	16.6	9.1	43.1	45.6
Luxembourg	n.a.	n.a.	n.a.	n.a.	95.2
Netherlands	57.3	60.3	45.8	n.a.	90.0
Portugal	n.a.	n.a.	n.a.	63.8	99.1
Spain	n.a.	n.a.	n.a.	n.a.	n.a.
Sweden	84.0	68.8	71.1	85.0	74.5
United Kingdom	20.5	27.6	24.0	35.2	71.7
DAC donors total	44.1	47.3	43.8	57.9	87.6

Source: Adapted from Hjertholm and White, 2000: Table 3.7, p. 96.

Table 15.6 Financial terms of ODA commitments[a] 1997–1998 average

	Grant element of total ODA Norm: 86%[b]		Grant share of:		Grant element of		
	1987–88	1997–98	Bilateral ODA	Total ODA	ODA loans	ODA to LLDCs	Bilateral ODA to LLDCs
Austria	71.7	95.0	80.8	87.4	55.4	100.0	100.0
Belgium	99.2	99.5	96.3	97.9	74.1	99.9	99.9
Denmark	99.5	100.0	100.0	100.0	—	100.0	100.0
Finland	97.7	99.8	98.0	98.9	43.9	99.7	99.5
France	86.5	92.2	77.2	80.3	53.7	98.8	98.2
Germany	88.8	96.0	77.2	86.1	71.0	100.0	100.0
Ireland	100.0	100.0	100.0	100.0	—	100.0	100.0
Italy	92.1	98.4	74.7	93.4	76.0	99.6	98.8
Luxembourg	—	100.0	100.0	100.0	—	100.0	100.0
Netherlands	94.2	100.0	100.0	100.0	—	100.0	100.0
Portugal	—	97.5	65.1	87.2	58.8	97.6	96.7
Spain	50.4	91.5	60.8	75.9	64.7	96.3	90.0
Sweden	100.0	100.0	99.8	99.9	—	100.0	100.0
United Kingdom	99.7	100.0	92.4	95.8	—	100.0	100.0
TOTAL DAC	89.7	92.7	70.8	79.0	63.9	99.5	99.1

Note: Excludes debt reorganization. Equities are treated as loans with a 100% grant element.

a   Countries whose ODA commitments as a percentage of GNP are significantly below the DAC average are not considered as having met the terms target. This provision disqualified Italy, Portugal, and the USA in 1998.

Source: OECD, 2000, Table 20, p. 208.

infrastructure is the largest sector receiving aid, taking 28.8 per cent of the total in 1997–8, for the DAC as a whole. The directly productive sectors of the economy—agriculture and industry and other production—received only 10 per cent of total commitments in 1997–8. Economic infrastructure increased its share of ODA over the period 1977–8 to 1997–8. As far as variations between EU members are concerned, of the larger donors,

Table 15.7 Major aid uses by individual DAC donors (% of total bilateral commitments)

	Social and administrative infrastructure		Economic infrastructure		Agriculture		Industry and other production		Commodity aid and programme assistance		Emergency aid		Other	
	1977–8	1997–8	1977–8	1997–8	1977–8	1997–8	1977–8	1997–8	1977–8	1997–8	1977–8	1997–8	1977–8	1997–8
Austria	17.4	44.3	31.2	1.9	25.5	3.6	19.2	2.3	–	0.4	0.3	8.0	6.5	39.5
Belgium	5.8	32.4	0.9	3.5	3.7	8.9	1.8	3.4	2.6	6.2	0.9	5.5	84.3	40.2
Denmark	13.3	28.2	3.6	12.6	14.4	8.8	15.6	0.8	12.1	0.2	1.9	8.5	39.1	40.9
Finland	9.4	35.4	32.2	5.2	18.9	10.7	16.7	3.4	4.4	0.1	1.2	13.1	17.2	32.2
France	56.9	43.8	12.5	8.5	7.6	6.7	14.7	2.5	4.5	3.2	0.2	0.3	3.6	35.1
Germany	23.0	39.3	24.8	16.2	11.0	8.2	19.7	2.2	4.5	2.1	0.4	4.0	16.5	28.1
Ireland	–	45.4	–	5.6	–	5.6	–	1.5	–	3.9	–	8.2	100.0	29.8
Italy	33.5	16.2	4.5	10.9	7.2	3.5	6.1	1.2	19.8	7.8	0.2	4.5	28.6	55.9
Luxembourg	–	60.2	–	2.1	–	8.6	–	5.1	–	1.4	–	13.0	–	9.7
Netherlands	30.8	23.2	12.3	6.3	23.9	7.2	8.7	1.3	6.2	1.4	1.3	10.8	16.8	49.8
Portugal	–	21.7	–	9.0	–	1.5	–	1.3	–	0.7	–	0.2	–	65.5
Spain	–	34.1	–	14.6	–	5.6	–	2.8	–	1.0	–	2.4	–	39.5
Sweden	20.0	33.8	4.5	12.7	8.5	7.7	16.4	1.4	1.6	2.7	1.5	19.7	47.6	21.9
United Kingdom	15.8	27.1	11.1	10.3	8.3	7.3	21.4	3.0	3.4	6.2	0.3	7.4	39.7	38.7
TOTAL DAC	20.0	28.8	15.7	21.4	10.2	7.7	10.7	2.4	12.6	6.5	0.7	5.8	30.1	27.3

Source: OECD, 2000: Table 18, pp. 204–205.

France and Germany devote the largest proportion of their aid budgets to social and administrative infrastructure. In the case of the UK, it is clear that there has been a shift in sectoral priorities, over the period covered in Table 15.7, from industry and other productive activities to social and administrative infrastructure.

The final point to be considered in this general overview relates to the geographical distribution of EU aid. The regional distribution is given in Table 15.8. Sub-Saharan Africa remains the major recipient of EU aid, although its share has fallen since the late 1980s. It is important to note that these figures are for gross disbursement (the total amount disbursed or spent over a given accounting period) and net disbursements (gross disbursements less any repayments of loan principal during the same period) would be lower.

Concern has been expressed in the Third World that the changes that have occurred in Eastern Europe and the former Soviet Union will cause a diversion of aid from developing countries as conventionally defined. Some of the countries of the former Soviet Union, such as the Central Asian Republics, have similar characteristics to developing countries. A small number of countries have been added to the list of aid recipients, including Albania, Kazakhstan, Kyrghizstan (now the Kyrghiz Republic), Tadjikistan, Turkmenistan, Uzbekistan, Armenia, Georgia, and Azerbaijan. From 1993, Central and Eastern European Countries, New Independent States of the former Soviet Union (CEEC/NIS), and countries in transition have been included in Part II of a new list of aid recipients (excluding those countries listed above) (OECD 1995: 126–7, A101). In general, DAC members have argued that so far there has been very limited aid diversion and it is difficult to predict how important an issue this will become in the future.[3]

Table 15.8 Regional distribution of ODA by individual DAC donors and multilateral agencies

	Sub-Saharan Africa			South and Central Asia			Other Asia and Oceania			Middle East, North Africa, and Europe			Latin America and Caribbean		
	1987-8	1992-3	1997-8	1987-8	1992-3	1997-8	1987-8	1992-3	1997-8	1987-8	1992-3	1997-8	1987-8	1992-3	1997-8
Austria	19.5	13.3	23.1	1.3	2.1	4.4	12.0	33.9	25.7	62.8	46.7	39.2	4.4	4.0	7.6
Belgium	75.8	57.5	63.6	2.3	4.0	1.8	9.9	13.2	9.6	5.1	10.7	8.7	6.9	14.8	16.4
Denmark	63.6	62.8	55.5	19.1	16.8	16.4	6.8	7.2	12.3	7.3	6.0	6.2	3.2	7.1	9.6
Finland	64.7	43.1	41.8	13.6	10.9	11.7	6.8	13.7	22.4	7.4	20.9	15.5	7.4	11.4	8.6
France	54.3	55.0	51.3	4.5	3.1	2.1	21.9	19.2	21.4	14.3	17.2	19.1	5.0	5.5	6.0
Germany	28.3	24.7	25.2	15.8	11.9	12.3	11.1	15.7	24.5	30.4	36.1	23.9	14.3	11.5	14.2
Ireland	94.7	85.0	86.6	3.0	2.7	2.9	1.2	3.5	2.7	0.4	7.4	4.7	0.8	1.4	3.1
Italy	65.5	39.7	54.6	5.0	2.2	0.9	6.6	14.4	3.7	12.5	28.9	20.7	10.4	14.9	20.0
Luxembourg	—	53.6	48.8	—	7.6	7.3	—	4.0	11.3	—	12.9	14.0	—	21.9	18.7
Netherlands	39.0	37.6	36.2	20.4	15.8	15.3	16.9	6.2	5.6	5.5	13.4	16.0	18.2	27.0	26.9
Portugal	—	99.7	98.3	—	—	0.1	—	0.1	0.4	—	0.1	0.7	—	0.1	0.6
Spain	19.2	10.6	24.5	—	0.0	2.1	12.1	22.1	10.2	6.4	18.7	19.3	62.3	48.6	43.8
Sweden	62.6	49.6	48.5	15.3	11.5	10.6	11.6	12.6	12.9	3.7	14.4	15.4	6.8	11.9	12.5
United Kingdom	49.1	45.4	43.3	27.6	24.4	21.6	10.1	13.2	8.6	6.2	8.9	6.9	6.9	8.2	19.6
TOTAL DAC *of which:*	32.1	28.4	29.5	14.8	10.2	13.3	22.2	24.7	27.3	18.8	23.2	16.4	12.1	13.5	13.6
EU Members	48.3	40.6	41.8	11.9	8.4	9.2	13.7	15.8	16.5	15.9	22.7	17.8	10.1	12.4	14.7
EC	58.3	55.6	40.4	11.0	5.6	8.1	9.5	5.4	6.1	10.9	24.7	32.7	10.2	8.7	12.7
OVERALL TOTAL	34.9	32.8	31.8	18.2	13.1	16.1	19.8	21.4	22.7	15.5	20.9	16.3	11.6	11.8	13.1

Note: Figures refer to percentages of total gross disbursements excluding amounts unspecified by region.
Source: OECD, 2000: Table 27, pp. 220–221.

Table 15.9 gives details of the major EC/EU aid recipients over the period from the 1970s to 1990s. Two points deserve special mention. First the percentage of total ODA accounted for by the fifteen largest recipients has fallen dramatically, from 52 per cent of the total in 1977–8 to 31 per cent in 1997–8. Secondly, there have been significant changes in the country composition of the 'top' fifteen recipients. New recipients appear in the list for 1997–8—Bosnia-Herzegovina, the Palestinian Administered Areas, and South Africa—which reflects the political changes that have occurred during the 1990s. More surprisingly, the top eight recipients (and Jordan) are not ACP member states, yet together they accounted in 1997–8 for 22.5 per cent of EU gross disbursements.

India, the largest recipient of EU aid in 1987–8 was no longer in the 'top fifteen' ten years later. Egypt has historically been a large recipient of EU aid, although its relative position has varied from year to year. Looking at the DAC as a whole, however, Egypt and India were respectively the third and fourth largest recipients of aid in 1997–8 (after China and Indonesia) (all data from OECD, 2000: Table 34, pp. 244–5). With the exception of Egypt, there was probably less correspondence between the DAC 'top fifteen' and the EU 'top fifteen' aid recipients in 1997–8 than in earlier years. This emphasizes the point made above that, although most attention is given to ACP member states, the EU has wider interests which encompass South Asia, the Middle East, and, to a more limited extent, Latin America. The geographical distribution of aid thus reflects a mixture of historical relationships, contemporary geo-political realities, commercial interests, and

Table 15.9 Major recipients of EC/EU aid, 1977–1978 to 1997–1998 (% of total ODA)

1977–8		1987–8		1997–8	
Bangladesh	5.4	India	6.0	Morocco	4.0
India	4.7	Ethiopia	5.8	Egypt	3.9
Vietnam	4.7	Côte D'Ivoire	5.5	Bosnia-Herzegovina	3.2
Senegal	4.3	Egypt	3.4	Algeria	2.7
Turkey	4.2	Senegal	3.3	Tunisia	2.2
Niger	3.7	Papua New Guinea	2.7	Palestinian Adm. Areas	1.8
Congo, Dem.Rep.	3.7	Sudan	2.7	Turkey	1.8
Egypt	3.1	Kenya	2.4	Bangladesh	1.5
Mauritania	3.0	Bangladesh	2.2	Mauritania	1.5
Burkina Faso	2.9	Mozambique	2.2	Ethiopia	1.5
Rwanda	2.5	Chad	2.0	Mozambique	1.4
Madagascar	2.5	Tunisia	1.7	Madagascar	1.4
Chad	2.4	Uganda	1.7	Jordan	1.4
Somalia	2.4	Tanzania	1.6	South Africa	1.4
Tanzania	2.3	Malawi	1.6	Senegal	1.4
Total	51.7	Total	44.8	Total	31.1

Source: Taken from OECD, 2000: Table 34, pp. 245.

humanitarian concerns. The EU, as a major multilateral donor, is perhaps less partisan than major bilateral donors (the USA and France, for example), but the geographical distribution of its aid nevertheless reflects its perceptions of regional and global interests.

15.5 The Europe–ACP relationship

Historical background

Table 15.10 details the evolution of the relationship between the EC/EU and the ACP. The evolving EU–ACP relationships reflect not only changes within the EC/EU itself (the accession of new members) but also changes within the global economic and political context—decolonization, the notion of a new international economic order (the Lomé model), the end of the Cold War (updated Lomé IV), and the effects of globalization (the Cotonou Agreement).

When the Treaty of Rome was signed in 1957, most of the countries that now constitute the ACP were still colonies. The Treaty of Rome provided for an element of aid to these colonies, however, in the form of an implementing Convention added to the Treaty. It provided for a form of unilateral association between the EC and its Member States and Overseas Countries and Territories (OCTs), through which trade and aid links could be maintained.

The first European Development Fund (EDF) was established in 1958 and gave grants for economic and social infrastructure projects largely in French-speaking OCTs. The 1960s was a decade of decolonization, and in 1963 the Yaoundé (Cameroon) Convention

Table 15.10 Evolution of the Europe–ACP partnership during the past 40 years

Year	Event	No. of countries		EDF Amount (€m.) (including OCTs)
		ACP	Europe	
1957	Association System			569,4
1963	Yaoundé I Convention	18	6	30,4
1969	Yaoundé II Convention	18	6	887,3
1975	Lomé I Convention	46	9	3.053,3
1980	Lomé II Convention	58	9	4.207
1985	Lomé III Convention	65	10	7.882,6
1990	Lomé IV Convention	68	12	11.583,0
1995	Lomé IV bis Convention	70	15	13.151,10
2000	Cotonou Agreement	77	15	14.300

Source: The Courier, Sept. 2000, Special Issue, p. 12.

was signed between the EC6 and 18 now-independent African countries (including Madagascar). A second EDF was established to give loans as well as grants, and the Convention included provisions for preferential trade arrangements and for the provision of financial and technical assistance. The Second Yaoundé Convention was signed in 1969, with a third EDF.

In January 1973 the UK joined the EC and some 20 Commonwealth countries were included in the protocol to the Act of Accession, opening the way to the negotiation of some form of special relationship with the EC—an opportunity also offered to those independent states in Africa that were neither members of the Commonwealth nor members of the AASM grouping (Association of African States and Madagascar) which had negotiated the Yaoundé Conventions. After a period of some uncertainty as to how newly independent ACP countries would view their position *vis-à-vis* Europe, the first Lomé Convention was signed in February 1975 in Togo, and, in June 1975, 46 ACP countries institutionalized themselves as a group with a permanent structure.

Lomé I has been described as a 'partnership of equals' and a number of joint institutions were created to administer the Convention. It introduced Stabex—a system designed to stabilize commodity earnings—and, at a time of stalemate in the global negotiations aimed at the creation of a New International Economic Order (NIEO), it 'appeared to offer an opportunity for a group of industrialised and developing countries to break out of the impasse . . . to establish a regional arrangement that would incorporate a number of items on the NIEO agenda' (Stevens, 1990: 77).

The optimism that characterized Lomé I was shown to be premature by events that followed the first oil-price shock of 1973–4. A brief boom in some primary commodity prices was followed by the second oil-price shock of 1979–80. The Sub-Saharan economies in particular were hard hit by global economic instability and began a period of stagnant or falling per capita incomes from which the majority of African economies have not yet recovered. Lomé II was signed in 1980, with a larger EDF and a Sysmin facility, but was regarded as disappointing by the ACP. Lomé III was signed in 1985, as the 'decade of structural adjustment' (see below) was beginning to emerge. Lomé III made a commitment to 'self-reliant development' on the basis of food security and self-sufficiency, enhanced by a broad-ranging 'policy dialogue' between EC Member States and the ACP states. Stabex conditionality was tightened up, however, and policy dialogue increasingly encompassed involvement in macroeconomic policy-making through the provision of resources through programmes of structural adjustment.

Stevens (1990: 84) argues that the first three Lomé Conventions did not lead to a radical transformation in the economies of the ACP. Lomé aid was widely criticized on two counts: first, it had been poorly used, financing projects either poorly designed or whose possibilities of success had been weakened by a hostile policy environment, and secondly, aid had been badly administered by the donor, with slow rates of disbursement. Donor procedures were allegedly slow and cumbersome, with duplicated appraisal procedures, over-centralization, and 'meddling' by Member States (Stevens, 1990: 85).

In addition, it was argued that the aid relationship had changed over time, with the EC attempting to impose a more orthodox donor–recipient relationship than was initially felt either necessary or desirable. 'Policy dialogue' had increasingly come to mean a shift in the balance of power for aid decision-making towards the EC to give it a greater voice in the selection of aid-financed projects and sectoral policies relevant to the success of those projects (Stevens, 1990: 84).

The Fourth Lomé Convention was signed in December 1989. For the first time it covered a period of ten years, although the Financial Protocol covered the first five years only with mandatory renewal provided for at the end of that time. The negotiations in 1989 anticipated the possibility of reviewing the actual text of the Convention midway through its term. This was not to be a global renegotiation and the emphasis was to be on a few essential points of mutual concern to the treaty partners. The mid-term review negotiations opened in May 1994 and were completed in June 1995. The results were formalized in the agreement signed in Mauritius in November 1995.

The 1990 Convention highlighted new areas of development aid policy which had been somewhat neglected in the previous conventions:

- Protection of the environment: the control of desertification and a commitment to ensure that economic and social development was based on a sustainable balance between economic objectives, management of natural resources, and improvement of human resources;

- Agricultural cooperation and food security: the emphasis was on the regional dimension of food security policies and the role of women in rural development;

- Industry and services: industrial cooperation and the promotion of services that support economic development were given new prominence. Such services included support for external trade, promotion of tourism, and development of transport and communications and information technology.

- Cultural and social cooperation: this was extended to new issues such as population, nutrition, and women in development;

- Other provisions in Lomé IV included a special programme of aid to the countries of Sub-Saharan Africa which had low incomes and large debts, and specific measures to assist the least-developed landlocked and island ACP states. As in previous conventions, there were provisions for emergency aid for the victims of natural disasters, refugees, and repatriated persons.

The review of the Lomé IV provisions in the mid-1990s was classified under four headings: institutional and political; thematic and sectoral; commercial; and financial (*The Courier*, 1996: 8). With respect to institutional and political issues, emphasis was placed on the recognition and application of democratic principles, the consolidation of the rule of law and good governance. Thematic and sectoral issues covered a range of activities including cultural cooperation, industrial cooperation, and Stabex (see below).

With respect to finance, programmable aid remained the central feature of ACP–EU cooperation within the context of agreed programmes of structural adjustment. In very broad terms, structural adjustment is a set of policies designed to reduce internal and external imbalances in an economy. Whereas stabilization policies are largely concerned with the reduction in aggregate demand, structural adjustment focuses on the increase in aggregate supply. Both sets of policies complement each other and both share many common elements—more liberal trade policy (removal of quantitative restrictions, reduction in tariffs), improved resource mobilization and allocation (through fiscal and monetary reform, removal of subsidies, reform of public enterprises, reform of agricultural sector pricing policies), and institutional reforms.

The Lomé IV provisions that covered structural adjustment emphasized that these policies were intended to promote long-term development in the ACP states, accelerate the growth of output and employment, and be consistent with the political and economic model of the ACP state in question. Adjustment had to be economically viable and socially and politically bearable. These were ambitious objectives, the achievement of which cannot be taken for granted. The record of structural adjustment programmes has been mixed, to say the least, and, although the EU argued that it would be pragmatic and realistic in its approach, it would be difficult to argue that these programmes have been successful overall.

The revised Lomé IV Convention made reference to the use of structural adjustment resources to encourage regional integration efforts and to support reforms leading to intra-regional economic liberalization. Support was to be given to the harmonization and coordination of macroeconomic and sectoral policies to fulfil the dual aim of regional integration and structural reform at the national level. It is important to keep in mind that trade policy probably has a greater economic impact on the ACP states than development cooperation policy. The ACP states have enjoyed free access to the EU market for the majority of their agricultural and manufactured products. The revised Lomé IV Convention signalled a change of emphasis, however, focusing on the role of trade in the development process and on measures to enhance the competitiveness of ACP exports both within ACP and EU markets and within wider global markets.

An important element of the four Lomé Conventions was Stabex (System for the Stabilisation of Export Earnings). This was a system aimed at remedying the harmful efforts of the instability of export earnings, and when it was introduced in 1975 it was welcomed for its innovatory approach, simplicity of operation, and the relatively rapid transfers that it provided. Lomé III saw a tightening in the restrictions placed on the use by recipients of Stabex transfers, and Lomé IV saw a further tightening of conditionality. Stabex was complemented by Sysmin, a special facility set up for those ACP states where mining sectors occupied an important position in the economy and which were facing difficulties for reasons beyond the control of the state or undertaking concerned. Sub-Saharan exporters of coffee, groundnuts, and cocoa and cocoa products, have been the major beneficiaries of Stabex transfers. The revised provisions to stabilize export earnings are described in Section 15.6 below.

15.6 The Cotonou Agreement, 2000

The Cotonou Agreement was signed in Benin in June 2000, between the 15 Member States of the EU and 77 countries of the ACP Group, together representing almost one billion people and more than half the member states of the United Nations. The ACP Group currently consists of 48 African states, 15 Caribbean states, and 14 Pacific states. France, the Netherlands, and the UK have a number of OCTs between them. (The full text of the Cotonou Agreement was published in a special issue of *The Courier* in September 2000.) The new partnership is for a period of 20 years, with a five-yearly review clause. It enshrines the principle of participative development, extending the partnership concept to a wide range of actors, including civil society, the private sector, and local authorities. Decentralized cooperation is an essential aspect of the ACP–EU partnership.

The Commission's new development policy spells out six key priority areas: trade, regional integration, support for macroeconomic policies with a particular focus on health and education, transport, food security, and institutional capacity building (*The Courier*, June–July 2000, p. 2). Three issues in particular are relevant to this discussion (see Box 15.2 for the broader developmental objectives and innovatory approaches): macroeconomic policy and poverty eradication, trade policy, and the role of the private sector.

In line with internationally agreed development objectives, the central objective of the ACP–EU partnership is the reduction and eventual eradication of poverty, within a macroeconomic context that emphasizes 'disciplined fiscal and monetary policies that result in the reduction of inflation, and improve external and fiscal balances, by strengthening fiscal discipline, enhancing budgetary transparency and efficiency, improving the quality, the equity and composition of fiscal policy' (Pt. 3, Title 1, Ch. 2, Art. 22). These, in principle, desirable and necessary macroeconomic objectives, are to be achieved within more liberal trade and foreign exchange regimes, but which, simultaneously, affect the socio-political background and institutional capacity of the countries concerned, and which give the ACP states the right to determine the direction and sequencing of their development strategies and priorities.

Apart from very likely conflicts between this multiplicity of objectives, two other factors need to be taken into account. Poverty eradication in ACP countries will depend on many factors that lie outside the ambit of the ACP–EU Agreement. Secondly, if the poverty alleviation targets are to be met, the major donor countries will have to increase their levels of ODA in real terms. We noted in Section 15.1 that there was a slight increase in both ODF and ODA in 1998, but when considering the aid record of the major donors presented in Section 15.4, it is clear that they were a long way from achieving the internationally agreed 0.7 per cent of GNP target for ODA. In the UK, for example, at the current rate of progress it is estimated that it will take 50 years to reach the 0.7 per cent target (*The Guardian*, 2 April 2001).

With respect to trade policy, the objectives of the new Agreement are to accelerate the smooth and gradual integration of the ACP states into the global economy, to help them rise to the challenges of globalization and adopt the new conditions of international trade (as being defined by the World Trade Organisation), and to enhance their production, supply, and trading capacities and improve the competitiveness of their traded goods sectors. The Trade Regime of the Lomé Conventions is not compatible with the WTO rules and the preferential treatment extended on a non-reciprocal basis to ACP countries will be phased out over a 10-year transitional period (*The Courier*, June–July 2000, p. 17).

Trade liberalization and greater openness to the global economy is a controversial area and raises a number of as yet unresolved issues. Given the low levels of development of many of the ACP economies, the lack of diversification of their productive and export sectors, and their low levels of global competitiveness, it is difficult not to conclude that the transition to a more open economic stance is going to impose significant short-term adjustment costs in exchange for more speculative longer-term benefits. The transition will be eased if financial and technical assistance is increased and if the private sector plays a more dynamic role.

The text of the Agreement (Ch. 2, Art. 21) emphasises the importance of creating a favourable environment for private investment and the development of a dynamic, viable, and competitive private sector. Cooperation between the EU and ACP countries will support, *inter alia*, the development of entrepreneurial skills, privatization and enterprise reform; the improvement in the quality, availability, and accessibility of financial and non-financial services to private enterprises; the development of a modern financial sector; and the support of micro-enterprise development. An investment facility to be managed by the European Investment Bank (EIB) has been established to provide risk capital and loans to support the development of the private sector.

The financial provisions of the Cotonou Agreement are highlighted in Box 15.2. The financial resources are allocated as follows: €13.5 bn. will go to the 9th European Development Fund (EDF), of which €10 bn. is for long-term arrangements, €1.3 bn. is for regional co-operation and €2.2 bn. is for the Investment Facility. In addition, it is estimated that there is €9.9 bn. left over from previous EDFs and an estimated €1.7 bn. of the European Investment Bank's (EIB) own resources (*The Courier*, No. 181, June–July 2000).

It has been recognized that, over the years, the system for the implementation of aid had become increasingly complex and subject to significant delays. The new Agreement is intended to emphasize coherence, impact, and flexibility. The instruments for providing aid in the form of grants have been rationalized and each ACP state will now get one single indication of a lump sum of resources for a five-year period, rather than a multitude of allocations from different instruments (*The Courier*, No. 181, June–July 2000). For example, it will be possible for the recipient to use these grants for macroeconomic support, sector programmes, traditional projects and programmes, debt relief, decentralized cooperation, or humanitarian aid. Grant assistance may also be used to offset the

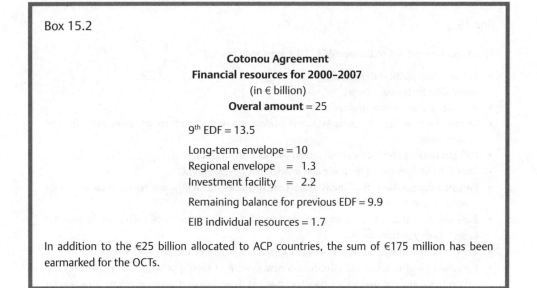

Box 15.2

Cotonou Agreement
Financial resources for 2000–2007
(in € billion)
Overal amount = 25

9th EDF = 13.5

Long-term envelope = 10
Regional envelope   = 1.3
Investment facility   = 2.2

Remaining balance for previous EDF = 9.9

EIB individual resources = 1.7

In addition to the €25 billion allocated to ACP countries, the sum of €175 million has been earmarked for the OCTs.

Source: The Courier, Sept. 2000, Special Issue, p. 7.

negative consequences of shortfalls in export earnings, replacing assistance previously channelled through Stabex and Sysmin (details of the new provisions are given in Annex II, Ch. 3). The starting point for each ACP country will be the establishment of a Country Support Strategy (CSS) which will: include an analysis of the political, social, and economic context of the country and outline the country's own development strategies; pay close attention to the activities of other donors; and, on the basis of this analysis, the focus of EU aid will be determined. In an operational Indicative Programme, attached to the CSS, the operations to be financed in the focal sector(s) will be spelled out (*The Courier*, June–July 2000, p. 24).

15.7 **Conclusions**

Few countries have had as much experience with foreign aid as the Member States of the EU (Panic, 1992). They were large recipients of aid during and after the Second World War (both relief aid and assistance under the Marshall Plan). With post-war reconstruction complete, they became the most important donors of ODA, along with the USA and, later, Japan. As we have argued above, the giving of aid, and the relationships between donor and recipient countries, raise a number of complex issues and pose problems which have no simple solutions. EU aid is no exception in this respect. The size, nature, and effectiveness of EU aid have been subject to criticism, and allegations of ineffectiveness, incompetence, and malpractice are not uncommon, if not always proven. From a more technical perspective, the EU aid programme has in the past been criticized for its

---

Box 15.3

The major innovations of the new ACP–EU Agreement aim to:

- Enhance the political dimension;
- Explicitly address corruption;
- Promote participatory approaches;
- Involve civil society in consultation on reforms and policies to be supported by the Community;
- Refocus development policies on poverty-reduction strategies;
- Improve the framework for trade and investment development;
- Enhance cooperation in all areas important to trade, including new issues such as labour standards and the links between environment and trade;
- Base the allocation of funds on an evaluation of the requirements of each country and the latter's policy performance;
- Create an Investment Facility to support the development of the private sector;
- Rationalize instruments and introduce a new system of rolling programming, allowing the Community and the beneficiary country to adjust their cooperation programme on a regular basis;
- Decentralize administrative and, in some cases, financial responsibilities towards the local level with the aim of making cooperation more effective.

Source: The Courier, September 2000, Special Issue, p.8.

failure to carry out adequate preliminary studies and to adapt projects to local conditions (Panic, 1992: 12) and for the long lag between commitment and actual disbursement of aid.

The EU itself has noted in the past the contradictions between political trends in some ACP countries and the centrality of the importance of respect for human rights, democratic principles, and the rule of law (*The Courier*, 1994: 10). In the 1990s a number of ACP countries faced aid sanctions, provisional suspension, or the slowing down of aid because of their failure to comply with the provisions of Lomé IV. Credit has also been suspended when countries eligible for structural adjustment support postponed or abandoned reform policies for economic or political reasons. Given the political realities of many low-income ACP countries, it would be misleading to presume that such issues can be avoided in the future.

These criticisms are not unique to the EU–ACP aid relationship, and by international standards, the EU is not a 'bad' donor. We have noted above the changing development priorities and policies as incorporated in the Cotonou Agreement, and in particular the focus on poverty reduction and alleviation should be highlighted. Even though it might well be the case that the EU has been slow in developing systematic operational strategies for poverty reduction and so-called people-oriented development (Cox *et al.*, 2000: 37), this is not a shortcoming unique to the EU, given the complexity of the issues raised.

Economic development is the outcome of many factors, both domestic and global, which interact in a complex way that is still not fully understood. The enlargement of the

EU, emerging relationships with the Central and Eastern European countries and the Newly Independent States of the former Soviet Union, the increasing importance of the WTO and the likely reform of the CAP, along with socio-economic and political change within the ACP countries themselves, will all influence the direction and pace of future development. The bilateral aid programmes of EU Member States will continue to be of importance, alongside the multilateral programme of the EU itself. Much will depend on the quality of the aid relationship between bilateral donors and recipients and the effectiveness of the EU–ACP partnership in creating a more favourable context for sustainable development and poverty reduction.

Discussion questions

1   Compare and contrast the record of the major EU aid donors during the 1990s.

2   What are the main factors which influence the 'aid relationship' between EU donors and ACP recipients?

3   Discuss the main changes that have occurred over time in the economic relationships between the EU and the ACP countries. In what ways do the provisions of the Cotonou Agreement reflect changes in development thinking and policy in the 1990s?

Further reading

DAC aid statistics are presented in the OECD *Development Co-operation Report*, published annually. This is the standard reference and also includes discussions of current aid and development issues. Cassen *et al.* (1986), Mosley (1987), and Hansen and Tarp (2000) contain excellent general discussions of aid and its relation to development. Hewitt (1983) is an invaluable reference on the first years of Stabex. The full text of the Cotonou Agreement is to be found in *The Courier* (2000). Cox and Healey (2000) provide a detailed examination of European development cooperation and its impact on poverty reduction.

Notes

1   Arguably, the EU's relations with non-member Mediterranean states have had a higher priority than those with ACP states. During the round of negotiations revising Lomé IV in 1995, most EU Member States would only agree the aid package for ACP once they were satisfied that the aid allocations to Eastern Europe and the Mediterranean were adequate (Parfitt, 1996).

2   The real percentage change between 1997 and 1998 was positive for Belgium, Denmark, Finland, Ireland, Italy, Luxembourg, Netherlands, Portugal, Spain, and the

UK. In the case of Italy, the net ODA rose by 78.4%, the figure for the UK was 8.6%. It is interesting to note that the two largest donors in absolute terms—Japan and the USA—both raised their net ODA significantly between 1997 and 1998—by 23% in the case of Japan and by 26.5% in the case of the USA (OECD, 2000: Table IV–I, p. 70).

3 Table 15.1A in the Appendix gives a different perspective on the regional distribution of EU aid (in €m.). Note that the share of the ACP countries in EU aid was at its highest in the period up to 1989. Thereafter it begins to decline, falling to a low in 1997 (43.2% of the total) and recovering slightly in 1998 (48.0% of the total). The share of the CEECs and NIS is 0.7% in 1989 and rises to 35.7% in 1997, falling slightly to 34.1% in 1998. This is not evidence of aid diversion, however. We would need to construct a counter-factual, that is, what would have happened to EU–ACP aid if the political and economic changes in Eastern and Central Europe and the former Soviet Union had not occurred. Only then could we reach any tentative conclusions as to whether or not aid diversion had occurred.

References

Bhagwati, J. (1967), 'The Tying of Aid', UNCTAD Secretariat, TDI7/Supp. 4, United Nations; repr. in J. Bhagwati and R. S. Eckaus (eds.), *Foreign Aid* (Harmondsworth: Penguin, 1970), 235–93.

Cassen, R. and Associates (1986), *Does Aid Work?* (Oxford: Clarendon Press).

Courier (1994), 145 (May–June, Brussels).

—— (1996), 155 (Jan–Feb., Brussels).

—— (2000), 181 (June–July, Brussels).

—— (2000), Special Issue (September, Brussels).

Cox, A. and Healey, J. (eds.) (2000), *European Development Co-operation and the Poor* (London: Macmillan Press Ltd for the Overseas Development Institute).

Department for International Development (DFID) (2000), *Eliminating World Poverty: Making Globalisation Work for the Poor*, White Paper on International Development (London; HMSO).

Frisch, D. (1992), 'The European Community's Development Policy in a Changing World', the Second Bradford Development Lecture, Oct., mimeo.

Hansen, H. and Tarp, F. (2000), 'Aid Effectiveness Disputed', in F. Tarp (ed.), *Foreign Aid and Development: Lessons Learnt and Directions for the Future* (London: Routledge), 103–8.

Hewitt, A. (1983), 'Stabex: An Evaluation of the Economic Impact over the First Five Years', *World Development*, 11/2 (Dec.), 1005–27.

Hjertholm, P. and White, H. (2000), 'Foreign Aid in Historical Perspective: Background and Trends' in F. Tarp (ed.), *Foreign Aid and Development: Lessons Learnt and Directions for the Future* (London: Routledge), 80–102.

Mosley, P. (1987), *Overseas Aid: Its Defence and Reform* (Brighton: Wheatsheaf).

OECD (1992), *Development Cooperation: 1992 Report* (Paris: OECD).

—— (2000), *Development Cooperation: 1999 Report* (Paris: OECD).

Panic, M. (1992), 'The Single Market and Official Development Assistance: The Potential for Multilateralizing and Raising EU Assistance', *Journal of Development Planning*, 22: 3–17.

Parfitt, T. (1996), 'An Analysis of the Euromed Relationship with Special Reference to Egypt', paper presented at a Conference on Restructuring Egypt: Policies, Implications and Strategies, University of Manchester, May.

Riddell, R. (1987), *Foreign Aid Reconsidered* (London: James Curry).

Singer, H. (1965), 'External Aid: For Plans or Projects?', *Economic Journal*, 75: 539–5; repr. in J. Bhagwati and R. S. Eckaus (eds.), *Foreign Aid* (Harmondsworth: Penguin, 1970), 294–302.

Stevens, C. (1990), 'The Lomé Convention', in K. Kiljunen (ed.), *Region-to-Region Cooperation between Developed and Developing Countries: The Potential for Mini NIEO* (Aldershot: Avebury), 77–88.

Tarp, F. (ed.) (2000), *Foreign Aid and Development: Lessons Learnt and Directions for the Future* (London: Routledge).

Thorbecke, E. (2000), 'The Evolution of the Development Doctrine and the Role of Foreign Aid, 1950–2000', in F. Tarp (ed.), *Foreign Aid and Development: Lessons Learnt and Directions for the Future* (London: Routledge), 17–47.

White, H. (1992), 'The Macroeconomic Impact of Development Aid: A Critical Survey', *Journal of Development Studies*, 28/2 (Jan.), 163–240.

World Bank (1998), *Assessing Aid: What Works, What Doesn't, and Why* (New York: Oxford University Press for the World Bank).

Appendix

Table 15.1A Regional distribution of EC aid, 1986–1998 (disbursements in €m.)

	1986	1987	1988	1989	1990	1991	1992	1993	1994	1995	1996	1997	1998
ACP	1,060	1,248	1,565	1,798	1,737	2,060	2,658	1,960	2,503	2,333	2,050	1,958	2,281
Asia and Latin America	191	197	226	417	426	457	531	537	493	644	506	485	421
Mediterranean and Mid East	311	164	249	331	285	1,012	468	594	581	578	439	467	427
CEECs and NIS	3	0	0	18	360	557	790	1,084	1,453	1,583	1,627	1,621	1,620
Total	1,565	1,609	2,040	2,564	2,800	4,086	4,447	4,175	5,030	5,138	4,622	4,531	4,749
ACP as % of total	67.7	77.6	76.7	70.1	62.0	50.4	59.8	46.9	49.8	45.4	44.3	43.2	48.0

Source: http://europa.eu.int/comm/development/cotonou/statistics/stat15_en.htm

Index

Note: Institutions and related concepts are indexed as far as possible by acronym (see Abbreviations on pages xvi–xx).